The Feminization of American Culture

ANN DOUGLAS has taught American studies at Harvard, Princeton, and Columbia University, where she is now professor of English and Comparative Literature. Her most recent book, *Terrible Honesty*, is published by Picador.

ANN DOUGLAS

The Feminization of American Culture

PAPERMAC

First published 1977 by Alfred A. Knopf, Inc., New York

First published in paperback 1988 by Anchor,
a division of Bantam Doubleday Dell Publishing Group Inc., New York

First published in Great Britain 1996 by Papermac
an imprint of Macmillan General Books
25 Eccleston Place, London SW1W 9NF
and Basingstoke

Associated companies throughout the world

ISBN 0 333 65421 8

A CIP catalogue record for this book is available from
the British Library

Printed and bound in Great Britain by
Mackays of Chatham plc, Chatham, Kent

for my friends

PETER WOOD

and

CHRISTINE STANSELL

LARRY GROSS

ELIZABETH KENDALL

CONTENTS

ACKNOWLEDGMENTS

I would like to express my gratitude to my teachers Alan Heimert and the late Perry Miller, who imparted to me their belief in the centrality of religion in the American experience. Their example taught me the meaning of exhaustive, committed, and heroic scholarship. Over my years of teaching at Harvard, Princeton, and Columbia, I have gained innumerable insights from various students, colleagues, and friends, but I would like to mention particularly Nancy Osterud, Barry O'Connell, John Stendahl, Don Whaley, George Forgie, Michael Bell, Peter Sacks, Gail Parker, and Elaine Showalter, all of whom helped me define and respect my special material. Sacvan Bercovitch was kind enough to read and criticize my manuscript; I have benefited greatly from his suggestions. Emile de Antonio helped to clarify my thinking; his courage in making difficult intellectual and political commitments forced me to re-examine and solidify my own convictions. My mother, Margaret Taylor, has been as important to this book as to my life; her encouragement and her strength have sharpened my desire to understand our common feminine heritage and to work for a better feminine future. Thanks are also due to the staff of the Schlesinger Library in Cambridge, Massachusetts, most notably Jeannette Cheek, whose helpfulness and expertise were invaluable. I am grateful for the invaluable aid provided by my editors at Knopf, Jane Garrett and Alice Quinn, and by my copyeditors, Deborah Zwecher and Stephanie Golden.

For Carl Schorske of Princeton University, whom I was privileged to know during most of the seven years I worked on this book, my gratitude and admiration are unbounded. His work and his discourse have provided me with an unparalleled model of intellectual richness and rigor which has at every turn quickened, clarified, and deepened my motive. Of the friends to whom this book is dedicated and who inspired and guided its creation, I can only say that I am grateful for their example and support; I am fortunate in having such companions and leaders in the effort to understand, resist, and vivify our culture.

ANN DOUGLAS
New York City
May 1, 1976

Preface to the 1988 Anchor Edition of
The Feminization of American Culture

Looking at this book from the perspective of just over a decade, I find that my ongoing feelings are still pleasure and satisfaction: pleasure that I engaged for nearly a decade in research and writing that was and remains vital to me as a cultural critic, an American, and a woman; satisfaction that the book was part, if a small one, of an ongoing tradition of theological study founded at Harvard University by Perry Miller in the 1930s, and part, if a controversial one, of an excavation and re-evaluation of American feminine nineteenth-century literature, then and since ably carried on by Jane Tompkins, Cynthia Griffin Wolff, Nina Baym, Mary Kelley, Madelon Bedell, and many other critics. Because this work landed to sink or float in what are turbulent and deep waters, a few words about my current thoughts on the debate in whose early stages this book played a role seem in order. "Canonical" values clearly supply the working assumptions of The Feminization of American Culture, much of whose material is extra-canonical. Yet the reliability and validity of the "canon" of almost exclusively male-authored, conspicuously shaped and achieved works is now rightly and forcibly questioned by feminist scholars and students of mass culture.

The canon controversy has taught me much over the last decade. As a result, I try in my current thinking, teaching and writing to distinguish between "canonizers," whether authors like Henry James or T. S. Eliot or critics like Yvor Winters, I. A. Richards and F. R. Leavis, who attempt to use work (sometimes their own) congenial to them to reorder,

revitalize and dominate the current notions of what ought to be valued
and studied within and without the academy, and the genuinely "canonized," authors ranging from "classics" like Homer and Aeschylus to
more recent writers like Dickens, Melville and Emily Dickinson, who
seem to have sheerly lasted, to possess an ongoing ability to engage
successive generations in the effort to create the next life of the text. I
hardly disavow the academy's role in keeping such canonized works
current; indeed, that activity seems to me the heart of the academy's
humanist mission. Yet in teaching for several decades, I have marked the
enthusiasm and boredom with which students resist a professor's attempts to convince them that they like what they don't. I can't believe in
the degree of passive submission among readers that the more extreme
critics of the canon (often precisely those who rely most heavily on
"reader response," the reader's uncheckable independent activity, to
make their critiques) tacitly presuppose. So I insist on the worth of
writers implicitly excluded by the "canonizers"—poets like Hart Crane
and Edna St. Vincent Millay who wrote in unappreciated opposition to
Eliot, novelists of shaky reputation like Gertrude Stein, Sinclair Lewis
and Jack Kerouac, whose work does not meet Jamesian or post-Jamesian
norms—*and* on the enduring value of most of the canonized texts, old
and new.

The male bias of all but the most recent canonizers is evident if
inevitable: after all, they were men. The teaching and studying of once
extra-canonical works, male- and female-authored, in traditional and
specifically feminist courses is rightly repopulating those broad (hotly)
negotiable margins of the canonized curriculum and redefining and re-
evaluating the meaning of the central canonized texts themselves. It is
my belief that as students and just plain readers we make similar demands on male- and female-authored texts. We ask them to awaken a
broad range of our faculties whose nature and interaction may differ
depending on the sex of the author; we also ask them to display strength
and sensitivity.

The most controversial aspect of *The Feminization of American Culture*
is the relatively low critical esteem in which I held the work of the
feminine authors (with the exceptions of Harriet Beecher Stowe and
Margaret Fuller) I considered. While respecting the very different evaluation of this material by other scholars, even believing that they may
have access to valid criteria I am temperamentally unable to appreciate,
I stand by my original assessment. The value of these Victorian feminine texts, while not negligible in a literary sense, is most crucial as a
sociological element in the cultural scene that it was the purpose of this
work to examine. If I underrated my women protagonists, and I believe

I did, the fault lay in my downplaying the long-term efficacy of many of their social goals and methods, pursued on platforms, committees, and editorial boards, as well as in their books: they ably initiated and assisted feminine advances in health, higher education and the professions, notably literature, teaching and medicine.

As I look back on this book, it seems, with the easy advantage of hindsight, that I misconceived and misannounced its underlying purpose. I thought I was addressing the issue of male versus female literary production and self-definition as much as, or more than, I was attending to the problem of a nascent mass print medium (here typified in popular clerical and feminine writing) and "elite" art and thinking (exemplified here in the work of Horace Bushnell, Margaret Fuller and Herman Melville). My sense of the pressing nature of the second issue, mass-versus-elite art, came late in the book's decade of development, and was written in, often crudely, in the later stages of its progress. Today, I have reflected on the fact that I was writing my Ph.D. thesis on popular medieval drama visions and their relation to ecclesiastical thought and institutional structure as I began research for *Feminization*; in the last decade, I have taught and published on "mass" art forms like rock and terror placed in a larger cultural and theoretical context; I am now completing a book-length study of the evolution and definition of what are still, with increasing dis-ease, called mass, middle-brow, and high literary art in New York in the 1920s.* I realize, in short, that my sharpest interest past and present lies with the interaction, interpretation and mutual redefinition of mass and elite art. Committed as I was and am to the proposition that culture is a process fully engaging both sexes, involved as I am with scholarship that entails exploration of my own (feminine) psyche, I also see that feminine issues and authors attract me because so-called "feminine" genres, like the domestic fiction of the Victorian era, have long been free travelers between the at times keenly policed borders of male and female, high and low art. The co-sexually authored genres, like humor and terror, are also such travelers; all-male forms, like the Western, usually a popular or mass form, and theological debate, traditionally confined to elite circles, are not. Such "free travelers" are central agents in the kind of cultural activity (the long-standing theological debate between free will and necessity is its origin) that is my ongoing concern.

Here I arrive at another controversy about the canon, intimately connected to the one in which feminist critics engage, but different in reach and aim: the debate devolved from the consideration of mass art.

* *Terrible Honesty: Studies in Secular Urban Culture 1919–1935;* forthcoming, Doubleday, 1988.

While I paid heed in *The Feminization of American Culture* to the pleasure
—surely itself no mean resource and reward—I had long found in the
sentimental Victorian feminine fare I discussed, I tended to call that
pleasure self-flattery or addiction. By this equation between pleasure
and addiction, I meant that I found myself reading Victorian sentimental fare, as today I find myself watching certain TV programs, past the
point that pleasure, in its truest form, which entails wide and various
vivification as well as reassurance, dictates, into a kind of mindless absorption. Such absorption can characterize response to first-rate art, elite
or mass; it is not its main feature. The difficulty of my facile equation lay
in the fact that I did not explore, nor had I ever done so, the many kinds
of attachment to literary and cultural artifacts that lie between addiction
and awed admiration and that alternate even within our response to a
single work, whether a masterpiece by Melville or a decidedly minor
work by Susan Warner. I wished to let extremes quarrel, to emphasize
antagonism, granting myself the prerogative of selecting, according to
my best judgment, the victor: here, theology, and highly masculine literary achievement.

Today I am interested in the full and varied spectrum of art from
mass to elite, the possible responses to its many incarnations, and the
widening (not the destruction) of the curricular canon as a result of such
response. After publishing *The Feminization of American Culture*, ready to
work more fruitfully on the discovery and exploration of such a spectrum, I found myself moving to the modern (and postmodern) periods,
to the points in American culture at which the media were full-blown,
or almost so, where this spectrum is widely extended and blatantly in
need of attention. The antebellum period, the subject of *The Feminization
of American Culture*, a period in which the first mass medium, print, was
just making its appearance, saw itself in terms more varied but not less
divisive and histrionic, than those I used and the terms used in the
earlier era were not dissimilar to my own. I persist in the hope that,
willy-nilly, I will be drawn to consider material my own resources and
liabilities best equip me to understand; I persist in the attempt to pick
up on, to amplify so as to analyze, the conversation and controversy in
which a given cultural epoch itself engages. A carefully researched and
qualified ethos of dramatics seems to me the heart of teaching, and the
most reliable basis and corrective for any methodology I may bring to
scholarship.

ANN DOUGLAS
April 1987
New York City

INTRODUCTION

THE LEGACY OF AMERICAN VICTORIANISM

The Meaning of Little Eva

Today many Americans, intellectuals as well as less scholarly people, feel a particular fondness for the artifacts, the literature, the *mores* of our Victorian past.[1] I wrote this book because I am one of these people. As a child I read with formative intensity in a collection of Victorian sentimental fiction, a legacy from my grandmother's girlhood. Reading these stories, I first discovered the meaning of absorption: the pleasure and guilt of possessing a secret supply. I read through the "Elsie Dinsmore" books, the "Patty" books, and countless others; I followed the timid exploits of innumerable pale and pious heroines. But what I remember best, what was for me as for so many others, the archetypical and archetypically satisfying scene in this domestic genre, was the death of Little Eva in Harriet Beecher Stowe's novel, *Uncle Tom's Cabin*.

A pure and beautiful child in a wealthy southern family, Little Eva dies a lingering and sainted death of consumption. Her adoring Papa and a group of equally adoring slaves cluster in unspeakable grief around her bedside while she dispenses Christian wisdom and her own golden locks with profuse generosity. The poignancy of her closing scene is in no way diminished by the fact that a good third of the story is yet to come, and must proceed without her. Little Eva's significance has curiously little to do with the plot of the book in which she appears. For Little Eva gains her force not through what she does, not even through what she is, but through what she does and is to us, the readers.

Of course any character in any book is peculiarly available to her or his audience and dependent on it. A book can be produced by the millions, as this one was. Simply as a character in a story, Little Eva is a creature not only of her author's imagination but of her reader's fantasy; her life stems from our acceptance of her and our involvement with her. But Little Eva is one of us in more special ways. Her admirers have always been able to identify with her even while they worship, or weep, at her shrine. She does not demand the respect we accord a competitor. She is not extraordinarily gifted, or at least she is young enough so that her talents have not had the chance to take on formidable proportions. If she is lovely looking and has a great deal of money, Stowe makes it amply clear that these attributes are more a sign than a cause of her success. Little Eva's virtue lies partly in her femininity, surely a common enough commodity. And her greatest act is dying, something we all can and must do. Her death, moreover, is not particularly effective in any practical sense. During her last days, she urges her father to become a serious Christian and to free his slaves; he dies himself, however, before he has gotten around to doing either. Little Eva's death is not futile, but it is essentially decorative; and therein, perhaps, lay its charm for me and for others.

Stowe intended Little Eva's patient and protracted death as an exemplum of religious faith, but it does not operate exclusively as such. Little Eva is devout, precociously spiritual in a way that would have been as recognizable to an eighteenth-century theologian like Jonathan Edwards as to the typical mid-nineteenth-century reader. Yet her religious significance comes not only from her own extreme religiosity but also from the protective veneration it arouses in the other characters in the book, and presumably in her readers. Her religious identity, like her death, is confused with the response it evokes. It is important to note that Little Eva doesn't actually convert anyone. Her sainthood is there to precipitate our nostalgia and our narcissism. We are meant to bestow on her that fondness we reserve for the contemplation of our own softer emotions. If "camp" is art that is too excessive to be taken seriously, art that courts our "tenderness,"[2] then Little Eva suggests Christianity beginning to function as camp. Her only real demand on her readers is for self-indulgence.

Stowe's infantile heroine anticipates that exaltation of the average which is the trademark of mass culture. Vastly superior as she is to most of her figurative offspring, she is nonetheless the childish predecessor of Miss America, of "Teen Angel," of the ubiquitous, everyday, wonderful girl about whom thousands of popular songs and movies have been made. Like her descendants, she flatters the possibilities of her audience; she does not quicken their aspirations. In a sense, my introduction to Little Eva and to the Victorian scenes, objects, and sensibility of which she is suggestive was my introduction to consumerism. The pleasure Little Eva gave me provided historical and practical preparation for the equally indispensable and disquieting comforts of mass culture. Perhaps Victorian sentimentality appeals to us not because it is so remote but because it is so near. Its products have the heightened and endearing vigor that comes from being the first of a line, but their line continues, unbroken if debased, to our own day. We treat Victoriana today with the same ambiguity we reserve for the consumer pleasures provided by our televisions, movie screens, and radios. Whatever our fondness for American Victorian culture, our critical evaluation of its most characteristic manifestations is often low. Terms like "camp" used to describe phenomena such as Little Eva socialize our ongoing, unexplored embarrassment. We Americans are, after all, the first society in history to locate and express many personal, "unique" feelings and responses through dime-a-dozen artifacts.

I will argue throughout this book for the intimate connection between critical aspects of Victorian culture and modern mass culture. Twentieth-century America is believed, if in pejorative senses, to be more "modern" than other modern cultures; nineteenth-century America was, in certain senses also usually considered pejorative, more Victorian than other countries to whom the term is applied. Even England, whose Queen was the source of the word "Victorian," was less entirely dominated by what we think of as the worst, the most sentimental, aspects of the Victorian spirit. It seems indicative, for example, that the Sunday School movement with its saccharine simplification of dogma found fewer obstacles and greater success in America than in England.[3] Putting it another way, I might say that Victorian culture in England represented a complex and intelligent collaboration of available resources unparalleled in America. My point can be clarified by glancing at Victorian literature in the two countries.

England's major writers—Charles Dickens, William Makepeace Thackeray, and George Eliot—dedicated their enormous talents to an exploration of Victorianism which, by the sheer fact of assuming its inescapability, complicated and enriched it. It was their treatment of their subject, not their subject, that distinguished them from other, less talented English writers. Even today they restore for us the context and possible seriousness of what are now more or less abandoned literary themes: feminine purity; the sanctity of the childish heart; above all, the meaning of religious conformity. In contrast, major American authors of the Victorian era like James Fenimore Cooper, Nathaniel Hawthorne, Henry David Thoreau, Herman Melville, and Walt Whitman turned their sights principally on values and scenes that operated as alternatives to cultural norms. Their subjects, as well as their styles, differed from those of many of their American contemporaries. They wrote dramas of the forest, the sea, the city. They sought to bring their readers into direct confrontation with the more brutal facts of America's explosive development. Thoreau, Cooper, Melville, and Whitman wrote principally about men, not girls and children, and they wrote about men engaged in economically and ecologically significant activities.[4] When they treated Victorian mores, with a few notable exceptions they either satirized them or lapsed into *pro forma* imitations of conventional models.[5] It was as if America's finest authors refused to redeem the virgin, the child, and the home from the isolation imposed precisely by their status as cult objects; they abandoned them to unreality. Here at mid-nineteenth century in America we see the beginnings of the split between elite and mass cultures so familiar today.

It is indicative of Victorian England's greater cultural cohesiveness that almost all the mid-nineteenth-century English authors we currently admire were admired by their contemporaries. In contrast, many of the American writers of the same period we now value were underrated and little read in their own time; those who, like Stowe, were highly esteemed are hardly studied today. Yet an examination of precisely what we dislike, at least theoretically, in the popular writers of the Victorian era—their debased religiosity, their sentimental peddling of Christian belief for its nostalgic value—is crucial for understanding American culture in the nineteenth century and in our own. The very ambiguity of our response is itself a motive for exploration. Such an examination will constitute the subject of my book.

Between 1820 and 1875,[6] in the midst of the transformation of the American economy into the most powerfully aggressive capitalist system in the world, American culture seemed bent on establishing a perpetual Mother's Day. As the secular activities of American life were demonstrating their utter supremacy, religion became the message of America's official and conventional cultural life. This religion was hardly the Calvinism of the founders of the Bay Colony or that of New England's great eighteenth-century divines. It was a far cry, moreover, from the faith which at least imaginatively still engaged serious authors like Melville and Hawthorne.

Under "Calvinism" we can place much of what rigorous theology Protestant Americans have ever officially accepted. Until roughly 1820, this theological tradition was a chief, perhaps the chief, vehicle of intellectual and cultural activity in American life. The Calvinist tradition culminated in the Edwardsean school:[7] most notably, Jonathan Edwards (1703–58) and his friends and followers, Samuel Hopkins (1721–1803), Joseph Bellamy (1719–90), and Nathaniel Emmons (1745–1840). The Edwardsean school has often been mythologized, but, whatever its very real faults, it undoubtedly constituted the most persuasive example of independent yet institutionalized thought to which our society has even temporarily given credence. Its members studied together; they trained, questioned, and defended one another. They exhibited with some consistency the intellectual rigor and imaginative precision difficult to achieve without collective effort, and certainly rare in more recent American annals.

For some time, roughly between 1740 and 1820, the rigor exhibited by the Edwardsean ministers seemed representative of the wider culture or at least welcomed by it. Edwardsean theology, however, outlived its popular support. In the eighteenth and nineteenth centuries, as in the twentieth, the vast majority of American Christians identified themselves as members of one of the various Protestant groups.[8] Yet the differences between the Protestants of, say, 1800 and their descendants of 1875 and after are greater than the similarities. The everyday Protestant of 1800 subscribed to a rather complicated and rigidly defined body of dogma; attendance at a certain church had a markedly theological function. By 1875, American Protestants were much more likely to define their faith in terms of family morals, civic responsibility, and above all, in terms of the social function of churchgoing. Their actual creed was usually a liberal, even a sentimental one for which Edwards and his contemporaries would have felt scorn and horror. In an analogous way, Protestant churches over the same period shifted their emphasis from a primary concern with the doctrinal beliefs of their members to a preoccupation with numbers. In ecclesiastical and religious circles, attendance came to count for more than genuine adherence. Nothing could show better the late nineteenth-century Protestant Church's altered identity as an eager participant in the emerging consumer society than its obsession with popularity and its increasing disregard of intellectual issues.

The vitiation and near-disappearance of the Calvinist tradition have been sufficiently lamented, and perhaps insufficiently understood. The numerous historians and theologians of the last four decades who have recorded and mourned its loss themselves constitute an unofficial school which can loosely be termed "Neo-orthodox."[9] In analyzing Calvinism's decline, however, they have not examined all the evidence at their disposal. They have provided important studies of the effects of the democratic experiment in a new and unsettled land, effects all tending to a liberal creed in theology as in politics: immigration on a scale unparalleled in the modern world, huge labor resources facilitating rapid urbanization and industrialization, amalgamation of diverse cultural heritages often at the level of their lowest common denominator. Yet they have neglected what might be called the social history of Calvinist theology. They have given scant consideration to the changing nature of the ministry as a profession or to the men who entered its ranks during the critical decades between 1820 and 1875. And they have overlooked another group central to the rituals of that Victorian sentimentalism that did so much to gut Calvinist orthodoxy: Little Eva's most ardent admirers, the active middle-class Protestant women whose supposedly limited intelligences liberal piety was in part designed to flatter. As if in fear of contamination, historians have ignored the claims of what Harriet Beecher Stowe astutely called "Pink and White Tyranny":[10] the drive of nineteenth-century American women to gain power through the exploitation of their feminine identity as their society defined it.

These women did not hold offices or own businesses. They had little formal status in their culture, nor apparently did they seek it. They were not usually declared feminists or radical reformers. Increasingly exempt from the responsibilities of domestic industry, they were in a state of sociological transition. They comprised the bulk of educated churchgoers and the vast majority of the dependable reading public; in ever greater numbers, they edited magazines and wrote books for other women like themselves. They were becoming the prime consumers of American culture. As such they exerted an enormous influence on the chief male purveyors of that culture, the liberal, literate ministers and popular writers who were being read while Melville and Thoreau were ignored. These masculine groups, ministers and authors, occupied a precarious position in society. Writers had never received public support; ministers ceased to do so after 1833 when the "disestablishment" of the Protestant Church became officially complete in the United States. In very real ways, authors and clergymen were on the market; they could hardly afford to ignore their feminine customers and competitors.

What bound the minister and the lady together with the popular writer was their shared preoccupation with the lighter productions of the press; they wrote poetry, fiction, memoirs, sermons, and magazine pieces of every kind. What distinguished them from the writer, and made them uniquely central agents in the process of sentimentalization this book undertakes to explore, is the fact that their consuming interest in literature was relatively new. At the turn of the nineteenth century, the prominent Edwardsean minister, Nathaniel Emmons, returned a novel by Sir Walter Scott lent him by a friend with protestations of genuine horror. A scant fifty years later, serious ministers and orthodox professors of theology were making secular literature a concern and even an occupation. During the same period, women writers gradually flooded the market with their efforts. While a female author at the beginning of the nineteenth century was considered by definition an aberration from her sex, by its close she occupied an established if not a respected place. The Victorian lady and minister were joining, and changing, the literary scene.

Northeastern clergymen and middle-class literary women lacked power of any crudely tangible kind, and they were careful not to lay claim to it. Instead they wished to exert "influence," which they eulogized as a religious force.[11] They were asking for nothing more than offhand attention, and not even much of that: "influence" was to be discreetly omnipresent and omnipotent. This was the suasion of moral and psychic nurture, and it had a good deal less to do with the faith of the past and a good deal more to do with the advertising industry of the future than its proponents would have liked to believe. They exerted their "influence" chiefly through literature which was just in the process of becoming a mass medium. The press offered them the chance they were seeking to be unobtrusive and everywhere at the same time. They inevitably confused theology with religiosity, religiosity with literature, and literature with self-justification. They understandably attempted to stabilize and advertise in their work the values that cast their recessive position in the most favorable light. Even as they took full advantage of the new commercial possibilities technological revolutions in printing had made possible, they exercised an enormously conservative influence on their society.

On a thematic level, they specialized in the domestic and religious concerns considered appropriate for members of their profession or sex. But content was not the most important aspect of their work, nor of its conservative impulse. Ministerial and feminine authors were as involved with the method of consumption as with the article consumed. Despite their often prolific output, they were in a curious sense more interested in the business of reading than in that of writing. Indeed, this book, while focused upon written sources, might be described in one sense as a study of readers and of those who shared and shaped their taste. Of course involvement and identification between authors and their readers was characteristically and broadly Victorian. Henry James could rebuke Anthony Trollope for his constant asides to the reader, for his casual admissions that he was making up a story to please an audience,[12] but Trollope was in the majority. To ask a Victorian author, American or British, not to address his readers was a bit like asking a modern-day telecaster to ignore his viewers. Literature then, like television now, was in the early phase of intense self-consciousness characteristic of a new mass medium: the transactions between cultural buyer and seller, producer and consumer shaped both the content and the form. The American groups I am discussing, however, showed an extraordinary degree, even by Victorian standards, of market-oriented alertness to their customers. They had a great deal in common with them.

The well-educated intellectual minister of the eighteenth century read omnivorously, but the dense argumentative tracts he tackled forced him to think, not to "read" in our modern sense; metaphorically speaking, he was producing, not consuming. His mid-nineteenth-century descendant was likely to show a love of fiction and poetry and a distaste for polemical theology; he preferred "light" to "heavy" reading. By the same token, numerous observers remarked on the fact that countless young Victorian women spent much of their middle-class girlhoods prostrate on chaise longues with their heads buried in "worthless" novels. Their grandmothers, the critics insinuated, had spent their time studying the Bible and performing useful household chores. "Reading" in its new form was many things; among them it was an occupation for the unemployed, narcissistic self-education for those excluded from the harsh school of practical competition. Literary men of the cloth and middle-class women writers of the Victorian period knew from firsthand evidence that literature was functioning more and more as a form of leisure, a complicated mass dream-life in the busiest, most wide-awake society in the world. They could not be altogether ignorant that literature was revealing and supporting a special class, a class defined less by what its members produced than by what they consumed. When the minister and the lady put pen to paper, they had ever in their minds their reading counterparts; the small scale, the intimate scenes, the chatty tone of many of their works complement the presumably comfortable posture and domestic backdrop of their readers. They wrote not just to win adherents to their views, but to make converts to literature, to sustain and encourage the habit of reading itself.[13] Inevitably more serious writers like Melville attempted alternately to re-educate, defy, and ignore a public addicted to the absorption of sentimental fare.

To suggest that problems of professional class or sexual status played a part in the creation and character of nineteenth- and twentieth-century American culture is not, hopefully, to suggest a conspiracy view of history. The ministers and women I am considering were intent on claiming culture as their peculiar property, one conferring on them a special duty and prerogative. They were rightly insecure about their position in the broader society; they sought to gain indirect and compensatory control. Yet they were not insincere, ill-intentioned, or simple-minded. It must be remembered how these people saw themselves, and with what reason: they were Christians reinterpreting their faith as best they could in terms of the needs of their society. Their conscious motives were good—even praiseworthy; their effects were not altogether bad. Under the sanction of sentimentalism, lady and clergyman were able to cross the cruel lines laid down by sexual stereotyping in ways that were clearly historically important and undoubtedly personally fulfilling. She could become aggressive, even angry, in the name of various holy causes; he could become gentle, even nurturing, for the sake of moral overseeing. Whatever their ambiguities of motivation, both believed they had a genuine redemptive mission in their society: to propagate the potentially matriarchal virtues of nurture, generosity, and acceptance;

to create the "culture of the feelings" that John Stuart Mill was to find during the same period in Wordsworth.[14] It is hardly altogether their fault that their efforts intensified sentimental rather than matriarchal values.

Moreover, whatever the errors of the sentimentalists, they paid for them. The losses sustained by the ministers and the women involved, as well as by the culture which was their arena, were enormous. The case of the ministers is clear-cut; they lost status and respect. The case of the women is equally painful, but more difficult to discuss, especially in the atmosphere of controversy that attends feminist argument today. I must add a personal note here. As I researched and wrote this book, I experienced a confusion which perhaps other women scholars have felt in recent years. I expected to find my fathers and my mothers; instead I discovered my fathers and my sisters. The best of the men had access to solutions, and occasionally inspiring ones, which I appropriate only with the anxiety and effort that attend genuine aspiration. The problems of the women correspond to mine with a frightening accuracy that seems to set us outside the processes of history; the answers of even the finest of them were often mine, and sometimes largely unacceptable to me. I am tempted to account my response socialization, if not treachery. Siding with the enemy. But I think that is wrong.

I have a respect for so-called "toughness," not as a good in itself, not isolated and reified as it so often is in male-dominated cultures, but as the necessary preservative for all virtues, even those of gentleness and generosity. My respect is deeply ingrained; my commitment to feminism requires that I explore it, not that I abjure it. Much more important, it does no good to shirk the fact that nineteenth-century American society tried to damage women like Harriet Beecher Stowe—and succeeded. It is undeniable that the oppressed preserved, and were intended to preserve, crucial values threatened in the larger culture. But it is equally true that no one would protest oppression with fervor or justification if it did not in part accomplish its object: the curtailment of the possibilities of growth for significant portions of a given community. Nineteenth-century American women were oppressed, and damaged; inevitably, the influence they exerted in turn on their society was not altogether beneficial. The cruelest aspect of the process of oppression is the logic by which it forces its objects to be oppressive in turn, to do the dirty work of their society in several senses. Melville put the matter well: weakness, or even "depravity in the oppressed is no apology for the oppressor; but rather an additional stigma to him, as being, in a large degree, the effect and not the cause of oppression."[15] To view the victims of oppression simply as martyrs and heroes, however, undeniably heroic and martyred as they often were, is only to perpetuate the sentimental heresy I am attempting to study here.

I have been more interested in the effects than in the conscious motives of the women and ministers under consideration, for there is no better indication of their dilemma than the often wide and tragic divergence between the two. In the process of sentimentalization which they aided, many women and ministers espoused at least in theory to so-called passive virtues, admirable in themselves, and sorely needed in American life. They could not see to what alien uses their espousal might be put. Sentimentalism is a complex phenomenon. It asserts that the values a society's activity denies are precisely the ones it cherishes; it attempts to deal with the phenomenon of cultural bifurcation by the manipulation of nostalgia. Sentimentalism provides a way to protest a power to which one has already in part capitulated. It is a form of dragging one's heels. It always borders on dishonesty but it is a dishonesty for which there is no known substitute in a capitalist country. Many nineteenth-century Americans in the Northeast acted every day as if they believed that economic expansion, urbanization, and industrialization represented the greatest good. It is to their credit that they indirectly acknowledged that the pursuit of these "masculine" goals meant damaging, perhaps losing, another good, one they increasingly included under the "feminine" ideal. Yet the fact remains that their regret was calculated not to interfere with their actions. We remember that Little Eva's beautiful death, which Stowe presents as part of a protest against slavery, in no way hinders the working of that system. The minister and the lady were appointed by their society as the champions of sensibility. They were in the position of contestants in a fixed fight: they had agreed to put on a convincing show, and to lose. The fakery involved was finally crippling for all concerned.

The sentimentalization of theological and secular culture was an inevitable part of the self-evasion of a society both committed to laissez-faire industrial expansion and disturbed by its consequences. America, impelled by economic and social developments of international scope, abandoned its theological modes of thought at the same time its European counterparts abandoned theirs; it lacked, however, the means they possessed to create substitutes. American culture, younger and less formed than that of any European country, had not yet developed sufficiently rich and diversified secular traditions to serve as carriers for its ongoing intellectual life. The pressures for self-rationalization of the crudest kind were overpowering in a country propelled so rapidly toward industrial capitalism with so little cultural context to slow or complicate its course; sentimentalism provided the inevitable rationalization of the economic order.

In the modernization of American culture that began in the Victorian period, some basic law of dialectical motion was disrupted, unfulfilled, perhaps disproved. Calvinism was a great faith, with great limitations: it was repressive, authoritarian, dogmatic, patriarchal to an extreme. Its demise was inevitable, and in some real sense, welcome. Yet it deserved, and elsewhere and at other times found, great opponents. One could argue that the logical antagonist of Calvinism was a fully humanistic, historically minded romanticism. Exponents of such romanticism appeared in mid-nineteenth-century America—one thinks particularly of Margaret Fuller and Herman Melville —but they were rare. In America, for economic and social reasons, Calvinism was largely defeated by an anti-intellectual sentimentalism purveyed by men and women whose victory did not achieve their finest goals; America lost its male-dominated theological tradition without gaining a comprehensive feminism or an adequately modernized religious sensibility. It is crucial that I be as clear here as I can. The tragedy of nineteenth-century northeastern society is not the demise of Calvinist patriarchal structures, but rather the failure of a viable, sexually diversified culture to replace them. "Feminization" inevitably guaranteed, not simply the loss of the finest values contained in Calvinism, but the continuation of male hegemony in different guises. The triumph of the "feminizing," sentimental forces that would generate mass culture redefined and perhaps limited the possibilities for change in American society. Sentimentalism, with its tendency to obfuscate the visible dynamics of development, heralded the cultural sprawl that has increasingly characterized post-Victorian life.

PART ONE

The Sentimentalization
of
Status

CLERICAL
DISESTABLISHMENT

A Crisis of Self-Confidence

Henry James, Sr., a religious maverick of no little waywardness and no less astuteness, judged that American Protestantism in the mid-nineteenth century was in a sad state of decline. In his words, "religion in the old virile sense has disappeared, and been replaced by a feeble Unitarian sentimentality."[1] Like most such sweeping generalizations, this is, of course, an oversimplification. Yet it is one worth examining, if only because it expresses an opinion shared by many of James's most intelligent contemporaries on a subject of vital concern to them: the changing nature of America's Calvinist heritage. James is indirectly making several very interesting points here. He surely knew that Unitarianism, an offspring of Congregationalism, had proved itself an extremely limited and even unpersuasive religious movement almost within decades of its inception in late eighteenth-century New England; he is implying, nonetheless, that its "feeble" and sentimental sensibility has pervaded or supplanted other forms of faith. Moreover, he suggests that Unitarianism is not itself a religion, but rather a kind of cultural substitute for religion; hence its triumph has been a victory for the forces of secularization. Finally, although clearly with no special thought or design, James finds it natural to talk of this process in what might be called sexual terms: he is saying that religion has been emasculated.

One needs to be careful in recording the sexual reverberations of words uttered by pre-Freudian Victorians, but it seems more than coincidental that post-Freudian historians writing of the vitiation of New England Calvinism to which James is referring have used language charged with similar connotations. These critics, the Niebuhr brothers chief among them, denounced the liberalism which had defeated the sterner orthodox creed as "sentimental" and condemned its persistent refusal to face the tragic nature of reality. In his seminal book, *The Kingdom of God in America*, Richard Niebuhr mocked the intellectual falsities and namby-pambiness of such facile theology by scornfully summing up its underlying credo: "A God without wrath brought man without sin into a kingdom without judgment through the ministrations of a Christ without a cross."[2] Niebuhr's accusation, with its implicit suggestion of a failure of nerve, is one that easily interlaces itself with sexual insinuations. Winthrop Hudson, an able historian of American Protestantism, could have been elaborating on Niebuhr's thought when he explained that "traditional theological insights [were] emasculated" by prominent nineteenth-century liberal thinkers.[3] Perry Miller, praising the dynamic and imperious New York revivalist Charles Grandison Finney, the *bête noir* of his early nineteenth-century liberal brethren, described him in terms which come close to equating religious and sexual prowess. Finney was "demonic": "among the evangelicals [he] was a Napoleon among his marshals." Only that other driving revivalist among Finney's contemporaries, Lyman Beecher, approached him in Miller's mind; only he was "man enough for the job" Finney performed.[4]

There is palpable masculine bias in these statements, an unexplored assumption that virility and more general worthiness are roughly synonymous. Yet I am interested in the persistent reappearance of such language less for the proof it provides of sexual prejudice distorting the business of historical analysis than for its potential usefulness as in itself historical evidence of a special, if difficult and not always reliable, kind. The language, first of all, highlights an obvious historical fact. American Calvinism possessed in the seventeenth and eighteenth centuries, and lost in the nineteenth, a toughness, a sternness, an intellectual rigor which our society then and since has been accustomed to identify with "masculinity" in some not totally inaccurate if circular sense. Moreover, in lamenting the vanished virility of Protestantism, critics like James or Miller have hardly stood alone. It is essential to realize that, consciously or not, they are echoing the self-condemnation of the men most involved. No one past or present has accused liberal Protestantism of effeminacy more seriously or more frequently than the nineteenth-century "liberal"[5] ministers themselves. For the moment leaving aside the question of on what grounds, valid or otherwise, their fears were based, let us look at the self-image of the Victorian liberal clergy. These ministers, usually Unitarians, sometimes non-evangelical Congregationalists, did not deny the genuinely progressive elements in their faith.

They produced their share of active reformers;[6] and, even while they might lament the vanished stern virtues of their predecessors, they considered themselves benefactors to the human race for their softened reinterpretation of the Calvinist creed. One Sunday in 1838, Charles Follen (1796–1842), a German-born Unitarian minister and a courageous advocate of a genuinely liberalized culture, had a "vision" as he was sitting in an empty church. His vision dramatized the considerable and justifiable optimism present in his wing of Protestantism throughout the nineteenth century. Follen saw a band of Pilgrim Fathers, "stern worshippers from another world," as he described them, displaced by a group of nineteenth-century Sunday School children innocently unaware of their ancestors' presence. The children's victory is effortless, for the Calvinists are apparently pleased to surrender: "here and there a smile, passing over their stern features, seemed like the reflection of the bright countenances of the little intruders as they stepped into the places of their great forefathers. The floor of the church was swarming with children." To complete this symbolic transfer of power, an eagle, perched proudly on the pulpit, his wings filled with "glittering swords and muskets," his eyes "fixed upon the morning sun" and "refulgent with the pious daring of the forefathers," is miraculously replaced by "the gentle form of a dove" who finally flies off to "heaven," borne upward on the Sabbath chorus of the children.[7]

Follen's view is positive: love and freedom have triumphed over fear and repression. Yet the picture he paints actually confirms rather than contradicts Henry James's analysis. The conscious force of church authority has given way to the unconscious influence of domestic affection; adult politics have succumbed to infantile piety, *Ecclesia* to a nursery. Masculinity is vanquished in the congregation and, even more significantly, in the pulpit.

Here was the rub. Few of Follen's contemporaries, whatever their attitudes toward the liberalization of their theology, were able to rejoice as wholeheartedly as he did over their own metamorphosis from "eagle" to "dove." We are learning nothing new about American culture when we discover that a male in the nineteenth century (like one in the twentieth), self-convicted of feminine qualities, was usually also troubled by anxiety that he might be a failure, non-functional, even non-existent. There were notable exceptions, Follen chief among them, but it is safe to say that, over the course of the nineteenth century, the liberal minister experienced increasing difficulty respecting his own vocation: a note of self-depreciation is heard again and again in the self-analysis which more and more occupied him.

Ralph Waldo Emerson (1803–82), the famous transcendentalist, was the son of a Unitarian minister and ordained in the clerical calling himself. A friend and a guide to Follen, he partially endorsed Follen's evaluation of the viability of their common Unitarian creed, yet he felt a nearly irreconcilable conflict inherent in the ministerial role. Like Follen, Emerson couched his argument in sexually connotative terms, although with reverse implications. In his view, the old Calvinist theology "tempts the imagination with a high epic (and better than epic) magnificence, but . . . sounds like nonsense in the ear of understanding"; the Unitarian belief, while intellectually tenable, is "effete." Faced with this impossible choice between vitalizing potency based on illusion and debilitating effeminacy grounded on reality, the modern clergyman was paralyzed; he could not be, Emerson concluded, "a man quite and whole."[8] As chief apostle of the emerging cult of self-confidence, Emerson would spend his life in a complex effort to shut out the voices of self-contempt. He began in 1832 by quitting the ministry.

During the Civil War, a struggle that called out the deepest anxieties of the largely pacifist liberal clergy, James K. Hosmer (1834–1927), another Unitarian minister, wrote a novel entitled *The Thinking Bayonet* which carries Emerson's definition of a clergyman as inherently effeminate to a new and frightening extreme. The Unitarian minister who is the novel's anti-hero hovers nervously on the edge of the battlefield and on the edge of the story; he is in every way a non-combatant. The observer-figures of Hawthorne, James, or Howells look robust, even strenuous, compared to this frail flower of Unitarian piety whose last name is appropriately the girlish one of May. Doomed always to a feminine role, May repeatedly contrasts himself with his closest friend, a brave and Byronic soldier, the "blue-eyed, fair-haired, muscular, thorough[ly] Saxon" hero of the tale. Significantly, the patronymic of this iron-jawed soul is that of the great southern general, Lee. May can only helplessly admire his friend with a wistfulness too deep for envy. He explains his feelings to his sister: ". . . to me he is grand. I think we always like what we do not have ourselves. . . . When he towers over me —little puny fellow that I am! when I hear his strong, rich voice, and see him, in a boat race, pull till his oar bends like a whipstock, and the people shout, my feeling is almost a hero-worship." The woman Lee loves and eventually wins, Leonora Otis, is of patriotic descent and military spirit. "A suitable mate for a Viking," as May describes her, she is the minister's superior in masculinity, and rides (the metaphor is his) with flashing eyes and dilating nostrils in "Amazonian fashion" "rough-shod" over the masochistic little man.[9] This is the idiom of one suffering such self-doubt that the only viable role he can envision for himself is that of victim. Given Hosmer's apparent estimate of the possibilities of the clerical profession, it is hardly surprising that, like Emerson, he left the ministry for a life of literary and academic pursuits.

By 1882, Joseph H. Allen (1820–98), a Unitarian clergyman of distinguished analytical powers, could write as a statement of simple fact that

American Protestantism over the last few generations had relinquished its "militant, heroic, aggressive" qualities, even while he acknowledged the gains accomplished by the humanistic values Follen had celebrated forty-four years earlier. It is important for the historian to note that Allen's pride in the Unitarian achievement (and he was hardly alone in this) was tentative and partial. The secularization of faith provided a rationale and an impetus for a number of liberal reforms, but it also involved changes and losses which weighed heavily on many of those concerned. Allen castigated his denomination for exemplifying and disseminating "amiable sentimentalism ... spiritual impotency, cowardice and self-indulgence."[10] Significantly, Allen himself, while he did not quit the clergy, redefined and relocated his ministerial role; an introspective man with antiquarian interests, he served as a historian rather than as an active practitioner for his denomination.

Allen's evasion of his clerical role was part of an increasingly typical pattern of behavior among liberal clergymen who did not, like Emerson or Hosmer, officially leave their pulpits. They de-emphasized their professional prerogatives in ways that would have perplexed and horrified earlier and more stalwart New England ministers. William Ellery Channing (1780–1843), the most famous of the Unitarian ministers in pre–Civil War America, disliked being addressed as "Reverend";[11] when a friend once reminded him that he was, after all, a clergyman, he retorted, "Yes, I know it, and always remember the disadvantage."[12] On one occasion, he rebuked his devoted admirer and unpaid secretary, the eccentric but extraordinarily intelligent Elizabeth Peabody (1804–94), for treating him too formally, too much as a minister.[13] His reprimand was not the sign that Peabody had been at last allowed into the inner sanctum on whose doorstep she had long and assiduously perched; it was rather representative of a deeply felt but generalized public position. In 1841, in an important address on the nature of "The Church," Channing denied that a clergyman possessed any special efficacy with God not vouchsafed to a devout layman. He rejected such an idea as "dishonorable to God" and totally foreign to the Bible.[14]

Channing had some of Follen's optimism. In part, he was downplaying his ministerial status in order to highlight his human credentials; he disdained to take a head start in the race. Several of Channing's Unitarian contemporaries, and more of his successors, in contrast, experienced their ministerial role as a claustrophobic form of entrapment which cruelly and paradoxically hindered them in the performance of the duties it entailed. Orville Dewey (1794–1882), an artistic, gentle, and supremely literate Unitarian clergyman from New York, could sound like a man dodging his own shadow when he spoke of his clerical function. Traveling from home, he chose always "not to be known as a clergyman." Like many of his peers, he dropped certain parts of the traditional ministerial costume; he replaced the customary stiff collar with a softer and more secular loose black tie. On one occasion, in painful conflict with obvious facts, Dewey insisted to a friend: "I am *not a clergyman*. . . . I question our position more and more." Dewey's own commitment to enlightened reform apparently did not allay his anxieties. He felt that as a minister he was "not fairly thrown into the field of life. . . . [but rather] hedged around with artificial barriers . . . a sort of moral eunuch." In 1852, Dewey wrote to his talented and equally insecure friend, the novelist and minister William Ware (1797–1852), about his experience as a visiting clergyman in Washington, D.C.: "The gayety passed him by; the politics pass him by. Nobody wants him; nobody holds him by the button but some desperate, dilapidated philanthropist. People say, while turning a corner, 'How do you do, Doctor?' Which is very much as if they said, 'How do you do, Abstraction?' "[15] Dewey fears his profession has consigned him to invisibility, to unreality. In his country's capital, he is a cipher.

Even allowing for Dewey's constitutional timidity, how does one explain his self-depreciation in the light of Alexis de Tocqueville's considered observation, made only two short decades before, that the American clergy possessed "immense power"?[16] To explain this discrepancy one needs to examine the situation facing the American ministry during this period and the differing responses available to different denominations. For it was precisely the ministers like Joseph Allen, James Hosmer, and Orville Dewey, members of the older, once state-supported, northern, non-evangelical denominations, who faced the most severe questioning of their economic, political, and cultural pre-eminence amid the turbulent religious developments of the first half of the nineteenth century. In what seemed the flush tide of American Protestantism, they often appeared the laggards, hesitant promulgators of feminine virtues in an era of militant masculinity, strangers in the promised land.

Disestablishment

By certain usually meaningful criteria, American churches gained immense strength between the founding of the republic and the outbreak of the Civil War. In the mid-eighteenth century, America had a smaller number of church members in proportion to overall population than any other Christian nation. In 1800 only one of fifteen Americans belonged to a religious society. By 1850 one of every seven Americans was a church member. This was apparently an impressive record of gain, but one that got very different reactions in different quarters. For the fact was that the large bulk of the new members were Catholics, Methodists, and Baptists, groups which had secured only the most precarious foothold in the New World at the time of the Revolution. At that earlier date, the leading denominations were the

Congregationalists, the Presbyterians, and the Episcopalians. By 1855, the Roman Catholic Church constituted the most important religious group in America. The leading Protestant sects were the Methodists, with some 1,577,014 members, and the Baptists, who could boast of 1,105,546 adherents. The Presbyterians counted 495,715 members, the Congregationalists, once so powerful, a mere 207,608. The Unitarians, originally comprising the influential eighteenth-century liberal or Arminian wing of New England Congregationalism and not officially on their own until after the turn of the nineteenth century, had 13,350 members.[17]

What had happened among the Protestants? It must be remembered that they had special circumstances to deal with in this period which their English and European counterparts faced only in part or not at all: territorial expansion and exploitation, immigration on a scale unknown abroad, and, equally significantly, the "disestablishment" of American religion. All these phenomena favored the Methodists and groups with similar organizations and creeds, and told against the Congregationalists and their allies.

In 1775, just prior to the American Revolution, nine of the colonies had "established" churches, comparable in status to the Anglican one in England. These were churches which citizens were required by their governments to attend and maintain, and against which so-called dissenting sects like the Methodists or Baptists were allowed only very limited overt powers of competition. In Connecticut, for example, where the contest between established and non-established groups increasingly dominated the political scene between the Revolution and 1817, dissenters or non-Congregationalists could not meet in churches for worship until 1770; they were forced to pay taxes to support the Congregational Church until 1777. The Connecticut Assembly, dominated by Congregational interests, as late as 1812 refused to incorporate the fully qualified Episcopalian Cheshire Academy as a college. In the remaining New England states, Congregationalism was also the established church. Episcopalianism, a "dissenting" sect in New England, was the official religion in the older southern states and New York. Predictably, the American Revolution brought disestablishment with it. New York went first in 1777; under Thomas Jefferson's urging, the Anglican Church in Virginia lost its official status in 1785; and, by 1833, when Congregationalism ceased to receive state support in Massachusetts, disestablishment was complete in the United States.[18]

It must be stressed that official "disestablishment," wherever it occurred and whomever it affected, was a symbol rather than a cause. It conveniently marks and represents a gradual course of events by which certain groups of ministers were severed from their traditional sources of power; this process began long before disestablishment proper and was to make the formal act of disestablishment possible and finally inevitable. Disestablishment, in other words, typified and accelerated a historical process with complex roots in the general democratization and industrialization of American culture. The result of the disestablishment process was an apparent triumph for the competitive, commercial, and individualistic spirit: a "voluntary" system in which no denomination had automatic precedence over any other and no person had any obligation to attend worship or to support religion beyond his or her own desire to do so. Between 1820 and 1875, the Protestant Church in this country was gradually transformed from a traditional institution which claimed with certain real justification to be a guide and leader to the American nation to an influential *ad hoc* organization which obtained its power largely by taking cues from the non-ecclesiastical culture on which it was dependent.[19]

Disestablishment represented, although it hardly caused, the formal capitulation of the Protestant churches to the American way, and both the objections to it as a proposal and the final virtually unanimous acceptance of it as a *fait accompli* turned precisely on this issue. While dissenting groups lobbied for disestablishment as an essential part of the promise of liberty offered by the New World, established groups questioned the freedom allowed by a tolerance which took competition as its ideal. Congregations had always chosen their minister, but they had also been legally required to support him and, more important, the church to which he belonged. The new voluntary system meant that the church itself, as well as any given minister, must curry favor in order to survive. In other words, the minister could take nothing for granted. Many Congregational and Unitarian observers feared that the newly disestablished minister, deprived of the traditional basis of his authority, would become too closely tied to the current needs and tastes of his congregation. Since he would be able to make his way only by bringing his people with him, it seemed all too likely that he would find his route in the paths beaten broad by his flock. America, the defenders of the status quo claimed, in abandoning established religion, would be giving up not, as the supporters of voluntarism asserted, merely a number of anachronistic privileges meted out to a few (and not over-deserving) ecclesiastical parties, but an example and a tradition of secure and independent church power with far-ranging and stabilizing influences on its culture. Conformity, such critics emphasized, was hardly liberty or its best safeguard. Lyman Beecher (1775–1863), a prominent Congregational clergyman, preaching fervently against the imminent disestablishment of the Connecticut church in 1812, predicted grimly if extravagantly that, under its dispensation, "we shall become slaves, and slaves to the worst of masters."[20]

Yet, in the first post-disestablishment decades, ministers of all sects and persuasions joined eagerly in vaunting their voluntary system. They stressed overwhelmingly that the clergyman was more rather than less powerful under its aegis. Even Lyman Beecher, who had devoted years of his life to fighting disestablishment and knew one of his most profound depressions after its victory in Connecticut in 1817, was later to condemn his gloom as folly and to declare voluntarism a kind of panacea for religious ills. With that Jacksonian thrust he was able to convey even in his most conservative utterances, he explained: "Before we had been standing on what our fathers had done, but now we were obliged to develop all our energy."[21] Less aggressive clergymen spoke also in support of voluntarism. Philip Schaff, the distinguished and astute theologian who came at mid-century from Germany to found the radically traditionalist "Mercersberg Theology" in a small Lutheran seminary in Pennsylvania, while noting the economic problems imposed by disestablishment, claimed that it produced no "unworthy dependence of the minister on his congregation."[22] Andrew Reed, a Scottish clergyman, announced in 1835 after an extensive visit to the United States that he could not find an American minister who opposed disestablishment.[23]

The causes of the apparent unanimity of American ministers on the success of disestablishment are complex. The newly disestablished clergy were hardly the Machiavellis many contemporary historians have painted them, but surely they possessed the modicum of political sense needed to recognize that no official trumpets abroad his fear and dislike of being totally at the mercy of those on whom he is indeed reliant. To do so is not only an insult to his constituents, but tantamount to a confession of impotence, an admission that he is weakly consenting to operate in a system whose very premises he dislikes. So the disestablished minister's ringing endorsement of the voluntary method was in part the old tactic of the bluff. His enthusiasm was meant to posit a control and to engineer a leadership whose actuality was problematic. His apparent approval of disestablishment was predictable in terms of the critique of disestablishment its opponents had put forth: it can be read with some justification as evidence of the spirit of dependency disestablishment fostered.

To put the same point more positively, one could argue that the disestablished minister's applause of the voluntary system was a sign not just of his compulsion but of his willingness and ability to work in its terms. Disestablishment indisputably forced the Protestant Church into aggressive and largely successful proselytizing; the figures I have already cited on the growth in church membership between 1800 and 1855 speak for this. Even the groups which lost, relatively speaking, gained considerable numbers of new adherents. Moreover, modern historians agree with contemporary observers that the pre–Civil War Protestant Church was able to create an unofficial establishment every bit as effective as its official pre-Revolutionary one.[24] Church property was still exempt from public taxation; legal restraints against blasphemy, Sabbath-violation, and outright atheism remained in force.[25] As Cushing Strout and others have argued, because the American government had severed its formal connection with the church and yet wished to employ religious sanctions in justification of its claims, the secular authorities were unlikely to challenge or defy the spiritual authorities; energy on both sides was employed in preserving and strengthening rather than in testing and redefining the links between them.[26] Lyman Beecher could talk frankly about the reform societies he helped make the dominant form of religious activity in the United States as "the providential substitutes for those legal provisions of our fathers."[27] There were undoubtedly hundreds of ministers like Beecher who had unconsciously been ready for the exhilaration of a free fight, who, with the advent of disestablishment, quickly took advantage of their new ability, enforced as it might be, to recast their thinking and their institutions in the liberal language of their culture.[28]

Yet the relative decline of the Congregationalists, Unitarians, and, to a lesser degree, the Presbyterians, those denominations least equipped for embarking on popular enthusiasms, cannot be ignored. It is a fact that, between the Revolution and the Civil War, the sects which were disestablished lost ground in every sense while the largest "dissenting" groups, which had never received state support, flourished. Even today we see a striking reversal of the original ecclesiastical settlement patterns of American life: while the formerly established Presbyterian, Congregational, and Episcopal sects now dominate no discrete geographical area of this country, the once-itinerant Methodists and Baptists presently control the South as firmly as the Congregationalists ever ruled New England. In the decades succeeding disestablishment, the groups whom the Methodists and Baptists had learned how to attract, namely the middle- and lower-class immigrants and frontier settlers, constituted precisely the fastest-growing elements of the population; they were the ones that any "voluntary" group would have to draw to maintain genuine power, if not prestige.[29] Hence, ecclesiastical practices already in use among the dissenting or non-established sects, most notably the Methodists and the Baptists, became perforce the logical methods, no matter how uncongenial, for the formerly established denominations to use to preserve or repair their authority.

This necessity pressed more painfully on certain of the disestablished groups than on others. It is important to remember that while the Anglicans had been established in New York and Virginia, they had operated, as we have seen, as dissenters in New England, most notably in Connecticut. In similar fashion, although the Presbyterians had been loosely allied in New England with the Congregationalists since the early nineteenth century and as a result had shared some of their privileges, they had played the role of outsiders in Virginia and other parts of the South where they settled in considerable numbers. Both denominations, in other words, had already faced competitive situations before disestablishment and had learned how to deal with them. Many evangelically oriented Congregationalists like Lyman Beecher, moreover, had worked with the Presbyterians under the "Plan of Union" to establish churches in the new communities of the opening West; indeed, Congregationalist critics of the "Union" claimed their ministers had been influenced and absorbed by their Presbyterian fellows. Such Congregational ministers, in any case, like Episcopalians in the North or Presbyterians in the South, had functioned as proselytizers in alien, rough, and difficult circumstances.[30]

The groups hardest hit by disestablishment were the non-evangelical Congregationalists and the Unitarians who were closely related to them. Confined almost entirely to New England, barely represented in states in which they were not established, they had never played the part of dissenters. They knew something of competition, since they had faced the increasingly powerful dissenting groups in their own territories, and they had fought—indeed, on occasion viciously—each other;[31] but they had viewed such struggles only from the conservative perspective of the threatened, never from the potentially more radical perspective of the challenger. The Unitarians, despite their status as rebels against the Congregational order, were hardly outsiders; they constituted the established among the established, and opposed disestablishment with particular fervor.[32] The Unitarians did not officially split from their mother denomination until a few years before disestablishment in Massachusetts, the only state where they exerted any real influence. Consequently, when they captured a Congregational church—as they frequently did between 1800 and 1825—they did not, like other dissenting groups, have to establish and finance a new operation; they simply took over the church's property,[33] leaving the unhappy minority to face the cost of going elsewhere. Moreover, the Congregationalists, with their Unitarian wing, were perhaps most dependent on the privileges of establishment simply because they had enjoyed them longest. The early seventeenth-century Congregational settlers had attempted a voluntary system, early discovered its limitations, and enlisted state support.[34] By the end of the Revolution, the only religious establishments surviving in America were those of New Hampshire, Connecticut, and Massachusetts; they were all Congregationalist, and they all had between twenty and forty years of life left in them.

If competitive commercialized democracy was the American way, the Congregationalists, including the Arminians among them who eventually labeled and organized themselves as Unitarians, had a history some several centuries old of opposition to it. Their adherents were more likely to be found among the middle and upper classes than among lower-class immigrants. Their appeal was to those who appreciated distinction and tradition, not to those who needed violently persuasive means to bring them within church portals. They stood for a settled ministry, for intellectual elitism; if they supported revivals at all, they wished to see them cautiously conducted in orderly fashion by ministers within their own congregations. The Methodists and the groups who resembled them had accomplished what they had by adherence to exactly opposite priorities. They had been able to expand with the country as the older groups had not, precisely because they sacrificed clerical security to evangelical mobility, ministerial education to zeal. With the loss of their "established" status, the Unitarians and non-evangelical Congregationalists were in a painful position. In a very real sense, they could afford neither to imitate nor to ignore their rivals. Their solution, or evasion, of their problem is important precisely because it would later offer a paradigm for the development of the formerly dissenting denominations; the membership and aspirations of these denominations became increasingly middle-class, more like those of the Congregationalists and Unitarians. At early mid-century, however, the disestablished groups could not possess even the small consolation of knowing that their predicament was prophetic, and would be shared.

The Economic Consequences

In one way, disestablishment enforced imitation of dissenting ways: the economic status of the disestablished denominations, whatever their actual monetary resources, was more or less on a par with that of every other religious group. Congregational ministers in Connecticut, for example, ceased in 1817 to have any automatic revenue from taxes. Henceforth, they were forced to raise the funds for anything they wanted to do, including building their churches. It is important to realize that even if disestablished ministers did not lose actual income by this shift, they lost stability, and that this loss was a crucial one for their economic identity. The American established ministry had been a profession comparable to that of school or university teaching today. It offered smaller wages but greater security than rival occupations did; from the seventeenth to the early nineteenth centuries it had operated on a lifelong tenure system. By mid-nineteenth century, however, whatever the theory of the once-established ministry, its practice was Methodist; willy-nilly, it was mobile.

Here again, one wants to avoid overestimating the consequences of disestablishment *per se*. The Congregational minister in America had never enjoyed the degree of financial security experienced by many of his English peers; the tradition of incumbency, the *sine qua non* of clerical security, had always been more fluid, more political, and more potentially democratic than in England. David Hall in his study of the seventeenth-century New England clergy notes a pattern of increasing mobility occurring as early as the second and third generations. This instability necessitated the development of a negotiated contractual agreement between preacher and parish.[35] American Congregationalists, while levying taxes for the support of their churches, had nonetheless customarily treated ministerial salaries as a matter to be decided between the particular minister and his congregation. As a result, financial quarrels had often played a large role in determining a clergyman's stay in a given place. While Joseph Bellamy refused to leave his small Connecticut parish for a much more prestigious and better-paid post in New York City, Jonathan Edwards broke with his Stockbridge congregation partly because they refused to raise his salary.[36] Some fifty years later at the turn of the nineteenth century, Lyman Beecher, always a fervent supporter of a settled ministry, made the first of three moves, each dictated by his need for more money than his parishioners felt they could offer him. Moreover, the controversy over ministerial tenure in New England officially began in 1770, decades before disestablishment, when the Congregational Church of Boston discharged Reverend Cross, an elderly pastor apparently too devoted to alcohol, over the protests of all the clerical councils consulted. The case was to be one of many.

Yet economic insecurity was undoubtedly an increasingly pressing reality for clergymen in the post-disestablishment years. Ministerial mobility accelerated with frightening rapidity. The more transient second-generation seventeenth-century pastor was likely to move only once.[37] One hundred years later his eighteenth-century descendant would move with only slightly more frequency; within the next sixty years, however, his nineteenth-century heir would move twice every decade. Daniel Calhoun has recently shown that the average tenure of a minister in New Hampshire in 1790 was thirty years, in 1804 twenty-five years, and in the late 1830s a mere four to eight years.[38] While no comparable study has been done of ministerial mobility in other northeastern states, non-statistical evidence suggests that the findings would be similar. *The Christian Examiner*, a monthly Unitarian periodical begun in 1813 and centered in Boston, ran a regular column in the pre–Civil War decades reporting all known recent moves among its clergy; the editor came habitually to prefix an apology for the large numbers involved. With sadness but with strikingly little sense of surprise, the Unitarian Sylvester Judd (1813–53) noted in 1851 that there was not one minister currently installed in Augusta, Maine, who had been there when he arrived eleven years before. Ezra Stiles Gannett (1801–71), a heroic Unitarian clergyman with strong Calvinist leanings, was an anomaly in Boston in 1870 for many reasons—not least because he had had a settled pastorate there for forty-five years.[39]

Moreover, the post-disestablishment minister tended not just to change place frequently, but increasingly to have no place, to be unattached to any particular pastorate. Preachers with short tenures in the formerly established sects were traditionally not officially "installed" in a church; this meant that they had not achieved full clerical status. In other words, Congregationalists, in direct contrast to the Methodists with their organizational stress on itinerant preachers, had traditionally discriminated against ministers who were unwilling or unable to make a long-term commitment to a congregation. The numbers of such uninstalled ministers, once insignificant, climbed sharply beginning in the 1820s, however; by 1865, the Congregationalists—as the Methodists had long done—formally and fully recognized as ministers all those who had been ordained, whether or not they had ever been locally attached. Leonard Bacon, a leading Yale theologian and preacher, announced the change on a ringing note of self-reliance: "The founders of the New England churches . . . did not see how to recognize any man as a minister of the gospel who was not an officer of the church. . . . We have outgrown that, and it is an inevitable necessity for us to outgrow it. . . . Our churches have grown to age, and can take care of themselves."[40] Necessity, however, was clearly as sharp a motive in this shift of Congregational policy as maturity.

Disestablishment intensified clerical impermanence for fairly evident reasons. The voluntary system meant that all sects were in open competition with each other. Each group was bound to do all in its power to attract converts, and with them, the necessary money to continue operations. The principle of competitive capitalism places a premium on novelty in ecclesiastical as in business affairs. Church members, increasingly alert to rapidly changing religious opinions, wanted to see such developments reflected in their pulpits; this might well mean a desire for a new and a young pastor. Then there were the so-called feeble churches, casualties of the voluntary system; their members, drastically decreased by the lure of competing sects, were often simply unable to support a minister. Clergymen were naturally eager to leave such poor and decimated parishes, and apparently did whenever they could.[41]

There may have occasionally been a rather unministerial desire to aggrandize at work in such moves, but the economic difficulties of many Protestant clergymen of the period seem unquestionable. Disestablishment promoted a kind of star system which gave much, perhaps too much, to a few, and very little to the many. An enormously popular preacher like the Congregationalist Henry Ward Beecher (1813–87) could make a comfortable fortune; yet, as one Universalist pastor complained, the average minister at mid-century earned about four hundred dollars a year, less than many manual laborers, not to speak of his fellow professionals, lawyers and doctors.[42] This figure is probably too low, but the fact remains that such complaints were common. The religious periodicals of the day were full of protests and rationalizations about low ministerial wages. Several wives of prominent clergymen published partial exposés (under pseudonyms) of the hardships of a pastor's life. In 1853, a reviewer for the *Christian Examiner* criticized *Sunnyside or the Country Minister's Wife;* in the reviewer's opinion, this depiction of an impoverished clerical family maintaining Christian cheer in the face of near-starvation was misleadingly optimistic.[43] Any chances to better such situations could hardly be ignored.

Furthermore, there was an apparent consensus among Protestant commentators on the ecclesiastical scene that, while the disestablished minister's wages, admittedly never high, had, if anything, decreased, expenses contingent upon his profession had increased. As J. H. Allen pointed out, the clerical mobility which disestablishment intensified was itself expensive in several ways. In past generations, the minister's official salary had been fleshed out by welcome unofficial offerings from his people with whom he often had a long-term and close understanding. Furthermore, he had other economic opportunities not available to his successors. The eighteenth-century pastor not infrequently farmed or at least tended an orchard, though stern souls like Hopkins and Emmons disapproved of such practices. Samuel Goodrich, the author of the popular "Peter Parley" books, was born the son of a Congregational minister in Ridgefield, Connecticut, in 1793. In writing his *Recollections* of his rural boyhood a half century later, he was at pains to emphasize the relative well-being of the clergy of the earlier period. Goodrich's father, who had no independent income, earned five hundred dollars a year, and left an estate of four thousand dollars to his eight children at his death. He farmed extensively, he hunted enthusiastically—a pursuit which "was not deemed a reproach at that time in a clergyman," Goodrich explains—and he mingled freely "with the people even in their labors and their pastimes."[44] Reverend Goodrich's successors, as Allen noted, were barred from such participation and such revenue by a changed public opinion which put tighter restrictions on ministerial activity. It was perhaps a mark of the now-transient clergyman's new isolation from his people and their concerns that it was no longer considered proper for him to pursue a secular vocation like theirs no matter how desperately he needed the extra funds. Besides, as Allen queried, what would be the point of planting fruit trees when the chances were good that the planter would be moving on to a different parish within five years?[45]

The new financial insecurity of the minister in the voluntary system went far beyond the loss of ecclesiastical taxes. Disestablishment, which could throw him psychologically on his congregation's mercy, might simultaneously remove him practically from its care. Furthermore, his particular prerogatives, his assumption of political and intellectual authority, had depended in large part on his now-vanished stability; his ascendency had been predicated on his permanent integration with his flock's communal life.

The Political Consequences

The seventeenth- and eighteenth-century minister had participated hotly in political debates.[46] On national occasions such as fast days, he had pronounced judgment on every aspect of current affairs. In earlier days, ministers like Jonathan Edwards and Samuel Hopkins could defy their congregations in the course of duty. Concomitant with the process of disestablishment, however, was an increasing tendency among ministers to substitute political rhetoric for genuine political leadership, to imitate rather than assert political authority. One historian has argued recently that the political parties as they emerged in New England during the early years of the republic, by nature and self-definition organized on a vote-getting or "voluntary" principle, were actually in rivalry with the religious sects, pre-empting many of the church's old communal functions and establishing perforce an operational model from which it could not escape.[47] The party leaders, in other words, usurped the role of actual societal leadership, leaving the ministers to borrow merely the trappings of the new political style. As early as 1796, Jeremy Belknap, a liberal clergyman from Massachusetts, bore witness to this competitive pressure in his uneasy observation that "there is a monopolizing spirit in some politicians which would exclude clergymen from all matters of state and government."[48] By 1825, a liberal writer for the Unitarian *Christian Examiner* revealed an almost complete assimilation of political creed and address on the part of ecclesiastical authority: "[the minister] is one of them [his people], and of them; and in no way or respect different from them but by their own wish and will. In short the form of our ecclesiastical like that of our civil institutions, is altogether republican. There is no more a divine right for ministers, coming down from ancient times, than there is a divine right for magistrates."[49] Style is as important as content here; this clergyman sounds suspiciously like a conciliatory politician addressing his constituents.

The northern disestablished clergyman was certainly in a politicized situation, but he was far from exerting political power. Strikingly, it was during the nineteenth century that the politically neutral term "denomination" replaced the more politically charged word "sect" to describe religious groups in America.[50] Any serious attempts on the part of seventeenth- and eighteenth-century ministers to interfere with government or business had always been liable to a rude check;[51] in the nineteenth century, such meddling met with a new and frank impatience. After the Revolution, several states moved to exclude clergymen from political office. Although this legislation proved impermanent, the attitude it presupposed did not. In 1825, a Senate committee, headed by future Vice President Richard Johnson of Kentucky, turned down a ministerial petition to bar mail-carrying on the Sabbath. The committee explained its refusal by reiterating the impropriety of the clergy's leaving their "proper sphere": political activity on the part of religious groups was "always dangerous"; they should trust to their "moral influence" alone to achieve their ends.[52] Two Baptist ministers, whose dissenting denomination had long crusaded for the segregation of church and state, helped Johnson to prepare his statement. More was at work here than the predictable desire of the young American republic to keep the various branches of power distinct. By 1854, when the New England clergy sent a memorial to Congress protesting the Kansas-Nebraska Act, politicians were infuriated less because the ministers were assuming rights which were not theirs than because they were speaking of matters on which they were pitifully uninformed. "I doubt," Stephen Douglas fulminated, "whether there is a body of men in America who combine so much profound ignorance on the question upon which they attempt to enlighten the senate as these same ... preachers."[53] The petitioning clergy were not debarred, Douglas implied, from intelligent expression of political opinions; they were incapable of it.

It is significant that this skirmish occurred over a piece of slavery legislation, for slavery provided the key test for the disestablished ministers' political power and integrity. Thrown into newly dependent economic relations with their society, clergymen were bound in the main to avoid any actual interference with the economic forces which ruled their culture. They could disguise their economic powerlessness from themselves and their society only if they never attempted seriously to interfere with the productive dynamics shaping their environment. For the northern clergyman, as for the southern one, this meant a fundamentally passive, if not favorable, attitude toward slavery, which the dominant northern merchants and businessmen had almost as much interest in protecting—Abolitionists were wont to point this out bitterly—as did the southern planters.[54] Yet public opinion in the North was for many reasons not totally in line with apparent economic interest; the disestablished northern minister, in contrast to his southern brother, had no sure guidelines, no self-evident and vulnerable dogmas or prejudices shared with his people and capable of transforming for him the demeaning pull of voluntarism into the more dignified propulsion of inner conviction.[55] He faced an unpleasant conflict between expediency and morality, and the result was a confusion painfully evident to observers then and now.

Most recent historians agree with the Abolitionists that the northern Protestant clergy, with important exceptions, notably failed to protest significantly the evil of slavery.[56] They also concur that the Methodists and Baptists evinced an earlier and more profound commitment to the anti-slavery cause than the other Protestant groups. Yet both of these denominations had large southern constituencies to lose by adherence to anti-slavery attitudes; and lose them they did.[57] The Congregationalists and the Unitarians, in contrast, as almost exclusively northern denominations, ran no such danger. One could argue that the established groups in the North, especially in the decades just prior to disestablishment, had become increasingly dependent on the economically conservative governing powers whose support was ever more vital to their embattled position; their original source of political power, a critical alliance with the status quo, became a source of its limitation in an increasingly diversified Northeast. The Methodists and Baptists, however, as outside groups with a less socially elite clientele, had formed different and more fluid political commitments: they had greater mobility for protest as well as for proselytizing.

Among non-evangelical ministers, Horace Bushnell (1802–76), a Congregationalist clergyman of Hartford, provides a case study of compromised opposition to slavery. In 1839, Bushnell formally opposed slavery; in 1850, he attacked the Fugitive Slave Law and urged northerners to "violate and spurn" it. In modern eyes, however, his attack on slavery reads suspiciously like a defense. To begin with, Bushnell was what we would call a racist; his views of the blacks were more or less identical with current white southern opinion. He considered them "not physiologically descended from the stock of Adam," "animals and nothing else." Like any southern apologist, he was sure that they could not survive the end of slavery, but would "dwindle toward extinction" without its protection. In fact, Bushnell— unlike a white southerner—could support emancipation precisely because, with the inevitable disappearance of the black people it entailed, Americans would "thenceforth" be "a homogenous universally free people." Bushnell's prejudices, unattractive as they are, were too common to be notable even in a man of his intellectual caliber. What is striking is the weakness and naivety of his grasp of the realities and facts of slavery. He insisted on couching the dilemma in personal rather than political or economic terms. The great evils of bondage were, in his mind, not the owning of human beings and the theft of their labor, but the "non-permission of the family state" among slaves and the neglect of their "moral or intellectual nature." Bushnell clearly felt more sympathetic toward the southern planters, men "involved in crime" but deserving "gentleness at the hands of the good," than he did toward the Abolitionists, "fiery ... agitators" who hurt their own cause. Clearly drawn to the slaveowners as somehow well-bred and apolitical men caught in an unpleasantly politicized situation, Bushnell advocated handling the matter as a problem in manners rather than as a confrontation between entrenched establishments; "one or two Christian gentlemen," sent as goodwill ambassadors to the South, would effect more, he suggested, than all the anti-slavery "associations." He refused to see the inevitability of conflict until it was upon him, not simply because, like any decent human being, he was opposed to unnecessary war, but also because the fact of war would demonstrate the utter inadequacy of his analysis.[58]

Of course one could name several prominent liberal ministers, such as Charles Follen and Theodore Parker, who were ardent Abolitionists, and one could certainly find numerous parallels to Bushnell's failure of perception and nerve among the clergymen of the evangelical Presbyterian-allied wing of the Congregationalists. Lyman Beecher's refusal to aid his former admirer Garrison is well known; even Charles Grandison Finney, who won away many of Beecher's followers through his more forthright commitment to Abolitionism, kept black and white students firmly segregated in the seminary he headed at Oberlin.[59] What distinguishes the liberal clergy from their more evangelically minded peers is less their cowardice on a complex and controversial issue than their de-emphasis of politics as a way of shaping and perceiving experience. Bushnell was opposed not just to Abolitionists in particular, but to "associations" in general. In contrast, Lyman Beecher, even while he denounced Garrison, was instrumental in forming several (very moderate) anti-slavery organizations to reflect his views. Beecher and his evangelical brethren, like Bushnell and his liberal peers, were most eager to support essentially private and personal causes—missions, prison reform, temperance—whose potential to hurt vested economic interests was real but limited.[60] Yet they did so through creating "moral societies" which then exerted considerable political pressure. The liberals, while hardly spurning such societies, tended to be less active in their formation and to play less conspicuous roles in the interlocking directorates which ran their operations. They depoliticized not just the content but the method of reform.

The differences between the two groups' political roles became clear in their responses to the Civil War. The evangelicals were anxious at least to simulate participation in democratic political life; the non-evangelicals were hesitant, doubtful both of themselves and the political life itself. For the more militantly evangelical northern Protestant denominations, the war offered an opportunity to confuse nationalist goals with the rather simplified millennial expectations their activist societies had been designed to nourish. In a sense, the evangelicals had kept themselves in training for political life through their voluntary organizations; they were more than prepared to make mileage out of the national struggle when it materialized. Their uncompromising and often mindless attack on the South during the war years signified that they had been at some level waiting for a polarized situation comparable to the one which had sustained the southern clergy for a generation or two; if they could not offer genuine criticism on an ambiguous political scene, they were more than capable, once sides were chosen, of hoorahing so vociferously as to appear protagonists rather than spectators. The liberal groups by 1860 had committed themselves too deeply to various forms of personalism and pacifism to make this kind of unanimous enthusiasm viable.[61] It was hardly altogether to their discredit that they refused to see the evangelical enthusiasm which could degenerate into moral coercion and jingoism as an adequate expression of political power or as a worthy substitute for it; yet it was essential to their dilemma that they could find no alternative.

The Intellectual Consequences

The liberal non-evangelical clergyman clearly faced special difficulties which confronted his evangelical peer with less urgency. Not least of these, and closely connected with his political dilemma, was the problem of his intellectual leadership in his community. In the period from 1820 to 1875, his parishioners first found those sources of stimulation and opinion which provide the average middle-class American today with his or her intellectual sustenance, such as it is. Unlike the southern Protestant congregation, which had its own reasons for skepticism—if not dislike—toward the fresh thinking and speaking brought by the burgeoning press and spreading lecture system to its doors, the northern congregation was, within its own terms, open and responsive to intellectual developments in the broader culture. Competition with new forms of public address and persuasion—the lending libraries, the lyceum lecture series, the periodicals, each relatively unknown in the eighteenth century but all-pervasive by the middle of the nineteenth—complicated and accelerated the process of disestablishment for northern ministers. As many of them were well aware, their audiences were both better educated and more difficult to please than those men and women who had gathered twice on Sunday a few generations earlier to get their weekly, and only, contact with literature, lectures, and, often, each other.[62]

Since the adherent of a revivalistic sect was likely to be and to remain less educated and less socially prominent than his non-revival-oriented counterpart, his minister did not confront the same challenge. Methodism and Baptism, both intensely evangelical sects, had hardly made their tremendous gains by converting Boston's Brahmins. Their success, as I have already suggested, was determined by the non-intellectual methods they evolved to meet the needs of a decidedly non-intellectual immigrant and frontier population. The violence of the revivals for which they were famous matched the violence of the life of those who were converted under their influence. At least until mid-century, the Methodists found little use for the arduous training and intellectual achievement the Congregationalists demanded of their ministry.[63] Peter Cartwright (1785–1872), popularly known as "the Methodist bulldog" and one of the most powerful of the early itinerant Methodist preachers, had nothing but scorn for the complex requirements of the older denominations: "illiterate Methodist preachers set the world on fire," he boasted, "while they were lighting their matches!" In his *Autobiography*, Cartwright tells many anecdotes of ineffectual and effeminate eastern ministers sent to evangelize out West with no weapon but overextensive book-learning. One of "these little home-manufactured fellows" was unlucky enough to share a service with Cartwright. The newcomer tried to read a sermon to the rather tough congregation, but, as Cartwright tells it, "the frame building we were worshipping in was not plastered . . . the wind blew hard," the candles flickered, and he could barely see the pages before him. Cartwright of course took over and preached a vigorous, searching, and successful sermon without notes. When the "hot house reader" was sent into the congregation to exhort the mourners, he did little better. His timid fear of the violent emotion of an all-out conversion experience—"Be composed; be composed," he kept telling the struggling sinners, while Cartwright contramanded him: "pray on brothers; there's no compromise in hell or damnation"—left him swimming feebly against the tide of salvation. Finally the "little preacher" was picked up bodily by a man in the throes of conviction and rushed around the congregation accompanied by delighted hoots and calls. Once released, he disappeared ignominiously and forever.[64]

Of course well-bred non-evangelical easterners, secure on their own ground, could be as scornful of rivals as Cartwright was of competitors on his territory; they lavished uneasy disdain on revivalists who, in their opinion, confused an insensitive tasteless anti-intellectualism with charismatic religious authority. Lyman Beecher's experience in Boston provides a case in point. A Yale graduate, Beecher was a far cry from Cartwright; he was a moderate who disapproved of many of the "New Measures" introduced into revivalism by Charles Grandison Finney. Yet he was unmistakably rural in speech and manner, and frankly vehement in his emotions. Beecher arrived in 1826 in his usual intense and heated state of sincerity, ready to "kindle a fire in all their [the Unitarians'] churches around Boston."[65] He hoped that his own impassioned, electric style of ratiocination would attract the liberal intellectuals of the hub-city, men who patronized and dominated the select and genteel literary and social clubs which were Boston's pride.[66]

Horace Mann, the great Massachusetts educator and a Unitarian of the most cultured, if reform-minded, variety, had heard Beecher preach in Litchfield, Connecticut, in 1822 and had written his impressions to a friend. Mann could hardly deny Beecher's fabled eloquence, but he clearly found the older man bigoted, provincial, even primitive:

> Dr. Beecher ... published ... a dolorous tale about the heathenish condition of the people of the U. States [*sic*], six sevenths of whom were, according to him, sitting in the ... shadow of death because ... they had not *hopkinsian* ... ministers to dispense the light of the Calvinist creed. ... I never heard such a sermon in my life. ... It produced as great an effect upon my feelings as it would have to have heard a great tragedy well performed at a theatre! *No more upon my belief*; for belief belongs to the understanding and should not be biased by hopes and fears.[67]

Mann was not alone in his response; Boston Unitarians went to hear Beecher, as one of them later confessed with a touch of pride, "on the watch for the amusing or the ludicrous."[68] In 1832 Beecher left Boston and its "fastidious" Brahmins to work out their own salvation; he was off to save the West from Catholicism.

The Unitarian or non-evangelical Congregational minister, however, facing the same audience Beecher confronted in Boston, was not always more comfortable. Their tastes and predilections were presumably his own, but this did not mean he automatically believed them adequate material for spiritual sustenance. Both minister and congregation were likely to be refined and highly literate. Cartwright stressed the foolish eastern novice's over-devotion to the written page; Catharine, Lyman Beecher's daughter, in explaining to Finney what made Boston's Unitarians so impervious to Beecher's brilliance, described them as "literary":[69] they oriented themselves through reading, through study, through conversation. Catharine Maria Sedgwick (1789–1867), a popular and fervently Unitarian authoress of the day, spent much time in Boston in the 1820s; her diaries reveal an earnestness of communal talk and intellectual pursuit that makes the Unitarian circle of Boston intelligentsia—the Channings, the Peabodys, and the Follens, to name Miss Sedgwick's special friends—sound like an extension of a Harvard Divinity School seminar.[70] Channing's parishioners, like Bushnell's in Hartford,[71] were people who expected less to be converted than to be socialized into religious awareness—no matter how superficially or crudely in many instances—by polite literature. Even their self-consciously limited emotional susceptibilities had a literary dimension: they did not expect or perhaps want their pastor to elicit from them a response more vehement than a book could create.

Living as he did in a country whose whole history was, as one foreign visitor noted, "the history of revivals,"[72] the liberal minister occasionally had trouble convincing himself that the relatively subdued interaction between himself and his congregation constituted genuine religious instruction; the techniques of Cartwright or Beecher could be ridiculed, but they nonetheless represented the only religious experience which an overwhelming majority of Protestant Americans accepted as authentic. Non-evangelical Congregationalists like Bushnell frequently expressed an intense desire to witness more passion in their hearers. There was hardly a single Unitarian divine of any prominence in the first half of the nineteenth century who did not privately or publicly express the fear that the Unitarian laity were, as their opponents often claimed, "cold," over-intellectualized, bookish, lacking in religious fervor. Nor did the liberal minister escape a similar charge. William Ellery Channing was troubled by the problem of "languor and insensibility" in his denomination;[73] other observers were troubled by the coldness they perceived in Channing himself. The acknowledged leader of American Unitarianism, despite his immense and apparently effortless pulpit eloquence, was capable of taking notes during an informal conversation—on his own words.[74]

Henry Ware, Jr. (1794–1843), born of a Unitarian family and later to become a professor at Harvard's liberal Divinity School, as a young man found Channing more than sufficiently persuasive, but he worried about the attitude of his fellow Harvard candidates for the ministry. "Our Cambridge students ... study religion too much as a science," he wrote his father in 1812. They "regard it as a subject to be reasoned upon ... and appear almost to forget that it is something to be felt." Even while Ware found revivals of the Finneyite variety "outrageous and vulgar fanaticism," incredible displays of "indecorum, ... profanity and blasphemy,"[75] he was troubled by the fact that he as a Unitarian minister inevitably played on a smaller emotional keyboard than the one on which a revivalist operated. He might achieve infinitely more subtle variations, but he was undeniably forgoing certain large and powerful effects. In disavowing violent manipulation of his parishioners' "hopes and fears," he renounced the use of terror and the longing for grandiosity, profoundly rich religious resources.

Using trauma as a basis for religious conviction can produce every kind of polarization.[76] Yet no one can dispute the efficacy of the nineteenth-century revivalist preachers in catching the ear and opening the purse of middle-class Protestant America. To say they were tapping non-religious anxieties and energies is a way of saying that they were aggressively but surely in touch with their times. And whatever the case with their motives, their energy was genuine. Here is Lyman Beecher describing the start of his first revival at East Hampton, Long Island, in 1807:

For some time there was no effect to anything I could do. I could not write any sermons that would take hold. Finally I resolved that I would preach the doctrine of Election. I knew what that doctrine was and what it would do.... My object was to preach cut and thrust, hip and thigh, and not to ease off. I had been working a good part of a year with my heart burning, and they feeling nothing. Now I took hold without mittens....

[He preached his sermon on Election on December 14, 1807.] At last I had found something that took hold. There was not an eye in the whole church but what glistened like cold stars of a summer's night....

I went home expecting; and word was sent up from the Springs that the Lord had come down the previous Sunday and that a meeting was appointed for Tuesday evening, and that I must not disappoint them. I went and preached. I saw one young man with his head down. I wanted to know if it was an arrow of the Almighty. I came along after sermon, and laid my hand upon his head. He lifted up his face, his eyes all full of tears; I saw it was God. Then I went to the Northwest and the Lord was there; then to Ammigansett, and the Lord was there; and the flood was rolling all around. Oh what a time that was![77]

Even if the non-evangelical clergyman was right in rejecting this kind of energy as a perversion of genuine intellectual concern, the crucial question remained here as in the political sphere: what did he have to put in its place?[78] Driven by the new sophistication of his audience and the rapid development of highly specialized fields of knowledge, he was forced to abandon the claim to terrain which his predecessors had been wont to regard as their backyard. His ministerial ancestors had seen themselves as intellectual experts: he had become the gifted amateur. He might enter areas his forebears would have neglected or banned—William Ware, Henry Ware's sensitive brother, wrote historical novels when he was not somewhat ineptly, if conscientiously, tending his New York City flock, and Orville Dewey patronized painting and sculpture; but both men were essentially outsiders in the field of art as Jonathan Edwards was decidedly not in the world of secular philosophy. The nineteenth-century liberal clergyman, checked intellectually, was simultaneously accepting, even courting, a kind of freeze on the emotional expenditure permissible in his flock and in himself.

The equally non-evangelical Episcopalian rector, addressing an equally educated, affluent, and reserved congregation, seemed to face a similar situation, and face it with success. It is no accident that the first church Unitarians captured in Boston was the Episcopalian King's Chapel; the two groups kept up a complex process of rivalry and imitation throughout the nineteenth century.[79] But the rector's position was in key respects different from that of his Unitarian or Congregational peer. The Episcopalians had always filled a special, discrete, and separate role. Their authoritarian ecclesiastical structure and ritualized worship might be construed as a threat to the American Way, but the denomination to which they adhered had not originated historically in this country as a protest-sect.[80] In contrast, the beliefs to which the liberal Congregationalist or Unitarian minister subscribed had developed in the course of opposing and redefining the New England Creed. By definition, the Unitarian clergy had fewer traditions of their own to fall back on. Unitarianism was criticized by its enemies precisely on the grounds that it was primarily negative in its animus, that it had nothing to substitute for the creed it defied except a half-hearted, literary piety and a weak imitation of Episcopalian ceremony.

The Personal "Sphere"

The central dilemma of the non-evangelical clergymen was that of increasingly limited resources. The introduction of the voluntary system had compelled the ministers of the Protestant groups most affected to disavow in their different fashions any public pretension to tangible "power" in favor of the claim of invisible "influence."[81] None of them had relinquished their former authority more entirely, however, than the non-evangelical clergyman. Fearful of openly challenging the economic forces of his society, compelled by unbeatable competition to abandon his former monopoly on culture, both scornful and afraid of the revivalistic reliance on fear and agitation, attracted but cautious before the lure of Anglican ritual, he was under a sometimes claustrophobic pressure from his fastidious and not always fervent congregation to be better trained, more skillful, and more versatile, while presenting a smaller number of topics and evoking a slighter intensity of feeling; he was asked to be more agile in an ever-shrinking space. One Maine clergyman, discussing "the magnitude of the ministerial work" in 1845, found the job's most painful demand to be on the sensibilities: it would be impossible, he wrote, to overestimate the tax exacted on the minister's "sympathies." In fact, "his heart must be a perfect barometer rising and falling according to the state of the atmosphere."[82] This metaphor suggests an extreme subjectivity which lacks even the merit of independence. The minister described here is doomed to perpetual activity within a fundamentally passive role; he is locked into an exhausting process of instantaneous responsiveness with no real sources of replenishment.

Not surprisingly, it sometimes seemed to interested observers that the non-evangelical clergyman's subject matter was disappearing, thinning out into literary platitudes and trivialized piety. There were innumerable pleas in the reviews and magazines of the liberal sects for greater force, vigor, and variety from their ministers. One writer in the *Christian Examiner* in 1840 complained that the real weakness of the clergy was the "sameness" and dullness of their sermons.[83] But monotony seemed inevitable when options were so limited. For the liberal minister was driven back on his own reactions, on himself, precisely at a time when, through an obvious vicious circle, his self-confidence was at its lowest. He was forced to professionalize the personal simply because he had lost any solid impersonal basis for his authority.

The liberal clergy gave clear signs of the anxiety produced by their increasing sense of self-immersion and cultural isolation. Nervous that their society was deserting them, they noted uneasily the increasing abandonment of their profession by the "best" young men.[84] Enrollment in Harvard's Unitarian-dominated and once-controversial Divinity School was low, sometimes shockingly so, during the second half of the century; those who did go were often not of the social caste that had graced its halls in earlier days.[85] Andover Seminary, once the school for Calvinists, at mid-century under the innovative liberal influences of Austin Phelps (1820–90) and E. A. Park, did a bit better; but half-jesting stories about a mythological student dedicated to the ministry by an uncle who found him "fit for nothing else" and so half-witted that he listed Benedict Arnold as one of the great Protestant reformers revealed that Andover had its dunces and its doubts.[86] Suspicion that American society was not consecrating its most talented sons to the ministry was exceeded by a powerful if less rational fear that it was ignoring, perhaps persecuting, those ministers it already possessed. Sentimentalized yet clearly felt accounts of ministerial destitution abound in the liberal religious press of the day. One clerical sob-brother painted a doleful picture of a small-town pastor, ill-paid, unheeded, eating his soul out in "agony," driven by necessity to teach school: "at last he occupies an un-minded grave in his own secluded churchyard, or he lives until another generation knows him not, knows nothing of the once glowing preacher in the old and jaded schoolmaster."[87]

This is soap opera, but it expresses a fear of cultural excision, a terror of living burial, which has its own very real historical significance. It is hardly accidental that soap opera, an increasing specialty of nineteenth-century liberal Protestantism, is a phenomenon which we associate with the special needs of feminine subculture. Cut off at every point from his masculine heritage, whether economic, political, or intellectual, the liberal minister was pushed into a position increasingly resembling the evolving feminine one. Who else was barred with him from the larger world of masculine concerns, who else was confined with him to a claustrophobic private world of over-responsive sensibility, who else but the American lady? Foreign observers in America were quick to draw the comparison between the situation and interests of clergymen and those of women. Harriet Martineau reported that the commercial classes treated the clergy disdainfully as powerless, ill-informed "people halfway between men and women."[88] Alexis de Tocqueville, who took a more optimistic view of the status of women and ministers in the New World, noted in both cases, however, that they carried authority only within their largely domestic and personal "spheres"; out of these "spheres," de Tocqueville noted, both were careful never to trespass.[89] Little wonder that so many non-evangelical clergymen between 1820 and 1875 expressed a terror of being constantly uprooted, then allowed to take even slighter hold in ever-poorer soil. Orville Dewey's trauma in Washington, D.C., comes into clearer focus. The liberal minister was losing his role among his society's leaders; his place was increasingly in the Sunday School, the parlor, and the library, among women and those who flattered and resembled them.

2

FEMININE
DISESTABLISHMENT

Feminine Hopes and Fears

Throughout the ante-bellum and Civil War period, liberal ministers were preoccupied with establishing and fixing the correct feminine role; equally important, they defined it in terms which strongly suggested clerical aspirations and anxieties. Horace Bushnell, writing to his young daughter in 1845, summed up the womanly ideal in one short statement: "a woman should be a Christian." A woman is by nature, he continued, amplifying on his theme, one "whose character can be finished only by assimilation to God."[1] Another minister, writing on the same subject a decade earlier in a popular Congregationalist magazine, had put the matter even more bluntly to his feminine readers: "religion is far more necessary to you than self-sufficient men. In you it would be not only *criminal*, but *impolitic* to neglect it." Your importance to society, the writer went on to warn, lies solely in your moral elevation.[2] Like the clergymen newly segregated in a strictly ecclesiastical realm, the women addressed by Bushnell and his Congregational contemporary are both flattered and threatened: stay within your proper confines, and you will be worshiped, their self-appointed mentors assure them; step outside and you will cease to exist. And feminine faith, like clerical piety, was to be of a peculiarly unassertive and retiring kind. Bushnell instructed his daughter to have no needs, almost no character of her own: as a woman, she should be "above all ... unselfish." "We demand," he explained, with a euphemistic flourish, "that she shall seem to have alighted here for the world's comfort and blessing ... all the ways of selfishness are specially at variance with her beautiful errand."[3] Whether or not Bushnell was aware of it, the part he sketches for the woman is, like that of the liberal clergyman, claustrophobically cramped, if sacred. She should prompt others rather than assert herself; she is to persuade passively by personal example.

The necessary, almost punitive connection between femininity and a certain kind of Christianity, while a favorite theme among liberal ministers, was a commonplace of the day, and one endorsed as heavily by women as by men. Sarah Hale (1788–1879), the editor of *Godey's Lady's Book* and the most important arbiter of feminine opinion of her day, frequently reprinted clerical injunctions to women with obvious approval. The willingness of literary-minded women like Hale and her readers to court such self-evaluation and self-restriction suggests that they were engaged in a struggle for identity and esteem as real and complex as the one which absorbed the liberal ministry in the same period. To document this feminine crisis in self-confidence, one cannot turn to direct or indirect statements of professional anxiety such as abound among clerical writers, for women of course had no comparable official profession. Yet many of them, the self-designated spokeswomen for the cautious among their discontented middle-class sisters, were intensely absorbed in trying to manufacture and defend a kind of pseudo-profession through the enunciation of a theory of female "influence." Not the most admirable among the self-aware American women of the mid-nineteenth century, they, like the liberal ministers among the clergy, are in a real sense the most significant historically. They were vastly more numerous than their overtly reformist feminine peers; Sarah Hale of *Godey's Lady's Book* always commanded more adherents than Elizabeth Cady Stanton, the suffrage leader. Moreover, the arguments Hale and others formulated, most notably the theory of "influence," were adopted not only by those who thought like them, but, eventually, by the suffragists and other avowed feminists.[4] Theirs was to be a winning strategy, although its victories were hollow. This is not to suggest that Hale and her followers did not advocate important reforms; they did, particularly in the critical area of women's education. I am admittedly downplaying such reform activities here and elsewhere because they were contained within traditional, if strategically rephrased, notions of the feminine role. Hale and her supporters pursued partially feminist goals by largely anti-feminist means; genuine success was hardly possible. Yet their caution was evidence not only of their short-term shrewdness, but of their very justifiable anxiety. At mid-century, articulate northeastern women, like liberal ministers, were profoundly concerned about what viable place they might find in their society.

As liberal ministers increasingly de-emphasized the traditional trademarks and actual facts of their calling, the feminine promulgators of the doctrine of "influence" habitually obscured women's biological and economic function; they displaced and relocated themselves by defining femininity always in terms of its effects, never in terms of its causes. Take, for example, this ecstatic panegyric on the well-bred female from the *Ladies' Magazine* in 1830:

> See, she sits, she walks, she speaks, she looks—unutterable things! Inspiration springs up in her very paths—it follows her foot-steps. A halo of glory encircles her, and illumines her whole orbit. With her, man not only feels safe but is actually renovated. For he approaches her with an awe, a reverence, and an affection which before he knew not he possessed.[5]

This apparent paean of self-love is actually a model of self-evasion; the dread of invisibility we saw at work in Orville Dewey inflates and mystifies the presented image. This is hardly an assertion of a full feminine ideal; physicality itself is painfully absent. The constant reiteration of feminine "purity" among the proponents of influence was not only a denial of patriarchal values, but of matriarchal ones. Reading this passage from the *Ladies' Magazine*, we have no idea of what this woman, or womanly ideal, is, except as something to be perceived and reacted to; she has no body and no personality. The opening sentence reads today like an advertisement for a versatile doll. The first word, and the key to the whole statement, is "See": look at her, believe in her, the writer is unconsciously urging, so she can exist. She is of value because she is able to work a kind of religious transformation in man; she represents nothing finally but a state of susceptibility to very imprecisely conceived spiritual values.

Dependent as this feminine creature is on masculine responses for her very being, she can as easily be man's victim as his "inspiration." Much of the contemporary writing on the stereotypic feminine figure suggests that, if woman precipitates and represents sensibility, she must inevitably prove this precisely by her sensitivity to pain. The relation between toiling pastor and indifferent flock, a frequent subject in the clerical fiction of the day, was echoed by the equally prevalent concern in feminine literature with the necessary but tortuous bond between wife and husband, mother and child. As one contributor to the *Ladies' Magazine* explained in 1836, a woman's husband may cease to love her, and she will be called to bear his neglect "in silence," only striving to win him back "by increased anxiety to please." Again, a child may fall ill, and she will, in an abandon of irrational but instinctive self-sacrifice, nearly kill herself in efforts to obviate its least pang of discomfort: "if but a slight cloud passes over its countenance, if but a disturbed motion gives evidence of suffering, she watches anxiously while others sleep, to soothe if possible, its slightest pain."[6]

Feminine suffering in the popular writing of the period could take distinctly more violent and active forms, ones which raised painful questions about its redemptive value. Indeed, paranoid terror that vulnerability would provide provocation only for brutality was as intense among women writing about their position as among clergymen discussing theirs. The temperance cause in which clergymen and women worked side by side provides a good example; it was often promoted as a covert crusade to salvage not the alcoholic but the woman at his mercy. The drunkard, usually a male, destroys by his debauches himself and the saintly wife, mother, daughter, or sister who loves him and would draw him from the saloon to the fireside. His defiant drinking serves as a reminder of the limits of female "influence"; he is willing to kill himself in order to attack its nearest representative.

Lydia Huntley Sigourney (1791–1865), once famous as the "sweet singer of Hartford," author of countless popular and pious tales and poems in the pre–Civil War era, published a collection of temperance stories in 1848 fittingly entitled *Water Drops*. Their message is overwhelmingly that man's brutality has no function but the torture of woman. In "The Widow and Her Son," the inebriate in question is a fatherless boy. When his devout mother pleads with him to mend his ways, he "revolt[s]." The hurt mother laboriously enunciates Sigourney's theme: "He despised my woman's voice, my motherly love." When the reprobate's pure sister touchingly admonishes him to reform, he spurns her advice as nothing but a veiled power play: "Always to be working under your orders, I suppose. No doubt that would be quite pleasing. All you women like to rule when you can."[7] He takes his revenge by choosing the totally masculine career of a sailor. For the rebellious male, the whole world can function as a refuge from feminine authority. Sigourney's most famous temperance tale, "The Intemperate," makes the same point. It opens with a description of a family trudging on the weary road from a New England farm to a new home in Ohio. We know at once that all is not well, for the wife is staggering along under the burden of her two children while her spouse is reeling under a quite different load. The drunkard eventually murders his delicate son, his wife's special favorite. His motivation for this and other lesser enormities is significant, if predictable: he strove to distress his wife and then *"visited her sensibilities upon her as sins."*[8] The happy ending is tellingly reserved for the real sufferer of the story; the "intemperate's" wife, finally freed by her husband's death, returns to the New England homestead from which he has uprooted her.

Even the determinedly moderate Sarah Hale, chief exponent of the doctrine of the feminine sphere, could occasionally describe the relation between the sexes in terms whose fierce extremism initially leaves a modern reader puzzled and disoriented: "Man the murderer and woman the mourner," "a fiend and an angel."[9] In 1834, when a Boston mob destroyed the Roman Catholic Ursuline convent, Hale found in their action not the excesses of bigotry but rather an extreme disrespect for women: "it is a cruelty, a wrong . . . to women," she exclaimed, "at which every female heart must revolt."[10] Hale was intensely sympathetic to all the overtly oppressed members of her sex: Mormon women compelled by the iniquitous system of polygamy to lead lives of sensual indulgence, Asian women forced into demeaning servitude in a society which had no notion of feminine worth, American wives committed to insane asylums by husbands eager to escape the grim example of their superiority.[11] Hale was usually supremely politic in her writings about male-female relations, but she was so precisely because she subscribed to a conspiracy view of history: women must engineer their well-being in a world dominated by a sex essentially hostile to it.

Whether she was being tactful or outspoken, hopeful or horrified, Hale, like the authors of the temperance tales, defined woman as the register of man's capacity for personal experience. The middle-class woman's fate in nineteenth-century America—rather like the minister's—depended in this view on the willingness and ability of her male peers, increasingly absorbed in the taks of settlement and competition, to recognize the values which their activities apparently denied. The well-bred woman was either essential or superannuated, a savior or a creature destined to speedy extinction. The narcissism at work in the very extremism of such alternatives could hardly disguise the fear which gave it birth.

The End of "Mother Power"

By the middle of the nineteenth century the northeastern well-bred woman was "disestablished" as surely as her clerical peers, although her disestablishment was hardly official. J. H. Allen, in discussing the effects of voluntarism in 1868, lamented that the church, which had once been the "meeting house" of the town, the center for the vital community activities of worship, education, and business, was now merely a house of prayer, and place for words, not deeds.[12] The middle-class northern woman had seen a similar transformation occur in her home: formerly an important part of a communal productive process under her direction, it had become a place where her children stayed before they began to work and where her husband rested after the strain of labor. Once her family had looked to her quite literally to clothe and feed them; now they expected a complex blend of nurture and escape from her "voluntary" care.

The difficulties of discussing feminine disestablishment, vital as I believe it to be to the understanding of nineteenth-century American culture, are enormous. First of all, the disestablishment of middle-class women was a very haphazard and proximate process, compared to the end of state-supported religion. No legislative acts banned home industries in early nineteenth-century New England, no feminine pressure groups lobbied for and against the change. Furthermore, the women affected, unlike the clergy, were not usually highly educated societal leaders accustomed to voicing and writing down their opinions. Few even of those who must have experienced or witnessed in their lifetimes the shifting status of the matron of the house from producer to consumer left detailed accounts of the transition. Unlike their clerical contemporaries, they had no awareness that their lives or their ideas were history: they were correspondingly careless of preserving their identities. As so often where women are concerned, sentiment was wanted, not facts. Literally hundreds of nostalgic memoirs were penned in the Civil War period about vanished rural ways, old New England farmsteads, and once-abundant country Thanksgivings presided over by all-capable and generically hospitable housekeepers; such reminiscences, while valuable as a response to cultural change, hardly give us a trustworthy account of it. Even today there is little accumulated research to depend on;[13] accounts and conclusions about the economic changes in the northeastern woman's life in the first half of the nineteenth century are inevitably tentative.

One must start by stressing that feminine "disestablishment" hardly affected all women in all parts of the United States. For the majority of American women living between 1800 and 1865, there was probably no economic dislocation and no concomitant "disestablishment" process comparable to that affecting the northern middle-class woman. For the countless girls who moved from a life of labor on a farm to a life of labor in a factory, for the feminine immigrants who came in increasing numbers straight from a ship to a northern sweatshop or a midwestern frontier, for the thousands of enslaved black women who served King Cotton, disestablishment clearly had little or no meaning. The southern white woman, who belonged technically in the same socio-economic category with her disestablished northeastern counterpart, found herself in many respects in a quite different situation during this period. Usually based on a farm or a plantation, the southern "lady" was still performing an important function. Responsible for the affairs of a complex household often including a number of slaves, she was economically essential to the agrarian system of the South. Slavery gave her, as it gave the southern minister, an important role which, while limiting her option and motivation for revolt, increased her opportunity for strategically placed support. It was not until after the Civil War that she had to deal with the problems arising from a modernizing urbanizing economy which had begun to beset her northern sister several generations before.[14]

In 1800, by any reckoning, America, North as well as South, was an agricultural nation. Only six percent of its population of five million lived in towns of 2,500 or more; only New York and Philadelphia could boast over 50,000 inhabitants. The common productive unit was the rural household; the processing and preserving of food, candlemaking, soapmaking, spinning, weaving, shoemaking, quilting, rugmaking, and many other activities all took place on domestic premises. Although extra income might be sought through the sale of produce and goods, such households were more or less self-sufficient. Buying and selling, when it occurred, was often conducted on a barter basis.[15] The system of household industry prevalent in the Northeast through the early decades of the nineteenth century meant that the majority of women in the area during that time were actively engaged in the productive activities of feeding, clothing, and equipping the nation.[16] Nowhere was their importance clearer than in the domestic manufacture of woolen goods, most notably "homespun," a coarse all-wool and usually undyed fabric from which most of the clothing worn in the Northeast was made.[17] The census of 1810 estimated that twenty-four of every twenty-five yards of wool produced in the United States was of domestic origin; during the Revolution and the War of 1812, when imported cloth was hard to come by, homespun was pushed on patriotic grounds and individual households were encouraged by bounties to prepare extra cloth for public sale.[18] Within the household, adult men traditionally handled certain difficult parts of the manufacture of cloth, but women were indispensable in spinning the wool and in many other stages of its production. Moreover, although from colonial days on professional workers had supplemented household procedures with skilled techniques, they were entirely dependent on the domestic industry. When the first labor-saving devices, like the carding machine and the spinning jenny, were patented at the turn of the nineteenth century, they were intended for and absorbed by household use.[19]

By 1830, the picture in the North was very different. Although the population was still over five-sixths rural and exports consisted largely of farm products, the industrial revolution, as modern economic historians tend to agree, was under way.[20] Commercial farming replaced subsistence farming; self-sufficiency was giving way to specialization. The urban population was growing faster than the population of the country as a whole. The War of 1812 and the embargoes, blockades, and tariffs which accompanied and succeeded it gave support to America's manufactures. When Jefferson, once the staunch defender of agrarian life, explained in 1816 that "experience has taught me . . . manufactures are now as necessary to our independence as to our comfort," political endorsement of the economic shift was complete.[21] Between 1820 and 1840 the number of people engaged in manufactures increased 127 percent, while those occupied in agriculture increased only 79 percent. Massachusetts and New York industrialized soonest. In 1836, a committee of the Massachusetts legislature acknowledged, although with little pleasure, that its inhabitants were "becoming essentially a manufacturing people."[22] By 1840, there were 1,200 cotton factories in the United States, two-thirds of them in New England. The wool industry, now subject to competition with cotton, had changed dramatically. Although one observer of the economic scene in 1839 estimated that domestic manufacture still accounted for as much cloth as factory production in America as a whole, the household was clearly losing out to the factory, especially in the Northeast.[23] Homespun had owed its success to primitive technological conditions and the absence of a real domestic market for more finished material. With the boom in inventions, the protection of the tariffs, and the opening of canals and railroads, the factories had within reach a low-priced woolen product and a market able and eager to buy it. By the time of the Civil War, homespun was common only in certain undeveloped parts of New England and in the western settlements. Middle-class women in the Northeast after 1830 were far more interested in the purchase of clothing than the making of cloth.

It is interesting to note that this economic shift was concomitant with a decided alteration in woman's position in society. Women lost a significant number of their legal privileges, among them the right to vote.[24] Despite their long record as expert midwives, they were barred from a newly defined and restricted medical profession. They vanished more or less entirely from a number of occupations; they appeared less frequently in public records as printers, blacksmiths, arms-makers, or proprietors of small business concerns. To put it simply and perhaps simplistically, the independent woman with a mind and a life of her own slowly ceased to be considered of high value. Widows provide a good index of this change in opinion. Since a widow is by definition a woman suddenly deprived of male support, the opportunities her culture affords her, the attitude it adopts toward her, are especially revealing of its stance toward women more generally. In colonial New England, a widow could be a powerful force in her community. "Widows" constituted a special order in the Protestant Church; even the tendency of the colonial mind to associate widowhood with witchcraft was a sign, if a negative one, of the presumed power of widows. A recent study of seventeenth-century Wethersfield, Connecticut, reveals that its widows actually tended to remarry less often and after greater intervals than its widowers; they apparently did so because they had greater options for full and busy single lives than did their male counterparts.[25] By the early nineteenth century, in contrast, widows were conventionally viewed as pitiful charity cases. Numerous organizations formed to relieve "widows and orphans"; stories turning on the pathos of the newly widowed bride or mother were popular.[26] There are no statistics available as yet on the rate of remarriage in the later period, but it seems highly unlikely they would reveal the same pattern of self-reliance which the study of Wethersfield highlighted. In common nineteenth-century conception, the widow waited for a man— a brother, a son, a new lover—to help her; any show of self-reliance was valuable chiefly as evidence of her worthiness of such aid. She had no communal tasks deemed appropriate to her widowed state; she was obligated to undertake nothing but the heavily self-involved business of mourning. The process of adjustment was seen as a private and psychological one. The widow had become a source of sentimentality; a woman without a man was an emblem of frailty and unproductivity.

Contemporary observers sensed and articulated a connection between the economic shift and the change in middle-class feminine status taking place in their society. In 1851, when Horace Bushnell came to Litchfield, Connecticut, to deliver an address in honor of the county's centennial, he testified that a major and complex upheaval had occurred since his own boyhood days on a nearby farm a half century earlier. By 1851, industrialization was a fact in Connecticut; between 1800 and 1850, manufactures had replaced shipping and agriculture as the state's chief source of wealth.[27] Bushnell's speech, however, was less a tribute to current progress than a lament for the "Puritan Arcadia" of the past. At the center of Bushnell's vision of the vanished era, which he tellingly entitles "The Age of Homespun," are the economically functional woman, the "frugal, faithful, pious housewife" spinning the clothes and linen of her family, and the organically productive household over which she presided: "[They were] harnessed, all together, into the producing process, young and old, male and female, from the boy that rode the plough-horse to the grandmother knitting under her spectacles. . . . The house was a factory on the farm; the farm a grower and producer for the house." The passing of the "Age of Homespun," in Bushnell's mind, has resulted in a "complete revolution of domestic life and social manners": a loss of self-reliance and social responsibility, the "severe" yet "sublime" virtues of the earlier day. Bushnell is aware that the "transition from mother and daughter power to water and steam power" is both so momentous and so final that "the very terms 'domestic manufacture' have quite lost their meaning." Domesticity itself is altered beyond recognition; women no longer marry to help their husbands get a living, but to help them spend their income.[28]

Bushnell's public words on the transformation of the socio-economic role of the New England woman are implemented by his private testimony, which, while more limited in scope, is more illuminating in its detail. His mother belonged to the old school, his wife to the new; he loved them both, but he loved and used them very differently. His mother, Dotha Bushnell, in her son's words, "had no advantages of wealth or family connection above the level of industrious respectability. Her field was in her family and there it was that she won her best honors." She possessed tremendous "physical endurance and tenacity" which enabled her to "bear severities of toil that would have reduced almost any other woman to the level of a drudge." To say that she was economically functional would be an understatement. She was, according to her son, economically indispensable:

> She was providing and training her six children, clothing her whole family in linens and woolens, spun, every thread, and made up in the house also to a great extent by herself. She had a farm-and-dairy charge to administer, also the farm workmen to board, and for five or six months in a year the workers, besides, of a homespun cloth-dressing shop. All this routine she kept moving in exact order and time, steady and clear as the astronomic year.... What mortal endurance could bear such a stress of burden! And yet she scarcely showed a look of damage.[29]

Mrs. Bushnell dedicated her son early to the ministry and was directly responsible for his final choice of a clerical career, but she never showed much overt religiosity; she trusted to the example of Christian habit rather than to devotional display to effect his conversion. She was reserved, even taciturn; it was her prudence, her industry, and her "tact" which her son found "sublime." She was "tender," "motherly," and "self-sacrificing," Bushnell notes, but her real greatness to his mind lay in her wisdom, her "wonderful insight and discretion."[30] As her son sees them, her strengths in spiritual and in secular matters were unmistakably at root economic ones. By his own account, Bushnell paid her the tribute one ideally only pays to genuinely factual experience: he took her word, more or less uncorrected and unaltered.

Bushnell's wife, Mary A. Thorp of Hartford, a descendant of the minister John Davenport and a woman of charm and education, in contrast seems less to have directed him where he should go so much as sustained him in his chosen course. Her role, as he at any rate liked to conceive it, was the nurturing one of affection, not the disciplinary one of authority. His mother was his leader, able to make him avoid error; his wife was to be his follower, instructing him as to his mistakes only by the pain they forced her to register. Insofar as she was to exert control over him, it was, as he once explained to her in a letter, to be as an "influence." She would be felt, but not heard: "[hers] is not an ambitious noisy power; it is silent, calm, persuasive, and often so deep as to have its hold deeper than consciousness itself.

... He loves her when he is too weary or too much bent on his objects to be conscious of his love.... She ministers and yet is seldom ministered unto."[31]

The causes for the difference in the roles played by Bushnell's mother and his wife are varied. Of course a man then (as now) expected to exert more authority over a spouse than a mother. Yet it is clear that Dotha Bushnell did not perform the same wifely duties for her husband that Mary Bushnell did for Horace. One remembers John Adams' remark on the stupidity of an English general during the American Revolution: "a smart wife would have put Howe in possession of Philadelphia a long time ago."[32] Adams clearly expected and got from his own intelligent and independent wife, Abigail Adams, what Bushnell looked for in his mother. In discussing the different functions of Dotha and Mary Bushnell, in other words, one must assume that the concept of wife has been itself the subject of change rather than a cause of change. It is also pertinent to argue, however, that the shift in identity between Dotha and Mary Bushnell was in part evidence of Bushnell's own social mobility. He married up. Even if Mary Thorp had lived in Litchfield a quarter or a half century earlier, she would not have been found spinning homespun; she would have lived in town, the protected and educated daughter of a man of local importance.

Yet Mary Thorp's self-definition as woman and as wife—and from the biographical information we have, it seems to have conformed fairly closely to her husband's image of her—was nonetheless dependent on the disappearance of women like Dotha Bushnell. The transformation in the feminine economic status did not mean that the same women turned from running the spinning wheel to playing the spinet; it involved, rather, a change in the concept of female labor which significantly altered the meaning of either occupation. When large numbers of respected and intelligent (if hardly upper-class) women like Dotha Bushnell were contributing by their work to their society's economic life, feminine labor, although unpaid, was necessarily judged essential, and women were inevitably defined, and allowed within limits to act, in essentially productive ways. When a dwindling proportion of the middle-class population engaged in farming and fewer farming families were involved in domestic production, when women increasingly either lived in relative ease tending the homes of their "productive" spouses or in relative discomfort working in newly established factories at low wages, female labor was devalued and the feminine identity was correspondingly reconceived. There was an enormous difference between the eighteenth-century matron tending her wheel and the nineteenth-century factory girl at her loom. The first was in a sense self-motivated, at the center of her productive unit; the second was the employee of others, a mere cog in a system of which she had little understanding.

It is important to be clear here. I do not wish to idealize the eighteenth-century middle-class woman's "productivity" or totally condemn the nineteenth-century middle-class woman's emerging, more leisured, consumer-oriented role; women in both centuries and in both capacities were engaged essentially, if in different ways, in service broadly defined—some of it, perhaps much of it, oppressive, some of it rewarding. The essential point is that feminine labor and its function in society were *visible* in the earlier period, and this visibility assured a minimal recognition, and a minimal degree of directness in the assessment of the feminine contribution. The mid-nineteenth-century middle-class "lady" I will be discussing was not necessarily as idle as her various critics and admirers on occasion painted her. She had many responsibilities; even servants, like the technological aid which succeeded them, could create as much work as they performed. It is rather that the lady's leisure, whether hypothetical or actual, was increasingly treated as the most interesting and significant thing about her; her function was obscured and intended to be so, and evaluations of her worth consequently tended to become exercises in indirection.

Eliza Farnham, a self-educated and active-minded writer from New York, had occasion to spend time in the late 1830s and early 1840s in the western states. As was customary in those days, she took advantage of her sojourn to publish an account which she called *Life in Prairie Land*. Despite the fairy-tale quality of her title, Farnham's book is actually the record of a confrontation between the new disestablished middle-class northeastern woman and the circumstances which had presumably shaped her grandmothers. As economic historians have noted,[33] the older methods of household production of commodities, particularly homespun, prevailed in the cruder western communities long after they had been discontinued in the more industrially developed East. This hardly meant, however, that the western woman enjoyed a position in society better than the one her eastern counterpart occupied. Indeed, the evidence suggests that the transplanted "pioneer" wife, forced to toil when feminine toil was equated with degradation, often had the worst of two worlds.[34] Eliza Farnham, a publicist for the superiority of women, faced with her overworked frontier sisters, clearly felt like a missionary among the heathens; she was indignant, pitying, condescending, didactic.

At one point, Farnham recounts a crucial conversation between herself and a farmer. The man, shrewd, tough, uncharitable, and unsentimental, reveals in answers to Farnham's questions how he found his wife, and why he values her. She is a good worker, and this, to Farnham's intense disgust, is all that concerns him. At the start of their exchange, she asks him if he is building his new house to protect his "bird." We the readers are of course supposed to realize that Farnham is referring to the farmer's wife; her little metaphorical flourish is a calculated way both of reminding us of her own literary good breeding and of instructing the farmer with what elegantly euphemistic terms he ought to honor any woman. The westerner, however, insists that he is not sheltering a delicate creature weaker and more sensitive than himself; indeed, he crassly compares his wife's physical strength to that of several of his beasts of burden. His clinching line is the edged remark: "I don't know what you Yankees call a 'bird,' but I call her a woman."[35] The farmer's attitude sprang inevitably from a frontier situation in which people were scarce and men far outnumbered women; whatever the value attached to it, woman's labor in the opening West was necessary. Farnham was a product of the East, where the work of settlement was past and women already outnumbered men;[36] women there might be indispensable but it was not their working powers which made them so. Such encounters could only make Farnham wonder whether the middle-class woman in the Northeast was in some sense superfluous. If she were, both the writer and her eastern reader were asking, might there not be a special worth potentially attached to superfluity in a utilitarian culture? What, they wondered, was to be the value of a euphemism?

Education for Exile

The confusion about the role of the middle-class northeastern woman, especially during the crucial years of transition between 1820 and 1840, was nowhere more apparent than in the efforts to train her, whether through advice books or actual schooling, for her part in national life. To counsel well, the counselor must usually have a definite goal in mind, a clear sense of what the purpose of the counseled should be; yet the advice and instruction profusely showered on the northeastern girl or matron during the 1820s and 1830s had no such end in sight. One might say not only that her mentors and teachers obfuscated her function, but that the function they urged on her was itself obfuscation of a culturally vital kind. To do her part in the sexual division, or redefinition, of labor in a modernizing society, the lady was decidedly expected to be a "bird" and not a "woman."

In 1830, Sarah Josepha Hale reviewed *The Frugal Housewife*, a "how-to" domestic manual written by the noted Abolitionist and reformer Lydia Maria Child (1802–80). Hale's reactions were both ambivalent and significant. Child's book, designed to ease the tension of economic transformation by rationalizing the middle-class woman's new domestic identity, was part of a growing effort Hale officially approved and aided. Catharine Maria Sedgwick, whom Hale consistently applauded, was just beginning her series of popular stories which would make a heroine of the housewife and discover drama in her struggles with her servants, her children, and her husband.[37] Catharine Esther Beecher (1800–78), another woman who had Hale's continuing support, was inventing and popularizing what she called "domestic economy," a phrase ideally suited to disguise the very disfunctionalism which called it into being.[38] Child's manual was, as all its successors would be, a cautionary book. Beneath a veneer of modernity, Child was sanctioning the genteel housewife's inevitably short-sighted economic struggles; she was urging her readers to cling to updated versions of their grandmothers' domestic methods as their best refuge in a sophisticated market situation beyond their control or comprehension.

Hale was well aware that Child was at least attempting to combine the virtues of the older feminine ideal with those of the newer model, to unite practicality and elegance. Indeed, Hale showered praises on Child herself as a kind of combination of Mary and Dotha Bushnell: "a lady of the first literary attainments, [who] yet shows herself acquainted with housekeeping in its most minute and closely calculated details." Yet Child's solutions to their common problems were not finally Hale's. Hale was palpably uneasy with Child's celebration of economic wariness and practicality, the legacy of the "Age of Homespun"; she was distressed, however, not because it offered a mere palliative to the modern housewife's profound confusion but because it might breed an over-concern and over-awareness of the value of money unsuited to women. "Our men are sufficiently money-making," Hale explained. "Let us keep our women and children from the contagion as long as possible."[39] Hale's priorities are clear. Male dollars must be ignored by female decorum; women should forget or at least appear to forget the sordid laws of acquisition and accumulation. The lady's role as spiritual exemplar to her competitive-minded husband is clearly more vital in Hale's mind than her function as his helpmate.

Hale's *sub rosa* conclusion was that the middle-class woman should be trained to play the part, not of a directly facilitating comrade, but of an indirectly beneficial laggard in the march of capitalistic progress. Other would-be educators of the northeastern lady agreed. Etiquette books of the day make it amply clear that women were to cultivate domestic piety behind closed doors while their male counterparts were to face, and if possible conquer, the competitive world of commerce. Charles Butler, author of *The American Lady* (1836), instructed his female readers on such subjects as "Female Influence," "Emulation," "Motives to Exertion," "Dress," "Operas and Concerts," "Dancing," "Storing the Memory," "Female Conversation and Epistolary Correspondence," and "The Duties of Matrimonial Life." The lady's preoccupation is to be with herself: her clothes, her manners, her feelings, her family. Butler feels no need to tell her anything about the larger society of which she is a part.[40] When Butler speaks to the "American Gentleman," however, he ignores domestic and religious concerns to focus on such topics as "Supporting the Dignity of the Commercial Character" and "Hints for Those Who Are Designated for a Mercantile Life." Twenty years later, Reverend Daniel Eddy, in *The Young Woman's Friend* (1858) and *The Young Man's Friend* (1855), reiterated Butler's sexual bifurcation. He grooms the "Young Woman" in the virtues appropriate to a tender wife, a solicitous mother, and a docile daughter, but he inculcates in the "Young Man" Industry, Frugality, Temperance, and Honesty, the "Four Sources of Success in Life." The "Young Man" is warned against the sins of the world, gambling, drinking, smoking, and so on; the "Young Woman" against the sins of the soul. There is a certain flattery for the lady here who is seldom even cautioned about the evils of liquor, for example; yet it is her ignorance, not her strength, which is complimented. Hers are to be the cloistered and untested virtues of the non-participant.

What formal education there was for girls in the pre–Civil War period enforced on them the same lesson of economic and cultural exile. Before the Revolution most middle-class American girls were frankly educated to be home-workers: their early and brief years at a "dame-school" and their occasional attendance at the summer session of a local academy were less important than the years they passed at their mother's side acquiring practical domestic skills. In the post-Revolution period, when they began to receive longer and more formal instruction, they did not, as one might logically predict, get even a modified version of the curriculum currently offered their brothers.[41] They received a special course, designed to meet a special situation. Margaret Fuller (1810–50), the famous transcendentalist, conversationalist, and feminist, complained that girls "run over superficially even *more* studies [than boys] without being really taught anything."[42] At the "Female Academies" which proliferated in the middle decades of the nineteenth century, young ladies studied modern languages, sewing, music, literature, history, and geography; they were seldom asked to tackle the masculine subjects of mathematics, theology, Greek, and the natural sciences. At a time when an apologist and defender for the feminine intellect could define woman as "the connecting link . . . between man and the inferior animals, possessing a central rank between the mysterious instinct of the latter and the unattainable energies of the former,"[43] it is hardly surprising that girls were sedulously protected from the more difficult disciplines. Education in general depended heavily on memorization, but numerous critics noted that girls were asked to do even less independent reasoning than boys. Explanatory visual aids, maps, and charts were common in the young gentlemen's academies before they reached similar institutions for young ladies.[44] Apparently, it was assumed that girls only needed to know the world by rote; they were not going to change it, so why should they need to understand it? If all education in mid-nineteenth-century America was by modern definitions casual, education for young women might be termed flippant. The typical female academy had no entrance examinations; since only a handful of girls stayed more than a semester or two, there were few tests and little curricular planning. The women heading such establishments were often social souls who enjoyed receiving students from the "best families," caring little about their pupils' advancement and rather more about their love lives.[45]

"Grace Greenwood," born Sara Clarke (1823–1904), a popular writer and reformer, analyzed the triviality of feminine education as a means of oppression: "I am convinced," she stated in the half-jesting tone which was her characteristic style, that "there is an alarming conspiracy formed by fathers and guardians to patronize only such institutions of female learning as are calculated to keep damsels in subordination, in order to prevent them from fulfilling their natural, lofty destiny—from aspiring to equal power and influence in Church and State."[46] Greenwood clearly had a point: in the superficiality was the specialty, for young ladies were being educated to be themes for thought, not thinkers; they were to be the muses not the practitioners of the arts, aesthetic or practical. Contemporary observers noted, some with distress, others with pleasure, the extraordinarily high cost of feminine education. Curiously, the price was its own justification. Girls' education testified to a widespread if contested conviction that middle-class females needed to know more about spending than about learning. The middle-class "educated" lady was on her way to becoming what Thorstein Veblen would proclaim her a half century later: an emblem of conspicuous consumption.

The educational trend in the training of girls toward costly superficiality was deplored with emotion and fought with energy. The ladies' magazines of the day united in denunciation of the meaningless gentility of current feminine training.[47] Emma Willard (1787–1870) of Troy, New York, taught her girls geometry in the 1820s even in the face of one male foe who remarked bitterly, "They'll be educating the cows next." Mary Lyon (1797–1849) knew her Mount Holyoke students in the 1830s and 1840s were fully as sharp and almost as well trained as their neighbors at Williams College. Catharine Esther Beecher founded more progressive female academies between 1822 and 1870 than she could possibly keep in operation. Yet these women, like Sarah Hale who vociferously supported them, were not in modern eyes altogether successful. Serious education for women did not make significant gains until the decade after the Civil War. In raising funds for their educational enterprises, Willard, Beecher, and even Lyon took self-conscious care to gather male patrons, to appeal to male authorities, and to couch their arguments in terms of male interests.[48] Feminine instruction, as they presented it, was simply a guarantee of masculine rights; the well-educated girl was advertised largely as a better and more understanding wife and mother.[49] The effort on the part of these women to camouflage their activities was understandable, and probably necessary, but it was nonetheless debilitating.

Behind all the efforts to train the young middle-class woman in the Northeast, then, whether on the part of conscious conservatives or announced reformers, was a common at least official assumption: she was to serve her male counterpart, not compete or even participate with him; her significance was to lie in her connotations rather than her actions. Her advisors and teachers purposely defined her role vaguely; it was a sketch whose details were to be filled in by a masculine hand. Yet the sketch had an outline which could not be altered. The ideal woman whom the counselors and educators wished to shape was to exert moral pressure on a society in whose operations she had little part, and to spend money—or have it spent on her—in an economy she could not comprehend. She was in embryo both a saint and a consumer. Naturally the lady and her advisors underplayed her status as consumer and overplayed her status as saint. They were largely ignorant of the developing economic situation of which they were a part; they were more aware of the sincerity of their conscious religious motivations than of the reality of the economic forces which partially determined them. Middle-class women, like those who counseled them, inevitably preferred to stress their moral and religious "influence" rather than their evolving importance as highly socialized and expert shoppers. In actual fact, however, the two roles, saint and consumer, were interlocked and mutually dependent; the lady's function in a capitalist society was to appropriate and preserve both the values and the commodities which her competitive husband, father, and son had little time to honor or enjoy; she was to provide an antidote and a purpose for their labor.

The Economic Value of the Euphemism: Finery as Flattery

Foreign travelers to the United States frequently remarked on the deference which seemed in their eyes to be a trademark of the middle-class American male's relations with the female. Isabelle Bird, a spirited English observer of the American scene in the 1850s, found this courtesy exaggerated and even ludicrous. Such chivalry, she commented, was not infrequently carried to "absurdity," and was seldom fully appreciated by its recipients: "The thousand acts of attention which gentlemen, by rigid usage, are compelled to tender to ladies, are received by them without the slightest acknowledgment, either by word or gesture."[50] Most travelers also noted the elaborately fashionable, sometimes tasteful, and often impractical clothes American women wore; they agreed with Timothy Dwight, a well-known educator and writer, that American "girls are taught to regard dress as a momentous concern."[51] Their elegant garments were presumably but another manifestation of the veneration in which they were officially held by their natural protectors. Yet Bird also observed that women, kept at home by the shortage of servants as much as by domestic devotion, were often neglected by their men, who, "immersed in a whirl of business, spent only short periods with their families."[52]

We seem to see a process of compensatory etiquette here, in which politeness suggests atonement as much as recognition. Charles Follen explained to his German relatives in 1826 that while "women and clergymen are most honored" in America, lawyers and businessmen have "the greatest influence."[53] Harriet Martineau summed up the situation of American women tartly: "Indulgence," observed the English radical, "is given as a substitute for justice."[54] Just as in certain matriarchal societies males are treated with elaborate and ceremonious deference by their feminine superiors, in the patriarchal middle-class culture of mid-nineteenth-century America the females were apparently being granted special status more as a substitute for power than as an acknowledgment of it. Yet such substitutes accrue their own prerogatives. Girls were encouraged to exact deference; their finery symbolized the flattery which was their due. Expensively educated, well-treated, and well-dressed, they could both advertise male earnings and compensate themselves for their own lost productivity. They did not make homespun; they displayed fine cottons and silks. Fashion was the back door through which middle-class northern women re-entered the American economy. Fashion was their form of reprisal, a contrapuntal commentary on economic productive processes; in its avowed disfunctionalism, it was capable of expressing, at its best, complex irony, at its worst, sheer hostility. The self-involved style favored by the Victorian lady—pinched waist, swelled bosom, and proliferating profusion of looped skirts and lacy petticoats—both obliterated and exaggerated the female body; it objectified and enforced the feminine function as euphemism.

Yet the supreme product of feminine fashion, the chief emblem of the emerging female consumer, was not found in the lady's clothing, but rather, odd as it may initially sound, in her reading and writing. The feminine proclivity for novels, the young miss's resort to the pen and the confidante, a standard theme for jest in eighteenth- and nineteenth-century fiction, had its serious side. A Marxist might argue persuasively that American girls were socialized to immerse themselves in novels and letters in order to make their powerlessness in a masculine and anti-humanist society more certain and less painful. In 1828, Sarah Hale, inaugurating *Godey's* predecessor, the *Ladies' Magazine*, shrewdly exploited this unstated dynamic. She assured the husbands and fathers of her prospective readers that her periodical would make for more loving, because less bored, wives and daughters. During the men's perhaps lengthy absences, the women would be reading avidly and profitably in Hale's pages.[55] Nathaniel Willis, the popular magazine writer, not infrequently commented on the increasing tendency of the American male to absorb himself in business and leave his wife to busy herself with practically dwindling if psychologically inflated domestic duties and cultural concerns too exclusively her own. Lydia Maria Child promoted a love of reading as an unspeakable blessing for the American female. She explained ominously, if honestly: "[reading] cheers so many hours of illness and seclusion; it gives the mind something to interest itself about."[56]

Sarah Edgarton Mayo (1819–49), the Universalist poet, provides a clear example of the feminine reader and writer. Raised as one girl among a host of brothers in rural New Hampshire, she read omnivorously. Later she wrote countless stories about young women who found lovers, social status, and personal significance through a well-designed course of reading. Mayo continued to read constantly and feverishly herself, and corresponded devotedly with a number of like-minded feminine Universalists. As one of Mayo's clerical friends noted, "She had a passionate love of letters, and seemed to live in the correspondence of her friends."[57] The Universalist ladies wrote to each other about the joys of literary friendship and about books from feminine pens: they enthused over *Corinne* and *Consuelo* and Mrs. Hemans. Like her Universalist sisters—the unhappy Mrs. Case, destined for the boarding-house life of a small-time divorced litterateur; Charlotte Fillebrown (1820–45), a lower-class writer of real talent who became insane and died at twenty-five; Sarah Broughton, starved in girlhood for stimulation in rural Vermont and forced in adulthood to glorify her role as feminine martyr in an ill-starred marriage to an alcoholic[58]—Mayo staked herself literally, utterly, and unsuccessfully on a life of letters. Fine-minded, genuinely devout, subject to depression, astutely aware of the limitations of her own work, she evinced symptoms of near-hysteria as she felt her life thinning out in her hands. She died in 1849 at thirty. Mayo was one of the first of that large class of women who, in Henry James's somewhat worried phrase of several decades later, lived "by the immediate aid of the novel."

Sentimental "domestic novels" written largely by women for women dominated the literary market in America from the 1840s through the 1880s. Middle-class women became in a very real sense consumers of literature.[59] The stories they read and wrote were themselves courses in the shopping mentality, exercises in euphemism essential to the system of flattery which served as the rationale for the American woman's economic position. Mayo and her successors found in the sentimental sagas of the day an icon of idealized if arrested femininity which forestalled the disappointments of maturation in a world uninterested at best in their intellectual and emotional adulthood. Indeed, this literature seems today both ludicrous and painful in the evidence it offers of the enormous need of its authors and readers for uncritical confirmation of themselves and instantaneous satisfaction of their appetites.

The typical heroine of such stories was, of course, beautiful. Her beauty was less a matter of looks, however, than a privilege of protection, a condition of invulnerability which camouflaged her needs as other people's demands and endowed her with almost superhuman powers. The transcendent heroine of *Bertha and Lily* (1854) by Elizabeth Oakes Smith (1806–93) habitually emits a faint radiance from her fingertips. In *Uncle Tom's Cabin*, Harriet Stowe's Little Eva manages to give away on her deathbed innumerable locks of her hair to her family, friends, and slaves, and still go apparently unshorn to the grave. The sentimental heroine could afford to be modest; without any special assertion on her part, her universe conspired as by Newtonian law to compliment her. Her image was inviolable; she did not need to face a candid camera. Whatever made her beautiful—her looks, her sorrow, her piety—was the one thing she would never be asked to give up. Her fictive fate might be harsh, but the person on whom she was ultimately dependent, her reader, would never reject her. She was a narcissist freed of the obsession of self-involvement. Metaphorically speaking, she never had to shop. In the streamlined emotional economy of the domestic novel, everything was delivered to her door. She never had to pay; she operated on an unlimited credit system. Special treatment was her destiny.

The Wide, Wide World, the first of the best-selling domestic novels for women, was launched in 1850 on its way to long-lived popularity by Susan Warner (1819–85) of New York. The story apparently turns on the unwillingness of the old-fashioned little girl, Ellen Montgomery, to participate in the "wide, wide world" of masculine competition and business into which a cruel fate thrusts her. All Ellen's miseries begin when her father is clumsy enough to lose a vital lawsuit, and with it, his income. Mr. Montgomery's surly incompetence and insecure aggressiveness threaten the idyll of feminine sensibility shared by his wife and daughter. Ellen makes a rather unfilial point of evading her father, but she cannot long escape the forces which he represents. When her ailing mother sends her off alone on her first adult mission to select some material at a store, a rude and busy clerk cheats, humiliates, and dismisses her because she is unused to the chicanery of commerce, because she is a child and a girl. Although a benevolent elderly gentleman indignantly intervenes and Ellen accomplishes her errand, Warner has made her point. The clothing-store setting seems important. Ellen is completely dislocated from her economic past; those who control the production of her apparel are utterly foreign to her. It is Ellen's distinction that she must be rescued from the world. She never requests or wishes in any way actually to function within her society. Brewing consolatory cups of tea for her several beloved and diseased lady friends is the full extent of her productive effort. Her undeclared hostility to her culture's competitive forces is too enormous to allow her to contribute to its economic life. The Bible and those who love it are Ellen's only business.

Yet Ellen's otherworldliness is not as straightforward as it seems. The actual buying under her mother's discreetly spiritualized supervision of an elegant little Bible features as prominently in her story as her perusal of it. In the bookstore, Ellen feels the quintessential pleasure of the consumer, the luxuriously difficult privilege of choice: "such beautiful Bibles she had never seen; she pored in ecstasy over their varieties of type and binding, and was very evidently in love with them all."[60] After a protracted period of happy indecision, she alights at last on a red leather-bound volume. The purchase of an ornamented writing table on the same excursion is an equally rapturous experience. Ellen's obvious love of the act of possession is here sanctified. Shopping for the necessities of food and apparel is painful, even unnatural; shopping to furbish the refined pursuits of religion and literature is delightful, and somehow not shopping at all. Ellen is constantly being orphaned and adopted, and the underlying question of her saga is, who can prove the best right to this jewel of a girl? Tellingly, the undeserving villains are those who force on her ugly objects; the deserving heroes those who pamper her delicate tastes. A cruel aunt at one point dyes Ellen's fine white stockings a coarse but durable brown: a reminder of the Age of Homespun. Ellen is mortally wounded. She is later taken in by rich relatives who lavish on her all the dainties she would not stoop to acquire for herself. Ellen is as grateful as her titular indifference to the goods of this world will permit. The truth is that luxuries are by definition her needs. She is to be decked out and adored. She expects, although she would never say so, the tribute of extravagance. Heedless as she is of economic realities, she has her very real place in the economy, if only because she is a symbol of expenditure.

At first glance, Ellen's extraordinarily single-minded ladylike proclivities appear to set her apart from other contemporary fictional heroines. These multifaceted ambidextrous maidens can usually run a household and save lives with the same quiet feminine spirit they bring to *belles lettres* and Bible-reading; they have what Harriet Beecher Stowe (1811–96), undoubtedly the most gifted woman writer of the period, called "faculty." As the decades wore on, however, this capability came to be curiously ornamental rather than functional. Aristocratic little Ellen might have hated to know how representative she was to be.

Stowe's female characters are emblematic of this trend, for they progressively lose their "faculty."[61] Mary Scudder in *The Minister's Wooing* (1859) is pure, delicate, even ethereal, perpetually framed in flowers and singing along with birds, but she can make the lightest biscuits and churn the creamiest butter in town. It is the men in her world who are, economically, at best unreliable, at worst downright shiftless. Mary's extraordinarily practical mother had supported her visionary and poetic father before his appropriately early death. When the story opens, Mary and her mother board and look after the local minister, Dr. Hopkins, who can write treatises on divinity but could not possibly get his own dinner. Mrs. Stowe is offering an economic critique here, if a symbolic one. The male poets and preachers think while their women work; men provide the community luxuries of ratiocination and feeling, women the necessities of food and clothing. And Stowe's sympathies at this point are with the laboring classes on whom she bestows all the rewards at her disposal. The enforced close contact of Stowe's early women characters with the real business of life makes them useful in every sense; in the long run they are not just the providers, but the true ministers and seers. It is Mary who brings the lost sheep of the book, the agnostic James Mervyn, back into the fold, not Dr. Hopkins.

Mary Scudder had many predecessors in Stowe's fiction and few successors. Mara Lincoln in the later novel *The Pearl of Orr's Island* (1862), like Ellen Montgomery, is absolutely addicted to pretty things. Her grandparents, with whom she lives, lavish money on fancy clothes for her to wear running around alone on the seashore. They incur community reproach for it, they feel guilty about it, but they persist in the extravagance, obscurely sure that they are only performing an act of justice. Mara, an artist of real talent, has no "faculty" of any kind, although she regards her lack as a regrettable deficiency. Stowe's own ambivalence is clear in her creation of a second heroine, merry Sally Kittredge, who has mastered all the skills Mara has missed. It is to Sally that Stowe reluctantly weds the story's somewhat insensitive hero after Mara's death. Eva van Arsdel, the heroine of the New York novels, *My Wife and I* and *We and Our Neighbors*, which Stowe wrote in the early 1870s, like Mara has no practical ability, but unlike her has no regrets. Her lovely clothes are her very essence. Henry, her husband, passes the honeymoon appropriately in literal worship of the mysteries of feminine dress; Eva and Henry, one might add, are hardly the last American couple to confuse female finery with female sexuality. Eva is proud to be a parasite. Her charming wardrobe, her success as the ideal wife and hostess she purports to be, indicate not how much she can do, but how much her charm can coerce others to do for her. Although Eva fixes up her home with a world of aesthetic taste and even practical ingenuity, she relies completely on her cook, the Irish Mary, to attend to all the real work of domesticity. She makes almost nothing; she buys almost everything. She is a "manager" because she stretches her presumably limited budget, not because she implements it. She creates nothing from scratch, as the women gifted with "faculty" did. She is a shopper rather than a worker; she wants her friends' admiration as much as their souls, and she tends to confuse the two.

We are watching here more than the evolution of the Stowe heroine: we are witnessing also Stowe's ongoing historical analysis of the changing societal and economic role of the middle-class northern woman over the preceding century. Mary Scudder lives a relatively self-sufficient existence performing certain important, even indispensable, tasks in a small eighteenth-century New England village; Eva van Arsdel plays a dependent if decorative part, not so much keeping a household as, in her words, "keeping up the poetry" in a post–Civil War urban metropolis. Stowe is explicit about the almost vindictive affection she feels for Eva in a way that Susan Warner and her ilk could never be about their over-involvement with their heroines. Eva is the apotheosis of all the saints who starred in the popular feminine fiction of the day; she is even, as her name suggests, Little Eva revisited. Eva van Arsdel is justified on the usual religious grounds—she has the customary number of male conversions to her credit; but she is also vindicated on economic grounds. In the newly commercialized and urbanized America of the middle decades of the nineteenth century, the woman consumer, Stowe demonstrates, is more important, more indispensable, than the woman producer; luxury items can and must function as necessities. With her usual acumen, Stowe had grasped the actual meaning of the sentimental heroine and her crucial role in the rise of consumer culture.

Advertising and "Influence": The Transformation of the Euphemism

David Potter has argued persuasively that the most important "institution" in a consumer society, dedicated as it is to the creation, multiplication, and satisfaction of artificial wants, is advertising; advertising instills "new needs" and values in those it addresses, thus "hastening their adjustment to potential abundance" and "training" them to act as consumers.[62] Most historians agree that America began its momentous shift from a productive to a consumer economy in the decades between 1860 and 1890. Certainly, this was the period which witnessed the first prodigious growth in advertising.[63] In the early 1870s, *Harper's Magazine* could turn down $18,000 offered by Howe Sewing Machine for the use of its back cover, but the magazine was fighting a losing battle. Daniel Frohman, involved in both advertising and theater, argued in *Hints to Advertisers* (1869) that "a man can't do business without advertising."[64] Available surfaces in cities were increasingly covered by advertisements in the 1860s; advertising agencies formed rapidly. Various well-known writers, including Mark Twain, Artemus Ward, and Bret Harte, lent their talents to the budding industry.[65] A reviewer for the *Galaxy* as early as 1867 labeled advertising the "monomania of the times."[66] By the

1880s, the advertising business had tripled its pre–Civil War expenditure; by 1900 it was spending $95 million a year.[67]

Advertising was more than a business, however; it involved a way of life and a theory of human nature. Both, moreover, had crucial links to the feminine subculture of which Eva van Arsdel was a representative. In 1871, the year in which the first of Stowe's New York novels was published, George Powell, a pioneer in advertising, directed the advertiser to "ignore every person, place or thing except yourself, your address, and your article"; "the great point," he concluded, "is of course to attract attention."[68] Despite the crudely theatrical aspect of the first stage of advertising, its theorists were early convinced that theirs was the technique of suggestion, of anticipating and even forming consumer tastes and needs without activating the consciousness of the potential buyer. Theirs, in short, was the technique of "influence" carried to its logical extreme. Unhampered by religious terminology or aspirations, advertisers could talk frankly about the economic purpose of such "influence." One writer explained that "a lack of ability to long concentrate the attention and disinclination to concentrated mental effort is a distinctly American trait"; the "busy pace" of American life means that anyone wishing to hold the attention of the public must be alert, flamboyant, and ready to take advantage of the slightest opportunity.[69] "Influence," whether exerted by advertising or anything else, in other words, is a technique adopted less to challenge than to seduce a competitive capitalist society too much in a hurry to get its tastes and values in any way but on the run, on the sly, and unawares. Indeed, "influence" is a form of flattery, if a dangerously insidious and ambitious one, for the advertiser studies the needs and wants of his potential market with extraordinary care and intensity. One could say that the late nineteenth-century advertiser was as ready as Freud, if for different reasons, to posit and explore the unconscious; forced to abandon the conscious life and mind of the American public, occupied as it was by commercial cares, he was proportionately eager to know and manipulate all the unconscious impulses of his subject.

Nor were the new advertising agencies unaware that their logical audience was feminine; they knew that, in some not altogether fanciful sense, women would operate as the subconscious of capitalist culture which they must tap, that the feminine occupation of shopping would constitute the dream-life of the nation. Nathaniel Fowler, the most important figure in early American advertising, asserted that all ads, even those for men's items, should be oriented toward women. "Although substantially all men are readers of advertisements," Fowler explained, "an advertisement has not one twentieth the weight with a man that it has with a woman of equal intelligence and the same social status. . . . Woman buys, or directs the buying of . . . everything from shoes to shingles."[70]

Harriet Beecher Stowe was aware as early as 1871 that the modern woman was particularly conditioned to be not only the most likely object of advertising, but its ablest amateur practitioner. Eva van Arsdel, as I have suggested, represents the proto-consumer mentality; formed by what are essentially advertising techniques, she is responsive to their pressure and skilled at their exercise. She is brilliantly adept at second-guessing the real wants of her friends and acquaintances; addicted to attention, she is as quick and as cute as any tricky billboard poster. The giving and getting of flattery is so basic to her that it functions as her epistemology. Domesticity, like religion, has become for her an aspect not of work or effort but of leisure, that manufactured utopia which advertising incessantly suggests. Eva's tastefully decorated home, into which she invites her special and especially admiring friends, stands as a sociological phenomenon midway between the Victorian home, a place whose (male) occupants were allowed to relax as a reward for working, and the modern home, a place whose resources provide their (male) residents with a reason for living and the only justification for working at all.[71] Eva van Arsdel is in every way the fitting successor to Little Eva. It is not just that Eva van Arsdel is as pampered and idle in her urban environment as Little Eva was among her slaves on a plantation in the Old South. Both are promulgators of "influence." And feminine "influence," no matter how genuine the religious convictions which inspired its formulation and exercise, represented the first appearance of what would be the most important means of forming and controlling opinion in fully developed capitalist culture: "influence" was ironically the mother of advertising, the only faith of a secularized consumer society.

The Moral Value of the Euphemism: Influence as Subversion

Most of the women engaged in the rationalization of the middle-class woman's role, the exponents of female "influence" who are of special interest to this study, unlike Stowe stressed the moral, not the economic, aspects of their suasion. Yet they encountered difficulties in doing so, for the plain fact was that they not infrequently unconsciously modified moral principle in the light of more pressing circumstances. "Influence" was ideally exerted in a world of gentlemen and ladies; it was most successful where its function, both overt and covert, was already understood and accepted. Its proponents, like the liberal clergy, avoided testing their grandiloquent claims on occasions where protest, not mediation, was unmistakably called for. At such moments, they tacitly confessed that they were, as Bushnell depicted his wife, followers, that their "influence" was most potent in persuading people to go in the direction they were already heading. This is hardly to suggest that their conformity was unmotivated or unmitigated. The situation at the heart of the temperance stories—women with few legal rights and relatively little physical force fearing and resenting men who ignored, exploited, or even brutalized them—was potentially a very real one.

Inevitably the pressure the formulators of "influence" exerted was less moral than psychological, less outspoken than insidious. They proudly claimed, without realizing what they were admitting, that they—like the advertisers—wished to address the unconscious as much as the conscious life of their audience. Their ethics were closely if unintentionally related to the ethics of the marketplace, the methods of acquisition and infiltration by which buyer and seller measure and manipulate one another. Conservative as Sarah Hale and the other exponents of "influence" seemed, they were in some sense extremists, inevitably untrained in public responsibility and accountability. Churchgoers all, they clung to Christianity; yet they were most attracted to its potentially subversive uses in a secular culture.

Participation in radical causes on the part of the practitioners of "influence" was strikingly low. Ladies, Sarah Hale had once tactfully reminded Lydia Maria Child, an early and courageous opponent of slavery, were not encouraged to deliver political views. Hale's closest allies, women like Catharine Beecher and Emma Willard, took neutral or conservative stands on crucial public issues. Beecher was the self-designated feminine apologist for the view that women had no business in politics. In the 1830s, she attacked the Grimké sisters for their public lectures on behalf of Abolitionism; in later years, she published several books to demonstrate that women had no need of the vote.[72] Willard's conservatism was equally pronounced, if more eccentric. On the eve of the Civil War, she argued in print that conflict could be avoided by making the slaves perpetual servants.[73] Her extraordinary suggestion found few backers. If the powers of euphemism could not avert national struggle, they could ignore it. Hale discreetly piloted a shaky *Godey's* through the perilous waters of the Civil War with nary a word about slaves or battles; she has the distinction of having "cut" the Civil War —and royally.[74] Harriet Farley (1813–1907), also an educator and an editor, was committed with Hale, Beecher, and Willard to the effort to extend women's dominion without running the risk of rewriting their charter. Farley, however, was forced to apply the politics of politeness directly to the relations of labor and capital. Her career consequently offers a case study both of the painful limits of "influence" as an agent of genuine social change and of its manifold possibilities as a means of devious social control.

In the 1820s, Francis Lowell designed the Lowell factories, to be located on the Merrimac River, on shrewdly semi-utopian and largely practical lines.[75] By the 1830s and 1840s, the factories were celebrated for their mill-girls; originally lured by relatively high wages and good living conditions, these girls came from farms all over New England and the central

Atlantic states. Bright, ambitious, literate, they were, as their best-known representative, Lucy Larcom (1824–93), later claimed, rather like the girls from the same area who would be going to Mount Holyoke and Vassar in the next generation. They were required to attend church at Lowell by their employers, as they had probably been required to do at home by their families; a number of them joined the "Improvement Circles" at the Universalist and Congregational churches. From these two groups, two very amateur magazines appeared in the late 1830s. They were soon merged as the *Lowell Offering*, edited in its most interesting phase by Harriet Farley and Harriott Curtis.

According to her own account,[76] Farley was the daughter of a poor and mobile Congregationalist clergyman and an eventually (and understandably) insane mother. She was one of ten children, most of whom died relatively young of consumption. She took the usual routes for an aspiring but impoverished New England girl of the period: although she picked up French and embroidery in a short stint in a nearby academy, she largely educated herself; she taught school; she wrote rather bad verse and fiction. Eventually she tended first a loom and then the *Lowell Offering* in the mills whose absentee owners boasted discreetly of their profits, and their periodicals. She does not tell us in the autobiographical revelations sprinkled à la Hale amid her editorials that by 1844 and for long after she was extra-salaried by Amos Lawrence, one of the most influential shareholders in the Lowell operation; she reveals only that she finds it rather hard, as indeed she must have, "to hear herself spoken of as a vile tool for aristocratic tyrants."[77] This was the charge being leveled in the mid-1840s against Farley and her *Offering* (whose circulation among the mill-girls, never high, was now almost non-existent) by operatives like the labor organizer Sarah Bagley, determined amid steadily worsening conditions to win decent wages and hours.

Farley had risen to prominence in 1840 when she publicly rebuked Orestes Brownson for his attack on factory conditions. She had then established a kind of confusion *engagé* as her specialty: "Neither have I ever discovered that any restraints were imposed upon us but those which were necessary for the peace and comfort of the whole and for the promotion of the design for which we are collected, namely, to get money, as much of it and as fast as we can."[78] Farley opposed strikes and approved "pic-niques" as suitable protest demonstrations for ladies.[79] It is too easy to assume, however, as Bagley sometimes did, that Farley was bought and sold. As she told it, her purpose had been to win respect for the class to which she belonged. She had known former mill-girls, she said, who spent their lives hiding or living down their former occupation. As though to substantiate Farley's defense, one operative years later was to reminisce in telling terms about the boost the *Offering*'s pieces once gave to factory morale:

"they appeared to us as good as anybody's writings. They sounded as if written by people who had never worked at all!"[80] To palliate work by literature was precisely Farley's aim. How could the operatives respect themselves if they were acknowledgedly accepting skimpy pay for long hours and poor accommodations? Farley's thinking here was much like that of the liberal minister lauding the voluntary system. A "picnique," like the *Offering* itself, was a traditionalized form of euphemism, a notice that one had already been treated well (how else the picnic or the periodical at all?) and would like, perhaps, to be treated a little better; a strike would announce flatly that laissez-faire policy had not worked, that one must now force one's due from a group apparently insufficiently impressed or intimidated to render it spontaneously. The painful trap Farley found herself in is obvious to her radical feminine descendants if not to her radical feminine contemporaries.

Farley had of course a rather different explicit political rationale for her conservatism. "To convince people," Farley explained, "we must gain access to them": to do this, we cannot assault them with opinions contrary to their own. We cannot alarm them by revealing the deprivation which could suggest our rage, and their danger. We must sugarcoat the proverbial pill. In an immensely telling, if trite phrase, Farley summed up her doctrine: we must "do good by stealth."[81] On the one hand, in this phrase as everywhere in her editorials, Farley was elaborating on the Christian prescriptions to which the proponents of female "influence" so often referred: turn the other cheek, return good for evil; reform by example not by protest. On the other hand she was, of course unconsciously, suggesting something faintly subversive in its connotations: "do good by *stealth*" has implications other than Biblical ones. Farley was advocating the decorous deviousness which was presiding policy in Sarah Hale's *Godey's Lady's Book*, from which ladies learned to cajole as well as obey their superiors, or in Catharine Beecher's Hartford Female Seminary, where girls were instructed always to "move in curves."[82]

The novels and poetry published by women between 1845 and 1875, in the great heyday of feminine authorship, continually manifest an apparent and sometimes actual confusion of moral standards. There are countless sentimental stories in which the heroine is accused of some fault or sin precisely because she is too naive or too pure to clear herself. Astrea Harmon, the heroine of Mrs. Bella Spencer's *Tried and True or Love and Loyalty*, a popular Civil War story published in 1866, is believed to be a spy for the Confederacy when she has in fact given up her family and fortune in the South to devote herself as a nurse to the Union cause. She arouses distrust only because she is attempting to shield her infamous husband, a rebel and, as it evolves in the rather extraordinary dénouement of the book, one of

Lincoln's assassins. With a reckless abandon not characteristic of her sister novelists, Spencer makes the fair Astrea guilty of bigamy and minor treason precisely to display the imperishable if constantly assailed quality of her innocence. Spencer's heroine is no longer subject to the law: the impulse of her heart is by definition holy.

Elsie Dinsmore (1868) and *Elsie's Holidays at Roselands* (1869), the most famous of the "Elsie" books turned out in a nearly endless series by Martha Finley (1828–1909), a bedridden single woman from Ohio, focus on a confrontation between feminine sanctions and man-made dictates. Elsie's widower father, the youthful Horace Dinsmore (usually mistaken by strangers for Elsie's brother), adores his saintly and tearful little girl, but he also demands absolute and unquestioning obedience from her on all occasions. Elsie is usually eager to comply with his demands, even to anticipate them, except when he requests her to do anything which conflicts with her interpretation of God's commands. Since Horace is not a real believer, he twice attempts to make her violate her conscience. Both incidents turn on the issue of the preservation of the Sabbath. On the first occasion, Mr. Dinsmore asks Elsie to play a secular air on the piano. Elsie refuses; her angered father determines to make her sit on the piano stool without food until she complies with his wishes. She does not relent; she falls off the stool in what proves a most efficacious faint. The second confrontation occurs when Elsie will not read aloud to her ailing father from a secular book on Sunday; her punishment consists of months of isolation, poor food, and, most important, the loss of her father's embarrassingly coveted kisses. Mr. Dinsmore claims on his side with some justification the sanction of Holy writ: "Honor thy father and mother"; Elsie is treated like an abject criminal by all the members of the large household in which she resides.

The fact remains that, even at age eight, the *little girl knows best.* So meek and mild, Elsie at bottom possesses a self-confidence as great as any of the Old Testament prophets she delights to read. She triumphs by a lengthy illness which terminates in her apparent death, the reading of her touching will, and a miraculous and timely resurrection into a thoroughly repentant and converted Papa's arms. Christianity with its messages of hope for the oppressed—"the last shall be first," "let him become a fool that he may be wise"—has been pressed into the service of the beleaguered feminine ego. It must have been difficult for Finley's fans to winnow out their conscious satisfaction at Elsie's adherence to the commandments of God from their unconscious delight at her resultant defiance of the commands, paternal or otherwise, of men.

Even when a pious female figure in the sentimental literature of the day is absorbed in virtuous actions or self-sacrificing feelings which her whole world unites to applaud, she is often still exploiting the paradoxical anti-morality of the New Testament in ways that reveal as much about mid-nineteenth-century American culture as about Christianity. The feminine self-abnegation lauded in the temperance tales and in so much of the popular fiction of the time is in some real sense immoral. In a poem by one "M. W." which appeared in *Godey's* in 1852, a distraught but determined wife promises her criminal husband, who has apparently asked (whether hopefully or despairingly we are not informed) if she is going to leave him:

> Forsake thee? Never! Though the mark
> Of Cain were stamped upon thy brow,
> Though thy whole soul with guilt were dark,
> Fear not that I will leave thee now.[83]

We notice amid this extravaganza of self-immolation that morality is strangely irrelevant. The wife has been (one assumes) unfairly treated; but, in a curious way, she is pledging to treat her sinful spouse equally unfairly. He has given less than what she has earned, she will pay him with more than he deserves, but the principle is the same. Each of them is self-involved, each is somehow impervious to outward influences and common sense. And her response is punitive in its mercy: he cannot shake her.

This strangely vengeful streak is visible not only in the feminine fiction of the day but also in innumerable "straight" comments made by women on public and private concerns. Sarah Hale, in one of the earliest issues of the *Ladies' Magazine*, explains with diplomacy and insight just what power is open to her feminine readers and what its gratifications are:

> Authority over the men must ... never be usurped; but still, women may, if they will, exert their talents, and [by] the opportunities nature has furnished, obtain an influence in society that will be paramount to authority. They may enjoy the luxuries of wealth, without enduring the labors to acquire it; and the honors of office, without feeling its cares, and the glory of victory, without suffering the dangers of the battle.[84]

This is a crucial passage for the history of middle-class northern women, for Hale is offering them and rationalizing for them the joys of vicarious livers, of parasites. These are their pleasures, not just (of course) as readers of Hale's periodicals but as readers, period—and as women. Hale would not have admitted or understood it, but the role she outlines for the lady is that of Eva van Arsdel, that of the consumer.

Hale was transforming feminine exclusion into exemption. In her monumental *Woman's Record* (1853), a vast collection of biographies of every distinguished woman from Eve down to George Sand, Hale calmly exculpated female criminals at the lenient bar of feminine understanding. She evolved a highly original interpretation of the Fall according to which Genesis was a testament to female superiority: woman's servitude to man was her punishment for sin precisely because she was made of finer and better stuff. A writer for the Congregationalist magazine, the *New Englander*, indignantly protested Mrs. Hale's whitewash job on Nero's mother, Agrippina II. Hale had acknowledged a few defects in this stock villainess, but pleaded eloquently that she was "still, above all and in all—*a mother*!" "Was it a mother's heart that murdered Lollia Paulina?" the reviewer demanded, with a certain justifiable sense of outrage.[85]

Yet Hale had hold of a well-nigh invincible argument in the prerogatives of maternity. The cult of motherhood was nearly as sacred in mid-nineteenth-century America as the belief in some version of democracy. Books on mothers of famous men, especially Mary Washington, mother of George Washington, poured from the presses in the 1840s and 1850s;[86] their message was that men achieved greatness because of the instruction and inspiration they received from their mothers. The motives of the often-divergent devotees of maternity were many and substantial. Praise of motherhood could bolster and promote the middle-class woman's biological function as tantamount, if not superior, to her lost economic productivity; imprison her within her body by glorifying its unique capacities; encourage her to outproduce her prolific, uneducated immigrant competitors. Moreover, such tributes acknowledged some potent facts. Mothers, while they were losing the power Dotha Bushnell had exercised, were in actuality gaining power of a different kind. In the mid-eighteenth century, Jonathan Edwards kept a stern fatherly eye on his flock and on his own offspring. Samuel Hopkins, who lived for several years with the Edwards family, described Edwards' close familial surveillance: "when they [the children] first discovered any considerable degree of self-will and stubbornness, he would attend to them til he had thoroughly subdued them and brought them to submit."[87] Edwards was a model of eighteenth-century paternal practice, although probably not representative of it. Yet it seems indisputable that paternal authority was a waning force in the middle-class American family in the century following Edwards' death. The American father, locked into tightening business patterns, was less and less likely to be at home: before the Civil War, for example, he usually went back to his house for lunch; after it, he was more likely not to. The middle-class mother had an increasing monopoly on her children's time, if not on their respect.

In her widely popular *Letters to Mothers* (1838), Lydia Huntley Sigourney explicated the omnipotent quality of maternal influence:

How entire and perfect is this dominion over the unformed character of your infant. Write what you will upon the printless tablet with your wand of love. Hitherto your influence over your dearest friend, your most submissive servant, has known bounds and obstructions. Now you have over a new-born immortal almost that degree of power which the mind exercises over the body.... The period of this influence must indeed pass away; but while it lasts, make good use of it.[88]

It is the lure of the total control found only in illicit authority planted within this apparent warning about the perils and pleasures of legitimate power which makes Sigourney's words so fascinating. A kind of heresy is once again the feminine subtext. Significantly, mothers increasingly took over the formerly paternal task of conducting family prayers.[89] When Nathaniel Emmons announced to his Franklin congregation that his son Erastus had lived and probably died "stupid" with sin, he clearly felt some obligation of judgment lay with himself; yet he was laying little if any guilt at his own door or that of Mrs. Emmons. Like his predecessor Edwards, he assumed the salvation of his offspring was finally a matter between them and their Savior. He could and did instruct, discipline, and evaluate them; Mrs. Emmons presumably aided him in the process; but they could do no more. Emmons never envisioned the Last Judgment scene which the theories of latter-day educators like Mrs. Sigourney, not to speak of Freud or Dr. Spock, would suggest: a scene in which the accused Erastus would pass the blame on to his family, and not so much to his father as to his mother! The American mother of the mid-nineteenth century, encouraged to breast-feed, oversee, and educate her child, was theoretically assuming, for better and worse, almost godlike prominence.

The cult of motherhood, like the Mother's Day it eventually established in the American calendar, was an essential precondition to the flattery American women were trained to demand in place of justice and equality. It offered them, of course, a very genuine basis for self-respect. It gave them, moreover, an innate, unassailable, untestable claim to charismatic authority and prestige, a sanction for subjectivity and self-love. The theories of motherhood promulgated by women like Sigourney generated important programs of child-raising, but they also found wide use as justification for conventionally unmaternal pursuits. American women over the course of the nineteenth century were able to exonerate almost any action performed in the sacred name of motherhood. During the Civil War, countless northern women demanded on the grounds of their maternal nature the right to follow, nurse, and occasionally harass the Union army. It was no accident that Clara Barton's "boys" liked to call their childless nurse "mother"; or that the most famous maverick nurse of the war, a middle-aged woman who left her Illinois family to "clean things up" on the battlefield and in the army hospitals, was christened "Mother" Bickerdyke. Elizabeth Blackwell was not the last woman doctor to argue for her sex's right to full participation in the medical profession, and even to guardianship over its moral and scientific development, with the simple time-worn reminder of their at least potential procreative capacities, what she liked to call, with ringing emphasis, their "God-given ... maternal nature."[90] Even the vote was claimed by many, including that most courageous and prolific pioneer, Elizabeth Cady Stanton, as a destined portion of the maternal inheritance.[91]

Neither medicine nor politics was to prove the most productive area for feminine influence. Perhaps the forum and the hospital still seemed too distant from the nursery fully to substantiate the maternal rationale. But grade-school teaching appeared a mere step away from cribside duty. The firm conviction displayed by many early nineteenth-century feminist pioneers in women's education that classroom control of America's primary-school system was as surely the divine prerogative of their sex as absolute sway over their children's unformed souls proved prophetic. Over the course of the nineteenth century, women gradually came to constitute the overwhelming majority of grade-school teachers in America's public and private schools, a feat they accomplished in no other country, and one which was to cause immense uneasiness in the men involved in American education by the turn of the twentieth century.[92] Typically, however, they gained their supremacy by working for a mere half of the salary customarily offered to men; despite their numbers they never achieved economic equality or leadership positions.

The pattern of defeat within victory which characterized the feminine takeover of America's schools symbolized women's more general position within their culture. If they had been spared the contagious corruption of public life—and the gains this exemption achieved for women were real— they had also missed the benefits, the education it offers. Barred from the manifest spoils and responsibilities of office, women understandably sought less legitimate rewards for their very real energies: psychological, emotional, what they called "moral" or "religious" control over the minds of their actual or symbolic offspring. Naturally desirous of seeing others in a state of ideal susceptibility to their "influence," they were inevitably conflicted about, sometimes hostile to, whatever diminished that receptivity: atheism, "demon rum," or the kind of scientific, intellectual, and artistic achievement from which they had themselves been painfully isolated.

The Feminine Advantage

Both liberal ministers and literary women had lost practical function within American society and were anxious to replace it with emotional indispensability; they turned of necessity from the exercise of power to the exertion of "influence." Both would in their own ways exchange dogma for prayer and knowledge, whether in the form of skills or of scholarship, for sensibility; they would substitute, in a sense, literature for life. Yet there were obvious and important differences between the position and reaction of the ministers and those of the women, differences which would be crucial to the development of modern American culture.

Between 1820 and 1875, neither the literary women nor the liberal clergymen I have been discussing had a room of their own. The saga of Harriet Beecher Stowe's creative efforts is a typical one in feminine annals. She was reported capable of tending a child, giving instructions to the cook, and dictating a new story simultaneously. The ministerial pattern was strikingly similar. Sylvester Judd, an innovative eccentric Unitarian minister, did all his writing while his children romped around his study; Horace Bushnell liked to work in the same situation; Henry Ware, Jr., actually composed his sermons with a child in his arms. Virginia Woolf has written with extraordinary perception of a woman's constant and constantly frustrated need to have "a room of one's own." Perhaps she understood less well why women, and others in a like situation, failed to achieve that goal, indeed often could not even formulate it as a goal. If a person feels, no matter whether consciously or otherwise, devalued, pushed aside, she or he craves first and foremost reassurance of her or his existence. So in mid-nineteenth-century America, women and ministers were not simply denied private rooms: they denied themselves. Given their cultural isolation, a demand for a room of their own could seem like further renunciation of an already slender claim on life, acceptance of solitary confinement. The professional women who got those little studies they supposedly coveted, ladies like the popular authors "Fanny Fern" (Sara Payson Willis, 1812–72) or Lydia Huntley Sigourney, obsessively reminded their readers of the incessant flow of interruptions which was their daily lot: a just reminder of the obstacles they faced and overcame, yet also a hint of the multitudinous nature of their indispensability. The ministers who designated their studies communal territory where the children played with toys, mother darned or read, and father wrote sermons, also feared the isolation of a room of their own; they too sought domestic importance as compensation for societal neglect.

Yet the ministers in forgoing their privacy were abandoning professional prerogatives as the women were not. Their Edwardsean predecessors had made of their studies protected sanctuaries; Samuel Hopkins and Nathaniel Emmons were shielded from their often-numerous offspring by their wives in ways still familiar to successful American males. They hardly turned to their children for occupational inspiration or camouflage. The mothers and grandmothers of women like Sigourney and Fern, in contrast, had never possessed any space for their own use. Hence, what was extraordinary about the vignette of Harriet Beecher Stowe could be that she was writing, not that she had a baby in her arms. What was notable about the picture of Sylvester Judd was hardly his literary activity but his domestic setting. In other words, the woman without a room of her own could still be advertising her new significance, but the minister in the same situation was calling attention to his new insignificance.

In certain ways, middle-class women were freed as well as enfeebled by the shift in their economic status; they were to have greater, if more questionable, powers as consumers than they had enjoyed as producers. Moreover, the domestic values to which they paid tribute represented no ethical transvestism on their part: they were women advocating the womanly, even if in aggressive ways. By locating their careers *en famille* in several senses, they were on one level making the best of a bad situation. They were by and large in the home; why not debunk the outside world not as indifferent but as unworthy? And the home could sanction rather than limit traditionally undomestic activities. It was a sign of the new self-conscious sense of upward mobility on the part of literary middle-class women that they coveted the elite prerogatives of their ministers, whose domain in so many ways seemed, if conspicuously more elevated than their own, yet tantalizingly contiguous to it. The liberal ministers were in a different position. Their economic loss did not necessitate any automatic compensatory economic gain. Certain of their traditional privileges had ceased to be efficacious or possible. As we shall see, they assimilated and catered to proto-consumer values; they coveted, even emulated, maternity and the illicit sanctions and real satisfactions it offered. Yet in modeling themselves partially on their women parishioners, whose sources of strength seemed less vulnerable to the forces of debilitation sapping their own prestige, they were patterning themselves on a group less publicly distinguished and professionally accomplished than the members of their own calling had traditionally been. And the feminine sources of strength were less substantial than they seemed.

The upward mobility of the women in question as natural proto-consumers gave them an edge in power; it is uncertain that it offered them genuine gains in status or self-esteem. This is not to say that there was no improvement in their lot and in their self-image over the mid-nineteenth century, but that it was perhaps significantly less than they thought it was.

Nothing is more distressing to the feminist historian than the atmosphere of flushtide self-congratulation that pervades the work of a woman like Sarah Hale; it is understandable, but nonetheless painful that, to groups whose potentialities are largely suppressed, any enlarged exercise of faculty seems, and probably is, at least in the short range an almost unmitigated good, whatever inner conflicts it creates, whatever limitations or long-term consequences it carries. It is as pointless to condemn the anticipatory complacency of women like Hale as to condescend to members of ethnic or racial minority groups who "waste" their money today on big cars and fancy clothes. The self-conscious if devious sense of social mobility felt by Hale and others was natural, yet it was delusive. Inevitably the uneasy alliance of ministers and women deepened their mutual entanglement in intricate and unperceived forms of dishonesty.

3

MINISTERS
AND MOTHERS

Changing and Exchanging Roles

The Data of Biography: Devotees of the Press

In discussing the ministerial and feminine impulse toward articulation and change, we need not rely solely on impressions gleaned from novels, magazines, memoirs, and tracts, invaluable as these are. By picking thirty liberal ministers and thirty middle-class women who were among the leading literary propagandists for a sentimentalized culture, and analyzing the relevant facts of career, geography, class, religious affiliation, family, and self-image in the context of a broader sample, it seems possible to obtain more precision about the causes and workings of the feminization process under discussion. (See Appendix A.)[1] I should disclaim here, however, any attempt at hard quantitative methods. I use the information gleaned from asking certain questions of my control groups to detail and explore the self-images already discussed here; I am admittedly clarifying the similarities and differences between ministerial and feminine groups rather than comparing them to groups in the larger culture.

To start with generalized collective characteristics, one might note that the sixty people in question were all, not just spokespersons, but self-conscious spokespersons; they formulated the problems and policies of the groups from which they came and they placed a tremendous, perhaps an inordinate, value on the process of formulation. They were dedicated to the active promulgation of liberal religious ends through literary means. The ministers of course were official representatives of the liberal wing of the

Protestant Church. A third of the women came from ministerial families, several married ministers, many were regularly reviewed in religious organs. Almost all of them were noted for their religious commitment, sermonizing intent, and the fervor with which they reinterpreted and softened Calvinism. Ministers and women alike saw themselves and the groups whose views they expressed essentially as members of a literary class. In 1869, Henry Bellows, a Unitarian minister and reformer, inquired rhetorically: "From what other body of men in proportion to their numbers, has this country drawn so largely its men of letters, its poets, its historians . . . as from the Unitarian denomination and even the Unitarian pulpit?"[2] Sarah Hale, collecting her *Record* of distinguished women of all ages, found, especially in her own era, a preponderance of authors.

A few of the clergymen and ladies under consideration wrote primarily reform- or religious-minded tracts—Joseph Tuckerman (1778–1841) and Catharine Beecher come to mind—but all had some ambition for a career of *belles lettres*. The women usually published primarily fiction and poetry; the ministers sometimes turned their hands to fiction or poetry—Andrews Norton (1786–1853), the Ware brothers, Sylvester Judd, Henry Ward Beecher, James Hosmer, and John Abbot (1793–1879) did so—but they were more likely to undertake less directly imaginative work. They might write literary criticism for the *North American Review* or the *Christian Examiner* or the *New Englander*, as Austin Phelps and the Peabody brothers did. Teaching literature was a possibility; Charles Follen instructed Harvard students in German letters, Bela Edwards (1802–52) introduced Andover pupils to the English classics. Some ministers published historical memoirs and studies with a strongly literary bent: the biographical sketches of Emmons and Hopkins by E. A. Park (1808–1900) are justly famous, as the tributes of Henry Bacon (1813–56) to Sarah Edgarton Mayo and "Charlotte" are justly forgotten. Clergymen might compose highly elegant and polished sermons very much designed for publication: Those penned by F. W. P. Greenwood (1797–1843) were snatched up by the "gemmy" ladies' annuals of the day. Ministers could edit a newspaper as Henry Beecher did in New York, or a denominational periodical as Horace Bushnell did in New Haven. Whatever aspect of literary activity these men and women practiced, they did so intensely, profusely, and more or less successfully.

It is important to realize that women and ministers alike were taking advantage of a revolution in the press which had occurred concomitantly with the process of clerical and feminine "disestablishment." No "profile" can be established for them without a discussion of the relatively new meaning of their literary activity. Until the early nineteenth century authorship had not been a profession in the modern sense of the word: it had been a matter of finding a paying patron rather than of pleasing a reading public.

In 1820, the books sold in the United States netted half a million dollars; in 1860, this figure had risen to twelve and a half million.[3] Publishing had become a business, and it operated increasingly under the laws of capitalist development; it was dependent on technological breakthrough, centralization of resources, strict attention to profits, and the creation and exploitation of a dependable large market through advertising and quick transportation facilities.

The Harper brothers offer a case study in the commercialization of northeastern culture. When the four young men, middle-class and ambitious Methodists from Long Island, gradually expanded their prosperous printing business to a full-time publishing effort over the course of the 1820s, they were making and heralding trends in their field. During the same period, they experimented shrewdly with new and quick methods of printing. They invested early in stereotypes, introduced in New York around 1813; by the 1830s, they had installed steam presses. By 1848, they could turn out twelve thousand copies of a page in an hour, a rate undreamt of a short two decades before. The Harpers, and those who were quickly to imitate them, had the machinery to support mass production.[4]

The brothers were of course in New York City, and, by the Civil War, so were most of the possibilities for highly lucrative, if not entirely prestigious, publishing. Before the 1820s, an author was likely to take his book to the local printer, often at his own expense.[5] In the years between 1800 and 1810, fifty percent of American fiction was published outside New York, Boston, and Philadelphia.[6] Small-town firms were to find it harder and harder to survive in the 1840s and 1850s; in the years between 1840 and 1850, only eight percent of American fiction was published outside New York, Boston, and Philadelphia.[7] And everyone knew which of these three cities had the commercial edge. Even the cultivated, philanthropic Careys of Philadelphia, the most important American publishers before the advent of the Harpers, did not achieve national circulation. Catharine Maria Sedgwick and Lydia Huntley Sigourney, known for their pious and evangelical works, in mid-career switched from New England publishers to a New York firm —Harper's, of course. At mid-century, Edward Everett, the great Brahmin orator, and Henry Ward Beecher, the famous Brooklyn preacher, drew fire when they published in Robert Bonner's spectacularly successful weekly, the *New York Ledger;* they ignored their critics, for the plain fact was that Bonner's paper, a pioneer in the use of advertising, was the most widely read, best-paying weekly in the country. Bonner was an educated if rakish man; the Harper brothers were neither. The eldest, John, liked to say, "I am only a humble maker of books," and, as his biographer adds, "he spoke the truth."[8]

The brothers were kind to writers by the rather unkind standards of their day, yet their primary interest, not surprisingly, lay in the public and its demands, not in the authors and their needs. The public was available to these new publishers as no public had ever been before. Reformers and educators were wont to lament the lag between America's rapidly increasing population and its educational facilities, but nonetheless schools at all levels —day schools, Sunday Schools, academies, high schools, and colleges—were proliferating in the 1830s, 1840s, and 1850s. A nation of democrats, its appetite whetted by burgeoning newspaper coverage of current doings, was willing to read different fare purveyed by the same cheap press. For various reasons, the southern readers sometimes eschewed the products of northern pens, but this loss was more than canceled by the opening of midwestern literary markets to eastern publishers with the advent of the railroads laid in the 1840s and 1850s.[9] In 1826, Cooper's *The Last of the Mohicans,* a popular book of the time, sold 5,750 copies; in 1853, Fanny Fern's *Fern Leaves From Fanny's Portfolio* sold 80,000 copies and was read literally from coast to coast.[10] Not inappropriately, a Pullman car was eventually christened with the successful author's name.

Given such a market, shrewd publishers naturally treated their business as just that—a business. The Harpers' motto was cheap prices and large circulation; they capitalized on religious family series and educational libraries. Like their competitors, the brothers encouraged writers to suit the supply to the demand.[11] In 1843, a reviewer for the *North American Review,* a prestigious periodical which the best minds of Boston could not save from dullness and poor circulation, complained bitterly:

> Literature begins to assume the aspect and undergo the mutations of trade. The author's profession is becoming as mechanical as that of the printer and the bookseller, being created by the same causes and subject to the same laws.... The publisher in the name of his customers calls for a particular kind of authorship just as he would bespeak a dinner at a restaurant.[12]

Drawing on the principles of the emerging and closely related advertising business, the new publishers encouraged high productivity in their authors: to keep up demand, the public must be constantly reminded that a particular writer existed. Such a policy was hardly helpful to a careful and slow creative author,[13] much less to a theologian, laboring for years on a "system." It helped prolific and careless souls like Henry Ward Beecher and Lydia Sigourney, as intent on acquisition as on art. Poe could point out unkindly, if truthfully, that Sigourney's enormous fame came not from writing great works, but by "merely ... keeping continually in the eye, ... by appealing continually with little things to the ear of the great, overgrown, and majestical gender, the critical and bibliographical rabble."[14]

Lydia Sigourney, like the equally successful Fanny Fern, was destined, as a contemporary put it, "to feed the multitudes on the plain ... rather than to pour nectar for the Olympians."[15] Henry Ward Beecher published his sermons in the weekly press almost as fast as he spoke them: then he collected them in volumes, like his "Lyceum" lectures, to garner extra profits. One commentator, tartly noting Beecher's shrewd instincts for publicity and cash, extolled him sarcastically: "Oh! most noble Mr. Beecher! ... Money has no charms for thee, never dost thou debase thyself by ... exhibiting [thyself] like a showman."[16] It was no accident, moreover, that Sigourney, Fern, and Beecher were all primarily magazine and newspaper writers.[17] Edgar Allan Poe, a brilliant analyst of a market he was never able fully to exploit for himself, realized that the "energetic, busy spirit of the age [tends] wholly to the magazine literature."[18] The decades between 1800 and 1865 saw literary magazines proliferating in ever-greater numbers; interestingly enough, they were in content and orientation predominantly domestic and religious.

In assessing the meaning of these changes in literary production for the activity of the ministerial and feminine groups, I should stress that the point is not that all clergymen and women who entered the literary field between 1820 and 1875 were intent on making a financial killing—many clearly were not—but rather that they turned to literature precisely at a time when it was becoming a business, and that the majority of them made a success of it. These facts inevitably colored their literary activity and their attitude toward it. Literature, with its apparent lack of professional requirements, could be treated as a hobby; most of the men and women in question preferred to define themselves as primarily ministers and theologians, women and housewives: Christians first, and writers second. In any case, whatever their actual predilections, current opinion forbade a clergyman or a woman to publish a work concerned with thoroughly secular themes or informed by secular ambitions for artistic excellence. Reverend William Peabody (1799–1847), praising Lydia Sigourney in the *North American Review* in 1835, demonstrated the conjunction of femininity, religiosity, mediocre literary skill, and clerical complicity in one loaded compliment. Because her genius makes no claim to "the very highest attributes of poetry," he points out, it is true feminine genius; for in contrast to man's "militant spirit" with its "fierce energy," "feminine creativity will always be found on religion's side."[19]

"Fierce energy" marked neither the practice nor the production of the men and women in question. The women refrained from the tactics of revival rallies if only because it was considered undecorous for a lady to exhort anyone for anything, even salvation; the ministers, because such methods were held to be equally inappropriate by their creed. As groups interested in working unobtrusively but all-pervasively by "influence," they could hardly ignore the lure of what one clerical commentator called the "continual droppings of the press";[20] the press was a very model of "influence."[21] Where a knock-down in-person plea would be out of place, a well-written "effusion" was by definition polite. A reader can regulate the effect of the printed page on him more easily than an auditor can control his responses to a speaker; it is always simpler to close a book than to walk away from someone openly intent on retaining his audience. The sheer facts of the literary medium posit a dependence on the reader's tastes and announce reading as a potentially consumption-oriented activity. The press offered liberal ministers and literary women an opportunity for long-distance preaching as a calculated display of good manners: a kinder God presented in a kindlier fashion.

Yet the literary and commercial success of the ministers and women in question is significant because it underlines the fact that they pursued less vocations than careers; they were professionals masquerading as amateurs. They evaded or at least mitigated just those restrictions imposed by pastoral and domestic duties which they celebrated in print; in disseminating praises of the private virtues, they gained access to the public realm. If they were confined to the kitchen and the church, they could sit down at the kitchen table or the desk and send out sermons, poems, and stories to compete, as they themselves were forbidden to do, in the markets of the masculine world.

The differences between the two groups, both committed as they were to literary self-definition, are as important, however, as the similarities. The majority of these ministers and women engaged in the feminization of American culture were prominent in the period between 1820 and 1875, but the clergymen were older than the women. Approximately two-thirds of the ministers were born before 1810, while two-thirds of the women were born after that date. There is a father-and-daughter grouping, so to speak. The ministers began the process of sentimentalization; the women, sometimes quite literally the daughters, often the admirers and disciples, of the older ministerial group, carried on and drastically accelerated the process. In the 1820s, 1830s, and part of the 1840s, the men were in charge; in the later 1840s, 1850s, and part of the 1860s, the women increasingly dominated their shared cultural terrain. The early period saw the initial liberalization of theology and its recourse to literature; the later, the assimilation and subordination of theology to literature. The first period marked the use of literature to implement reform, if hardly of a radical variety; the second, the absorption of reform as literary inspiration. Both theology and reform were subsumed in the accelerating and complicated clerical and feminine need of self-justification, for which literature provided the best vehicle.

This shift in emphasis is apparent even within the confines of the two separate groups. While the first generation of women, born usually before 1810, devoted themselves to religious and social betterment, the second generation, born after that time, although hardly without societal purpose, defined themselves more entirely in literary terms. Both feminine generations were adverse to theological speculation, but women like Catharine Esther Beecher and Lydia Maria Child were more likely to cast their very objections in the form and language appropriate to doctrinal debate; younger women like Harriet Stowe or Elizabeth Oakes Smith used basically literary modes. Catharine Beecher, born in 1800, always harbored a conviction that she could have been an inspired imaginative writer; her production, however, consisted largely of tracts devoted to the causes of liberal Protestantism, feminine education, and home economics. Her sister Harriet, born in 1811, thought of herself with justification as a moral crusader. The themes of her works remained closely tied to Catharine's concerns, but the works themselves were almost exclusively novels and stories.

Ministers born after 1810 were also significantly more interested than their clerical predecessors in avoiding theological argumentation and in exploring the possibilities of the essay, the poem, even the novel as apt conveyances for their views; there is reason to think, however, that they were in large part following the women's example. First-generation women like Catharine Maria Sedgwick (1789–1867) or Lydia Huntley Sigourney, who began to publish in the 1820s before book-writing could be realistically conceived in sheer business terms, were likely to depend in theory and practice on male advisors, frequently men of the cloth, and their writing reflected this alliance; second-generation feminine authors like Susan Warner or Fanny Fern, in direct and profitable contact with a new mass literary scene largely consisting of feminine readers and periodicals designed to please them, could and did bypass clerical sanction even while they usurped clerical authority. Andrews Norton might with some cause think of himself as a patron of female letters; Austin Phelps, thirty-four years his junior, observed the omnipresent feminine novel as a phenomenon over which he exercised no authority but felt considerable envy.[22]

Literary sentimentalism, as it established itself in its extreme form in the late 1840s and 1850s, was definitely—despite its masculine backers and mimics—a feminine concern, and one potentially indifferent to assertive responsibility in either the secular or sacred realm. Significantly, the northeastern women born after 1810 who engaged themselves primarily with reform are not included in my sample precisely because they tended not to use literature as a vehicle of expression.[23] Neither Elizabeth Blackwell (1821–1910), the first woman doctor, nor Elizabeth Cady Stanton (1815–1902), the leader of the suffrage movement, nerved as they undoubtedly were by the strategic narcissism of feminine literature, cast medical abuses or feminine wrongs in fictional guise.[24]

The liberal ministers born after 1810 who were active in social causes or in the formulation and defense of dogma, in contrast, are included in my sample. As clergymen and simply as men, they had at their disposal a broader range of sophisticated and demanding literary forms suited to the expression of essentially social and political opinions than did Blackwell or Stanton: they did not need to disavow literary aspiration to espouse reform. Nonetheless, it is striking that, even while those ministers committed to some genuine criticism of their society could write elegant and forceful prose, even subject theology and reform to literary ideals, they minimized, by and large, their overt preoccupation with *belles lettres*. Unpleasant as it is to observe, the social commitment of a given liberal clergyman often seems inversely related to his direct involvement in popular literature. Horace Bushnell, who was rumored to browse through fiction in bookstores, would never have written a novel; and despite his liberal theology and his conservative, occasionally naive politics, his intellectual and social integrity was and is unassailable. Henry Ward Beecher, whose sermons were as racy as stories, published *Norwood* (1867), a best-selling novel of village life. Beecher's posturing, his at times indiscriminating interest in popularization, have rightly seemed more solid and more interesting to posterity than his principles. Moreover, the cultural irresponsibility of feminized sentimentalism was revealed by its eventual fate. After the Civil War, no longer backed by any significant segment of the male (or female) cultural elite, feminine literary sentimentalism became by definition lowbrow; it had begun its downward trek in public esteem to its present degraded position as the staple of the poorer religious press, saccharine greeting-card poetry, and the weakly soulful lyrics of certain popular singers.[25]

The majority of the ministers and women under discussion would have been deeply disturbed if they had fully foreseen the religious, literary, and even political consequences of the sentimentalizing process they helped to initiate. The ministers obfuscated their profession and its duties, but they remembered enough of their past to be at least nostalgic about clarity, and they felt responsible enough for the future to preserve a minimal commitment to actual possibilities. Their finally more influential feminine collaborators, who intended to elaborate the clerical position and make it more fully consonant with feminine needs and ideals, in actuality transformed it. Examples are numerous. Edward Payson (1783–1827), a Congregationalist preacher of Portland, Maine, magnified the religious importance of prayer, which he likened to poetry; his daughter Elizabeth Prentiss (1818–78), a well-known novelist and religious writer, made this devotional and anti-dogmatic exercise the absolute center of Christian life. Austin Phelps of

Andover Seminary developed, as he wrote, "a concept of heaven as a place"; he testified to a fervent belief in the reassuring promise of a concretized afterlife, a belief which was his refuge and solace in a very troubled life. His daughter, the popular writer Elizabeth Stuart Phelps (1844–1911), entertained a "concept of heaven as a place" in an extraordinarily literal sense. In her novel *The Gates Ajar,* published in 1868 and dedicated to her father (to the horror of the collective theological world and probably to his dismay), heaven was very much a "place," with houses, streets, pianos, food, and clothing, just like earth, only better—Kansas with hills, as one character sums it up. What in the father's strained but brilliant mind was a concept borrowing the consoling indistinctness of fantasy, in the daughter's equally overwrought and sensitive consciousness became fantasy usurping the authoritative outline of a concept. If the ministers gathered the firewood, the women applied the match.

Ministerial and Feminine Profiles

The ministerial profession, as we have already seen, held an increasingly conservative, even retrogressive status in American society. Certain liberal clergymen attempted to rob such criticism of its sting by anticipating or intercepting it. They courted a privileged oblivion; a peculiar ministerial modesty became fashionable. Even Horace Bushnell felt compelled to begin his autobiography with a deceptive disavowal: "My figure in this world has not been great."[26] Bushnell was ambitious in every sense; many of his clerical peers, however, were as retiring as Bushnell only claimed to be. This is not to suggest that they were unsuccessful: success and aggression are of course by no means synonymous, and most of the liberal ministers under consideration did extremely well by the standards of their profession and by broadly conceived humanistic standards. But the majority of them, desiring to avoid the competition for which they were permanently out of practice, sought victories which were by definition theirs. They were by and large not men given to chances or changes.

With notable exceptions, the clergymen in question placed relatively little value on sheer bodily energy, and increasingly assumed a conjunction between their profession and poor health. As early as 1826, "Clericus," writing for the *Christian Examiner,* reported that it was notorious "that the health of a large proportion of clergymen has failed or is failing them"; they suffer from dyspepsia, consumption, and a "gradual wearing out of the constitution."[27] In 1847, another writer for the same periodical warned the consumptive away from the ministry, admitting that "there is much illness in our profession. Many of its brightest ornaments have died young. Others have been compelled by ill health to seek different employments."[28] In listing current resignations of ministerial posts, the editors of the *Examiner* frequently gave "insufficient health" as the reason.[29] Carlos Wilcox (1798–1828), the poetic preacher who preceded Bushnell at Hartford's Second Congregational Church, knowing full well the hazards of a minister's lot, felt sure it would bring early death to him. In 1839, Sylvester Judd, a student at the Harvard Divinity School, liked to wander in Mt. Auburn Cemetery and muse on "the clergy all sick and dying. What is the disease?"[30]

No clerical commentators attempted to check ministerial mortality against mortality rates in other masculine professions and I am not equipped to argue that clergymen in actuality died in greater numbers than their non-clerical peers. Several points do, however, seem clear. The death toll among prominent and relatively youthful members of the liberal clergy in the period between 1820 and 1860 was at least conspicuous, and highly publicized within clerical ranks. Wilcox died shortly after assuming ministerial duties; Judd was dead a decade after his Mt. Auburn ruminations. The Unitarian imagination was struck by a constellation of deaths in 1842–43: F. W. P. Greenwood, Henry Ware, Jr., and William Ellery Channing all passed away within months of one another; the first two, struck by tuberculosis, were still in their forties. Literally dozens of promising young liberal ministers found early graves during this period: Joseph Buckminster, Levi Frisbie, John Abbot, William Peabody, Oliver Peabody, Charles Follen, Samuel Thacher, William Thacher among the Unitarians; and Daniel Temple, Chester Islam, Oliver Alden Taylor, William Bradford Hames, Mathew Rice Dutton, James Richards, Levi Parsons, and Daniel Poor among the Congregationalists come to mind, almost all victims of consumption. A third of the ministerial group under consideration suffered from a tubercular condition. It is unlikely that the ministry had developed new perils for the potentially consumptive in the nineteenth century, but it may have possessed a stronger claim on them; it may have seemed more appropriate to associate the ministry with ill health, and to dramatize the connection. We must remember that religion was increasingly associated with feminine influence and disassociated from masculine activity. Boys with weak health or indoor tastes, likely to be introspective and sensitive, stayed at home. Of necessity more closely drawn to their homebound, religious, and supposedly "weaker" mothers than to their more secular-minded, active fathers, they were naturally attracted to the clerical profession. In other words, a poor physical constitution could be linked to, even confused with, interest in "feminine," domestic, and religious pursuits. The conjunction of the idea of ill health with the clerical image is nonetheless significant.

The social and vocational patterns of the clergymen under examination confirm the lack of aggression which their health condition indicated and enforced. Most were middle-class; most were, if anything, socially mobile but hardly dramatically so. Although a small but solid minority were sons of farmers, the jump from agriculture to the ministry was a traditional one in New England. Few of them considered alternative callings or worked seriously at other kinds of jobs. From a religious point of view, they were a homogeneous and stable group. Fourteen were Unitarian, five ultra-Unitarian or transcendentalist, six liberal Congregationalist, one Congregationalist, two Universalist, one liberal Presbyterian, and one Unitarian-turned-Episcopalian. All but two of them adhered to the faith in which they were reared. They tended to marry women strikingly similar to themselves in social and cultural background, women raised, so to speak, to marry them. Channing wed a cousin; the Ware brothers, Henry and William, picked two devoted and like-minded sisters. At a time when America was on the move, these liberal clergymen were, in the main, apt to remain in the area in which they had been raised. Spokesmen for the disestablished clergy, they were able to protect themselves from the most obvious perils, and opportunities, of the voluntary system; they were both fortunate and anachronistic. Henry Ward Beecher, born in Connecticut, settled in Brooklyn; James Freeman Clarke (1810–88), the son of an old New England family, spent several years in Kentucky; Edward Beecher (1803–95), a Connecticut man, served for a while as president of the College of Illinois. Even such limited mobility, however, was hardly typical. Channing, Ware, Jr., and Greenwood, to cite just a few examples, spent the majority of their lives in the Boston area. Furthermore, many of the ministers under discussion promoted lack of mobility as an ideal: they delivered panegyrics on the more stable rural, village-centered past; they took the lead, as we shall see, in the new nostalgic antiquarianism of mid-century.

The self-appointed role of the liberal ministers was the conservative one of cultural custodian.[31] In the literary realms which they increasingly entered, they were more respected than popular. There were exceptions. Channing's sermons were destined to an extensive circulation that depressed Matthew Arnold, and Henry Beecher achieved a hit with *Norwood* even though, he liked to joke, it proved conclusively that he could not have ghost-written *Uncle Tom's Cabin* as some critics had once thought. Such literary success in clerical ranks was not only unusual, but perhaps unnecessary. The ministers in question were in the main not dependent on the crass evidence of numbers and dollars to establish their claim to literary life. Their very profession gave them at least minimal educational background and status. They could head the nation's most prestigious schools and colleges, edit its most important magazines. They functioned as spokesmen for their country's cultural aspirations, although they were often unwilling or unable to meet its actual literary needs.

Caretakers for their culture, dedicated to taste rather than creativity, apparently disdainful or incapable of the competitive mobility of contemporary life, the ministers under examination approximated rather closely the conventional feminine ideal. As the century wore on, they were described more and more frequently by themselves and by contemporaries in terms that stressed their softer susceptibilities. Eliza Buckminster Lee (1788–1864), the sister of the eloquent Unitarian prodigy Joseph Buckminster (1784–1812), said her brother had always seemed "an angel in disguise"; angels were commonly depicted as feminine.[32] J. H. Allen, speaking of Channing, praised his "almost feminine" "native sensitiveness of organization" and his "womanly temperament."[33] Henry Bellows found in his friend Orville Dewey an "almost feminine sensibility."[34] F. W. P. Greenwood remarked in James Freeman, the founder of the King's Chapel, the first Episcopalian church in Boston, and later Greenwood's colleague there, an expression as "bland and gentle as a woman's."[35] William Thacher, a Unitarian minister who died young, was apparently characterized by a "winning and almost feminine gentleness of demeanor."[36] Even when the words "feminine" or "womanly" were not used to praise a given minister, the adjectives which were employed suggested traditionally feminine virtues: "sweet," "meek," "gentle," "sensitive," "poetic," "delicate," come up again and again. Carlos Wilcox, for example, was remembered as "a most gentle, amiable, and loving spirit, with much of the ethereal in his countenance"; he had "poetry in his countenance and manners as well as in his mind and heart."[37]

In sum, the most literate and articulate of the Unitarian and non-evangelical Congregational clergy courted, with whatever ambivalence, a feminized image which echoed and rationalized their conservative career and family patterns.[38] What about the women who were both their supporters and their rivals? Most of the women under consideration propagated and sanctified the feminine stereotype which the liberal ministry was appropriating. Indeed, they espoused and swore by the passivity appropriate to their sex. Many may have been skeptical about its efficacy; only a few bold ones like "Fanny Fern," who enjoyed dressing up in men's clothes in private and baiting the male world in her public column for the *New York Ledger*, attempted to make capital of their skepticism about the efficacy of feminine helplessness. Even the spirited Grace Greenwood fell meekly into line when she defined "true feminine genius" in 1850 as "timid, doubtful and clingingly dependent; a perpetual childhood."[39] The difference between the women and the clergymen lies less in the image they projected than in the reality which underlay it and the uses to which they put it. The women, unlike the ministers, were in certain ways, as we have seen, a rising group, and they reveal the aggressive characteristics of one. They sought power; they did not defend or analyze it.

Let me start with the question of health. The literary women sampled here made no claim to physical vitality. Feminine health was reputedly as poor as clerical health. In *Physiology and Calisthenics* (1856) Catharine Beecher warned her readers that "there is a delicacy of constitution and an increase of disease, both among mature women and young girls, that is most alarming, and such as was never known in any former period."[40] In *Letters to the People on Health and Happiness*, Beecher attempted to back up her apocalyptic rumblings with statistics. She had asked all of the numerous women she knew in cities and towns across the United States to make a list of the ten women each knew best, and rate their health as "perfectly healthy," "well," "delicate," "sick," "invalid," and so on. Her report, which covered hundreds of middle-class women, was as "alarming" as Beecher could have desired. Milwaukee, Wisconsin, provides a typical example:

> Milwaukee, Wisc. Mrs. A. frequent sick headaches. Mrs. B. very feeble. Mrs. S. well, except chills. Mrs. L. poor health constantly. Mrs. D. subject to frequent headaches. Mrs. B. very poor health. Mrs. C. consumption. Mrs. A. pelvic displacements and weakness. Mrs. H. pelvic disorders and a cough. Mrs. B. always sick. Do not know one healthy woman in the place.[41]

Just as many liberal clergymen were convinced that it was the peculiarly demanding nature of their profession which made it so hazardous to the health of its practitioners, Beecher was sure that in the sexual and domestic duties of middle-class women lay the secret of their physical suffering. As in the case of the ministers' fears, there was an undoubted reality behind Beecher's exaggerated statements. A certain number of liberal ministers did die young, usually of consumption; and the constant pressure to talk and preach, endemic to clerical life, could hardly have been helpful to those with an incipient tubercular condition. In an age whose medical knowledge was primitive even by modern standards, many women did undoubtedly suffer chronic infections attendant on menstruation, intercourse, and childbirth. Moreover, "attention" to a problem in a given period is as telling as its actual "incidence," which may be almost impossible to determine; American women and clergymen of the eighteenth century may have been in fact more sickly than their supposedly frail nineteenth-century successors, but they did not define or talk of themselves as sick, and their descendants did. The cultural uses of sickness for the nineteenth-century minister and lady are undeniable. To stress their ill health was a way for both punitively to dramatize their anxiety that their culture found them useless and wished them no good; it supplied them, moreover, with a means of getting attention, of obtaining psychological and emotional power even while apparently acknowledging the biological correlatives of their social and political unimportance.[42]

Yet there is a real difference between clerical and feminine complaints of sickness, at least as they are revealed in the sixty individuals under consideration. While almost all the ministers and women expressed their concern with the physical trials to which their profession or sex was subject, the women were in actuality a somewhat healthier group than the clergymen. Approximately one-half of the ministers experienced chronic and occasionally disabling illness; one-third of the women did. Ten of the clergymen died before fifty; six of the women. Twenty-three of the women lived past seventy; twenty of the ministers. The women, whatever their strength or longevity, were as valid and sincere spokespersons for the very real physiological problems of their sex as were the ministers for the trying difficulties besieging those in their profession. The issue is in no simple sense one of hypocrisy; it is a matter of unconscious, sociologically determined strategy based on a psychological conflict, even bifurcation, which was undoubtedly a source of pain and anxiety to the women who experienced it. The women perhaps talked about ill health rather more than they experienced it; in doing so, they were trying to palliate not only their failures in their society, but their successes. Feminine modesty, broadly conceived, was an apology for new strength. It assured its public that its possessors, if they had come so far, would come no farther; they would not presume. Ministerial humility at any level, whether physiological or professional, was a means of covering and conceivably bettering a newly weakened position.

The majority of the women in the group under consideration lived out a display of competence while they talked and wrote of the beauties of incompetence. Sarah Hale, an astute self-apologist, was given to dropping little personal explanations in the midst of articles on varied subjects. A consideration of Anne Boleyn, for example, leads somehow to this dignified statement: "It is only in emergencies, in cases where duty demands the sacrifice of female sensitiveness, that a lady of sense and delicacy will come before the public, in a manner to make herself conspicuous. There is little danger that such an one will be arrogant in her pretensions. These remarks may be considered as allusions to our own case." Hale engages in her literary and editorial work, a pursuit "foreign to the usual character and occupations of her sex," only in order to "obtain the means of supporting and educating her children in some measure as their father would have done." Clearly anxious that she has somehow usurped her husband's role, she stresses that her only real source of happiness in her fame is the sweet thought "that *his* name bears the celebrity." Hale's culturally imposed self-alienation is real and distressing; her mimicry of industrial split-level consciousness, frightening. She is not above using her declared maternal motivation for a shrewd bit of advertising. The public is given the "surest pledge" that she will deserve its patronage: "the guaranty of a mother's affection."[43] Hale was a mother but she was also a businesswoman. Femininity was too valuable an insurance policy to be openly abandoned.

The similar life patterns of the women under consideration suggest the aggressive nature of their underlying motivation. Like the ministers, they came predominantly from solid middle-class backgrounds, yet they showed a mobility and a resourcefulness often absent in their clerical peers. Several of them eventually rose in the world from rather modest beginnings. Lydia Sigourney, for example, the daughter of a provincial gardener, married into a wealthy mercantile family. Sarah Hale came from a small New Hampshire farm to become the arbiter of American taste through her editorial job at *Godey's Lady's Book*.[44] In the course of their lives, almost half of the women changed their religious affiliation; only two of the ministers did. Eleven of the women were Episcopalians, and all eleven had been baptized in another denomination. Although it was clearly more momentous for a minister to leave his church than for a lay person to leave his or hers, such a change was treated as highly significant by any devout nineteenth-century American Protestant. Furthermore, most of the women, including those who remained with their original denomination, experienced a shift in their religious opinions; this represented a genuine change, although one less conspicuous and culpable for anyone, lay or clerical, than switching churches. Fewer of the clergymen fundamentally modified their creeds.

Religious mobility of course does not necessarily imply intellectual activity. Two-thirds of the men, and only a quarter of the women, were Unitarians; Episcopalianism was the most attractive denomination to the women, and not to the men. Without impugning the sincerity of either group, several points can be made. Both Episcopalianism and Unitarianism were distinctly upper class, but Episcopalianism, due to its English association and relative antiquity, probably had the edge in prestige. Moreover, Unitarianism could and often did require a complicated commitment to certain demanding, if limited, forms of self-scrutiny. Episcopalianism, in contrast, with its de-emphasis on preaching and its emphasis on ceremony, could offer a haven to those more able to display than to examine themselves.[45] The bifurcation I have already noted in the feminine self-definition made certain kinds of self-scrutiny painful, if not impossible. Moreover, for anyone involved in the process of upward mobility, advertisement of achievement is as essential as achievement itself. Women like Sarah Hale, Emma Willard, and Lydia Sigourney converted to Episcopalianism in part to demonstrate that they had attained status and to insure its possession; they sought in religious affluence a respite from the very real if unexamined struggles they had fought, not a continuation of them.

Such women were perhaps reserving their combative energies for what they deemed more strategic arenas. The women were more assertive and more independent than the ministers in their careers. Whatever their claims, they tended to adjust their personal lives to the needs of their work, rather than the reverse. In contrast to the ministers, only a bare majority (seventeen of thirty) of the women in the sample married,[46] and half had children. Several of those who did marry, like Ann Stephens or Elizabeth Oakes Smith, married men engaged in literary work who were helpful in promoting their own efforts. Others, like Margaret Fuller, "Fanny Forrester" (Emily Chubbuck, 1817–53), Elizabeth Phelps, and Harriet Farley, took husbands relatively late in life, after the bulk of their important work was done. A number, like Fanny Fern and Sarah Hale, did not begin their writing careers until they were widowed. Most of those who were unmarried supported themselves financially, and the majority of those with husbands (nine out of seventeen) were more successful than their spouses and, by most effectual tests, acted as the heads of their households.

The women made more major geographic shifts than did the ministers. In part, one could argue, they were simply following their husbands: Harriet Stowe had little choice about her repeated moves in Ohio and New England as her husband sought to improve his pedagogical and clerical fortunes. Yet those who were free to make their own choice, like Sarah Hale, Fanny Forrester, Alice Cary, Fanny Fern, and Margaret Fuller, actively sought out the urban centers of culture where they could market their talents to best advantage. Twenty-four of the thirty had tried other occupations in addition to writing; six had engaged in manual labor, twenty-one in teaching and/or editorial work. Those who worked with their hands did so from necessity; and teaching was one of the few respectable forms of employment available to women. Their editorial activity perhaps possesses a deeper significance. One must remember here that editorship, a common and traditional prerogative among members of the ministerial group, was a novelty for women. To be an editor is at least to try to get hold of the reins of power, to acquire the means to push one type of literature over another. It is, in a sense, a way to control the actual literary market for one's own benefit. Sarah Hale, Lydia Huntley Sigourney, and Ann Stephens (1810–86) had a hand in some of the most popular, if hardly the most prestigious, periodicals and annuals of the day and filled them with work by themselves and by other writers (usually female) pursuing similar lines.

The simple selection of a literary career meant something very different for these women than did the choice of a clerical and literary profession for their ministerial counterparts. Of course it was an open and often-debated question whether or not outspoken women such as Margaret Fuller and Lydia Maria Child were "unsexing" themselves by publishing their controversial opinions on public affairs in the newspapers of the day. Yet even the directly imaginative work slated for magazine and book publication which occupied the vast majority of the women in my sample was enough to brand its producers as both aggressive and competitive. It was no accident that Louisa May Alcott (1832–88), drawing the characters of the March girls in *Little Women,* made Jo, the rebellious tomboy who liked to whistle and talk slang, the writer of the family. Women writers in the early and mid-nineteenth century were in a sense tomboys poaching on male preserves. Henry James, observing the dominance women writers exercised over the field of fiction in the 1880s, was well aware that a revolution had taken place; fifty years before, feminine authors had been few and frequently challenged.[47] I have already said that both women and ministers had special reasons for being attracted to a literary career, yet it is nonetheless true that such a career gave the women, as it did not the ministers, a first glimpse of the privileges that professional life could bestow: an independent income, a group of friends outside the family circle, and self-sufficient creative activity beyond the procreation of children. Before the Civil War, authorship was the only profession open, no matter how grudgingly and fearfully, to women other than the infinitely less conspicuous business of teaching; the literary world was the logical arena for the display of feminine ambition.

If feminine motivation for a literary career was by definition more assertive than clerical aspiration in the same area, so was feminine performance. The minister's work, as I have said, was influential rather than irresistible; the woman's, while often treated with critical seriousness, was decidedly popular. All of these women, in some very real sense, commanded the audience they had marked as their own; Catharine Beecher's *Domestic Economy* was the classic in its rather new genre. Over half the women produced near best-sellers or best-sellers. It is worth remembering that the sales of all the works by Hawthorne, Melville, Thoreau, and Whitman in the 1850s did not equal the sales of one of the more popular domestic novels.[48] Stowe modestly hoped to get a new dress out of the proceeds of *Uncle Tom;* despite a bad copyright situation and a disadvantageous publishing arrangement, she netted thousands of dollars, a mansion in the Northeast, and an orange plantation in Florida. The ministers had a certain range of literary forms available to them: tracts, "systems" of divinity, sermons, essays, sketches, even poetry and fiction. With the exception of Bushnell, Norton, Park, and Edward Beecher,[49] all the clergymen under consideration avoided the most challenging genre at their disposal, the serious theological treatise. The women had some variety of choice too, although a rather more limited one: they could write tracts, sketches, poetry, and fiction. Their selections tended to be more adventurous than the men's. Women like Catharine Beecher or Lydia Maria Child actually overstepped feminine boundaries by writing reasonably sophisticated political and religious polemical treatises.[50] Beecher in particular was undoubtedly as skillful a religious casuist as any of the ministers except Bushnell, Park, and her brother Edward. The majority of the women interested in fiction wrote primarily novels rather than short stories; and they were usually able to sustain their level of achievement, such as it was, through a number of exceedingly fat volumes.[51] The women, in sum, aimed at the biggest rewards possibly available to them; the men at the surest. The women took the more active, the ministers the more passive part.

The Feminine Congregation

The similarities and dissimilarities between ministerial and feminine roles were exposed and exaggerated by the potent fact that the two groups perforce kept company: the nineteenth-century minister moved in a world of women. He preached mainly to women; he administered what sacraments he performed largely for women; he worked not only for them but with them, in mission and charity work of all kinds. His dependency was, moreover, a relatively new one. Certain ecclesiastical changes had occurred in the seventeenth century which foreshadowed later trends: the minister had gradually taken over the once-civil services of marrying and burying his parishioners; [52] the old style of church seating, men on one set of benches, women on another, gave way to family pews. Both developments suggested a domestic iconography in the minister's congregation, an involvement on his part with private and familial affairs which anticipated his later custodianship over essentially feminine concerns. It was not, however, until the end of the eighteenth century, with the weakening of the establishment system and the development of the voluntary societies, that the liberal minister began fully to experience his deeper reliance on an audience which was increasingly active, assertive, and feminine.

Female "influence," whether he liked it or not, was the minister's chief support; maternal power was a model of action with complex relevance to his own performance because it was his prime channel of communication. The Unitarian prodigy Joseph Buckminster reminded his feminine hearers "how little" the minister could do without their aid.[53] Reverend Daniel Wise put the matter in a way both flattering to the feminine ego and expressive of ministerial fears: the pulpit alone is not sufficient to accomplish the immense task of social conservatism he saw as its duty. "There is," he announced thunderously, a "POWER BEHIND THE SCHOOLROOM AND THE CHURCH which is capable of neutralizing the effects of both: maternal influence."[54] Harriet Martineau stated the situation equally dramatically but a good deal more baldly; no one listened to American ministers, she claimed in her celebrated study of New World society, except "women and superstitious men."[55] After all, only if those women who appeared at Sunday services and weeknight prayer meetings, America's chosen delegates to the Protestant Church, carried back the Christian message to their sons, brothers, husbands, and fathers, would the ministerial voice reach the ear of the masculine forces which dominated American society. American businessmen supported churches in large part because they thought they were protecting the social order in doing so, but social order is a complex concept. As everyone increasingly realized, feminine demands had much to do with the uses of masculine income.

The church, like the faith it was meant to embody, was apparently a feminine preserve. There was a shared consensus among mid-nineteenth-century clergymen, voiced most vehemently by the liberal ministry, that the Protestant congregations of America were becoming increasingly and preponderately feminine. In 1833, Sebastian Streeter, an early and fervent Universalist, could say with every evidence of stating a commonplace that "Christian churches are composed of a great disproportion of females"—so much so that in certain quarters it had become a joke.[56] Three decades later, Frederic Dan Huntington (1819–1904), shortly before deserting his pastoral post at Unitarian Harvard for an Episcopalian rectorship, admitted that "in many cases, the Church [or the communicants] is a lean minority of the congregation, composed chiefly of females and aged men."[57] Another convert to Episcopalianism, Reverend William Gage, in the semi-exposé he wrote of Unitarianism in 1859, explained, "The church was almost without male members."[58] Even the Episcopalians, as one of their historians tells us, evinced concern at this time over the "alarming" preponderance of women in their churches.[59] Henry Ward Beecher, whose ability to draw women was to become too widely known, seemed to find nothing depressing or unusual in the fact that his first church in Laurenceburg, Indiana, consisted of nineteen women and one man. Howard Allen Bridgeman, a liberal Congregationalist, writing for the *Andover Review* in 1890, posed the ecclesiastical question of the day succinctly: "Have we a Religion for Men?" After quipping that "the women naturally gravitate to the prayer-meeting, and men as naturally to the penitentiary," he expressed in more serious vein his dismay that his gospel appeared "limited by sex distinctions."[60]

Modern historians have often accepted the view[61] that the nineteenth century saw a numerical shift from a male-dominated to a female-dominated Protestant Church, but the conclusive demographic and statistical work which would substantiate it has not yet been done. What evidence we have in contemporary evaluations by earlier clergymen as to the sexual composition of their church membership points in the opposite direction. Let me cite several typical examples. In the late seventeenth century, Cotton Mather noted as a truism that more women than men were church members, and that they were more active members to boot.[62] In the mid-eighteenth century, Samuel Hopkins had only one or two men in his rather scanty congregation.[63] Ezra Stiles, minister of the rival Congregational Church in Newport at the time and later president of Yale University, had more communicants but not many more men, proportionately speaking: fifty-six of his seventy members were women, although only the men here as elsewhere were allowed to vote on ecclesiastical matters.[64] Samuel Mather, a liberal Congregational divine of the same period, had 110 men and 246 women in his Boston congregation.[65] In other words, until more and different evidence becomes available, we have reason to assume that the nineteenth-century liberal ministers moaning over their largely feminine flocks as a signal and new disaster are telling us as much about their own anxieties as about any actual statistical developments. What is clear is that they felt increasingly dominated by their women members who had in the proliferating "societies" new arenas of activity available to them in the church; the ministers also perhaps felt increasingly drawn to their feminine congregation, and an issue of power or of attraction which was decidedly present became confused with an issue of numerical change which may or may not have been valid.

The bonds of nineteenth-century liberal clergymen with their female parishioners were apt to be close ones which formed early, and held. It is important to remember at this point that a significant number of non-evangelical ministers had been delicate, even sickly, homebound little boys. Ministers often exalted the maternal impulse because it had been a key force in their own lives. Earlier generations of clergymen had surely been subject to the same type of suasion. John Smalley of Connecticut, a pupil of the New Light divine Joseph Bellamy, recorded that the two most profound religious experiences of his youth were hearing George Whitfield preach and watching his mother pray.[66] The fact remains, however, that eighteenth-century preachers did not normally stress these experiences. They may have felt, and acknowledged, maternal example, but they did not define themselves in its terms, as their successors were most decidedly to do.

Horace Bushnell attributed his choice of the ministry, which he later described eloquently as the decision that he "should finally be," to maternal guidance.[67] Henry Bacon and Henry Soule (1815–52), Universalist pastors who worked on *The Universalist and Ladies' Repository* in the 1840s, claimed that their ministerial vocations were dictated by maternal influence.[68] Theodore Cuyler (1822–1909), a New York Presbyterian divine of a liberal and literary stamp, told the world in his autobiography that "God made mothers before he made ministers." "There is a ministry that is older and deeper and more potent than ours," he elaborated; "it is the ministry that presides over the crib and impresses the first gospel influence on the enfant soul." His words apparently had a personal application, for his own mother had a great impact on his religious development. He eventually put a memorial window in his Brooklyn church depicting Hannah and Samuel and dedicated to his mother. According to Cuyler, when he was attending Princeton Seminary, a professor on one occasion asked those students who had praying mothers to rise; nearly all the hundred and fifty young men present leaped to their feet.[69]

In innumerable cases contemporaries stressed that a given minister had not only been influenced by his mother, but had inherited almost exclusively her temperament and her looks; they almost imply that his father had no share in his conception or formation. Ephraim Peabody, a Unitarian clergyman who died of consumption at fifty in 1857, received from his mother, in the words of his friend Reverend Bartol, his "exquisitely delicate nervous sensibility and . . . inward composure of spirit."[70] Dr. R. S. Storrs, eulogizing Edwards A. Park at his funeral in 1900, explained that although Park's father was also a minister, he did not really resemble him; Park drew his character, and his greatness, chiefly from his "gentle and dignified" mother, who was "not fond of theological debate [but] . . . a lover of poetry."[71] Such claims and descriptions are too often repeated in memoirs and commemorative sermons on liberal clergymen to be ignored. It seems highly likely that, in a period when religion was more and more the province of women, many of the young men drawn to the church were seen to be deeply attached and even similar to the women they knew best, namely their mothers.

Moreover, as an adult the liberal minister, unlike the average middle-class American professional man, through the very nature of his work was apt to count among his closest friends a significant number of women. Some commentators on the clerical scene found in such enforced and perhaps courted proximity to female parishioners the source of the proliferating ministerial sex scandals which would fill the popular press in the 1860s and 1870s. In 1837 Harriet Martineau had been distressed by "the evil" she witnessed in America "of women being driven back upon religion as a resource against vacuity; and of there being a professional class to administer it."[72] The English writer Frances Trollope, whose racy book on American "domestic manners" insulted the young republic in 1832, gave a highly colored but probably not altogether inaccurate vignette of clerical-feminine relations:

> It is from the clergy only that the women of America receive that sort of attention which is so dearly valued by every female heart throughout the world. With the priests of America the women hold that degree of influential importance which in the countries of Europe is allowed them throughout all orders and ranks of society . . . and in return for this they seem to give their hearts and souls into their keeping. I never

saw or read of any country where religion had so strong a hold upon the women or a slighter hold upon the men.[73]

A few decades later, Henry Ward Beecher, dropping in to read his novel-in-progress *Norwood* to the charming Libby Tilton in her husband's absence, was planting the seeds for one of the biggest scandals of the 1870s, but he was only doing what many a less prominent and more innocent minister of the day must have done: he was, after all, a professional talker, inevitably seeking the most available if not the best-trained ear.

It is difficult to be sure, but one guesses that Beecher's clerical predecessors found their male parishioners, if no more numerous, more accessible than those of Beecher and his contemporaries; and perhaps the message of the earlier pastors was more relevant to masculine concerns. Samuel Hopkins, best remembered for his friendships with the two other great American theologians of his day, Jonathan Edwards and Joseph Bellamy, led a female prayer circle in Newport whose members were among his dearest parishioners. He even wrote the biography of one of them, Susan Anthony, in a spirit of great admiration.[74] Yet much as he needed and valued the support of such women in the hostile situation he faced in Newport, he was not emotionally dependent on them.

A generation later, Joseph Emerson, an orthodox clergyman particularly interested in female education, found the stimulation of an admiring woman indispensable for his best thinking, writing, and conversing. His self-pitying and didactic letters to his various sensitive but short-lived wives are unappealing examples of the parasitic interaction between ministerial and feminine egos. Writing in 1802 to the girl, then his pupil, destined to be his first wife (and to die shortly thereafter of consumption), he tells her that, after reading Mrs. Steele's hymns, he was in a "melancholy transport. It seemed almost too great a luxury to enjoy alone. I most ardently wished for the presence of one or two sentimental females with whom I might read, with whom I might admire the pious, the melting effusions of an angelic soul." His need to set himself up as a model of taste, piety, and sensibility before an appropriately enthralled female spectator is so intense as to make his pedagogy suspect. Capable of inspiring the affection and respect of insightful women like Mary Lyon and Zilpah Grant, he seems nonetheless in his correspondence to be perpetually posing before a mirror. After the death of his first wife in 1804, he wrote a (female) friend: "today I think my happiness has exceeded everything that I have ever before experienced.— The bell is now tolling for the funeral of my departed Nancy.—Never before was a knell so pleasing."[75] It is difficult not to find in Joseph Emerson's tenacious claim to constant feminine attention a vanity willing to tyrannize a presumed inferior rather than compete with an equal.

Several decades later, Sylvester Judd felt the same craving for womanly sympathy. As a divinity student at Harvard, he wrote voluminous letters to female friends; his awkward posturing is often touched by a real pathos missing in Emerson's effusions. He confides to one correspondent in 1839, after rhapsodizing over the pleasures of a meditative stroll in Mount Auburn cemetery:

> There is but little of the genuine emotion in our [sex]. The habits of men are too commercial and restrained, too bustling and noisy, too ambitious and repellent. . . . Women are the bonds of society. . . . Men are like mountains, bold, icy, moveless, that woo the winds and worship the stars, but frown an eternal defiance at each other.[76]

Judd is hinting that he is not suited for male society; that he, insignificant and shouldered aside by men in the marketplace, can only swell and expand his powers in female company. He is very much asking for "tea and sympathy": only when the fear of criticism is removed will he be an object worth criticizing. He wants the warm fostering of home, the intimacy bestowed by the sex trained, as one of their self-styled mentors urged, to admire, never to envy.[77]

Even Theodore Parker (1810–60), the militant reformer, drew steady sustenance from a close group of female admirers.[78] William Ellery Channing found more than sustenance in the intense devotion of gifted women like Eliza Cabot, Dorothea Dix, Catharine Maria Sedgwick, or Elizabeth Peabody: some of his best sermons came from their conversation and letters. Peabody survived her mentor to write the fascinating if sentimentalized *Reminiscences of Reverend William Ellery Channing* in 1877. There she tells with relish the story of Channing's relations with two slightly insane and very senile old ladies. Possessed by a paranoid fear of poisoning, they would take food only at Channing's hands.[79] Peabody clearly intends her vignette as a parable: otherworldly and saintly, Channing automatically inspired trust in these women excluded from the larger world and hostile to it. But the story could work in reverse, for Channing was dependent for stimulation and support on the very same feminine forces so dependent on him. Significantly, when Channing underwent conversion at age fifteen and burned, as he later recalled it, "to do something worthy of [his] great thoughts," he turned his mind to the conversion of women; he knew that women "were the powers that ruled the world, and that if they would bestow their favor on the right cause only and never be diverted . . . triumph would be sure."[80]

One could argue that the minister's "congregation" should be defined more broadly than I am doing here. Indeed, I have suggested that ministers, like women, turned to the press in part to reach a larger audience, to find a wider congregation. Yet the readers that both groups found awaiting their productions were middle-class women.

It is no accident that the burgeoning libraries which catered to the new mass reading market began under clerical auspices, only to pass in certain real respects into feminine hands.[81] One historian of American libraries lists a new interest in history among causes for their development in the Jacksonian period. This in turn he attributes to the fact that young New Englanders who would have gone into the ministry a generation earlier were now turning to historical and literary pursuits.[82] Yet many of the movement's most active promoters were not clergymen manqué, but liberal men of the cloth. The select Athenaeum library of Boston was established by a discreet coalition of business and ministerial investors.[83] In 1833 Abiel Abbot, a Unitarian minister, founded the pioneering public library in Peterborough, New Hampshire; Abbot was prominent in the library movement in New England over the next two decades.[84] Women, in contrast, played a much more modest role in initiating libraries. At the turn of the nineteenth century, milliners like Mary Sprague and Kezia Butler in Boston,[85] whose clientele was almost exclusively feminine, sometimes rented out books. Later, women associated informally to buy and share popular fiction.[86] By the end of the nineteenth century, however, several women's organizations campaigned actively for the establishment of free libraries; library managers noted that a good percentage of their customers were female, as were many of their employees.[87]

Women's omnipresence in the libraries was but one sign of their new cultural power. As early as mid-century, it was clear to a perceptive observer like the fashionable writer Nathaniel Willis who it was that ruled the literary world: "It is the women who read. It is the women who are the tribunal of any question aside from politics or business. It is the women who give or withhold a literary reputation. It is the women who regulate the style of living.... It is the women who exercise the ultimate control over the Press."[88] Joseph Emerson, wishing for a feminine companion to share with him the sentimental pleasures of poetry, and Henry Ward Beecher, reading his novel aloud to his devoted young parishioner, Libby Tilton, were dramatizing the simple fact that the liberal minister wrote, as he preached and talked and acted, largely for women.

Imitation and Rivalry: Pulpit Envy

The liberal clergy faced a difficult situation. Middle-class churchgoing and reading women had genuine control, no matter how limited, over their ministers; and some of them, moreover, were at least partly aware of their power. Catharine Esther Beecher warned the ministry in 1857 that God had "designed that woman should have the leading power as the *educator* of mind," and, as a natural corollary, "it is designed that *she* should be qualified to gain by her own independent powers all that is revealed by God." As "the heaven-appointed educator of infancy and childhood," she is inevitably opposed to the (Calvinist) "theological theories . . . as seemingly opposing the moral sense and common sense of mankind."[89] In effect, Beecher is cautioning the clergy to heed the wishes of their most important constituents. Her threatening, even possessive attitude is hardly atypical. Ministerial characters figure prominently in nineteenth-century novels by women; moreover, within the terms of a given story, the clerical figure is clearly accounted feminine property. His housekeeping, his selection of a wife, his choice of a cravat, are the concerns of the neighborhood women, married and single, as surely as if he were a member of their own families.[90] Women writers and historians took an increasingly proprietary interest in ministerial biography. Few ladies in the eighteenth century presumed their capacities equal to the task of narrating a clergyman's life; thousands in the nineteenth century did. The minister was their material.[91]

The authors of such memoirs explain their own temerity precisely by the stress they place on the diminishing prestige surrounding the ministerial office. Samuel Hopkins, an impressive though by no means a skillful preacher, used to make one of his youngest female hearers sob on a Sunday with fear, because, as the little girl said, "I look up and think I see God in the pulpit."[92] Her reverence, while extreme, was not unusual. Catharine Maria Sedgwick, writing of her early reactions to Dr. Stephen West, the orthodox minister in her girlhood home, Stockbridge, Massachusetts, records she had felt "the painful . . . awe . . . which the New England clergyman then inspired." But she outgrew this, she adds, because she realized he had the "most tender and gentle heart" that ever beat beneath a "stern exterior."[93] He is not, in other words, so very different from her feminine self. This was a comparison which could function in two directions: if the minister was like a woman, why shouldn't the woman be like a minister? Sarah Edgarton Mayo, known to her friends as the "Angel of the *Rose*" (the Universalist gift annual she edited), once wrote a friend: "I sometimes wish I were a man and a minister."[94] A similar desire was evident elsewhere in the feminine subculture of which Mayo was a minor representative.

Most of the genteel periodicals for ladies which covered the coffee tables of the period espoused the cause of female education. Their contributors protested consistently, as we have seen, the current emphasis on the "gilded cheat" of accomplishments and advocated a more rigorous curriculum. The elevated educational aspirations these writers evinced, however, were perhaps less interesting to their readers than the rationale they presented for such ambitions: American girls should be well educated because they were themselves to be the teachers of America. And the office of pedagogue, filled by a female, as one writer for the *Ladies' Repository* explained, might well accomplish "the regeneration of mankind."[95] Catharine Esther Beecher in her lifelong crusade to get adequate funds for the training of women teachers was wont to address her appeals for money and support to the Protestant ministry. This was only reasonable to her mind since she saw women teachers as engaged in "missionary" work and inspired by "religious faith,"[96] and consequently as ministerial allies if not ministerial substitutes. Beecher herself had been educated in Miss Sarah Pierce's famous school for young ladies at Litchfield, and was, like her early preceptor,[97] as interested in saving souls as in teaching mathematics and moral philosophy. With the help of paternal advice Beecher conducted several quite successful revivals at her Hartford Seminary in the 1820s. She eventually tried without success to hire the evangelical but ladylike Zilpah Grant, Mary Lyon's co-worker at Ipswich Seminary, specifically to quicken the religious life of her school.[98]

Mary Lyon's legendary revivals, first at Ipswich in the 1820s, then at her famous Mount Holyoke College in the 1830s, represent the extreme in the feminine fusion of clerical and pedagogical roles. Lyon, a devout Baptist, was convinced that all the ministers in the land could do nothing without the aid of "self-denying female teachers" (234).[99] Indifferent from the first to financial profit for herself and intent on salvation for her students, she measured her success in exclusively evangelical terms. In 1827, reviewing a school year in which a revival had begun only to leave the majority of her pupils untouched, she wrote: "I have a pleasant school, but one thing is wanting and when I think of that, my heart is sad. Amidst all my blessings, I feel that the frown of God rests on me" (53). She seldom had such cause for despondency. The self-educated daughter of a New England farmer, uncouth, vital, genuine, she yearned to rescue young women from what she called the "empty gentility" (245) of middle-class feminine life. If a student was unhappy, Lyon was wont to tell her that she was so only because she had failed that day to have "large desires for the conversion of the world" (89). Lyon's own desires were as large as her extraordinarily generous soul, and when she founded Mount Holyoke in 1836, she conducted it, in her words, "on the principles of our missionary operations" (188). Mount Holyoke sent out and financed hundreds of women missionaries during Lyon's presidency.[100]

Lyon herself became a beacon and an inspiration to women all across the United States. Sarah Hale of course championed her in polite editorials for the *Lady's Magazine* and later for *Godey's,* and Lucy Larcom, the millworker and writer, was to report later on the admiration Lyon had evoked among the Lowell factory girls.[101] Not inappropriately, Lyon also attracted a ministerial following. The famous Dr. Alexander of Princeton Seminary told a student sagely that "Mary Lyon had the right idea."[102] Edward Hitchcock, a distinguished geologist and the president of Williams College, wrote a biography of Lyon whose tone was one of frank envy for her evangelical achievements. An example of "moral sublimity" (471), as Hitchcock viewed her, she possessed a power as a preacher comparable to that of a "practiced mesmerist" (446). Indeed, Hitchcock intended his *Memoir* of Lyon, published in 1852, as a guide and a prod to ministerial ambition: "Why should even ministers be ashamed," he inquires, "to learn wisdom on a subject so important from a woman, especially from one so eminent for wisdom and piety and whose experience in revivals was so extensive? ... Who does not feel desirous," he adds, "of catching at least a portion of her falling mantle?" (483–4).

Few were destined, however, to wear that mantle. She was one of the extraordinary personalities of her day, but her inspirational power came precisely because she succeeded just where so many wished to shine. Thousands of nineteenth-century American women contributed what would amount to enormous sums to the missionary effort.[103] In such legendary figures as Mary Lyon or Ann Judson, a much-loved missionary to Burma, the women who stayed at home found a projection, amplification, and sanctification of their own domestic duties as well as a vicarious release from them. Educators like Catharine Beecher might promise housewives that their occupation was to "form immortal minds,"[104] but it must have been hard in the multitudinous press of ordinary life to feel the vocation behind the labor. Feminine missionaries actively, manifestly, and prominently engaged in saving souls from terrible ignorance dramatized and vindicated the housewives' importance. Lyon and Judson lived adventurously, but their appeal was that they apparently did so by realizing, not rejecting, their feminine role. Judson used her knowledge of Burmese to write a catechism for children; Lyon, a skillful housekeeper, regularly converted her help and invested domestic lore, required knowledge at Mount Holyoke, with the lure of religious discipline. Both achieved masculine visibility through feminine self-sacrifice. Such women were very much housewives become ministers.[105]

Popular fiction for women depicted the same assimilation of ministerial and feminine functions implicit in women's educational and missionary work. There were countless sentimental tales of maidens effortlessly and unsuspectingly performing ministerial feats in the natural course of their domestic duties; just doing what came naturally as a capable and devout young girl apparently involved saving souls as a kind of unintended although by no means unwished-for byproduct. Adeline D. T. Whitney

(1824–1906), a friend of Harriet Beecher Stowe's and an established author
of books for girls, painted a classic vignette of the glories of girlish ministry
in *The Gayworthys* (1865). With an imploring glance and a sweetly spoken
request, young Sarah Gair persuades an ill-used, embittered, but fundamentally noble-hearted sailor, Ned Blackmere, to attend church for the first time
in twenty years. Once there, he finds the sermon preached on the doctrine
of limited election by the ominously named Reverend Scarsley confusing
and repellent. After the service, Sarah takes him outside the church to the
more congenial churchyard where they wander among the ancient tombstones and she shyly but surely disagrees with her minister. By explaining
that election really means that "everybody" is "elected—to their own particular life, and death, and all,"[106] she converts Blackmere to a truly religious
state of mind in which Sarah's benign God and Sarah's innocent self pleasantly contend as suitable objects of worship.

The fantasized feminine assumption of clerical office was not always so
easy nor so unconscious. There was an entire sub-genre of historical fiction
which focused on a conflict between the Puritan fathers and a young girl.
The fathers attempt to stamp out opposition to their rigid creed; the innocent and saintly heroine engrosses the sympathy of her readers by suffering
harsh seventeenth-century penalties for humane nineteenth-century beliefs.[107] In *Naomi* (1848) by Joseph Buckminster's sister, Eliza B. Lee, the
heroine is a beautiful and persecuted young Quaker in colonial Massachusetts. Her American milieu is one where the feminine sex is constantly
victimized: Lee even stops to focus movingly on a lovely doe slaughtered
by careless Indians to fill out her picture of feminine enslavement. Although
we are told that Naomi is merely "receptive" and lacks a "powerful imagination" (252)[108]—in other words, she is thoroughly feminine—she manages to
outtalk a conclave of New England's most learned ministers specially gathered to test and condemn her. Her real sin, Lee informs us, is not so much
her dismissal of Calvinism, which she terms "little less than blasphemies and
curses" (415), as her disavowal of pastoral guidance; she "dared to think for
herself." Her final statement avows, "I must live by my faith, not that of my
church" (413). She does so, gets away with her life, and her lover, a convert
to her theology.

Outside the historical genre, other feminine novelists on occasion depicted a frank and even bitter contest between minister and heroine for
spiritual leadership in a given community. The classic example is *Bertha and
Lily*, published in 1854 by Elizabeth Oakes Smith. Smith, author of the
poem "The Sinless Child" so admired by Poe, had disavowed Puritan
theology with "a sense of horror" at six and claimed to be sinless herself: "I
was good." Her religious heritage was mixed, including both Calvinism and
Universalism, but the die was cast when Smith chose the Unitarian Reverend

Nichols of Portland with his "ideal sweetness" over the fiery orthodox Edward Payson of the same city. Her choice of a liberal pastor was the first step in a career which was to remove her from clerical control altogether. In 1877, after an unhappy marriage and a distinguished career as a writer, feminist, and public speaker, she became the pastor of an Independent congregation in Canastota, New York.[109] *Bertha* more than anticipated her own clerical eminence.

Bertha is a brilliant, beautiful, and radical young woman who gradually takes over the role of religious leader in the little town of Beach Glen. The youthful liberal minister officially established there, appropriately named Earnest, initially resents her superior spiritual gifts. "Bertha should preach," he notes in his journal (55),[110] but he is a little disconcerted when she does, outdoors, drawing far larger crowds than he can command. He confesses to envy: she talks to him "as if I were a stupid boy" (66) and makes him painfully aware by her untutored triumphs that "half the learning stowed away in my brain was so much useless lumber" (199). Professional training is no substitute for feminine instinct and sensitivity, both of which Bertha has in abundance. This incipient rivalry is nipped in the bud by Earnest's total capitulation: he marries Bertha, revolutionizes his church according to his wife's principles, and grows, in Bertha's words, "a lovely, inspired child-man" (325), while she becomes, in his eyes, like Christ in her "new revelation of womanhood" (332-3). Sarah Hale once expressed her conviction that "to bring about the true Christian civilization, which only can improve the condition of our sex, the men must become more like women, and the women more like angels."[111] In Smith's novel, the woman has indeed become more like an angel—it is Bertha, remember, who gives off that faint glow from her fingertips—and the man has become more like a woman. What Hale neglected to say but what Smith makes clear is that in the process the man will apparently lose power while the woman gains it. Bertha is the minister, Earnest the parishioner.

The fictional takeover of clerical powers by women was as significant in its form as in its content. The sheer fact of the novel itself was one more threat literary women offered to ministerial hegemony. In the 1680s, fiction and romance constituted only about three percent of the reading matter of Americans; half of the works in circulation were theological.[112] In 1793, Thaddeus M. Harris, a liberal minister and Harvard librarian, published a *Selected Catalogue of Some of the Most Esteemed Publications in the English Language Proper to Form a Social Library* and recommended only thirty-four titles in theology out of 227. He endorsed thirty books of poetry and drama, eleven of fiction, forty of history and biography.[113] Harris' modest claims for theology's circulation were probably optimistic; a study of the Providence Social Library in 1753 reveals that even then theology was among the least-read subjects.[114] Royall Tyler in *The Algerian Captive* shows his hero returning to Boston in 1795 after a long absence to discover that fiction and "books of mere amusement" have captured the attention of all classes: his countrymen have forsaken "the sober sermons and practical pieties of their fathers for the gay stories and splendid impieties of the traveller and the novelist."[115] Educational and clerical leaders were drawn to the early nineteenth-century library movement because the libraries apparently offered a way of replacing unsavory books in public favor with wholesome ones.[116] Yet from their inception, it was clear that libraries tended to circulate a good deal more fiction than theology. Tentative figures for the Harper Brothers firm between 1820 and 1830 suggest that theology formed the least significant category of their published books.[117]

Moreover, feminine fiction was competing with strictly theological and religious work in frighteningly direct ways. Many of the ladies who penned the best-sellers of the day saw themselves in quasi-clerical terms. Susan Warner claimed that she wrote *The Wide Wide World* "on her knees"; Harriet Beecher Stowe told the world that "God wrote" *Uncle Tom's Cabin*.[118] What minister could ask for better inspiration? Sarah Edgarton Mayo was quite frank in her wish to accomplish by her writing "the same amount of good to one individual that I have received from a single sermon."[119] William Ellery Channing, noting the advent and proliferation of female novelists, described them as "evangelist[s]," "teacher[s] of nations."[120] He was perfectly aware that their purpose was similar to his, and their tactics perhaps superior: "Woman, if she may not speak in the church, may speak from the printing room, and her touching expositions of religion, not learned in theological institutions but in the schools of affection, of sorrow, of experience, of domestic charge, sometimes make their way to the heart more surely than the minister's homilies."[121] A writer for the *Christian Examiner* frankly labeled Catharine Maria Sedgwick's didactic novels "sermon[s]."[122] James Freeman Clarke, considering Bushnell's *Vicarious Sacrifice* in the same periodical in 1866, warned his readers that enormously popular novels like those of Susan Warner which propagate "the crudest forms of the doctrine of the atonement"[123] must be taken seriously, if only as menaces to the preservation of genuine religious doctrine. Elizabeth Oakes Smith was preaching through her heroine Bertha in a double sense.

Imitation and Rivalry: Pulpit Paranoia

The clergymen's answer to the complex challenge of their feminine congregations was not so dissimilar to poor Earnest's. Ministers vacillated between resentment and flattery, yet both responses underscored the inescapable facts of their dependency on feminine attention and their tendency to assimilate feminine models. At the one extreme, in the realm of fancy, clerical claims for feminine virtues crescendoed at times dangerously near heresy. One clergyman, writing in 1854 on "The Woman Question," not content with asserting that the "womanly element predominated" in Christ, likened woman very specifically to the Messiah: "She must open the long disused page of the beatitudes among us, for manly energy rots among its husks, having dismissed reproving meekness and poverty of spirit. Let woman offer them an asylum; let her rise and take the beautiful shape of the Redeemer."[124] Nor was the Deity safe from such comparison. Horace Bushnell in the late 1860s found it perfectly natural to speak of falling back "into God's arms," to be pressed to his breast "even as a child in the bosom of its mother."[125] Henry Ward Beecher, who, like all his siblings, made his dead mother the rationale and center for a feminized theology, told his hearers that a mother's love is "a revelation of the love of God."[126]

To identify the female with God and the Savior made it possible even for the touchy clerical ego to associate her in rash moments of enthusiasm with the minister as well. "If man is the warrior, woman is the priestess," one Unitarian writer exclaimed in 1858. Edwards A. Park began his seminal and controversial sermon on "The Theology of the Intellect and the Theology of the Feelings" in 1850 by a tribute to the superiority of maternal to paternal instruction as a guide to pastoral ministrations.[127] By a natural analogy, the family, the special congregation of the woman, was viewed by clerical eulogizers as comparable to the church. Daniel Wise, a Connecticut clergyman and author, tells a little parable for the benefit of the conscientious female readers of his *Young Lady's Counsellor* (1852). A minister visiting a lady parishioner catches her, to her embarrassment, in the middle of her housework. He interrupts her apologies by his heartfelt ejaculation: "Let Christ, when he comes, find me so doing!" Wise, in elaborating his lesson, likens the "moral importance" of her "humble task" to that of "the missions of Gabriel to the ancient prophets."[128]

At the other extreme, in the realm of fact, ministers blocked the practical implementation of those feminine virtues they lauded so energetically in print. Ministers opposed the outright and by definition unholy demands for political equality posed by the women's rights movement,[129] but they also bitterly feared and fought feminine assumption of conspicuously Christian tasks. Clerical hostility was a form of territorial imperative springing from an uneasy sense of a too cramped common space. Ministers suspected—and rightly—that women had more chance of capturing the church than the Senate; and they reserved their fiercest powers of resistance for such a possibility. Of course women could not be ministers—all ecclesiastical authorities were agreed on that. Horace Bushnell, in the letter in which he enjoins the Christian virtues so vehemently on his daughter, reminds her that her very piety should forbid her to be either a soldier or a minister: a conjunction of taboos flattering to their promulgator. For a long while it appeared that women could not even be missionaries, if ministers were to decide the issue. Women, who were eventually to be absolutely indispensable to the missionary effort, won the right to enter, then to organize, mission work over repeated and widespread clerical objection.[130]

Other shared feminine-ministerial concerns give ample evidence of the ambivalence of the minister's reactions to the pressures toward feminization he increasingly experienced. Sunday had long been the minister's special day. Increasingly, as the century progressed, it seemed to be his only day, and his right to it did not remain undisputed. The day when by custom and sometimes by statute ministers were asked to perform and all other adults decreed to do nothing, it was the ordained time for a momentary and perhaps token redressing of the balance between the competitive and contemplative forces of American culture. Various groups in the ministry fought at different times in the first sixty years of the nineteenth century to keep this claim on their society's attention. They protested the profanations of commerce, the interference of the mails. But they had another competitor: the churchgoing American matron. Sunday also symbolized her spot in the sun, her moment for possible magical transformation from neglected Cinderella to courted princess. The Sabbath came to be heralded as a sort of weekly Mother's Day. After all, Sunday was the one day of the week the American male was supposed not only to go to church but to stay home.

Sarah Hale described the Sabbath as the very cornerstone of the invisible *imperium* of womanly persuasion: "What opportunities these days of rest at home present to the wife and mother [she exults]! The whole family are then brought under the sweet ... feminine influence which, like the power of gravitation, works unseen but irresistibly over the hearts and consciences of men."[131] Catharine Maria Sedgwick, in her widely read fictionalized tracts on the Christian family of the 1830s, chose always to emphasize the domestic rather than the ecclesiastical side of Sabbath worship. It is the instructive books perused by thoughtful children resting on maternal laps, the devout conversation and prayer with which parents and offspring refresh and edify each other, not the sermons delivered in church, which make Sunday a sacred day in Sedgwick's stories.[132]

The opening and proliferation of Sunday Schools dramatized the ministerial and feminine struggle for possession of sacred territory. Sabbath Schools, begun in England in the later eighteenth century as a means of educating, and controlling, lower-class children, spread rapidly in America in the early nineteenth century. In 1817–18 the Sunday School Union had forty-three schools and 5,970 pupils; a scant six years later, it could boast 723 schools and 49,619 pupils. From its inception, the Union was funded largely by businessmen, but the most active promoters and organizers were ministers and women. In 1804, a number of women from different denominations formed the Union Society in Philadelphia to educate poor girls; the Society, with twenty-six female members, incorporated in 1808. Isabella Graham, a devout Presbyterian, organized the Female Union for the Promotion of Sabbath Schools in New York in 1816; her daughter, Joanna Bethune, was to carry on her work. The feminine groups in New York and Philadelphia worked closely with ministers and other interested men, but their co-operative effort in no way obviated—indeed it underscored—their heightened power. The experience of organizing and administering funds and people intrinsic to the running of any of the female voluntary societies was a heady and educational novelty for the women involved; it raised their importance in other people's eyes and in their own. The Sunday School movement, however, offered women special opportunities. Women constituted the bulk of teachers; as the Sunday School system gradually came to include middle- and upper-class children and assumed its modern function as an indispensable institution of the Protestant Church, feminine pedagogical control had genuine competitive thrust.[133] Children who had once been required to sit, no matter how restlessly, through the regular adult service, might now receive their earliest religious instruction from a woman rather than from the minister. Some clergymen objected to the dilution of doctrine inevitable in this catering to the childish mind; none protested the deleterious conjunction of feminine instruction with intellectual pabulum. Many frankly resented feminine encroachment on clerical power. In Medway, Massachusetts, the local minister and his deacons fought a women's group agitating to establish a Sunday School: "These women will be in the pulpit next," their opponents claimed.[134]

Yet ministers by and large tolerated, even welcomed, the Sunday Schools. The schools did not of course confer on women automatic *entrée* to the pulpit; indeed, they brought more people into what could still be defined as ministerial territory. The business of writing and publishing was a somewhat different and more serious matter. Liberal ministers were very aware, as we have seen, that feminine writers were angling for their congregations. Here, as everywhere, women complimented and frightened ministers by imitating them. The fluid situation of the press stood, however, in marked contrast to the still relatively hierarchical structure of the church. Few of the controls which blocked feminine mobility in the church existed on the literary scene: the minister could prevent direct in-person feminine access to his adult congregation, but how could he dictate the reading of his parishioners? They might listen to him one day a week, and read his feminine rivals the remaining six.

The liberal minister tended increasingly to depict his deepening involvement in literary activity as an effort to define and control resources both necessary and potentially dangerous. He justified his course, when he did, in terms of defensive maneuvers. In 1865, one Unitarian minister frankly urged his brethren to make their sermons as wide-ranging, engaging, and polished as possible: otherwise "the most intelligent and earnest men and women will go to literature instead of to church for inspiration, guidance, and culture."[135] The liberal clergyman was hardly unaware that by engaging on the enemy's territory, he inevitably ran the risk of contamination or capture. Bushnell's rival in Hartford, Joel Hawes, an old-style Congregationalist, argued against literary preaching, and he couched his complaint in a telling image of transvestism: "The sword of the spirit [is] . . . so muffled up and decked out with flowers and ribbons as no longer to show what it is."[136] Such a blunt image was unlikely to turn up in a liberal minister's prose, but the idea behind it was hardly foreign to him. Henry Ware, Jr., warned that a literary life could lead to "the *careless indulgence of the imagination*" which in turn would produce "self-indulgence . . . voluptuousness . . . effeminacy."[137]

Clerical critical response to feminine literary production was predictably mixed; poetry was one thing, fiction another. Andrew Peabody, a well-liked Harvard Unitarian, could sincerely rank Mrs. Hemans over Homer because the latter neglected "heart sorrow" and seemed ignorant of "sublime tranquillity."[138] Andrews Norton, an important Unitarian critic and polemicist, praising the same poet, complained that Milton lacked the "pure religious sentiment" and showed God through "colossal forms that repel our human sympathy." It is precisely Milton's self-conscious greatness which antagonizes Norton. He claims that Milton is in a sense disqualified from true eminence because he did not understand "domestic life, that life in which now almost all our joys or sorrows are centered,"[139] that life which is Mrs. Hemans' chosen theme. Peabody's and Norton's absurd judgment that Hemans is greater than Homer and Milton is understandable; they were defending themselves. For they too, as ministers, were pledged in some sense to similar nurturing values; equally important, they too could write domestic poetry. Norton's learned controversial tracts make better reading today than his saccharine verse, but the point is that he considered both suitable displays of his clerical and intellectual eminence.

The rise of the novel was roughly coincidental with the commercialization of the press; unlike poetry, the novel was a relatively new and secular form, and one which many clergymen long considered inappropriate for their use. Yet the liberals were significantly more tolerant of fiction (though hardly more prolific in writing it) than their evangelical and dogmatically minded peers; its possibilities came too tantalizingly near providing an answer to their own needs for it to be ignored or uncriticized. When Samuel Miller of Princeton's Presbyterian Theological Seminary expressed his wish that he could ban novels, Henry Ware, Sr., of Harvard Divinity School defended the genre, even arguing that it could be permissible and beneficial for ministers to read fiction. Liberal clerical commentators were fully cognizant of how much fiction women read and wrote,[140] and they were equally aware that the fiction women preferred was the sentimental tale or romance.[141] They saw the significance of the new form precisely in its ability to interest, to attract easily. The novel was the key emblem of the advantages and abuses inherent in "influence." In 1859, a reviewer praising Bushnell's *The Natural and the Supernatural* called it "the chief theological work of the time" and added tellingly: "its strong current, as though we were on the surface of a novel, swept us through all the crooks in a day."[142] A novel persuades without argument, without labor: it suggests a credo of leisure. William Peabody, reviewing Fredericka Bremer's novels in a laudatory notice for the *North American Review* in 1845, recognized that the very young could be reached best by stories: "fiction is the first thing [the young mind] learns to love."[143] Fiction creates a kind of birthright church of its own such as the non-evangelicals dreamed of: no struggle, no conversion experience are necessary.

For the same reasons, of course, novels were dangerous. If feminine fiction was to induce or substitute for religious faith, what was to become of the church, of dogma? Clerical critics incessantly compared the effect of fiction to that of alcohol and tobacco.[144] William Peabody warned his son against excessive indulgence in novels: "It is to the mind like drinking to the body: it intoxicates and destroys the power of the mind for any strong and useful exercise."[145] It was a standard complaint that fiction allowed the reader to be "passive"; as Peabody pointed out in his review of Fredericka Bremer's novels,[146] the entranced reader is like a traveler gradually falling asleep in a snowdrift. An anonymous reviewer of "New Books of Piety" for the *Christian Examiner* in 1863 elaborates brilliantly on Peabody's thought. "Novel-reading," he explains, involves "the cultivation of a single set of feelings"; "all the organs seem to be on the point of becoming rudimental again, under the tyrannical development of a single inner sense." Novel-reading thus produces "hypocrisy and shameful insensibility of the actual world."[147] In tones strikingly similar to those of present-day critics of television, these spokesmen are struggling to formulate and define the rapt, autistic, regressive state of the member of the modern mass audience. Peabody had put the clerical apprehension succinctly: it is because of novel-reading "that so few people *think*."[148]

We have already seen the stress placed on memory and the insignificant value attached to independent observation in girls' education. Emma Willard's talented sister, Almira Phelps, also a teacher, complained that a young lady on a ship would fall into a romantic revery while her male counterpart would try to find out how the boat worked. Phelps was making an implicit critique of female instruction: if one knows the world only by memory, only by rote so to speak, the only possible imaginative exercise available is fantasy, the excursion into the unreal.[149] A reviewer for the *Christian Examiner* in 1839 castigated "female novelists" for overdoing "introspective auto-biography."[150] Another critic in the same journal a few years earlier had referred offhandedly but significantly to "the adventure of some hero or the sentiment of some heroine."[151] "Heroines," who naturally predominated over "heroes" in a fiction written largely by women for women, did not act or observe: they *felt*. Orville Dewey in a Phi Beta Kappa oration delivered in 1830 articulated his claustrophobic conviction that American letters fostered a hothouse rather than a schoolroom atmosphere. Novel-reading is the pursuit of idle ladies and of men who are fast becoming "effeminate" as a result. American literature is no longer "public" but "private": Dewey sensed in feminine fiction the personalism of the liberal clergyman carried to its extreme limits. Novels are "luxuries"—a word Dewey repeats several times—not "substantial food";[152] literature has become a form of consumption rather than of productivity. Dewey understood that fiction was to be the special property of Susan Warner's Ellen Montgomery.

The Clerical Dilemma: The Recourse to History

The contradictions in the clerical response to the feminine presence and challenge are as obvious as they are explicable. The ministers were caught in a vicious paradox. The women were their principal supporters. Accepting feminine help meant in part prolonging their own exile from masculine concerns; refusing it hardly guaranteed new and different adherents. On the one hand, to praise feminine virtues, or books, was to encourage women to look upon clerical prerogatives as their rights. On the other, since ministers were in fact drawn ever more closely to feminine models, to exalt womanhood and its efforts was to enhance themselves and their own claims to authority. For most of the clergymen involved there could be no real resolution to this profound difficulty, although a number of them, as we shall see, attempted to find one. The simplest attitude for them to adopt about their feminized position, one which in part obviated the problem of evaluation, was what one might call historical. On the vexed issue of fiction, many non-evangelical clergymen acknowledged that novels were here to stay, with or without ministerial approval. Austin Phelps began reading novels late in life "as a sedative"; he soon concluded that fiction "is not only one department [of literature], but is fast becoming *the* department overshadowing all the rest."[153] On the closely related question of the essentially feminine nature of Christianity itself, the minister occasionally took a similarly historical overview. One Unitarian clergyman writing for the *Christian Examiner* in 1858 announced that while "the ancient world was emphatically masculine," "Christianity [had] proclaimed the Gospel of the 'Ever Feminine' " and showed "the utter nothingness of masculine self-sufficiency."[154]

William Ware, a distinguished historical novelist as well as a less distinguished Unitarian pastor, amplified and complicated this analysis in his romance *Zenobia*, published in 1836 and destined for long popularity. The story recounts the conflict in the third century between the warlike Roman emperor Aurelian and the ambitious and proud mistress of the eastern kingdom of Palmyra. More important, the book represents Ware's carefully researched, rather timid, yet deeply felt imaginative projection of a pre-Christian civilization. This is a world in which a capacious and unpolarized sexuality sets the ideal. The noblest men are fighters, philosophers, and lovers of beauty; the finest women lead armies, and handle weapons as skillfully as they do lutes. In one of the most fascinating scenes in the book, Zenobia, her daughter Julia, and her closest friend Fausta play at a sport which involves shooting a spear through a ring so that it lands on the ground beyond. One woman after another accomplishes this feat with nearly perfect success while the narrator Manlius applauds. It takes no knowledge of Freud to realize that Ware is exalting the powerful attractions of a profoundly bisexual culture. Christianity, however, is waiting like a character in the wings for its cue. Manlius, soon to be a neophyte, interprets the nature of the new faith to his Roman friends. Christianity is "feminine" although not "weak or effeminate." It is characterized by "its gentleness, ... the suavity of its tone, ... the humanity of its doctrines, ... the deep love it breathes toward all of human kind, ... the high rank it assigns to the virtues which are particularly those of women."[155] Of necessity, it will be opposed to the aspiring spirit of Palmyra as surely as to the militarism that is Rome. *Aurelian* (1838) and *Julian* (1841), the two successors to *Zenobia* Ware wrote, concentrate, interestingly enough, more on the persecutions of the Christian converts than on their eventual triumph. Ware's hesitation about the modern feminized religious culture which will succeed the heroic pagan society is apparent not only in the point at which he focuses and stages his story, but in the form he chooses for it; the scholarly romance, first widely popularized by Sir Walter Scott, was the most "masculine" of the fictional forms, yet it was indisputably fiction. Ware wants it both ways, if he wants it at all.

Lurking behind Ware's books and the pronouncement of the *Christian Examiner* reviewer is an attempt to find in historical necessity an escape from the dilemma of the clerical profession. The modern historian, with the easy advantage of hindsight, can see the line of thought which contemporary clerical writers were barely beginning to enunciate. Beneath the conjunction of femininity and Christianity lies a probably unacknowledged assumption that the modern age in some sense would belong to the woman; and hence, hopefully, to the minister who accommodates and imitates her. Indeed, whether or not clerical observers fully knew it, the middle-class woman's place in the emerging industrial order was assured; if neither autonomous nor respected, she would be, at the least, its most carefully watched, skillfully programmed, and rewarded victim. In espousing feminine values, the minister could become a middle-man of history, a participant, or a puppet with his feminine peers in the rather cowardly new world of consumer culture. The historical rationale, no matter what its validity, no matter how fully it exculpates the woman and the woman-bound minister and releases them from the impossible task of self-judgment, leaves two absolutely critical questions unanswered: where will the process of feminization, and fictionalization, stop? And whose interests does it ultimately serve?

PART TWO

The Sentimentalization
of
Creed and Culture

4

THE LOSS
OF THEOLOGY

From Dogma to Fiction

Atonement: The Descent of God

Certainly the forces of sentimentalism would alter the doctrinal beliefs of liberal Protestants, and in dramatic ways. New England Calvinism had long centered itself on the concept of the Atonement. Let me outline briefly this doctrine so crucial to the northern mind and imagination. I will use as my *locus classicus*, *True Religion Delineated* by Joseph Bellamy, a follower, in some sense a popularizer, of Jonathan Edwards. Bellamy published his theological masterpiece in 1750, with Edwards' explicit endorsement, to "distinguish true religion from false."[1] The more "liberal" or "old light" branch of New England Calvinists disapproved of it from the start; Bellamy's essentially Grotian theory represented the first skirmish in a long battle in which the Calvinists were to try, not altogether successfully, to fight the increasingly powerful liberals with liberal weapons.[2] Yet whatever its concessions viewed from a mid-eighteenth-century strict Calvinist viewpoint, Bellamy's tract represented the last major formulation, or reformulation, of the older idea of the Atonement to prove itself acceptable and effective for large numbers of American Protestants. If we can trust Harriet Beecher Stowe, and she is speaking here on matters she had every reason to know well, *True Religion Delineated* was one of the most popular non-fictional books in New England in the eighteenth and early nineteenth centuries.[3] To read Bellamy's treatise even today is to be caught up in its trenchant logic and superb rhetoric.

Bellamy's first premise is, quite simply, that God is the author of evil but that man is totally responsible for sin. There is an apparent contradiction here, but not to Bellamy, who feels confident he is dealing with "plain fact." God *is* omnipotent, and the world *is* full of evil. God could of course have done things differently had he so chosen. Therefore, he did not so choose. There you have it. Yet how can man be punished for sin that God has willed? Bellamy's answers grow less direct here, though nonetheless powerful. Man or Adam, he argues, had an "infinite obligation" to love God. Therefore, the slightest deviation from obedience was deserving of "infinite" punishment. In fact, Bellamy explains, "a whole eternity of perfect obedience would do just nothing towards making the least amends for the smallest sin." As it is, far from being obedient, man is infinitely depraved, with a heart longing to destroy his creator: indeed he *cannot* will good. Nathaniel Emmons with merciless candor would acknowledge what many of his colleagues evaded or worked out by complex theories of differing kinds of "ability":[4] God requires something of man (virtue, obedience) that he has not given him.[5] God asks the impossible. Bellamy pointed out that God is capable of willing sin to bring about good—thus he hardened Pharaoh's heart so that the Hebrews might leave Egypt while its ruler drowned in the Red Sea—but man can only will evil for the sake of evil, and hence is culpable.

In the main, however, Bellamy avoids such rationalizations of God's behavior as in themselves impious. He stresses bluntly and repeatedly that man has no claims on God at all: every man has deserved eternal damnation if only because God wants it that way. God is to judge man, not to be judged by him: "when it is a plain matter of fact that God does such a thing, we may thence conclude that it is most certainly right for him to do so, although we cannot understand how it is" (154). In fact, Bellamy is perfectly willing to admit that what "would be infinitely wicked for the highest angel in heaven," much less man, to do, is "infinitely becoming to God" (19). God, in other words, is absolutely entitled to commit what humanity calls crimes and account them benevolence; mankind must abide by his values. "O, but for God to damn a whole world for one sin!" Bellamy imagines his reader exclaiming, and then reproves him: "But stay; does not this arise from mean thoughts of God and high thoughts of yourself?" (156).

It cannot be too much stressed how supremely *other* Bellamy's God is; from the human perspective that William Ellery Channing would espouse so passionately in his seminal 1819 address at Jared Sparks's ordination, God is utterly lawless. His motive is indeed love, but it is self-love. The universe is his mirror. God is a narcissist, creating a world as an actor might write a play—so that he can have the starring role. And he wants a big part, calling for a characterization that will run the gamut of emotional possibilities. He has written the story of man's damnation and salvation because it will fully reveal and exercise his gifts. "What will he get by it all?" Bellamy inquires. "He will excite and display every one of his perfections to the life and so ... will exhibit a most perfect and exact image of himself" (44). Regenerate man will be so magnetized by the spectacle of God's glory that he will happily consent to play any bit part in the cosmic drama. He will, as Samuel Hopkins was to explain, be willing to be damned if God so wills it; he will rejoice, as Emmons liked to emphasize, in seeing once-cherished friends and relatives tossed into hell-fire by a justly incensed deity.[6]

What can be the meaning of Atonement, the part of mercy, in such a ritual of eternal exhibitionism? Bellamy makes it crystal clear that God was under no obligation to give his son to suffer for man's misdemeanors; nor is he compelled to forgive man's sins because Christ has died. Christ was sacrificed not to take away sin, but to display God's dislike of it: not to show God's clemency, but to stress his punitiveness. Bellamy's God, ever histrionic, puts on a sort of spectacular temper tantrum controlled only by his divine and innate didactic purpose: he reveals his hatred of his creatures, not his love of them (267). He in no way responds to man's needs; he is following out his own laws of self-expression. Yet there is another element in this action, for, by Christ's death, God is making it possible for himself to forgive man if he should choose to do so. Christ in dying satisfied God's "honor" (269–70). The Savior died, in other words, to pacify the Lord's pride. God can now feel justified in saving, if he so chooses, men from the damnation they still richly and infinitely deserve.[7] Curiously, the Atonement has changed neither man nor God nor the basic relations between them. On the one hand, it seems a mere facilitating maneuver, a face-saving operation; on the other, its token quality is a testimony to the eternal rightness of God's order. A radical turnabout in God's attitude would have indicated a need for alteration, would have hinted at imperfections; for a being so tremendous, action must be merely symbolic, merely display. The Atonement represents only a different expression on the unchangeable divine countenance; God is God and man is man still, despite Christ.

This doctrine of the Atonement is in many ways a horrifying one. Yet it clearly once possessed immense imaginative and intellectual appeal. Unfair as it undoubtedly is, it operated as a model of majesty; crushing, humiliating as it may appear and often was, it could be a source, almost uniquely so even among Western religions, of energy. It provided its adherent, no matter how it belittled him, with a supreme and commanding object of worship. According to popular lore, a black man who had long attended Bellamy's church was asked after the retirement of that powerful and eloquent preacher how he liked his successor; the parishioner found the newer man satisfactory, but not so exciting or stimulating as Bellamy had been. Bellamy "made God so great—SO GREAT," he explained.[8] The terror and the thrill of obeying, partially identifying with, even being punished by such a mighty being must have been enormous. Furthermore, Bellamy's claim that he was presenting the "plain facts" was a potent one: Calvinism, resting on its stern ideas of the Atonement, squarely faced the presence of evil, of sin, of injustice in life. In the Calvinist view, things are inevitably one way and not another. Consequences are to be respected. All men suffer from Adam's sin as surely as a child singed by the fire is burned.

The idea of the Atonement which gradually came to replace the Edwardsean or "New Divinity" theory among liberal Protestant ministers and theologians in the early and mid-nineteenth century represented a shift from this basically paternal (or gubernatorial) and authoritarian view to a fundamentally maternal and affective one. God is no longer expressing hatred of sin in his sacrifice of his son but love of man; he ceases to govern by the direct imposition of his will and begins to sway by the influence of example. In certain ways, the change was, and is, obviously a welcome one. Yet the difficulty for modern thinkers in the newer, "softer" theory is not that it opposes the older, male-dominated concept of the Atonement, but rather that its opposition is incomplete and finally unimaginative; patriarchy is denied, but truly matriarchal values are not espoused. Strength, as essential to genuinely feminine as to genuinely masculine social and intellectual structures, is absent; weakness itself, no matter how unintentionally, is finally extolled.

This shift in the doctrine of the Atonement was already under way in various forms in the eighteenth century within the liberal wing of the Calvinist clergy, but it surfaced dramatically and decisively in the next century with the Universalist attack on the Atonement in 1807 by Hosea Ballou (1771–1852), the Unitarian assault begun by Channing in 1819 and consummated by Noah Worcester (1758–1837) in 1830, and the Congregationalist redefinition of the doctrine under the skillful command of Horace Bushnell in 1866. In a sense all of these thinkers were playing variations on the same theme. Ballou was well aware that Channing was echoing him; the *Christian Examiner* welcomed Bushnell's work as Unitarian in spirit, and queried whether the Hartford theologian had read (and failed to acknowledge) Worcester. The successive adoption by these thinkers of an increasingly liberalized and sentimentalized Atonement was immensely significant if only because it symbolized the deeper and deeper penetration and acceptance of formerly denounced heresy into the citadels of orthodoxy.

Ballou's seminal and simply titled *Treatise on the Atonement* was written in a vigorous and trenchant style that Bellamy would have understood even while he would have abhorred the doctrines the book contained. Ballou begins by saying that sin is only the result of "the imperfect knowledge men have of moral good." Since this knowledge is itself incomplete, in other words, finite, sin itself must be finite, not infinite as Bellamy had argued (15).[9] If sin were infinite, Ballou points out, it would be by definition uncheckable, even by God (18). Because it is finite, so is its punishment; there is no final and complete damnation such as Bellamy envisioned as the fate of a large portion of the human race. Ballou, like Bellamy, argues that God is the author of sin, but he is so only because "it is intended for [man's] good" (36). Here Ballou gives the story of Joseph and his brothers. The brothers' treachery led to Joseph's elevation and their own final redemption, thus providing an example, to be much used in Universalist annals, of the beneficent consequences of sin. God nowhere, according to Ballou, requires more of his creatures than they can perform, for his aim is not self-assertion but accommodation to men, the working out of their salvation in terms comprehensible to them. Ballou mocks the very idea that God could want either to preserve or to add to his glory, for such a wish would imply that it is not already eternal and immutable. God would never punish men eternally because endless torment by definition cannot heal or reclaim them; and their spiritual growth is his preoccupation.

The Atonement had what meaning it did in Bellamy's scheme precisely because man, through his inability to appease God's honor or his wrath, needed, although he in no way deserved, Christ's sacrifice. Ballou has removed this rationale; he even ridicules the self-involved nature of Bellamy's god whom he imagines as a creditor finally, and ludicrously, paying the debt to himself which he insists must be paid and which man the debtor cannot pay. Ballou's translation of a divine dilemma here into its human analogue —which he then uses as an unimpeachable test of truth—is typical. God's privileged, absolutely non-human status is gone; he is to be judged very much in mortal and moral terms. "It is profane," Ballou explains, "to attribute a disposition to the Almighty which we can justly condemn in ourselves" (88). He always feels it a fair and pertinent question to ask about any divine action: is it the way a parent would treat a child? While Bellamy started from the premise that it is obvious that God does *not* treat man as a father treats his son, Ballou assumes the reverse.

It is precisely from this implied familial affection that Ballou draws his own explanation of the Atonement, which he illustrates repeatedly and tellingly by the parable of the prodigal son. God does not need to be reconciled to man, for his love because divine has been unchanging; it is rather man who is to be reconciled to his maker. Ballou is careful to explain it as part of Adam's sin that he (wrongly) thought the Lord was angry with him; he projected his own evil passions onto God. The undeniable fact remains that God, far from feeling any need for appeasement, is wooing man, winning him by a display of affection and conciliation. Furthermore,

God, like any good parent, loves all his children equally (178); he wants the happiness of all of them; he will save them all. Ballou utterly rejects Bellamy's notion that man could so far forget himself in God's glory as to rejoice in anyone's damnation, for human feeling, trifling in Bellamy's powerfully logical system, has become the supreme value in Ballou's scheme. Ballou "had rather," by his own emphatic confession, "be possessed of that *sympathy* which causes [one man] to *feel* for *another*, than to *enjoy* an *unsocial pleasure* in a *frosty heaven* of misanthropy!" (182).

Man has displaced God on center stage in Ballou's vision, but God, though relegated to the wings, is still God, still authoritative. Ballou gladly sacrifices free will, though his Universalist followers were not always willing to join him, in order to retain some vestige of God's sovereignty. Man, according to Ballou's plan, has no more choice about being saved than he did under the Calvinist dispensation about being damned. When we come to Noah Worcester's tract, *The Atoning Sacrifice, A Display of Love Not of Wrath*, the changed title indicates the further metamorphosis the doctrine has undergone since it left Ballou's hands.

Worcester, unlike Bellamy or Ballou, was no controversialist. A leader in the pacifist movement, an editor of the *Christian Examiner* and dedicated to eradicating the spirit of sectarian strife from its pages, he was distinguished, in the words of a contemporary, for his "dignity and sweetness," his "almost feminine gentleness," and his capacity for "gratitude"; he began every blessing by placing his hand on his heart and invoking the Lord with heartfelt emphasis as "Indulgent Parent!"[10] In *The Atoning Sacrifice* Worcester, like Ballou, basically rests his argument on anthropomorphic and familial analogies: "to every Christian who knows by experience the feelings of a tender father, the following appeal is made," he explains (6).[11] Like Ballou, he views the Atonement as "the means of effecting changes in *us* not in God" (12). But his interest is no longer in a sovereign God, or in God at all except as he manifests himself in a "submissive, meek and forgiving" Christ. The Atonement has become for Worcester, the self-styled "Philo Pacificus," "a PACIFIC MEASURE . . . made from love to enemies and on the gospel principle of overcoming good with evil" (3). Ballou had wanted to minimize, even ignore, suffering precisely because he saw it as punishment for sin, and he did not believe God would punish sin with undue severity. Worcester transforms the very nature of suffering itself: it is often, even in this life, not "of the nature of punishment" but the result of "well-doing," for the "virtuous frequently . . . suffer for the guilty" (113–14).

This is the rationale for the suffering of the victim: the innocent civilian depicted in Worcester's pacifist propaganda, massacred or mutilated in a war for which he or she has no responsibility; the guiltless wife dramatized in the temperance literature of the day, chained to an alcoholic brute; and now Christ himself, winning both God and man by the patience and forbearance he exhibits in his ordeal. Bronson Alcott, a brilliant if erratic transcendental educator and philosopher, refused to discipline his pupils in the accepted way. The only use of the rod he condoned was in the hands of his guilty students. The punishment he inflicted for an infraction of rules, in other words, was to force the offender to hit him, the teacher. According to Alcott's daughter, Louisa, this treatment produced deep, lasting remorse because the boys were forced to display and feel their own brutality; they saw the consequences of their misdemeanor in the pain it literally and figuratively caused their loving and concerned instructor. Alcott was giving his students a lesson in the meaning of the Atonement as Worcester understood it; he, like Christ, was martyring himself to express and exorcise the sinfulness of his charges.[12] God is no longer acting out his own drama, but man's. Bellamy's God was a commander and a logician; Worcester's Savior is a creature of feeling, passive rather than active, invoking not displaying.

Bushnell's contribution to this evolving reinterpretation of the Atonement was entitled *The Vicarious Sacrifice*. His substitute of the word "vicarious" for Worcester's "atoning" is highly indicative of the increasingly parasitic and indirect quality he finds in God's action. Bushnell's theory is the same as Worcester's but his stress is different. He emphasizes even more heavily God's love of man; God "clings" to his creature, "feeling afflicted for him, ... encountering gladly any loss or suffering for his sake" (280).[13] A reviewer for the *Christian Examiner* pinpointed the newest and most radical development Bushnell had initiated. "The purpose of the incarnation was not to meet man's need but God's," Bushnell's critic summarizes his argument. "God could not reach man; therefore he 'broke into the world' to get at his last offspring. He came to acquire with man a character, and thus to secure the influence of character," or what Bushnell calls "moral power."[14] With the incarnation, God has ceased to be an "abstract excellence" and become a "person." He is not just consenting to act out man's passions, as in Worcester's vision; he is expropriating them.

Bushnell's concept is more complex than I am suggesting here.[15] He felt and provided for God's glory as neither his predecessors nor his followers did. Eight years after the publication of *The Vicarious Sacrifice*, Bushnell wrote *Forgiveness and Law Grounded in Principles Interpreted by Human Analogies* which, as its title suggests, was designed to correct what he had come to see as the over-liberal, too anthropomorphic bias of the first treatise. In the later treatise, Bushnell stressed that the Atonement was necessary not just to win man but to pacify God.[16] Yet Bushnell was not as influential in his revision as in his first presentation. And in his earlier work, God has in a real sense abdicated. Bushnell's deity, like some celebrity dissatisfied with his totally public existence, has yearned for, and found, a private life. It is the fantasy, often not without rationale or validity, of the weak that the strong will spontaneously give up the pre-eminence which their inferiors would be forever incapable of wresting from them because they suddenly feel its emptiness. It is a fantasy offering a double compliment to the dreamer, honoring his enforced passivity, vindicating the validity of his portion even while bettering it. God has justified his creatures in Bushnell's scenario simply by envying them. He has found it lonely to be God up there with all that power and no love. He prefers earth to heaven, feeling to logic. Bushnell repeatedly stresses Christ's "sensibility," his "sympathy"; he points out that the Savior's suffering can be "nothing strange" to us because we witness it daily in the responses of a mother to her child.[17] It is not just that God wants to become man; he wants to become woman.

In a sense we are back with Sarah Hale who wished men to become more like women and women to become more like angels. Not surprisingly, Hale evolved a theological doctrine of the Fall in which woman was cast in the role of Bushnellian Savior. Hale presented her theory, an attempt to translate the drama of the Atonement into sexual terms, as the preface to her *Woman's Record* in 1852. Asserting that God created woman last as the crowning and best part of creation, she explains that woman was indeed made "for man," but not in the sense in which the words are usually understood: "She was not made to gratify his sensual desires but to refine his human affections and elevate his moral feelings. Endowed with superior beauty of person and a correspondent delicacy of mind, her soul was to 'help' him where he was deficient, namely in his spiritual nature." To complete the parallel between Eve and Atoning Christ, the effect of original sin (for which Hale assigns Adam almost total responsibility) is inextricably to entangle woman with the fate of her inferior, man. She is to suffer vicariously for his sins, and to try to work out through the "influence" her new proximity at least assures her the "salvation [of] . . . the race."[18]

Hale was not only anticipating Bushnell, but formulating the essential drama of contemporary feminine fiction. In its pages, a woman did not need to be tied to a drunkard to suffer a Christlike martyrdom. Mara Lincoln of Stowe's *The Pearl of Orr's Island* acts out Bushnellian and Halean concepts of the Atonement. She converts the novel's black sheep, the rather brutish though attractive Moses Fennell; but she accomplishes this not by marrying him as he wants her to do, but by dying. Always ethereal in mind and "delicate" in body, shortly after her engagement Mara goes first into a decline and eventually into a lengthy sequence of edifying deathbed scenes. Like all the dying heroines in the popular fiction of the day, Mara offers both a reproach and an inspiration to the masculine mourners gathered to watch her demise. Mara sickens, symbolically, when Moses is away on a long trip and she has not yet completely won his heart. As a boy, he had been brutally indifferent to her feelings. As a young man in love with her, he revealed little more sensitivity. He regarded her religious faith, utterly crucial to her, half-contemptuously, as a suitable possession for a woman but irrelevant to a man: in his view, someone (a woman) ought to spend her time treasuring this obsolete belief whose value is currently next to nothing, on the off-chance that the market will alter. In a sense, Moses prized Mara precisely because he could dismiss her. Mara worried even before her illness that she should not unite her purer nature with his coarser one, but her "sympathy," like Christ's, made the link between heavenly and earthly beings; in a curious way, her illness is the result. Sinless herself, she is suffering for his offenses. But she tacitly lures even while she accuses him. In her weakness is her strength; last, she is indeed first. Death has put her on center stage in a lead role for the first time. She is finally able to reveal fully the beauties of faith and devotion (and herself) in what becomes a tantalizing display; for like a smart salesman, she is snapping shut her case and walking out the door just when her customer is ready to pull out his wallet. Moses, newly and power-fully convinced of Mara's value, is destined to a lifetime role as a faithful and unsatisfied devotee.

Yet Mara has done nothing spectacular, nothing dramatic. Her death, like her life, is quiet, gradual, graceful. In *The Vicarious Sacrifice*, Bushnell says of Christ's triumphs that they did not come from "the heat of encoun-ter"; the Savior earned "no title of honor such as the world's great men have achieved." Indeed, Bushnell reminds us, until Christ was thirty, he did "noth-ing more than to beautifully and exactly fulfill his duties."[19] How like the gently conscientious Mara the Lord sounds! Both of them operate in what-ever historical time is suggested by the atmosphere of home, not in a con-tinuum of destiny determined by the events of the forum or the field. In *Little Foxes* (1866), Stowe encouraged the housewife to see herself as engaged in a small-time but crucial process of daily self-sacrifice, to "look at her domestic trials as her haircloth, her ashes, her scourges—accept them—rejoice in them—smile and be quiet, silent, patient and loving under them. . . . [she] is a victorious saint."[20] In "Living to God in Small Things" (1839), Bushnell had urged his readers in similar fashion not to be misled by love of fame to overlook "influence," "at first . . . not felt because . . . noiseless," but gradually all-pervasive. He directs them to the example of God, who "descends to an infinite detail." If God merely attended to the thunder and forgot the dew, "his works would be only crude and disjointed machines."[21] Again in an important sermon of 1846 called "Unconscious Influence," after defining the nature of influence—by a "law of social contagion . . . we overrun the boundaries of our personality, we flow together"—and stressing its all-important role in family life and child-rearing, Bushnell points out that men "dislike to be swayed by direct, voluntary influence. They are jealous of such control, and are therefore best approached by conduct and feeling, and the authority of simple worth which seems to make no purposed onset." This, he adds, was precisely Christ's method.[22]

The special realm for ministers as for women was that of the little, the overlooked but indispensable detail; by an obvious compensatory process, they were believers in the adage that "a stitch in time saves nine," tellers of the tale about the finger in the dike. They were pledged, professionally, to the insignificant and its crucial effect on the unconscious. Sarah Edgarton Mayo, explaining her predilection for what her contemporaries called the "beautiful" rather than the "sublime," exclaimed: "I love little scenes and things the world all over. There is a sublimity in space but beauty is made up of little parts. A tree, a knoll of flowers, a singing brook, a bud, a butterfly, a bee—are not these a picture? I love things *near*."[23] Sylvester Judd was describing the same predilection when he remarked, "Nature, like art, seems to require a border in order to be finished." Judd preferred a view of a distant mountain framed and contained by neighboring woods to the broad and open view from a summit.[24] He too avoided the big. Both Mayo and Judd promise and ask for protection, permanent residence amid objects that will neither threaten nor dwarf. They anthropomorphize their world, they make it accessible; they translate foreign texts into their own language; they give and ask for the flattery of imitation. Their commitment to the little, the near, is one with their commitment to a Bushnellian or Worcesterian Atonement by "influence."

The new Bushnellian Christ, meeting men on mortal terrain, shaping himself to human needs, offering himself as a model not as a governor, is very much Mayo's and Judd's representative. He has become a being who tactfully refuses to overwhelm those whose favor he courts; he wisely prefers to prove his power of infiltration than to test his capacity for onslaught. Newly sensitized and feminized in image, defined as a lover of all the world's "little ones," the liberal Jesus too is interested in discovering and tapping the unconscious; he too is adept at the small gains which can pass unnoticed. Like a character in a story, very much in fact like Stowe's Mara, Bushnell's Christ is connotative, even derivative; he must suffer rather than command precisely because he is dependent for his reality, not on his "readers'" abilities to perceive objective truth, but on their capacities for subjective impression and reaction.[25]

Conversion and Church Membership: From Testing to Playing

The personalized, feminized, literary Bushnellian view of the Atonement was, as we have seen, a non-crisis-oriented one, and it implied and presupposed a tranquil theory of religious development in man as well as in God.

In the older Calvinist scheme, some persons were saved, others were not, and the difference was a momentous and hopefully visible one. God's ways were both unknowable and exact; momentously, one person *was* taken, another *was* left, although the why of it might not be clear. There was an immense incentive for thought-filled precision in this creed with its imperious and legalistic Atonement. Repressive as it was, Calvinism was empirical, even scientific, in the special objectivity it fostered and demanded in its most faithful believers. If God had few soft spots in his heart, little sympathy for man, the good minister owed it to his flock to be equally harsh, equally factual, and equally determinate. The only antidote for divine wrath at a clergyman's disposal was ministerial wrath; the only immunity to punishment was in its anticipation. Calvinism could give to those who believed it a confidence, which at times merged unpleasantly with arrogance, that they were at least fully armed, if not invulnerable.

The greatest figures of New England Calvinism showed an ability to examine and judge religious states which was to become legendary. Samuel Hopkins was noted for the kindly meant cruelty with which he discouraged even dying parishioners who he believed to be entertaining a "false hope." In 1755 called to the deathbed of a woman "full of joy and comfort supposing she had saving discoveries of Christ," he was satisfied "upon examining her ... that she was deceived; that it was only the workings of her imagination. She was confident, but I told her my fears." With resigned insight he concludes: "How exposed to the delusions of the devil are ignorant persons! especially those whose understanding is shattered and their imagination lively by a fever."[26] Nathaniel Emmons brought the same relentless spirit of investigation to the consideration of his son Erastus, who died in 1820. He had found little that was promising there, and with the more than Roman rigor, the spare severity which ever characterized him, he told his congregation so in the funeral sermon he preached on the occasion:

> He lived stupid, thoughtless and secure in sin, until he was brought to the very sight of death. ... But whether he did ever heartily renounce the world and choose God for his supreme portion cannot be known in this world. In his own view he had become reconciled to God. ... But it is more than possible that like others on a sick-bed, he built his hopes upon a sandy foundation.[27]

Emmons, like most of his persuasion, expected the Lord's workings in the human soul to be marked and momentous; no easy assurances of inner peace, whether given on a deathbed or elsewhere, could satisfy him. Throughout the nineteenth century, the more theologically conservative and revivalistically oriented denominations kept the earlier Calvinist emphasis on a pronounced, even violent, often sudden conversion experience; revivals themselves were of course premised on the reality of such an experience. Lyman Beecher's attitude toward conversion was typically evangelical. His own religious awakening, as he remembered it in later years, was quick and powerful, possessing obvious and conscious parallels to Paul's epiphany on the road to Damascus. At the age of twenty, Beecher was deeply struck by a remark of his mother's on a passing drunkard who had once been "under conviction" but had since lost all religious inclinations.

> There was no perceptible effect from these words, only, after she left the room I felt a sudden impulse to pray. . . . I was not in the habit of prayer. I rose to pray, and had not spoken five words before I was under as deep conviction as ever I was in my life. The sinking of the shaft was instantaneous. I understood the law and my heart as well as I do now or shall in the day of judgment. I believe the commandment came, sin revived, and I died, quick as a flash of lightning.[28]

Beecher remained faithful throughout his career to his own conversion experience as a model. In 1829, he wrote a friend testifying to his belief in "instantaneous" as opposed to "gradual" conversion;[29] and he was always willing to analyze and defend the "conviction" he had thus received.

Beecher's awakening was implicitly a testimony to God's power as well as to Beecher's own importance, a tribute to divine ability to intervene massively and decisively at a given instant in an individual's life. Beecher's most famous children belonged to a very different generation theologically, and none of them were able, or willing, to achieve a similar experience. From the start, Beecher urged his sons and daughters to "agonize, *agonize*" to enter in at the strait gate; certainly he himself agonized over them and regularly subjected their hearts to a scrutiny almost as piercing as Emmons'.[30] Beecher's happiness in his revival work was deeply alloyed by the realization that none of his own family were "safe." Edward stalled almost endlessly and never knew a full saving experience. Catharine was unable to undergo conversion at all despite a barrage of letters written to her (and published) by her father in the 1820s;[31] Harriet defied most of the rules of Edwardsean theology by coming into her father's study at a very tender age full of happy confidence that the Lord had simply taken her to be his own; she felt no anguish, only infinite calm and joy. Henry Ward as a boy was puzzled and troubled by the whole process, pressured constantly by demands he could neither meet nor dispute.

Significantly, the Beecher children, with the possible exception of Catharine,[32] did not want their father as the engineer of their conversion or their intercessor at the throne; they longed rather to see their mother, Roxana

Foote Beecher, in that role. Henry Ward, explaining his childhood religious perplexity, wrote significantly: "I wanted to be a Christian. I went about longing for God as a lamb bleating longs for its mother's udder."[33] Henry Ward was barely three when his mother died of consumption in 1816, but even then, according to family legend, he made an effort to run away to "Ma" in "heaven," and he talked of her his whole life. Harriet, in explaining her mother's role in family life, later wrote that "her memory and example had more influence in molding her family, in deterring from evil and exciting to good than the living presence of many mothers." She represented for her children a "blessed" figure, a "saint in heaven." Harriet recalled vividly waking from a virulent, nearly fatal fever as a child to hear her father praying thankfully to his dear wife now with the Lord. As Harriet paints the scene, there is a clear sense that Roxana Beecher has saved her daughter's life by her holy mediation, just as she stood "as a sacred shield" between her sons "and the temptations of youth."[34] It is worth remembering that Charles Beecher, Roxana's youngest born, dedicated his Bushnellian work on the Atonement, *The Redeemer and the Redeemed*, to his mother, whom, as he said, next to his Savior he most hoped to meet at the Resurrection.

Roxana Beecher has both special and representative significance. By all accounts an extraordinarily gifted and intelligent woman, reserved, quiet, evincing fine breeding and even elegant manners, with artistic tastes and a keen interest in science, she came from an Episcopalian family and never essentially changed her faith. Indeed, in the early days of their courtship and marriage, Lyman, fresh from his theological training and preparing for his first ministerial assignment on Long Island, kept trying to test, à la Hopkins or Emmons, the soundness of his fiancée's religious hope. He was essentially anxious because she confessed to none of the negative aspects of the traditional conversion experience: she did not acknowledge "a disposition so horrid as even to curse God to his face," such as Bellamy had posited; she did not seem to love God's glory "disinterestedly" without reference to the good he had done her. Roxana summarized her belief, and her opposition to her future husband, in a letter written on September 1, 1798, which was to become in many ways a key document of her children's experience and to serve as the basis of their own declaration of independence. Drawing on her Episcopalian and her feminine heritage, she dismisses a non-human God by the simple evidence of her own feelings:

> How ... can I help loving God because He is good to me? Were I not
> an object of God's mercy and goodness, I cannot have any conception
> what would be my feelings. Imagination never yet placed me in a
> situation not to experience the goodness of God in some way or other,
> and if I do love Him, how can it but be because He is good, and to me

good? Do not God's children love Him because He first loved them?
. . . In contemplating the character of God, his mercy and goodness are
most present to my mind, and, as it were, swallow up his other attributes.

Almost sixty years later, her husband touchingly and characteristically endorsed this letter "Roxana beloved still this Dec. 5, 1854, Lyman Beecher."[35]
There is little evidence to show that Roxana's epistle changed his thinking,
however, although his children sometimes liked to think so.

Roxana Foote, anticipating Ballou and Bushnell in her stress on the
primacy of God's love, on the Deity's intent to win her by giving her what
she needs and wants, is obviating the necessity of a painful or sudden conversion experience. There is nothing disagreeable or difficult for her to contemplate, only God's love. There is nothing disagreeable or difficult, or new, for
her to do; God has been continuously sustaining her by his affection and
gradually bringing her closer and closer to him. The religious awakening
Beecher advocated was a violent and immediate one essentially because it
assumed the confrontation of two enemies, God's grace and man's sinful
nature, and the absolute conquest of the latter by the former. Man is being
assimilated into something not-like-him; violation as well as regeneration is
at work. Roxana's implied view of conversion, which was to be Bushnell's,
is not that of a battle between two antagonists, but an evolving mutual
assimilation of two similar if unequal beings. Edward, Henry, and Charles
all concluded by adopting Roxana's view while officially staying within
their father's church (despite repeated protests and efforts at expulsion on
the part of that often bewildered and antagonized church); Harriet and
Catharine espoused their mother's testimony and her denomination.

More and more religious thinkers and activists of the generation succeeding Lyman Beecher's sidestepped or redefined the traditional conversion experience. Even Edwards A. Park, who would show strong revivalist
proclivities and a decided admiration for Finney, at eighteen decided to
become a minister although he had experienced no special religious awakening; he tested himself, and felt that he not only believed but loved the Biblical
doctrines and that this was sufficient.[36] Austin Phelps passed a sensitive—not
to say morbid—boyhood in the grip of "religious despair." His father, a
rather stern Congregational minister, forced the boy for his moral edification to attend funerals and look at the corpses. At twelve he was almost
converted in the traditional Calvinist way: he "longed for . . . [and] *waited*
for some sublime and revolutionary change of heart." In later years he found
his earlier agonies pathetic and totally unnecessary. He adopted a Bushnellian belief in religious "*nurture*" and "unconscious growth" based on a
domestic model: "The family is the nursery of [faith], and the Church is but

the family on an extended scale." Phelps even speculated that he might have been far happier had he been raised an Episcopalian.[37] Orville Dewey, also reared a Calvinist, repudiated his early training with equal vehemence: he came to feel that "Infidelity" was more defensible than Calvinism. Dewey found his youthful conversion regrettable: "it is lamentable that it ever should be an event in any human life."[38]

It is significant that both Phelps and Dewey intensely protested the way their orthodox parents had treated them as children. The Calvinist child went to church with his or her family twice on Sunday to sit in a pew often so constructed that few adults—and certainly no children—could see out of it and to listen to long, detailed, often highly abstract sermons written by adults for adults. Perhaps he or she was allowed to play with the strings of mother's purse, to look through the prayerbook, or at best to eat some treat specially brought along to reward or pacify younger members of the family. The child as such was an often uncomfortable hostage from another moral state, an impressed and ignorant recruit. In the eighteenth century most New England Calvinist churches had demanded of their full members baptism (and that often at a fairly advanced age when the subject would presumably be able to understand the meaning of the act) and a public testimony of conversion.[39] In the nineteenth century, an innovative evangelical like Lyman Beecher might repudiate infant damnation but he still insisted flatly: "Baptism in infancy does not constitute adult membership in the visible church." Beecher deplored the Unitarian "attempt ... to confound the scriptural distinction between the regenerate and the unregenerate."[40]

Prerequisites for church participation were squarely based on the conviction of innate depravity and an expectation of the significance of maturity; Calvinists assumed that a struggle was to be fought by the Christian which would require a certain amount of time, awareness, and skill. God could pour his grace out on a mere child—the legendary conversion of four-year-old Phoebe Bartlett under the ministration of Jonathan Edwards was evidence of the fact—but he was unlikely to do so. The paradox of Calvinism was its absolute stress on God's sovereignty with its equally firm emphasis on human preparedness. The Lord appeared to the ten virgins because he so desired, not because they were waiting (or not waiting) for him. But woe to them whose lamps were not ready to shed light on his coming![41] At its best, Calvinism represented a complex set of values which fostered both achievement and humility; it demanded that its adherents be both children and adults.

If one believed, however, with the liberals that the soul came into the world already prepared, already converted, why delay or complicate admission into a church society which could only benefit by the presence of young Christians? Channing liked to praise "the mild beauty of children": God would not, he believed, do anything so "repulsive and unamiable" as to damn them, as Calvinists had once held he did, or give them souls deserving of damnation.[42] Horace Bushnell found no opinion "more essentially monstrous . . . than that which regards the Holy Spirit as having no agency in the immature souls of children who are growing up helpless and unconscious into the perils of time."[43] Bushnell did not deny the presence of evil in children, but he denied its dominance, and in doing so, he, like Channing, repudiated the essential presupposition of Calvinism: that God rightly demands something of man that it is in some way impossible for man to do.

In Bushnell's view, it is precisely when the individual is least amenable to and capable of conscious control—namely, in childhood—that he or she is most assimilable to God. The great point is never to jar the child's sensibility, never to disturb the infant soul, which, like the needle of a compass, points unerringly and instinctively toward its maker. Children are to be encouraged, even imitated, not broken. Bushnell wanted early baptism and, like Sylvester Judd, he wished the baptized infants then to grow up Christians in the church, free to partake in communion, the standard test of adult membership, without any special profession.[44] Piety was to be the result of "habit," not of effort.[45] In this way, ministers could gain adherents without recourse to revivals, and very uncritical adherents at that. By a logical extension of the idea that God would accommodate himself to man, and gain from it, adults were to please children for the profit of their churches and their souls. If Christ in the Atonement acted on the unconscious, not the conscious, nature of men, ministers emulating him should logically address themselves to toddlers as well as grown-ups; they too should practice the techniques of maternal "influence" as formulated by women like Sigourney and Hale.

The permeation of the Protestant Church by children, which Charles Follen saw in a vision one Sunday afternoon, was a statement of fact as well as a fantasized ideal. Liberal ministers increasingly wooed the souls of children under their pastoral care. Sylvester Judd, in his "Account" of his conversion to Unitarianism, explained that his intellectual perplexities were solved, or rather obviated, by a little girl's intuitive understanding of the Sermon on the Mount: " 'I should not be happy in Heaven with God if I had a wicked heart,' " the child told Judd.[46] He later wanted to make his Augusta, Maine, parish into an extended family. He wrote to absent parishioners, especially the younger ones, as regularly and familiarly as if they were indeed part of his hearthside circle, always signing himself "Your affectionate friend and pastor";[47] he arranged special excursions and treats for the children in his congregation.[48] Judd was sincere, but he was setting and anticipating a trend; love of children would become almost a professional requirement for the ministry. The provision later in the century for recreation rooms and secular amusements within the church was part of an effort to assimilate the church to the home and the playground.

The old Calvinist way of church induction presupposed a struggle for maturity that implied distancing from the mother and conflict with the father, and drew on an implicit and anticipatory analogy with Oedipal development. It assumed, and expected, pain: not the passive suffering of deprivation and martyrdom, but the active distress of assault and achievement. The most obvious metaphor for the newly opened church as Bushnell and Judd conceived and tried to implement it, however, was that of a mother with her offspring, obviating their faults, smoothing their path—never letting them go. Domestic novelists, like liberal ministers, reveled in depictions of infantile piety gently and easily coasting from the nursery into the safe harbor of the church. Susan Warner, in a fascinating late novel entitled *Daisy Plains* (1885), which documents her own theological liberalization, shows two small girls, one white, the other a black servant, seeking church membership at the precocious age of ten. The father of the family, as always in Warner, has been a failure in every sense, but the mother has nurtured the children gently and incessantly in trust of Jesus as well as in reliance on the Bible. Symbolically, they go to examination at the hands of a number of initially skeptical and hostile clergymen straight from mother's arms. After their simple and heartfelt answers to the tricky questions of their increasingly impressed interlocutors have demonstrated that little girls best understand that true theology is but loving feeling, they return to her proud embrace.[49] Mother and church are one. Judd summed up the liberal ideal when he described the conversion experience, ideally unconscious, as a return, a "go[ing] home."[50]

Liberal theology and literature increasingly downplayed the importance of pain and effort in the conversion process. In the liberal view, self-torment and self-denial were flawed not because they were bad in themselves but because they could not really achieve their own goals. In Chapter Two I talked about Eva van Arsdel of Harriet Beecher Stowe's *My Wife and I* and *We and Our Neighbors* as the representative of the new impractical heroine increasingly popular in the fiction of mid-nineteenth-century America. Herself self-consciously childlike, not to say childish, Eva is an emblem of play, of leisure, of carefree gaiety, and a symbol of the increasing trust Stowe, in common with her culture, was putting on these qualities as instruments for the new Bushnellian kind of regeneration. Eva has nothing that she has to do; her time is essentially recreational, and she passes her days by making friends and saving souls. Among her special flock is a colleague of her husband's, a sensitive and conscientious journalist called Bolton who, because of a single bout of youthful intemperance, in adulthood still considers himself an alcoholic. In true Calvinist fashion, he judges himself "lost" and unfit to marry the woman he loves although she is spending her life pining for him. Eva firmly counters his opinion as "morbid," and engineers his wedding to the girl of his dreams. A sense of sin and the stringent self-discipline it recommends represent false, if sincere, heroism: Bolton is not only happier, but more securely protected against his special failing, with a loving and beloved wife by his side. Again, the daughter of Eva's Irish cook Mary falls, through little fault of her own, into a life of prostitution. While her mother's denunciation and reproaches only upset and anger Maggie, while the stark costume and silent piety of the sisters of an Episcopalian order with whom she stays for a while awe but distance her, Eva's inexpensive finery, vivacious talkativeness, and affectionate ways lure her to Christ. Eva poses no threats, awakens no fears, raises no defenses; she makes children of all who will play with her.

Exponents of this new belief in play and of its importance in the conversion experience ranged from the religious hedonist to the theologian. Henry Ward Beecher, who asserted that to be a Christian was "to be the happiest person in the world," told Yale students in 1872 that he "studiously refused to entertain anxieties." In the partial physicalization of respectable Protestantism which was his most interesting achievement, Beecher, finding it best to put Calvin aside, redefined the "elect" as the healthy; he said, and demonstrated, that such would have "an insatiable love of play."[51] Beecher loved to watch fine horses; he collected old books and rare gems. Like other prophets of the mind-cure movement,[52] he sensed that mid- and late-nineteenth-century Protestant America wanted religion to provide an antidote to work as well as a spur to toil. He made religion an agent of personal liberation and fulfillment, a means of self-expression for *l'homme sensuel* as well as for *l'homme spirituel:* he revealed religion as a facilitator of leisure.

Henry Ware, Jr., had already tried to grapple with the problem of "How to Spend Holy Time" and had toyed fascinatedly with the possibilities of leisure implicit in the Unitarian emphasis on what Channing called "self-culture";[53] it took Beecher to say that spending time was itself holy. In Beecher's novel *Norwood,* Dr. Wentworth, a shrewd, humane, and aesthetic-minded physician, acts as his spokesman. At one point Frank Edel, a broken-hearted rejected lover, decides to turn from art to preaching to express his new-found conviction of life's tragic nature; when he consults Dr. Wentworth, however, the older man advises him to stick to painting. Dr. Wentworth points out that the Christian artist preaches, and to a far larger congregation than the minister, but his real message for Edel is: dodge "pain" and "self-denial." Beecher at this point is hovering tantalizingly between the idea that suffering is the easy way and the proposition that the easy way is the best one. Whatever his rationale, however, he wants his characters comfortable with themselves, self-acceptant, self-loving, ample. *Norwood* is unmistakably a tedious book, composed of little action and much rambling and discursive talk. Beecher claims at the start that the pace of what he tellingly calls his "leisurely narrative" is intentional. He doesn't want his readers to devour the novel feverishly in a sitting as they might some highly colored romance; he asks that they pursue it meditatively, reflectively, over a period of time, to taste, to relish, to savor.[54] The novel is to be, in other words, a (Beecherian) religious experience, an exercise in consumer pleasure.

Horace Bushnell, who brought to the rationalization of a post-Calvinist culture much of the intellectual responsibility and massiveness of the Calvinist theological tradition, published a study on *Work and Play* in 1864. He begins by saying that his primary example and his motive for the investigation was the sight of "his children and kitten playing on the floor together." The unconscious and spontaneous ways of children are his starting inspiration, although by no means his stopping point. He considers their play "muscular," and goes on to a consideration of the "hard struggle of [adult] work" which can peak into a realm of "inspired liberty and spontaneous beauty." His conclusion is that "we are to conceive that the highest and most complete state of man, that which his nature endeavors after and in which only it fulfills its sublime instinct is the state of play. To say that a man labors is to say that he fails."[55] Bushnell here anticipates Beecher who would explain, "Whoever thinks without thinking is in fact a genius."[56] Bushnell admired Beecher's vitality but found him theologically primitive, not to say barbaric, and his own thinking is much more complex than the Brooklyn preacher's. Both are advocating a post-romantic theory of organic development, both call for the "whole man." Both urge, in intelligent opposition to the old Calvinist ethos, the resourcefulness of trust: to play is to offer testimony to the possibility of safety. Yet Beecher wants to obviate the necessity of work altogether; Bushnell is urging instead that its final end is mastery, harmony; work losing consciousness of itself as effort passes from determination into delight. He is in actuality engaged in a complex restatement for his modernizing society of the ancient Calvinist dilemma over the relation between the use of "means" and the passive awaiting of God's arbitrary grace. Bushnell hypothetically establishes a streamlined process by which neither is lost but one becomes the other; it is a message of renewal, and arrival, which in no way ignores the necessity of the passage. He summed up his ideal of faith, and hinted at all his differences with Beecher, when he said, "Abiding in Christ is to abide; it is not to *bask*."[57] Nonetheless, his emphasis is on joy not pain, play not work, leisure not effort. The unkindest cut history gives to human achievement is that the effects of our actions are often so much simpler than the intentions behind them; different as their aims were, Bushnell and Beecher finally moved Americans in similar directions.

Bushnell habitually delivered sermons whose length and argumentative density humiliated his little daughter, well aware of the predilections of his Hartford congregation; he continued to publish even denser treatises, although his sermons sold better. Nonetheless his most fascinating and most successful attempt as a religious thinker was his effort to introduce leisure as an element into theological thought. He once said that "if I had my life to lead over again, there is one thing I would not do—I would not push,"[58] and, like Beecher, although at an incomparably more profound level, he tried to teach theology the art of relaxation. Having undergone a prolonged period of religious anxiety and uncertainty in early manhood, he later used to advise others involved in a similar ordeal:

> Never be in a hurry to believe; never try to conquer doubts against time. Time is one of the grand elements in thought as truly as in motion. If you cannot open a doubt today, keep it til to-morrow; do not be afraid to keep it whole years.[59]

In his most difficult theological work, he urges his readers to take it easy. A bit like a guide leading a group of amateurs on an arduous expedition, he promises his readers there is "nothing too abstruse or difficult" in what he asks them to understand; they are proceeding "along open ranges of thought," rapidly bearing "a considerable continent already . . . behind us";[60] they can stretch, they can breathe. Territorial imagery occurs as naturally in Bushnell's prose as physical metaphors appear in Beecher's more heated periods.

Bushnell believed that "forgiveness is man's deepest need and highest achievement":[61] the forgiveness he has in mind is like that which Stowe's Eva van Arsdel urges on Bolton in *My Wife and I*— self-forgiveness. Man's conversion experience is no longer an acceptance of God so much as an acceptance of himself, and Bushnell understood this as a function of happiness, of nurture, and of process. Ministers of an older day like Johathan Edwards, or even latter-day revivalists like Charles Grandison Finney and Lyman Beecher, stressed the inexorable press, the immediate need of conversion: the crisis was now, the decision was now, time was running out, which was to be your destination, heaven or hell? Tomorrow you may wake up, Edwards intoned in his correct precise voice, his eye fixed habitually and calmly on the back of the room, in hell. Bushnell, like Henry Ward Beecher, is arguing that time is on your side. Time is no longer God's, days and years marshaled toward the relentless revelation of the divine will, but man's— moments running freely into space, like a stream pooling into a lake. Expansion, cultivation, flow is the mortal task, not contraction, discipline, and strain. Nathaniel Emmons, a theological innovator despite (he claimed because of) the strictness of his creed, was under genuine pressure as he dryly pursued truth: thinking for him was a matter of finding clues to a vast design planned by someone else; ratiocination was a string leading in and out of the divine labyrinth. Thinking for the much less scholarly although more brilliant Bushnell was to be inspiration, play, creativity. Austin Phelps, perceptive as always, understood that for Bushnell "work was *discovery*"; he was "a seer, not a reasoner,"[62] and he could ignore predecessors with a fine disdain. Self-expression for Henry Ward Beecher had become posture, gesture; for Horace Bushnell it was insight, vision; but both posited as the goal of religious experience and development, assimilation, ease. In downplaying the Calvinist over-emphasis on effort with its reification of pain, Beecher and Bushnell tended also to downplay the inevitable role agony plays in human experience. Trust is not a good in itself; it must take account of obstacles and define its objects. Both Beecher and Bushnell helped to create the rationale for Eva von Arsdel and her calculated oblivion, anticipatory of the consumer's amnesia.

Anti-Intellectualism and the Theology of Feeling

The new view of God's plan and man's part in it, with its stress on the emotions, the unconscious, and the resources of leisure and literature, undoubtedly fostered in the clergy an anti-intellectualism which came in time to have troubling effects on the profession and on the broader culture.[63] We have seen that many ministers, in the midst of their most extravagant statements about the "feminine" nature of Christianity or the Christlike role of women, insisted upon female unfitness, indeed incapacity, for the trials and duties of the ministry. In *Woman Suffrage: The Reform Against Nature* (1869), Bushnell, after saying that men and women could not be more "unlike" if they were two different species, explains that the male is the "law," thundering forcefully from Sinai, the female the "gospel," subject to law but bringing "grace." Bushnell then goes on to proclaim the superiority of woman, couching her pre-eminence in terms of the Atonement: she "goes above the law in doing everything for it, and overtops it in giving by submission to it." Clearly feeling that he has implicitly raised an obvious question, he answers it by saying that women are not to be ministers because "ministration is one thing, and the question of administration another."[64] Women lack the brains necessary for executive action. Feminine sentimentality, ignorance of the world, lack of scholarship, precisely those qualities which made women more Christian—and which were named increasingly in any rationale of the liberal ministerial role—were, paradoxically, held against them. This apparent contradiction is eloquent. Even while liberal ministers sabotaged their intellectual heritage, they wished to hold on to it, and they feared that in women and in feminization lay its most formidable antagonist.

Women did not attempt to undermine clerical scholarship: as wives and housekeepers, they provided the labor which made it possible; as church members, they constituted the audience which received its fruits in sermons, prayers, and discourses; as intelligent and sensitive individuals, many of them exerted an important and constructive influence over the thinking of their ministerial husbands and friends. Yet, as we have seen, disbelief in female capacity for scholarship and real intellectual or artistic achievement was widespread in American culture. The clergy, anxious to preserve their claim to distinction from those they imitated, fostered such skepticism; its effects on women and on their attitude toward religion were largely and predictably negative. The gravest irony of the ministers' position was precisely that in defending themselves they armed their enemy.

The reactions of the two most talented Beecher sisters to the pervasive, clerically endorsed misogyny of their society were representative, if extreme. Both women were unusually well versed and interested in Protestant theology; both played a major role in vitiating its intellectual content. Their options were painfully limited. In Harriet Beecher Stowe's novel *My Wife and I*, the frivolous Eva van Arsdel is set against her older sister Ida. Eva, as I have noted, is a pretty little coquette. She reads little besides magazines and likes to get her "ideas" by talking to men who have read more than she. Her "study" boasts few books and is decorated to give the illusion of what Eva calls "my Italy"; the room sports copies of works by Bushnell's favorite painter, Fra Angelico.[65] At one point Eva explains her Anglican faith with a superficiality which fascinates and horrifies: " 'I long for the dear old prayers of my church, where my poor naughty little heart has learned the way and can go on with full consent *without stopping to think*.' "[66] Ida van Arsdel, in contrast, is doctrinally free-thinking, but temperamentally a Puritan; she fixes her study up like a room in an old New England farmhouse. Scholarly, bright, hard-working, Ida is determined to be a doctor and a lifelong spinster. She is clearly the more admirable of the two sisters, yet Stowe pretty much drops her from consideration in *We and Our Neighbors*, the sequel to *My Wife and I*. Stowe chooses to focus her attention, with whatever ambivalence, on the feminine opponent rather than on the feminist upholder of the New England way. One can hardly fault her; Stowe's society had given her little incentive or hope in plotting Ida's future. Ida was the rare exception, not the rule, and unlike her equally improbable, saintly fictional predecessors, Ida's appeal to readers was limited. Stowe as a novelist and a person was far too sociologically alert—indeed, almost punitively so —to waste her time on sheer highmindedness.

Harriet's own sister, Catharine, at first glance seems closer to Ida than

Eva. Easily the intellectual equal of her most brilliant brother, Edward, Catharine Beecher was capable of producing theological tracts which (if published anonymously with no hint of the sex of their author) won the respect and response of some of America's ablest divines. As a young woman, however, while her brothers went to Yale or Amherst, she stayed at home. Her adult life was spent in an ever-sanguine, ever-frustrated search to raise the funds necessary to endow a woman's college, staffed by women and designed to satisfy her biased yet high standards. Beecher was too restless ever to become truly bitter, but her heart burned at times when she contemplated the magnificent financial resources of Harvard and Yale and thought of her own multiple failed educational endeavors. Despite her temperamental self-righteousness and excitability, her claim that she could have succeeded if she had only had more money seems a fair one: a good portion of her frantic over-activity was an effort to substitute human ingenuity for economic backing. Beecher suffered from hysteria and occasional paralytic afflictions. One hardly needs recourse to psychoanalysis to sense that she was suppressing a massive hatred of the male world which had denied her her colleges, denied her, in a very real sense, her mind.

All Catharine Beecher's antagonism surfaced in an extraordinary book published in 1850 entitled *Truth Stranger Than Fiction*. This work purported to be a defense of Delia Bacon (1811–59), formerly Catharine's student at the Hartford Female Seminary, later a talented lecturer and writer somewhat in the line of Margaret Fuller. Bacon had been engaged to Alexander Mac-Whorter, a Yale graduate, a minister, and a man significantly younger than herself. In 1847, MacWhorter had rather humiliatingly refused to marry her. At this time, Delia's brother Leonard, a distinguished New Haven preacher and a Yale professor of divinity, had brought MacWhorter to trial for breach of faith before the local Connecticut convocation, and had lost the case. Both MacWhorter and Bacon enlisted backers whose interest was not sparked solely by Delia Bacon's plight. The contest was in reality one between the older ministers, many of them colleagues or pupils of Lyman Beecher's closest friend, Nathaniel Taylor, and the younger clergymen, led by Bacon; the former were professors and theologians, the latter were chiefly less learned men from the county parishes.[67]

Catharine Beecher contributed two lawyers and herself to the trial, and then wrote her indignant account of it. She was fully aware that the conflict was between what Edwards A. Park would call "the theologian" and "the pastor" (194, 235, 293),[68] and her book was assertively dedicated to the "Parochial Clergy" of America. She knew that she was attacking not just, as she melodramatically emphasized, "*The grey hairs of my father's friend* [Taylor]!" (294), but the Calvinist intellectual tradition and the elitist male institution most heavily endowed for its propagation (12, 290–1). Her rally cry was the sanctity of the domestic claims which MacWhorter had violated and which Yale University, in exonerating him, had despised. She was positive that the adverse decision could only have been the result of a "MALIGNANT CONSPIRACY!" (249), but she was determined, as she told Leonard Bacon, to oppose it: "*Such* a woman with *such* a calumny affixed to her by *such* men is, and must be, the center of a perpetual warfare. There is no peace to her or to one whose destiny is now united with hers, till this wrong as far as it can be, is righted" (287). Unfortunately, to Delia Bacon's distress, Beecher kept her word. If she did not alleviate Delia Bacon's situation, she did express her rage and display her revengeful alliance with the forces of sentimental morality against those of theological scholarship. The most serious motive for her rage is one she omits from the book. Critics laughed at the excesses of Beecher's tirade, yet her anger was admirable. The fact that she had little constructive advice to offer was the best justification of her passion. She had been barred all her life from access to the training necessary to fully solve the problems she exposed.

The forces of anti-intellectualism Catharine Beecher invoked were destined to win the day in clerical ranks. In 1853, a few years after Beecher's outburst, Bela Bates Edwards of Andover Seminary lamented that people considered "an intellectual clergyman . . . deficient in piety and an eminently pious ministry . . . deficient in intellect."[69] Clerical ability to unite piety with intellect—and thus to win wide respect—came to seem more and more elusive. By 1883 President Eliot of Harvard could say that the ministry had declined greatly in the preceding forty years principally because educated men no longer found the "intellectual qualities" in the clergy which they expected in a guide.[70] One clear sign of the dilemma of the ministry was the increasingly youthful age of men assuming pastorates. By the mid-nineteenth century, especially in large towns, congregations tended to select men in their thirties, often more youthful than the most influential members of the church.[71] In 1859, Reverend C. van Santvoord, president of the Synod of the Dutch Reformed Churches, complained: "churches of present times . . . show so strong a proclivity toward calling young men in preference to teachers of riper experience and more solid attainments . . . that a man happening to be prematurely bald . . . or gray, . . . may reckon on almost certain discomfiture" when competing with a younger candidate.[72] In van Santvoord's opinion, churches hoped thus to pay little, to get men up with the times, and to have "a fair countenance" to contemplate on Sunday morning. Congregations were seeking in their ministers the ideal of feminine labor—namely youth, good looks, and cheapness; they were insuring the lack of lengthy training also characteristic of women employees.

Seminaries inevitably reflected congregational demands. Between 1850 and 1895 the number of Yale's graduates doubled, yet the proportion of those who entered the ministry decreased by more than sixty percent. Of those who joined the clergy, fewer came from the best colleges; fewer came from colleges at all.[73] Within the seminaries themselves, whether Harvard or Andover or Yale, there was a shift of emphasis in requirements for ministerial candidates which presupposed a change in theological outlook at least correspondent to the altered intellectual level of the young men applying to such schools. In 1726, the massively well-read Cotton Mather, writing his *Manductio ad Ministerium (Directions for a Candidate of the Ministry)*, said that he believed "learning" of a general kind the second most important qualification for a clergyman after piety. He recommended that a well-trained minister should know Latin, Greek, Hebrew, Rhetoric, Logic, Natural Philosophy, Mathematics, Astronomy, and Divinity. The purpose of all this erudition was clear to Mather; he stressed that "it is of the last importance that . . . [the candidate] should be a good casuist."[74] Mather was extolling the inquisitional and controversial skills Hopkins and Emmons possessed in such eminence: the ability to discriminate false from true, and defend the correct against the incorrect. Mather assumed that the truth was to be had, if with difficulty, labor, and argumentation.

Emmons and Hopkins, who trained hundreds of young ministers in the days before seminaries opened, upheld Cotton Mather's standards. They themselves labored twelve hours daily at their desks; their impractical absent-mindedness about affairs of this world, in which antiquarians would delight, was cultivated, not innate. Emmons refused to work in his garden lest it distract him from more urgent responsibilities. He believed that the duties God required of men were so many and so diverse that the true Christian would find no time for mere amusements; Emmons had no concept of leisure.[75] Little wonder if, according to popular lore, such men occasionally rode off on the wrong horse after service or even occasionally made themselves at home in the wrong house: they had more important things on their minds than such mundane distinctions. Reverends West, Whitridge, and Hopkins used to meet together regularly and talk theology for hours. On one occasion, just as night fell, Whitridge came out to see West to his horse. They fell again into theological debate and were absorbed until they thought they detected a fire in the east—it was the rising sun.[76]

Timothy Dwight, heir of Jonathan Edwards by lineal descent and by creed, as a tutor at Yale in the late eighteenth century pursued the ascetic commitment to learning which had characterized his predecessors. He limited himself to two mouthfuls of food at dinner (usually potatoes), slept on the floor, and studied heroically long hours. Probably partially as a result of this regimen, he almost lost the use of his eyes. In later years, he was never able to work for prolonged periods of time. He professed to be thankful, since he had been forced to the discovery that "real knowledge" was only to be drawn from life. His style as a teacher and a preacher training future ministers at Yale was consequently very different from that of his fore-bears.[77] In the words of a contemporary, Dwight "broke up the metaphys-ical mode of discussion so prevalent at that time in the pulpit, and introduced a more popular and instructive method of address."[78] One can hardly regret Dwight's partial loss of vision; it led to the masterly *Travels in New England and New York*. Dwight's shrewd practical powers of observation are dis-played to the fullest in this lively narrative, which is far superior by almost any criterion to his dull if solid four-volume treatise, *Theology Explained and Defended*. Dwight's changed course undeniably marks, however, an unwit-ting turn in the New England Calvinist tradition. Increasingly after Dwight, ministers were pastors, even writers, before they were theologians.

The fate of Andover Seminary illustrates the shift in American Protes-tantism away from dispute, doctrine, and scholarship. Founded in 1808 as a bastion against Harvard, which had recently capitulated to the then-insurgent Unitarian forces, Andover was intended to preserve and perpetu-ate the New Light Divinity of Edwards and Hopkins. All professors at the school swore opposition not only to Atheists and Infidels, but to Jews, Papists, "Mohametans," Arians, Pelagians, Antinomians, Socinians, Sabelli-ans, Unitarians, and Universalists; they renewed this oath in public once every five years. Students, conducted through a supremely rigorous course which heavily emphasized Biblical exegesis, indisputably essential to devel-oping controversial skills, were examined once a year by trustees, visitors, and faculty, also in public.[79] The clear assumption was that theological truth was indeed a fortress, but one in constant need of defense. Moses Stuart, who taught at Andover, delivered his learned broadsides against the Unitarians in the earlier part of the century; other, more liberal scholars like Edwards A. Park and Calvin Stowe were to succeed him at the task of ingenious debate. Calvin Stowe reiterated emphatically in 1852 that "the right inter-pretation of Scripture" was the cornerstone of religion, but students did not always agree.

By the 1870s students, abetted by the younger members of the faculty, demanded, and got, less Biblical exegesis in their middle years. Park, after a long and unsuccessful struggle against their demands which his own liber-alism had unwittingly fostered, resigned in 1881; unable to appoint the Hopkinsian scholar he had wished to see in his place,[80] he was destined to spend the next twenty years working on a never-assembled biography of Jonathan Edwards. The students' revolt against Biblical criticism was cru-cial because it revealed their endorsement of Orville Dewey's observation that "the main, the almost exclusive object of the ... modern pulpit is religious impression."[81] The great revivalist preacher Edward Payson of Maine was reputed to believe that "doctrines should be like sugar in tea—

only tasted in the cup"[82]—and who needed a full year of close Biblical study just to provide "flavor"? Even the Biblical criticism which Park and others had gone to Germany to study failed to take hold in America; in 1847, the scholar George Noyes published a despairing article in the *Christian Examiner* entitled "Causes of the Decline of Interest in Critical Theology"; Noyes concluded that seminaries might fail for lack of public support.[83] Andover, like Harvard and Yale, survived, but the preoccupation of later generations of divinity students was increasingly to be either with themselves and the cult of self-nurture, or with the changing, conflict-laden world and the creed of the Social Gospel—not with learned explication of the Holy Scriptures.

In 1850 Park himself had instigated the second major nineteenth-century controversy among the liberal Protestant clergy over their intellectual role. The first had occurred in 1839 when the transcendentalist Unitarians of Boston and Cambridge, led by Ralph Waldo Emerson, George Ripley, and Orestes Brownson, split from their more orthodox Unitarian brethren ably marshaled by Andrews Norton of Harvard Divinity School. Norton was a parishioner of Henry Ware, Sr., a Brahmin intellectual possessed of genuine if conventional acumen. His dedication to scholarship and reason was extreme, for, as a fervent social conservative, in these alone he found potentially civilizing forces for the democratic chaos around him. It was characteristic of the man and his spirit that his son, Charles Eliot Norton, very ill at ten, worried only that he would die and not be able to "edit father's works."[84] Norton was bitterly opposed to transcendental subjectivity and the incipiently democratic notion, as he put it, "that the mind possessed a faculty of intuitively discerning the truths of religion."[85] Utterly distrustful of the common people or even the less common people, he wished to see "religion ... taken out of the hands of divines ... and its exposition and defence ... become the study of philosophers as being the highest philosophy."[86] These philosophers were to possess "extensive learning." Norton's response to the implicit attack on the clergy's elite status was, as his transcendental opponents fully recognized, to become more elite, to assert the challenged claims ever more assertively. The historian Richard Hildreth, one of Norton's ablest critics, realized that Norton was essentially arguing that "religion consists in knowledge."[87] To be a religious leader, in other words, was to be a professional and safely out of the range, if also out of earshot, of the untrained. If there was a choice to be made between popular appeal and intellectual pre-eminence, Norton at least had no hesitations.

The case was very different for Park, who was twenty-two years younger, considerably more brilliant, and infinitely more imaginative, although every bit as scholarly as Norton and equally concerned about the clergy's dwindling intellectual stature. Norton was slated to be a partisan, a self-believer, able to defend and see only one side of a historical conflict; Park was destined by temperament and talent to an attempt to bridge the fissures of his culture. He tolerated intellectual mediocrity with great difficulty. When a student, after delivering a peculiarly spiritless and dull sermon, asked Park what hymn would best accompany it, Park snapped back, with the acerbic irony which Puritan discipline fostered and could not always check, "Now I Lay Me Down to Sleep." Driven abroad by the nervous prostration and insatiable curiosity which would dog him all his days, he experienced a profound depression in Germany; the advanced Biblical scholarship and the extensive libraries he found there made him ashamed and afraid for provincial Andover. Like Cotton Mather, he firmly believed that a minister—who filled, to his mind, the greatest place in God's creation—ought to know everything. He intensely admired Moses Stuart, a colleague who exemplified the martyrdom and the glory of a learned clergy:

> A Christian scholar, contending with the infirmities of an emaciated body, leaving his sleepless couch that he may discipline himself for the studies of an anxious day, and closing his volume at evening that he may gain some intermittent sleep for the relief of his wearied frame ... keeping aloof from the haunts of men that he may search out new motives for winning them to a life of godliness.[88]

Stuart had indeed kept "aloof," and Park could not finally accept this as a valid alternative for the modern minister. In his memoirs of Hopkins and Emmons, whose scholarship Park helped to make legendary, he dwells fascinatedly on the inability of either man to attract a broad audience. Both achieved their impact in a manner traditional for a member of an intellectual elite: by educating students who were able to spread their doctrines as they themselves were incapable of doing. Park was impressed by their ability to adhere to and believe in truth, without the confirmation supplied by followers: he perhaps exaggerates their isolation to throw into bolder relief the fine quality of their intellectual integrity. They had no need, no conception of a public in the modern sense. Yet at the same time it is clear that Park finds such pristine and tenacious virtue in itself a guarantee of very limited popularity. He keeps stressing that both men put their beliefs harshly, boldly; he hovers between an apology for such tactless and impolitic overstatedness and an admission that a minister cannot say what he believes to be the truth and appeal. Everywhere he implies that no latter-day minister could fully follow their relentless course. Park himself was a powerful revivalist preacher who was able to awe and thrill even Emily Dickinson, a superb scholar whose biographies and studies still stand; he solved the clerical problem of his generation in his own life. Yet he was always pressed by that urge which tormented and inspired Matthew Arnold, to make the "best culture *prevail*"; he was always searching for a way to democratize what he hardly recognized as his own achievement, always anxious to rationalize and make accessible a clerical creed and lifestyle which would permit both learning and popularity, or, in his terms, "intellect" and "feeling." His religious and intellectual ideal was in the best sense a bisexual one, and he wished it to be not an isolated ideal, but part of Christian practice. He failed finally in this aim, but his failure is one of the most interesting phenomena in the history of nineteenth-century American theology if only because, occurring in such a quarter, it demonstrates that success was hardly possible anywhere.

Park knew that to engage men's minds is to enlist their hearts—he said so, and demonstrated so—but in his numerous writings about the clergy he repeatedly sets up, or recognizes, a split between the two faculties. As so many of the ministers of his time were to do,[89] Park envisioned and longed for a theology in which virile energy was to be united with "refined sensibility."[90] In a crucial address entitled "The Theology of the Intellect and the Theology of the Feelings" delivered in 1850, he described the former as precise logical doctrines developed and supported by the reason, and the latter as the form of belief "suggested by and adapted to the wants of the well-trained heart"; in a telling illustration, he linked the first with a "father," the second with a "mother." Of course, some version of this distinction had been familiar to Christian theology since the church fathers; it is the definition and respective value Park gives the terms which is striking. Although Park's ostensible purpose is to argue that the two are both indispensable to the Christian minister, who must have "all the sensibility of a woman without becoming womanish, and all the perspicacity of a logician without being merely logical," his opening remark stresses that the appeal to the heart and the imagination can be successful when the reason and judgment have been addressed in vain; and throughout, his special plea is for the feelings.[91]

Park's discourse was at once recognized as epoch-making and controversial, and few were unaware which "theology" had emerged the victor. A reviewer for the *Christian Examiner* applauded Park; obviously thinking that he expressed agreement with the Andover leader, he wrote: "We are free to confess that much as we honor logic and the intellect, we would prefer a hymnbook and a heart."[92] Charles Hodge, a brilliant Presbyterian theologian at Princeton Seminary and the self-chosen defender of orthodoxy, in the lengthy and stunning debate which ensued between Park and himself, showed himself not only disapproving of Park, but more aware of the implications of Park's argument than Park himself. Ironically sounding a great deal like the deceased Emmons whom Park so venerated, Hodge insisted that one "theology" must be true, the other false, or there could be no explicit or implicit contest between them. He was doggedly conscious that Park, in most un-Calvinist fashion, was *refusing to choose*, and in doing so, "enabling a man to profess what he does not believe." He was convinced that Park was finally, from no matter what motives, fostering sentimentality: allowing people to regret what they themselves have destroyed, to confuse fact with fiction. In his single most penetrating thrust, he accused Park of believing that the central tenets of the Protestant creed were "merely intense expressions"—while Hodge knew them to be "true as doctrines."[93]

Hodge argued that Park was not so much impressing literature into the service of religion as turning religion into literature: he believed that the escape Park was trying to find for himself was that of language. Emmons and Hopkins, by Park's own account, were men capable of few linguistic effects and interested in fewer. Emmons asserted: "I never thought of my style; I wrote as I thought."[94] Jacob Ide, Emmons' nineteenth-century editor, speaking of Emmons' style, praised its "perspicacity"; his thoughts were "perfectly naked."[95] Emmons was a man absolutely sure that he had "obtained certainty upon all points which would admit of it,"[96] and few, apparently, did not. He wanted his thoughts "naked" precisely because he knew the thoughts were there and he wanted them in the spotlight. Park called attention to the words, in Hodge's opinion, because he was substituting them for the thoughts. There is undeniable evidence for Hodge's interpretation. Park said openly that the theology of the feelings provides "visible and tangible images" rather than "abstract thoughts," that it is suited not to controversy but to poetry;[97] and he continually implied that the Scriptures offer imaginative language not statements of fact, that the Bible is a literary text. He came perilously close to saying that religion is metaphor.

In a passage which perhaps shows the influence of Bushnell's Coleridgean treatment of language in *God in Christ* (1849), Park explains "that liberal doctrines of theology are too vast for complete expression by man, and our intensest words are but a distant approximation to that language which forms the new song that the redeemed in heaven sing."[98] Park is acknowledging the timeless truth that expression cannot match realization; he is also subscribing to more specific romantic notions of the inexactness and richness of language. Hodge charges that this is a credo more suitable for a poet than a minister. Hodge metaphorically pulls the rug out from under Park; he denies to Park the consolation of aesthetics, he asserts the ugliness and primacy of dogma. He accuses Park, in several brilliant phrases, of "playing with words," of performing "pirouettes" on words;[99] Park is substituting the leisured art of literature for laborious commitment to truth. It is the same issue we have already seen in the changing concepts of the Atonement and of the conversion process. God does not assimilate to man nor man to God easily or pleasantly or beautifully, Hodge insists: sobriety, struggle, pain, the intense awareness that comes with realization and ratiocination not laced with emotion, the bareness of "plain facts," are essential ingredients in the genuine religious experience and calling.

Hodge indubitably had logic on his side; he was in the invincible position of meaning exactly what he said and being fully aware that his opponent did not. Hodge was incapable of seeing the sincerity and importance of Park's effort to revitalize dogma with the creative forces of literature; Hodge himself here and elsewhere seems to have issued a personal veto against the imaginative life. Yet he saw correctly the drift of Park's thinking; his essentially institutional mind apprehended the potential over-personalism of Park's approach. The victory of exposure was Hodge's, but the *Christian Examiner*'s allegiance to Park's more moving if less solid arguments was symbolic of the trend Hodge so tenaciously combated. Park had history on his side; the sentimental appeal, which he endowed with an intellectual integrity and conviction it was seldom to display again, won the day. Park's own students would de-emphasize the historical and scholarly work of Biblical exegesis in the Andover curriculum.

In 1852, two years after Park's address on "The Theology of the Intellect and of the Feelings," the liberal Congregationalists, in a new effort to collect and define their forces, held a Synod. It was the first official Congregational gathering since the one in 1646–48 at which the Cambridge Platform was formulated and ratified. The concern of the participants, unlike that of their long-ago predecessors, was not with theology. They made plans to found the Congregational Library Association in Boston—Bela Edwards and Park were particularly influential here—and laid the groundwork for the inception of the *Congregational Quarterly*. A National Council called in 1865 only further dramatized liberal discomfort with orthodox theology. The representatives vaguely endorsed "the faith and order of the apostolic and primitive churches held by our fathers"; on a special and rather ironic excursion to Plymouth Rock, however, they voted to delete the word "Calvinism" from the traditional Congregational statement of self-definition.[100] The penultimate chapter in a book on the triumphs of Congregationalism published in 1894 was entitled "Congregational Literature."[101] Hodge's cynical suspicion about Park's direction, if not his motivation, was more than vindicated. Attention to the claims of the press and interest in a rather nostalgic obfuscation of the past were pre-empting commitment to the older New England theology for which Hodge claimed with justification to be a latter-day spokesman. Liberal Protestantism had moved one step nearer to the feminine subculture it both courted and feared.

Anti-Institutionalism: The Pastor and the Sentimental Heroine

The anti-intellectualism which had begun to pervade the non-evangelical minister's theology by mid-century inevitably affected his concept of the institution to which he belonged and of the role he was to play in it. J. H. Allen astutely remarked that the voluntary system had produced "spiritualism [and] sentimentalism," but that it had failed "and must always fail in building up an *institution*."[102] The liberal clergyman promoted, if ambiguously, a personalized and de-professionalized church. He lost confidence in the special and established claims of his own denomination; he habitually joined forces, or tried to, with Christians of all beliefs in worship and recreational activities. He evaded ecclesiastical self-definition.

The most extraordinary and inspiring expounder of anti-institutionalism within the liberal ranks was Joseph Tuckerman (1778–1841). Born of a Boston patrician and mercantile family, from an early age Tuckerman was known for his blameless conduct, his intensely emotional nature, and his "devotion to . . . literature." In many ways Tuckerman, dominated, as he himself said, by his "affections" rather than his "thoughts," was prototypical of the new liberal minister. Channing explained: "His strength did not lie in abstract speculation . . . His heart was his great power."[103] Tuckerman joined with his sensibility a concern for the urban poor shared by few of his equally sensitive clerical contemporaries. Forced by ill health to abandon a regular Unitarian pastorate in 1826, he founded the much more strenuous "ministry at large," a small, interdenominational, and *ad hoc* band of "free" ministers, tackling economic, social, and spiritual ills wherever they found them in whatever ways seemed most appropriate. Deeply troubled by the fact that by his count almost half of the 13,320 Protestant families in Boston had no religious affiliation at all, Tuckerman lamented the exclusiveness which characterized the majority of urban Protestant churches. Pews could only be occupied by those who bought or rented them; the impoverished were consigned ignominiously to special seats. Churches were organized, in other words, to congratulate the rich rather than to save the poor.

Tuckerman became increasingly suspicious of all organized religious effort. He hated official charity as fiercely as any proud pauper: a crusader against centrally controlled state philanthropy, he wanted the local communities voluntarily to care for their own deprived. The only part he would have allowed the state to play was in penalizing towns that failed to erect workhouses and other necessary facilities. The essence of Tuckerman's philanthropic style was personal service and care. He claimed to be "of no party," and he spoke to and for those who had no interest in being members of a church, for those who had no interest in hearing a minister but who felt a genuine need for what Tuckerman called a "Christian friend." He wanted to enter the homes of the poor rather than to draw them into church. True religion for him was impossible without the "sympathy, interest, respect, love" which the poor so seldom received; the only church which mattered existed anyplace where these qualities were in operation. Tuckerman underplayed his clerical role; he believed fervently in the sanctity of the ministry, but he saw its virtue precisely in its self-disavowal, in its intrinsically unprofessional nature. "It is character only which gives any power to office," he asserted.[104] In Tuckerman's eyes, the minister possessed but one valid creed: that contained in his personal example.

It is difficult even today to read Tuckerman's *Ministry at Large* with its stress on local control, its relatively enlightened analysis of the causes of poverty, and its eloquent language, and not feel its author's impassioned, intelligent, and crystalline concern and love for the people of whom he writes. Tuckerman was some sort of saint, if a minor one. He was not alone, however, in his disinterest in ecclesiastical institutions. Henry Ward Beecher, who clustered more naturally with the sinners than with the saints, showed the same anti-institutionalism and anti-professionalism later in the century; but he substituted a manufactured intimacy for principled care. Tuckerman disavowed institutions to protect the social community, broadly conceived; Beecher was an exemplar of the force of sheer personality, and personality dedicated to the needs of an audience, not to the purposes of a community.

Lyman Beecher, every inch a "churchman," fought Atheists, Unitarians, Episcopalians, and Roman Catholics to the death; he did everything (short of abandoning his own heresies) to preserve the precarious unity of the Congregational-Presbyterian "Evangelical Front"; his most famous son appealed to Congregationalists and free-thinkers alike. Finding what close friends he had among businessmen, journalists, and lawyers rather than among clergymen, Henry Ward Beecher advised candidates for the sacred office to "avoid a professional manner" and reminded them constantly that they were "men" before they were ministers. In the sometimes embarrassingly overt sexual language he habitually used to describe the successful minister's performance—he was to "thrust," and "lunge" and "pour his manhood" out over his congregation—Beecher makes the clergyman sound more like an exhibitionist than an ecclesiastical dignitary. He preached without a pulpit, standing almost within touch of his audience. He advocated that ministers not write out their sermons but speak *extempore;* he was after impression as much as truth. Lyman Beecher, anxious to get his first revival under way in East Hampton, had taken "hold without mittens"; Henry Ward characteristically wished metaphorically to extend from the pulpit a "warm and glowing palm bared to the touch." He was intent on seduction, not compulsion. He seldom talked of the church; he almost never spoke of doctrine except to debunk it. To be a minister, to belong to a church, was only to court definition and claustrophobia: preachers are "all partialists," he warned; "a man's study should be everywhere." The only authority Beecher craved was that of omnivorousness; he wished to be as pervasive, and as intimate, as appetite.[105]

Tuckerman and Beecher represented the two extremes of the new anti-institutionalism developing in the liberal clergy between 1820 and 1875, and many of their colleagues ranged between them. An admiring acquaintance said of Ezra Stiles Gannett, one of the most conscientious, hard-working, earnest, and fervently Unitarian ministers of the early and mid-nineteenth century, that he was among the last clergymen to have a sense of "ministerial brotherhood."[106] Gannett was associated with Channing at the Federal Street Church in Boston, and he was often troubled by Channing's publicly stated dissatisfaction at being confined within one creed, even the notoriously loose Unitarian one. "I belong to the Universal Church," Channing proclaimed in 1841; "nothing shall separate me from it." The founder of American Unitarianism felt "the spirit of sectarianism" was "from hell."[107] Charles Follen, a prophet of the ecumenical trend of the later transcendental-Unitarian clergy, claimed with Channing to be a member of the "universal church," sympathizing even with Jews and Catholics.[108] Edwin H. Chapin, one of the most popular preachers in New York City, was thought to be a Universalist only because it was impossible to tell what he was.[109]

Such ministers stressed the devotional and practical, rather than the doctrinal or ecclesiastical, aspects of faith. They were not without feminine models and adherents. Women like Lydia Maria Child or Catharine Maria Sedgwick repudiated sectarianism and partialism as fervently as Channing himself. Even as they proliferated their own associations, organizations, societies, and clubs, middle-class American women revealed a deep-seated and extreme distrust integral to their envy of the professions and institutions which excluded them. Catharine Esther Beecher's crusade against Yale was only part of a larger campaign in which she had many sisterly assistants.[110] Of these Dorothea Dix (1802–87) was perhaps the most talented and significant.

Dix was born in 1802 to an ill-assorted couple; her father was an alcoholic and a fanatic convert from Congregationalism to Methodism, her mother an uneducated woman some eighteen years older than her husband. Dix spent a miserable childhood mainly with her grandmother, whom she likened to Medusa.[111] She said in later years that she "never knew childhood,"[112] and her short career as a brilliant but excessively demanding and inflexible teacher proved her right. Until her late twenties, she was devoured by literary ambition of a conventional variety; she could write a confidante on one occasion about paying her "watery tribute to the genius of L. E. L.," a popular poetess.[113] Dix turned out the usual volumes of Sunday School fiction and sentimental poetry bearing predictable titles like *The Garland of Flora*. A convert to Unitarianism, she took care of Channing's children in the early 1830s and received all the benefits of his affection, discipline, and respect. With her consumptive tendency and her literary sensibility, she seemed in early womanhood, as a friend said, "an invalid, a very gentle and poetical and sentimental young lady."[114] In the mid-1830s she went abroad for her health, and returned in 1838, thirty-six years old, unmarried, unknown, an unhappy, aimless, rather typical minor lady-litterateur. Then, by a near-accident, she saw the inside operations of a neighboring jail; the rage and conviction this visit inspired in her led to a highly motivated career of prison, hospital, and asylum reform which lasted almost until the century's close.

Dix was very much a "minister at large." Reading her Bible aloud to quell the madmen, Dix was taking on (at the least) a clerical role. One of her biographers has noted perceptively that her Massachusetts memorial has certain similarities to Edwards' famous sermon, "Sinners in the Hands of an Angry God."[115] Lydia Maria Child christened her a "God-appointed missionary to the insane."[116] Dix rebuked strangers, and presidents, with absolute self-confidence, and proclaimed herself "the Hope of the poor crazed beings who pine in cells and stalls and cages. . . . The Revelation of hundreds of wailing suffering creatures."[117] Like Tuckerman, moreover, Dix always worked on an essentially individualized, maverick, *ad hoc*, although tightly controlled, plan. Whether consciously or not, she exploited the doctrine of female "influence" to the hilt. Beautiful, well-educated, socially conservative, politically tactful, welcome in both North and South before and after the war, she besieged state legislatures and important personages with impassioned appeals still well within the limits of decorum. One admirer remarked that he had seen in chapels of asylums Dix had founded or visited portraits of her placed and adored as one might expect an icon of the Virgin to be. Dix grasped the potential force of the veneration accorded the lady in place of power: she could be unique, autonomous, the arbiter not the subject of moral judgment, the holy opponent rather than the inmate of all merely man-made institutions. It was symbolic that on Dix's crusading trips abroad in later life she was actually to boast of her inability to speak a foreign tongue—and of her ability to accomplish exactly what she wanted anyway.

Dix's charge against the prisons, hospitals, and insane asylums of her day had many motives, the most important of which was the criminally inadequate conditions which prevailed in them.[118] Like Tuckerman, Dix, for all her occasional (and self-sustaining) posturing, had a sense of a wider community which never left her; it was her distinction that she pledged herself never to forget those her society was determined to ignore. In a very real sense, Dix's chosen foe, like Tuckerman's, was organization *per se*. Once asked at an asylum to inspect the superintendents' suites, she replied, "Oh no! doctor, I have never found any suffering among officers of an institution."[119] During the Civil War, an older and more paranoid Dix, appointed superintendent of nurses and determined to help soldiers since she could not be one, revealed new extremes of distrust for professionalism and professionals. She required no nursing experience for her volunteers (though she did demand that they be thirty or over and homely), and she calmly instructed them to obey her rather than the doctors for whom they were actually working. A one-woman vigilante squad, she refused to take off a single day during the whole course of the war; she attempted to cut off the doctors' liquor supply and to oversee, and correct, every branch of wartime medical practice. As an observer remarked, she could not work within any system, "for she belonged to the class of comets."[120]

Dix irritated military authorities by being, in the words of one exasperated official, in a perpetual state of "breathless excitement." George Templeton Strong, a sanitary commissioner, seized on the absurd and hysterical aspects of her over-concern:

> She is disgusted with us because we do not leave everything else and rush off the instant she tells us of something that needs attention. The last time we were in Washington she came upon us in breathless excitement to say that a cow in the Smithsonian grounds was dying of sunstroke, and she took it very ill that we did not adjourn instantly to look after the case.[121]

Strong was annoyed at that inability to establish proportions that understandably crippled many of Dix's sex. What he failed to note was that her anxiety rose from her horror, here focused on a petty but symbolic detail, that all these professionally trained, wage-earning men might quite simply be incompetent. After Dix had opened the door of her first state-run jail and seen the enormities of neglect and maltreatment there, she doubted. In a sense, she enjoyed the doubts, because they implied that if men were apparently not helped, were even disabled, by their training for the task of running the world, the burden fell on her, and her apparent (and feminine) lack of qualifications became a positive asset for the task. Yet the intense, distorted, but oppressive sense of unending obligation which resulted from her frightening conclusion that she was the only wakeful passenger on a ship headed for certain wreck was real too.[122]

It may at first glance seem strange or unexpected that Dix should have turned from youthful aspirations to be a literary lady to adult ambitions to be the unassisted savior of her nation, but her progression was in reality a natural one. Tuckerman too as a young man fervently loved literature; he too found his mature identity in a less hyperbolic but no less maverick missionary endeavor. Dix had liked to read sentimental fiction, and a number of her admirers described her in terms which suggest the heroines of such stories. From Washington Horace Mann wrote his wife, the former Mary Peabody, that he was happy to be Dix's "lackey" and to fight in her cause: he "loved to picture her," he continued enthusiastically, "entering alone realms of darkness where man did not dare to set his foot . . . or with a hymn upon her lips quieting the fiercest raging of madness."[123] Like Florence Nightingale, the English "Lady of the Lamp" who would so resemble her in temperament and achievement, Dix translated readily into automatically charged conventional pictures and ideas. Dix enabled or inspired Mann to draw on the stereotypes of ideal feminine virtue prevalent in his society; he found it natural to fictionalize her. And it is easy to see why.

The heroine of sentimental literature is typically, as we have seen, an amateur minister handily outdoing her established clerical competitors. Whether she is outside the church or spiritually at its helm, she cannot be a mere parishioner, a mere party-member, a mere cog. The reader seldom learns her exact religious affiliation. Like Dix and Tuckerman, she works alone, as a one-woman unit. I cannot think of a single heroine in the hundreds of sentimental novels I have read whose basic identity is tied up with a philanthropic group. These heroines are all, of course, incessantly engaged in charitable missions, dispensing cold jellies, warm stockings, and prayers, but they are always alone. In such stories, women who belong to do-good associations are usually villains; it is as if to join a benevolent society is to abandon one's femininity. Rose Clark, the suffering heroine of a novel by Fanny Fern, meets harsh treatment at the hands of Mrs. Markham, a cold, grasping matron who runs the orphanage where she lives; Mrs. Markham cuts off Rose's hair, locks her in dark closets, even whips her.[124] In most sentimental novels, however, institutions of any kind are not so much attacked as ignored. Not infrequently, the heroine will engage in activities which the historian-reader knows were the object of powerful reform-minded organizations, but she will never, apparently, think of joining or mentioning them.[125] Eva van Arsdel in Stowe's New York novels, for example, rescues prostitutes, redeems drunkards, returns lost animals, and provides an *ex officio* neighborhood community center, but never involves herself in a purity campaign, a temperance drive, an anti-vivisection league, or a settlement house. We seldom learn of a fictional heroine's activities even in a school or in a store: like Tuckerman's, her chosen philanthropic arena is the home, whether someone else's or her own. Furthermore, she never attacks poverty or intemperance or prostitution as social phenomena: that would in itself presuppose a degree of abstraction which she would find abhorrent and irrelevant. Her attempt, like Tuckerman's, is always to "improve conditions to the greatest possible extent by improving character."[126] And she offers the sight of her own example to inspire her beneficiaries.

The differences between the sentimental heroine or those who created and imitated her and figures like Tuckerman and Dix are obvious and important. Tuckerman and Dix had an intellectually defined and morally vivid purpose to which literature was subservient. Tuckerman, throughout his book on his ministry at large, addresses his reader personally and speaks always to him "as an individual." He refuses to allow his audience to escape into its collective irresponsibility. Every truth, he feels, is by nature *ad hominem;* he wants to convey the privacy of intense conviction. The domestic novelist also personalized her readership; but she was as interested in manufacturing a privatized experience for her readers as in awakening their consciences. She was concerned with the isolation created by fantasy rather than the solitude imposed by moral commitment. Tuckerman was using literature as Dix used her tracts and petitions, to re-establish essentially communal values; the domestic novelist was plying her trade to convey an illusion of community through the shared consumer pleasures available in a mass society. Tuckerman grew up decades before the vogue of the sentimental heroine was full-blown; Dix's girlhood barely coincided with the heroine's rise. At most, one could say that Tuckerman anticipated certain of her qualities, and that Dix borrowed her invulnerability in order to engage in crucial societal tasks. Yet the conjunction, and progressive degradation, of minister, lady-reformer, and sentimental heroine is unmistakable; and the process of assimilation imperiled the passionate precision which alone can edge and validate antipathy to institutional and professional life.

We can elaborate on this process of deterioration by looking at another aspect of the minister's professional self-image. In *Truth Stranger Than Fiction,* Catharine Beecher had espoused her "parochial clergy," the ministers or pastors, as part of her attack on the clerical scholars and theologians, and with good reason: the pastor, as he was increasingly defined, was in several senses a sister. Tuckerman had never been a particularly forceful or scholarly minister, and he tended always to see himself as a pastor rather than a preacher or a theologian. The distinction became an even more frequent and crucial one in liberal ranks. In an interesting series of sermons on the "Duties" of the ministry, Edwards A. Park pointed to a bifurcation between the theologian, who is to "cherish learning as a mark of status"[127] and "discriminate between the authority of *the mass* of believers and the authority of a few leading minds,"[128] and the pastor, who is if anything to conceal what scholarship he has and to attend and speak to the "domestic griefs" and "private joys" of his congregation.[129] Interestingly enough, Park saw the theologian as a masculine figure—one of his key words for Moses Stuart, for example, was "manly"—while he viewed the pastor as feminine: "so gentle and well nigh domestic is the pastor's vocation," Park explains, "as in the view of some to steal away his manly energy."[130] Stuart, as Park well knew, belonged to an older generation of ministers. Nathaniel Emmons, like Samuel Hopkins, in his effort to keep himself free from temporal cares, courted ignorance not only of his own personal affairs but of his parishioners as well: he made no pastoral calls except in cases of emergency. Channing's colleague Ezra Stiles Gannett, who idolized his fervently devout mother and found his father, a liberal minister, inaccessible, who always needed to lean on an "arm of love," as his son wrote, was convinced his pastoral work was his most important duty. He called on his numerous parishioners in their own homes at least once a year, and sometimes more. In his view, the pastor's task, like the woman's, lay in the home, and like hers, it was composed of telling minutiae, of *"particulars."*[131]

Henry Ware, Jr., was the Unitarian *beau idéal* of a pastor in the first half of the nineteenth century. Like Gannett, he idolized his mother and found relations with his kind, but very reserved and strict father difficult. Ware later analyzed the repressive effect Ware, Sr., a prominent preacher and scholar at Harvard Divinity School, had had on his emotional development: "My father's dislike of ostentation in religion has, I fear, [been] ... injurious. It has made me silent on the subject, backward to introduce it; has made it difficult for me to speak of it with warmth, much as I love it." Ware, Jr., did not, however, like "very ardent and fervent devotional exercises," which he felt made as tyrannical demands on the individual's emotional capacities as his father's intellectualized and restrained style of worship did on his mental resources.[132] He wanted affection, not passion: his was very much a religion of gentleness. Never effusive, never intimate with anyone outside the circle of his family and a few chosen friends, he personalized the abstractions of his creed into a new clerical lifestyle.

Unlike his father who was a skilled controversialist able to quell the doughtiest anti-Unitarian opponents, Ware, Jr., was hardly a brilliant student; of a literary bent, he always lacked the "thorough discipline of an accomplished theologian." His object was never to display great "audition" nor even striking "talents" in the pulpit. Ware thought both of these finally hindrances to the minister's true task, his "private duties," the pastoral visits and ministrations in which he exerts the "most real religious influence" on the *"characters* of men" by promoting "personal religion." The ministerial role as Ware conceived it, in contrast to Hopkins' or Emmons' view, was that of a nurse rather than a doctor, a mother rather than a father. Henry Ware's biographer and brother, John, describes a fascinating scene in which Henry's wife urges him to take on some single great work and cease dissipating his talents in scattered poems, sketches, sermons, and pastoral calls. Ware gently rebukes his wife for such masculine sentiments, answering with the standard feminine rationale for inconspicuous achievement: "I am glad to do the little good that I can in any way that presents itself."[133]

In 1829, the first professorship of Pulpit Eloquence and Pastoral Care was created at Harvard Divinity School. Significantly it was specially ear-marked for Henry Ware, Jr. In 1816, Ware had ministered to the smallest Unitarian society in Boston, and, although he had done extremely well there, it was with the assumption of the Harvard post that he came fully into his own. He had been chosen precisely for his purity of character, his emphasis on pastoral work and personal religion, and he was expected in his new role to be, as he well knew, a great "influence" for good not only on his students but on other ministers. He had been set on a hill very much so that his light might shine before the world; his example was to permeate the clerical ranks. His appointment signalized Harvard's skillful attempt to assimilate and rat-ify the anti-institutionalism increasingly characterizing the liberal faith Har-vard represented. By all accounts, Ware was successful in just the terms he was meant to be. He invited his students to tea, got to know many of them well, encouraged them to engage in philanthropic activities. As one student later wrote, "he raised the standard of ministerial character."[134] In 1831, he published *On the Formation of the Christian Character*, his most significant work and a fitting manifesto and rationale for his new position.

Ware wrote his wife in 1831 that he was surprised to learn "how strongly people feel" about the book: "They speak to me of it with tears in their eyes."[135] In his tract, Ware takes the usual Unitarian line, but more radically. He steers entirely clear of dogma; he heads straight for sensibility, if at a suitably gracious speed. The institutional aspects of religious life are underplayed; in discussing the "Means of Religious Improvement," Ware gives only a third of his allotted space to the activities of attendance at preaching and partaking in communion. The book is a how-to manual addressed very much to the private individual. Intimacy of tone is height-ened by the fact that, as Ware makes clear from the start, he speaks only to those who already agree with him; he writes "only for those who are desirous of knowing themselves and are bent upon forming a religious character." Conversion and controversy are irrelevant here; the issue is the necessity, and pleasure, of further assimilation among those who already resemble one another. In a loaded metaphor, one could say Ware's book signalizes the transition from family ties to incest; intellectual discrimination is by definition impossible. Ware explains that religion is "a matter of per-sonal application and experience," "a sentiment or affection of the heart," an affair of meditating in "habitual thoughtfulness of mind" and performing "simple and blameless tasks." Faith is entirely consonant with human nature:

the devout Christian walks "in communion with another sphere." All is harmony, unity, tranquillity for him: "His duty and his inclination are one. ... to him heaven is already begun."[136] Like Henry Ward Beecher, Ware, to use Bushnell's phrase, is basking rather than abiding; the pastor has become the advocate of self-love.

Ware advises keeping a diary and undertaking daily self-scrutiny and examination for the best "formation of Christian character." Of course such self-investigation was an integral part of the Puritan tradition, but the emphasis is different here: this is a leisurely counting over of one's emotional resources rather than a strict balancing of one's quotidian account with one's maker. Ware is also especially concerned with Christian conversation, a topic which he claims preoccupied the Savior and his disciples. Again Ware's interest is divided between the value of self-control and the lure of self-display: "let your example of cheerful, innocent, blameless words exhibit the uprightness and purity of a mind controlled by habitual principle, and be a recommendation of the religion you profess," he tells his readers. Under the guise of a justified self-approval, Ware subtly offers the pleasures of the mirror: self-communion. Ware urges his followers not to ignore "the abundance of books" among which "God has graciously ordered that your lot shall be cast." He suggests at least an hour of reading a day, and, although the Bible is of course to his mind the primary text for study, he recommends getting a list of other books from a minister; he states his belief that "no work of truth and science, or of elegance and taste, which does not tend to corrupt the morals or create a disrelish for serious thought, need be prohibited to a religious man."[137] Ware's ideal Christian, metaphorically and literally speaking, reads rather than acts.

The assiduous friend of various notable women writers such as Maria Edgeworth and Joanna Baillie, Ware was himself a minor poet and litterateur; he wrote about the beauties of nature, village funerals, and other matters of the heart as aids and corollaries to the "formation of Christian character." Interestingly enough, he had provided in his popular tract, which forms the apotheosis of his pastoral mission, an exact theological rationale and description for the behavior of the heroine of sentimental literature. Jane Elton, the heroine of Catharine Maria Sedgwick's first novel, *A New England Tale* (1822), written to defend and advertise the Unitarian creed, is an anticipation of Ware's thinking. An orphan, living with an uncongenial Calvinist aunt, she is modest, quiet, intelligent, affectionate, pious, grave, and reflective. She breaks one engagement because her fiancé Edward Erskine is not a believer. Her text might well be "Be ye not yoked with unbelievers," but she seems less motivated by adherence to doctrinal purity than by the realization "that my most sacred pleasures and hopes must be solitary" if she marries him. She firmly believes in the central tenet of the liberal creed—that God has "in his wisdom implanted the principle of self-love in our bosoms"—and she finally weds a like-minded Quaker.[138] The pleasures of self-contemplation as well as of congeniality are insured by their similarity.

Sedgwick was a close friend of Ware's; he read, admired, and even directed her writing, and their shared preoccupation may be in part attributable to their common faith and their personal intimacy. Yet later fictional heroines, whose creators never knew Ware or shared his creed, conform as closely as Jane Elton to the dictates of *On the Formation of the Christian Character*. Fleda, the successor to Ellen Montgomery and the star of Susan Warner's second best-seller, *Queechy* (1852), inhabits a world very much like the narcissistic one envisaged in Ware's tract: it exists not in or for itself but only to discipline and create moral character; it is there only so that the sentimental heroine may become a Christian and make others so. Fleda finds her little world "a vale of soul-making," if in a rather limited way. An orphan, she is living at the start of the story with her very elderly and venerable grandfather, Mr. Ringgan, notable for his "womanly sweetness" and impracticality.[139] He dies and she, like Ellen Montgomery, sets off on her travels. Fleda is serious, well-read, constantly looking on the spiritual and moral side of life, thoughtful, devotional. She has a young guardian some twenty years older than herself called Mr. Carleton, who anticipates Elsie Dinsmore's famous sire. At the story's start, Carleton is well-to-do, handsome, brilliant, charming, but proud, defiant, even Byronic; he has not found religious certainty, or Fleda.

Fleda effects Carleton's regeneration with relative ease; Warner, like Ware, is less interested in conversion than in congratulation. The pair then proceed along a heavy and uninterrupted course of common improvement. Their conversations, conforming precisely to Ware's injunctions, inch forward in a step-by-step process of observation, testing, and displaying reminiscent of the absolute earnestness of conversation that women like Catharine Sedgwick and Eliza Follen reported in the 1820s in the Boston Unitarian circle of which Ware was a part: their discourse is a liberalized catechism in which both teacher and pupil are instructed, fostered, buoyed. One could say they take turns playing pastor to each other. Here is a typical example of Fleda and Carleton moving inexorably from the trivial to the profound, their supposedly acute critical faculties only sharpening the rigidly unscrutinized pleasure of total mutual and self-esteem. They are walking arm in arm along a city street:

> "How pretty the curl of blue smoke is from that chimney," he said. It
> was said with a tone so carelessly easy, that Fleda's heart jumped. . . .

"I know it," she said eagerly—"I have often thought of it—especially here in the city."

"Why is it? What is it?"

Fleda's eye gave one of its exploratory looks at his ... before she spoke. "Isn't it contrast?—or at least I think that helps the effect here."

"What do you make the contrast?," he asked quietly.

"Isn't it," said Fleda with another glance, "the contrast of something pure and free and upward-tending with what is below it." ...

"To how many people do you suppose it ever occurred that smoke had a character?," said he, smiling.

"You are laughing at me, Mr. Carleton? Perhaps I deserve it."

"You do not think that," said he, with a look that forbade her to think it. "But I see you are of Lavater's mind, that everything has a physiognomy?"

"I think he was perfectly right," said Fleda. "Don't you, Mr. Carleton?"

"To some people, yes!—But the expression is so subtle that only very nice sensibilities, with fine training, can hope to catch it."

Thus basking even in such tepid rays, ever ascending, they reach and revel in the ether of religious observation, until Carleton can exclaim, " 'How very much religion heightens the enjoyment of life' "—to which "Fleda's heart throbbed an answer."[140] Elitists of spiritual sensibility, they find all the world food for their calmly voracious intelligences. The life of the mind, of which Fleda and Carleton clearly consider themselves devotees, is not in evidence in the pages of *Queechy*.

Henry Ware, Jr., died in 1843, almost a decade before the publication of *Queechy;* he was spared seeing the fruits of his tract. Yet just before his death he was at work on a sequel to *On the Formation of the Christian Character* entitled *Progress of the Christian Life;* what there was of it appeared posthumously in 1847. As the title suggests, Ware's later tract was intended, like Bushnell's second work on the Atonement, to correct the excesses of his first statement. He stresses repeatedly that "the life of contemplation" is only valid if it produces "the life of action." He particularly compares "religious affections" to "sentimental reading"; both, misused, can "consume and waste the sympathies" by "awakening the impulse" to action without "gratifying" it. Ware's solutions to the threatened bifurcation between "sensibility" and realization, however, only reveal the diminution of the intellectual resources at his command. He finds the most persuasive argument for the necessity of action finally to be that *"action is an essential and all-important means of religious growth"*; action, in other words, is important chiefly because it can save religious sensibility from its own excesses; it is subordinate to the "formation of the Christian character." Despite Ware's acknowledgment of a "certain vagueness" which clouds the idea of "Christian progress," he cannot clear it away; he offers almost no specific examples of pious "action" and prefers to stress only that it must be a matter of "habit."[141] Ware, determined to construct the framework of a full Christian life without recourse to theology—the second tract, like the first, absolutely, almost obsessively, avoids doctrine—is like a carpenter working without his tools: precision utterly eludes him. Ware did not live to finish *Progress of the Christian Life;* Susan Warner went on to produce numerous sequels to *Queechy.*

5

THE ESCAPE FROM HISTORY

The Static Imagination

Teachers Without Texts

In truth, to publish serious theological work was to go against the increasingly anti-intellectual temper of the times; few liberal Protestant clergymen had the training, inclination, or courage for such an attempt. With notable exceptions, they were apologists, not preachers. Temperance men indeed, they diluted their doctrines to suit the taste of their listeners. Over the course of the nineteenth century, the Protestant minister became the only professional other than the housewife who ceased overtly to command, much less monopolize, any special body of knowledge. His self-esteem depended more and more on the hope, even the genuine attempt, to *be* better, and less and less on the claim to have learned certain skills which would allow him to *do* better.

One is reminded of the housewife of today's television ads. She is presumably obsessed with putting the right detergent into the laundry; yet even if her choice is effective, she expects no more from her family than a kiss or a compliment whose offhandedness stresses that it is no act of recognition. Her bold sons and husbands and less bold daughters, putting on their sparkling clothes, are uninterested in the why of it: they simply feel better. Her family is on the move, on the go, while "mom" is stationary; she functions like scenery affecting the mind of the traveler. Her interaction with her family must appear accidental, if fortuitous. The housewife's submerged and dubious expertise is expressed only in the tip-off glance she exchanges with her equally weary and indispensable feminine audience. She is "in the know," but barred from the conceptualization of what she knows. Mothers and ministers with their undetected skills keeping their bustling families and congregations more decent than their bustling should permit ... Despite their secret supremacy, even despite the real service they perform and the satisfaction they may take in it, they have abandoned any right openly to participate in the process of change or fully to understand it as a phenomenon.

Whatever the causal relationship between ideology and events, it is clear that ideas play a crucial part in the comprehension and enactment of personal and social change. Dogma, the commitment to a certain set of ideas, creates precision not because it fosters the illusion of certainty on all points, but because it can help its subscribers to pick the right chance and nerve them to take it. We induce people to alter partly by urging them to think, and to think from a different perspective than the one they normally adopt. No one who wishes to effect change can cease to be an educator; no educator can do his work by starting exactly where his hearers are, nor with their assumptions. If he does so—and the majority of liberal Protestant ministers, like the majority of American middle-class mothers and housewives, have increasingly done so in the last century—his educative role has become part of what the historian Daniel Boorstin terms a "pseudo-event":[1] an event designed and arranged so that people will notice it and believe it to be happening, though it will in fact not take place: a trick of public relations which proves only the existence of a performer and an audience—proves, in other words, only that the embryo market situation does indeed exist. Such an educator provides, no matter how unwillingly, merely window-dressing for the forces which control his society. An ideology[2] can represent a significant mode of resistance to economic determinism; it is a way of giving the vote, so to speak, to that part of oneself, no matter how small, which has withstood for whatever reasons the pressures to conform.

We have already seen why an occasionally hostile lack of interest in theological thought was inevitable among educated and literary Protestant women and what they had to gain from the demise of theology; unlike the ministers, the women had never been involved in the formation or perpetuation of Protestant dogma. This does not mean, however, that they had a better substitute for it than did the ministers. Their efforts to make other women experts in "domestic science" were robbed of vitality by the intrusion of technology into the kitchen; mother-at-home was forced to play hostess to male inventions. Their hopes to make women into professional mothers were diminished by the appearance of (male) child psychologists and educational experts who guided rather than followed feminine practice. Yet educated nineteenth-century American women, like ministers, wished to see themselves as missionaries and teachers. The sincerity of the dismay which they expressed as women and Christians when they contemplated a world irreligious and basically antagonistic to feminine concerns can hardly be questioned; who does not want in some way to change a society which denigrates her? Their choice to capitalize on the subversive, even subliminal aspects of their faith rather than to emphasize its strength as a sustaining ideology for protest was logical and inescapable,[3] but this is another way of saying that they were in certain ways doomed to failure. If the women under discussion disavowed openly strident feminist methods, the goals they worked for were feminist ones: better education, more opportunities, and more respect for their sex. The progress of women's rights in our culture, unlike other types of "progress," has always been strangely reversible, in part because historical circumstances have always made it impossible for significant numbers of women to adopt an ideology appropriate to their position. As nineteenth-century women neglected Protestant dogma to point out the undeniable, yet often overlooked, nurturing values contained in their religious heritage, so twentieth-century women thus far have stressed emotional "supportiveness" rather than the (usually Marxist) doctrines which elsewhere buttress communal thinking.[4] Nurture and supportiveness are essential values in any feminist-humanist vision, but they need some structure to inform them if they are to be achieved rather than espoused. The Victorian lady with her dislike of theorizing set an example which has proved compelling even to her more overtly politicized descendants.

As a preacher of the gospel, the liberal minister was presumably committed to the hope of changing men; yet he renounced the right to educate his congregation into his nominally chosen system of conceptualization. Unlike his predecessors, he seldom delivered a series of sermons on a selected knotty theological problem such as the doctrine of election. His sermons tended instead to be, in the broadest sense, occasional. Henry Ware preached, to take some examples at random from his *Works*, on "The Duty of Improvement—A New Year's Sermon" and "The Parallel Between the Jewish and Christian Passovers." Little wonder that the Protestant Church during this period magnified and proliferated religious "occasions" in ways that would have appalled its Puritan originators, who austerely disregarded even Christmas and Easter: the Victorian church, in multiplying holidays, the intrusions of stasis into the realm of change, was simply honoring and extending the only valid license of its preachers.

Skills gain their authenticity from the recognition of unavoidable facts presumably entailed in their acquisition. A lawyer, a doctor, even a psychiatrist, whose function is closest to the minister's, asserts that his ability to help his client is largely independent of the worth of his own personality; he knows what passes for law, or medicine, or the psyche. The liberal minister who abandoned theology lost his right to start from the "facts" of the Bible as his predecessors understood them: that God made man, man sinned against him, and God had and has the right to assign any punishment he judges fit for the offense. Men in this older view live in a world not of their making in which they are, in momentous and ultimate senses, not at home; the minister is the only specialist in the knowledge they need to locate themselves. Abandoning theology, the minister lost his expertise in the realm of what the psalmist called "God's thoughts"; he was inevitably forced to seek the lowest common denominator in the minds of his listeners: some loosely defined preoccupation with spiritual, social, and personal matters. The sermons of liberal Protestants inevitably became a bit like today's horoscopes—"You will want love this month, but you may not find it; trust your old friends"—designed to fit any set of circumstances and lacking the corrective bite provided by a sense of historicity.

The intellectual failure of which I write is all too apparent to need belaboring; what is perhaps more important is the failure of the majority of ministers and women involved to achieve genuine success, as opposed to popularity, in the forms with which they attempted to replace theology. Any contemporary chronicler of American historians acknowledges the numerical supremacy of clergymen—and sometimes of women—among the nineteenth-century authors of biographies and local histories, and then goes on to dismiss their productions in a few pages. Any modern student of popular American fiction and *belles lettres* in the same period is forced to mention a host of names, usually those of women, occasionally those of ministers, which are unfamiliar to the general reader. The clerical and feminine authors whose works are so largely forgotten today were caught in a double dilemma. A minister might initially reject a theological form (the treatise) as unpopular and uncongenial even though he felt guilty at his reluctance to undertake it. Unhappy and constricted within the secular or secularizing form he had chosen to alleviate his original anxiety, however, he might well end by reminding his readers that it was only his didactic religious purpose that prompted him to embark at all into poetry or biography. A female writer, putting suitably feminine piety into unsuitably popular and public modes, went through a similar cycle of self-assertion and self-doubt which left her, perhaps by design, too preoccupied to devote her energy to the problems inherent in her chosen vehicle and all too willing to use her original religious intent largely as self-justification. Ministers and women, unable to own up fully to the demands of either their subject or their form, subverted both.

The literature thus produced, whatever its actual merit, is important for the mass culture it helped to bring into being because of its fundamental and complicated obsession with mediocrity. Authors feeling a confusion of purpose such as I have just described were by definition and by choice amateurs, not professionals. They could hardly wish to call attention to themselves, to boast of achievement in any usual sense; they could hardly fail to produce a partially genuine critique of the prominent and a defense of the unskilled, the forgotten, and the common, the mass-produced items of modern life. They were of necessity interested in those multitudinous situations, events, and persons which they could deceptively portray as lying outside the process of conspicuous historical change but which served in actuality to absorb and mute it.

The Romantic Historians: History as Protestant Religion

Though a nation of churchgoers, Americans were not concerned with theology. What, if anything, did hold their intellectual attention? The answer in varying forms until the eve of the Civil War seemed to be history. By 1860 there were 111 active historical societies in the United States; 90 of these had published some "proceedings." And this in a country where there were only fifty-five towns with a population larger than fifteen thousand.[5] Between 1800 and 1860, 90 of the 348 best-sellers in America, over one-fourth, were either histories or books on historical topics; the seven most influential periodicals of the day devoted fully thirty percent of their contents to historical subjects. By 1840, history was widely taught at the elementary-school level; as early as 1790, Noah Webster, in his popular textbook, *The Little Reader's Assistant*, allotted half his space to historical material. The formal study of the past made its way slowly but surely into high-school and college curricula.[6] Moreover, American fascination with history at least initially stimulated and gained strength from the growing American absorption in fiction.

To put it quite simply, history itself provided the most suitable subject for literature in post-revolutionary America. As English critics were all too fond of pointing out, there seemed to be a dearth of new literary work in this new country. "Who reads an American book?" the British wit Sydney Smith inquired in 1821. His query was snide but not jesting. Was there a lack of literary material, or motivation? Innumerable nationalist literary *apologias* flowed from the pens of anxious defenders of American culture or proto-culture in the early and mid-nineteenth century to quell such anxieties. Their authors argued that American energy was necessarily in large measure devoted to the development of a continent, not to the pursuit of the arts. Such arguments blossomed logically in the proclamation that America itself was the "greatest poem" and its exploitation hence an act of the imagination as of the body.[7] America's material was clearly in its extraordinary and, hopefully, providential history: "a city on a hill" had one obvious subject

—itself, and those civilizations which paralleled, threw into relief, or prepared for its progress.

It is a commonplace to remark how "literary" the great American historians of the early and mid-nineteenth century were; the popular works of William Prescott on the Spanish conquest of the New World or the studies by Francis Parkman of the wilderness struggle between French and English were frankly formed on dramatic models and organized around carefully contrived flights of rhetorical eloquence. History was sometimes touted as a kind of antidote to fiction, exciting but not enervating.[8] The demand on the historian, however, to write well, to be accessible, to provide entertainment, to focus on character, to orchestrate events—in short, to remember Sir Walter Scott and the Waverly series—never flagged. A critic writing for the *Atlantic Monthly* in 1859 urged frankly that a work of history should be as pleasurable for its readers as the "airiest novel."[9] In his young manhood, Prescott tried his hand at genteel light literature; Parkman, like John L. Motley, the historian of the Netherlands, produced a novel; even George Bancroft, the Jacksonian celebrator of Manifest Destiny, began by publishing a volume of poor Byronic verse. All four men saw themselves throughout their careers as practitioners of *belles lettres*.[10] The real progenitor and rival of the new history was less literature than theology.

The quickened American interest in history was, of course, part of a major intellectual shift which involved all of Western Europe, particularly Germany. To put it simply, people began to believe that the most profound and meaningful way of viewing life was as a series of events unfolding uniquely in historical time; man's growth, and his measurements of it, in other words, took on enormous new significance.[11] The attitude of the seminal German thinkers with whom several of the best of the American historians studied was not necessarily or apparently anti-Christian or anticlerical. Indeed, their philosophy of history represented a complex transformation of Protestant dogma. One could almost say that the German romantic historian-philosophers were performing a complex intellectual operation by which they transplanted the heart of Protestant theology into the body of secular society.

G. W. F. Hegel, perhaps the most important philosopher of the nineteenth century, like many of his competitors and followers, was as willing to find in the dialectical historical patterns he elucidated what another great German historian called "the loftiness and logic of the development [of] . . . the Ways of God"[12] as ever John Winthrop, the seventeenth-century governor of the Massachusetts Bay Colony, had been to see the design of God in the suffering of a band of colonists on the Massachusetts coast. It seems obvious that the great dialectic of Calvinism[13]—God versus Man reconciled in Christ—was in part responsible for the concept of historical progression as thesis, antithesis, and synthesis worked out by German philosophers like Hegel. Moreover, the combination of a sense of tragedy with millennial hope, a combination frequently attendant on dialectical thought, was common to Hegelians and to Calvinists. Hegel stressed continually the waste of history; he eloquently referred to history itself as a "slaughter-bench."[14] The mass of men, in Hegel's theory, do not further the great historical design, and even those who do advance it count less for their motives and aspirations than for the effects they produce, effects often contrary to their intentions. Winthrop, like his Calvinist brethren, understood historical waste too; Winthrop's Deity also elected his instruments with a fair degree of arbitrariness to serve his purposes.

Yet Hegel believed—as John Winthrop or Jonathan Edwards did not —that the dialectic operates only in time; as a result, in apprehending whatever reality means, it is more essential in the Hegelian view to perceive the differences than the similarities between historical epochs. Hegelian philosophy, committed to this relativistic assumption, concerned itself less with the discovery and meaning of the immutable laws of God's universe and more with the definition of the ways by which men perceive or project such laws, and how these perceptions alter over time. The German thinkers most directly responsible for the inception of the intellectual presuppositions with which we still live—Herder, Hegel, Schlegel, Fichte, Schiller, and Goethe, all partly available in English by 1850[15]—characteristically began their work with an attempt to formulate the distinctions between the classical, the Christian-medieval, and the modern periods. Hegel described philosophy as "its age comprehended in thought."[16] Philosophy was now chained to history, not to theology. St. Augustine, the greatest of the early church fathers, had believed, as others did after him, that the Christian should direct his thoughts toward the eternal "City of God" and ignore the flux of his earthly home. St. Augustine's nineteenth-century German successors, equally fascinated with constructing a historical-theological world view, disagreed. They saw the fundamental philosophical task as the comprehension of the significance of change—a phenomenon which, we do well to remember, interested St. Augustine relatively little.

By a paradox essential to Calvinism, history for the Calvinist had represented not only God's immortal plan, but mortal life experience; the end, God's glory, was foreordained, but the means, whether furthered in a given individual's salvation or damnation, meant as much as that end. Although it was not, according to the older Protestant view, in man's power to determine whether or not he personally was saved, his spiritual state was nonetheless justifiably and rightly his most momentous concern. Hegel's was a view of history which, in a way unthinkable to Winthrop and those who thought like him, discounted the state of a man's soul. Hegel started and ended with what actually happened, the "accomplished end, and its result as operative upon the actual world,"[17] as Winthrop could not. Even as he tried to save himself from entrapment in matter, in what he called "the madness of what has happened," by amplifying a teleological view of events, a "final aim [for which] these monstrous sacrifices have been made,"[18] Hegel subordinated means to ends. Winthrop could never have used the word "sacrifices"; every life has, to his mind, *served*. Hegel's perception of the relentlessness of change in human life produced in him a fascination with force potentially separable from any awareness of God's design. His conception of history was inevitably both intellectual and elitist; finally, the only consolation for the sheer magnitude and waste of historical motion lay in philosophic perception of the patterns it formed.[19]

The young American scholars who went to Germany expressly to approach thinkers like Hegel or Goethe made sure to let their friends back home know that they were dutifully sorting out the wheat from the chaff. George Ticknor, the future professor of Romance Languages at Harvard, acknowledged that the Germans "are a people who at this moment have more mental activity than any other existing," that among them are the handful of intellectuals who define the issues of the day; but he was also convinced that they frequently misdirect and even "pervert" their enormous talents.[20] Goethe might be a genius, but George Bancroft, future author of the most popular history of the United States ever written, found him "dirty" and "bestial."[21] Such New Englanders hoped to gain intellectually while keeping their religious commitment intact. This was of course not possible, nor probably desirable. Of the seven most important figures in the development of post-Revolution American history—George Ticknor, Edward Everett, Jared Sparks, George Bancroft, William Prescott, John Lothrop Motley, and Francis Parkman—none were untouched by the new German historiography and the transformation of theology integral to it.

Everett, Sparks, Bancroft, and Parkman were all either the sons of ministers or ministers themselves, and these four made a conscious choice against the ministry and for the historical profession. Bancroft, the son of a Unitarian minister, came back from his sojourn in Europe determined, after prolonged struggle, on the career of a clergyman; yet he seemed unconsciously set on defeating his own decision. He wore outlandishly foppish velvet clothing; he dropped affected phrases like "our dear Pelican Christ" from Cambridge pulpits, to the dismay of his listeners.[22] He soon left the ministry..After a stint as a teacher, he became a full-time politician and historian. Edward Everett was not officially an historian, but he made his name through orations on the American past, on Adams, Jefferson, Washington, the "Fathers" and their deeds. He too gave up a clerical career, and one which began far more brilliantly than Bancroft's. Hard-working, eloquent, capable of everything, as his student Emerson astutely recognized, except of finding a mission in life,[23] Everett took over Joseph Buckminster's Unitarian pulpit at the tender age of twenty. A few years later, without breaking openly with the ministry, he made, like Bancroft, a step sideways toward the academy; he joined the faculty of Harvard College as a professor of Greek. By the age of twenty-six, he could write his sister about the "natural disdain" he felt for many of the concerns of the ministry and express scorn for the much-celebrated sermons of the prodigious and sainted Buckminster: "their puerility of style and . . . affectation of literary correctness . . . [were] calculated to do the least good to those who most need it."[24] Four years later, in 1824, Everett was elected to Congress, and, like Bancroft, he abandoned the ministry altogether for politics, diplomacy, and history.

Jared Sparks, the editor of the multi-volume *American Biography*, made no such formal shift. He gradually redirected his energies from the duties of a Unitarian minister (which he had transformed largely into editorial work in any case) toward those of a talented eulogizer of the American past. It was Parkman, the youngest and perhaps the greatest of the group, who most defiantly chose history as a protest against what he considered the effeminacy of the liberal church. His father, a clergyman also named Francis Parkman, was a disciple of Channing; witty, gentle, ineffectual, melancholy in temperament, he insisted on observing fading clerical proprieties and aided groups like "The Society for the Relief of Aged and Indigent Clergymen." He apparently aroused little respect in his son. In later years, the younger Parkman liked to recount a childhood scene whose hostile implications he clearly cherished. His father was talking with a sentimental feminine parishioner while the little boy sat unobtrusively sketching nearby. When asked politely to show the grown-ups his picture, he revealed a tableau in which three devils were carrying away a minister! The sketch was clearly Parkman's translation of the feminine-clerical dialogue on which he was eavesdropping. Throughout his life, he referred to ministers as "vermin."[25]

Not one of the new American historians, however, altogether disdained the clerical-theological profession. All of them, whether consciously or otherwise, expropriated and rescued a number of its most vital traditions for their own use. Even those historians who had never considered the ministry as a profession embraced the career of historian with what at times seemed appropriated zeal. Prescott, the son of a lawyer, and Motley, the descendant on the paternal side of merchants, underwent what can only be called conversion experiences. Prescott, wealthy and charming, was known among his acquaintances as an idler almost up to the moment when *Ferdinand and Isabella* was published in 1838. George Ticknor, in his biography of Prescott, takes care to show his readers Prescott's stern self-control, to share with them the examining journals, the reiterated resolves which nerved Prescott in his struggles to produce.[26] Motley as a young man represented a more desperate case than Prescott; he was considered less gay than dissolute. Reputedly beautiful after the Byronic fashion, he possessed the elegant insouciance of a Bulwer-Lytton dandy. Motley had been well educated by Bancroft himself at his Round Hill academy, but at Harvard the reading he pursued was chiefly fiction. When a tutor reproached him for such superficial tastes, he answered with all the nonchalance of a determined trifler: "I am reading historically, and have come to the novels of the 19th century. Taken in a lump, they are very hard reading."[27] Further study in Germany prepared for but did not precipitate his destiny. By 1839, at twenty-five, he knew, however, that the study of history offered him the discipline he apparently despised but secretly craved. The hero of his first novel, *Morton's Hope*, is made tellingly to confess: "The ground work of my character was plasticity and fickleness. I was mortified by . . . my ignorance and disgusted with my former course of reading [largely poetry]. I now set myself violently to the study of history."[28]

Motley's *Rise of the Dutch Republic* did not appear until 1856, but by the mid-1840s he had discovered the therapeutic value of the research involved in the new history. For all its literary qualities, early nineteenth-century historiography prided itself chiefly on its disavowal of impressionism, its obsession with the "facts," with the object, as the German historian Leopold von Ranke put it in an immortal phrase, "wie es eigentlich gewesen war" (as in itself it truly is).[29] Prescott, reviewing Washington Irving's *Conquest of Granada* in 1829, writes happily of the factual impulse of recent history: "Poetry [is] confined to her own sphere."[30] Prescott, Motley, Bancroft, and Parkman did extensive work in European and American archives; like their Calvinist predecessors, they solaced themselves with the belief that their labor was putting them in touch with, and was even itself equivalent to, truth. Behind their commitment to research lay their trust in work. "Be occupied always," Prescott admonished himself;[31] Sparks, whose career was an exemplum of effort, warned others that "idleness and dissipation" will never purchase their devotees "a seat in the temple of fame."[32] Prescott and Motley both spent a decade preparing their first major studies. History offered these pioneering historians what theology had offered their fathers: the resource of exhaustiveness. They tended to conceive of their work in terms of a massive life plan. Bancroft and Sparks meant in their different ways to treat all of American revolutionary history, Prescott to detail Spanish-American relations in their entirety, Motley to document the Germanic-Dutch impulse to liberty, Parkman to cover the struggle of England and France in the New World from start to finish. They undertook their monumental tasks in the same spirit in which Edwards and Hopkins dedicated their futures to the consolidation of their theological systems.

Research for the historian, as formerly for the theologian, could involve not just labor but martyrdom. Parkman's chosen subject, the American forest, and the fervency with which he pursued his experience of it, remind one of the arduous missionary forays of earlier Calvinists like John Eliot or David Brainard. Parkman wrestled, as did Prescott, against lifelong illness: Parkman's "enemy," as he called his disease, was an incapacitating disorder centered in the head; Prescott's was incipient blindness. But both men battled on in a spirit Hopkins or Emmons would have recognized and appreciated. Everett, Ticknor, Bancroft, Prescott, and Motley, during their student days and long after, habitually worked ten to fourteen hours daily, a regimen reminiscent of that which men like Hopkins and Edwards had imposed on themselves. Timothy Dwight and William Ellery Channing confessedly injured their health by their zealous over-commitment to the study of God's word; Parkman admitted that he had done "violence" to his constitution in preparing for his career; Prescott knew he could regain vision in at least one eye if he would stop the reading necessary to his work, but he never seriously considered such an abandonment of his vocation.

The transfer of energy formerly assigned to theological tasks into the service of history is as apparent in the work as in the career patterns of the most prominent nineteenth-century historians. With Hegel, they appropriated from Protestant theology a notion of dialectical relationship and development which they used to understand the phenomenon of change; in every sense coming after Hegel, they became more interested in the fact of change than in the laws which tried to explain its purpose.

At first glance, the underlying preoccupation of the romantic historians appears to be not only a secular, but a political one:[33] the rise and spread of liberty. It is important to remember here that the beginning of modern historical writing in the United States coincided with the winning of independence and the consequent debate and controversy over the form of government appropriate for this exemplary new nation. The burst of historical activity was thus part of the scramble among towns, states, sections, and parties for a controlling voice in American affairs. Jefferson was sure that Judge Marshall's Federalist *Life of George Washington* was designed to influence the election of 1810. A southern reviewer objected to Bancroft's stress on New England; he was fully cognizant that, if northerners wrote the nation's history, they would "become our masters."[34] American history was thus politicized and political from its inception; it naturally tended to stress the importance of politics, and of the special American brand of politics. George Bancroft, while always maintaining devoutly with Hegel that God directs human progress, argued consistently that the religious "liberty" the Pilgrims had sought was, intentionally or otherwise, the precursor for the political freedom of which their nineteenth-century descendants boasted; despite his lifelong love of Jonathan Edwards, he became vividly interested in the ministers among his subjects only when their aspirations most transparently took on a directly political cast.[35] Motley, writing several decades after Bancroft began to publish his *History*, found the meaning of the struggle of Protestant Holland against Catholic Spain in the Dutch quest for political independence. Even Prescott, justifying the Conquistadors' conquest of Mexico, pointed up the despotic nature of Aztec rule—ignoring for the moment the equally dictatorial regime to be imposed by the Spaniards.[36]

Yet the persistent theme of the romantic historians was not finally politics, deep as their involvement was in political affairs. They would each have defined the term "freedom" differently to begin with: Bancroft was a Jacksonian democrat who considered himself "radical to the heart's core,"[37] while Parkman, Prescott, and Motley were in varying ways patrician in their allegiance. Parkman was clearly not as politically oriented as the others, yet he was definitely of their school; it is as if in Parkman's work the political focus, with its rather spurious optimism, can be dropped as adventitious. Whatever their very real flaws of attitude and judgment, romantic historians saw too deeply into the meaning of their country to concentrate on its democratic mission. Although they might not have been willing to say so, their common interest was less in liberty than in "the course of empire," the phenomena of discovery, expansion, struggle, conquest, and exploitation of which politics is but one reflection. Whether it was Cortez defeating the Aztec leader Montezuma, or La Salle planting the French flag in the American wilderness, the drama which fascinated them was that of imperialism. Their work is finally, in the broadest sense, not political but military history; they were profoundly if inconclusively involved in the study of violence. Jared Sparks, apparently the least biased member of the group, the one most determined to be fair, in compiling his popular twenty-five-volume *Library of American Biography*, which he intended as a kind of biographical history of America itself, notably stressed adventurers over saints. The vast preponderance of his *Lives* are devoted to explorers, soldiers, and politicians, those who manifested above all energy.[38]

Despite the fact that Sparks selected his biographers from every walk of (intellectual) life including the ministry, the portraits which emerge are strikingly similar: whether the subject is William Phipps or Alexander Wilson, whether the writer is the minister William Peabody or the scholar Alexander Everett, the focus is on the problem of masculine ambition. Captain John Smith, whose "life and adventures" are given by the literary critic George Hillard in the second volume of the series, could serve as a prototype of those whose lives succeed his: he is one "among the adventurous spirits whom a restless love of enterprise called from the bosom of repose in England to new scenes and untried perils in our Western wilds"; he was fortunate enough to "live in striving and eventful times" and to find in America "an object attractive enough to keep his imagination perpetually kindled and vast enough to task all his powers."[39] Such words suggest that their author does not live in such times, does not have such an object. Men like Hillard, or Sparks, are warming their hands very self-consciously at fires they have not kindled. This is clearly the value of history to them: it permits their vicarious participation in the massive energies at work in their society; it allows them imaginatively to invoke and to control the ungovernable spirit animating capitalist culture, change itself.

Sparks used his role as historian to re-enact the drama of discovery and enterprise which so fascinated him. Like his major peers a pioneer in archival research, he traveled thousands of miles and examined innumerable hitherto-unseen manuscripts in the course of his work. He felt himself "an explorer ... in the ... untrodden fields of American history."[40] The letters he wrote to friends in 1827 from Mt. Vernon, where he was going through the Washington papers, read a little like those of a general engaged in military operations sending dispatches to his civilian contacts. Most of Sparks's stable of writers for the *American Biography* series engaged in no such strenuous forays; yet they are consistently uninterested in those who overtly most resemble their own scholarly selves; they dismiss "sedentary" pursuits with consistent scorn. They lust for the event, which they implicitly define as the moment of impact. The relatively short shrift given to clergymen in the *American Biography* is explained when Convers Francis, the biographer of John Eliot, apostle to the Indians, passes rapidly over Eliot's lengthy, settled ministry in Roxbury: "There is not much to be told; for the life of a clergyman as such, though full of toil, is not full of events."[41] Francis concentrates rather on Eliot's missionary work with the Indians, and he is primarily interested in the fact that it was largely a failure. Christian piety cannot integrate the natives into modernizing society. To convert the Indians as the Puritans originally intended to do, in Francis' narrative as later in Parkman's, only hastens their demise; faith all by itself is a sign of passivity and of approaching obsolescence.[42]

Sparks, Prescott, Motley, Bancroft, Parkman, and their followers were writing what Nietzsche would call "monument" history: the commemoration and celebration of significant masculine achievement, all the more impressive to these authors for its evanescence and futility. The vastness of the topics and the periods they covered, as well as the organic theory of history as a process of conflicting and resolving forces which they had appropriated from the German school, made imperative an epic panorama and synthetic sweep from which by definition only the mightiest figures—those, in Hegelian terms, possessed of the "spirit of the age"—could detach themselves and emerge with clarity. The works of the romantic historians are marked by a sense of unending motion which both parallels and finally contains the aspiring will of the chief protagonists.

Motley clearly enjoyed writing the "Historical Introduction" to his *Dutch Republic*, in which he compressed a millennium into its most significant details; the necessity of condensation makes him an aggressor, an historical hunter stalking the ages for his prey. His excitement gradually mounts; at the close of the introduction, he switches into the present tense. As he prepares to usher in his story proper, the narrative, released, can dilate momentarily. This beginning is not deceptive. The overall rhythm of Motley's *Dutch Republic*, like that of Prescott's *Fall of Mexico*, is a counterpoint of movement and collection, force and resistance: the spectacle of the ever-turbulent masses, the ever-moving ages, is periodically broken by the set portrait of the hero or villain, whether Philip II of Spain or Cortez. The arrest involved in these moments of portraiture is deliberate and self-conscious: the historian honors his hero, no matter how he may abhor his principles, by exempting him briefly from the flow of his narrative, just as Cortez or Philip fought to impress his nature upon his times. The sea metaphors Motley uses again and again are appropriate and telling beyond their obvious relevance in a history of Holland. In Motley's narratives, as in those of his fellow historians, the heroes inevitably drown in the flood of the account, but they are allowed vivid and full flashbacks before they do drown. The logic of the narrative suggests that their energy is less only than that of the process it attempts to alter.

The style the best of the nineteenth-century American historians employed—a highly rhetorical, oratorical, grand style—illustrates the same law of motion which governs the narrative form: exhibitionism struggling heroically to arrest the attention of an utterly mobile universe. Bancroft was known, even criticized, for the profusion and extravagance of his descriptive powers; in revising his early volumes, he felt bound to engage in what he called "slaughtering adjectives."[43] Yet it was the later writer Francis Parkman who produced the most highly crafted "purple" prose; he spoke of Hennepin's discovery of Niagara thus: "On his left sank the cliffs, the furious river raging below; til at length, in primeval solitudes, unprofaned as yet by the pettiness of man, the imperial cataract burst upon his sight."[44] This is a style which places a high value on conspicuousness and waste. What is prominently displayed is in the same moment thrown away. The effect of restlessness in Parkman, Motley, or Prescott is heightened by a profusion of metaphors whose occasional confusion seems the result of the quickening pace. Motley describes Philip the Fair, the father of Charles the Fifth, as "the bridge over which the house of Hapsburg passes to almost universal monarchy, but, in himself, nothing."[45] The reader's half-realized impression that one cannot be both a "bridge" and a "nothing" is lost in the tide; Philip is both precisely because even before the close of the sentence the perspective, invincibly progressing, has necessarily shifted. Motley has not revealed any literary incompetence here, but he has demonstrated his lack of interest in what could be called a stable metaphor situation. Characters, places, scenes are subjected to a kind of transformational grammar of events.

There is constant and complex lip service paid in these works to the Hegelian dialectic. Motley can refer almost clinically in passing to the rules of historical change: "even as in all human history the vivifying becomes afterwards the dissolving principle."[46] The invincible impression held by the reader that these narratives are not altogether "dialectical" comes less from a questioning of their authors' sincerity in using such phrases than from an unavoidable awareness of attention directed just barely elsewhere: philosophic concern with the dialectical process is lost in fascination with its sheer momentum. The dialectic becomes self-consciously absorbed in its own pace. Parkman, Motley, and Prescott are masters of the art of flashback and anticipation, and the obvious but rich ironies to be garnered by this method. Edward Everett in an 1853 oration on "The Discovery of America," speaking of the 1492 proclamation by the Spanish throne that all lands found in future by Columbus will belong to Spain, notes ominously: "Thus was America conquered before it was discovered."[47] Everett's perception here of the fundamental law of imperialism, as of capitalism—that appetite can be so strong as to presume digestion before the fact of consumption—is a recurring and controlling one in the historical work of Everett's friends. Dialectical fate is present; the oppressor will die, the oppressed will rise, only to oppress in turn. But the motion which accompanies and accomplishes this process tells far more than the outcome.

Look, for example, at the magnificent closing paragraphs of Parkman's *Conspiracy of Pontiac* (1851). Parkman has just described the assassination of the Indian leader after the defeat of his attempt to expel the English from the lands of his tribe:

> Thus basely perished this champion of a ruined race. But could his shade have revisited the scene of murder, his savage spirit would have exulted in the vengeance which overwhelmed the [Indian] abettors of the crime. Whole tribes were rooted out to expiate it.... over the grave of Pontiac more blood was poured out in atonement than flowed from the veins of the slaughtered heroes on the corpse of Patroclus....
>
> Neither mound nor tablet marked the burial-place of Pontiac. For a mausoleum, a city has risen above the forest hero; and the race whom he hated with such burning rancor trample with unceasing foot-steps over his forgotten grave.[48]

The point here is of course the irony; one should note how thoroughly in Parkman the dialectical process has been detached from its benign Hegelian end. Even more important, however, is the aimlessness, the omnivorousness of the irony: Pontiac's death ironically leads to more Indian revolts; the Indians, however, by a further irony, destroy principally themselves rather than their white conquerors; by a last and most wrenching irony, the Indians' beloved forests have been replaced by cities which Parkman, no sympathizer with the Indian cause, clearly dislikes almost as much as Pontiac himself. Tied to the inexorability of history in the Hegelian sense, committed to the *fait accompli* which yields a vivid tableau but little explanation or moral resolution, Parkman has been forced to resort to ambiguity as in itself artistically and philosophically conclusive; in a multitude of unsatisfactory and limited possibilities simultaneously presented, Parkman has discovered a suitable ending. In the *Conspiracy of Pontiac*, there has finally been no winner but the ever-alert principle of irony, the spirit of change itself.

The Antiquarians: History as Sentimentalism

The collective output of the romantic historians even with its oppressive bias toward masculinity and force, constituted an undisputedly serious effort toward American self-realization. There were important reasons why ante-bellum America was vitally receptive and suited to the Hegelian and post-Hegelian outlook. As we have seen, the new history represented the use and transformation of the structures of America's oldest intellectual tradition, Protestant theology, in the service of a modernizing time- and change-conscious culture. Furthermore, the belief in progress so common in America, a belief based on enormous industrial and technological development, made palatable and even necessary the idea, central to the historicism which Hegelian thinking inevitably created, that events occur uniquely and irredeemably in time. To put it another way, only a high degree of materialist optimism such as America habitually suggested could permit men to live without benefit of the notions of compensation inherent in older non-Hegelian and cyclical theories of history.[49] America was a civilization whose rapid and apparently promising intellectual, economic, and social development necessitated the at least partial adoption of historicism.

I have suggested that the romantic historians, like so many of those who have come closest actually to dealing with our culture, were in part absorbed by the phenomena they attempted to analyze. They held the mirror to the fundamental impulse of their society; inevitably they themselves were also reflected and contained therein. Yet, it is important to remember that Prescott, Motley, and Parkman immediately commanded European audiences; history was largely responsible for what share of intellectual respect

America evoked abroad before 1850.[50] As was later the case with the novels of Hawthorne and the work of the southwestern humorists, foreigners interested in America were even quicker than United States citizens to hear and listen to an authentic voice; they were alert to note when the ratio between propaganda and information shifted the critically essential degree. If the work of Bancroft, Prescott, Motley, and Parkman is imperialist, at times repellently so, it nonetheless represents a significant clue to a critique of a society which was itself absorbed in conquest. And the romantic historians, as we have seen, intermittently sensed and expressed the corrosive and seeping ambiguity of American success, although they could present no alternative to the cult of progress.

Others did try, if in vain, to find an alternative. The four major American historians were widely admired in their own time and since. Although their work continued to appear and to be read throughout the later half of the nineteenth century, the historical writing of which their work was the most significant outcome had passed its peak by 1850. Indeed, the proportion of histories or historical novels among best-sellers, the percentage of historical material in the contents of the more popular magazines and reviews, began to diminish in the 1840s.[51] Just as critical exegesis, whose models were also largely German, failed to take firm hold in the ante-bellum period, romantic history enjoyed a rise and a fall during the same time; important historical work, like major Biblical criticism, did not re-establish itself until several decades after the Civil War, and then in more scientific, more technical, and less synthesized form.[52] This does not mean, however, that history was not written in the United States between 1850 and 1875. Although fiction swept the American market as never before, histories and biographies continued to pour from the press. The period witnessed the rise of lyceums and libraries, many of them interested in the preservation of local history and monuments; the collection and publication of genealogies; and the founding of magazines like the *New England Historical and Genealogical Register* and the *New Englander*.[53] What had happened was not even the temporary demise of history, but the temporary defeat of one wing of the emerging historical profession by another: the triumph of sentimental, local, antiquarian, "social," and, loosely speaking, religious history, written mainly by clergymen and women, over-romantic, national, prophetic, "political," and secular history produced principally by well-to-do amateurs.[54]

The earliest historical research in America had been done at the local level, if only because, as I have remarked, towns and states and sections were initially interested in history as a means of self-inflation and self-advertisement which could justify their claim to a bigger piece of the new national pie. In other words, the historical impulse in early nineteenth-century America was as natural to those who felt unjustly neglected as to those necessarily involved in the problem of conspicuousness. The men and women who wrote local, antiquarian, or biographical history at this time were fascinated by the meaning of obscurity. The cliche they most frequently used to describe their motive was the phrase "to rescue from oblivion." They did not claim the title of historian but referred modestly to themselves as those who filled "the humble office of a compiler." They were anxious to find "those minor points . . . which have escaped the notice of historians" and "the smaller matters of individual experience" which more pretentious historical narrative "in its stately march could not step aside to notice."[55] These chroniclers discovered their mission in redeeming what was discounted as waste by imperialist Hegelian history, and in many ways their effort was potentially admirable and farsighted.

The majority of what I will call the "antiquarian" efforts which were under clerical and feminine auspices reveal a justified anxiety among ministers and women that their society was as indifferent to their past as it was to their present. One writer, speaking on "Ministerial Biography" in the *New Englander* in 1854, urged New England towns to discover and publish the history of their former ministers and churches. He anxiously cites an example of neglect: "There are large portions of the state [Conn.] in which nothing has been done to rescue from oblivion the memories of the early ministers."[56] Clerical commentators could be perfectly frank about the special importance of the past for them. Whatever the past actually might be, it can function in the present as an emblem of changelessness and thus provide a corrective to a society obsessed with change. As one rather florid commentator wrote in 1859:

> We idealize the past, and recall it in the placid moonlight of romance, set off in the form of imagination, and seen through the haze of softening regrets and holy tears. Its domain, so sweetly peaceful, whence most of the evil has been eliminated and where all the good has been touched with consecration, contrasts with the turmoil and haste of the present.[57]

Ministers wanted to dwell on the past, but the past which concerned them was hardly the one presented by contemporary romantic historians. They were often uninterested, occasionally hostile, before the supposedly heroic exploits of the colonial and revolutionary periods. Sylvester Judd lost his position as chaplain to the Maine legislature when he felt compelled to preach against the American Revolution.[58] Noah Worcester, despite his strong Federalist reverence for Washington, also found the Revolution morally disturbing; Penn was the only one of America's early heroes he praised unstintingly. In 1815, Worcester straightforwardly, if heretically, disavowed those archetypal American models of masculine endeavor, the Puri-

tan Fathers: he found them "a class of men assuming the most hostile attitude
. . . brave in battle, but . . . [always] in a state of alarm, anxiety or hostility."[59]
Horace Bushnell took a similar view of his theological progenitors. In his
depiction, they resemble titanic figures in a fresco by Michelangelo. They
are imposing and inhuman: "they took hold of the iron pillars that held up
the theological heavens, and climbed and heaved in huge surges of might and
kept their gross faculties in exercise. . . . They looked upon the throne, they
heard the thunder roll." They provided a "grand massive character" for
American religion, to which God now means to add the needed "softer
shades of feeling."[60] Edwards A. Park was never able to love Jonathan
Edwards, although he devoted the last decades of his life to a memoir of his
famous ancestor. Park venerated Edwards, but he wished Edwards had been
able to be "something more of a brother and somewhat less of a champion."[61] "Champion" suggests an overpowering figure, a combatant, and a
winner. Devalued by his culture, the mid-nineteenth-century liberal clergyman evaded rather than courted comparison with his weighty predecessors.
Equally important, he insisted that current historiography, in ignoring less
conspicuous experience like his own, was perverting its task of record keeping and record evaluation.

The liberal minister was aware of the slight place his profession was
accorded by contemporary historians. Park noted that "the name of a pastor
is seldom mentioned by an historian."[62] William Ellery Channing remarked
that history "has not a place even in its margin for the minister and the
schoolmistress."[63] We have seen what short shrift Jared Sparks gave clergymen in his *Library of American Biography*. It was perhaps Sparks's neglect
which spurred his friend Reverend William Sprague of Albany to compile
his massive nine-volume *Annals of the American Pulpit* between 1857 and
1869. The titles of the two series are significantly inappropriate; Sparks's
"Biographies" or "Lives" usually present studies of an entire place and period, while Sprague's *Annals* are actually a compilation of short biographical
sketches which supply the reader with little historical background. Sprague
can omit the background because of the growing disassociation between the
mission of the minister and conventional historical action or importance.
The minister was increasingly seen as belonging to what Horace Bushnell
eloquently called the "dead history" of "oblivion"; "dead history" consists
of those deeds and people which live on in their unrecognized influence
rather than in the articulated memories of their fellows. "Do the vegetable
growths repine or sicken," Bushnell asks, "because they cannot remember
the growths of the previous centuries? Is it not enough that the very soil that
feeds them is fertilized by the waste of so many generations moldering in
it?"[64] Edwards A. Park explained, with some point, that "the real unwritten
history of the race is not, in the main, made up of war and of diplomatic

manoeuvres, but of those domestic griefs which the pastor assuages and of those private joys which he hallows."[65]

The implicit assimilation of clerical and feminine "history" here under the rubric "domestic" and "private" is striking and understandable. Women too felt with justice that their story was both "real" and "unwritten." Middle-class women were by definition less responsible for America's industrializing present or its heroic past than their secular male peers. They had had their share, more than their share some felt, of the democratic work of settlement. One feminist historian, writing for the radical reform periodical *The Lily* in 1853, quipped angrily that she was tired of hearing of the hardships the Pilgrim Fathers had endured: the Pilgrim Mothers had suffered all the same trials—plus the Pilgrim Fathers![66] Women had had less than their share, however, in the elitist business of law-making and constitution-composing. Feminine work has always been ahistorical by the definition of male historians: raising children and keeping house have customarily been viewed as timeless routines capable of only minor variations. In a country like America whose historical identity rests on a short series of self-conscious crises, the exclusion of women from the historical life of the culture is particularly acute. American history does not reach back into an irrecoverable past; hence it nowhere takes on in retrospect the aspect of process which interweaves it inexorably with social life. We have marble busts of all our great leaders, original copies of all our important documents; we even have photographs which cover a third of our entire span. Men keep public records; women seldom figure in them, much less keep them. American history by any comparative basis afforded in the Western world is an extraordinarily recorded affair and hence an extraordinarily masculine affair. In America, history has functioned as a kind of literacy test which women automatically fail.

Women who undertook the writing of history at mid-century did so with a revisionist aim, whether acknowledged or not. Elizabeth Ellet, a New Yorker and a poet, dedicated her considerable skills to the reinterpretation of the American past. She was well aware that there existed an "abundance of materials for the [masculine] history of action" and little for the (feminine) history of "feeling,"[67] yet she determined to redress the balance. In her most important work, *The Women of the American Revolution*, published in three volumes between 1848 and 1850, Ellet tried to turn her readers from their preoccupation with the Revolution's "leading spirits," the founding fathers, to a concern with the founding mothers, who provided "the nurture in the domestic sanctuary of that love of civil liberty which afterwards kindled into a flame and shed light on the world."[68] When women wrote historical novels, they did so to express discreetly veiled hostility to the very history they were apparently extolling. I have already discussed works like Eliza B.

Lee's *Naomi* as protests against the ministry, but they were, perhaps more importantly, protests against a peculiar definition of American history. The mission of the heroine in these novels is to free the hero from history: she rescues him paradoxically from the historical novel, which she transmutes to a domestic tale. Naomi and her loyal lover eventually desert the Puritan faith and the Puritan community which persecutes those belonging to their Quaker persuasion: they marry and go off into a sylvan idyll. The book ends precisely and appropriately when we pass out of the prison of male chronicles into the domain of unrecorded feminine grace and family life. It is, of course, a convention of the novel that it closes with a dismissal of its characters into their private lives where they will no longer be subjected to the readers' scrutiny, but this convention has double force in a book like *Naomi*. The author does not so much drop the historical lifeline as cut it. Her characters have gone into a realm where history cannot follow them.

Catharine Sedgwick's historical work is equally ambivalent. Occasional protests from America's male critics, who felt a woman could not deal adequately with history or government, apparently found an echo in Sedgwick's understandably confused conscience.[69] In *Hope Leslie* (1827), a romance set in seventeenth-century New England, Sedgwick's high-spirited heroine represents benign feminine anarchy wreaking charming havoc with official records. As she defies the stern edicts of Governor Winthrop and his peers, frees witches, and defends Indians, Hope Leslie suggests counter-history; she is an *ex post facto* protest against the masculine solidities of the past. In later books, Sedgwick evaded rather than subverted American history. She prefaces *The Linwoods* (1835), a novel about the American Revolution, with an avowal that she has omitted any real consideration of the Revolution itself on the grounds that she is but a "weak and unskilled woman."[70] She tastefully substitutes for such analysis the delineation of several rather dull love affairs and a few fervent panegyrics on Washington's nobility of character. Only the heroine, Isabella Linwood, an impetuous patriot who continually regrets she is not a man and thus able to defend her country, suggests Sedgwick's frustration at her sex-determined exile from her own material. By the later 1830s, Sedgwick had turned to thinly fictionalized domestic manuals and religious tracts. Her apostasy from history, even from subversive history, was little noted but immensely significant. Unable as a woman to find a perspective from which she could adequately treat the past, she turned her very real talents to a depiction of the pleasures and trials involved in running the modern household, and she took her large feminine following with her. Works like Sedgwick's *Home* (1835) and *Live and Let Live* (1837) represent in embryo form the romance of domestic management which would become the staple fare of the profoundly anti-historical women's magazines of the twentieth century.

In the generation of women authors which succeeded Sedgwick's, Harriet Beecher Stowe is the only major figure who could be said to have devoted her finest talents to the historical novel. It seems hardly accidental that the great vogue and success of female authors in what Fred Lewis Pattee has called "the feminine fifties" coincided with the end of the dominance of historical fiction. The chosen *noms de plume* of several of the most important of these authors suggest their anti-historical bias in its least constructive guise: "Fanny Forrester," "Fanny Fern," "Grace Greenwood"—not to mention "Minnie Myrtle," "Lily Larkspur," and, somewhat later, "Jenny June." Such names, flirting coyly with suggestions of vegetative process, are decorative advertisements of luxury items. Even while they flatter the authors' femininity, they define it as superfluous; they are purely fictional. By such self-baptism, feminine authors become characters in their own sentimental effusions: hothouse products, they are self-announced refugees from history.[71]

Literary women and liberal ministers joined in their antipathy to the military subjects which obsessed the romantic historians. Many of them were pacifists, and their commitment to peace was clearly motivated by their dislike of "masculine" history as well as by their hatred of violence. Pacifism was most prominent and viable in the period between 1815 and 1850, after the partial national disillusion with the catastrophe of the War of 1812 and before the heated and belligerent sectionalism which preceded the Civil War. Pacifism, unlike temperance, never had the official support of the major Protestant churches; it was launched in 1809 by a layman, David Low Dodge.[72] Yet from its inception, the American Peace Society numbered a very high percentage of clergymen among its members and many women among its supporters. One of the movement's historians estimates that a third of its initial supporters were in the ministry;[73] another scholar stresses that in 1828 the peace societies drew more adherents from the ministry, and especially the Unitarian clergy, than from any other profession.[74] By 1852, when the movement was in definite decline, it was a clerical concern limited to New England: of its 307 life members, 168 lived in Massachusetts and 93 were clergymen.[75] Women were always active and eager in the pacifist cause. Where we have records for any given peace society, they reveal a significant feminine presence; at Portsmouth in 1826, the group included 18 men and 17 women.[76] Women were more likely, however, to evince their concern by less direct and conspicuous means. They could urge their minister to join the American Peace Society or to preach at least once a year on the subject of pacifism, and many did so. Most of the ladies' magazines of the day were avowedly and almost automatically in favor of non-belligerence. In the *Ladies' Magazine* of 1836, Sarah Hale had applauded the formation of the "Boston Ladies' Peace Society."[77] *The Ladies' Wreath: A Magazine Devoted to Literature, Industry and Religion*, edited by Mrs. S. T. Martyn, opened with a spirited attack against the "Tendencies of War";[78] *The Ladies' Album* also editorialized indignantly and frequently on "The Evils of War."[79]

Protestant ministers, unlike Protestant women, had taken an acknowledged and respected role in the American Revolution.[80] Thirty-six years after the struggle for independence, however, Noah Worcester, a Unitarian minister, himself a veteran of the Revolution but destined to become the single most important figure in the early peace movement, denounced military glory in his one-man pacifist organ *The Friend of Peace* as absolutely un-Christian, not to say unclerical; he exclaimed that a fighting minister "at this day would be regarded as a *madman!*" Worcester was frank from the start of his anti-war career on his alignment with feminine principles. He outspokenly sought the support of women, promising any future feminine adherents: "By thirty years of faithful and united exertion on the part of the females of Christendom, war might lose all its fascinating charms, and be regarded by the next generation with more abhorrence than the people of today look on the gladitorial combats of Rome."[81]

The view Worcester took and dramatized of war in his attacks on it was the minute and essentially domestic one that television—whose advent represented the apotheosis of social history—enables us to hold today; he was skillful at the close-up picture in which besieged towns become groups of families and soldiers become men, husbands, and fathers. For him there was no such thing as military history; there was only the outrage of humanitarian values. Under the *nom de plume* of "Philo Pacificus," Worcester described "The Horrors of Napoleon's Campaign in Russia" in 1815. He felt that the reader is only "diverted" from the true issue by the customary "encomiums on the bravery of fighting men and the glories of victory." The point about war for Worcester lay in civilian consequences rather than in military actions. He directs us characteristically not to the battlefield but to the sidelines, where the greatest and least deserved suffering is taking place: "On one side was an old man just expiring. On the other, an enfant whose feeble cries, the mother, worn down with grief, was endeavoring to hush."[82] His concern is with the innocent victims, the women, children, and elderly who can only be martyrs in the masculine arenas of conflict and aggression. In 1816, Worcester's friend and admirer William Ellery Channing voiced his protest against the exaltation of the "hero," with his "love of excitement," his "passion for superiority, for triumph, for power." Channing was perfectly conscious of what his demand, like Worcester's *ex post facto* reporting of Napoleon's Russian siege, implied—a new history. "Let the records of past ages be explored," Channing urged, "to rescue from oblivion, not the wasteful conqueror ... but ... the benefactors to the human-race" engaged in philanthropy rather than destruction.[83]

Those women who joined peace societies or urged their ministers to join shared many of Worcester's preoccupations. They too deflected military into social history; they too were concerned less with the actions than with the effects of war, and particularly with those effects which touched family and feminine life. An anonymous lady pacifist in the *Ladies' Album* explained that "the female portions of society are the greater sufferers in war. Theirs is a domestic life. ... War breaks up the domestic circle. It calls the husband, the father, the brother and the lover from the endearments of home to the field of carnage."[84]

One of the most popular novels of the Civil War, *The Gates Ajar* by Elizabeth Stuart Phelps, a novel which reached and touched thousands of female readers, never recorded a battle scene or presented a soldier. The author's concern, in her words, was with "the women—the helpless, outnumbering, unconsulted women; they whom war trampled down, without a choice or protest."[85] Phelps's story focused on Mary Cabot, a young and insignificant girl in a small Massachusetts town who is overwhelmed by grief at the loss of an idolized brother in combat. Mary finally accepts the war and all its dreadful consequences only by denying its reality. Following an obvious process of compensation, she ignores earthly existence to focus on a heavenly land where family felicity is exaggerated into eternity. Domestic peace, a world of women and womanly cares, is seen to be the abiding order, not the aggressive and senseless militarism of men. For Phelps as for Worcester, heaven, like history itself, is a civilian affair, a matter of individuals and their tastes and needs.

Clerical and Feminine Biography: From History to Biology

The biographies women and ministers wrote in increasing numbers about themselves and each other over the middle decades of the nineteenth century mark the consolidation of the clerical-feminine history, or flight from history. In 1839, Jared Sparks formulated a definition of the different types of biography current in his culture. The first kind is the "historical biography which admits of copious selections from letters and other original papers"; the second is the "memoir" whose method is "more rambling and relating more to affairs of a private nature."[86] Almost all of Sparks's American biographies are entitled "Lives" and belong to the first category;[87] the vast majority of the clerical and feminine biographies under consideration here are self-styled "Memoirs."

The antiquarians were attempting to create both a social and a re-Christianized history; they certainly avoided the arrogance inherent in the grand view of Hegelian intellectual history, and this is very much to their credit. The pacifist impulse I just described here is a profoundly sympathetic one. From the antiquarian perspective as from the traditional Protestant viewpoint, every life *serves*. The number of books written on relatively obscure people, usually ministers or literary women, in the mid-nineteenth century is enormous. Theoretically, they are valuable just as unused television footage could be useful to our descendants: they offer a quotidian record. Partial anticipators of the Braudelian and Eriksonian methods,[88] the clerical and feminine biographers sought to convey what could be called the psychological topography of their era. Yet one cannot help feeling that this is neither their main purpose nor their principal achievement. To begin with, a number of these narratives manage to convey no genuine information at all. It seems a general rule in the development of social history that the excision of conceptualization can go only so far before significant detail —whose importance ironically is the *raison d'être* of social history and the titular reason for the exclusion of theory—also begins to disappear. Moreover, there is little development of any kind operating in the feminine-clerical accounts. The primary impulse of the antiquarians is neither to confront man with God as the Calvinists did, nor to explore the laws of man's internal growth as more recent, what we might term anti-patriarchal psychologists and anthropologists have done; they wished rather to protect their subjects from competition, whether emanating from men, God, or the movement of time itself. Bancroft, Prescott, Motley, and Parkman were always concerned with the individual, but they refused to sever him from the context of historical change which both created and overcame his heroism. The antiquarians, like Sprague in his *Annals*, usually excluded the historical panorama; it could only serve to dwarf their less enterprising subjects. They bestowed a curious immunity from history on those they commemorated.

I wish to be as precise as possible here. There is an enormous and vital distinction between an interested, respectful acceptance of the full human condition and a glorification of the death of the critical instinct—between acknowledging human limitations and celebrating them. This is not a difference merely between good and bad social history. The first is a religious impulse, the second is finally a commercial one, and eventually involves the preparation of the individual for the role of consumer. For the consumer is by definition the man with no interest in theorizing, the person possessed of only the haziest powers of discernment. There are notable exceptions, but as a genre, one must say that the clerical-feminine biographies represent the first, although hardly the last, use of the biographical form as calculatedly therapeutic indulgence in the experience of ordinary human personality.[89] As such they marked a significant break in the tradition of ministerial biography.

In 1796, Samuel Hopkins wrote an account of one of his most devout parishioners, a fervidly prayerful woman called Susanna Anthony. He was hardly the first or the last minister to memorialize feminine devotion to God, and to himself.[90] It was more striking, however, when, almost a century later, women began to preserve clerical lives for posterity. We have already seen that Elizabeth Peabody published her *Reminiscences* of William Ellery Channing in 1880. Sylvester Judd's confidence in feminine ability to appreciate was not ill-placed: one of his best correspondents, his cousin Arethusa Hall, gave his story to the world in a most sympathetic memoir published in 1853. Interchanged letters and intimate conversations were only a prelude to a more prominent exchange in which clerical and feminine sensibilities interacted for posterity. Women like Hall or Peabody were indeed the caretakers they had been chosen to be. Popular sermonizers loved to dwell on the picture of the Three Marys at Christ's Tomb, and the deceased liberal minister usually had his feminine grave-watchers and believers also. "Let the poor, the widows, and the orphan write [the minister's] epitaph," one clergyman exhorted in the *New Englander* in 1845;[91] and sometimes they did.

Beginning approximately in the 1840s, the authorship of clerical biography underwent a decided shift. The most prominent ministers of the eighteenth century were usually memorialized by their brethren, their intellectual peers, whether contemporary or later. Hopkins wrote the life of Jonathan Edwards. Edwards A. Park did biographies of Hopkins and his ablest heir, Nathaniel Emmons. The nineteenth-century clergyman, especially if he belonged to a liberal group, was apt to have a feminine biographer: not only Channing and Judd, but Horace Bushnell, Orville Dewey, Austin Phelps, Charles Follen, Joseph Buckminster, and Frederic Dan Huntington come to mind as genuinely prominent clerical figures whose lives were written by feminine friends and relatives. Of my sample group of thirty ministers, twenty-one had at least one full-scale biography written about them in the generation after their death. Fifty percent of these were by women. Not surprisingly the biographies of ministers from feminine hands were somewhat different in nature from their predecessors. In a novel appropriately entitled *Papa's Own Girl* (1874), Marie Howland, a feminist writer and utopian thinker, summed up the credo of the new feminine biographers with more frankness than most of them would have relished:

Women are beginning to see the folly of allowing their "Lords" to write the biographies of great men, and are gradually taking the task upon themselves. When they do their full share of this work, there will be found in history many pigmies that would have swelled to colossi under the pens of their own sex; for their claims to the honor of greatness as moral forces will be judged by the way they treat women, specially and generally. A man may be great in a particular sense, if he is nothing but a military or political leader ... but he can never be great integrally as a man if he lacks tenderness, justice or faith in humanity. Men who are very tender as lovers, and deeply sensitive to the influence of women, usually have the reputation among brutal men of being "hen-pecked" —a word never found in the vocabulary of refined people.[92]

Domestic setting and domestic motivation dominate the memoirs written by the daughters, wives, and friends of Unitarian and Congregational clergymen. These men are presented, naturally, as they are viewed—from a feminine perspective: they appear primarily as fathers and husbands. Elizabeth Stuart Phelps emphasized her father's emotional and more particularly his family life. Orville Dewey's daughter quotes much more extensively from his family letters than from his theological works. Charles Follen's wife Eliza, in an exceptionally fine memoir, pays ample tribute to her husband's pioneering efforts in education and theology, but she stresses above all else his kindness and consideration to family and friends.

Earlier ministers, and their biographers, had not emphasized their domestic needs as predominant. Thomas Shepard's moving account, penned in seventeenth-century Massachusetts, of the loss of his wife through childbed fever was intended to instruct the reader on the fallibility of earthly relations, not to display his own capacities for familial feeling. By the turn of the eighteenth century, however, a split was noted (or created) between ministers' public and private selves by their biographers. Jonathan Edwards, Jr., for example, who could be "irresistibly impressive and even terrible" in the pulpit, was "mild and affectionate" at home.[93] Stephen West in church seemed a herald "sent down to denounce God's wrath upon a guilty world"; in his family his manners were as "bland as those of a refined and lovely woman."[94] There is a hint here that the true self is the private non-professional one, that West was, as Catharine Maria Sedgwick liked to imply, somehow unable to display his winning pastoral qualities once on his feet delivering a sermon. Later ministers, according to their own testimony as well as that of their biographers, drew professional inspiration from their domestic affections, which they counted all-important. Women were allowed, indeed encouraged, to confess that to love and be loved was their most important mission in life, even the start of their religious faith. Bushnell apparently felt equally eager to admit that "it is the strongest want of my being, to love," and his daughter was ready to domesticate his statement further: "it was in family life that he shone brightest."[95] Sylvester Judd testified to the same hearthside creed: "Though I am a minister ... I can never forget that I am a man, a lover, a husband. The sentimental part of my nature is deep, strong, pervasive. It is to me almost religion."[96]

Ministers were granted, and they courted, other traits which they elsewhere recognized as peculiarly feminine and domestic. Nothing reveals the parasitic relationship between women and ministers better than their mutual habit of commemorating their commemorators, and in strikingly similar terms. I wrote in an earlier chapter about the modesty, the ostensible lack of ambition, clergymen and ladies increasingly claimed for themselves and those they admired. Eliza Follen, Elizabeth Phelps, and Mary Bushnell Cheney all stressed the humility, the self-effacement, of the men whose biographies they were writing. Bushnell himself, we remember, began his autobiography with the modest if inaccurate statement: "My figure in this world has not been great.... I have almost never been a president or vice-president of any society.... Take the report of my doings on the platform of the world's business and it is naught. I have filled no place at all. But ... in my separate and *merely personal* ... life, I have had a greater epic transacted than was ever written or could be."[97]

Bushnell is here paying himself not simply the same compliment his daughter gives him but the favorite tribute clerical biographers offered their feminine subjects. Reverend Daniel D. Addison, a liberal clergyman, opened his memoir of Lucy Larcom with the standard obeisance to her apparent insignificance: "Her life was one of thought, not of action. In their outward movement, her days flowed on very smoothly. She had no remarkable adventures; but she had a constant succession of mental vicissitudes, which are often more dramatic and real than the outward events of even a varied life."[98] Henry Bacon's biography of "Charlotte" follows a similar pattern. Bacon, a Universalist pastor and editor-in-chief of *The Universalist and Ladies' Repository,* first recognized Charlotte's fictional and poetic gifts while she was working at fifteen at a bindery in Boston. A working-class girl of undoubted force and talent, Charlotte Fillebrown died in 1845 aged twenty-five. Bacon begins:

> Our record here is of a pure hearted and heroic woman;—not heroic because of any wonderful exhibition of female intrepidity but because of a sustaining and persistent energy, that made the best of life as it came, not refusing to do little in the way of culture because a great deal could not be done. The truest heroism is that which seldom finds a place in history, and to proclaim which the trumpet of fame is too brazen.

She had "no very striking qualities ... [to] command the attention of the world"; she "lived to love."[99]

This tribute, like Bushnell's evaluation of his place in the world, does not represent quite the Christian humility of Jonathan Edwards, who could account himself a worm and wish to lie infinitely low before God. It suggests rather the complex art of apology in which abasement and exaltation intertwine. The self is not being humiliated as it is in Edwards' journals: the public self—in the case of Bushnell, Larcom, and Jerauld a very interesting one—is effaced in order to bring forth the private self for attention, celebration, and caressing. It is the over-emphasis, not the emphasis, on the personal which is distressing. The fascination of the ministerial and feminine biographies lies precisely in their intensely and consciously privatized mood. One might argue that their insistence on the obscurity of their subjects is a necessary part of their calculated secretiveness: only in learning about those who theoretically have no reason to believe their private lives will be a public concern can the reader respond most fully as a voyeur; only if the subject is someone ostensibly no better than herself can the reader's voyeurism function as an introduction to her own sensibility and as a narcissistic enmeshment in herself. The aim of these memoirs is to establish an atmosphere of intimacy so strong as to replace historical awareness with what seems almost biological consciousness; the biographer's obsessive stress on his subject's capacities for suffering and for sympathy with the world of process draws the reader into the innermost sanctums of personality.

Bushnell's life, as his daughter described it and as he probably actually lived it, was a Christian struggle with pain. He fought consumption for years before the end: lying awake during sleepless nights coughing, he would rise the next day and work at a book or some task; almost dying on a mountain-climbing expedition, he barely recovered, not to go home but to get up and reach the summit; existing finally with one lung, he began a theological treatise on "Inspiration" only months before his death just to draw, as he wrote, "a little sense of being from it." His own bodily weakness made him preoccupied with "forgiveness," which he described as "man's deepest need and highest achievement."[100] Austin Phelps, according to his daugher, endured a lonely and miserable childhood. As an adult, he patiently suffered tortures from the neuralgia and insomnia which many of his colleagues and critics blamed on a weak will rather than a flawed constitution; he felt forced to a great "sacrifice," as he described it, in abandoning pastoral work; early in his career, while tending two wives in fatal illnesses, he became a compassionate and loving nurse. Naturally Phelps brooded increasingly on the meaning of the act of intercession, on the special abilities granted to the disabled. Charles Follen, as his wife memorialized him to fulfill a duty to the world which she found a "crucifixion" for herself, was a timid and frail child, never "sympathetic with boys." Later in America, he spent himself for Harvard students only to be defrauded and turned away by the university authorities. He prepared brilliant lectures and delivered them conscientiously and enthusiastically to an audience of two or three persons. He labored for an often-indifferent congregation whose final unreasonable demands resulted in his untimely death in a shipwreck. Follen learned the lessons of "disinterestedness," the value of "devotional feelings" and "tenderness."[101]

Follen's role, like Bushnell's or Phelps's, is the immolated one assigned the pious woman in contemporary fiction and biography. Mary Clemmer Ames, a noted journalist and writer, published a memoir of her friend, the genuinely talented if minor poet Alice Cary (1820–71), in 1874. As for Eliza Follen, the very task of writing was painful for Ames: "Every line coming from memory has deepened the wound of irreparable loss," she begins. Describing Cary's deprived childhood, her early disappointment in love, her rich but secluded life filled with illness, self-doubt, and unachieved aspirations, her intense but mournful love of her own sex and her indignation at their wrongs, Ames reveals, as she intended, what Cary "as a woman could be, and was, to another."[102] Although Cary courted death by prolonged periods of toil in overheated rooms, when it came in 1871, she fought it. Cary longed perhaps for a fuller life than she had ever had, for a fuller release of her unmistakable though stunted creativity; but Ames makes of her final fierce reluctance a kind of feminine Gethsemane. She stresses that, dying in summer in a hot city, Cary missed the countryside where she had been born and bred. In her last hours, Cary was happy, according to Ames, only when hearing those portions of the Gospel which recount Christ's love of women.

Henry Bacon, in his memoir of Charlotte, takes a similar line. "Five years have passed," he begins, "and on the anniversary of Charlotte's death we begin this memorial. The heavy rains are falling, and the sultry air of this August day [is] oppressive; but the sunlight penetrates the clouds." Bacon sounds as if Charlotte has become a saint: God marks her day with special signs. In telling of Charlotte's death, Bacon, like Ames, stresses her "longing to get into the country, to smell the green trees and the fresh air," her sorrow, and her extreme and significant attachment to a passage in a sermon by F. W. P. Greenwood called "Christ Our Fellow Sufferer." With no justification but the logic of the martyrdom he is bestowing on Charlotte, Bacon hypothesizes her special fondness for passages like this: "loving him ... and comforted by his sympathy when I weep and fear, I am better prepared to follow and imitate him when he submits, endures and triumphs." Like Christ, Charlotte did not "wrestle with her Maker, as though she was wronged by suffering"; she consented to her pain.[103]

These accounts vary greatly in style and value. The Bushnell and Follen biographies are broad and still indispensable studies. The Charlotte biography does no justice even to its rather slight subject. Yet all these narratives imply that their protagonists are performing a ritual of (Bushnellian) Atonement; and that this ritual assimilates them to a natural world whose law of development and decay usurps the prerogatives of time. The preoccupation with suffering in all six memoirs, the references to the country and the weather in the narratives about Charlotte and Cary, the intrusion of the pain experienced by the authors in the Follen, Cary, and Charlotte books, highlight a tendency common to ministerial-feminine biographies of the period, although hardly equally present in all of them: an avoidance of the prominent use of dates and a replacement of these by what could be called the organic markers—birth, conversion, marriage, aging, and above all, illness and death. These markers are the lowest common denominators of human life. In the weaker of these volumes, the average life cycle is treated here as of greater historical importance than any extraordinary achievement; the phenomena of biology are applauded as comprising the history of the average. Historicity is dissolved in atmosphere; a potentially cyclical pattern dislodges a linear one. "Masculine" attempts at domination and demarcation give way to "feminine" abilities for assimilation and absorption. The active force of public example is lost in the persuasive rites of protection and dependency established by the nurturing power of memory. Biography is merged with something close to a vegetation myth.

The clergyman himself, as he is described in the reminiscences penned by literary women and liberal ministers, increasingly resembled a benign and patriarchal god, at home and at one with a natural setting.[104] Nowhere is this transformation clearer than in the treatment of the very old minister, the survivor from the grimmer days of Calvinist theology, by his younger successors and his feminine admirers. A test case for the new sensibility, the "patriarch," as he was called in a spirit almost antithetical to the one in which we use the word today, was softened and subsumed into the organic rites of life.

Edwards A. Park in his memoirs of Emmons (1861) and Hopkins (1852) continuously makes both sound like very aged men. In a sense, this is understandable: Hopkins and Emmons lived to extremely advanced ages; both were in youth as in maturity sober and serious individuals; Park drew many of his impressions of Emmons from his meetings with him at the very end of his long life. There can be little doubt, however, that Park wants to picture his predecessors primarily in old age; that age is in his memoirs part of their very essence rather than a temporal condition. The figures are as fragile, in Park's delineation, as old manuscripts. In his biography of Emmons, Park includes a vignette, relayed by another minister, of the later Emmons preaching to his elderly congregation. His theme was "Men Are More Merciful to Their Enemies Than God Is to His": "I saw one old man after another who had grown gray under the patriarch's ministrations, bending forward in breathless silence, rising at length from their seats and gazing with eagerness to catch every word that fell from the lips of their teacher. . . . an old man who held his manuscript before his face, and read it in a low monotone."[105] This is a ministerial dream: a like-minded (masculine) congregation compelled by the sheer force of truth as presented by God's clerical envoy. Yet the point here is that the aged are addressing the aged. They are striking mementos of past virtue, but they are also fossilized, weakened, sentimentalized. The emotions they arouse in us are more important than the emotions they feel; they have been deflected precisely through their gray hairs and silvered piety from subjects to objects.

Hosea Ballou, the most important figure in early American Universalism, also suffered a mysterious change of character in the hands of his memorialists. Ballou, despite his conviction that "holiness and true happiness are inseparably connected," his love of nature, his sometimes maudlin hymns, his distrust of learning, and his faith in an essentially untrained ministry, was no sentimentalist. He found the ministry a "spiritual warfare," and conducted himself accordingly, attacking Calvinists, Unitarians, and, when provoked, fellow Universalists, with vigor and acumen. Like Hopkins and Emmons, he lived to a ripe old age, and long before his death he was being hailed as a "patriarch." He wore his white hair long, and, according to his son, had a "remarkably venerable appearance"; his face was a "benediction," his feelings were "tender."[106] Caroline M. Sawyer, the wife of a Universalist pastor, and herself a leading figure in the little literary coterie which put out the genteel publications of her denomination, *The Ladies' Repository* and *The Rose of Sharon*, wrote a poem after hearing Ballou pray in 1843, a decade before his death at the age of eighty-one. She entitled it "The Pleader at the Throne": Ballou is a mediator, not a commander. On another occasion, Mrs. Sawyer described in prose Ballou's memorable effect on his audience:

> No-one who was present then and there can ever forget the impression made by the saintly white-haired old man as he arose in the pulpit, looked slowly around upon the vast congregation, most of whom saw him for the first and last time there, and then meekly but fervently breathed out the tenderest prayer that ever reached the ear of the good father.[107]

There is something very unsubstantial about the figure of Ballou here: he breathes rather than speaks, he is seen for the first and last time—vanishing into the realm of memory which is his only kingdom. At Ballou's funeral in 1852, his colleague and successor, Reverend Alonzo A. Miner, also a contributor to *The Ladies' Repository* and *The Rose of Sharon*, extolled him again and again as "our venerable patriarch," "our venerable father," "our father in Israel." According to Miner, Ballou's great contribution to liberal theology had been his stress on the "paternal spirit" of God; he "effected a very general redemption from that state of orphanage to which so large a part of the world felt itself doomed."[108] There is little in Miner's eulogy to remind the hearers that Ballou was ever young, that, despite his humane and generous spirit, he was almost always aggressive. Ballou has been canonized in old age, frozen in a benediction. He dwindles in the reader's imagination even as he accrues significance. Sawyer and Miner look on him like departing travelers gazing back on a figure which gets smaller and smaller, and then is lost to view. Ballou, like Hopkins and Emmons, is becoming a relic, precious, talismanic, culturally crucial—but obsolete.

Let me say a little more about the connotations around the "patriarch" figure in the contemporary subculture which was claiming these ministerial figures for its patron saints. The patriarch appears again and again in the sentimental literature of the ante-bellum period; he is always, in every respect, the opposite of the so-called Victorian father.[109] Lydia Huntley Sigourney did the classic sentimental studies of false and true male dominance, one entitled "The Father," the other "The Patriarch," and both published in *The Young Lady's Offering* in 1847. Symbolically "The Father" opens the 1862 collection of tales, but "The Patriarch" closes it. The last word is his.

"The Father" is a brilliant, cultured, and driving businessman, Byronic in character, tempestuous and excitable in disposition, rigid and proud in will. He spends his life increasing his fortune and educating his delicate, chaste, and adored daughter. Occasionally laying the classic female hand on his classically fevered male brow, she provides a needed antidote to his unspecified but highly successful activities in the world. Ostensibly, he is the commanding one in the relationship; he stays up whole nights planning her reading, he gloats over her like Pygmalion over Galatea: " 'Was it strange that I should gaze on the work of my own hands with ineffable delight?' " he inquires.[110] It is the male committing the ultimate heresy: he imagines *he* can create life. Sigourney has chastisement waiting, however, in the wings. The daughter dies unexpectedly; the father goes through an agony of grief, until, positively rigid with hysteria, unable to sleep or to weep, he throws himself on her grave and even tries, apparently, to exhume her. Finally, on her burial mound, he cries, and Sigourney can forgive him. For he weeps that he has lost a woman, that he is not a woman able to create life, and, in weeping, he is like a woman. Curiously, Sigourney has made no mention of the "mother" in the tale; her place is empty, waiting to receive the "father" when he resigns his rule.

Sigourney's "patriarch" is a dummy figure set up for compensating worship in place of the deposed father. He is the ancestor comfortably stowed away in the rocking chair, the male softened by the kindly touch of time. His reign is a tribute to the sensitivity and receptivity of his subjects, not to his own powers of direct exertion. He rules by his example and by their regard for tradition; possessing no force but "influence," he is essentially connotative. The small self-sufficient rural community which he heads is what Sigourney calls "hermetically sealed." This spot is "swamp-encircled";[111] iconographically, it suggests very feminine territory. Cut off from civilization, its occupants do nothing but hold primitively simple and pious outdoor religious services and venerate their elders. At school, they learn only the three Rs and the Bible. There is no story here; in this timeless and totally self-involved world, there can be no dialectic, no progress of any kind, nothing but ceremonious repetition. Progress smacks of excitement, of masculinity; a feminine ripeness is all Sigourney, or the patriarch, desires. Appropriately, the narrator-observer is a minister, who helps establish a chapel for the little society and attends the patriarch's funeral at the sketch's close.

Of course Mrs. Sigourney is not here writing history or biography, yet I might point out that it is almost impossible to separate her historical from her fictional work.[112] It is not unfair to see Mrs. Sigourney's "father" and "patriarch" as roughly analogous to the subjects of romantic "biography" and the ministerial-feminine "memoir." Sigourney's "father," like the Pilgrim Fathers, the founding fathers, and the heroes of Hegelian history, stands for energy, enterprise, virility, direction, hybris; his sin is to try to change nature. Taut with unreleased grief, tearing futilely at the closed earth, the father, as Sigourney describes him, is sterile—until he acknowledges the limits of his authority. Sigourney's "patriarch," in contrast, suggests the aged minister of the memoir. He is less the impregnator than the pregnant; he suggests the precondition for futility. Absolutely not a leader, he belongs to his community only because he embodies its shared and common feelings and aspirations. Fit representative of clerical and feminine hopes and anxieties, he is the ultimate, almost parodic emblem of "influence," of totally consensus and conformist thought. The only authority he seeks and possesses is, figuratively speaking, biological. His corpse goes into the earth from which the community's sustenance will come.

We are back with Bushnell's rationale for the "history of oblivion": "Do the vegetable growths repine or sicken because they cannot remember the growths of previous centuries? Is it not enough that the very soil that feeds them is fertilized by the waste of so many generations moldering in it?" Bushnell's Hegelian interest in organic imagery does not conceal his un-Hegelian philosophic emphasis. The "waste" so essential to Hegelian notions of historicity has not simply been redeemed; waste, as the reject of time and change, has been elevated in importance above the forces which define and throw it off. The intimate atmosphere of the memoirs is attendant upon the private act of *boarding* which is their essential dynamic. The genuine lessons of compassion the antiquarians would teach cannot obfuscate the enormously tenacious importance they placed on personal possession, broadly defined. On Worcester's battlefields, in Elizabeth Phelps's heaven, in the memoirs devoted to Austin Phelps, Alice Cary, and others, nothing can happen, because there are no events, only objects and emotions—which increasingly merge together—on display. There can be violation or preservation of order, but not genuine change. In their well-founded fear of historicity, the feminine and clerical historians substituted space for time as the fundamental dimension of human experience. As is the case with modern telecasters, they paid attention to groupings rather than progressions. They were interested in the relationship of the individual with what he or she owns, with what in an almost biological sense belongs to her or him, whether family, home, job, or even the sense of self. In their vision, the forging, severing, and re-creating of such attachments substituted for the dialectic of the Hegelians.

6

THE DOMESTICATION
OF DEATH

The Posthumous Congregation

The Fascination with Death and Mourning

To say that the memoirs of women and clergymen were concerned with
death is an understatement; to a degree that requires special consideration,
they were exercises in necrophilia. They revealed as much of the art of the
mortician or the gravestone-cutter as of the craft of the biographer. Contemporaries on occasion described the memorialists' efforts in strikingly
literal funereal terms. The Unitarian George Ellis, reviewing Sprague's *Annals of the American Pulpit* in 1857, called Sprague a "sepulchral artist"
carving the gravestone of his ministerial predecessors. Ellis was particularly
moved by the fact that at least eighty of the ministers who contributed
biographical information to Sprague's first two volumes had died by the
time of publication; six of these contributors were between the ages of
ninety and one hundred. Ellis described the letters various clergymen wrote
in tribute to deceased colleagues as "the dewy flowers and the green grass
growing over graves where tears have been freshly shed."[1]

Nothing shows more clearly the underlying motive of the memoirs
than the fact that a moving death rather than a stirring life provided the
suitable qualification for treatment. Children, veritable infants, became a
conventional subject not just of poetry but of full-scale biography. Tots like
Agnes Adams and "little Georgie" Cuyler, the respective protagonists (if one
may use the word in this connection) of *Agnes and the Key of Her Little Coffin*
(1857) and *The Empty Crib* (1873), were notable, understandably, less for

their lives which were usually short, than for their deaths which were often protracted. Even in the memoirs devoted to adults, life gains its interest chiefly as a prelude to death. The reader is reminded from the outset that the memorialized is going to die—perhaps young, certainly well.

A host of examples comes to mind, but none is more striking than the biography of the Reverend William Peabody written shortly after his death in 1847 by his brother Oliver. Peabody was a fervent Christian, an opponent of "controversial divinity,"[2] a defender of the Sabbath, and a pioneer in the cemetery and Sunday School movements. A literary man of real, if minor, talent who contributed to the *Christian Examiner*, the *North American Review*, and *The Token*, he published rather gentle pieces on autumn and death. His best poem began with characteristic euphemistic melancholy: "Behold the western evening light!/ It melts in deepening gloom;/ So calmly Christians sink away/ Descending to the tomb."[3] From the start, Oliver Peabody depicts William as one too good to live, the kind of pale, serious, sickly, pious little child that wise old women were always clucking prophetically over in the domestic novels of the day. William survived childhood, however, to marry an extremely devout woman whose resolve to give "all the power of . . . [her] soul to a private intercourse with God" had an immense impact on her husband.[4] When she died at an early age in 1843, he told himself that she had been called first so that he might learn through sorrow to be more worthy of her. Cherishing his grief, he liked to sit by moonlight near her grave. His links with this life were further attenuated when his eldest daughter died suddenly only four months after his wife.

At this point in the Peabody biography an extraordinary thing happens. A new and anonymous writer explains, "the pen fell from the hands" of Oliver Peabody just as he approached his brother's moving deathbed scene. As William might have said, Oliver had "calmly . . . sunk away." The consumptive Oliver had originally been a lawyer; he found himself unsuited, however, to enforced contact with a quarreling and litigious world and turned to the ministry in middle life; the step from the ministry to the grave was apparently the only logical one at this point in his spiritual history. Oliver felt that, in writing his brother's story, "he was carving the letters on his own gravestone."[5] Oliver's successor, the second biographer, luckily survives his task, describes William's saintly and gentle death, and includes a memoir of Oliver for good measure.

A memoir like this is not only a biography; it is a part of what can be called contemporary consolation literature. This enormously popular genre included obituary poems and memoirs, mourners' manuals, prayer guidebooks, hymns, and books about heaven. Such writings inflated the importance of dying and the dead by every possible means; they sponsored elaborate methods of burial and commemoration, communication with the next world, and microscopic viewings of a sentimentalized afterlife. Their authorship was typically, although not exclusively, clerical or feminine. The causes for the widespread success of consolatory literature were many and complex. At this point, what is clear about the readers' demand is largely negative: consolation literature probably does not reflect an actual increase in the death rate of children or adults, although it may point to changing expectations about mortality.[6] More can perhaps be ventured about the author's motivation.

I have already said that women and ministers, in an effort to rationalize and glamorize their position, were engaged in subordinating historical progress to biological process. Barred by external taboos and internal anxieties from elaboration on the overtly sexual acts of impregnation and childbirth, they concentrated on illness and death: they were more interested in the moments at which crude energy failed than in those at which it accelerated. The glorification of death offered the final crucial strategy in the effort to anthropologize historical inquiry: as Mrs. Sigourney's "Patriarch" suggests, forgotten lives are remembered by mother earth. The tombstone is the sacred emblem in the cult of the overlooked. It is hardly accidental that the ornate statuary which increasingly decorated Victorian graves has some resemblance to enlarged victory trophies; symbolized and congratulated by stone angels, the dead were not losers but winners. Mid-nineteenth-century cemeteries were the paradoxical progenitors of a later generation's halls of fame. The clerical-feminine commitment to stress and exaggerate the value of those apparently wasted and insignificant "ordinary" lives which patriotic history and industrial development too often neglected reached its logical culmination in an imaginative reinterpretation of the doctrine of the "resurrection" of the dead. If the insignificant could be proved to be the significant, if the dead could live, ministers and women could establish a new balance of power in the free-for-all, intensely competitive democracy of American culture. Like politicians engineering egalitarian triumphs by stumping fresh territory, drumming up new votes, and even inventing voters, they multiplied the numbers and enhanced the resources of their supporters. Some might see the election as rigged, but the victory was theirs. And they were hardly the last participants in the drama of popular American culture partially to invent the public they captured.

Lydia H. Sigourney, in one of the more striking among her almost countless obituary poems, "Twas But a Babe," rhetorically upbraided an unspecified urban male passerby, apparently absorbed in his commercial profit-mongering and indifferent to a sad funeral procession wending its way behind a little coffin to the local graveyard. "Poise Ye, in the rigid scales/ Of Calculation, the fond bosom's wealth?" she inquired bitterly.

Sigourney's implicit point is that the private rituals of mourning should outweigh the public demands of business, that the claims of home and church should count for more than the imperatives of the marketplace. Her initial tone of indignation suggests her awareness that, in plain fact, most competitive middle-class American men did not share her priorities. When Mrs. Sigourney turns, however, to detailing the imagined grief of the bereaved parents, she notes with particular approval and sympathy the "mute" father with his grief-worn and "pallid brow." By the poem's close, revitalized by imaginary contact with such domestic scenes and sentiments, Mrs. Sigourney is preaching with full ministerial confidence to a more general audience, all "who mourn" a "vacant cradle."[7]

The pattern of Mrs. Sigourney's little poem is characteristic of most of the consolation literature of the period: an explicitly or implicitly hostile protest against the competitive, aggressive, non-familial society; a chastened reminder that everyone will be forced sooner or later by the death of a loved one (or by his or her own death) to turn from public to private considerations; and a tactful hint as to where the needed comfort at such hours can be found. Mrs. Sigourney anticipates the modern undertaker. Her poem is a way of leaving her card: "if you should need my services . . . and you will." The world of consolation literature is a domestic and personal one, a place where the minister and the mother become at last the only genuine authorities.

Elizabeth Prentiss, who wrote the best-selling *Stepping Heavenward* (1869), a classic of nineteenth-century consolation literature, once gave an interesting and revealing definition of the function of "a pastor's wife," a position she herself occupied. There was an obligation, or rather an opportunity, "to feel the *right* to sympathize with those who mourn, to fly to them at once, and join them in their prayers and tears." She continued: "It would be pleasant to spend one's whole time among sufferers, and to keep testifying to them what Christ can and will become to them, if they will only let him."[8] Clearly such moments gave unusual power not only to Christ's word but to those who conveyed it—the minister himself, or his wife. His literary efforts were often veiled reminders of the last hour—and of his own crucial role in it. We have seen that Hopkins was never more the teacher than at the bedsides of dying parishioners; the liberal pastor, in contrast, was the comforter, winning entrance which at other times was denied to him. Intercessor between God and man, heaven and earth, he was the supplicant, the "pleader at the throne," as Caroline Sawyer described Ballou. His power came from the fact that at such a moment supplication is the only possible mode of expression. The clergyman's chance, like the woman's, was now coincidental with the weakest moment of his parishioners. No longer confident that he could meet his congregation at their strongest or impress its ablest representatives—the men of intellect and talent in their stores, counting-houses, and courtrooms—the minister increasingly fell back upon an inner parish of women and those men who had been reduced to playing the woman's role; his congregation consisted of those who were feeling rather than thinking.

The sensitized mourner was clearly of vital and new significance in this domestic drama. The authors of mourning manuals directed their books toward the actually and recently bereaved parent, husband, or wife seeking reassurance. Private, particular grief, in other words, was their declared starting point and *raison d'être*. Of course the ordeal of the Christian survivor forced to realize that he has "idolized" a loved one taken from him by a chastening God was traditional in New England religious writing. The seventeenth and eighteenth centuries, however, had no real cult of mourning literature. The griever was seen as culpable, if human. His condition was hardly considered one of particular fascination in the same way, for example, that the state of a sinner on the eve of "conviction" might be. Thomas Shepard, a prominent seventeenth-century divine, devoted only an eloquent page and a half to the loss of his adored wife, and he concluded his account with a characteristic stroke of partial self-condemnation: "Thus god hath visited & scourged me for my sins & sought to weene me from this woorld, but I have ever found it a difficult thing to profit even but a little by the sorest & sharpest afflictions."[9] Anne Bradstreet, writing in 1665 on the death of a grandchild, explained the irrelevance of what later generations would call mourning: "Blest babe, why should I once bewail thy fate,/ Or sigh thy days so soon were terminate,/ Sith thou art settled in an everlasting state."[10]

In sharp contrast, the bereaved nineteenth-century authors of tributes like *The Empty Crib: The Memorial of Little Georgie* and *Agnes and the Key of Her Little Coffin* quite frankly assumed, and apparently got, the engrossed attention of significant portions of their society for their emotional and moral state. Reverend Theodore Cuyler, the prominent New York clergyman who wrote *The Empty Crib*, received thousands of more than sympathetic letters from kindred mourners. Cuyler appended some of these epistles in *The Empty Crib*. I will quote from one to give the flavor of all:

My dear Sir,—If it ever falls in your way to visit Allegheny Cemetery, you will see there "a flower" on *three* "little graves." "*Anna*, aged 7 yrs; *Sadie*, aged 5 yrs; *Lillie*, aged 3 yrs;" all died within six days, and all of scarlet fever! [Cuyler's "Georgie" died of scarlet fever also.] It sometimes may reconcile us to our own affliction to hear of one still greater elsewhere; and this is the reason why I, a perfect stranger, venture to trespass upon you in your sore bereavement, and to tell you of my heartfelt sympathy.[11]

There is no escaping the sense that grief is not being used here as discipline, in the way Shepard and Bradstreet used it, but as therapeutic self-indulgence. Mourning is still intended clearly to foster spiritual development, but a curious exhibitionism seems to be doing the work formerly expected of self-scrutiny. The bereaved shall be the gainers if not of the world's goods and positions, at least of its concern. Even if the mourner figure is neither a minister nor a mother, he is a possible stand-in for them: grieving entails an experience of powerlessness which unites them all. The attention the mourner is so lavishly granted by his authors compensates him for more losses perhaps than he has consciously suffered.

In these annals of grief, the deceased, like the mourner, shows striking if unacknowledged affinities with the author. The dying or dead child is the most conspicuous exemplar of the new turn to the old prophecy, "the last shall be first." "Agnes" and "Georgie" were supposedly guides to their adult supervisors in ways that must have been both suggestive and flattering to their maternal and ministerial biographers, many of whom knew well what it was like to be treated, even to function, as children in a world of unheeding adults. Furthermore, these small household saints, according to their biographers, usually chose their mother or their minister as their model. Little James, an early deceased son of the Universalist minister Sylvester Cobb, was memorialized by his mother Eunice Hale Cobb in 1852. According to her account, he was a clergyman in embryo. As a very young child, he disliked "to mingle with the boys [at school], so as to hear their profane and vulgar language." He advised "respect of the aged" and once rebuked a man who referred to his father as "the old gentleman." He loved the Bible, took communion at age seven, and was wont to argue with fellow passengers on boats and trains against the use of tobacco. If he emulated his ministerial father, he adored his mother. During his last sickness, he expressed his wish to her that "we could die with our arms around each other's neck."[12] The dying infant was made supremely to flatter his feminine and clerical biographers: he shared their weakness while he dignified and extended their authority.

The process of extension often took on nearly supernatural characteristics. The special quality of a biography like Oliver Peabody's memoir of his brother lies in the rather sepulchral sense it gives the readers that they are listening to a posthumous voice. During William Peabody's last months, he seemed to his loving congregation to be increasingly "standing on the confines of the eternal world, as one ready to be offered; permitted just before entering its gate to point out to those he loved, with the failing accents of a dying voice, the way to reach its blessedness."[13] Mrs. Sigourney played daringly on the enticing boundaries between life and death where the Peabody brothers apparently lingered. In her poetry she was apt, as an everyday matter, to overlook the apparently trivial distinction between the living and the dead female. She pictures one deceased maiden lying "In calm endurance, like the smitten lamb,/ Wounded in flowery pastures."[14] Is the girl dead, or merely stricken? Even Mrs. Sigourney's narrative posture betrays the same fascinated confusion. Her only attempt at a novel, *Lucy Howard's Journal*, the story of a Christian housewife's progress in piety and family life, purports to be the diary of a dead woman presented to the world by her rather guiltily surviving spouse. Lucy Howard speaks from beyond the grave. As luck would have it, Mrs. Sigourney's own autobiography, *Letters of Life*, which she began in the early 1860s, was almost complete when she died in 1865. The book, finished by other hands, has some of the same otherworld posthumous authority which she granted Lucy Howard's infinitely less interesting account.

Mrs. Sigourney's last recorded words were the benignly all-inclusive ones, "I love everybody."[15] A few decades before, Mrs. Sigourney had published a sentimentalized biographical sketch entitled *Margaret and Henrietta* (1835). According to her account, Margaret had died with the same phrase on her lips.[16] Could Mrs. Sigourney have mentally noted the appeal of such a last line, stored it up, and finally re-enacted a deathbed scene which she had in part invented? Long before she uttered her last words, Mrs. Sigourney was prone to usurp the authority of the dead. Prior to her marriage in her late twenties she had been a distinguished schoolteacher in Hartford. In later years, she liked to keep up with her former pupils through annual spring picnic-processions in the woods near Hartford. These rituals were clearly extraordinarily important to Mrs. Sigourney's psyche: she maintained them for decades, graciously including pupils' children as well as pupils. She wrote a regular account of them—perhaps the only thing she penned that she never published—entitled "A Record of My School."[17] The attraction of the reunions for their organizer seems obvious: here she could play out the funereal fantasy she had developed in her poetry, her novel, and finally in her memoir. The girls, later to be middle-aged women, marched to the sylvan spot ceremoniously dressed in white, flanked by processions of handicapped children from Hartford's deaf and dumb asylum (a special interest of Mrs. Sigourney's). Once arrived at the "glade," they presumably ate in picnic fashion (though Mrs. Sigourney characteristically downplays such healthy and gross activity), and listened to their former preceptor's yearly talk. Mrs. Sigourney's focus was always the same: she dwelt lovingly on whomever of the original group had passed away during the preceding year. That death at a young age from consumption or childbirth complications was frequent among Mrs. Sigourney's pupils can hardly be denied by anyone who looks over the statistics which she, a sentimental Madame La Farge, accumulated in her "Record"; that Mrs. Sigourney was doing more than recording obvious and tragic facts is equally clear to anyone reading through the actual obituary sermons she delivered on the lost "floweret" of the year.

Even more striking, however, is Mrs. Sigourney's penchant for talking as one who has herself barely escaped the perils of death. At the first reunion in 1822, presumably in her usual plump and ruddy good health, she nonetheless urges her listeners to go on meeting annually even if "the voice that now addresses you should be silent, the lip that has uttered prayers for your welfare should be sealed in the dust of death." In 1823, she tells her hearers that since they last met she has been sick, has been "(at least in thought) on the confines of the abode of spirits," and has brought back solemn words of wisdom. Mrs. Sigourney has assumed a clerical role; more important, she has become her own medium.

The Fox sisters did not begin their table-rappings in upstate New York until 1848, but Mrs. Sigourney had in several senses anticipated them.[18] She was straining for the authority conferred on the Peabodys, the power granted by the privilege of extraterrestrial communication. Several of the little saints whose early deaths drew so many sympathetic tears showed extrasensory abilities similar to Mrs. Sigourney's. It was not just a matter of the conventional little finger pointing upward, the smile on the once-rosy lips, the last gasped "Mother" or "Jesus." A dying child like James Cobb enjoyed extended communications with the spirit world: he watched angels dancing in anticipation of his speedy arrival, saw various deceased members of his own family, and relayed their messages back to the living. He was quite literally a medium, and after his death he continued to appear to his relatives.

Death, province of minister and mother, instead of marking the end of power, had become its source. Spiritualism in its most generalized and most specific senses was a manifestation of a complex retransfer of force from the living to the dead, from the apparently strong to the apparently weak. Books on spiritualism and the afterlife like Elizabeth Ellet's *Watching Spirits* (1851), Mrs. H. D. Williams' *Voices from the Silent Land* (1853), Daniel Eddy's *Angel Whispers* (1855), and William Holcombe's *Our Children in Heaven* (1868), conveyed the clear impression that death widened rather than limited the ministerial and maternal sphere of influence. These sainted dead hovering around their old haunts, whether women, ministers, or pious children eternally firm in the virtues inculcated by their mothers and their pastors, were so many witnesses, even spies, for the church and the home. At work here is the compensation process I spoke of earlier: if you cannot make converts among the living, declare them among the dead. Death must become, not exactly life, but a controlled extension of the feelings, and property rights, of the living.

The Rural Cemetery Movement

Before the early nineteenth century, Americans buried their deceased in the local churchyard. The relative absence of ostentation in these simple graves, the abandonment of the distinctions of wealth or birth which had presumably interested those buried there when alive, suggested forcibly that the dead were no longer concerned with this world. By the 1830s, a new and very different method of treating the dead, what would prove to be the modern method, began to find acceptance.[19] The intramural churchyard was replaced by the landscaped "garden" or "rural" cemetery, located away from the church on the outskirts of town or village. Developing awareness of the laws of hygiene in part motivated the shift from the old crowded churchyard to the spacious lawn cemetery; this awareness in no way accounts, however, for the new conspicuous elaboration which characterized the layout and development of the new cemeteries. It is hardly surprising that the same groups who produced the consolation literature of the period promoted and extolled the rural cemetery and the innovative modes of burial which accompanied it. The rural cemetery movement officially began in America in 1831 with the opening of Mt. Auburn, the first garden cemetery in the Western world except for Paris' Père Lachaise. New York, Philadelphia, Baltimore, and Salem were among the many American cities quickly to follow Cambridge's lead. The pioneering Boston enterprise was distinctly Unitarian, Brahmin, sentimental, and literary. Among the founding fathers were the Unitarian lawyer and writer Joseph Story, the antiquarian author and temperance reformer Lucius Sargent, the Unitarian clergyman and poet John Pierrepont, and the ex-Unitarian clergyman and prominent orator Edward Everett. At the consecration of the cemetery in 1831 Henry Ware, Sr., led the prayer and Judge Story gave the address.

The new, planned, and picturesque rural cemeteries, unlike their intramural predecessors, were dedicated to the idea that the living, and the dead, still "cared." Paths with pastoral names, gentle rills, green slopes, and newly popular graveside flowers flattered the presumed docility of the deceased. The severe tombstones of seventeenth-century New England with their stark reminders of the fact of death—a cross, a death's-head, or an hourglass—had given way in the late eighteenth century to new anthropomorphic designs. Actual if crude portraits of the deceased appeared; allegorical pictures of the Resurrection, tastefully adorned with willow trees, were in evidence by 1800.[20] By the 1840s, statues of what one popular graveyard guidebook calls "weeping female figures"[21] marked various family plots in Mt. Auburn: Mrs. Sigourney had been immortalized and mass-produced in marble. Lachrymose verse à la Sigourney decorated ornate gravestones. "In Jesus' arms we laid her down/ A lovely jewel for his crown," were typical lines inscribed on the gravestone of a young girl in Princeton, New Jersey; "asleep in Jesus" was a popular caption for children's tombs everywhere.[22] Reverend Cuyler, passing an afternoon at New York's Greenwood cemetery near the grave of his "little Georgie," bid his son a by no means final adieu: "The air was as silent as the unnumbered sleepers around me; and turning toward the sacred spot where my precious dead was lying, I bade him, as of old, '*Goodnight!*' " Greenwood was to Cuyler "simply a vast and exquisitely beautiful dormitory."[23] It is not so much that the dead are alive as that they are altogether accessible to the living.

Developing funeral customs carefully fostered the same illusions the cemetery created. The dead person was reincarnated as a kind of hideous euphemism for a living one: it seems no accident that corpses were increasingly made to resemble dolls. There was a growing de-emphasis on somber mourning clothes and gloomy funerary practices. Sylvester Judd left directions for his own laying out: he was arranged for viewing "in apparent comfort upon his couch, as if in quiet natural slumber. A winter rose lay by his side." According to his biographer, "gloominess and dread" were banished.[24] The deceased were to compliment and imitate their survivors rather than threaten them. Elaborate and highly differentiated metal caskets replaced wooden ones in the early nineteenth century, although many protested their use. The metal casket, unlike its predecessor, insured that neither it nor its contents would disintegrate or return to the earth for a long time. The actual designs of the new coffins were clearly intended to please the taste of the living. Nehemiah Adams began his account of *Agnes and the Key of Her Little Coffin* by explaining that there had been a great improvement in the design of children's coffins. They no longer had "broken lines and angles. . . . They look like other things, and not like that which looks like nothing else, a coffin." He added, rather maladroitly, "You would be willing to have such a shape for the depositing of any household article." There was apparently a soft lining and a nameplate inside the box, and a "lock and key" had replaced the old "remorseless screws and screwdrivers."[25]

While eighteenth-century American families generally prepared their deceased for burial at home in simple and straightforward ways, outside organizers began to proliferate in the early nineteenth century: first the midwife or the livery-stable keeper or the sexton, and finally the professional undertaker. The undertaker's art took a gigantic stride forward with the practice of embalming, initiated during the Civil War though not widespread until the twentieth century. The new funeral directors of the later nineteenth century, with their double emphasis on business and sentimentality, were the heirs of the liberal ministers and lady authors who had helped to create the sensibility of mid-century. By the 1880s, there was a National Funeral Directors' Association with a representative organ called *Sunnyside* (it competed successfully with a rival periodical entitled *Shadyside*) which could issue touching and ludicrous statements to the press like the following:

> Funeral directors are members of an exalted, almost sacred calling. . . . The Executive Committee believed that a cut in prices would be suicidal. . . . A $1,000 prize was offered for the best appearing corpse after 60 days. . . . A resolution was passed requesting the newspapers in reporting the proceedings to refrain from flippancy.[26]

Of course, the "best appearing corpse" was the most lifelike one.

Nothing speaks more clearly to the transformation of death the rural cemeteries promulgated than their promotion as places of resort, well suited to holiday excursions. They functioned as a Disney World for the mortuary imagination of Victorian America. Sylvester Judd, in his days as a student at Harvard Divinity School in the late 1830s, was fond of a stroll among the tombstones. For him, Mt. Auburn was "that place of beauty and death, of melancholy and delight."[27] In 1859, one young man from Connecticut made a special pilgrimage to the spot. His reactions ranged from borrowed aesthetic piety to indigenous class-consciousness: "What a vast lot of money I saw piled up in monuments. . . . Oh what pleasure there is in walking among the dead. So say the people."[28] By 1876, James Cabot Lowell could write rather unkindly about his fellow Bostonians that their idea of proper hospitality automatically included a dinner with uncongenial and ill-sorted people and "a drive in Mt. Auburn cemetery where you will see the worst man can do in the way of disfiguring nature."[29]

Hamlet went to the graveyard in a mood of alienation from his kind, of philosophical despair; he resorted to the churchyard to confront some ultimate reality. The mid-nineteenth-century American went to the cemetery rather in the spirit in which his twentieth-century descendant goes to the movies: with the hopefulness attendant upon the prospect of borrowed emotions. The rural cemetery's camouflage of death was so entire that its purpose came paradoxically to seem the creation of the *illusion* of death for the vicarious edification and stimulation of the living. The cemetery functioned not like experience but like literature; it was in several senses a sentimental reader's paradise. The Sunday stroller could peruse the saccharine inscriptions which I have already mentioned. Moreover, hundreds of official and unofficial literary guides to the various graveyards appeared during the middle decades of the century. The *Picturesque Pocket Companion and Visitor's Guide Through Mt. Auburn* was out by the late 1830s, when the cemetery was less than a decade old. It included Judge Story's address *in toto* and a detailed description of the most interesting among the monuments, and

closed with "Miscellanies," a collection of prose and poem pieces on death
and graveyards; there were pieces by the sentimental litterateur Willis G.
Clarke, the famous English poet Mrs. Hemans, and the gifted young Nathaniel Hawthorne. In 1844, Caroline F. Orne, a very minor talent, helpfully
published a book of poems entitled *Sweet Auburn and Mt. Auburn with Other
Poems*. Of the six stories Mrs. Sigourney included in *The Young Lady's
Offering* in 1847, five close with graveyard scenes and funeral processions.
The visitor to Mt. Auburn and other cemeteries was clearly intended to stop
under an inviting willow, or pause near an artificial pond, and read aloud.

The funerary literature and the rural cemeteries themselves did not
present death merely as provocation for the sensibility of the living, however; they advertised it in curious ways as matter for actual appropriation
and acquisition. The topography of the cemeteries, like the language used
to describe them, suggested a utopian preservation, literalization, and even
objectification of a conservatively conceived past.[30] They were the emblem
and the site for the biologically oriented, cyclical history promoted by
women and ministers which I discussed in the last chapter. One commentator explained that graveyards provide the common man with his only lesson
in biography. According to a critic for the *New Englander* in 1831, the rural
cemetery demonstrated to observers that "in the mighty system of the
universe, not a single step of the destroyer, Time, but is made subservient
to some ulterior purpose of reproduction, and the circle of creation is
eternal."[31] The originators and supporters of the rural cemeteries had intended them to serve as negotiable sanctuaries from the present. An advocate
analyzed their appeal: "The retirement they afford to surviving friends in
their visits to the graves of loved ones; the quiet precincts of the sacred place,
made beautiful by the embellishments of artistic tillage and the inspiration
of natural scenery, combine to make attractive and sacred the city of the
dead. They become places of respectful and reverent resort."[32] In accor-
dance with their name and in contrast to the intramural churchyards they
replaced, the rural cemeteries were located out of town, away from the
urban bustle and noise: they were to be uncrowded, pre-industrial, privatized.

The quiet atmosphere of the cemeteries was strictly enforced. Those
responsible for the development of Mt. Auburn in 1831, for example, laid
down careful regulations about the planning and use of its grounds: the
trustees of the spot had the right to remove "offensive and improper" monuments; no "vehicles" were allowed but those owned by "proprietors" (owners of plots); no one was allowed within the gates on Sundays and holidays
except proprietors.[33] As such restrictions suggest, the sentimental impulse
ostensibly responsible for the creation and policing of the rural cemeteries
was in part a disguise for an impulse of ownership like the one motivating

the new ministerial and feminine history. Nostalgia, here as elsewhere, functioned as a spiritualized form of acquisition. Until the 1880s, proprietors disfigured their plots by the erection of iron railings. Cemeteries bristling with such jealous markers gave evidence of squatters' rights rather than of mourners' grief.[34] Francis and Theresa Pubszky, a foreign couple visiting America in 1853, objected to the custom in frank language: "Exclusiveness little befits a cemetery; the idea of private property carried even into the realm of the dead ... has something unnaturally strange."[35]

Observers were particularly fond of describing the rural cemeteries in terms which likened them to that emblem of the possibilities of ownership, the middle-class home. One commentator on "The Law of Burial and the Sentiment of Death" for the *Christian Examiner* in 1836 expressed his belief that the graveyards could foster "the sentiment of retrospection and reverence" and draw their visitors from "the busy competition" and "hurried ... ambitious spirit" of the day.[36] This of course was also the language used in the period to describe the ideal American home, also by definition pre-industrial. In the words of a popular domestic manual by a Reverend Phillips, the home was the "heart's moral oasis"; like the cemetery, it was a "refuge" for the "bereaved and disappointed."[37] Another writer for the *Christian Examiner* made the comparison explicit: thoughts provoked by the cemetery "give a new aspect to all our social relations and confer upon our homes particularly, where these relations are the most intimate, a peculiar sacredness."[38]

It was no accident that the same architectural thinking underlay the new proto-suburban domestic architecture and the new rural graveyards. The idea of the "picturesque" as formulated by Andrew Jackson Downing dominated both. A landscape gardener and an architect, Downing was also a man of letters and a close friend of polite literary men like George Curtis and Nathaniel Willis; he edited a magazine entitled *Horticulture* and wrote several books. Socially conservative, of the genteel school in every sphere, he attempted to civilize, moderate, and control the taste and homes of America's business-minded middle class; as one contemporary put it, Downing wished "to infuse a spirit and a grace in forms otherwise admirable only for their usefulness."[39] Downing's architectural theories rested on what he called the "theory of association." In the "cultivated country life" which his proto-suburban styles were meant to emulate or approximate, in his words, "everything lends its aid to awaken the finer sensibilities of our nature. ... The heart has there, *always within reach*, something on which to bestow its affections. We begat a partiality for every copse that we have planted." Downing's style was meant, as his friend Nathaniel Willis perceived, to foster "a most careful culture of *home associations*," to strengthen "memory," not ambition.[40] This "theory of association" is the familiar doctrine of "influence" which we have already seen used to rationalize and recoup feminine and ministerial powers. Architecture, whether in cemetery landscaping or suburban homes, became one of the ways in which the less aggressive purported to correct the sensibility of their competitive society.

As a gentleman should, Downing took his artistic principles from England, but in doing so he avoided the grandiose as inappropriate to a democratic country. He classified domestic homes and grounds under two headings: the "beautiful," characterized by a gentle and flowing style, and the "picturesque," dominated by a more abrupt and irregular one. The picturesque, generally preferred by Americans, was in actuality a debased version of what German writers and scholars at the turn of the century had called the "sublime." By this term, they designated the wild and almost anarchic elements of the natural and mortal landscape perceived and assimilated by the human mind only at great peril to itself. The excitement and challenge of the sublime was precisely what Downing chose to ignore. Unlike the productions of the "sublime," the "picturesque" landscape or building is not an illustration of the laws of motion. The difference is that between a torrent and a rill, a rushing waterfall and a babbling brook. Change in the "picturesque" world is merely decorative. One of Downing's supporters and helpers explained that he wished to counteract the "restlessness and disposition to change which is characteristic of our people."[41]

The "picturesque" cottage-style home was to be modest but delightful; the surrounding land was groomed by judicious planting into a carefully controlled mimicry of natural abundance.[42] The new cemeteries looked as if they were extended grounds for such domiciles. The *Picturesque Pocket Companion and Visitor's Guide Through Mt. Auburn* rightly points to the "unusual variety" of trees, the "beautifully undulating" surface, the "flowers and ornamental shrubs," the carefully measured paths of Mt. Auburn as evidence of "picturesque . . . landscape gardening."[43] The rural cemetery plot, like the proto-suburban home, gains significance solely through its owner's fond appreciation. The cemetery plots, like their descendants, the suburban homes, manifest just enough variety to pay tribute to the fact of distinct ownership and to perpetuate the romance of individual reduplication of an utterly standard theme. The dead and their places of rest have become very much the property of the living.

Prayers and Hymns: Exploration of Another World

The act of acquisition did not stop with the graveyard. During the middle decades of the nineteenth century, America was busy taking over territory on its boundaries. The studies of past conquests by the romantic historians were paradigms for current aggression. A number of Americans, however, not apparently engaged or interested in these dramas of imperialism, were sighting and colonizing territory theoretically of infinitely greater importance than the Southwest: heaven itself. Consolation literature of all forms between 1820 and 1875 became preoccupied not just with the last scenes and earthly resting places of the dead but with their celestial destination and doings. William Holcombe, the author of *Our Children in Heaven*, expressed the need of "some great spiritual telescope to bring [the dead] . . . near to us in all their beautiful reality," the need of "a clear, consistent, philosophical authorized revelation of the life after death."[44] This was easier to provide than at first might be imagined. Heaven was apparently as real, as concrete, as Texas; and heavenly prospects turned out to have many affinities with domestic scenes.

It is possible and even appropriate to describe this spiritualist annexation of heaven in the language of the modern media. The sub-genre of consolation literature dedicated to the definition and promulgation of praying and hymn-singing formed what we might call channels of communication to the other world. The writers of consolation literature established contact with the next world through prayers and hymns; then, like modern television reporters, they purveyed news of the heavenly realm back to earthly audiences. The authors of such accounts had enormous authority, for who could question their reports? No matter how genuine the need and belief of its proponents, the new domestic heaven was unquestionably the earliest—but in some sense the most perfect—"pseudo-event" in American history: totally fabricated, yet uncontestable.

Prayer manuals, which appeared in ever-greater numbers at mid-century, taught thousands of Americans, in the phrase of a later mind-cure expert, to "tune in with the infinite."[45] An examination of the lives and motives of the authors of two of the most famous among them, *The Still Hour* and *Stepping Heavenward*, may help to explain their proliferation in this period. Typically, the earlier manual is a treatise by a man and a theologian, the second is a novel by a woman and a mother.

As we saw in an earlier chapter, Austin Phelps had a close personal acquaintance with sickness and death. According to Elizabeth Stuart Phelps, her father was possessed of a "divine instinct to relieve suffering," and he tended a succession of dying wives as well as his frail daughter. He founded the "Improvement Association" for the graveyard of his town. In his own view, he was a victim, early consigned by a conspiracy of ill-health and neurosis to the role of disestablished among the disestablished.[46] As a young man, Phelps's frail constitution forced him to relinquish active pastoral duty in Boston; in middle age, he was seldom well enough to achieve the perfect fulfillment of his teaching and writing obligations at Andover Seminary on which his conscience insisted. He wrote a self-pitying yet genuine piece entitled "The Premature Closing of a Life's Work" which begins: "Look around: you find the world full of those arrested, rebuffed, disappointed though willing—oh, how willing!—workers."[47] A number of Phelps's contemporaries apparently believed Phelps courted an invalid state. Certainly there are questions to ask about a man who, after nursing one wife in a fatal illness, would within a few years marry her sister, clearly marked as tubercular, and nurse her through the remaining eighteen months of her life.

What is clear is that in Phelps's mind his suffering conferred on him a special status, even a special occupation. He liked to hope that, while he was excluded from the work of "busier manhood," he gained in "spiritual vitality." It is not surprising that over the years Phelps developed a stronger and stronger belief in the reality of the heavenly life, and in the reality of prayer. He was open about the meaning of prayer in a life like his, as an anticipation of powers not yet gained, a compensation for powers lost, as solace for the sick and therapy for life-prisoners: "The value of prayer [is] as a means of usefulness to men whose life's work like ... mine is mainly finished. This oppressive sense of useless living is relieved by it."[48] In 1860, a few years after the death of his second wife, Phelps published *The Still Hour: or, Communion with God*, intended to help others learn how to pray. He frankly admitted that prayer was finally for the passive, that it was "in its highest conception, a *state* rather than an *act*."[49] But he was also convinced that "prayer has command of an immense reserve of yet undeveloped resources."[50] In a later work, Phelps recounts a significant story about a sick and solitary woman who made a career of praying for everyone she knew. Again, like so many semi-spiritualists, drawing on a pseudo-scientific analogy, Phelps explains: "Her daily life ... is a line of telegraphic correspondence between this world and heaven."[51] Her greatest triumph came when she prayed incessantly for a young man she had never met but whose accidental presence in a railroad car with her had revealed to her his religious crisis. She learned later that he had converted within a year and joined the ministry. Prayer allowed those excluded from the challenges of human history to participate in the miracles of divine providence.

In his later years, Phelps was peculiarly impressed by the work of Elizabeth Prentiss. Prentiss' father, Edward Payson, a famous preacher in Portland, Maine, in the early nineteenth century, was himself noted for his spontaneous and heartfelt praying, what he called "a kind of devout poetry."[52] He died when Elizabeth was still a little girl of eight. Although she later fiercely resented comparisons between herself and her father, she cherished the memory of him all her life as a "hero and a saint." Admitting that she had been particularly influenced by his "devotional habits," she traced her own real spiritual development from the childhood moment when she had inadvertently rushed in on him "prostrate upon his face—completely lost in prayer." Like her father, Prentiss was constantly subject to ill-health, insomnia, and intense emotional conflict; she too was a creature of real talent, perhaps of genius. Unlike him, she had the full-time job of mother of a large family and knew the frustration consequent upon repressing very genuine and powerful artistic and ministerial impulses until nearly the end of her life. In the 1850s, Prentiss lost a daughter and a son, and she sought comfort in books like *Light on Little Graves, The Folded Lamb, The Broken Bird*, and *Christian Consolation*. Increasingly, Prentiss found her outlet, like her father and like Austin Phelps, in prayer. She prayed incessantly on every subject, never stopping to think, as she said, "if such and such a matter [was] sufficiently great for his [God's] notice." Prentiss' last words to her husband, shortly before she left for the Bible-reading at which she would have her final collapse, were a slow and emphasized injunction: " '*You pray one-little-prayer for me.* ' "[53]

Prentiss' most popular novel, the partly autobiographical *Stepping Heavenward*, a book which Phelps read repeatedly with great admiration, is as surely a prayer manual as *The Still Hour*. "Every word of that book," Prentiss later explained, "was a prayer." A clerical admirer described its impact: "It was one of those books which sorrowing, Mary-like women read to each other, and which lured many a bustling Martha from the fretting of her care-cumbered life to ponder the new lesson of rest in toil."[54] The story concerns an over-burdened doctor's wife, whose piety is tested by her husband's insensitivity, her in-laws' selfishness, and the agonizing death of one of her children. Its genuine force comes from Prentiss' clear perception that the housewife's work is never finished, and hence never fully successful, satisfying—or rewarded. Katy Elliott masters one practical or familial problem only to have another crop up; the static moment of achievement, the well-earned narcissistic pause for applause is by definition impossible. Prentiss depicts the middle-class mother's life as one of harassment whose rewards are genuine but obscured. The motto of *Stepping Heavenward* can be summed up in the words of the heroine's mother: " 'Go on praying—pray without ceasing.' " Prayer provides at minimum a little leisure, time off for self-involvement no matter how lofty; but it is more. Significantly, Katy does not learn the true meaning of prayer and closeness to Christ until she is cut off from all household work by a painful seven-year illness which, the reader assumes, terminates in her death. Needless to say, her family does not fully appreciate her until she abandons her status as semi-skilled wife and mother for the spiritual superiority of sainthood. Katy's last utterance, which closes the book, is, appropriately, a prayer expressing her thankfulness for God's grace.[55]

It is important that Katy's final prayer is also a poem couched in the stanzaic form of the hymn. As I have already said, Elizabeth Prentiss' father,

Edward Payson, had believed that prayer was "devout poetry." Prentiss loved hymns so much that at one time she felt herself in danger of preferring them even to the Bible. Discipline overcame this excessive predilection, but the passion for hymns remained. During Prentiss' lifetime, American churchgoers came increasingly to identify prayers, poetry, and hymns. There are several points to be noted about the hymns which proliferated and were welcomed in American homes and churches during this period: first, their relative novelty as an important part of American Protestant worship; second, their largely non-evangelical and feminine authorship; and last, their liberalized theology, poeticized form, and growing obsession with heavenly life.[56]

In Puritan days, congregations chanted "hymns" which were drawn closely from the psalms. Indeed, respect for the sacred word and a crude system of rhyme apparently necessitated a certain disrespect for easy comprehensibility. The *Bay Psalm Book*, first published in 1640 and standard in New England for nearly a century, rendered the opening lines of the Twenty-third Psalm in rather literal fashion: "The Lord to me a shepheard is,/ Want therefore shall not I." Richard Mather, a member of one of New England's most illustrious clerical families, in the *Psalm Book*'s Preface: "God's altar needs not our polishing." Another representative of the same family, Cotton Mather, who had done his own translation of the psalms, thought "a little more of Art"[57] not inappropriate, and watched with interest the changes that took place in hymnology during the late seventeenth and early eighteenth centuries.

The great event for English hymnology during this period was the appearance of Isaac Watts's *Hymns* in 1707 and his *Divine and Moral Songs* in 1715, works destined to dominate hymn-writing for nearly two centuries. Watts used only the suitable portions of psalms for his hymns and on occasion loosely paraphrased those. His predecessors had felt committed to every scrap of God's word; his successors were on occasion to desert Holy Writ altogether for secular sources. Watts, an English Anglican who tended toward proto-Unitarianism, was perfectly aware of the transformation he was encouraging: he admitted that he had "brought down the royal author into the common affairs of the Christian life." If men were to sing about God, it must be in terms and tunes they understood, and enjoyed. Initial approval of Watts was cautious in the colonies. The first American edition appeared in Boston in 1739; Philadelphia issued one in 1742, New York in 1752. Cotton Mather was very enthusiastic about Watts's hymns, but thought them suitable for private rather than public services.[58] Indeed, it is crucial for understanding the role of hymns in the changing American Protestant Church to remember that they were originally conceived as best adapted for domestic and familial rather than communal and ecclesiastical uses. It was only when the church itself had been redefined in domestic terms that hymns could be central to their forms of worship. A conservative Congregationalist like Joel Hawes, Bushnell's rival in Hartford, bowed to the new fashion with extreme and open reluctance. After a hymn had been sung, Hawes customarily announced with some acerbity that divine service would now recommence.[59]

Watts became the standard authority, but his very example inspired successors and imitators. He had demonstrated, as the Wesley brothers also did in the mid-eighteenth century, that hymn-writing was a human endeavor, a form of literature, of authorship. The Congregationalists of Connecticut put out *The Hartford Selection* in 1799; Timothy Dwight, the Congregationalist "Pope" of Connecticut, published his very popular selections in 1807, mainly drawn from Watts and his school. With the end of church establishment and the spread of denominational rivalry as the American Protestant *modus vivendi*, every sect had its own hymnbook. Even Adin Ballou's Universalist and communal followers had their special collection, entitled *The Hopedale Collection of Hymns and Songs* (1845).

The fact remains, however, that from the start of the nineteenth century, certain sects were clearly dominant in the writing and publishing of hymns in the Northeast. The Episcopalians, for obvious reasons, tended to be conservative in their choices. The Presbyterians, who retained a clearer emphasis on the sermon and the spoken word than many of their rival Protestant sects, were not particularly fruitful in hymns. The Baptists developed a compelling brand of emotional folk-song hymn, but its popularity was largely in the South and Southwest. All historians of the subject seem in agreement that the Unitarians, aided and abetted by liberal Congregationalists and what Theodore Cuyler called "godly women" writers,[60] produced more popular hymns of high quality than any other sect.[61] Between 1830 and 1865, the Unitarians published fifteen separate hymnbooks. Henry Ware, Jr., William Peabody, and F. W. P. Greenwood were among the editors and authors; in 1855 Henry Ward Beecher helped to put together *The Plymouth Collection*, probably the most important hymnbook of the mid-century period. More and more Protestants were singing more and more hymns written by Unitarians, like-minded Congregationalists, and women. The special trademarks of these hymns were their literary quality and their tendency to stress the more cheerful aspects of Protestant theology. Changing funerary practices were intended to rob death of its proverbial sting; hymnology facilitated the process by ignoring hell and highlighting heaven.

Hymns were increasingly viewed as performing a very different function from that of the sermon they might accompany. Austin Phelps, who helped to write the single most important treatise on hymnology in America in the nineteenth century, explained to his readers that the subject of a sermon is not necessarily appropriate to a hymn. Hymns, in his opinion, express "the *heart* of the church." As such, they should not have "an excess of the analytic element," they should be well-written, tasteful, beautiful. Their purpose is to inspire, uplift, and cheer: they are to act as a kind of "tonic to the worshipper."[62] Hymns were not, in other words, to be intellectual. Phelps was using hymns to further and define that split between the "theology of the intellect" and the "theology of the feelings" which his colleague at Andover, Edwards A. Park, had enunciated.

If Phelps found all conceptualizing foreign to a proper and successful hymn, he held one brand of speculation uniquely inappropriate: that which deals with hell or damnation. Reminding his readers that "the Scriptures inculcate a faith which worketh by love," he urged that "comminatory" or threatening hymns should be very rare.[63] Earlier hymnologists had hardly agreed. In 1758, Samuel Davies, the president of Princeton, had penned a hymn containing these grim lines on the fate of the damned: "In vain for mercy now they cry;/ In lakes of liquid fire they lie."[64] Phelps was able to quote numerous lines from Watts which he pronounced unfit for a "Christian hymn": lines about "Eternal plagues and heavy chains,/ Tormenting racks and fiery coals," or lines entailing enforced confessions on the part of the singer that

> Twas I that shed the sacred blood;
> I nailed him to the tree;
> I crucified the Christ of God,
> I joined the mockery!

Calmly overriding the examples of Dante and Milton, Phelps explained that "actual and tangible horrors do not belong to poetry"; no Christian could "*revel* in song on such a theme" or "clutch at *details* of modes and instruments of torture."[65]

Phelps wrote that "sacred song instinctively looks heavenward." Phelps also noted that "hymns on heaven are innumerable,"[66] and a study of dozens of the most popular hymnbooks of the period confirms his opinion. In 1818, Congregationalist William Tappan wrote a popular hymn called "Heaven, A Place of Rest" whose title might well have served for hundreds of the popular hymns which succeeded it. The kindest remark an admirer could apparently make about a hymn-composer was the one Dr. Charles S. Robinson made about Thomas Hastings: "His poems breathe the very air of heaven!" Reverend Cuyler praised William Muhlenberg, an Episcopalian rector who wrote the well-loved hymn "I Would Not Live Always," for his "heavenlymindedness." In "Like Noah's Weary Dove," Muhlenberg exhorts his soul (the dove) to fly through "the open door" into "the ark of God." Fanny Crosby, the blind poet who wrote hymns for Moody and Sankey later in the century, emoted joyously in 1858:

> We are going, we are going
> To a home beyond the skies,
> Where the fields are robed in beauty,
> And the sunlight never dies.[67]

The subject of such hymns is not simply heaven, but its accessibility. The "home" of which Crosby writes was to be taken in a rather literal sense by many of her contemporaries. In *The Still Hour*, Austin Phelps explained that "an astronomer does not turn his telescope to the skies with a more reasonable hope of penetrating those distant heavens than I have of reaching the mind of God by lifting up my heart at the Throne of Grace."[68] Phelps's analogy suggests again the pseudo-scientific spirit of assurance which the writers of consolation literature brought to the subject of heaven. Somewhat as we might follow on television the lunar expeditions of our modern astronauts, mid-nineteenth-century Americans mourning their dead were encouraged to follow their journey to heaven in minutest detail; to inquire what they ate for breakfast, who they met, how they lived. The consolatory books of the afterlife increasingly promised them that such facts were part of available knowledge. In the 1880s, Elizabeth Stuart Phelps, carrying her father's analogy to its logical extreme, produced two novels, *Beyond the Gates* and *Between the Gates*, which set forth the eating habits, occupations, lifestyles, and methods of child care and courtship current in heaven. She even described with some care an oratorio Beethoven had just composed for a celestial audience. The only inquiry she could not answer was the natural one "touching the means" by which her deceased narrator, a male physician, was "enabled to give this record to the living earth." That is the only "secret" which, as she says in the last line of *Between the Gates*, she decides to let "remain such."[69]

Heaven Our Home: The Colonization of the Afterlife

The debate over the afterlife to which the consolation literature made such an interesting contribution had a complex history in American and European thought. Medieval Christians had shown an intense interest in the next world, an interest which created a special, popular, and long-enduring literary genre, the monastic vision.[70] Yet built into this tradition was the notion that heaven itself was finally forbidden to human eyes. During and after the Reformation, Christian thinkers and believers showed an increasing preoccupation with the doctrine of the millennium, that period of a thousand years before the Last Judgment in which Christ and his saints would rule on earth.[71] Millennial speculation was particularly intense in America: many could not help associating the birth of this new nation with more general and religious possibilities of regeneration. Jonathan Edwards was not alone in hoping that America might be the chosen site of the millennial rule.

Before the Civil War, American Christians tended to be millenarians, although they split into two deeply opposed camps: premillenarians, usually members of the less educated and more evangelical sects, who believed that Christ would come to earth suddenly, even unexpectedly, at the start of the millennium to supervise its unfolding; postmillenarians who held that Christ would not appear until the end of the thousand-year period, leaving men to guess and execute his wishes in a more gradual and less dramatic fashion.[72] In 1878, a special convocation of clergymen from more traditional groups met in Chicago to uphold premillennial views. Strikingly, those responsible and those attending were almost entirely of the evangelical sects: Presbyterians, noted for their orthodoxy here as elsewhere, dominated. There were few Episcopalians, few Congregationalists, and no Unitarians.[73] Unitarian thought on the subject is typified by F. W. P. Greenwood, who, several decades earlier, had dismissed the millennium altogether and referred to the Judgment Day as "figurative," emblematic only of Christ's "coming in our hearts."[74]

The proponents of premillennianism could be very astute about analyzing the thinking and motives of their postmillennial foes. George Duffield, a Presbyterian minister and hymn writer, in his 1842 treatise on the "Second Coming of Jesus Christ" notes that every postmillennial organizer of missionary work hopes "to see his church assume ascendant influence and lead the way to the millennium."[75] In 1840, Reverend J. W. Brooks, fighting those who disregard the millennium because they cannot see the "practical use" of the doctrine, reminds them that utility is ultimately irrelevant: "Men do not recognize the chief and all-important feature of the Bible," he thunders—that it is not the word of man, but "THE WORD OF GOD."[76] Nathaniel West, who attended the Premillennial Conference, also lamented "the mistaken system of spiritualizing and accommodating Bible language."[77] It is Charles Hodge versus Edwards A. Park once again: is man dependent finally on God, or God on man? Is God's word dogma or literature?

Yet the differences between pre- and postmillenarians were not as great as they seemed. Both groups had increasingly confused the millennial period with the heavenly afterlife, and in doing so had sacrificed the Augustinian and Puritan stress on the importance of the Last Judgment and the commanding role an autocratic and even alien Diety played in it.[78] Furthermore, both groups increasingly shared a conviction that this earth, purified and transfigured, would be the locus of the millennium. Henry F. Hill, writing in 1853 on "the world to come," staunchly attacks the postmillenarians. He reminds his readers that the world is still full of evil and will require dramatic, and divine, aid to achieve millennial status; he warns that even ministers may be mistaken, and that "the Preaching of Peace [is] a snare." Yet he believes, and claims most ministers believe, that the earth "purified indeed and beautified, but retaining its materialism" will be the site of our millennial and heavenly existences. Despite his orthodox stress on God's will, he is still willing to admit that it is enacted totally in man's sphere and in man's terms. Hill, for all his premillennial zeal, was careful to promise his readers: "the faculties of the mind are not to perish with this mortal life . . . the indescribable love of home planted in the human heart . . . rendering even trivial things around the homestead sacred and endearing . . . will not only live but increase in the resurrection state."[79]

If millennial and heavenly lives were not clearly separated, this world and the next were inevitably more and more closely, if unintentionally, assimilated to one another. The millennial debate became part of a larger discussion over the nature of heaven: kingdom or home? American ministers of the seventeenth and eighteenth centuries had given relatively little attention to the subject. When they spoke of the next life, it was hardly in terms to attract the carnal heart. Nathaniel Emmons had remarked in one of his grimmer sermons: "The truth is there is nothing which God requires men to do in this life in order to go to heaven that is harder to be done, than to be willing to be in heaven."[80] Emmons attributed this aversion to men because he looked upon the next world as the Lord's possession, and as such a landscape inevitably foreign to mortal eyes.

There were men and women to uphold at least a portion of this view in the northeastern United States at mid-century, but they were in the clear minority, and confused at best. George Cheever, a popular and reform-minded Congregationalist minister of New York City, in his book *The Powers of the World to Come* (1853) stressed the "glory" of the afterlife. Putting the Judgment in central place in his celestial picture, he visualizes the regenerate souls passing eternity in the active worship and praise of God in the most traditional theocentric way. Yet, despite all his highlighting of God's omnipotence, Cheever still tries to reconcile divine glory with very human domestic needs. He promises his readers that heaven "is not the dim incomprehensible universality of omnipresence merely, but a place for our abode, as determinate as place is for us now, and with as intimate a home circle, as the dearest fireside on this earth can have, nay incomparably more intimate and personal and definitely local in our Father's House in Heaven."

Heaven is to reunite families; it even offers nurseries for children who die before their parents.[81]

Among non-evangelical groups, the out-and-out supporters of a domestic heaven were dominant. Andrew Peabody, F. W. P. Greenwood, the Wares, Charles Follen, William E. Channing, and Austin Phelps, to name just a few, believed that heavenly life satisfied the human heart as presently constituted, that it offered homes restored, families regathered, and friends reunited.[82] Intimate speculation about heavenly scenes became common in the consolation literature of the period.[83] In the later 1850s a few daring souls began to write novels about heaven.[84] Given the tradition of the novel, to write a novel about anything was in a sense to domesticate it, to bring it from the church congregation to the family circle. No one was better aware of this than Elizabeth Stuart Phelps, who took heaven as her fictional specialty, to the delight of hundreds of thousands of Americans and the scorn of Mark Twain.[85] Phelps's best-seller *The Gates Ajar* was published in 1868; two other books on the same subject followed it in the 1880s but she was able to claim, rightly, that her views were still what they had been in 1868 when she was only twenty-four.

Phelps was the descendant, not just of Austin Phelps and Moses Stuart, but of ten generations of Congregational ministers and deacons.[86] She would undoubtedly have been a minister if such a path had been open to her.[87] In girlhood, while her two brothers played at mock-sermons, she turned to literary preaching. Self-consciously plain, reform-minded, over-earnest, nearly an invalid from neuralgia and insomnia, she did not marry until forty-four, and the world laughed, for her husband Herbert Ward was seventeen years her junior, an aspiring writer clearly more drawn to her literary success than her personal charms. The marriage was not happy. In *The Gates Ajar*, Phelps quotes from a Scottish divine who speculated that "Heaven may be a place for those who failed on earth."[88] Though Phelps was hardly a failure—her books sold well throughout her life—she had missed not just love, but fulfillment. Seldom likable, always a sentimental writer, often a sloppy one, her formidable talents sapped by her need of self-justification, she received little real personal or critical esteem. She came increasingly if comprehensibly to see herself as a vehicle of suffering. In 1889 she wrote in a clear mood of self-revelation about the point when pain ceases in any real sense to be profitable: "there comes a limit . . . beyond which the best that Fate could offer could not atone for the worst she had inflicted." Believing that God has chosen to impose on his creatures "the final test of love[:] . . . trust under apparent desertion,"[89] Phelps also stressed with a certain bitter animus that he has pledged them all the redress in his power. If earth is an orphanage, heaven surely must be home in every sense of the word..

No one was more committed to the denial of death as a separate state than Phelps. In 1885 she published an extraordinary volume entitled *Songs of the Silent World*, filled with reassuring poems supposedly written by dead people to their living and grieving relatives. An imaginary trusting survivor expresses Phelps's credo in the best poem of the book:

> There *is* no vacant chair. The loving meet—
> A group unbroken—smitten, who knows how?
> One sitteth silent only, in his usual seat;
> We gave him once that freedom. Why not now? ...
>
> Death is a mood of life. It is no whim
> By which life's Giver mocks a broken heart.
> Death is life's reticence. Still audible to Him,
> The hushed voice, happy, speaketh on, apart.[90]

The Gates Ajar is posited on this hopeful, literal-minded assurance, and it constitutes the apotheosis of the consolation literature of the day. The book appropriately focuses on the conflict among the would-be consolers of Mary, a New England girl who has lost her adored brother in the Civil War. On one side, there is Dr. Bland, the local Calvinist minister, who preaches of a cold and abstract heaven as " 'an eternal state' " where the regenerate " 'shall study the character of God.' "[91] On the other is Mary's Aunt Winifred who believes in a thoroughly concrete and domestic heaven where dead soldiers will chat with President Lincoln and culturally starved young girls will have pianos to play. Heaven, in Winifred's view, is a consolation prize.

Mary herself is an easy convert to this view. After long talks with her aunt in the local graveyard, she is reconciled to the loss of her brother precisely because she realizes that she has not lost him at all: adopting the confusion of heavenly and earthly spheres which is Winifred's credo, Mary comes to believe her brother is watching her, waiting for her. It only takes a domestic tragedy to bring Dr. Bland, following the rest of the town, into Winifred's camp. When his wife burns to death, he craves comfort, and only Winifred's belief can supply it. Winifred, like her author, is not satisfied, however, with the control of the souls of her townsmen; she wants the souls of her readers as well. All the logic of *The Gates Ajar*, as of the consolation literature of which it is the culmination, suggests to the reader: you are going to end up, if you are well-behaved and lucky, in a domestic realm of children, women, and ministers (i.e., angels), so why not begin to believe in them now? Phelps has at her disposal a bid for power which, if ignored, could become a threat of revenge.

Phelps's bid is formidable, however; the bribe she offers her readers is the enormous, intimate domestic detail of her heaven. Reading the book is somewhat like window-shopping outside the fanciest stores on Fifth Avenue. It is the confidently precise information about the rewards of celestial life which makes this book and its successors such extraordinary documents of American religious and cultural history. Aunt Winifred predicts with assurance that her hair will no longer be gray "in heaven," that heaven will look (at least to her) like Kansas, the state she loves best. She teaches her little girl Faith to talk confidently to her dead father and to expect that God will give her everything she wants, even her favorite cookies, in heaven. Phelps's sequels to *The Gates Ajar* prove Winifred's staggering assurances to be modest understatements. The narrator of *Beyond the Gates* finds herself (after her death) in a lovely semi-rural graciously suburban landscape. A kindly angel escorts her to her new house, which is in every sense a home:

> We stopped before a small and quiet house built of curiously inlaid woods. . . . So exquisite was the carving and the coloring that on a larger scale the effect might have interfered with the solidity of the building, but so modest were the proportions of this charming house that its dignity was only enhanced by its delicacy. It was shielded by trees . . . there were flowers—not too many; birds, and I noticed a fine dog sunning himself up on the steps. . . . I . . . strolled across the little lawn, and stood, uncertain, at the threshold. The dog arose as I came up, and met me cordially.

Inside, she finds "much of the familiar furniture of a modest home" as well as beautiful objects which are strange to her. Her deceased father, who has long been living there and waiting for her, comes to meet her. He is glad, in a tellingly bourgeois phrase, to have " 'somebody to come home to.' "[92]

Earlier in this chapter I compared the authors of consolation literature to politicians campaigning for new votes in fresh territories and to imperialists annexing new continents. But the sentimentalists, invading as they did a totally imaginary land, had in one sense an easier time of it than either politicians or imperialists usually do. They did not have to win over or subdue a hostile populace; their new supporters were just like themselves, their new country was home. They had no obstacles to overcome, and their imaginary kingdom reflected that fact: ownership, not acquisition or effort, is its law. Therein lay the source of its widespread appeal to Victorian and post-Victorian America. Phelps, like the other authors of consolation literature, had an immense interest in visualizing the afterlife as being scaled to domestic and pastoral proportions, as a place where she would dominate rather than be dominated. In doing so, she documented the enticingly effortless and inevitable pre-eminence of the average. She dilated heavenly time, she blew up that anticipated moment whose meaning she could legislate; an early practitioner of the art of soap opera, she was fascinated by the inertia of the prolonged close-up. The anthropomorphizing instinct can go no further, for the next world is here known with an intimacy which only possession can bestow. Spiritualism is paradoxically the logical façade of materialism. The unknown objects and possibilities of the "modest" house in *Beyond the Gates* suggest no break with its earthly counterpart, but rather the mysterious glorification inherent in the process by which an impermanent object becomes permanent. The occupants of Phelps's heaven—engaged in good works, keeping up with earthly news, redecorating their homes, falling in love, and gratifying their various tastes—live in a celestial retirement village; they constitute a consecrated leisure society. The carefully contrived world of the dead in heaven, as in the rural cemetery, a world created in protest against the larger competitive society, in actuality served to transfer, isolate, and protect what would become the most essential ritual of that society: the chaos of productivity is eliminated in order to insure the pleasures of consumption.

~~◇~~

THE PERIODICAL PRESS

Arena for Hostility

The Uses of Confusion

I have been describing a cultural situation of enormous tension and even some malignity: influential groups working apparently at cross-purposes with their society, in actuality at cross-purposes with themselves, perpetuating a complicated series of deceptions and self-deceptions. Of course simply to describe this pattern is to exaggerate it and to distort human experience. Close-range biographical studies of figures like Sarah Hale, Lydia Sigourney, Catharine Beecher, Henry Ware, Horace Bushnell, or Edwards A. Park would reveal not only great differences among them but a common mundane reality. Yet this is only to say that individuals of any class or group have experiences whose meaning is not exhausted by an analysis of their class or group but is rather determined by broader human possibilities and limitations. Whatever their individual motivation, the collective impulse of these people was toward self-flattery, self-aggrandizement, and an irritation occasionally almost homicidal in intensity.

As is so frequently the case with the members of subcultures, the ministers and women in question did not in actuality expend their most intense energies combating those they officially designated as their opponents. Indeed, it is a measure of the strength of the emerging industrialist-capitalist order in the Northeast that its clerical and feminine critics were systematically and half-willingly confused; they adjusted to a chronic state of confusion and were rewarded for this adjustment. They were the unconscious progenitors, as I have suggested, of modern American mass culture, a culture in which comics routinely insult their audiences and themselves, disk jockeys toss out wisecracks whose casualness partly hides, partly enhances their sadistic tone, popular interviewers investigate their subjects with a curiosity that intentionally borders on malice, advertisers downgrade their rivals in order to precipitate popular patronage. Our so-called democratic interest in competition, in "sport," is culturally engaged by the spectacle of submerged hostilities which serves the purpose of obfuscation rather than of challenge or criticism. For there is only one real issue between the combatants, whether reviewer and reviewed or disk jockey and hit singer: which of them will engross more of the public's attention.

The clergymen and ladies in question were engaged in just such mockencounters with each other. When we look at the imaginative writings, especially the popular journalistic works, which they wrote and admired, we find in them a testament of sexual tension, of covertly stated hatred of women by men and the reverse. There was, and is, need of discussion and conflict on the subject of the relations of men and women in our society, but the clergymen and women were offering neither. Rivals for the new mass audience increasingly addicted to popular magazine fare, they were expressing the diversionary anger of groups antagonized by competition for gains which neither fully respected. They both imitated and undermined one another; even as they consolidated their shared hegemony, they damaged its integrity and viability. In the end, they conducted no exploration of the genuine differences, whether imposed or innate, between masculinity and femininity, although a number of them genuinely wished to do so. They exploited and played with stereotypic sex distinctions somewhat in the spirit in which modern advertisers attempt to differentiate their products: to gain the competitive edge. In their work, implicit sexual dislike provides provocation, innuendo, titillation, not analysis. No one wins, no one can win, no one really wants to win. It seems no accident that the mood of clericalfeminine literary production is distinctly incestuous; subject and object, public and private, are indistinguishable. Its dynamic is generated by a closed system of competition to which no judges are allowed. The point of incest as a topic or a mood is that it has a conspicuously disappearing subject: two do not become one, they become less than one; they emblematize confusion, not union.

Ministers and Magazines: Divided Aims

I discussed in Chapter Three how threatened the liberal minister felt by the competition feminine writers of domestic fiction posed to his religious hegemony. Nowhere were his fears more formidable and more justified than in the sphere of periodical publication. Nathaniel Willis shrewdly analyzed

the well-nigh dictatorial power middle-class women exerted over their culture as the result of their role as "the real constituency" of all periodical
literature.[1] Given the tastes of the female audience women and ministers
shared, they were compelled to promote or criticize the publication of
fiction in popular magazine form—to respond, in other words, to literature
in its most transparently mass-commercial incarnation.

   In the burgeoning if perilous world of popular magazines and monthlies, women's periodicals had taken an early and easy lead. *Godey's Lady's
Book*, seconded by its imitators *Graham's* and *Peterson's*, long outdistanced
all masculine rivals. As late as 1860, when *Godey's* was in decline, it claimed
150,000 subscribers to *Harper's* 110,000. The *North American Review*, edited
and supported by the Adamses, the Nortons, and other New England wor-
thies, never drew more than a few thousand patrons. Equally distinguished
religious periodicals did not fare better. Family magazines, however, which
attracted many of the same feminine readers who liked *Godey's*, proliferated
in the decades before the Civil War.[2] *Godey's*, *Graham's*, and *Peterson's* were
known and feared for a telling combination of lachrymose fare and hard
economic astuteness: they led the way in the signing of articles, the use of
copyright, and the cultivation of advertising on a large scale—all developments which were to underpin the financing of later American magazines.[3]
Predictably, several of the prosperous periodicals managed by men imitated,
with varying degrees of guilt and anxiety, the themes and style of their
feminine rivals. At times they looked like rather small minnows swimming
in the wide wake of the matronly *Godey's* whale. Fashion plates à la *Godey's*
appeared in surprising places. Even *Harper's Monthly Magazine*, which began in 1850, had a few fashion plates tucked at the back of each issue for
good measure.

   Many clerical commentators purported to be, and probably were,
deeply troubled at this state of affairs. The originators of the Congregationalist journal, the *New Englander*, derided the male editors and co-editors of
such periodicals as *Godey's* and *Graham's*, who "so far as they are men, . . .
have given up their manly appetites and devoted themselves to the amusement of our citizen ladies."[4] Other ministerial critics expressed discontent
with the very prevalence of periodical writing. In 1847, a reviewer for the
Christian Examiner panned *Alderbook*, a collection of magazine stories by
"Fanny Forrester." He deplores her "flowery sentimental" style, which he
trusts is not "attractive to the sober-minded." What bothers him most, however, is that "Fanny Forrester's" tales were originally magazine publications,
typical contributions to the coy light-hearted pages of Nathaniel Willis'
Home Journal; as such, they should hopefully have been, if not of solid
literary worth, at least safely ephemeral. He bemoans the countless readers
—he compares them to "locusts"—who support such periodicals; once again

he has recourse to the "sober-minded" who "mourn" the "invention of periodical literature." To collect feeble pieces like Chubbuck's into a volume which will take its substantial place on library shelves, "among books to be perused . . . is an additional evil," subjecting the public to "a double deluge." We "must set up what dikes and breakwaters we can," he concludes grimly.[5]

The dikes erected by liberal clergymen against the flood tides of feminine sentimental periodical literature were often disturbingly flimsy. The reasons are obvious. Most liberal ministers were extremely hesitant to publish novels; and a volume of sermons, no matter how literary and sentimental,[6] could not command the same market as a work of fiction. Appealing periodical fare, however, was theoretically within their sphere. From the start of the magazine business in America, religious journals and papers had numerically dominated the periodical market.[7] By one historian's count, there were ten religious journals in 1800, eight hundred and fifty in 1840.[8] At mid-century, religious periodicals still outnumbered ladies' magazines, although none of them were as successful as the best of their feminine rivals.[9] Their editors and contributors could vindicate themselves by the claim that they were providing a corrective to the secular feminine journals; like modern preachers who skillfully employ television to spread their message, they felt compelled to make use of the powerful means of mass communication all too available to their opponents. Yet the historian examining these liberal clerical publications discovers a marked if conflicted progression from intellectual, religious, belletristic material to popularized, sentimental, and fiction-oriented writing, and a tone of mounting confusion and hostility in the face of a public which can apparently be neither entirely ignored nor won.

The takeover of Harvard by the Unitarian forces in the early years of the nineteenth century marked a crucial and enduring coalition between Cambridge *belles lettres*, scholarship, and liberal theology. This coalition gave both Harvard and Unitarianism their special character and produced several of the most distinguished ante-bellum periodicals in America. In 1803, the fastidious Unitarian prodigy Joseph Buckminster and a group of like-minded cohorts began to publish the *Monthly Anthology*, which theoretically emanated from witty and elegant dinner-club conversation in the most approved English fashion. The club in question, the Anthology Society, also founded in 1803, consisted largely of liberal-minded ministers, but its aims were not ministerial in any traditional sense. Buckminster, the son of a Congregational clergyman who frowned on novel-reading, was, by his sister's account, ever "fond of reading romances, but rarely indulged himself in so pleasant a pastime."[10] His private journal testifies, however, that while he was ignorant of Aristotle, Bacon, and Newton, he was devoted to the works of the celebrated Mrs. Radcliffe.[11] The periodical which he founded was unsuccessful financially, going through five publishers in its eight brief years of life and never attracting more than a few hundred subscribers—a failure which seems appropriate in light of the repeated professions of dislike for commercial America made by its contributors. Buckminster and his friends John S. J. Gardner and Samuel Cooper Thacher hoped to find in "the delight and charm of literature ... a refuge from the tumults and contentions of active life." The journal, devoutly literary, for the most part ignored theology, a subject, in Buckminster's urbane opinion, "upon which much of our genius and learning has been always employed, and not seldom wasted."[12]

The *Anthology*'s most impressive successor was of course the *Christian Examiner*, which ran under Unitarian and Harvard auspices from 1813 to 1869. Originally a strongly sectarian organ, under the aegis of editors like Noah Worcester, Henry Ware, Jr., and William Ware, it gradually became more neutral theologically, and more oriented toward *belles lettres*. In the 1850s, articles on the decline of the liberal clergy jostle uneasily but significantly with half-grudging reviews of popular works of domestic fiction. By the 1860s, its closing decade, the journal was decidedly literary and secular: volume seventy-three for 1862 includes seven articles on religious subjects, four on moral and political issues, twelve on literary matters. This balance, or imbalance, is typical. The *Christian Examiner*'s demise came from many causes, not the least of which, one suspects, was the increasing competition of the *Atlantic Monthly*, begun in 1857 under the avowedly secular management of Boston's loosely Unitarian Brahmins Oliver Wendell Holmes and James Russell Lowell. That such was the *Christian Examiner*'s successful rival speaks volumes for its changed and confused purpose. Unlike its predecessor, the *Monthly Anthology*, the *Christian Examiner* had to combat not simply the business forces of American society, but the commercialization of the culture itself. The *Examiner*'s move to the more competitive atmosphere of New York in 1866 only hastened its demise.

From the earliest days of magazine publication ministers had contributed in large numbers to secular magazines and even to ladies' magazines;[13] on occasion, they edited them. Theodore Cuyler sent in pieces to *Godey's Lady's Book* while a student at Princeton Theological Seminary, with no apparent sense of contradiction.[14] The popular gift tokens of the period, themselves the lightest cream of sentimental magazine fare, offered a meeting ground for ministerial and feminine pens. Sarah Edgarton Mayo solicited poems and sketches for the Universalist token *Rose of Sharon*[15] not only from sister scribblers like Broughton, Case, Scott, and Fillebrown but from ministers of her denomination like Henry Bacon, Henry Soule, E. H. Chapin, and Thomas Whittemore. Sarah Hale began her editorial career when

Reverend John L. Blake, an Episcopalian clergyman who was the principal of the Cornhill High School for Young Ladies and a *Godey's* contributor, invited her to come to Boston in 1827 and edit a ladies' magazine;[16] the *Ladies' Magazine* began under clerical auspices. From ministerial participation in feminine journals it was but a step to the creation and control of religious journals clearly designed to tap, and educate, the public which read the magazines tailored for female and family consumption.

The *New Englander* came out under Connecticut and Congregational auspices from 1843 to 1892. Horace Bushnell was among the notables involved in its founding. Like the *Christian Examiner*, it was to be a prestigious religious and critical journal, eschewing any creative contributions, but it was a much more confident, aggressive, and militant organ than its Unitarian model. Open war was soon declared on "the fashionable monthlies" and "our lady literature." One early reviewer was happy to name his enemies: *Godey's*, *Graham's*, *The Lady's Companion*, *Miss Leslie's Magazine*. He explained: they contain no good literature, nothing to "provoke thought," no "rational information," only "foppery and nonsense" donated by "third rate" authors adept at salesmanship rather than art.[17] The *New Englander*, as its title suggests, intended to remind its readers of their more substantial and virile past. One of its first issues contained a eulogy of tough-minded Nathaniel Emmons; apparently he was especially to be praised for "adhering to his proper business as a preacher and not turning aside to the business of book-making."[18] The campaign against cheap periodical fiction continued in the 1850s. A lengthy article on "The Editorial Profession" demanded that magazine editors receive rigorous and extensive scholarly training covering the natural sciences, modern languages, philosophy, history, theology, and literature, and possess the virtues of "versatility," "alertness," "natural energy," "tact," and a "high tone of moral philosophy";[19] the *New Englander*'s ideal editor sounds more like the highly educated saintly minister of Cotton Mather's *Manductio Ministerium* than a mere journalist.

Yet by the mid-fifties, the *New Englander* was devoting increasing space to criticism of novels from feminine pens: *Vara*, *Ida May*, and *The Lamplighter*, for example, were allotted, although clearly begrudged, attention. By the late 1850s, the *New Englander*'s principal contributors were more and more uncertain about the boundaries between its religious and literary interests; this uncertainty erupted in an irate 1859 review of Holmes's *Autocrat of the Breakfast Table*, then running in the new *Atlantic Monthly*. Holmes's critic of course disliked the "spirit of indifference or levity" to religion which in Congregationalist eyes marked Holmes's essays. He most strongly objected, however, to the *Atlantic Monthly*'s printing any work which dealt, as Holmes's decidedly did, with religious matters. The *New Englander* reviewer argued that once Holmes turned to religious material, he should have published in a religious periodical—like the *Christian Examiner*. After this sly slap at the lax standards of the Unitarian journal, the critic explained that the *Atlantic Monthly* should deal with "Literature, Art, and Politics" but not with religion.[20] It is a mark of its failure of purpose that the *New Englander* could assert its right to comment on secular literature while denying the corresponding privilege of religious discussion to an avowedly secular magazine.

Other liberal religious periodicals made more direct forays into the realm of feminine fiction, only to compromise their original aims more completely. The *Universalist* began under the editorship of Reverend Sebastian Streeter in 1833. Its first volume displayed the usual run of pro-Universalist theological articles and more general moralizing essays. By late 1833, the journal had changed hands. Streeter was succeeded by two other Universalist ministers, Daniel Smith of Boston and Matthew Smith, later to be a vociferous and despised traitor to the Universalist cause. The periodical had also changed name and direction. An editorial of November 2, 1833, announced that from henceforth the *Universalist* would be called the *Universalist and Ladies' Repository* and devoted to the causes of literature and of women—a telling conjunction.[21] The editors were perfectly frank about the fact that the switch had been made to broaden their power base, to reach the Protestant women whose kindly feminine natures (the editors claimed) should make them easy converts to the charitable doctrine of the salvation of all men;[22] and the editors were well aware that the way to attract lady readers was to offer stories. The *Universalist* indeed provides a telling case study of the need of the various Protestant sects to supply their female adherents with suitable reading. But the matter was not a simple one. Thirty years after its inception the magazine was still alive, although supported by a relatively low number of subscribers. Its contributors were Universalists, principally women. Its editors, however, were now also women, its contents almost purely fiction; it even sported fashion plates.[23] It had become more or less indistinguishable from the secular ladies' magazines of the day.

The *Christian Parlor Magazine*, which a group of Congregational clergymen began in 1844, provides an even more striking example of the attempt by the religious press to compete with the women's magazines. Evangelicals like Lyman Beecher and the Abbott brothers donated their efforts; Mrs. Sigourney lent her aid. So did Timothy Shay Arthur, destined for fame as the author of lurid temperance novels like *Ten Nights in a Bar-Room* and *Woman to the Rescue*. Yet the periodical lasted only ten years, a victim apparently of its own ambiguousness of intention. It set out to be didactic: moralizing travelogues, pious and non-sectarian accounts of eminent Christians, popularizations of Biblical stories accompanied by illustrations, all underlined its mission of instruction. Various writers inveighed against fiction, especially in the early numbers, although a few cautious reviews of religious novels were included. The proprietors and contributors could not bypass fiction altogether, but they limited themselves almost exclusively to tales designed to precipitate the religious sensibility: these turned out to be almost entirely stories of death and the graveyard. To take the issues of 1846–7 as an example, one finds nine stories about dying maidens and their resting places, five sketches of pious females, five reminiscences of an idealized past, four cautionary pieces preaching by negative example, and one temperance tale. Most of the poetry for the same years is devoted to death or heaven. There are articles on specific graveyards, Mt. Auburn and Greenwood among them, with maladroit titles like "Wonders of a Buried World." Several of the tales begin quite literally with a tombstone: first we have a descriptive pan of a cemetery ("our graveyard is a lovely spot," etc.); then the narrative voice spells out the inscription on some particular gravestone, and we are off into the touching life of "Mary Wilson" or the sad story of "Henry and Louise."[24]

A sepulchral monument apparently marks the allowable meeting place of religion and art. Neither is trespassing, but the common ground is too restricted to allow either any creative mobility or scope. The result, even for those accustomed to the monotony of the average gift book or ladies' magazine, must have been stupefying. The self-defeat involved in the *Christian Parlor Magazine*'s effort to use feminine material in the service of clerical interests is ludicrously apparent in the engraving which provided the frontispiece for the June 1846 issue. The picture is entitled "The Good Shepherd," a title which presumably indicates that the subject is Christ, an identification the accompanying poem makes explicit; but the picture itself unmistakably shows a small girl with a crook, resembling nothing so much as Little Bo Peep. The *Christian Parlor Magazine* has achieved a kind of apotheosis of clerical-feminine confusion; it has objectified the feminine heresy, and traveled farther into the realms of unreality than *Godey's* or *Graham's* ever cared to go.

Masculine Sentimentalism and the Problems of Dependency

It is striking that reviews in clerical periodicals damned Herman Melville and R. W. Emerson, both of whom they associated with German romanticism, and praised Washington Irving, Henry W. Longfellow, Nathaniel Willis, the early Nathaniel Hawthorne, "Ik Marvel," and George Curtis, all in some sense followers of the English authors Laurence Sterne and Charles Lamb. When ministers like Henry Ware, Jr., and Orville Dewey turned to *belles lettres*, they wrote whimsical, light, epistolary sketches à la Lamb and

Irving, not romances à la Melville. Henry Ware, Jr.'s sketch "The Village Funeral" owes everything to Irving's "The Pride of the Village," although Ware's heroine, unlike Irving's, is merely deceased, not sexually abused.[25] Orville Dewey carried on a highly self-conscious literary correspondence with his good friend, the novelist and minister William Ware; he could mimic Sterne ("Here's another new day, William; and I wish I were a new man") and jest pointedly, "I have none of the Lamb-ent light which plays around your pen."[26] Such members of the liberal clergy were acknowledging and fostering an important split in American letters, in some ways comparable to the one I have already noted in American theology and historiography. They were drawn as critics and writers not to the few serious non-commercial writers, romantics like Melville[27] dealing with religious issues in sophisticated narratives which commanded little public attention, but rather to the essentially secular sentimental authors of the genteel Irvingesque school, who wrote for the magazines and sold well with the predominantly feminine American reading public. In a sense, the "intellect" was once more undervalued for the sake of the "feelings."

Ministerial commentators of course had their reservations about the price their most cherished secular authors had paid for their popularity. A reviewer for the *Christian Examiner* in 1844 worried uneasily that Willis, despite his manifold gifts, was lacking in "manliness of thought and dignity of sentiment."[28] Longfellow, who usually received raves in the religious press, was accused by one critic in a religious magazine in 1848 of producing a "Goody two-shoes kind of literature . . . slipshod, sentimental stories told in the style of the nursery, beginning in nothing and ending in nothing."[29] Yet it was perhaps the highly ambivalent preoccupation of the male sentimentalists with feminine taste, even their partial feminization, which made them so interesting to liberal ministerial observers. In many ways secular counterparts of the liberal ministers, the male sentimentalists played a crucial role in making the periodical literary scene a testing ground for covert social and sexual hostilities.

Washington Irving summed up the American author's dilemma: "Unqualified for business in a nation where everyone is busy; devoted to literature where literary leisure is confounded with idleness, the man of letters is almost an insulated being, with few to understand, less to value, and scarcely any to encourage his pursuits."[30] Like the minister, the writer was essentially "disestablished," but unlike him, he had never had an "established" place in American society. Rough political alliances like the one between poet-journalist Philip Freneau and the Jeffersonian party at the turn of the nineteenth century were the only approximations early American letters had to offer to the complex, if inadequate, system of patronage which had evolved between men of wealth and men of literature in Europe since the

early Middle Ages. Matters were not entirely improved by the commercialization of literature which began in the late eighteenth century and was
full-blown by the middle of the nineteenth. Nathaniel Willis, running the
popular *Home Monthly* in the 1840s and 1850s, cautioned his sister Sara
Payson Willis, eventually famous as "Fanny Fern" but then just beginning
her literary career, to stay away from New York, the "most overstocked
market in the country for writers." He claimed that he had tried "to find
employment for dozens of starving writers in vain," and added that the *Home
Monthly* perforce paid its contributors nothing.[31] Willis himself, however,
made a financial success out of writing as few other males did in his day.
The reason may be detected in his realistic description of himself and his
peers, no matter how creative their enterprises, as journalists "trying to make
a living by being foremost in riding on a coming turn of the tide." In his
view, literary men wrote for the "middle class" and were middle class.[32]
Unlike Nathaniel Hawthorne, who complained bitterly about the low tastes
of the feminine reading public, Willis and his popular sentimental brethren
set themselves to please the ladies. But to acknowledge, even to court, such
dependency was not always to find it palatable.

The best-known sentimental male writers in ante-bellum America were
the magazine writers—Washington Irving, Nathaniel Willis, Donald Mitchell (known as "Ik Marvel"), and George Curtis. They revealed a personal and
professional profile strikingly similar to that of the liberal clergy.[33] With the
exception of Curtis, they had stern fathers of orthodox persuasion who made
them feel belittled and unproductive; they claimed to be following their
mothers in adopting a sunnier creed.[34] All four suffered from ill health[35] and
showed an indecisiveness about their careers which betrayed the fact that,
if they had in theory rejected their fathers' ways, in practice they found it
difficult to discover meaningful alternatives. They chronically postponed
adulthood. Irving tried law, the family business, travel abroad. Apparently
destined to be an author, he let ten years elapse between the successful
publication of *Knickerbocker's History of New York* and the appearance of
The Sketchbook of Geoffrey Crayon. Curtis experimented with utopianism,
putting in a stint at Brook Farm, then traveled abroad, and gradually began
to produce sketches.[36] Willis seemed a pretentious foppish idler to others as
he followed the footsteps and mimicked the ways of the *beau monde* in New
York and Europe. He had, however, a happy conviction, proved right in the
gossipy pages of the fashionable papers he would edit, that his social advancement was synonymous with his literary career.[37] Mitchell found resolution on a life work acutely difficult. Like Irving, he tried law, without
enthusiasm. His friends began to worry; he himself exclaimed in 1845 with
self-pitying despair: "All the world intent upon their peculiar business. I
alone without it! When, when will it be otherwise?"[38]

All four became men of letters with real importance in their society: Irving was also an ambassador and an historian, Curtis an active reformer; Willis, Mitchell, and Curtis edited several of the most influential periodicals in New York. Yet their writing displays everywhere their fear of paternal condemnation. The male sentimentalist showed as much guilt about writing as his feminine counterpart, perhaps because he believed it, or knew his society believed it, to be increasingly a feminine occupation. Women authors were anxious because their literary activity questioned the convention that only men should write; they nonetheless knew that the convention was fast becoming an illusion which served merely to save face for their male rivals. In an important story Irving included in his *Tales of a Traveller* (1824), the "hero," Buckthorn, confesses with a mixture of shame and bravado to poetic aspirations—"that is to say I have always been an idle fellow and prone to play the vagabond." He is disinherited by his father on the grounds that poetry is "a cursed, sneaking housekeeping employment, the bane of all true manhood"; when he later regains his legacy, he fittingly repents and renounces "the sin of authorship."[39]

All four writers discovered their calling in travel: the first important works of Willis, Mitchell, and Curtis were travel sketches modeled on Irving's ever-popular *Sketchbook*.[40] This contiguity of travel and writing was not accidental; it expressed the fact that these authors built their professions on a form of evasion—of their country, of their own identity, and of their occupation itself. They made of apparently aimless wandering a vocation, a vocation which perforce always retained amateur rank. They emphasized the casualness of their journeys, the haphazardness of their impressions, the uncollated quality of their notes. They escaped censure because they did not take themselves seriously. They confessed to indolence. They pleaded implicitly for a special status, that of perpetual child, of the observer licensed only because he is incapable of participation. They dodged achievement, and could be surprised and elusive in the face of success: they wished to be considered amateurs, even idlers, not men working hard to achieve their literary goals. Willis early created a brilliant *persona*, the "Idle Man," an epicure and a dandy who in the summer "eats ... with an amber handled fork to keep his palm cool."[41] Mitchell's most long-lived contribution to American letters was appropriately the Editor's "Easy Chair" column in *Harper's*. Curtis, who took over this department in 1855, had already established his own appropriate literary *persona*, the idler who narrated travelogues like *Lotus-Eating: A Summer Book* (1852). We are reminded of the liberal clergy's disavowal of their official roles, of the women writers' modest disclaimers of professional status and motivation.

The sketch—the literary form these authors took from European and English sources and which was destined to become the magazine form *par excellence*—ideally expressed their anxieties about their status. The sketch has few pretensions; it is humble, self-deprecatory. *Pencillings, Fun-Jottings, The Rag-Bag*: these were some of the titles Willis gave to his collected "ephemera." The sketch is by definition short; part of the convention behind it is the assumption that it was produced at a sitting, even carelessly, that the feeling or thinking was everything, the writing nothing. Perfectly adapted to commercial periodical publication, it makes no claim to last; it is ultimately dispensable. It concerns itself with the small, the "picturesque."[42] It is the literary analogue to the architectural style its promulgators would choose for their semi-rural, semi-suburban homes.[43] Irving acknowledged at the start of the *Sketchbook* that he was not interested in the "sublime." In mood, the sketch is unmistakably personal and subjective. Its narrator is never omniscient; that would be to grant him too much power. In a piece by Irving entitled "The Stout Gentleman," the narrator becomes more and more curious about a portly man who occupies an English inn with him.[44] The sketch closes abruptly and comically when the narrator sees only the posterior of the stout gentleman as he gets into a coach to leave; none of the narrator's questions are answered. The Lockean empiricism which formed the intellectual underpinning of the sketch as it developed during the eighteenth century in England in the hands of Sterne, Goldsmith, and Lamb here highlights the narrator's impotence in narration: he is apparently as helpless as a child, trapped in himself, a prisoner of his perceptions.

The tone of apology so essential to the career and art of the male sentimentalists, like the attitude of humility adopted by ministers and women, was not, however, a simple one. Their form, the magazine sketch, despite its apparent timidity, is self-indulgent in mood and shrewdly commercial in purpose. Like any potentially mass-produced object, its lack of pretension as art makes it more appealing as an article of consumption; it can be read casually, then forgotten. Its very insignificance frees the consumer from guilt. Again, the *personae* of the male sentimentalists are teases, loiterers, given to disappearing around corners, gently dodging shadows of their own making, men with a vanishing act. Their evaporation complex seems a sign of self-effacement—as, indeed, it partially is; it is also a covert and self-congratulatory manifesto of irresponsibility. Their docility is deceptive; in the midst of their humility lies a hidden animus against the forces which humble them. The gentlemanly narrators are not quite as kindly, as insignificant, as assimilable to feminine tastes as they seem on first glance. It is as if they publicly disarm themselves of all dangerous weapons in order not to be suspected of carrying poison. They submit partly in order to gain the chance to be at close range, intimate with the enemy. Irving in *The Sketchbook*, Willis in *Pencillings by the Way*, Mitchell in *Reveries of a Bachelor*, and

Curtis in *Prue and I* (all works originally serialized in the periodical press) inherited and enhanced a male *persona*, overtly emasculated and covertly vengeful, whose ambiguities reflected their own aspirations and conflicts.

Irving's Geoffrey Crayon is a bachelor; his existence is built on explicit and implicit envy of the domestic state, yet he never seriously seeks to alter it. Mitchell's "Bachelor" too dreams of matrimony; ironically, however, he has little hostile run-ins with his vigorous housekeeper, who almost sweeps him away as he weaves his idle fancies by the fireplace. Curtis' narrator is happily married, and the ordering of characters in the title *Prue and I* is symbolic. Prue is a tactful and devoted wife, but we never forget that she could have married an extraordinarily successful businessman by the side of whom the narrator seems in every way insignificant. She darns, and cooks, and thinks, and loves, while her spouse meanders. Yet the point is that Prue's husband, like Mitchell's and Irving's bachelors, does meander: the book is largely the record of his fantasies about other younger, richer, and more beautiful women. No matter that he and the Bachelors officially belong to the domestic domain; in their secretive dreams they are wide rangers and even furtive opponents of the regime of which they appear the most secure and abject subjects. "Paul Pry[s],"[45] they are vampires of sensibility, lacking vitality of their own and especially equipped to tap that of others. At one point, Mitchell's Bachelor pictures himself conducting an idle flirtation with a charming girl in Europe and writing of his inconclusive amours to his lovely cousin at home. The cousin, who worships him, is occupied in tending a dying parent and not far from the grave herself. He returns, having wooed but not wed the European girl, to discover the American one is dead. She has left a packet of forgiving letters filled with evidence of the suffering his foreign peccadilloes caused. Again, when he imagines himself married, it is only to linger fondly over his fictional wife's demise from consumption: "and now the hand that touches yours," he inquires almost salaciously, "is it no thinner, no whiter than yesterday?"[46]

The relationship between the sentimental narrator and the diseased maiden about whom he fantasizes is extremely complex and richly revelatory. He courts identification with her because her feminine resources are precisely the ones he needs. Her emotional susceptibility, her subjectivity are his inspiration. He comes as near as he can to the suffering of the female while still savoring the titillation involved in identifying with the male who caused it. Her weakness and isolation are in a sense his own and thus he both exploits and rejects her. The sentimental author was dependent on female suffering for his material just as he was dependent on female readers for his livelihood, but he resented and subtly tried to reverse this subjugation.[47] The women in his pages exist only to give the narrator, otherwise idle and useless, something to do: they provide him with a vocation.

Like that of Irving's *Sketchbook*, the world of *Reveries* and *Prue and I* is virtually depopulated: its creatures are those of the narrator's fancy. The characters are pale and derivative like members of some family in which generations of inbreeding have weakened the stock almost unbearably; they have listened only to each other for too long. Their models were from the start literary ones; they are faint with nostalgia for their predecessors in the pages of Addison, Steele, Sterne, and Goldsmith. Literature and its creations are never forced in these works into rivalry with life. There is no competition to the narrator's imagination. Prue's husband explains the peculiar advantages of his position: "I am the guest who, for the small price of invisibility, drinks only the best wines and talks only to the most agreeable people."[48] He is sure that he enjoys a certain Miss Amelia more in fancy than any of her actual male escorts do in fact. Mitchell's Bachelor inquires pointedly: "can any wife be prettier than an after dinner fancy, idle and yet vivid, can paint for you?"[49] The sentimental narrator's ever-present consciousness that he is but dreaming, and dreaming dreams he can at any moment disperse, is a subtle reminder that he is the dictator as well as the servant of his feminine readers' imaginative needs. He never forgets that he has the author's power—which becomes all-important when literature is commercialized—of withholding; he can interfere with the reader's range and rate of consumption.

The clerical critics who enjoyed such magazine sketches in the 1850s were to find in the 1870s an infinitely less welcome and more spectacular example of the same veiled masculine exploitation of genteel femininity in their own ranks. In 1869, Henry Ward Beecher published *Norwood*, one of the crucial documents of its period, although a perusal of it today might not at once explain its significance.[50] It was as commercial as any of Curtis' or Mitchell's productions and designed for a similar audience. Beecher revealed little of the anxiety which had troubled his clerical predecessors undertaking fictional work. He wrote *Norwood* for a huge sum of money paid him by the enterprising editor Robert Bonner. Bonner serialized the novel in his widely circulated weekly, the *New York Ledger*. *Norwood* was a magazine work replete with village scenes and a conventional love interest. The main figure in the story was not a minister but a doctor, one Dr. Wentworth, who confused Christianity with Darwinism and duty with spending money on oneself[51] very much in the style of his author. The book sold well, but its tale aroused little controversy; it was rather the circumstances surrounding its writing which produced high conflict. In characteristic fashion, Beecher acted out the drama of ambivalence his secular and clerical colleagues preferred to confine to print; perhaps only Beecher was shrewd enough to know that, by the late 1860s, no amount of overtness could break the stranglehold commercial literary stereotypes held on experience. Perversely,

Beecher was as well protected from life as Mitchell's Bachelor; his scandal was from start to finish a literary affair.

Beecher had a very specific audience in mind for his rambling work, namely Libby Tilton, wife of Theodore Tilton, Beecher's closest associate in his various reform-minded religious enterprises. Beecher had difficulty in getting started on the project; he had never written a novel, and he did not altogether share Robert Bonner's interesting conviction that fiction was his natural métier. As he himself said, he needed "somebody ... that would not be critical, and that would praise it, to give me the courage to go on." Libby, in her husband's words, was "sympathetic to a very rich degree."[52] Tilton and Libby were not altogether congenial. Tilton explained at the trial in which he accused Beecher of committing adultery with his wife[53] that he had gradually come to disbelieve in the divinity of Christ, while Libby was "almost an enthusiast"[54] for the opposing view. He mocked her for her physical petiteness, her penchant for saccharine devotional art. Tilton's words at the trial, as well as his journalistic and fictional work,[55] reveal him to be a strong, vigorous, not altogether astute, rather self-righteous, and combative man. He prided himself on his moral purpose, on his principled frankness; Beecher's apparent *bonhomie* originally seemed a complement to his own temperament. Libby Tilton was inclined to tears and melancholy; she was recovering from the death of a child and drawing on her pastor's helpful powers of consolation when Beecher "seduced" her.

Attractive, charming, not particularly bright, emotionally unstable and immature, Libby Tilton was a devotee of literature, a follower of the religious press. Susan Anthony, the leader of the suffrage movement and a friend of Libby's, described her generously as "a woman of wide reading and a fine literary taste."[56] A few decades earlier Libby would have been an admirer of Mrs. Sigourney; she read the novels of Mrs. E. D. E. N. Southworth with avidity. Libby showed the squeamish fastidiousness inculcated by such ladylike mentors; despite a serious flirtation with the New York women's movement, she was upset and disgusted by Victoria Woodhull, a flamboyant advocate of free love and a self-proclaimed candidate for the presidency. It should be noted that The Woodhull, as she was known, had her revenge on Libby and her lover; her public proclamation of the affair, made appropriately enough at a meeting of the American Association of Spiritualists, forced Tilton, several years after the event, to bring suit against Beecher. Libby was of a different stamp; she emulated the exaggerated and euphemistic rhetoric characteristic of Mrs. Sigourney and her sisters. She referred to Christ as "The Great Lover" in her letters. She felt and tried to instill in her children a "reverence" for the clergy. She regretted greatly that Tilton himself was not a minister—which, he commented characteristically, "is the only virtue I possess."[57]

According to her husband, Libby initially felt no guilt about her affair with Beecher. Her pastor had coyly called their relationship "nest hunting," a phrase borrowed from his novel-in-progress, and an evasion to which only Libby's peculiar literary socialization could have lent any credibility. She passed hours on her knees in prayer; she was, as Theodore Tilton summed her up, "sentimental."[58] As a prolific letter-writer she had something in common with Richardson's Clarissa. She and her pastor exchanged innumerable notes whose indiscretion later haunted them. She even read her rather histrionic letters to Theodore aloud to Henry Ward, who expressed "great admiration" for them.[59] And, let me stress it, she was a reader. She began to view her illicit relationship with Beecher differently, as Tilton tells the story, only when she read a novel which presented a character in a position similar to hers. Libby was distressed and interested to discover that the author clearly found such a situation to be cause for remorse, penitence, and final spiritual elevation. Libby confessed to her husband in part because she had found another role to play.

This is not to condemn her. It is only to scrutinize at painfully close range the barrenness of her possibilities. Libby was reported to have complained bitterly at one point during the protracted controversy around her private affairs: "I have always been treated as a nonentity—a plaything."[60] The scandal hardly bettered her lot. Tilton forced accusations against Beecher from her; Beecher demanded retractions; their various intermediaries extracted other contradictory statements from her pen. Beecher had begun by believing that his innocence depended on hers; initially, he referred to Libby tenderly as a pure "child." Later he realized he could clear himself by damning her, and took to rebuking her "excessive affection."[61] When, after the trial was long over, she published a plain statement of the truth of their love affair, simply, as she said, with unconscious pathos, to satisfy her "quickened conscience,"[62] it was too late. Her identity was already lost. Finally abandoned by both husband and lover, she died essentially of confusion, without a life, without a literary model to give her the illusion of life.

Beecher had an easier time of it. He had written his book, had read it chapter by chapter to an eager Libby in intimate *tête-à-têtes* held in her husband's absence, just as he had done everything since his arrival in New York City from Indiana in 1847: to be seen, to be heard, to have an audience. His success protected him. Plymouth Church, where Beecher served as pastor, was big business; pew rentals alone pulled in $60,000 a year.[63] There were men indifferent or disdainful toward Beecher personally who were eager to save such a profitable concern. As a writer, as a preacher, Beecher was indispensable; he was the central attraction at Plymouth Church. Libby was as fascinated as Beecher with the possibilities of exposure; with her ill-placed confidences and prolific letters, she courted attention as surely as he did, but she knew infinitely less well what to do with it. Beecher was not Machiavelli or probably a follower of Don Juan despite Victoria Wood-hull's maliciously hopeful claims for his vast "physical amativeness."[64] He practiced a debased version of Whitman's trick of substituting love of everyone for love of anyone. Unlike Libby, however, he could capitalize on his confusion and maneuver through it with embarrassing skill.

Beecher's occasional blubbering and frequent obfuscation at his trial demonstrated his ability to exploit his own amorphousness. He claimed he had not seduced Libby. Tilton accused him of "sexual intimacy"; he admitted to "improper advances." What kind of defense was that? What, after all, was seduction anyway? But in a sense Beecher's confusion was genuine, no matter how manipulated. Had he seduced Libby, or was it just "nesting"? If you close your eyes, does anything really happen? Did he read her a novel, or act out a novel? The trial itself supplied excitement for half a year to all Americans who read the papers or the magazines. One commentator for *Leslie's Magazine* noted enthusiastically that "we are reading the most marvellous of human dramas; greater in plot, dénouement and effect" than Hawthorne's *Scarlet Letter* or Eliot's *Romola*.[65] Little wonder that Beecher on trial increasingly talked in literary terms. He spoke of a kiss given him by a woman friend as "a holy kiss as I sometimes have seen it in poetry";[66] he justified his physical prowess (or what he confessed of his physical prowess) in terms reminiscent of the standard rationale of the polite lady-poets: "When you shall find a heart to rebuke the twining morning-glory, you may rebuke me for misplaced confidence. . . . It is not my choice; it is my necessity."[67]

Here is the fascination of the fateful conjunction of Libby Tilton and Henry Ward Beecher avid over the pages of *Norwood*, a duller drama by far than the one which unfolded during its reading. The minister-writer and the lady-reader have indeed found their common ground. It is their mutual foray into fiction which is of such interest—a foray in which they must be utterly parasitic on each other and whose success depends on an entire exclusion of the forces of American society—an exclusion brutally shattered by the protracted Beecher-Tilton trial. The trial called to the bar not so much Henry Ward Beecher and Libby Tilton as sentimental fiction itself. The characters of Mr. Beecher and Mrs. Tilton were on trial in a double sense; not just their lives but their roles were at issue. Although the jury was essentially unable to reach a verdict, Beecher's own church exonerated him. The liberal minister had shaped his female parishioners' tastes and fantasies, then borrowed the powers they attributed to him. Beecher enacted the fantasy with which the male sentimentalists had flirted: exploiting the feminine reader and then excluding her.

Feminine Sentimentalism: The Bitterness of Harriet Beecher Stowe

Unmistakably, this was a game that two could play as well as one. The women I have been considering were hardly unaware of the hostility emanating from their clerical and literary brethren, and they returned it with interest. Examples are plentiful, but none is more compelling than the one offered by Harriet Beecher Stowe. Among the most gifted women of her generation, Stowe fiercely defended her adored brother Henry Ward in his hour of need, but there can be no doubt that in a larger sense his cause was not altogether hers. During the years of Henry's affair, Stowe published two important novels—*My Wife and I* (1871) and *We and Our Neighbors* (1874), to which I have referred in earlier chapters. Both appeared originally in the *Christian Union*, a weekly of which Henry Ward was editor, and they are very distinctly magazine writing as none of Stowe's earlier serialized novels were. Neither of them is up to the level of her previous works, *Uncle Tom's Cabin, The Minister's Wooing, The Pearl of Orr's Island,* and *Old Town Folks.* In their pages, Stowe is solving, or coming close to solving, her own problems as a woman, a writer, and a religious believer, but her solutions are not commendable. If Henry Ward had unconsciously presented the tableau of women at men's mercy, Harriet triumphantly displayed the scene of man abject under feminine rule. She managed to analyze and mock the futilities inherent in the position of the liberal minister and the male sentimentalist; she recorded an enormous scorn for masculinity itself. Harriet had more to lose than Henry did. Both brother and sister were in a real sense geniuses; while Henry's true calling, however, was commercial, Harriet's was ethical. To take her revenge on an unjust society, she abandoned a romantic, essentially historical style for a sentimental approach to which historical concerns were painfully peripheral.

Harriet Beecher, like all the Beecher children who made their mark, started her career riding on her father's coat-tails. Lyman Beecher was always enthusiastic about "Hattie's" gifts; before she was ten, he pronounced her a "genius" and only wished "she was a boy."[68] Stowe repaid her father's admiration by memorizing dozens of hymns as a small child and composing *bona fide* sermons at various points over her long life.[69] We have seen how Stowe clung to her mother's memory, but it was, after all, a memory. She was five when her mother died. She was very much her father's daughter, if not his superior, and in ways for which one admires and likes her. Of Beecher's children, only she relished the vernacular as he did; she outdid her father in her shrewd instinct for comedy, and became the only major feminine humorist nineteenth-century America produced. She had Beecher's ear for dialect, his eye for realistic detail.[70] With this relish for the actual Stowe combined, like her father, a genuine sense of the sublime. Lyman and Harriet grasped the essential Calvinist truth which Melville understood so well: that sin itself is the sublime, and that only its enormity puts men on speaking terms with God. In adolescence, Stowe emoted properly and passionately over that archetype of the sublime, Niagara. In adulthood, on her first tour of Europe, she promptly rejected the "effeminate" beauties of Raphael for the excesses of "all-powerful" Rubens.[71] In a spirit her father could have understood, she exulted that Rubens' "triumphant, abounding life" had dragged her "at his chariot wheels," and proceeded to articulate her rather peculiar aesthetic demands: "Art has satisfied me at last. I have been conquered and that is enough."[72]

Stowe thought that "the very pain" Rubens caused her proved him "a real living artist."[73] She takes for granted here that great art is a form of onslaught. That was indeed the art of Calvinism, of Lyman Beecher—and of *Uncle Tom's Cabin.* Stowe wrote her masterful anti-slavery novel in part to show up the faint-hearted American clergy of which Lyman Beecher was in this case a conspicuous example, and she picked a form they were sure to recognize. *Uncle Tom's Cabin* is a great book, not because it is a great novel, but because it is a great revival sermon, aimed directly at the conversion of its hearers. In subsequent years, in a series of sometimes rambling, sometimes sentimental but always witty and alert narratives Stowe conducted the most brilliant exploration of New England Calvinism as a theology and a lifestyle ever conceived by an American. No one understood better Calvinism's repressive aspects, especially in relation to women; no one saw more clearly the inevitability of its decline; but Calvinism was nonetheless the subject of Stowe's best work. The little girl whose father had complimented her by wishing she were a boy grew up to be a woman and an artist whose achievement was to beat daddy at his own game, and, more important, to realize far more fully than he the meaning of the religious vocabulary they both employed. Her tragedy was that, when she rejected this vocabulary, as, in the quest for self-expression incumbent on a temperament as creative as hers, she inevitably did, she found nothing fully adequate with which to replace it. Her failure is a revealing one.

In 1869, the Countess Guiccioli, once Lord Byron's mistress, published her *Recollections of Lord Byron;* she whitewashed the English poet and damned his wife as censorious, cold, and vindictive. The Byrons had parted at Lady Byron's insistence a half century earlier; both of them were now dead; but interest in the old scandal still ran high and largely in Lord Byron's favor. Stowe, who had become Lady Byron's confidante in several revelatory sessions in England in the 1850s, rose at once to her friend's defense in *Lady Byron Vindicated.* She knew (from Lady Byron, she claimed) what later biographers have confirmed, that Byron never loved his wife and married to cover his love affair with his half-sister Augusta. As Stowe saw it, Lady

Byron had had no choice but to leave him, and her subsequent silence had been an act of compassionate nobility. In trying to destroy Lord Byron through her hysterical panegyric on his wife, Stowe was undermining a poet who had fascinated her father;[74] Byron had, moreover, long held immense personal significance for her.

In her basically sympathetic portrayal of the very Byronic Aaron Burr in *The Minister's Wooing* (1859), Stowe had pictured him as an apostate from the Calvinist tradition of his famous ancestry, yet one still paradoxically enmeshed in essentially Calvinist thought patterns. Her Burr is finally Calvinist precisely because he knows he is damned, and this awareness is the source of Stowe's concern. His self-disdain as well as his good breeding advertise him a gentleman, if not a Christian. The story closes, at some cost to the narrative to which he has been largely peripheral, with an account of the erection of a simple monument on Burr's neglected grave. Stowe cannot shut him out altogether from the circle of redemption. Her reading of the same character in *Old Town Folks* (1869), Ellery Davenport, is much harsher. This Byron-Burr figure is less a sinner than a cheater and a deceiver; he almost destroys the happiness of the gay and childlike heroine, Tina. At the end of this line of development, the Byron of *Lady Byron Vindicated* is a tormented voluptuary who commits incest because he "longed for the stimulation of a new kind of vice." He is still a believer (" 'The worst of it is, I *do* believe,' " he reportedly told Lady Byron)[75] but he no longer engrosses Stowe's interest or compassion.

Stowe is identifying less with the Byronic hero than with the woman he inevitably wrongs; she has developed a sharper and more self-conscious sense of sisterhood.[76] Yet the price Stowe pays for it is fearful, and reveals a great deal about the sexual polarities of her culture. To defame Byron was not only to censure a traducer of her sex, but also to defame rebelliousness and its products—the "remorse" which Stowe rightly perceived as the inspiration for Byron's obsessive creativity. His pain was at least kin to that she herself had once felt before Rubens and defined as essential to Calvinism and art. Byron was regarded by Lyman Beecher and by Stowe as the poet of the sublime. To praise Lady Byron, no matter how unfairly she was maligned, was to laud a denial of creativity and to extoll conformity. A reserved and dignified philanthropist, Lady Byron was an exemplar of Anglican benevolence, not of Puritan guilt. The writing of *Lady Byron Vindicated* was an important event for Stowe. The book antagonized thousands of readers; but more important, it advertised Stowe's new-felt freedom in the early and mid-1870s. She was adopting the self-worship inculcated by sentimental feminine antinomianism which her extraordinary intelligence had prevented her from fully assuming all her insecure and chaotic life. She was beginning to boast rather than analyze.

Narcissistic rage is at the heart of Harriet Beecher Stowe's writings of the late 1860s and early 1870s. She wrote *My Wife and I* and *We and Our Neighbors* in part to regain the public she had alienated with *Lady Byron Vindicated;* yet these two novels pulse with essentially the same hostility, no less intense for its new coyness. In neither of these works has Stowe given up her long-standing attempt to supplant her father and obtain his ministerial authority; she has rather displaced him entirely by tacitly redefining the true sacerdotal office to exclude him. Stowe's earlier heroines had all been ministerial stand-ins—Mary Scudder in *The Minister's Wooing,* for example, makes many more converts than Dr. Hopkins—but they had been recognizable ones. Like Mara, her successor in *The Pearl of Orr's Island,* Mary palpably wants—in her fashion, just like Lyman Beecher in his—"to save souls," and her whole life is a clear preparation for her mission. She is a church member, an assiduous and thoughtful reader of the Bible. Stowe's frivolous later heroines no longer need any resemblance to the usual ministerial pattern to claim its sanctity. They are completely unschooled and totally secularized. They are ministers who are anti-ministers, prophets of the culture-bound family faith which was to dominate America's religious future. Harriet Beecher Stowe's new credo could be summed up thus: salvation comes through the agency of the *average* woman. And her heroines are "average" with a vengeance, for how else can Stowe demonstrate that *any* woman is better than *any* man? Her creative impulse has narrowed perilously near a scorn of any real accomplishment as, by definition, masculine, and rejection of the effort, privatization, and suffering she knew were attendant on it.

Stowe's disintegration as a writer is evident in the New York novels; and her curious relish at the thinness, the mediocrity of these stories is equally apparent. Not long after publishing *My Wife and I,* Stowe, with astonishing condescension, could remark to her great contemporary George Eliot that *Middlemarch,* fine as it was, lacked "jollitude." With a note of breezy reproach, Stowe informs the English author that she writes on "so high a plane! It is all self-abnegation."[77] Stowe's failure of insight seems almost deliberate; she could not be making it clearer that her own days of "self-abnegation," and great achievement, are triumphantly over. By a similar and equally painful logic, in the New York novels Stowe for the first time in her career totally abandoned historical and recognizable models for her characters. The *Key to Uncle Tom's Cabin,* a collection of historical documents that purported to substantiate the story of *Uncle Tom,* proved Stowe's not entirely conscious veracity in her first masterpiece; Nat Turner, Samuel Hopkins, Byron, Savonarola inspired several of her finest later portraits. Her feminine characters, for obvious reasons, had seldom derived from prominent historical sources, but until 1871 they had always played, and often forcibly, against masculine characters drawn from "real-life." In *My Wife and I*, all characters are fictional. Moreover, *We and Our Neighbors* is the first actual sequel Stowe ever wrote; like the male sentimentalists, including her brother, she was newly fascinated with the possibilities of art lovingly imitating art, with the excision not only of competition, of standards, but of experience itself.

Calvinism itself is predictably the first male achievement which Stowe is intent on demolishing. It is important to remember that these novels and sketches are Episcopalian and, equally important to add, Episcopalian as Stowe understood the term. She, with many other intelligent Americans, had turned to the Anglican Church in the mid-1860s. It had much to offer her. One should not overlook the fact that Stowe's move to Episcopalianism in part bore witness to her broadening religious and social vision. She genuinely welcomed the potential catholicism of the Anglican Church in an immigrant and urban culture; she was cognizant of the ways its organization and its orders allowed it to work more effectively in the exploding cities in which her father's denomination (Presbyterian-Congregationalist) was failing to take real hold. Yet it seems undeniable that in her religious realignment, Stowe was confirming and hastening her flight from self-criticism and from the authority of vital experience.

Despite sometimes bitter internal debate over the growing use of ritual initiated by the Oxford Movement, the Anglican Church was, comparatively speaking, a model of non-conflict in a very conflicted society. It was crucial to Stowe that the Episcopal sect, alone among Protestant denominations, claimed a history of organic evolution from the primitive church. Certainly in American life the Anglican Church put a premium on continuity and serenity. The Baptists, Presbyterians, and Methodists all split officially and deeply on the slavery issue prior to the Civil War, and the fissures were in some cases well-nigh unbridgeable. The Episcopalian Church never divided, because, as one of its historians has pointed out,[78] it simply refused to recognize the issue. The style of Anglican ecclesiastical ceremony confirmed the church's image in Stowe's eyes as a model of tasteful self-approbation. Of course the Episcopal Church, despite its participation in the urban revivals of 1857 and 1858, was non-evangelical; the kind of total self-examination which supposedly accompanied the conversion experience in other sects was never demanded of its members. Moreover, the Episcopalian rector was wedded to his prayerbook and to a fixed service which de-emphasized the sermon; his language was the conservative one of public ceremony. It is important that Stowe joined the church just at the time when rituals were proliferating: despite "low church" protest, crosses, candles, saints' days, daily matins and vespers, choral services, weekly communion, even sacramental confession and absolution and elevation of the host were borrowed from Catholic practice by Episcopalians.[79] Stowe's New York novels show that she heartily approved of most of these practices, and with sure instinct dismissed only those which posterity has also rejected. As we will see, these rituals had significant narcissistic potential for her.

The Protestant (non-Anglican) ministry is not presented as a viable option in the New York novels and sketches. Henry Henderson, the narrator of *My Wife and I* and *We and Our Neighbors,* is the son of a small-town New England clergyman who has much in common with Lyman Beecher. Absorbed in theological controversy, "naturally impetuous though magnanimous" (35),[80] Reverend Henderson has love but limited time for his offspring. When Henry is born, he takes a short break from his work:

> "God bless him," said my father, kissing me and my mother, and then he returned to an important treatise which was to reconcile the decrees of God with the free agency of men, and which the event of my entrance into this world had interrupted for some hours. The sermon was a perfect success I am told and nobody that heard it ever had a moment's further trouble on the subject. (6)

Little Henry naturally devotes himself to his loving mother and fantasizes about a day when his father will be old and unable to preach. After Reverend Henderson's death, his closest friend explains that his greatness was not in his theology, into which he poured all his energies, but in his benevolent heart, which he in the main ignored. In other words, in so far as he was lucky enough to resemble his wife, he was successful: what he thought to be his achievement was largely a rather touching waste of time.

Stowe displays even less sympathy for the more timid clerical souls whom Lyman Beecher had fought decades earlier in Boston. Reverend Henderson may have been an anachronism, but at least he was a man. *My Wife and I* opens with a section entitled "The Author Defines His Position" which is in part a cruelly piercing attack on the often pathetic attempts of the contemporary liberal clergy to rationalize and popularize their predicament. A few lines will give the flavor:

> The Rev. Dr. Cool Shadow will go on with his interesting romance of "Christianity, a Dissolving View"—designed to show how everything is, in many respects, like everything else, and all things lead somewhere, and everything will finally end somehow, and therefore that it is important that everybody should cultivate general sweetness, and have the very best time possible in this world. (2)

Faced with such options, it is hardly surprising that Henry Henderson never considers the ministry seriously as a possible profession. He knows he lacks the faith necessary to meet its demands and challenges, and he spends no time agonizing about his deficiency. Instead he chooses a career in the popular press that is competing so handily with the religious one, and becomes a reporter for a New York newspaper.

The male sentimentalists come off no better than the ministers in Stowe's acerbic pages. The very title of *My Wife and I* reminds the reader of George Curtis' *Prue and I*. The episodic narrative and the male narrators of all the works Stowe turned out between 1868 and 1874, with the exception of *Pink and White Tyranny*, suggest the same source. *Little Foxes* (1866), *The Chimney Corner* (1866), and *House and Home Papers* (1865), the preparatory works for the New York novels, are collected sketches which originally appeared in the *Atlantic Monthly*. Christopher Crowfield, their narrator, is reminiscent of Prue's husband. "A literary man, with a somewhat delicate nervous organization and a sensitive stomach,"[81] he is bald, fastidious, domesticated, and effete. Like Mitchell's Bachelor, he loves to lie "back in my study chair with my heels luxuriously propped on an ottoman"; this is "my cloud land where I love to sail away in dreamy quietude, forgetting the war, the price of coal and flour"[82] until his strong-minded practical wife briskly reminds him of approaching deadlines. Crowfield embarrasses the reader with the apologetic excesses of his self-dislike: palpably afraid of the women he propitiates by imitation, he deprecates himself as a "clumsy, old, blind vulcan."[83] Since he is Stowe's puppet, he is in part expressing her own sentiments about him, but Stowe is also getting at the lack of self-respect which was so crippling in writers like Curtis and Mitchell.

Henry Henderson, though neither a minister nor an author, seems weak in every sense. When as a child he first leaves home to go to day school, he is in terror of the big boys who threaten to bully him. Then Daisy, the first love of his life, whom, with precocious anticipation of the domestic state, he calls his "child wife," comes to his rescue: she has his place moved to the girls' side of the room. "I was a blessed little boy from that moment" (11), he tells us. He is completely dependent on little Daisy, as he will be on Eva van Arsdel, his legal wife. And no wonder. Males in these books are either awkward brutes, stumbling amid feminine subtleties, or wistful would-be transvestites. In either form, they are by nature failures, just as the women are by nature successes. It is quite clear that Henry Henderson has no other function than to provide an audience, a mirror, an adorer for his wife (or wives). The crucial point is that his subjugation, unlike that of Prue's husband, is not apparent but real. Henry, presumably spending a good deal of time writing about Eva and all her little doings, is advertising his sexual disadvantage.

And Eva's doings are very little indeed. Stowe was much too intelligent not to have doubts about her new fashionable heroine, whom I have already described as the proto-consumer. *Pink and White Tyranny*, which appeared in the same year as *My Wife and I*, reveals the superficiality, the coldness, the utter small-mindedness of Lillie Ellis, a society belle who to the casual eye might seem very similar to Eva van Arsdel. But if Lillie represents Stowe's fears about the modish modern girl, Eva suggests her hopes, and in *My Wife and I* and *We and Our Neighbors*, she indulges them to the uttermost. Before her marriage, Eva is a pretty society flirt with somewhat higher aspirations than the wealthy loveless match which seems clearly in the offing. She is a regular churchgoer, but her theology, as we have seen, is a trivial and subjective know-nothingism. She prefers the Biblical explanation of the creation to the Darwinian one because, as she says, " 'I think it a good deal easier to believe the Garden of Eden story, especially as that's pretty and poetical, and is in the dear old Book that is so sweet and comfortable to us' " (322). A quote like this suggests accurately not only the thinness of her personality but the impoverishment of her language. She talks as James was to make Daisy Miller talk just a few years later. Stowe, who could exult ov∙ · the "curlie-wurlies" of Eva's lovely younger sister Angélique, was clearly past the point of being critical of her slight heroine.

Eva's great charm for everyone, including her author and her husband, apparently lies in her tasteful wardrobe. Admiring her, Henry feels compensated for "those severe edicts" which decree that male dress should be dull. Like some kind of bird, the female of the species is apparently destined to brilliant plumage, the male to drab. Henry's wits seem as dull as his clothes when he gapes over her finery; yet it is clear he is undergoing a religious experience, and more particularly, an Episcopalian one. Eva's clothes and the process by which she adorns herself are at some level for Stowe analogous to the rituals of her new-found church. In the two novels in which Eva figures, Stowe lingers fondly over scenes in which young couples adorn and re-adorn little chapels at appropriate seasons. Not too surprisingly, the young men always fall adoringly in love with the young ladies on such occasions. In *We and Our Neighbors*, St. John, a devout Episcopalian rector, has redecorated his church in blue and gold. He is stunned when Angélique van Arsdel conducts her Sunday School class in a matching blue and gold outfit. Of course, although hitherto absorbed in his church, he now falls in love with her. In Stowe's narcissistic imagination, the woman has herself become the church, and the man is a rapturous communicant. Eva is quite frank about her ambitions. In *We and Our Neighbors*, counseling her sister to abandon her vague girlish dreams of a hero-husband, she explains sagely: " 'your heroes like to sit on pedestals and have you worship them. Now, for my part, I'd rather have a good kind *man* that will worship me' " (403).[84]

Her emphasis on the *"man"* here, however, is somewhat misleading. She is all for marriage, eager to make matches for her sisters and friends at every

turn, but her motive is not finally respect for the value of the male. Her aim
in life is the essentially narcissistic one of multiplying her image by creating
little domesticated replicas of her life. She holds her Thursday evening
get-togethers to implicate her friends at once in the domestic process; they
are to participate, admire, and do likewise, and six of them do. Eva's own
marriage is absolutely without content or meaning except as a model. It is
an advertisement, not a product. After the honeymoon, her husband's adora-
tion is assumed but not expressed. At one point, we see them going to bed
together in a classically sexless scene. He, exhausted from his day, is half
asleep, while she is chatting on about subjects which don't interest him. The
vignette closes with her superior acceptance of his indifference and her
amusement at his rather gross physical fatigue: " 'Oh, you sleepy-head!
Well, never mind. Good night' " (85). (There is no evidence in either novel
that the female of the species ever needs sleep. She is on a perpetual,
sprightly alert.) Needless to say, the couple has no children. It is apparent
that Eva has no time for childbearing: she is too busy showing off. It is as
irrelevant to expect children from her as to expect a doll to talk. Henry is
generally absent from home. He is like a character always off-stage, for
Stowe increasingly omits any information about his job. When at home, he
is a factotum figure. Furthermore, we almost never find this model couple
alone in the home they love so much: either guests arrive, or one of them
goes out, Eva to "visit," Henry to work or to his "club." The reader is
thoroughly sympathetic with their apparently inconsistent dread of privacy: it is all too evident that, once alone without an audience, they would
cease to exist.

One must say, to do her credit, that Eva, in chatting with her potential
mimics, is never base enough to insinuate that romance or even love has
much to do with marriage. There is a businesslike air lurking behind these
matchmaking *tête-à-têtes*. She is always enticing her feminine friends by the
possibility that they can "make" some man by taking him up as a matrimonial investment. The arguments she uses on her sister Alice in favor of her
suitor Jim, a cheery young reporter, are typical. " 'Your influence might
help him' " in his career, she points out. Alice agrees. " 'Jim ought to be
married, certainly,' " she says "in a reflective tone. 'Just the right kind of
marriage would be the making of him.' " But Eva's clinching argument is
an interesting version of the "let's keep it in the family" approach. " 'I do
think it would be a nice thing for us all if you could like Jim, for he's one
of us; we all know him and like him . . . you might settle right down here,
and live near us, and all go on together cosily' " (403). Jim's main selling point
is apparently that he is already familiar, already domesticated; he sounds a
bit like a prefab house, ready to be put up. In marrying Jim, Alice can
quickly dispose of him, and get to the real business of female life; setting up

an "easy," "nice," "cosy" home for others to envy and imitate. Needless to say, she accepts him.

Eva exults over their prospective marriage and two others she has skillfully engineered in a letter written to her mother-in-law. These letters, which punctuate the narratives at regular intervals, are in themselves rather curious affairs. They seldom tell us anything we have not already learned through the direct narrative. Their purpose is not to inform but rather, by the narcissistic process on which the book operates structurally as well as thematically, to re-reflect, to gloat. As Eva redescribes the trivia which comprise her life, she repossesses her kingdom, and replicates it once again for her somewhat weary readers. Here, at her peak as a matrimonial entrepreneur, in the key sentence of the book she unabashedly demands her due pound of praise: " 'Mother, doesn't it seem as if our bright, cosy, happy, free-and-easy home was throwing out as many side-shoots as a lilac bush?' " (462). The natural, even floral, connotations of Eva's metaphor seem insidiously deceptive. One has a vision of an unending assembly line, mass-producing thousands of these homes, essentially empty like Eva's and Henry's, each existing only because the others do. Incest has been commercialized.

The Loss of Romanticism

Stowe's late novels hint painfully at the tragic dead end of Victorian American culture. There is the viciousness between the sexes. There is the triumphant drift toward a consumer and mass-media society: Eva the shopper, Henry the newspaper reporter, Stowe herself at least momentarily the advocate of the superficial, the replicable. Equally important in these books, however, is what has been lost: theology, feminism, and romanticism—to all of which Stowe, like others in her culture, was logically the heir. Stowe herself is not to blame for this profoundly disappointing end to a brilliant career.[85] She did what she did in a half-understood effort to vindicate women in the most effective way in a society that she sensed undervalued them. But it was a costly vindication, for to accomplish it she had to debase all that was best in her religious heritage, repress all that was strongest in her own creativity—and then, boast of it.

A period which produced Nathaniel Hawthorne, Herman Melville, Walt Whitman, Henry David Thoreau, Ralph Waldo Emerson, Edwards A. Park, and Horace Bushnell, among others, produced no women, with the exceptions of Margaret Fuller and Stowe, who could match their claims even if the standards used were appropriately rephrased and redefined. Edward Beecher, the most impressive of Lyman's sons, was, if anything, less gifted and less intelligent than either of his more famous sisters. His achievements cannot match Harriet's and are no greater than Catharine's. He was every bit as eccentric as they were. He still had a balance, a restraint, a dignity, even a decency, which they lacked. I could make Edward Beecher sound ridiculous by paraphrasing his wildest notions about reincarnation; but I would only need to quote a few lines from the most excessive statements in his monumental *Conflict of Ages* to make my reader know that she would not laugh to his face, that Edward Beecher must be taken seriously. To quote Catharine Esther Beecher, however, ludicrously grim with moral rage in *Truth Stranger Than Fiction*, or to read from Little Eva's death scene in *Uncle Tom's Cabin*, is, first of all, at some level to amuse; only later can one ask for reflection and analysis. Edward Beecher was perhaps misguided; but his sisters were inflated, overdone, and the difference is vital. He was not always balanced, but they occasionally lacked all sense of proportion. This has nothing to do with propriety. Once, when Horace Bushnell was in London, he felt neglected and unknown, but he consoled himself with the thought that "anything which sets a man practically in his place, is a mental good, a good of manners, of feeling—dignity itself."[86] It was precisely this precondition to intellectual honesty—a sense of proper place, the true and indispensable "room of one's own"—that the middle-class northern woman, no matter how intelligent, lacked.

Both exalted and ignored, was the lady the savior of her nation, or a slave to an unappreciative master? Defined in unexplored extremes, she inevitably often dealt in them herself, and encouraged those segments of her culture most committed to the avoidance of self-examination. Inevitably she was profoundly disaffected from politics. It was not simply that she was barred from the polls and her rights; she had little to gain from the sense of placing, the awareness of class and interest, of societal structure, which genuine political consciousness fosters. When she obtained the vote in 1920, she used it with indifference; she voted with her men, not because she was sheeplike as various commentators claimed, but because, paradoxically, politics were not *her* politics. Sentimentalism had for too long served her needs better; for sentimentalism might be defined as the political sense obfuscated or gone rancid. Sentimentalism, unlike the modes of genuine sensibility, never exists except in tandem with failed political consciousness. A relatively recent phenomenon whose appearance is linked with capitalist development, sentimentalism seeks and offers the distraction of sheer publicity. Sentimentalism is a cluster of ostensibly private feelings which always attains public and conspicuous expression. Privacy functions in the rituals of sentimentalism only for the sake of titillation, as a convention to be violated. Involved as it is with the exhibition and commercialization of the self, sentimentalism cannot exist without an audience. It has no content but its own exposure, and it invests exposure with a kind of final significance. Little wonder that

Harriet Beecher Stowe closed her career as a show-off. And she had plenty of company.

It is fitting, I think, that my chosen period—which covers the "feminization" or sentimentalization of northeastern culture—ends with a series of scandals, most notably, as we have seen, Harriet Beecher Stowe's notorious exposé of Lord Byron's relations with his half-sister Augusta and Henry Ward Beecher's much-publicized affair with Libby Tilton. Incest underlay both scandals: brother and sister, minister and parishioner were advertising in bed as in print their rather unhealthy, and not altogether willing, need of one another. Like Stowe's New York novels and the writings of the male sentimentalists, these affairs suggested what could be called the mirror-phenomenon increasingly dominant in American life. Replication of the self, absorption in the self, disguises confusion as to the purpose of the self; politics yields to publicity. Many newspapermen and cartoonists rebaptized their trade during the years of the Beecher-Byron controversy and the Beecher-Tilton trial: some papers devoted as many as ten reporters to the coverage of the Brooklyn imbroglio. In a self-immersed and self-congratulatory culture unable to generate the genuine tensions and purposefulness of criticism, only scandal remains to provide the sense of ritual excitation without which mass communal life is intolerable.

The triumph of sentimentalism in nineteenth-century America is never clearer than when one realizes the relatively small number of romantic writers and theologians, male or female, this country produced.[87] For, however one defines the romantic impulse—and I do not pretend to be doing that adequately here—it clearly involves a genuinely political and historical sense, a spirit of critical protest alien to the sentimentalism so often confused with it. Romantics such as Goethe, Schiller, Keats, Shelley, Coleridge, or even Byron never lost touch with ethical concerns as the mainspring of their inspiration. Byron's once-celebrated death in the cause of Greek liberty may seem self-glorifying, even diversionary, to some of us now; it is still today —as it was to the Greeks then—a profoundly different matter from staying at home, writing odes to Greece, and dying in bed. The unmistakable exaltation of the self found in the works of the romantics was a desperate effort to find in private resources an antidote and an alternative to the forces of modernizing society; it was not, like sentimentalist self-absorption, a commercialization of the inner life.

The test which distinguishes romanticism from sentimentalism is that its language, its rhetoric, no matter how strained or foreign to modern ears, has not—to use Hemingway's phrase—"gone bad"; language, like that of the sentimentalists, which has utterly capitulated to the drift of its times invariably "goes bad." Perhaps we would not write today in the way Shelley, for example, did. Lines like

Hail to thee, blithe Spirit!
  Bird thou never wert,
That from heaven, or near it,
  Pourest thy full heart
In profuse strains of unpremeditated art

may ring a bit grandiose. But we understand that the relationship of such language to its age is fundamentally healthy, is one we might wish in our very different fashion to approximate. The language of Victorian religiosity, whether it appears in the pages of Dickens or of Mrs. Sigourney, we at once reject, at least consciously, as a useful model. Mrs. Sigourney wrote about birds too:

Beautiful boy, with the sunny hair,
What wouldst thou do with that birdling rare?
It belongs to the sky—it hath wings, you know,
Loosen your clasping, and let him go.[88]

We find so much of this rancid writing in our nineteenth-century literature. Mrs. Sigourney's present disrepute by no means obviates her enormous popularity among her contemporaries. And where is our Goethe, our Schiller, our Hegel, our Byron, our Shelley, our Keats, our George Eliot? One could go on, but the point seems evident. Our romantics were opposed and conflicted, prone to compromises and failures of productivity in ways different from, if not more intense than, anything known by their English and European contemporaries. Yet in literature as in theology, there were such figures. And without some discussion of them, the story of Victorian sentimentalism in America would not be complete. They are all the more heroic, all the more valuable to us, precisely because their achievement was so rare and so threatened. Their romanticism was inevitably characterized and defined by their defiance of sentimentalism and of incipient mass culture. They had to try to move in straitjackets, and motion, not unpredictably, often became contortion—stunted, incomplete. Yet it was motion, and all the more significant because it took place under conditions and against odds that would increasingly prevail in America and elsewhere.

PART THREE

Protest

CASE STUDIES IN
AMERICAN ROMANTICISM

8

~❦~

MARGARET FULLER AND
THE DISAVOWAL OF FICTION

"A Sharp Identity"

In July 1850, Margaret Fuller was returning to America after participating
in the ill-fated Italian struggle for liberty. She never reached land; her ship
foundered on a rock just off Fire Island and she drowned. Her body was
not washed ashore. Ralph Waldo Emerson, Fuller's friend from earlier days,
lamented that America had been waiting to welcome her.[1] Elizabeth Barrett
Browning, a more recent acquaintance, believed that Fuller, as a woman
who had dared to hold profoundly unconventional views, would have met
with little sympathy and less understanding in her native land. Browning,
a strong admirer of Fuller, concluded the American feminist was, in fact,
better off dead.[2] In any case America was denied, or spared, a confrontation
with one of its genuine heroines, a woman uniquely equipped and determined to challenge the political, artistic, and sexual assumptions of her
society. A crucial moment of reckoning was indefinitely postponed.

We know who she was, more or less.[3] Emerson's difficult and homely
friend, the brightest woman in ante-bellum New England, she edited the
transcendental periodical *The Dial* and invited Boston's blue-stockings to
take part in efforts at self-education called "Conversations." Increasingly
radical in her maturity, she worked as a journalist in New York, eventually
joined the patriot cause in Italy, had a child by an Italian count much
younger than herself, and died at forty. We know her story, but genuine
recognition has been slow and intermittent. Margaret Fuller is not an easy
woman to face.

Fifty years after her death, she was profoundly to trouble Henry James as he tried to write about the period of Italian history she had known at first hand; he claimed that the "Margaret-ghost" haunted him as no other could.[4] In elucidating her strange power over him, he brings us very close to Fuller and the issue she poses. She suggested for James the boundary between fantasy and reality, literature and history, a distinction fraught for him with sexual connotations. One critic has described James as the "great feminine novelist of a feminine age of letters";[5] certainly he was preoccupied with the sexual identity of the novel and the novelist. From the start of his literary career in the 1860s, he had insisted to the reading public, and himself, that fiction, the traditional province of women, be accorded all the seriousness of history, the customary province of men.[6] In 1903, when he made the statement about Fuller, James was ostensibly engaged in writing actual history, a biography of William Wetmore Story. Story, an American sculptor, lived with his wife in Rome in the late 1840s during Fuller's stay there. The city was then in an active state of siege; Rome was crucial in Italy's unsuccessful fight for independence, a fight to which Fuller made an active and impassioned contribution. Significantly, James concentrates on a nostalgic invocation of a lost gracious Europe and largely ignores the military and political events taking place. His biography is, in a sense, as much fiction as history.[7] Yet the figure of Margaret Fuller, a close friend of the Storys, keeps disrupting the leisurely and protected idyll James creates. She interrupts the Storys' breakfast hour with news of the war; she diverts them from a stroll to visit a hospital for wounded Italian soldiers; she constantly suggests some crisis the Storys and James, with their shared preference for peacetime occupations, are evading. James plays with the possibility of dismissing Fuller as a minor, even a comic figure, but he cannot do it. As he was aware, Fuller herself was engaged at the period he covers in writing a journalistic history of the Romans' struggle against their French invaders. Fuller is allowed on stage as James's conscience; she questions his self-announced and reiterated role as "historian." He was disturbed by her because he realized that, legendary as her "eloquence" had been, she was fundamentally interested (in his words) not in "talk"—his own creative obsession—but in "facts." As Perry Miller has noted, James knew Fuller was a "heroine," but it seems unlikely that he ever used her, as Miller has suggested, as a model for any of his female characters.[8] James knew there was a radical disjuncture between Fuller and the heroine of fiction—a creature who mattered as vitally to him as to any woman living by "the immediate aid of the novel," to use his famous phrase—and he respected that disjuncture; she was too "angular" to exist comfortably in any world he might create. Indeed, it is greatly to James's credit and central to his genius that he could acknowledge Fuller's importance, threatening as it was to him; she might not, one suspects, have been capable of an equal generosity of perception toward him. James was struck by the major "fact" about Margaret Fuller: her achievement of a "sharp identity," an effort, he noted, "unaided and ungraced."[9]

James's instinct that Fuller did not belong to his material is important and provocative. Fuller was and is so disquieting because she does not lend herself to the fantasy life, to the essentially fictional identity, associated with women. Her image can be attacked or ignored, but it is not malleable. Fuller was finally not even metaphorically a heroine of fiction, though it was a part she coveted and explored. I said in Chapter Two that the essence of the fictional heroine is her ability to attract flattery without having to solicit it. But Fuller was palpably and embarrassingly unpatronized; "unaided and ungraced" as James recognized, she obviously did all her own advance work, and it was hard going. "I now know all the people worth knowing in America, and I find no intellect comparable to my own," she reportedly told a group of friends.[10] She had to flatter herself or teach others how to do it for her, and that made her resentful. A past-mistress of the innuendoes of martyrdom, with an air both exalted and exhausted, she advertised her vulnerability by her intermittent querulousness. She cut an acquaintaince when he talked to her, by his own confession, "as I talk to others."[11] She openly demanded everything from anyone who knew or would know her; an ultimate effort was the simple price of admission to the sanctum. She expected a "friend" to provide her with "the clue to the labyrinth of my being."[12] The very assumption of the difficulty of approach implied in her metaphor might well repel. Unlike Mrs. Hale or Mrs. Sigourney, Fuller did not talk of herself in terms of "influence"; she saw herself as a complex, rich, and perhaps hopeless problem whose confrontation might precipitate and tax her friends' finest resources. She could not be absorbed; she had to be dealt with. One can hardly imagine Fuller adopting a sprightly *nom de plume* like "Fanny Forrester" to advertise her assimilability. In a culture which was beginning to identify femininity with male relaxation, Fuller found few takers.

Fuller was inevitably drawn to the romanticism which found no home in her native land. Here again names are important. It is striking that Fuller was the only American woman of the nineteenth century known—like the heroines of contemporary romantic European fiction ("Consuelo," "Corinne")—by her first name alone. In an age when female writers were politely referred to as "Mrs. Sigourney," "Mrs. Stowe," and "Miss Warner," Fuller was called by friends and acquaintances "Margaret." By implication, there could be many "Fannys" or "Harriets" or "Catharines"; there was only one "Margaret." She was a romantic. Fuller's great romantic peers and predecessors abroad, Madame de Staël and George Sand,[13] however, had special precedents, sanctions, and abilities denied their American counter-part for making their intricacies in some sense part of their allure. Fuller might emulate and claim their position; she could not approximate the circumstances which made it tenable. It was her often debilitating distinc-tion that she proudly fought the same battle in which de Staël and Sand engaged without the same armor. De Staël and Sand were beautiful, well-born, wealthy; they had access to a sympathetic milieu, and dozens of devoted lovers. Fuller was not good-looking, and it galled her to be "ugly";[14] she did not know a man's love until she was thirty-seven, although she often sought it; she did not possess or inherit wealth and social standing, and most of her major career decisions were determined, and constrained, in part by monetary considerations;[15] she was as brilliant as Sand or de Staël, but America provided none of the traditional means of utilizing and rewarding intellectual women which France offered. Her "Conversations" could not rival de Staël's or Sand's salons; Fuller's parties of the intellect were pioneer-ing efforts, not accepted rituals. Covert revolt, not overt acculturation, provided what vivacity they could boast.

Fuller's special quality was her invincible historicism; she had nothing to give nor to rely on but herself. Her case was significant and fascinating because it rested perforce solely on its own merits.[16] As a young woman, she wished desperately to be adored, idealized. From necessity and tempera-ment, in the end, however, she sought achievement more than flattery. She lacked some of the attributes appropriate to the status of literary heroine, and the discovery of this fact gave her intense pain, but she also came to recognize that the status itself was not equal to her needs or her rights. Fuller's life can be viewed as an effort to find what she called her "sovereign self" by disavowing fiction for history, the realm of "feminine" fantasy for the realm of "masculine" reality. She recognized, moreover, that such an opposition reflected culturally imposed polarities which she disdained, al-though she did not always have the energy or the resources to define, or redefine, her terms adequately.

Fuller felt, with justice, that her life was immensely difficult, if not impossible. How, as a woman living in her society, was she to sail safely between Scylla and Charybdis; reject the narcotic of narcissism on the one hand, and escape the penalty of exile on the other? Fuller was often histri-onic and over-solemn in her expressed sense of impending personal doom. She took the measure of her world when she assumed that her suffering would equal her aspirations and her achievements; her air of martyrdom was shrewd analysis, if in somewhat sodden lyrical disguise. One adoring young woman noted that Fuller's face was "full of the marks of pain";[17] Fuller was barely thirty at the time, but, whatever her vanity, she proudly exhibited the scars of suffering. Fuller protected and sanctioned herself by commiserating profusely with the cost her life exacted of her; but she never thought she had done, could have done, or should have done, otherwise. Self-pity never became sentimentalism; it never seriously sapped her boldness.

Fuller did all we can ask of an individual living in a historical context mainly repressive of the best in her. When she could, she walked toward what she sensed as the opening area of significance; when she could not, she dragged herself, crowded herself, edged herself, into new territory. If that meant falling over a cliff, she fell. Like Harriet Beecher Stowe, she could not do away with what was weakest, most culturally damaged in herself; unlike Stowe, she held it as a curious kind of hostage to what she believed strongest, most respectworthy in herself. The laughter that Fuller's claims for herself inspired in her own day and since is instructive. She nags the American imagination; immortalized in a curious oblivion, left in the stocks of history, she seems to suggest the perils for women of insisting on attention for their integral selves. You don't get it by insisting, she discovered, but she also raised the question as to whether you get it if you don't insist. She could never fully admit or believe that she expected to survive, but she picked the place where she wanted to go down. She never wavered in her determination to live her own life and not someone else's. In this determination was comprised whatever genuinely clarified meaning she gave to the rejection of "fiction" or "fantasy" for "history" or "reality"; she would not be bought off with vicarious experience or power. If she could not always find the first-hand material she sought, she could always reject the second-hand. Her energies were in part consumed in the struggle such an existence entailed, but she had no choice; Margaret Fuller's business was salvaging her opposition intact. She found some aid and much resistance in her effort.

The Legacy of Timothy Fuller: The Will to Action

By her early twenties, Margaret Fuller had the reputation of being the best-read person, female or male, in New England. In a sense, this was a reputation which was planned for her before her birth by an eccentric father as ambitious for his first-born as he was for himself. Timothy Fuller was an active influential politician and lawyer until his well-known opposition to Andrew Jackson cut short his career in 1832; before and after his fall, he always had time and energy to spare for the personal supervision of Margaret's education. He trained her rigorously and exhaustively in the classics and history.[18] Her young life was devoted, Fuller recollected later, to studying and demonstrating what she had learned for the most exacting of instructors. "With me," Fuller concluded dramatically, "much of life was devoured in the bud."[19]

When Fuller wrote this around 1840, she was recording changed concepts of child-rearing as well as self-pity, but her assessment of her childhood is not altogether a fair one, nor one to which she herself always subscribed. It is possible that, despite her honesty, she occasionally preferred to stress her father's aspirations for her rather than admit her own ambition. At age eleven, away at school, she wrote home to Mr. Fuller: "Be assured that I will do my utmost to acquit myself well. I think of nothing else."[20] She was soon in first place in the academic rolls of Dr. Parks's school, if not in the hearts of her fellow-students. The German scholarship and literature she read in her early twenties, in a successful effort to become one of the leading experts on contemporary German culture in America, she mastered on her own. A major quarrel arose between father and daughter in 1832 when Mr. Fuller wished to retire after his political defeat to rural Groton and Margaret wanted to remain in Cambridge to consolidate and display her scholarly achievements. Margaret always regretted the terse enmity in which the two lived in Groton shortly before Mr. Fuller's unexpected death in 1835, but nothing could have better underscored their essential similarity. In any case, whether she was the object or the heir of her father's obsessive intellectual ambition, Margaret Fuller acknowledgedly benefited by his training in major ways.

For there is another perspective from which to view Timothy Fuller's schooling of his daughter other than the one which highlights its very real brutality. As a contemporary noted, there was nothing unusual about the work expected from the six-year-old Margaret by her father—except that it was demanded from a girl. Frederick Hedges, later a friend of Margaret's, and early destined by his family for Harvard and the ministry, underwent a similar educational ordeal.[21] The point is less that Margaret's father wished she were a boy than that he treated her with as much seriousness as if she were one. Although Timothy Fuller had married a lovely-looking woman and was to have one beautiful daughter, Margaret's younger sister Ellen, he asked of Margaret not feminine grace and imprecision but masculine fidelity to fact, to "common sense." In an age when women were taught to appropriate a special language of politeness and complaisance, Mr. Fuller forbade Margaret the use of phrases like "I am mistaken" and "it may be so."[22] He forcibly cut her off from the feminine subculture of etiquette books and sentimental novels.

Fuller felt her father's training had suppressed her "dreams," her tendency to "infatuation,"[23] but she always remembered he had paid her the final compliment, one which ages of chivalry had seldom accorded women, of criticizing her. It was only when she was terribly and apparently fatally sick in her mid-twenties that he expressed his opinion of her, and it was a characteristic blend of exuberance and judiciousness: she had her "defects," he believed, but no real "faults."²⁴ As Fuller later acknowledged, he taught her what almost none of her feminine peers possessed: "self respect," "self reliance." He subjected her to none of the "bewildering flattery"²⁵ which makes its recipient dependent on its donor for her sense of identity. She had, no matter how precariously, what Horace Bushnell found so helpful: a sense of her place. Although Fuller would court and receive flattery, even homage, in her later years, she tried to use it to sustain her in her pursuit of truth, not to deter her from it; she continually sought ego-confirmation in order that she might learn to do without it. In 1842 she wrote a friend: "I would have my friends tender of me not because I am frail but because I am capable of strength:—patient because they see in me a principle that must, at last, harmonize all the exuberance of my character."²⁶ Mr. Fuller fostered in Margaret his own passion for accuracy, a passion which in the more unstable, imaginative, and brilliant daughter deepened into a profoundly ethical concern for veracity, for reality itself. "Give me truth; cheat me by no illusion,"²⁷ she once wrote; and the words could have served as the motto of her life.

Timothy Fuller set "masculine" ideals of character for his daughter, and he gave her "masculine" subjects to study. First at Harvard and later in his legal and political work, he had deeply imbibed the rhetoric and philosophy which the generation who fought the American Revolution had drawn from classical Rome. At a time when the "accomplishments" of music, art, domestic crafts, the polite languages, and *belles lettres* were stressed in feminine education, when it was a moot point whether Latin, much less Greek, should be included in the young lady's curriculum, Mr. Fuller made the classics, especially those of Rome, Margaret's staple fare. She responded with intense and long-lived enthusiasm. In her fragmentary autobiography, she tried to sum up the lesson of Latin antiquity as she had understood it. "History" was more important than "literature." "It was degeneracy for a Roman to use the pen: his life was in the day. . . . The will, the resolve of Man! It has been expressed—fully expressed!"²⁸ The books she venerated urged their readers not to read or write, but to live. Mr. Fuller, as Margaret proudly noted in later years, was no mere "word-hero";²⁹ he, like the Romans they both admired, was a speaker and man of action, a man conscious of history. Margaret drew close to her father during their unhappy Groton years only when she helped him in his researches in the American past. Thomas Jefferson, who struck her as being as many-sided as Goethe, was a major discovery; his achievement, she wrote a friend, reconciled her to America. All her life, Fuller liked to identify herself with the American eagle, and to do so was not mere self-dramatization; it testified to the fact that she had been trained in the rhetorical and political tradition of the American Revolution. Unlike many of her peers, she felt no need to minimize or exalt the founding fathers. She squarely defined their legacy as the struggle for independence, by violence if necessary, and she expended her finest adult energies in rescuing it from obsolescence.

The difficulty for Margaret Fuller from the start was in reconciling her historical consciousness with her feminine identity. It was her pride to claim open access to the whole world of achievement, and she learned enormously from a series of outstanding men: first her father, later Emerson, Goethe, Mickiewicz, and Mazzini. Yet she always felt incumbent on her an act of sexual translation which she found sometimes hard to make: there were masculine words and actions she valued for which she could find no readily available equivalents in the feminine vocabulary. "I love best to be a woman," she lamented in her early thirties, "but womanhood is at present too straitly-bounded to give me scope."[30]

Since there was no overt institutional encouragement or acknowledgment of Fuller's intellectual progress, it had to appear both self-motivated and subversive. Harvard, in whose vicinity Fuller lived until her early thirties, of course excluded women. Since she handily outtalked and outthought Harvard's finest graduates, she suggested the possible superfluity, for the genuinely gifted, of the male-created and male-servicing system of higher education which was New England's pride. No one who met her during her lifetime—and she encountered many of the formidable intelligences of her day—failed to leave on record his impression that he had met one who took the measure of his mind, one who was literally "peerless."[31] Even as a young woman, Fuller was tutoring and inspiring some of Harvard's finest students. In the early 1830s, James Freeman Clarke, a close friend of Fuller's and destined to become a leading Unitarian minister, wrote her that he expected her to head a great new school of American letters, of which he would gladly be a humble member.[32] In Victorian America, however, to acknowledge Fuller's astonishing intellect was at least in part to condemn her. Clarke repeatedly told her, to her clear chagrin, that he considered her far too superior to the rest of her sex to be the object of his romantic affections.[33] Later James Russell Lowell parodied her intellectual superiority and self-involvement: "I myself introduced, I myself, I alone, I to my land's better life authors solely my own," he makes his absurdly pretentious "Miranda" assert in "A Fable for Critics."[34] Emerson acknowledged that every time he saw her she had palpably grown and advanced since their last encounter.[35] Every step she took, she took alone; every step seemed to prove something about feminine potential and masculine privilege which most of New England's male elite did not want to know. Viewed from their perspective, her progress was an insult. Hawthorne was not alone in his vicious hope that this woman who had tried to be "her own Redeemer" would prove "a very woman after all," no better than "the weakest of her sisters."[36] It was immensely difficult for Fuller not to internalize this kind of condemnation as a will to failure; indeed, she quite literally exhausted vital powers in trying to evaluate such rejection and respond to it rightly. The difficulty was that her critics were in at least one sense right. Her accomplishments did define her as an outcast, even as a freak; she had almost no feminine precedents or models to help her believe in what she was and discover what she wanted to become.

Among women of her personal acquaintance, Fuller found no one whose life could serve as a blueprint for hers. Her mother, a self-sacrificing, gentle woman who tended her garden and her numerous offspring with affection if not astuteness, clearly counted for little in Fuller's childhood. As a child, she had ambiguous dreams about her mother dying; only much later did she find in Mrs. Fuller's placidity a resource.[37] In an effort to supplement Mrs. Fuller's maternal image, Fuller was persistently drawn to women older than herself. In girlhood, she attached herself to a charming and cultured visitor from England. Later she became intimate with the childless, English-born Mrs. John Farrar. The well-bred and intelligent wife of a distinguished Harvard professor, Mrs. Farrar was the author of the best etiquette guide of the day, *The Young Lady's Friend*. She was a friend indeed to the young but not always ladylike Fuller, correcting her manners and offering to take her abroad in 1835. A woman, however, who believed the "great business" of feminine life was "shopping," and who cautioned her readers to beware lest their voices be "heard above the gentle hum around you, either in laughter or conversation,"[38] had only limited usefulness as mentor to a girl whose wit was to make Emerson laugh more than he liked and whose compelling conversation was destined to silence professional talkers.

Looking for models outside her own circle of personal acquaintances, Fuller found, especially in America, a relatively barren field. In a period when ambitious American women were increasingly seeking careers in literature, she disavowed fiction. Despite her admiration for the imaginative work of George Sand and Madame de Staël, Fuller only once directly essayed a work of fiction, a short story which has since disappeared.[39] Refusing to write for the increasingly powerful *Godey's*, she condemned the magazine literature typical of contemporary feminine subculture as "flimsy beyond any texture that was ever spun or dreamed of by the mind of man," a mere "opiate." Her sense of mission was too intense and too entirely self-centered to allow her to try fully to understand the causes of these deficiencies. There were real limits to Fuller's sisterliness: she seldom talked long with those who functioned—whatever their reasons—as opponents to her precariously held sense of superiority. She summed up her utter disavowal of the burgeoning ladies' culture in a word: it lacked "reality."[40] Feminine literature as it was beginning to flourish in Fuller's day offered, to her mind, an evasion of American history, not an entrance into it. The only American woman author Fuller ever paid tribute to was the novelist Catharine Maria Sedgwick, and she bestowed on her very tempered praise. Fuller liked the older writer's freedom from sentimentality, her common sense, her interest in history.[41] The "domestic" novel, the specialty of the women who succeeded Sedgwick, had little to say to Margaret Fuller. Fuller felt no special hostility toward domestic life and labor, but she had no animus driving her to exalt its claims. She wanted to write critical and political essays, an ambition never widespread among literate American women, and in Fuller's day fast disappearing altogether.

Not surprisingly, Fuller was most drawn toward women who had participated actively in the making and the talking of history; she admired the heroines of revolution and rhetoric, women who, like the founding fathers, had acted, spoken, and written for the furtherance of a cause. It tells us a good deal about Fuller's implicit analysis of the role of women in America that the only women she found at least in part worthy of emulation were all foreigners: Madame Roland, Madame de Staël, and George Sand. Madame Roland wrote her Girondist husband's tracts and lost her life during the French Terror for her commitment to the distinction between republicanism and anarchy. Her memoir, written in prison, was a model of the classic art of apology. Fuller found her an exception to her sex, of "Roman strength and simpleness of mind," not "sentimental," able to see beyond "mere personal experience."[42] Madame de Staël interpreted and publicized the new romantic German culture in France, although Napoleon banned her books. When de Staël asked her close friend Talleyrand if Napoleon was as intelligent as she, he responded, "he isn't as brave";[43] and on numerous occasions, Madame de Staël made this compliment appear simple observation. Fuller decided young that she wanted to resemble the "brilliant" de Staël, rather than the "useful" Maria Edgeworth.[44] George Sand left her husband in 1830 to come live in Paris with her first lover just when, as she put it, "the Revolution . . . [was] in permanent session."[45] It was a many-sided and prolonged revolution, which Sand as a woman and an artist never ceased to support during Fuller's lifetime. Her novels, as she was the first to admit, were novels of ideas, propaganda on a high level. Fuller followed Sand's career with passionate interest; her friends constantly compared the two women, who were only six years apart in age. When Fuller met Sand in Paris in 1847, the older writer looked at her and, with her usual instinct for the right words, said slowly and distinctly, "C'est vous."[46] Fuller loved her then, but she had long defended the French novelist in a provincial culture which read her to condemn her.

Madame Roland was dead before Fuller's birth, however, and neither de Staël nor Sand fully satisfied her needs. She scented in both, and not inaccurately, self-indulgence; they had been "fed on flattery." They were not Romans: sensibility vitiated their rhetoric. They had allowed themselves to exploit the weaknesses traditionally permissible, even encouraged, in their sex. Of de Staël, Fuller noted in 1844: "while she was instructing you as a mind, she wished to be admired as a woman; sentimental tears often dimmed the eagle glance."[47] Discovering the same failing in Sand, she queried with anguish, "Will there never be a being to combine a man's mind and woman's heart, and who yet finds life too rich to weep over? Never?"[48] Fuller was hypercritical on many occasions, but this was not one of them. Her tone was one of anguish, not condemnation. She needed desperately to believe that a total integrity, the only goal she saw as worth attaining, was attainable; and how could she believe it if there was no woman who had ever achieved it? She was never unaware that the narcissism to which the absence of models would temporarily drive her was finally more limiting than liberating.

The Transcendental Years: "Eloquence" as Narcissism

In 1835, at twenty-five, Margaret Fuller was in many respects at an impasse. Released from the pressures of Timothy Fuller's dictatorial rule, she assumed many of his responsibilities, but the role of head of the family was for her a duty, not a vocation. Marriage seemed unlikely; she disliked teaching. Her ambivalent awareness that she had few models to imitate, her confused predilection for life over literature, her fascination with rhetoric and talk, drew her naturally to the transcendental group in Concord. She was closely associated with them until 1843. Almost all the members of the group were, like Fuller, rebellious Unitarians, elitists dedicated to preaching and proselytizing, interested in romanticism and many varieties of liberal, even radical, reform. Most fundamentally, however, transcendentalism represented an at least theoretical commitment to experience over erudition, and, by this definition, Fuller was a transcendentalist *par excellence*. Transcendentalism was for Fuller as for few of her fellow-transcendentalists, however, a bridge, albeit a shaky one, from literary to historical consciousness.

When Fuller heard Emerson proclaim his scorn for over-reliance on reading, when she assisted at Bronson Alcott's Temple School where conversation, not memorization, was stressed,[49] she observed closely and seriously. Her growing distrust of New England bookishness and its oppressive role in the process of feminine socialization is abundantly manifest in this period. Although she had trained herself to be a scholar of monumental proportions and was gathering materials for a major study of Goethe, she kept evading actual scholarly achievement. She told Emerson she preferred to do a sketchy and imperfect work on Goethe rather than allow herself to linger too long under his influence.[50] She finally contented herself with a short, brilliant essay on the German writer. She required no reading of the participants in the "Conversations" she held for interested women every winter from 1839 to 1843. This gave an air of insubstantiality to many of the discussions, which ranged loftily but vaguely over vast topics and ideas. The nature of the Greek religion, the meaning of "life," were questions that apparently could be debated on the spot with no external aids or preparation. During one of the 1841 Conversations, Fuller told her class "she could keep up no intimacy with books. She loved a book dearly for a while but ... she was sure to take a disgust to it, to outgrow it." Having gleaned what an author had to give, she "tired" of him—even in the case of Shakespeare.[51]

There was bravado in this remark, of the kind essential to the liberating therapy the "Conversations" were intended to provide for Fuller and her feminine friends.[52] Fuller's involvement in women's education, as well as her observation of her culture more generally, had convinced her, as we have seen, that while girls were taught even more subjects in school than their brothers, they learned next to nothing because they were not called upon to "reproduce," to use what they knew.[53] In her Conversations, Fuller was addressing women who had read too much, listened too much, and thought for themselves too little. She could not teach them, as Goethe advised, to study the natural world, for she herself had little bent that way; but she could at least help them to observe the workings of their own minds, to be critics rather than consumers. And her partly assumed iconoclasm was a way of throwing them back on themselves, of making them take themselves seriously, if only because she allowed them to tap no other resource. Sarah Clarke, one of Fuller's friends, explained perceptively the cause of the legendary and fanatic love which younger women yielded Fuller: "You felt exhilarated by the compliment of being found out, and even that she had cared to find you out."[54] Fuller acted as if what her pupils felt and said was not merely decorative, but consequential. The revolt against books, against the role of reader, which she enacted for her feminine pupils, and herself, was a symbolic protest against the derivative lives to which their society consigned them; they, Fuller insisted, were *originals*.

Yet, if Fuller was clear during her transcendental period about what she was rejecting, she was much less sure about what she was putting in its place. No one can read the accounts of the Conversations, not to speak of the correspondence with Emerson, and escape the realization that Fuller did not yet know her true direction. She was in a state of acute opposition; and her answer, not finally a successful one, was to offer herself repeatedly, insistently, even belligerently, as the living example, as if attention to her presence would generate or dictate the content of what she was to represent. Fuller's pretensions at this time were enormous. Her friends, following her example, called her a "sibyl," a "seer"; and she was, for she was desperately engaged in trying to prophesy—herself. Emerson, James Freeman Clarke, and William Henry Channing (1810–84) all found Fuller similar to de Staël's romantic heroine Corinne in her abilities as an "improvisatrice."[55] Julia Ward Howe called her "grandiloquent."[56] Yet Fuller was not "acting" in any artificial sense: she fell into a form of behavioral rhetoric partly as a natural translation of the classical prose she had memorized in girlhood; partly, and more importantly, as a complex means of self-anticipation.

Fuller had no real models, as we have seen, close at hand; so, as she apparently imitated "Corinne" or de Staël, she was actually using grandiose gesture as a way of objectifying herself in order then to have a model. At this point in her career, she was trying, in a rather special sense, to be a literary heroine. Fuller's rather heavy insistence on suffering and her mystic powers[57] in the late 1830s and early 1840s was part of her claim to this role. It was narcissism, but a narcissism born of utter necessity and one that was somewhere intended to self-destruct, if only through its own excesses. Emerson saw astutely that Margaret wanted to be a "living statue"—and one always placed to best advantage.[58] He failed altogether to see that she had to be her own precedent, that she had first to embody what she somewhere wished to transcend; he had little compassion for the terrors inherent in such a procedure. Her "mountainous Me"—to use Emerson's description of her self-importance—her monotony of self-magnification, were necessary defenses: she had to claim tragic stature. Witty on occasion herself, she always found it painful to be the object of wit. Staying at the Emersons' in 1840, she was troubled by her charming but ne'er-do-well brother-in-law, the poet Ellery Channing, also a visitor, who liked to amuse himself at her expense. Teasing her for her seriousness, he criticized: "You are too *ideal*. You make every body restless by always wanting to grow forward. Now I like to grow backward too." Emerson was intrigued with such lightheartedness, which made Fuller's earnestness appear lumbering. Fuller resolved somberly and ponderously in her journal: "I must not let him [Ellery Channing] disturb me. This child of genius must not make me lay aside the armour without which I had long since lain bleeding on the battlefield. I am what I am."[59] She could tire of her "earnestness," but she was too beleaguered; she could not afford to laugh at herself.

De Staël's heroine, Corinne, to whom Fuller was so often compared, was an artist gifted in many directions, but chiefly she was a brilliant spontaneous talker, an "improvisatrice"; she displayed "eloquence."[60] There was no other aspect of the narcissistic role of romantic heroine which Fuller found so congenial. "Eloquence" certainly offered partial solutions to Margaret Fuller's most basic problems as an American, a woman, and an artist; yet it was an answer she inevitably strained to the breaking point. It is important to remember that the "eloquence" so prized by Emerson, Fuller, and their friends meant to them public speaking, a high form of that rhetoric on which Fuller had been raised. Emerson found "eloquence," although rarely, in the impassioned speeches of Daniel Webster.[61] "Eloquence" was in essence oratory, a meeting place between literature and life, and a genuine flourishing American form[62] which Timothy Fuller, lawyer and politician, had doubtless taught and exemplified to his daughter. The American Revolution which they had studied together had begun with just such rhetoric: schoolchildren then as now believed that the statement "Give me liberty or give me death" was equivalent to the onset of hostilities. In a country as new and as absorbed in material progress as America, spontaneous "eloquence," which took less time and training than the production of an epic or a novel, was bound to win highest honors. To be a talker, to be "eloquent," was to be American.

Both Margaret Fuller's detractors and her admirers in her own day and since knew that she could talk incomparably better than she could write,[63] although few of them understood why. Emerson, contemplating a biography of Margaret Fuller, recorded his fear that he and her other male friends lacked the "courage" to confront her life, a life whose activity, audacity, and integrity made theirs seem cowardly and trifling.[64] Nevertheless, he let himself dismiss her finally in his journal as representing "an interesting hour" in New England culture.[65] Already the author of dozens of immortal essays and poems himself, Emerson judged that Fuller's "influence" would not outlive her. She had talked, while he had written. Fuller's failure as a writer was not as entire as Emerson liked to believe, but it is true that her early poetry was, as she said, "all rhetorical and impassioned,"[66] and the didactic critical prose she produced in her transcendental years awkward and incomplete. Yet during these years she was consolidating her reputation as one of the greatest talkers in America. And her masterful late prose would demonstrate that her problem was not a simple lack of talent for writing.

There are many possible reasons for Fuller's over-reliance on the spoken medium during much of her adult life in America, not least of which was the fact that she was a woman. In a society that offered little encouragement for intellectual women, Fuller needed the stimulus of a present audience to dare to display her full powers. She had been denied the self-confidence needed for long-term productivity, for working without the reassurance of immediate attention and approval. William Story called Fuller "her own worst enemy,"[67] but he forgot that this role can be itself a punishment imposed by society on its deviants and rebels. Could she have been able to imagine, as she took up her pen, an American audience willing to accept philosophical, political, and ethical instruction from a feminine mind? The presence and popularity of *Godey's* and its ilk were hardly encouraging. "When I meet people," she explained, "it is easy to adapt myself to them, but when I write, it is into another world."[68] She could only believe such an audience existed when she saw it in front of her. Utterly dependent on the live "inspiration" which provided an unacknowledged cover for sexual rebellion, Fuller penalized herself for her superior intelligence by sabotaging its reliability and narrowing its range of impact. Not surprisingly, Fuller did her finest writing before 1843 in the informal, personal mode of the letter. There she could best sustain the illusion of an actual audience. She wished, as she wrote Emerson, to be and portray "a soul ever rushing forth in tides of genial life."[69] She wanted to embody herself in her words: as a result, all writing to a certain extent failed her. Only as a talker did she feel entire confidence and conviction.

Yet even Fuller's legendary "eloquence" was poured forth during her transcendental period as much to testify by its force that she was right as to reveal what she was right about. She lamented to her closest friends that she had found no one sufficiently capacious and challenging to draw out her full conversational powers. This was no boast, but a plea and one with real pathos. She felt tormented that she could procure so little help in knowing herself; she still half-believed that if she could *talk* well and long enough she would find herself in the dazzling flow of words. But she only half-believed it. Her Conversations suggested that the experience which was to replace erudition was to be "eloquence," itself a form of parasitism; and Fuller felt the paradox. Through her "eloquence," she could only attempt to stress and embody the primacy of experience she was aware she had not known. In one of her Conversations, Fuller remarked that " 'eloquence was a kind of thieving!' "[70] She had long realized that her greatest temptation was to "profane life with rhetoric";[71] she asked too much of herself not to feel that "eloquence" was for her a form of pretense—at its best a pledge, at its worst a lie. To be "eloquent" was apparently to be outside, and above, the feminine subculture as it existed in the Northeast; but was not "eloquence" nonetheless a higher form of "influence"? Self-advertisement, no matter how magnificent or strident, was not self-actualization, and ultimately Fuller would be satisfied with nothing else. Her lament that she had found no one able to bring her out as a talker only highlights the vicious circle she was in during her late Concord years. Since she had no refuge at this time but the myth of her "eloquent" grandiose self, she was drawn to those who also needed to believe in it; she was attracted precisely to those who might eventually damn or abandon her, but who would never creatively share the doubts about herself which constituted her most important hope of fulfillment. She was drawn, in other words, to Ralph Waldo Emerson.

The Transcendental Years: The Relationship with Emerson

Fuller's relationship with Emerson from 1836 until 1844[72] provided her with her ultimate opportunity to exploit and attack the metaphorical life which depended on the substitution of "eloquence" for experience. There has been much speculation, scholarly and otherwise, about whether or not she was in love with him. Probably she was initially, in some sense, but this was never the real issue between them. Emerson was firmly married, and Fuller was devoted to his family. Her challenge to him was graver even than a demand to be loved.

Fuller's appeal was inevitably most forceful for those undergoing a crisis of self-confidence like her own chronic one. Members of her own sex, especially the more gifted ones, were her natural parishioners; so were liberal non-evangelical clergymen self-consciously suffering the status oppression familiar to women. In a sense, Fuller was the most important of the nine-teenth-century American women who challenged clerical prerogatives. Timothy Fuller was the son of a minister, although he and his four brothers turned decisively to the law. His daughter borrowed many tactics from ministerial precedents. She corresponded with her pupils in Providence, R.I., and marked one pile of their letters "under conviction," another "obtained a hope";[73] her searching scrutiny of friends and acquaintances resembled the inquisitional methods the Edwardsean clergy of the eighteenth century had employed to distinguish "true religion" from false; her heroic labors of scholarship recalled Samuel Hopkins' daily twelve-hour stints on his *System of Theology;* even her Conversations developed in part from the techniques of the informal prayer- and discussion-groups liberal churches increasingly sponsored. She represented the best of the older Calvinist and the newer liberal religious traditions in New England. James Freeman Clarke and William Henry Channing, Unitarian ministers intimate with Fuller, felt shamed by her example, and avowedly learned from her as preachers and pastors. Clarke and Channing were probably not cheered, however, by Fuller's astute assessment of the difficulties under which formally ordained ministers like themselves, weakened by disestablishment and overly depen-dent on congregational approval, labored. She refused to live at the experi-mental Brook Farm, although its occupants proposed to demand no work from her. They simply wanted the inspiration of her "genius." Quick to realize that they were looking for a Fourierist minister, she refused at once: "Where would be my repose, when they were always to be judging whether I was worth it or not. It would be the same position the clergyman is in, or the wandering beggar with his harp. Every day you must prove yourself anew. You are not," she concluded in an important phrase, "in immediate relation with material things."[74]

Fuller first set her sights on Emerson as the "only clergyman of all possible clergymen who eludes my acquaintance."[75] When she finally met Emerson in 1836, he had just left the ministry because he believed, as we have seen, that as a minister he could not speak or feel freely, he could not be a "man quite and whole." He had quit his profession precisely in order to get into closer touch with the experience of life—the "immediate relation with material things"—that Fuller needed to believe she represented and did indeed in part represent. In a sense, he needed and courted liberation from the feminine subculture of his society as surely as Fuller's feminine students did. He was, at least in theory, peculiarly susceptible to her. Like Anne Hutchinson with John Cotton, she could argue that she was merely taking her mentor at his word. She could lay siege to him—paying long visits to Concord, teaching him German, winning the devotion of his mother, his wife, and his son, barraging him with the letters and company of her own coterie of adoring friends, demonstrating on every level the abundance and provocation of her resources—and claim as she did so that she was responding to his own call for reinforcements. He had left the ministry, he had turned from a scholarly and traditional profession to the less defined role of talker, writer, poet; she appeared on his doorstep as the first member of his new congregation.

Fuller's aggressiveness with Emerson has obscured the fact that he did indeed ask her to lay siege to what he once called his "chicken coop." Although he endorsed an early letter from her as "shocking familiarity,"[76] after her first visit he expressed his pleasure to a friend: she was, he said in a significant phrase, "a great refreshment."[77] Later, when Emerson pleaded to Fuller his normally cold constitution, his inability to be productive if subjected to much emotional excitement, he always took on the role of apologist: he was in the wrong in his retreat from her, he implied, though he could not help it. The essence of Fuller's challenge to Emerson was her demand to know whether or not he meant what he said, whether or not his life was finally metaphorical. She rightly pressed him with none of the sympathy she showed the feminine attendants of her Conversations: did he exist in literature, or history? She understood that her sisters needed to be led to formulate the question; Emerson should answer it. She forced the issue with passionate intensity precisely to camouflage and overcome her own temporary inability fully to define or answer the same question about herself, but her instinct that this was the question to direct to Emerson was unerring. Emerson asked Fuller to personify a part of himself he had to express, and repudiate. He needed her to play his Muse; he even wished at times to be victim to her fury. He needed her as an expression of his guilt —that he lacked passion and political concern, that, even as he urged his countrymen to create an original bold literature, he was not somehow quite an American, that he was committed to metaphor, an experiment with life, rather than to life itself, that he was still not a "man quite and whole."

Fuller's friendship made Emerson feel dissatisfied with his creative efforts in ways whose beneficial or damaging consequences on his work he struggled confusedly to evaluate. Referring to himself as a "mute," he repeatedly expressed frustration with his inability to communicate. He wished to live "with people who love & hate, who have Muses & Furies"; he begged for "once in my life to be pommelled black and blue with sincere words"; he wanted to be "electrified" by her "eloquence."[78] When he wrote her that he wished he could live with those "who have Muses & Furies," he added that then he could write "Romances & Tragedies." Significantly, it did not occur to Emerson that any amount of communication with "Muses & Furies" would make him stop writing, but he did envisage writing differently. Emerson was well aware that his chosen and ordained vehicle was the address; all his essays were versions of the commencement oration. His literary vocation consisted in telling people that they must want to live, and how, not in showing people living. Exhortation substituted brilliantly for experience in his essays, and Emerson knew it as well as Fuller did.

Their relationship was built on the shared assumption that she had something to give which he was unable to receive. Yet in a sense neither wanted to complete the gesture; each depended for self-definition on the frustration inherent in his or her role. Early in the friendship, Emerson explained Fuller's effect on him: "It is like being set in a large place. You stretch your limbs and dilate to your utmost size."[79] Tellingly, this is the kind of imagery of expansion he would use years later to express his complex reaction to heroes whom he would call "representative men."[80] His reservation about Fuller is already implicit in his praise: she made him feel bigger than he normally was; who long wants to be tasked to the utmost? It is hard not to give our sympathies to Fuller who craved, no matter how confusedly and violently, contact, rather than to Emerson who finally demanded, no matter with what justification, distance. Yet Emerson is not to blame; Fuller used him as surely as he used her. If he needed to play the diminished hero who cannot respond when he is reminded how much he has been offered, she needed to be the rejected heroine, the all-abundant giver with no one capacious enough to welcome her generosity. De Staël's brilliantly spontaneous Corinne is abandoned, after all, by her cold reserved lover Oswald. Rejection can be experienced as the ultimate ritual of narcissism: one is left alone with oneself, too good for the world. The parallels with the Oswald-Corinne affair seem important. The Emerson-Fuller relationship was literary, and self-consciously testing and accusing itself as literature.

The tensions of the Emerson-Fuller relationship began to ease as the two worked together on the transcendental periodical *The Dial*, between

1840 and 1844. Fuller was a far better editor and journalist than Emerson would ever be, or care to be, and he acknowledged and admired her tremendous yet cautious efforts on the *Dial*. When he took over the nearly impossible responsibilities of the editorship from her in 1843, he realized as he never had before and never would again the practical resourcefulness and drive of her nature. Fuller continued to review and admire his work, although with reservations. Peace came, not simply because at bottom they cherished and respected one another, but because their joint enterprise clarified and finalized their conflicts. In theory at least, Emerson wanted the *Dial* to be a "fruitful Cybele," not "purely literary" but speaking on matters of "property, government, education as well as on art, letters, & religion."[81] In practice, Emerson wished to see the *Dial* an elitist organ, filled with high-quality poetry and essays. Fuller knew well that the transcendental group could not fill up even four issues a year with first-rate material; more important, she approached the magazine with different aims. She told Emerson at one point that when he had criticized her for welcoming "talent" and not holding out for "genius," she had been flattered. She wished to be more catholic, more open-minded and democratic than she was, not less.[82] She conceived the *Dial* as a representative publication, open to all who thought along similar high-minded lines. In the brilliant critical papers she was writing for the *Dial* during this period, she made it clear that her view of literature was not aesthetic and philosophical like Emerson's but sociological, historical, and political. Literature was not to be an asylum, but a marketplace and a thoroughfare. In her words, literature should "be regarded as the great mutual system of interpretation between all kinds and classes of men. It is an epistolary correspondence between brethren of one family."[83]

The shared responsibility of the *Dial*, in other words, paradoxically did away with the illusion of a common territory. Through her work on the magazine, Fuller found a channel for her "eloquence" more viable than confused antagonism or endless self-inspiration. She wanted to write about her culture and address herself to the major issues of her day. So of course did Emerson, but with a caution so pronounced as to inflame Fuller's wrath long before she was certain of her own commitments. Moreover, despite her autocratic insistence on the highest standards, she wished to be widely read. Emerson shared her ambition, yet unlike Fuller he would not go so far as to write for those organs which were already widely read. Emerson's and Fuller's reactions to New York City in the early 1840s highlighted the differences between them. When Emerson went to lecture in the metropolis in 1842, he wrote Fuller in a most ambivalent spirit about this "realm strange to me." He had met the self-educated and vigorous editor of the *Herald Tribune*, Horace Greeley, "who listens after all new thoughts & things but with the indispensable New York condition that they can be made available." "What can I do," Emerson queried helplessly, "with such an abettor?" The "endless rustle of newspapers" made him feel "not the value of their classes but of my own class—the supreme need of the few worshippers of the Muse—wild & sacred—as counteractions to this world of material & ephemeral interest." Yet, as in his responses to Fuller, he was finally critical of himself, not of the city. It is his "poorness of spirit" which forces his retreat, he apologizes. In his next "transmigration," he would "choose New York." In her reply, Fuller asked to hear more of "those dim New Yorkers";[84] within the year, she was to move to the metropolis and work for Horace Greeley's newspaper as a reporter and critic.

Fuller had long desired to travel. Her frustration in sacrificing a long-anticipated trip abroad in 1835 to what she viewed as her family's needs was intense. An instinct had told her all her life that she was not living in the place nor with the people best suited to her, that she could find herself in finding the world.[85] When Fuller was setting out on her trip to the West, a trip which was to produce an extraordinary travel book, *Summer on the Lakes*, and to crystallize her new sense of vocation, Emerson wrote that he envied her "this large dose of America; you will know how to dispose of it all. We have all been East too long. Now for the West!"[86] His tone of exhortation is telling for its futility: after all, Fuller is indeed heading "for the West." They are mercifully going their separate ways. In plain fact, Fuller, unlike Emerson and Thoreau, could not "travel widely in Concord." She could not foster her creativity nor nourish her life upon a paradox.[87] To her perception, traveling widely in Concord was finally just that—traveling widely *in Concord*. Concord was many things, but it was most emphatically a tiny part of the world. Her appetite for the actual was so constituted that she starved on experiences that sufficed genuinely to sustain and richly to inspire Emerson. What was for Emerson wise restraint was for her damaging repression. A policy of self-involvement which was therapy and inspiration for Emerson spelled dangerous self-inflation for Fuller. The frequent failure of condensation in her style, in pointed contrast to the sometimes over-condensed, epigrammatic style of Emerson (a contrast Emerson noted), revealed that she could not find eternity in a wild flower, or the history of the world in the history of herself, although she had tried. Her essential vision was not literary, not metaphorical, but historical. Unlike Emerson, Fuller had to recognize experiences for which there were absolutely no analogues or substitutes.

None of the transcendentalists, except Fuller, had any talent as a journalist or any real bent for history. One of Fuller's chief trials as editor of the *Dial* lay in Bronson Alcott's contributions. Alcott admired both Fuller and Emerson enormously. Emerson returned the compliment. Fuller, while she felt and defended Alcott's undeniable integrity of purpose and purity of soul, had reservations. Alcott's "Orphic Sayings," which Fuller printed in 1840 with total reluctance, Emerson with mixed enthusiasm, drew ridicule on the fledgling journal. When Fuller confessed in her diary her inability to overcome her "distrust of Mr. Alcott's mind,"[88] perhaps she was thinking of a passage like the following on "Thought and Action," a topic close to her heart: "Great thoughts exalt and deify the thinker; still more ennobling is the effect of great deeds on the actor. The dilation and joy of the soul at these visitations of God is like that of an invalid, again inhaling the mountain breeze after long confinement in chambers: she feels herself a noble bird, whose eyrie is in the empyrean."[89]

There is nowhere in "Mr. Alcott's mind" the tension that comes from awareness of the crucial distinction between potentiality and actualization, the tension that made Fuller write passionately in 1841, "I must die if I do not burst forth in genius or heroism."[90] Alcott had worked with his hands on and off all his life, and worked hard, a fact for which Emerson and Fuller respected him. Yet the theoretical and the practical lay in comfortable embrace in his expansive intelligence. He had absolutely no sense of history. Self-taught, he had perused the classics of literature and philosophy intent on his own quest for truth. His question about any author, whether Plato or Shakespeare or Mrs. Sigourney, was always "What does he or she say to us *now*?"[91] He never recognized, as Fuller unflinchingly did, that the writers of the past may have something to tell us which we do not want to hear, but must. She expressed on several occasions her wish that the transcendentalists—to whom she always referred in the third person—would "learn how to make use of the past"[92]—and of the present, she might have added. She herself was learning fast.

New York and Italy: Experience and Commitment

Emerson had found Horace Greeley estimable but unassimilable. Fuller, who went to work for Greeley on the *Herald Tribune* and to live as an intimate in his family, respected him and got on with him. Greeley's rather nervous and discontented wife was an admirer of Fuller and had urged her husband to offer this New Englander a job. Greeley, greatly impressed by Fuller's *Woman in the Nineteenth Century*, a book for which Emerson promised but failed to write a preface, needed little persuasion. In *Woman in the Nineteenth Century*, Greeley recognized a commitment to human rights as profound as his own and a gift for searching analysis couched in persuasive prose which would distinguish his columns. Fuller's work on the *Tribune* increased his esteem. He saw that she fulfilled his own professed ideal: she wrote for the people without pandering to them. With obvious sincerity, Greeley pronounced her the most brilliant woman in America.[93]

There were, of course, differences between the two. In part, Greeley simply did not understand his employee. The necessities of fortifying her own position had led Fuller to stress woman's special "Muse"-like "magnetic" and "intuitive" qualities,[94] to demand homage even while she expected equality of opportunity for her sex. The shrewd and enterprising Greeley, more alert to her inconsistencies of thought than her consistency of need, occasionally thought it witty to leave her to open a door for herself while he declaimed from *Woman in the Nineteenth Century:* " 'Let them be Sea-Captains if they will!' "[95] Fuller was doing much more than rationalizing her own isolation when she explained in *Woman* that "celibacy" was the great fact of her era, that "many minds deprived of the traditionary or instinctive means of passing a cheerful existence must find help in self-impulse or perish." She was noting the beginning of a cultural crisis which is still with us when she stated her reluctant belief that "at present," women could not rely on men to guide or respect them, that they had to be themselves "the best helpers of one another."[96] Greeley, more alive to Fuller's loneliness than to the insights it granted her, commented: "great and noble as she was, a good husband and two or three bouncing babies would have emancipated her from a great deal of cant and nonsense."[97] He was distressed that Fuller did not change her diet to suit his notions, surprised that she could not turn out the same number of words per hour that he did.

Yet Greeley's very carping and his occasional lack of sympathy revealed that he assessed Fuller by his own standards, not by hers; and in certain respects his values were the ones she had looked for and been unable to find in Emerson. Greeley wanted to know: could she work effectively, could she speak cogently to the issues of the day, did she mean what she said? He was not susceptible to Fuller as her Conversation students, or Emerson for that matter, had been; he distrusted the coterie of admirers she immediately drew around her in the metropolis. By being blind to "Margaret," paradoxically, Greeley inadvertently helped her see herself; he did not reinforce her chosen image and thus imprison her more firmly in it. He facilitated her transition from a world where intensity of impression was counted almost everything to one where effects were constantly, if not always accurately, calculated and examined.

With her usual insight, Fuller grasped perfectly Greeley's significance to her: "He teaches me things which my own influence on those who have hitherto approached me has prevented me from learning."[98] Yet Fuller did not wish to abandon her grandiose self altogether so much as to redirect its energies to something more productive and substantial than its own advertisement. At some level, she clearly sensed the crippling narcissism of her transcendental years. As a journalist in New York, she altered her concept of her audience; they were less the people she wanted to have see and hear her, than the people she wished to talk to about something. And, significantly and appropriately, she began, though with little awareness of it, to change her style.

Fuller was no happier with herself as a writer in New York than she had ever been. Yet her most perceptive friends noted a difference—a welcome simplification, force, and point in her prose. I have said that in her transcendental period she was using her writing too entirely as a vehicle for herself for it to be successful. This is not to imply that she was obsessed with the personal in a helplessly subjective fashion, although Emerson and other male friends at times hinted such was the case. It was rather that her aspirations were in some not altogether illegitimate way Messianic; and she had nothing for a Messianic vehicle but herself, even while she was rightly convinced of her own inadequacy. Journalism both satisfied and deflected Fuller's need for personal communication. Its relative informality was congenial to her; she believed it to be in style and tone very close to "conversation."[99] The compulsion to meet a daily deadline freed her from the fears entailed for her in consciously attempting a large-scale achievement. Her instinct for self-defeat was incorporated into the conditions of success: she could not really look at what she was doing; she wrote it, and it was printed. And she had a subject outside herself. As a newspaperwoman, Fuller's attention could be less on the struggle between Margaret-in-person and Margaret-on-paper, and more simply and powerfully on what she wanted to say. Finding a form of indirection, she found direction.

Woman in the Nineteenth Century is journalism in the best sense, as the more consciously reporting yet more romanticized *Summer on the Lakes* is not. When Fuller finished it, she felt for the first time that she had left footprints which time would not erase. She was right. Emerson realized at once its quality: it is "a piece of life," he wrote her—for Fuller, from Emerson, the ultimate compliment. Thoreau recognized, in a telling phrase, that it was "rich extempore writing, talking with pen in hand."[100] For many reasons, these two men were less willing to acknowledge that Fuller was discovering not just her style, but her material. Significantly, Fuller's subject was current events—history, not literature. The literary criticism she did for Greeley represents some of her best work, but she had done excellent literary criticism for the *Dial*. Her new sense of excitement is felt most vividly in the *Herald* pieces on slavery, prisons, labor. As she extended and deepened her perception of national life, she became increasingly aware that current American pre-eminence was based on abuse of various classes of people, most notably blacks, immigrants (who formed the bulk of the working classes), Indians, and above all, women. She spoke for these groups with force and indignation; her subject was oppression.

Fuller's deepest concern, moreover, lay with the subtle forms of status oppression that she as a woman had always known rather than with brutal and overt economic exploitation. She is at her most compelling and astute in *Summer on the Lakes* when she analyzes the cause of the white man's low estimate of the Indian. "The aversion of the injurer for him he has degraded,"[101] Fuller calls it. She was acutely alive to the tragic irony that the whites, in order to justify their own inevitable rapacity and destructiveness, were determined to destroy the Indian's sole remaining possession, his self-respect. *Woman in the Nineteenth Century* revealed that she saw male-female relations as another version of the same dynamic. She was most sensitized, and most indignant, before that part of the rationale of oppression which tells its victim, whether Indian or woman: you merited no better. Her characteristic crusade was against the myths so integral to status oppression: that all Indians are by nature lazy and drunken, that all women are incapable of intellectual effort and naturally seek domestic life. Herself tentatively disavowing an image which she had long confused with her identity, as a journalist Fuller naturally took on a kind of muckraking role: her desire and her claim was to have seen for herself, to be able authoritatively to separate hard "facts" from self-serving "talk."

Fuller's new capacity for self-analysis was manifest in her increasing dislike of the popular forms of "eloquence." As she became more aware of the discrepancy between myth and reality in her society, she grew equally convinced that most Americans did not want to be enlightened; they welcomed a culture of sheer verbosity. The proliferating July Fourth orations of florid self-congratulation infuriated her. On the national birthday in 1845, she issued a counterblast: America has shown "that righteousness is not her chief desire, and her name is no longer a watchword for the highest hopes to the rest of the world,"[102] she announced. She was still Timothy Fuller's daughter; her standard was always that set by the American Revolution. In 1845, she lamented: " 'More money! more land' are all the watchwords they [modern Americans] know. They have received the inheritance earned by the fathers of the revolution, without their wisdom and virtue to use it. But this cannot last."[103] Fuller was calling for historical rebirth, "not merely . . . revolution but . . . radical reform,"[104] such as she increasingly realized her country could neither provide nor tolerate. Her battle against her culture's substitution of rhetoric for action could not be fought at home.

In 1846 Margaret Fuller set sail for Europe. She planned to visit England, France, and Italy and hoped to support herself by sending back dispatches to the *Tribune*. This trip was the most important act of her life.

What most people remember about her foreign sojourn is the liaison she established with Angelo Ossoli and the fulfillment she found as a woman. These are of course of enormous significance. Ossoli, whom Fuller wedded sometime after the birth of their son in September 1848, was an Italian nobleman eleven years younger than herself. By all accounts, he was physically beautiful, kind, gentle, unintellectual, unpretentious, and utterly devoted to Fuller. Deprived of his own mother at six, affectionate and docile by nature, Ossoli was not threatened by her authority: indeed, he needed it.[105] His attachment was in many ways profoundly new and beneficial to Fuller. She undoubtedly understood his limitations,[106] but she loved him deeply; and she loved their son, in whom she found the "only real happiness" she had ever known, more. Fuller's marriage was finally inseparable, however, from the historical events which she was witnessing and aiding. Fuller and Ossoli were drawn together in the first place by their shared political sympathies. Later they repeatedly chose temporary separation and even risked the life of their child Angelino because of their over-riding commitment to the destinies of the short-lived Italian republic. Italy, for a variety of reasons, came first.

One must remember that the trip abroad for Americans contemporary to Margaret Fuller was very much a literary pilgrimage. In France and England, where she visited before going to Italy, Fuller was painfully conscious that all the "stock" sights and personages she saw had been described so frequently by earlier travelers as to be stripped of any historical reality. Her accounts written for the *Tribune* insinuate again and again that she knows her readers are already familiar with the places and people she is reporting on—from other reporters, from other books. Her comment on Sir Walter Scott's ancestral home is typical: "This pilgrimage [is] so common that there is nothing left for me to say." The essential repetitiousness and superficiality of well-read tourism was a perpetual irritant to her; she was conscious of being unwillingly trapped in the most worn-out and derivative of literary conventions. Everything was, in her word, "hackneyed," derivative.[107]

There was no country Americans had traveled to so often, loved so much, and written about so verbosely as Italy, where Fuller arrived in March 1847. Cooper, Hawthorne, Emerson, Story, James, and most of the American tourists who left records of their travels testified to the fascination Italy exerted on them; but the needs they expected it to serve were rather special ones. They concurred in slighting the political, intellectual, and domestic habits of the Italian people, even while they praised and envied the Italians' love of art and capacity for leisure. They unanimously resented the encroachments of the present on the classical past.[108] Emerson's initial expression of disillusion on his first Italian trip is typical. Hoping to "come suddenly in the midst of an open country upon broken columns and fallen friezes" standing in "solemn and eloquent" solitude, he found instead ruins "carefully fenced around like orchards" and filled with "this vermin of ciceroni and padroni."[109] Emerson, in other words, expected Italy to look like the prints of Italian scenes so in vogue in America; he wanted it to arouse the emotions Byron's and Goethe's poetic tributes to Italy provoked; he expected not a country but a museum, not life but art. We are back with the Italy James liked at least to imagine that the Storys had found. It is striking that while American criticism of Italian literature and painting flourished in the nineteenth century, no reputable historical study of Italy came out of America until the work of William Thayer; and even he, it must be noted, was trained by Charles Eliot Norton, a distinguished Italianist but in no sense a professional historian.[110] In the same period, Americans, as we have seen, were producing superb histories of aspects of Spanish, English, French, and Dutch civilizations. In American eyes, Italy was an artistic resource for capitalist culture, and by definition both effeminate and ahistorical: it was to serve a higher version of the need met by the "Fanny Forresters" and "Grace Greenwoods."

Fuller responded passionately to Italy from the moment she arrived. The thought of earlier tourists did not trouble her here. She "found all familiar ... and yet all new as if never yet described." "Nature" in Italy has "a charm unhackneyed, unhackneyable." She felt "the fulfillment of a hope!"[111] For Fuller's Italy was not the Italy of her predecessors or her contemporaries. Indeed, the culmination of her life work was in her protest against their view of Italy, in her monumental effort in her *Tribune* dispatches and her now-lost history of the Roman republic to translate Italy for Americans from the realm of "literature" back into the realm of "history." In 1848 and 1849 Italy was in revolt against its Bourbon and Austrian overlords, and the oppression against which the Italians struggled was the one Fuller as a woman best understood. They were fighting to vindicate their psychological as well as their political rights.

In the Italian people, contemptuously dismissed by their rulers and by visiting Englishmen and Americans as charming, artistic, and emotional ne'er-do-wells, cowards incapable of preserving—much less regaining—the heritage of their titanic Roman ancestors, Fuller rightly found victims of the kind of status oppression which most inflamed her. Like women and children, the Italians were assumed to live for and in their feelings. Fuller knew all too well what it was not to be taken seriously. The Italians were striving for what her father had taught her, what she had wished to convey to her Conversation students, what she had tried to embody as a challenge and a provocation for Emerson. They wanted to be more than decorative and pleasing: they wanted to be free, independent, and strong. When they demonstrated nobility of thought and forcefulness of action in their brief days of political independence, Fuller noted triumphantly that no one could say now that Italians only "boast" and do not "act." The Italians were "learning to prize and seek realities."[112] Symbolically, their leader, Giuseppe Mazzini, a man of limited practical shrewdness but of enormous and skillful idealism, had renounced a life of literary pursuits to lead the campaign to unite and free Italy. He was not an "orator," Fuller noted, and praised his "conversational" style.[113] Not surprisingly, Fuller found in him not only a personal friend, but the "Great Man" she had sought in vain in Emerson. The Italians, in short, were doing what Fuller the woman wished to do, what she feared her country was never again to do: they were turning words into deeds.

Never had Fuller's sense of the possible falsity of words been so painfully sharp. She had to fight stubborn past misconceptions of Italy and rapidly proliferating present ones. She grew to detest many of the major newspapers, most notably the London *Times*, which depicted the surprisingly successful Roman republic as the work of a small group of ill-trained, self-interested, and incompetent men imposing their confused will on an unwilling and disorganized populace.[114] During the days of the siege in June 1849, her journal entries diminished to several lines of tense commentary, but she was still sending her accurate and impassioned accounts to the *Tribune*. She reminded her readers that she was "not a person to be kindled by a childish, sentimental enthusiasm,"[115] and her evolving style testified that her words were what she claimed them to be—"sincere." Believing as she did that the Italian struggle for independence paralleled the American Revolution, that the "spirit which made it [America] all it is of value in my eyes . . . is more alive here [in Italy] at present than in America,"[116] Fuller wielded the oratorical tradition in which she had been trained with new skill and authority. She had never been more rhetorically impressive than when she passionately redeemed the legacy of the founding fathers by translating it in terms of the socialism which had become her creed:

> There is no peace. . . . It would appear that the political is being merged in the social struggle: it is well. Whatever blood is to be shed, whatever altars cast down, those tremendous problems must be solved, whatever be the cost! . . . to you, people of America, it may perhaps be given to look on and learn in time for a preventive wisdom. . . . You may, despite the apes of the past who strive to tutor you, learn the needs of a true democracy. You may in time learn to reverence . . . the true aristocracy of the nation, the only really nobles—the LABORING CLASSES.[117]

At her finest moments in her late dispatches, Fuller went beyond rhetoric to achieve an "eloquence" more genuine than any which had marked her transcendental period. Here is her memorable description of Rome after the French occupation:

> I ... entered the French ground, all mapped and hollowed like a honeycomb. A pair of skeleton legs protruded from a bank of one baricade; lower, a dog had scratched away [the] light covering of earth from the body of a man, and discovered it lying face upward all dressed; the dog stood gazing on it with an air of stupid amazement.[118]

The change is a simple but crucial one. Fuller is no longer wordy. More confident of her identity, she no longer needs to flood her subject with herself. She has learned the style of understatement in which facts are allowed to speak for themselves.

In the last years of her life, Fuller no longer thought of her work as critical or even journalistic, but as "historical."[119] She never fully defined these terms, but it is possible to guess at her meaning. She was always moved by the great achievements of art, and the architecture and painting of Italy gave her intense pleasure. Yet she was proud to measure the distance between herself and her culture when she could write a friend at home that she, a woman, found "art ... not important to me now."[120] To judge this remark rightly, one must put it in its cultural context. At the time Fuller was working on her (now lost) account of the Roman Revolution in 1849 and 1850, other American feminine writers had already published travelogues like Lydia Huntley Sigourney's *Pleasant Memories of Pleasant Lands* (1842), thin pastiches of quotation-laden eulogies and reminiscences of encounters with literary lions. Fuller's old friend James Freeman Clarke, in many ways an apostle of Mrs. Sigourney's genteel culture,[121] was abroad in the late 1840s, intent on viewing "the Alps," "fine ... picture galleries," and "old cathedrals" in that order; despite the dramatic events taking place around him, he found "the world's history" did not affect him.[122] Little wonder that Fuller exulted that she would return to America from revolution-torn Europe, not perhaps more "cultured," but "possessed of a great history."[123] In her mind, "art" was somehow bad, "history" somehow good; that she felt little need to amplify such a painfully simplified view is a measure of her society, her own antagonism to its values, and the energy she devoted to the expression and maintenance of her anger. She clearly believed that "art" was increasingly functioning in American culture as a diversion from the pressing problem of the socio-economic order, and that "history" suggested active participation in the revolutionary changes necessary to transform and better that order. For distinctions more complex and more profound than these, she had no time.

Epilogue

By mid-summer of 1849 the short-lived Roman republic had fallen to the French. When Pope Pius resumed his occupancy in Rome in June 1850, Fuller had already made plans to bring her small family back to America. She had uncanny premonitions about the trip; Ossoli had been warned to fear death by water, she herself expressed reservations about the ship in which they took passage. Her worst fears were prophetic. An epidemic of smallpox spread on the ship, taking the captain's life and almost proving fatal to Angelino Ossoli. The ship went on, only to strike a rock and founder off Fire Island. Most of the crew and passengers waited for hours on board, expecting the lifeboats visible on the shore to come momentarily to their rescue. One by one the passengers struck out for land by whatever means they found available. Fuller, insisting that she and her family must live or die together, refused to make the attempt. Shortly before the vessel sank, her child was taken off board by a crew member; his body was later washed up on the beach. Fuller was last seen before the boat went down standing alone near the mast.

Biographers have debated, to no avail, whether or not Fuller was committing suicide in her decision not to try for shore. It is clear that she was enormously apprehensive about the return to America, and that she felt drained and embittered by what she had recently undergone. Despite the inspiring courage displayed by the Italians, despite their righteous cause, they were defeated, and Fuller was "sickened" by the utter injustice of their failure. In a prophetic image, she wrote Emerson shortly before she left Italy that she was sinking and did not want to be buoyed up any longer. She had found fulfillment only to have it taken from her. Adam Mickiewicz, the great Polish poet, sensed there was a strain of defeatism in Fuller which he deplored even while he understood and sympathized with its causes. The quality that he kept enjoining on her was "gaiety." At one of her darkest hours, he promised her: "You can still regain all your health and live robust and gay. Believe it."[124] Quite simply, Fuller did not believe it.

In *Woman in the Nineteenth Century*, Fuller had demanded passionately: "And will she not soon appear?—the woman who shall vindicate their birthright for all women, who shall teach them what to claim, and how to use what they obtain?"[125] Fuller wanted to be that woman, and, in part, she succeeded. Rebecca Spring, a friend of Fuller's, recorded that fifty years after Fuller's death she still dreamt of her and all she had done: "Let our sex never forget Margaret Fuller," she prayed.[126] Margaret Fuller was arrogant; at times she assumed her demands were equal if not superior to the resources of the universe. She was self-pitying; she did not fully back her ethical judgments by analysis nor adequately express them in significant art; the difficulties of her life made her both more and less honest than she might otherwise have been. She craved affection and attention absolutely; her needs were as sharp and ominous as ice cracking in winter. Her preoccupation with herself was constant and monumental. Yet her achievement was great: she was able to save herself amid the partial collapse of a culture she increasingly distrusted and dedicate herself to the serious support of an opposing way of life. She found what Adrienne Rich has since termed "the treasure in the wreck."

9

HERMAN MELVILLE AND
THE REVOLT
AGAINST THE READER

The Masculine Inheritance

On March 20, 1846, Margaret Fuller left a note on Horace Greeley's desk asking for a copy of *Typee*, Herman Melville's recently published narrative of South Sea adventure. Evert Duyckinck, a prominent New York literary man and a friend of Melville's, had brought the book, Melville's first, to Fuller's attention. Her review appeared in the *Tribune* on April 4. The conjunction of critic and author was a fortuitous and significant one. Melville was to be, with Fuller, among the few genuine romantics America produced in this period; he was to share both her dislike of the dishonesty of sentimentalism and her pervasive concern with the meaning of history.

Fuller's review of *Typee* stands out among contemporary appraisals. They were largely favorable, and hers was no exception; but she especially commended exactly what other readers condemned. After superficially praising Melville's "pretty and spirited pictures" and "arch manner" she endorsed, with obviously quickened interest, Melville's skepticism about the value of the missionary effort in the Pacific. In Melville's opinion, the do-gooders, in their ignorance and scorn of indigenous culture, were corrupting, not converting, the natives. Fuller agreed. Indeed, only Margaret Fuller, with her brilliant tactlessness, could have counseled, as she did here, that the ladies' sewing societies engaged in outfitting missionaries read this book aloud "while assembled at their work."[1] Impatient as ever with pious endeavors conducted with more attention to the self-esteem of their subjects than concern with the needs of their objects, Fuller, like Melville, wanted her society to face, at the very least, what it was doing. Fuller ignored the art of *Typee* and the complex personality in ambush behind it to focus on the book's possible didactic and corrective intent; but she at once grasped, and met, Melville's preoccupation with veracity.

Although Melville was a New Yorker, and in the city shortly before Fuller left it to go abroad, there is no evidence that he met her. There is reason to believe, however, that he would have respected her and her work, had he known them. Traveling to England in 1849, he amused himself with *Holidays Abroad* by Caroline Kirkland, a pragmatic, witty, and gifted writer, and commented enthusiastically: "She is a spirited, sensible, fine woman." Melville did not expect intelligence in women—in curious ways Fuller did not either, under existing circumstances; but he felt the dearth of discernment in his environment too sharply not to prize it wherever he found it. Later, Melville read Madame de Staël with deep pleasure, noting in his journal: "It is delightful as well as wonderful to see ... such penetration of understanding in a woman who at the same time possesses so femininely emotional a nature."[2] Melville could here be paraphrasing more calmly Fuller's anguished cry: "Will there never be a being to combine a man's mind and a woman's heart?" Fuller was a feminist, Melville was not; yet both saw the tragic segregation of the sexes in America as evidence of a deeper and even more troubling bifurcation in their culture: that between what Edwards A. Park had called "the intellect" and "the feelings."

Melville confronted this bifurcation with a particular kind of skill which Fuller's special needs and circumstances had not left among her options. On the most obvious level Melville, unhampered by Fuller's almost compulsively strident ethicality and her culturally imposed difficulties with literary production, was a creative writer, and a great one, as she was not. While he distrusted fiction no less than she, Melville could, by complex and brilliant tactics of displacement, use and expand the narrative form itself to express his hostility to it. Both Fuller and Melville were constantly experimenting as writers in radical ways: Fuller tried poetry, fiction, scholarly essays, critical journalism, history; Melville produced reviews, romances, sketches, narratives of every kind, short stories, verse. Yet where Fuller seems to be picking up a series of disparate modes and trying each in turn, Melville is apparently engaged in one continuous process of evolvement, to which the varying forms are subordinate. Fuller is like someone trying on different articles of clothing, Melville like someone making alterations on a single garment.

Fuller, as I have tried to show, was persistent in her search for authenticity; but she was capable, and fortunately so, of discarding almost entirely a solution whose limited potential she had exhausted. She could talk to Emerson, she could work with the transcendentalists, she could engage in protest against American apathy, she could write fiction, poetry, or criticism —only so long; she had finally to put herself first. If such activities or people were not ultimately going to further her goal of self-fulfillment, she had to abandon them. She disengaged from Emerson, she broke with the transcendentalists, she expatriated, she failed to perfect a literary technique. Like a person running from a burning building, she took what she could, the essentials; she consigned much to inevitable destruction. She was embattled in ways that made it imperative for her to turn ideas into slogans. This is hardly to criticize Margaret Fuller: on the contrary. What revolutionary does not simplify? And what could display more intelligence than Fuller's profound understanding that the only viable role for a woman like herself at the juncture at which she lived was an essentially revolutionary one? Melville's case, and his consequent greatness, however, were different. It seems natural to me to discuss Fuller's achievement in large part in terms of her life, Melville's in terms of his books. I am aware of the disparity in my treatment of these two, to use one of Melville's favorite words, "phenomenal" people; and I do not mean to suggest that Fuller's work was not integral to and representative of her life, or that Melville's life was not intricately responsible for his creative effort and exemplary in itself. Melville's life was difficult as surely as Fuller's writing was daring. With his once-prosperous father's death in 1832 when he was thirteen, Melville was precipitated into the American experience of (downward) social mobility in a way unique among the major writers of his generation. His early and wide-ranging career as a sailor, his subsequent settling into a curiously unimaginative marriage and his increasing commitment to a literary career which he invented with a radical fierceness unparalleled in American letters, his struggles simply to support himself and his large family, his touchingly truncated literary friendships, most notably with Hawthorne, his growing personal and professional isolation, his mounting anxiety occasionally bordering on insanity, his final occupation as a New York customs official which blanketed the last three decades of his life—all these facts comprise a history integral to the often painful story of our culture's potentiality for self-realization. Yet, given the limits of space, I think my emphasis—Fuller's biography, Melville's opus—is right. Indeed the emphasis is less mine than America's. Melville's identity was conflicted and precarious, but he did not have to make it up in the same way that Fuller was forced to hypothesize hers: there already existed in American thought an ambivalent concept of the (masculine) original "genius" for which there was no genuine feminine equivalent, and which Melville could adapt, if at great cost, to his own ends. Melville's cruelest critics mocked his clear determination to be a "genius";

they called him insane; but they never suggested—as Fuller's enemies, and her friends, did—that he was a freak.[3]

Melville persevered in the argument he understood to be his own; he refused to alter the terms, for that would be to alter the problem, and the problem itself was what he had to solve. His identity was bound up with it, but finally his identity was distinct from it; he possessed, in some professional sense not altogether culturally available to Fuller, work. During Melville's visit to Hawthorne in Liverpool in 1856, the two men took a walk by the sea and resumed an old discussion on the possibility of belief. Hawthorne was struck with Melville's characteristic tenacity, on this subject as on every other, a tenacity that clearly came less from hope than from a sense of respect for the issues he raised:

> It is strange how he persists [Hawthorne wrote]—and has persisted ever since I knew him, and probably long before—in wandering to and fro over these deserts, as dismal and monotonous as the sand hills amid which we were sitting. He can neither believe, nor be comfortable in his unbelief; and he is too honest and courageous not to try to do one or the other.... he has a very high and noble nature.[4]

One remembers Thomas Carlyle's similar tribute to Fuller's "truly high" nature, her "chivalrous nobleness à toute epreuve" after meeting her in London in 1846; yet the reasons for Carlyle's admiration were different from those Hawthorne adduced in his praise of Melville. Carlyle had never, he wrote Emerson, witnessed a desire as intense as Fuller's to consume the universe as if it were her oyster, "to be absolute empress of all height and glory in it that her heart could conceive."[5] Fuller's emphasis was on possession, Melville's on comprehension. Melville as a man was surer of his inheritance than Fuller could be as a woman; his effort was to deal with it. The essential dilemma in all Melville's work is that of responsibility. It is clear to Melville always that he has a legacy, although it may be a useless one, like Redburn's outdated guidebook, or even a murderous encumbrance, like the water-logged and over-conspicuous "white jacket."

It is perhaps grandiose, yet I think essentially accurate, to say that Melville conceived of America itself in some genuine sense as his inheritance, and his burden. America was the problem he had to comprehend. Like Fuller, Melville felt profound bitterness on occasion about his country; it is impossible, nonetheless, to imagine him relocating his patriotism as she did. Fuller apologized at various points for having apprenticed herself to European rather than American minds. She never truly shifted her intellectual allegiances, however; she knew the European minds were the best minds, and her commitment to the best was precisely analogous to her commitment to herself. Although Melville's serious career began when he immersed himself in reading the great European masters past and present, although he absorbed voraciously what they had to teach him,[6] he did not write directly about them or from their models.

Indeed, no American author clung more tenaciously to American material than Melville. Whitman of course is as consistently wedded to American subjects as Melville, more so in fact, but the connection is experienced as inevitable, assumed. Whitman's work does not revolve, as Melville's in part does, around the felt denial of the impulse to abjure America. Melville's later narratives, most notably *The Confidence Man*, cleave to American materials with almost punitive vengeance: "This, *this*," one feels Melville saying, "is my subject!" All of Melville's writing is alive with his at times outraged conviction that he cannot produce a work significantly better than his culture. With the exception of portions of *Redburn* and *Israel Potter*, Melville debars himself in his major works from the use of European settings. The only alien civilizations Melville allows his readers contact with are those of the South Seas, precisely those which Americans (and Europeans) were then in the process of destroying. The non-American world Melville shows us is the arena for American acquisitiveness: the seas are the locale where Americans conduct their fishing industries and their wars, the South Sea Islands are the places to which they send their missionaries and their sailors. The non-American world of Melville's narratives is one by definition mutilated by America. Through his main semi-autobiographical characters, usually American sailors and soldiers, Melville acknowledged himself as protagonist and victim of America's imperialism; he denied himself use of the resources of older and richer cultures.

Melville defined the test which every formidable American author in his day and since has had to impose on himself: how to exploit and resist the crude American material which both enriches and impoverishes the writer; how to take the exact measure of the reader who belongs to and is that material, how to know him utterly and intimately without being absorbed by him. Before Melville started to write, Edgar Allan Poe had dramatized the dilemma in his detective tales. Poe's detective figure, Auguste Dupin, explains on one occasion that in trying to solve any case, he must put himself precisely in the place of the criminal involved: trace his footsteps, think his thoughts. Little wonder that Dupin, impoverished, obsessive, secretive, resembles the insane and criminal narrators of Poe's horror tales; the only difference between Poe's detective and his criminal is that while both imagine the crime, the detective does not commit it. Increasingly over the course of Melville's career, his protagonists—Ishmael, Pierre, Captain Amasa Delano, the lawyer in "Bartleby the Scrivener" come to mind—become proto-detectives, and Melville's own undoubtedly hostile conception of the

American writer's task becomes exactly that of imagining his society's crime without enacting it.[7]

In paradoxical fashion, Melville committed himself to a self-selected crime to insure himself against the crimes of sentimentality and effeminacy which he was recording and protesting in his society. I would like to argue that the crime Melville picked as his own was masculinity itself—just as Fuller, I might add, chose femininity, as she conceived it, as her sin. This was possible precisely because of the fact that, when sex roles are as utterly stereotyped as they were in nineteenth-century America, genuine sexual identity becomes by definition—and perhaps this was the point—illicit. Certainly Melville was as deeply and broadly concerned with manhood as Fuller was with womanhood; she used her life as her main vehicle of definition, he his work, but the concern was the same. Fuller perceived that women would be afraid to think when thinking made them outcasts. Melville came to see more and more clearly the other side: that a culture which gave feminine antinomianism privileged status would be forced to treat, and distort, masculinity as a species of outlawry, whether opposed as immoral or abetted as titillating. This is not to suggest that masculinity was Melville's only preoccupation or that he conceived of it in simplified and primarily sexual terms. Melville's essential struggle was to widen and make complex definitions which his culture conspired to narrow. He conceived masculinity, as Fuller understood feminism, essentially as resistance to sentimentalism, as an effort at a genuinely political and philosophical life.

Melville was never unaware that the American reading public consisted largely of middle-class women whose domesticated and at times insidious piety was buttressed and catered to by large segments of the clerical and literary establishment.[8] In *Pierre* (1852), Melville presents a savage study of the conspirational interaction between genteel religion, feminine morality, and polite literature against the interests of genuine masculinity. Early in the book, Melville introduces us to a clergyman called Reverend Falsgrave, a self-made, elegant temporizer, a lover of choice female companionship, and the author of "various fugitive pieces upon subjects of nature, art and literature" (139).[9] Falsgrave is totally dependent upon his female parishioners, most notably the widowed Mrs. Glendinning, Pierre's mother, whom he wishes to marry; by necessity he must fail the male members of his congregation. Pierre is involved in a special crisis: he has discovered, or so he thinks, that his father secretly sired an illegitimate daughter before marrying his mother. What should he think of his dead father, revealed as a seducer? How should he treat that daughter, now discovered? The case is complicated by a neighborhood scandal: Delly, a lower-class girl, is pregnant and unmarried. The local community, indifferent to the wrongdoing of the man involved, wants to drive her away. Pierre can hardly miss the analogies with his father's past: Delly might be his father's mistress, hounded and persecuted while he was allowed to go free. Pierre poses his dilemma, suitably disguised as concern for Delly's case, in front of his mother to Falsgrave. Falsgrave cannot handle this problem, partly because he is too weak to possess any genuine ethical system of values—his arena is social and literary, not religious—and partly because he must follow Mrs. Glendinning's lead. And she refuses to deal honestly with the situation since to do so would be to remind herself of the limits of her power: precisely those imposed by the complex imperatives of male sexuality. Easier simply to condemn Delly, the woman in the case, as Mrs. Glendinning does, than to scrutinize what she cannot control, the male seducer. The woman and the minister conspire to ignore the facts.

Pierre is totally disillusioned with both of them, yet he himself has exemplified Melville's awareness of the special taint of American culture. Before his encounter with his illegitimate half-sister, Isabel, he publishes a number of sentimental "effusions" in polite periodicals. Critics praise Pierre's productions for their "smoothness and gentleness" (342), their lack of "vulgarity and vigor," and their suitability to the "family circle"; the enterprising editors engineering the sentimental market ask to publish his collected works in a fashionably thin volume. Pierre modestly considers himself as yet too young for such a proceeding, not realizing, Melville bitterly adds, that most popular writers are "legal minors forced to go to their mammas for pennies to keep them in peanuts" (349). Countless young ladies send their "albums" for Pierre's autographs; he dismisses a stack of such volumes with a graciously cavalier kiss. Like any genteel poeticizer of the day, Pierre pens sentimental obituary verse; he dedicates one poem to "the Late Reverend Mark Graceman" (345). Pierre abandons this conventional literary career, and his popularity, when he flees to New York to live with Isabel, but Melville has successfully exposed its effeminate, juvenile, hypocritical, and essentially mercenary nature.

Pierre's first work is a sonnet entitled "The Tropical Summer," clearly a satiric reference to Melville's early successful South Seas narratives. Yet Melville had never tried to court the feminine market as Pierre does. From the start of his career, he expected an indifferent or hostile response from women readers. Writing to Richard Dana in 1849, he acknowledged that *White-Jacket* was "man-of-warish in style—rather aggressive I fear."[10] The source of his fear is clear when he expressed his surprise to Sophia Hawthorne a few years later that she should like *Moby Dick*: "for as a general thing," he wrote her, "women have small taste for the sea." He cautioned another feminine acquaintance to have nothing to do with the same novel:

Don't you buy it—don't you read it when it does come out, because it is by no means a sort of book for you. It is not a piece of fine feminine Spitalfields silk, but it is of the humble texture of a fabric that should be woven of ships' cables & hawsers. A Polar wind blows through it & birds of prey hover over it. Warn all gentle and fastidious people.[11]

Significantly, Melville received less critical and popular support than any other major American writer of his day or since, nor did he court it. He dismissed *White-Jacket* and *Redburn*, two of his finest early works which were well received, as mere trash written to get money. He wanted, he said, to write those kinds of books which are "said to fail"—and he did.[12] We see here a version of the narcissistic rage which propelled Harriet Beecher Stowe into the publication of *Lady Byron Vindicated*. Both Stowe and Melville felt profoundly hostile before a culture whose most basic assumptions opposed their full maturation. But while Stowe in her anger tragically if inevitably on occasion lumped the best of her oppressors with the worst of them, Melville never lost sight of who his enemy was. It was always the absence of critics whose judgment he could respect which triggered his rage. Stowe's dilemma was such that she was forced to be willing to settle for an audience; Melville held out hopelessly, even vindictively, for an audience of his peers. Nor was his preoccupation with failure finally kin to that of the male sentimentalists. They advertised the modesty of their ambition in part from guilt, in part from a desire to redefine success to fit their own image. Melville soon acknowledged his ambition—to write great books which would fully utilize the most demanding and ambiguous material America offered; but he flatly proclaimed that there were few in America to aid or appreciate his attempt. Melville regarded the reception of his books as a test which would ascertain what genuine masculinity, or, as he tacitly defined it, what health and independence of mind, remained in American culture. The content and style of his work were to register his increasingly bitter disillusion with his experiment. Melville's subject came to be his readers, and his disappointment with them.

The Early Works: The Uncontested Space

Melville's early narratives, *Typee* (1847), *Omoo* (1847), *Redburn* (1849), *White-Jacket* (1850), all enjoyed a real if limited popularity; they represent Melville's original acceptance by one segment of the American reading public (those interested in "adventure" stories), his gradual need to complicate and explore that acceptance, and finally his incipient desire to question an audience whose comprehension and tolerance proved painfully inadequate.[13] All four books are set at sea, which was for Melville what the safari or the bullfight would be in more simplistic ways for Hemingway: an arena for the male occupations of acquisition and combat and a preserve for specifically masculine vices and virtues. Sea narratives were attractive to Melville, as they were to the Brahmin Richard Henry Dana, because they offered their author an opportunity to introduce tough low characters without going outside the confines of respectable literature. In the preface to *Omoo*, Melville explains to us that whaling is "a business ... peculiarly fitted to attract the most reckless seamen of all nations ... [and] to foster in them a spirit of the utmost license."[14] The narrator, the Melvillean *persona* in the early books, is, of course, better educated than his comrades, but, with the exception of Redburn, he gives his loyalty to the crew. If he is going to change at sea, it will be in only one way; the "tough training" of a sailor's life, according to Melville, makes a "thorough-bred tar" out of any "boy."[15] Although Melville's viewpoint on this process is complex and compassionate, it is nonetheless true that his weak sailors, most notably Redburn's sensitive and wild English friend Harry Bolton, fail and even die. Melville does not triumph in these facts; he regrets them, yet he records them.

There are no women of any kind to speak of in *Redburn* and *White-Jacket*, and the only women in *Typee* and *Omoo* are Polynesians who pose few challenges to the protagonists. The famous Fayaway of *Typee* is a charming and sympathetic creature. Lovely to look at, uninhibited, tender, sensual, she understands better than any of the other Typees Tommo's needs and desires. She offers exactly what the American Victorian lady would deny her male counterpart: unmoralized pleasure. In *Omoo*, when a native girl resists the advances of a white ship doctor, she does so clearly in a spirit of mischief and on the grounds of personal predilection. There is no moral issue involved. Melville takes pains to point the contrast between "the artless vivacity and unconcealed natural graces" of the Polynesian maidens and the "stiffness, formality and affectation" of the women back home: "It would be the Venus de'Medici placed beside a millener's doll!"[16] *Godey's Lady's Book* praised *Typee;* the reviewer had clearly missed the challenge Melville directed to its readers.

These early works, however, are only at moments conscious of feminine America at all. The issue is resistance or obedience not to female authority but to male rule. Part of the essential Calvinism of these narratives is Melville's implicit insistence—an insistence that divides him from most of his contemporaries, including Hawthorne—that the fundamental struggle in American culture is the Oedipal one of son against father, not that of son against mother. Melville stresses everywhere the tyrannical authority the American sea captain exercises. In *White-Jacket,* he compares Captain Claret to Henry the Eighth and informs us that a captain has far more power over his crew than the American president exerts over his constituents.[17] The sly and dishonest captain of Redburn's ship is aptly named "Riga," the Latin word for "stick" or "rod." Melville's captains seldom fail to use the weapons which are metaphorically associated with them. In *White-Jacket*, what story there is turns on several whipping incidents. Captain Claret relishes floggings. At one point, it momentarily appears that the narrator himself is going to be whipped; determined to avoid such a humiliation, he seriously contemplates killing Claret by pushing him overboard. The Oedipal iconography could not be clearer.

It is important to notice at this juncture, however, that the whipping incidents seldom center merely on a personal "Oedipal" confrontation between the captain and a specific sailor. In every case, Melville depicts the captain as unjust; therefore, the issue becomes whether the shipmates of the victim are going to band together to defend him or keep a cowardly peace. White-Jacket is rescued from his beating, and from committing murder, by another sailor who dares to speak up and clear him of the offense with which the captain has charged him. Earlier in *White-Jacket*, a man is beaten for defending a friend whom the captain is intent on flogging. At the close of the narrative, the captain willfully and unfairly orders all the crew to shave off their beards. One noble old sailor absolutely refuses; he is whipped and confined, yet still he holds firm. The other men admire him, they know his resistance is right, but they do not stand by him. It is a measure of the corruption which the prospect of shore life represents to Melville that the crew, eager to land without delay or interference, obeys the captain. In sum, the issue underlying the flogging scenes is paternalism versus fraternity, capitulating to the oppressor versus organizing the oppressed. Melville is suggesting, in profound opposition to the tendencies of his culture, that the real "plot" on shipboard—and in the American society which shipboard life for Melville always symbolizes—is essentially political and class-oriented.

This is a difficult problem, but it seems to me Melville was perhaps the first major American author to sense that the essential question for the American writer and intellectual was whether he was going to subscribe to what would be the Freudian or what would be the Marxist analysis of his culture—whether he would focus on personality or on societal structures as causal agent. It is worth noting that in all the narratives from which (American) women are excluded—*Typee*, *Omoo*, *Redburn*, *White-Jacket*, *Moby Dick*, "Bartleby the Scrivener," "Benito Cereno," *Israel Potter*, and *Billy Budd* —Melville is interested primarily in questions of class: the clash between employer and employed, master and slave, government and soldier. Partly in response to his own failed career, Melville was increasingly preoccupied with the lost, the overlooked, the forgotten, the obscure, and the inaccessible. So, as we have seen, were many of the sentimental and religious writers of the day; but Melville's emphasis was on economic facts, not on nostalgic evasion of them. In a country as highly commercialized, as totally oriented toward publicity as Melville's bombastic newspaper-addicted America, he realized that fame and recognition were a sign not so much of achievement as of status; he understood that the cause of disposal was class. The class problem does not seem to exist in America, Melville was aware, precisely because the lower classes are the unscrutinized—a situation he brilliantly attempted to rectify in his depiction of common sailors, immigrants, blacks, and city clerks.

The narratives which include women—most notably *Mardi*, *Pierre*, "Jimmy Rose," "I and My Chimney," "The Apple-Tree Table," and *The Confidence Man*—are, in contrast, primarily psychological. The most basic questions in these works are not about class but about emotional and spiritual health and disease, about the possibilities of communication and trust. The protagonists are mainly of the same social class—the middle class. Delly, the only lower-class character in *Pierre*, is a very minor character. The "Confidence Man" in his various disguises ranges from black lower-class to white upper-middle-class. The whole point of his masquerade, however, is that he is exposing and exploiting not the class realities of America but his fellow middle-class passengers' sentimentalized response to the trappings of class: "Black Guinea," the Negro beggar, receives pity and contempt; the more affluent-appearing "Cosmopolitan" usually gets a respectful hearing. I would note also how differently Melville treats the question of money in the psychological as opposed to the class-oriented works. In the latter, money is usually spoken of frankly and specifically. We know, for example, exactly how much money Redburn and Harry Bolton are supposed to get from Captain Riga; Melville describes in detail the process by which Ishmael's and Queequeg's wages are determined. In the psychological narratives, economic facts are almost entirely obscured; their suppression is actually one of the common themes of these works. "Jimmy Rose," for example, concerns a wealthy and charming man's fall from prosperity. His former friends, more or less ignoring his plight, let him drop over for tea and pretend they are not aware that such apparently casual repasts constitute his main support. In his sick old age, he is tended by a pious young girl who visits the needy in most approved sentimental fashion: she relieves Jimmy's suffering with jellies and religious tracts. Despite his habitual courtliness, one day he throws her books into the corner, muttering: "Thinks she to solve a gentleman's heart with Poor Man's Plaster?"[18] He himself cannot admit the truth about his utter deprivation, but he can no longer tolerate lies.

My distinction between Melville's "Marxist" and "Freudian" work is of course imprecise, since all the works show the influence of both kinds of thinking,[19] but I believe it is roughly accurate. Why does this rough distinction correspond to works without women and those with them? At some level, Melville seems to have grasped the at least outward disavowal of economic issues which we have seen as essential to the role of the American lady. In order not to make conspicuous her lack of economic productivity, she had to ignore economics altogether. In 1836, Catharine Maria Sedgwick, whom Melville later knew in the Berkshires, published a cheery little study of the upper and lower classes entitled *The Poor Rich Man and the Rich Poor Man*. Its moral was that wealth has nothing to do with happiness and genuine success. Incensed at such sentimental evasion, Melville published a bitter parody in 1854 which he mockingly called "Poor Man's Pudding and Rich Man's Crumbs." In *Pierre*, Melville explores feminine ignorance of economics more explicitly. Isabel, Pierre's sister, and Lucy, his fiancée, are living with Pierre in New York; both are utterly reliant on him to support them. When the upper-class Lucy first moves in, she has apparently no conception of the financial difficulties her arrival causes the pinched little household. She decides to paint portraits to earn money, and Pierre lacks the heart to tell her how little difference her ladylike efforts can possibly make. If Lucy lacks class-consciousness, Isabel lacks class altogether. An orphan who grew up in a series of totally anomalous situations, Isabel has only the vaguest notions of societal life, much less of economic necessity; she of course is incapable of doing anything to help affairs. Her superb guitar-playing is the product of inspiration à la Stowe or Sigourney—God does it, not Isabel. It is untutored and unteachable. Only Pierre has enough economic sense to feel their poverty and ignominy. In other words, class-consciousness is minimized in *Pierre* and the other narratives I have grouped with it simply because the women whose awareness provides the male protagonist's claustrophobic arena are themselves incapable of it.[20]

And hence it is a significant part of the "masculine" quality of the early works that the conflicts on which they turn are largely ones of class. The crucial scene for all these narratives occurs early in *Redburn*. Impoverished young Redburn is crossing to New York by ferry. Humiliated by the public disclosure that he has not adequate fare for his passage and must travel as a kind of charity case, he brandishes his ludicrous old hunting piece at the other, prosperous passengers whose cold stares he detests. He frightens them as he intends, and then goes to stand alone and sullen in the rain on the deck. "Such," Melville summarizes grimly, "is boyhood."[21] Popular American literature in Melville's day and after was dedicated—and not totally without cause—to the effort of substituting moral, sexual, generational, and even geographical definitions for economic and class-determined ones: the good characters and the bad, the women and the men, the maid and the matron, the boy and the adult, the young and the old, the northerner, the southerner, the easterner, the westerner. Redburn's "boyhood," that supposedly idyllic period, is empty and useless as a category, Melville implies; his age counts for less than his economic status.[22]

Melville's early narratives are as unyielding to the demands of sentimentalism in form as they are resistant to it in content. Over and over, Melville assures us that he will "set forth things as they actually exist";[23] he writes to correct "high-raised romantic notions" about life at sea; no "sentimental" illusions motivate him; he will give us "facts."[24] At one point in *White-Jacket*, he describes his purpose thus:

> I let nothing slip, however small; and feel myself actuated by the same motive which has prompted many worthy old chroniclers, to set down the merest trifles concerning things that are destined to pass away entirely from the earth, and which, if not preserved in the nick of time, must infallibly perish from the memories of men.[25]

Melville of course did not actually follow the facts of his own sea adventures in quite the literal-minded fashion he suggests here; he relied at times heavily on accounts of other travelers, and selected and edited his own experiences with care. Yet Melville is accurate in the *White-Jacket* passage at least in so far as he is suggesting that the impression his narrative should convey is fidelity to fact.

Melville was from the start profoundly distrustful of fiction; he wrote fictionally chiefly in what I have called the psychological works. In other words, he used fiction to write about women or worlds which had been formed by their presence, and he always used it as a mode of irony. The term *fiction*, as I am applying it to Melville's works, is a complicated one. *Mardi* and *Moby Dick*, for example, are neither factual chronicles nor fictions; they are rather romances of a special kind, heightened imaginative explorations of significant events and emotions. It is crucial to Melvillean romance that both books apparently begin as accurate narratives centered in a realistic character's consciousness: they take off, quite literally, into the realm of story—with Mardi's quest and Ahab's appearance—from this factual basis. The "story," the more palpably inverted part of the book, acts as a heightening, a continuation, and a transformation of the at least avowedly factual narrative; it is always for Melville a type of necessary hybris. As such, it threatens the narrative's existence—in the unsuccessful *Mardi*, it kills it—but it is essentially dependent on it; the story can be called to account by the narrative: Ishmael in part determines our responses to Ahab. Melville's "fictions," in contrast to his romances, are those works such as *Pierre* and *The Confidence Man* which are deliberately irresponsible, which are at no point harnessed to a narrative sensibility we can trust. Fiction is to Melville a form of deceit. Unlike Margaret Fuller, he found brilliant uses for it, but he employed it only in works like *Pierre* and *The Confidence Man* which are profoundly concerned with sentimentalism and self-hatred. By a process of reversal typical of Melville, fiction is in a sense Melville's way of imitating and punishing his "fiction"-hungry audience.

Among the four early books, the first two, *Typee* and *Omoo*, represent Melville's happiest and surest if not his most profound examples of the narrative form. They advertise their factual accuracy, and they reveal a total structural dependence on the nature of actual experience. What is off-stage is always acknowledged. The demands of what "story" there is are never absolute; they never impinge on reality. If Tommo in *Typee*, for example, does not know what happened to his comrade Toby after Toby left the valley of the Typees, we will not find out either, although by any of the laws of fiction, we could expect to. In particular *Omoo*, Melville's second South Sea book, reads like an exercise in unmanipulated narrative; Melville writes in ether. All events have equal emphasis: it is the hardest of Melville's books to recall in any detail. Melville seems to be gamboling in the pleasures of objectivity. If *Moby Dick* was to be a "wicked, wicked book," *Omoo* is an extraordinarily innocent one. Most narratives, fictional or factual, work by a process of becoming burdened with themselves; they become curiously guilty, and this guilt is part of our at times almost compulsive involvement in them. *Omoo*, in contrast, is relatively eventless and what events there are never accumulate. Each chapter seems to begin again like a new morning. In contrast to the parasitic quality of Melville's "fiction" from *Pierre* through *The Confidence Man*, *Omoo* is a model of narrative independence: a collage of reported experience. Melville clearly does not yet feel that he must bargain with his readers and manipulate their reactions. *Omoo*'s innocence is finally dependent on its blissfully assumed ignorance of its own commercial identity.

Not all the early works are so structurally joyous as *Omoo* or even *Typee*. In publishing the wild metaphorical romance *Mardi* (1849), Melville gambled that the audience he had won with *Typee* and *Omoo* would be interested in what he considered his development; he lost. Despite their relatively straightforward quality, *Redburn* and *White-Jacket*, which come after the critical debacle of *Mardi*, are more complicated and conflicted in their forms, although not in their themes, than their predecessors. This disjuncture between form and theme deserves comment. It is part of Melville's special and radically inventive identity as a writer that, while he can be uncomfortably Victorian in his ideas and rhetoric, he is always incalculably if equally uncomfortably modern epistemologically. When we speak of experimentation we usually mean that the experimenter is taking only eighty percent of his material (rather than 100 percent) as a given and playing with the rest. Melville was disturbingly capable of dropping almost all assumptions, of taking nothing for granted. Whatever his literary debts, he wrote often as if no other book had ever been written or ever would be. This refusal to accumulate formally makes Melville less stable, and on occasion more disappointing, than any other writer of his stature, but it is essential to his lifelong purpose. Structure rather than content was his most responsive register and indicator: every change in his sensibility showed up at once as formal instability and transformation. Form was thus sensitive with Melville in part because he increasingly grasped that the author meets his reader's expectations or doesn't, earns his reader's trust or fails to, punishes or rewards the reader, through form rather than through theme: in other words form, and the arousal and satisfaction of audience appetite it controls, provide the negotiating ground for writer and reader.

Redburn's form is indicative of Melville's post-*Mardi* uncertainty as to who his audience was and how he should treat it. The book reveals a confusion of tone and *persona* which makes even the work of "Ik Marvel" or Harriet Stowe look uncomplicated. Melville alternately informs us, condescends to us, shows off to us, and satirizes us;[26] Redburn is on one page a prig who calls a gentleman a "wight" (à la Spenser), refuses to drink or smoke, and generally mimics the reader's presumed prudery; on the next page, he is an embittered rebel who talks bluntly and assaults the reader's complacency. Melville cannot here wed consistency of characterization with consistency of attack. *White-Jacket* presents a different and somewhat more skillfully handled formal problem. The protagonists are coherent; the plot is not. The "story" occurs—as it will always do in Melville but here with unusual force—in segments, as pieces that the reader cannot quite fit into one puzzle. The noble and gay sailor Jack Chase, who is above his station, the rather sad poet Lemsford attacked by the rest of the crew, the episodes of the whipping, the enforced shearing of the sailors: they all form a partial pattern; they do not constitute events. The story seems to be mysteriously absorbed, as it will be in *Moby Dick*, into symbolic objects, most notably the nearly lethal jacket itself, whose meaning is never fully articulated. Melville was always more creative with nouns than with verbs; he was more likely to make up nouns from verbs than the reverse.[27] In some roughly analogous fashion, objects in his later narratives soak up events and refuse to yield them in any accessible form. It is as if they can only give them up in the form of a highly imaginative and difficult "story": the white whale's unfathomed meaning somehow secretes the Ahab section of *Moby Dick*. In *White-Jacket*, no "story" takes off. The narrative refuses to precipitate itself, to give birth: it is curiously sullen. As in *Redburn*, Melville is temporarily blurring the distinction between "Marxist" and "Freudian" material; a kind of tormented and self-conscious stasis, different from the freely willed eventlessness of *Omoo*, intrudes almost unsought on the potential narrative development. In spots *Redburn* and *White-Jacket* become signs of suffering rather than studies of it. The causes of Melville's pain were many, but not least among them was his growing dislike of the "public." The partial artistic failure of *Redburn* and *White-Jacket* is both involuntary and voluntary. Melville reveals his increasing distrust of his audience by withholding his book, by refusing to perform the authorial tasks of development and reconciliation.

Moby Dick and *Pierre*: *The Struggle for Possession*

If Melville was performing an act of formal repression against his readers in *Redburn* and *White-Jacket*, he was also staving off open expression of his conflict with them. In *Moby Dick* and *Pierre*, Melville allows this conflict to surface, and, in doing so, he summons and exploits all his creative energies to a degree unique in his career. The two books are, however, radically dissimilar. While Melville acknowledges his challenge to the sentimental culture of his reader in both works, only in *Moby Dick* does he still hope to make good on it. As a result, the book operates thematically and structurally as a conversion process; Melville plots brilliantly to bring his audience to his side.[28] *Pierre*, in contrast, is Melville's document of despair. Revenge, not conversion is his aim; Melville punishes his readers in advance for their inevitable failure of comprehension.

We have already seen how Melville specifically warned women away from *Moby Dick*—"Don't you buy it—don't you read it." The book was written for men, or at least from a self-consciously masculine viewpoint. Early on in the story, Ishmael and Queequeg attend a chapel service for sailors where they see a number of women whose countenances suggest "unceasing grief" for their men lost at sea. When they appear in *Moby Dick*, women are the mourners and the losers: they have no other role. Never before has Melville emphasized so heavily the acquisitive brutality of the fishing enterprise: we witness the horrible killing of an old sperm whale, we see the beating of his bloody fins. Melville's attitude is hardly simple here; yet his criticism of the whaling industry, real as it is, functions less significantly than his need to face the facts, paint the whole picture, as part of an exemplary process of disciplined total perception. Melville is giving the reader lessons in honesty, not in pity. Melville never denies in *Moby Dick* the value of the domestic virtues of piety or morality; he does deny such virtues the right actively to justify themselves in the narrative. Their place is negative; they are what is forgotten, over-ridden, whether for good or bad. On board the *Pequod*, the first mate Starbuck constitutes himself the spokesman for the softer, more "human" values; it is he who, just before the chase of the white whale, speaks to Ahab of his own family waiting at home and of Ahab's young wife and new-born son. Ahab has a moment of weakness; he thinks of the mother he never knew, he even weeps, but he is finally adamant against all softening impulses. The most impervious and dictatorial of all Melville's captains, Ahab will not help the captain of the *Rachel* look for his lost son, he disavows the black boy Pip whom he had befriended, he turns from Starbuck. Important as the relations among various crew members are to Melville, he subordinates them, as he did not in his earlier narratives, to the phenomenon represented by his captain. Both newly embattled and released at this point in his career, Melville wishes to explore rather than challenge the meaning of masculine authority.

It is interesting that, unlike Melville's earlier protagonists, Ahab cannot be understood at all without some knowledge of Calvinism: it is essential to his masculinity. In the works preceding *Moby Dick*, Melville dealt with the Christian religion in large part negatively, by a critique of the missionary effort; in *Moby Dick* and the books which succeed it—all of which are essentially located in America as the earlier narratives were not—the critique continues, but it is accompanied by an intermittent yet vital exploration of the Calvinist heritage Melville's contemporaries were abandoning. As Hawthorne's comments in his Liverpool journal indicate, Melville was in no conventional sense a believer; but, as his own artistic ambition was activated in its most serious form, he apparently found it necessary to utilize the ideas and structures of Calvinism. Its hieratic form, its preoccupation with pain, defiance, and grandiosity, its complex confrontation of the human and the inhuman, give Melville a suitable object for imitation, exploration, and attack. In *Moby Dick*, when Queequeg is signed up for the *Pequod*, Bildad, one of the ship's owners, wishes to convert the pagan harpooner to Christianity. The other owner, Peleg, at once protests: " 'Pious harpooners never make good voyagers—it takes the shark out of 'em' " (89).[29] One could say that in *Moby Dick*, Melville is putting the shark back into religion.

At one point, in speaking of the white whale's beauty, Melville explains: "real strength never impairs beauty or harmony, but it often bestows it." Melville is of course defending the "sublime" against the tacit resistance of a society which espouses the "beautiful" and the "picturesque." He continues by comparing the "robustness" of Michelangelo's "God the Father" with "the soft, curled, hermaphroditical" Christ of later Italian painters, and—as Melville must have been aware although he does not say so here—of nineteenth-century American representations. Such pictures of Christ show "nothing of any power, but the mere negative, feminine one of submission and endurance, which on all hands it is conceded form the practical virtues of his teachings" (372). Melville was never really concerned with Christ—certainly not the Christ of his culture; for him as for Lyman Beecher, although in a more terrifying sense, "everything was swallowed up in God." Although the God of *Moby Dick* is hardly the specific theological entity of earlier Calvinist creeds but rather an "inscrutable thing"—the presence which Ahab defies and the white whale suggests—he is hardly less terrifying, less impressive, or even less Calvinist for his amorphousness and inaccessibility. *Moby Dick* is, in fact, an implicit critique of liberal Protestantism. Starbuck's death, which occurs when the white whale overwhelms the *Pequod*, is a demonstration of the inefficacy of the sentimental creed. Imploring "Ye sweet powers of air," whom Melville has specifically linked with feminine influences, to "hug me close," Starbuck goes down to destruction ironically exclaiming "My God, stand by me now!" (562–63). Melville's God is as indifferent to mortal needs and aspirations for happiness as Joseph Bellamy's. Like the God Bellamy preached whom one of his parishioners found " 'SO GREAT!' " the divine presence in *Moby Dick*, whether malign or benign, by definition stretches the human mind almost past endurance. Ahab's acknowledged insanity is a measure of his recognition, however inadequate, of the force that rules the universe. The "class" struggle in *Moby Dick* is no longer between crew and captain; the men back Ahab in his pursuit of the whale. But the "Marxist" struggle has been transformed, or abandoned; *Moby Dick* concerns the archetypal conflict between the rules and the ruled, between God and man.[30]

Moby Dick opens with a powerful revival service conducted by Father Mapple, a former seaman. His sermon sets the tone for the book. Ahab, damned as he is, will convert the entire crew, with the exception of Starbuck, to his Calvinist view of life, his obsession with what Melville elsewhere called "the power of blackness"; in a very real way, I believe, he will convert the reader. The crew's concern and our concern will increasingly be Ahab's confrontation with his destroyer. This is not to suggest that Melville totally approves of Ahab any more than he entirely disapproves of the domestic virtues which Ahab cannot heed. Yet it would have been so easy for Melville to turn us against Ahab; if the noble self-possessed Bulkington remained on stage longer, if Ishmael, or indeed any crew member we thoroughly respected, genuinely resented and protested Ahab's despotic lack of concern for the crew's interests, we could contextualize and distance Ahab more readily. None of these things happen. Bulkington disappears; Ishmael, despite his disapproval, is swept up by Ahab. Ishmael launches the "narrative," but only while it deals with events on shore; he tells us of his friendship with Queequeg, the preparations for sailing. Once at sea, Ishmael's voice exists in a complex counterpoint with Ahab's and is at times even supplanted by it. Ahab gives us, indeed embodies, the "story," and his voice represents the extreme of public performance and revivalist art. Ahab is probably the greatest orator, the finest preacher in American literature; if Margaret Fuller had been alive in 1851, she would have appreciated his language; if Stowe had read *Moby Dick*, she would have understood his style and his subject.

In taking over the narrative voice, Ahab moves it from the personal to the impersonal; Ahab's mind may be diseased, but it is a sickness he caught from God, not man. Nor can the movement from the particular to the abstract be reversed. After Ahab's death, the closing paragraphs before the "epilogue," presumably given us by Ishmael, are in a narrative mode which is significantly more mannered, more grandiose, than Ishmael's opening style. Here is the start:

> Call me Ishmael. Some years ago—never mind how long precisely—having little or no money in my purse, and nothing particular to interest me on shore, I thought I would sail about a little and see the watery part of the world. (1)

Note the frightening connotations of a plethora of undistinguishable possibilities, Ishmael's hypothetical unwanted but insistent personal perspective. Here is the (penultimate) ending:

> Now small fowls flew screaming over the yet yawning gulf; a sullen white surf beat against its steep sides, then all collapsed, and the great shroud of the sea rolled on as it rolled five thousand years ago. (565)

The tone is detached but magisterial, even orchestrated. Certain things are no longer possible: history has happened. Ishmael is no more "important" than he ever was, but his attitude toward his task of reportage has shifted. Ishmael survives, although he inhabits a universe which stands defined as the wake of the whale and the grave of Ahab. His return is necessary, for he represents the possibility, no matter how randomly available, of taking responsibility for experience, even for experience beyond our control. He suggests if not a commitment, a continuity on the part of the author, and a lesson for the reader.

Ahab's implacability offers a clue to his literary as well as to his religious significance. His moral value is ambiguous, as I have said, but I do not think this ambiguity is central to Melville's design as, say, the uncertainty about Lord Jim's courage is essential to Conrad's. Melville is not drawing the reader close to Ahab in the sense that he is urging the reader as a man to emulate or even evaluate Ahab as a hero. The levels of Melville's literary self-consciousness here are numerous and uncannily "modern," as we like to say in praise of writers of former ages. He grasped the fact that a reader identifies with a fictional protagonist not only as he represents a "real" person, but also purely *as a fictional character*. Melville brings the reader close to Ahab because he wishes the experience of Ahab *as a hero in a book* to educate the reader not simply as a person but *as a reader*. Ishmael is not only an observer and an actor in the book, he is a model for the reader. It is important that Ahab is a deliberately old-fashioned, even anachronistic, character; his bombastic, self-consciously literary rhetoric is that of the American drama of the 1830s; his very insanity is a kind of cultural throwback; his intensely romantic view of the universe—which his "monomania" frees him to find compact with meaning, if a diabolic one—is not that of Ishmael, our contemporary. Ishmael, with his utter lack of cultural roots and his terror of a potentially empty, meaningless universe, needs to identify with Ahab as well as to survive him. Ishmael is not asked to become Ahab —finally he cannot, although he is tempted to try—but he is asked not to deny that he knew him. Melville is insisting that art is not a product to be consumed and thrown aside, as the "sketch" suggested, but an experience which can and must alter the participant's view of life and himself. Ishmael cannot regain his pre-Ahab voice because Ahab has happened. The reader is denied the usual cycle of vicarious involvement, readjustment, and rejection. *Moby Dick* is the most powerful attempt made by an American author on the eve of the commercialization of literature as a part of mass culture both to find a wide audience and to restore the indispensability, the essentially religious dignity, of the literary work.

In an age which expected its authors to be accessible and easily assimilable, Melville advertised the difficulty of his book. When Ishmael arrives at the Spouter Inn, he finds on the wall "a very large oil-painting" whose subject it is almost "impossible to decipher." There are "such unaccountable masses of shades and shadows," such "portentous" masses, that it is "enough to drive a nervous man distracted." The painting possesses an "unimaginable sublimity" which freezes the viewer to the spot, until he "involuntarily" takes "an oath ... to find out what that marvellous painting meant." Only by "much and earnest contemplation, and oft repeated ponderings," however, can Ishmael make out an image: that of a whale impaling itself on the three masts of a ship—a picture very close to the final scene with Moby Dick and the *Pequod* (10, 11). Melville is both acknowledging and justifying the intricate sustained effort he demands of his reader: as Margaret Fuller asked of her friends, he expects his readers to be productive. The reader is asked to move from the passivity of the "sub-sub," the Irvingesque *persona* who opens *Moby Dick* with his erudite but uncollated series of definitions, the consumer of literature who is always more a reader than a writer, toward the philosophy of Ishmael, who is pre-eminently engaged with experience, and finally to the passion of Ahab, whose imagination encompasses and creates the enormities of adventure. The reader is urged to deal with the ambiguities of Ahab's moral status precisely because to deal with ambiguity is, in Melville's mind, to deal with danger. Melville asks the reader metaphorically to risk his life to explore the necessities of the imagination; he invites the reader to help him write the book—if he dares.

The reader of *Pierre* is exposed to endless "ambiguities"; that is, indeed, the book's subtitle. But the danger is not educative here, for Melville allows his readers no real way into the novel; the story is an insult, not a dare. In the same letter to Sophia Hawthorne in which Melville expressed his surprise that she had liked *Moby Dick*—"for as a general thing women have small taste for the sea"—he promised her that his next work, presumably *Pierre*, would be a "rural bowl of milk," a book for the ladies.[31] Instead, in *Pierre*, Melville turned decisively and openly against the middle-class sentimental-minded feminized reading public he had essentially tried to evade or educate in his previous work. It is as if their interference with his creative effort has become so troubling that he must deal with it, and he does so by making it, in curious ways, the actual subject of his book.

The forces of domesticity which were excluded in the earlier works and intricately contained in *Moby Dick* have overwhelmed the world of *Pierre*. For the first but not the last time, Melville limits himself to a claustrophobically inland setting. Wealthy young Pierre Glendinning, the hero, grows up on a lush country estate. There is nothing wild in the landscape; it is all blossoms and birds, a model of the picturesque. It suggests the ideal feminine setting, and, fittingly, its other principal inhabitants are women, Pierre's masterful mother Mrs. Glendinning and his innocent young fiancée, Lucy. Their polite Episcopalian faith is, at least in theory, Pierre's. Pierre's father is dead; he is the first, but again not the last, of Melville's heroes who does not have to struggle with a living paternal authority, actual or symbolic. His essential conflict is with his mother.

Imperious and beautiful Mrs. Glendinning is the daughter of a general, and, beneath her calculated façade of dignified charm, she reveals the habit of command. Discreetly wielding her sexual attractions to keep her son close to her, she envelops Pierre in what Melville tellingly calls a "fictitious" relationship. The two evince a confusion between life and literature as deep as any that Henry Ward Beecher would display. They pretend coyly that they are brother and sister, and their conversation is studded gaily with literary allusions. Mrs. Glendinning wants Pierre to marry a timid, retiring girl, such as she believes Lucy to be, one who will pose no threat to herself. Her playful decorum hides a desire to repress all genuine excitement in her son. On one occasion, she reproves Pierre in the style of an etiquette manual: " 'Never rave, Pierre, and never rant' " (14). In her musings about her son, the word Mrs. Glendinning uses over and over again to describe him is "docile." Indeed, she frankly admits to herself that she hopes he will resemble "a fine woman" in possessing a swelling chest, abundant hair, and docility (26). Mrs. Glendinning has all the authority usually associated with the man of the family, and she uses it to keep Pierre in innocent and amiable ignorance of the real world, her rival. Melville seems to be cynically suggesting that the Victorian lady, and reader, will use all her "influence" to keep her men, and her authors, as "feminine," and as restricted, as she is supposed to be. The distractions Mrs. Glendinning permits Pierre are precisely those which perpetuate her power: dabblings, as we have seen, in trivial fashionable verse, and sentimental flirtation with his fiancée. Pierre is the only male heir in his branch of the family. The line is disappearing, and dwindling; when Pierre tries on the clothes of his grandfather, a noted leader in the Revolution, they are much too large. Pierre's distance from any heroic military ideal is clear from his jesting description of himself as "First Lady in Waiting to the Dowager Duchess Glendinning" (17).

Pierre has been raised to venerate his dead father as a perfect gentleman —what else would be an adequate compliment to his mother's "influence"? When he learns of the existence of his illegitimate half-sister, an important crisis in his thinking inevitably occurs. It cannot be over-emphasized that this discovery does not disillusion Pierre primarily with his father; it is his mother's falsifications which come under his most severe scrutiny. The revelation of Mr. Glendinning's sexual transgressions provides Pierre, curiously enough, with his first real opportunity to replace his mother's idealized mannequin with a flesh-and-blood man: to conceive of virility. We never hear anything really detrimental about Mr. Glendinning beyond the fact of his illicit liaison and its fruit. Pierre recalls his father's deathbed remorse, his calling for "my daughter"; Isabel remembers his kindness and generosity with her. What Pierre has learned is not that his father was "bad" so much as that he was not altogether satisfied to live a prisoner in his wife's home and mind. Ironically, Mr. Glendinning becomes at this point just what Mrs. Glendinning claims he should be to his son: a model.

Pierre's first reaction is to test out in a covert manner his mother's response to the possibility of Isabel's existence. In other words, he tries, by discussing Delly's case, to find out if her mind, what Melville carefully describes as "a fine mind of medium culture" (3), is capable of encompassing and dealing adequately with his father's experience. That experience constitutes exactly the reality Mrs. Glendinning wished to keep from Pierre; of course, she treats Pierre's hypothetical case with fear and anger. He gives her no second chance; he clearly does not want to. Instead, he enters into an alliance with Isabel which affirms his father's affair with her mother. So far is he from wishing to attack his father that his only justification for his cruelty in refusing to explain matters to his mother is his repeatedly stated desire to protect his father's reputation. He is shielding, even cherishing, precisely his father's "sin," the masculine right of self-expression, against his mother's censorious standards.

Pierre fondly hopes that in running off to New York City with Isabel, he is performing an act of "heroism," a word he and Melville use often in the first half of the book as a possible description of his course. Yet he does not become an adult, much less a hero. Simply by ceasing to acknowledge her existence, Pierre can kill his mother; she dies of grief and rage, and he rightly takes responsibility, describing himself as her "murderer" (403). But killing his mother is not the same thing as finding the father his mother has so totally obfuscated. And without a father, Pierre can find no focus, no real significance for his rebellion. He can destroy, but not create. His father's sophisticated protest against contemporary mores, which is Pierre's unacknowledged incentive, was real precisely because it had a consequence: a daughter, presumably Isabel. Pierre's much more extreme revolt is a failure in all its aspects, religious, literary and personal: there is no outcome, no fruit.

Pierre abjures the liberal Episcopal faith in which he was confirmed, yet he finds no way back to the Calvinist epistemology and structure which gave shape to Ahab's vengeance and his rhetoric. In New York Pierre lives in an old church whose former members gradually deserted it when the neighborhood in which it was located became *déclassé;* at the time Pierre moves in, the building is inhabited chiefly by poor artists and intellectuals. Yet the symbolic transfer of activity is not substantiated in fact. Melville, unlike Matthew Arnold, found art no substitute for religion, because art without dogma is sensibility or rhapsody, incapable of form. The only religious authority Pierre encounters among the "Apostles" is the calm and dry Plinlimmon, more anticipatory of F. Scott Fitzgerald's T. J. Ecklesberg than reminiscent of Joseph Bellamy's Deity. Plinlimmon's theories are the opposite of any "dogma" Melville, and his characters, have found useful in the past: the philosopher hypothesizes an utter discrepancy between heavenly and earthly time, facts, and values. In other words, the system of analogy which was essential to the dignity of Ahab's blasphemy has totally broken down. Meaningful art is impossible. Before he leaves home, Pierre destroys the polite poetry he wrote earlier; he no longer reads novels, finding that they utterly falsify existence. In the city, steeping himself in Dante and Shakespeare, he toils on a "blasphemous rhapsody" (497) (in the phrase of the publisher who indignantly rejects it) as persistently and painfully as any of the great Edwardsean ministers worked on their systems of divinity. Yet, although Melville is clear on the worthlessness of the "popular novels" the publisher and the public favor, he never tells us whether Pierre's work is of genuine value or even coherent. In any case, it will never see the light.

This pattern of futility is reiterated in Pierre's personal revolt. He has defied his mother's conventional ethics, he has run off with Isabel. Melville makes no bones about their strong sexual attraction, but they apparently do not sleep together. His father chose sex without marriage; Pierre picks marriage without sex. It is one of the greatest ironies of the novel that Pierre, while revolting officially against Mrs. Glendinning's code, is himself the Virgin Absolute of the story. None of Melville's earlier heroes, except the boy Redburn, had been particularly continent. Pierre, in contrast, is not just a virgin; he is obsessed and defined by his virginity. Redburn, interestingly enough, unlike Melville's other sailor narrators, had no close friends among his fellow crew members; Pierre too has no intimate male friends. It is as if his virginity is a pledge of his allegiance to feminine values, a pledge he desperately wishes to break, but cannot. Lucy's decision to follow Pierre to New York, and his decision to welcome her there, bring down on him the hatred of her brother and of Pierre's cousin and former dear friend, Glen. At the end of the book, Pierre welcomes a challenge from Glen and Lucy's brother; he kills them, then commits suicide. In the earlier works, as I have said, the "sons," usually crew members, banded together in fraternity against the "father," usually a captain. In *Pierre*, since there is no father whose real power must be opposed or supported, the sons in pointless rivalry merely for feminine attention turn on each other. In the essentially political world of *Moby Dick*, most of the characters die, but it is for a *purpose* which we may like or dislike. In the domestic psychological world of *Pierre*, the main characters die for no real reason. If Ahab was a "monomaniac," Pierre is a neurotic.

Pierre is of course fictional as none of Melville's earlier works were. There is no moment when we feel we are getting straightforward description of a place or an experience. The grandiloquent rhetoric of *Moby Dick* has given way to a hothouse language of exaggeration. *Pierre* may actually be a parody of the legendary and tempestuous best-sellers cranked out by women like Mrs. E. D. E. N. Southworth in this period.[32] Certainly, Melville makes the sentimental domestic romance into a cage in which he deliberately confines his main character—and himself—both to define the limits of the form and to test the possibility of breaking out and destroying it. A kind of prisoner of fiction, Pierre is trying to get out of his book or to make it something else. His struggle forces the reader to know the form as one knows a cell in which one has been frantically seeking an egress. But there is no exit, only a final and desperate exhaustion.

There are so many straight lines, metaphorically speaking, in the narrative of *Moby Dick*: Queequeg and Ishmael signing for the *Pequod*, the chase of the whale itself, the thrust of the harpoon. The action proceeds and cannot be reversed: it is historicist in the Hegelian sense. The plot lines in *Pierre* are all circular, ending dismally at their starting point, canceling themselves out: if Pierre leaves Lucy in the country, she comes after him in the city; if Isabel settles on one candidate as her actual father, she later discovers another equally plausible one. Like Mrs. Sigourney's tales and sketches, *Pierre* takes place in the mind, and so nothing can happen; there is no narrative, and no history. Isabel is symbolically the most important character in the book. Her very presence destroys Pierre's concept of his history and of his father's, and she has nothing to put in its place. Everything Isabel tells Pierre is pure conjecture. Her amnesia is at times ludicrous; she seems retarded, a bit like Faulkner's Benjy in *The Sound and the Fury*, as she dissolves what must have been events into dim sensations. She admits: " 'Always in me, the solidest things melt into dreams, and dreams into solidities' " (165). Isabel's dreams are a manifestation of the insidious female sexuality of which Mrs. Glendinning's drive for power was a very different representative; both act to conceal and distort the past.

I have tried to argue elsewhere in this book that the American women of Melville's generation were trying to replace the masculine vision of history as a series of political and economic facts enacted and marshaled by men with a feminine view of social and biological process. *Pierre* represents Melville's horror at this substitution and what it meant for the possibility of masculine maturation in his society. Pierre cannot become an adult, much less a hero; it could almost be said that he cannot be born. Narrative time has been replaced by psychological time and by biological time. Pierre works on his book in a cold room; Isabel wishes to keep the door between his study and her bedroom open, "so the heat of her room might bodily go into his" (414). Pierre refuses. It is the ravishing, suffocating heat of her body that he is trying to escape; he is literally trying to enter the proverbially cold world of reality. In vain. He dies, symbolically enclosed in a prison cell, and Isabel reclaims him. " 'Ye knew him not!' " she exclaims rather unkindly to Millthorpe, Pierre's only loyal, if simple-minded, male friend. She has made her point, however; Pierre has been separated from his last masculine ally. Dying, Isabel falls on Pierre's dead body, and "her long hair ran over him, and arboured him in ebon vines" (505). Pierre has suffocated in the feminine sensibility.

The Magazine Pieces: Going Underground

Pierre was a critical and popular failure of an order that made *Mardi* look like a success. Melville's implicit hostility to his readers and critics was sensed, and returned in spades. After labeling *Pierre* "the craziest fiction extant," one critic went on to say: "The amount of utter trash in the volume is almost infinite—trash of conception, execution, dialogue and sentiment." Another critic fulminated against the "supersensuousness with which the early relations of the family are described," and warned the author: "Mother and son, brother and sister are sacred facts not to be distorted by sacrilegious speculations." Significantly, *Godey's* picked up on the fact that the book was a satire of "modern literati."[33] It is hardly surprising that in the works which succeeded *Pierre*, Melville went underground. After finishing *White-Jacket*, he had written a friend "what a madness & anguish it is that an author can never—under no conceivable circumstances—be at all frank with his readers."[34] Melville became distinctly less "frank" later in his career; he grew increasingly adept at the art of withholding and innuendo. In *Moby Dick* and *Pierre* there is a frequently felt Hamletlike "antic disposition," as Melville dangles and twitches possible gratification before his audience; in the works which succeed *Pierre*, this process of manic tantalization is missing. The vitality of desperation has been replaced by the cunning of deceit. Melville has dispossessed his readers without totally destroying his own rationale for writing: indeed, the dispossession itself becomes his motivation. Reading the earlier works is like rocking in a ship on a stormy sea; reading the later ones is like sitting becalmed in ominously still waters.

In the period between 1853 and 1857 Melville produced some of his undoubted masterpieces: *Israel Potter*, *The Confidence Man*, "Bartleby the Scrivener," "Benito Cereno," as well as half a dozen tales of genuine interest and power. Significantly, he intended them all for two magazines, *Harper's* and *Putnam's*, and all but *The Confidence Man* actually appeared in their pages. Of course Donald Mitchell, the "Ik Marvel" who wrote *Reveries of a Bachelor* and founded the legendary "Easy Chair" in *Harper's*, and George Curtis, author of the sentimental pastiches *Potiphar Papers* (1853) and *Prue and I* (1856), were the editors of *Harper's* during Melville's association with it. J. H. Dix was editing *Putnam's*, a newer periodical, but it was well known that he followed Curtis' advice and lead in every possible instance.[35] As we have seen, both Curtis and Mitchell were skillful, trivial, and wittily self-doubting "magazinish" writers working in the graceful tradition of Laurence Sterne and Washington Irving for a largely feminine audience.

That Melville designed his own magazine tales to pass muster with the same genteel handkerchief-reaching audience these men attracted seems very clear. The fact is that, without winning acclaim, they did pass muster. *The Piazza Tales*, a collection of a number of these pieces published in 1856, received favorable reviews: one critic complimented Melville for having regained "much of his former freshness and vivacity."[36] Strikingly, the great American public chose precisely from among Melville's magazine works to perpetuate the once-immoral author's fame. A *McGuffey's Reader* of 1888 actually anthologized Melville's account of Benjamin Franklin's pro-temperance comments delivered to a skeptical Israel Potter[37] for the edification of the American young. Melville was undoubtedly writing satirically, but *McGuffey's* didn't notice. More tellingly, the reserved but secretly warm-hearted clerk Titbottom in Curtis' *Prue and I*, a shy but benevolent little refugee in the bureaucratic ranks, actually owns himself a friend of Bartleby's.[38]

Ahab and Pierre, vast as were the differences between them, had both been rebels against their society. It is an indication of the seriousness with which Melville still considered his culture that their revolt was open and expensive: it cost them their lives. The lesson that Melville learned from the likes of Curtis and Mitchell, and one which by 1853 he was sufficiently alert and bitter to absorb and elaborate, was that there was no need to pay such a price. His readers did not demand or understand it. Ahab's death, Pierre's immolation, were like conflagrations kindled in situations for which a match would have been sufficient: ludicrous. The excesses of their efforts at masculine stature were beside the point, outmoded, passé. Melville's newly lowered estimation of his audience was evident in the doll-house proportions of the work he offered them; he deceived his readers, he veiled his insults, partly to demonstrate to them how little worth the effort of attack they were. In the mid-1850s Melville, in whose writing speech was always to be key, turned for his models from the stage, where bombastic actors like Edwin Forrest paced and postured before mixed audiences in half-sincere struggles to idealize America's barbarity, to the "Easy Chair," where editors pontificated, jested, flattered, and equivocated for parlor consumption. In order to create, Melville always needed close contact with the nightmare central to the American psyche: in the mid-1850s, he found its dynamic was not anguish, but affability; its subject was not the death-throes of masculinity but the vicious coquetting of the feminine or effeminate.

The stories Melville wrote for the magazines between 1853 and 1857 are all, in form, variations on the "sketch," and the central figure in most of them is the "Ik Marvel" character, descended from Irving's Geoffrey Crayon. In *Moby Dick*, Melville had quickly dismissed the Irvingesque "sub-sub" who opens the book; in the sketches, the indolent, smug, dreamy, timid, sentimental observer, toying with the tragedies of life, precipitating and disavowing them, rules.[39] Let me start with the narrator of "Bartleby the Scrivener," the earliest of Melville's more important magazine tales. This prosperous complacent lawyer clearly owes much to Sterne, Irving, and Marvel, and probably influenced Curtis' conception of his narrator in *Prue and I.* The story is really his not only because he is as barren as the scrivener he pities, but also because we cannot get at Bartleby's story except through him. In a sense, he is the reader, screening out whatever fails to flatter him; he is the editor choosing and rejecting what he will print. It is the contrast between Bartleby's meaningful inaccessibility and the narrator's sometimes meaningless garrulity which provides the heart of the tale.[40]

Bartleby's employer is clearly, like all the narrators of these sketches, liberal in religious belief. He attends the fashionable Episcopalian Trinity Church, and he is so ignorant of theology that he is capable of grouping together the well-known free-thinker Joseph Priestley and the orthodox

Jonathan Edwards (130).[41] He has no real equipment to understand Bartleby's economic and spiritual dilemma; what he wants, and what he succeeds in doing despite some genuine twinges of uneasiness, is to sentimentalize his clerk's story, to make it resemble those he has read in magazines like the one in which "Bartleby" itself appeared. Melville is dramatizing here the process by which an essentially mass sensibility transforms and assimilates the alien to its own needs. The narrator is clearly a literary facilitator, a conveyor belt to his culture. At the start, he assures us that he could "relate divers histories at which good-natured gentlemen might smile and sentimental souls might weep" (103). A would-be memorialist in the clerical feminine style, he is regretful that he lacks the materials for a full "biography" of Bartleby: it is "an irreparable loss to literature" (103).

This lawyer has already had several rather eccentric clerical employees and apparently willingly accepts their peculiarities. Although he unwittingly allows us to understand that these copyists are by small and futile oddities of behavior rebelling against the routinized and monotonous quality of their work, his own sympathy for them seems rather to come from their willingness to appeal to his emotions than from any real comprehension of their position. Turkey, who is wont to blot his afternoon copying under the influence of his lunchtime drinking, disarms his employer by an "appeal" to his "fellow feeling": they both are getting old, he points out (107). The two men are not really alike: one is relatively secure and prosperous, the other in a position of insecure dependency. But it is this sentimental illusion of brotherhood, this obfuscation of an essentially class situation, which the narrator demands as the price of his sympathy, and it is precisely this which Bartleby denies him.

The narrator is constantly trying to use Bartleby's plight to touch off his own emotions. "His poverty is great," he ruminates, with the kind of sadistic pity of which Mitchell's Bachelor was a past master, "but his solitude how horrible! Think of it!" (120). He is lost in "fraternal melancholy," a perversion of the word "fraternal" to which Melville was as sensitive as Whitman could have been. He tries to extract Bartleby's story from him (122); he attempts to force the scrivener to express gratitude for his own benevolence (123). The apparently morose clerk in Curtis' *Prue and I* who claims cousinship with Bartleby does finally tell his employer about his past; Bartleby does not. Faced with his only possible biographer, his final and most important preference—and Melville knows just how recessive if inevitable it must be—is for oblivion. Bartleby's revolt is against the literature of his day; he is refusing, essentially, to be a character. "Ah Bartleby! ah Humanity!" How easy, how ironic; how hard that Bartleby's life, potentially so defiant in its meagerness, should become indeed another "dead letter." The narrator, having "placed" Bartleby's story within the context of the biographies of oblivion we have examined, has finally got his "emotions"; with onanistic indulgence he hastens to share his pity: "hardly can I express the emotions which seized me" (140)—he has almost, but not quite, got us too. Melville reminds us, however, that the narrator's final solution, his interpretation, rests only on a "rumor" that Bartleby had worked as a clerk in the Dead Letters Office at Washington; his silence, no matter how coaxed, how massaged, how mangled, persists. Bartleby prefers to destroy history rather than to distort it.

Melville's distrust of the narrator figure, the occupant of the "easy chair," in the tales of this period never flagged; he came, however, increasingly to sense and exploit the hostility of this character to the very audience that he had been formed and maimed to serve. In Melville's two latest and in certain ways most interesting magazine stories, "I and My Chimney" and "The Apple-Tree Table," Melville puts himself behind the antagonistic possibilities of his sentimental male narrator, even while he grimly predicts the eventual success of those this personage both flatters and resists.

In the first tale, which Curtis praised particularly as "capital, genial, humorous" and, the final compliment, "thoroughly magazinish,"[42] we find the Melville narrator closest in character to the narrator in Curtis' *Prue and I*, recently serialized in *Harper's*. "A dozy old dreamer," given to a pipe and to "indolently weaving [his] vapors" (154),[43] he lives in a world of women, father of two daughters and husband to a strong-minded positive-thinking lady who almost totally intimidates him. In describing his subjection, the narrator slips in an astute analysis of the political possibilities of the current notion of woman's "sphere" for those women willing to pay lip service to it: "By my wife's ingenious application of the principle that certain things belong of right to female jurisdiction, I find myself, through my easy compliances, insensibly stripped by degrees of one masculine prerogative after another" (133–34). He has made his stand, however: his wife and daughters wish to tear down the tremendous central chimney, "a huge, corpulent old Henry VIII of a chimney" (109) as he proudly describes it, which dominates the architecture of the house, but he steadfastly refuses.

The issues here are many, and complex. The women want the house redesigned along the recent convenient proto-suburban pattern, best suited to feminine needs and ideals:[44] timid himself, the narrator nonetheless defends the chimney as a bastion of phallic, assertive, and aggressive masculinity. The fate of most of Henry VIII's spouses is well known. The story takes a new twist when the wife calls in an architect named "Hiram Scribe," who is paid by her to claim that the chimney has "a reserved space, hermetically sealed" (148) possibly containing hidden treasure, and therefore must be torn open. Scribe is suggesting in veiled fashion by this womb imagery —an inner space with a "treasure," i.e. a child, in it—that the chimney is feminine. The narrator is able to dispose of this interpretation by offering Scribe more money to support his own case. Among other things, the architect is possibly a "hired scribe," emblematic of the writers and litterateurs bribed by the feminine populace to invalidate and destroy the masculine experience.

The story closes on a deceptively light note. The narrator has learned that if he leaves for a day, his womenfolk will call in laborers to tear down the chimney. So for seven years, he has not moved from home: "Some say that I have become a mossy old misanthrope while all the time the fact is, I am simply standing guard over my mossy old chimney; for ... I and my chimney will never surrender" (166). Melville has come a long way from the "mossy man," the great American writer he had in 1850 hoped Hawthorne, and himself, to be. It is Redburn with his gun, but aged and weakened. The narrator can merely fend off his destructive audience, and perform a custodial role toward an artistic achievement which he knows is only a decaying relic, and one in whose making he could never have had a share.

In "The Apple-Tree Table," the struggle for appropriation, the conflict of interpretation which we have already seen in different guises in "Bartleby" and "I and My Chimney" continues. The basic question remains: who will determine the content and form of American culture? Once again there is antipathy to domesticity planted in the midst of a domestic tale. The narrator is the narrator of "I and My Chimney," although apparently in a different and smaller house, with the same bustling wife and the same genteel daughters. This time the object quarreled over is an old "apple-tree table" with a devilish hooflike leg which the narrator finds in his attic. Apparently acting from the most benevolent and sentimental impulses, he determines to bring the table into the parlor. His tone is positively missionary: he wishes to surround "this sad little hermit, so long banished from genial neighborhood with all the kindly influences of warm arms, warm fires, and warm hearts, little dreaming what all this warm nursing would hatch" (15). His daughters fight his plan to "domesticate" the table, destined to become a source of terror to them.

The table soon gives off a persistent ticking noise. The daughters, undoubtedly influenced by the recent wave of Spiritualism,[45] attribute the noise to ghostly presences; it is actually, as they eventually discover, the result of two incarcerated bugs working their way out of the wood. The girls still claim a sort of "spiritual" interpretation, rationalizing, in pious fashion, that the insects symbolize Christ's and man's resurrection. One daughter closes her explanation with a trite moral: " 'Spirits! spirits!' she exclaimed, with rapture, 'I still believe in them with delight, when before I thought of them with terror' " (51). Melville assumes his readers are feminine—he speaks at one point to "whatever lady doubts this story"—and he apparently lets them have the tale, for the daughter's speech pretty well ends it. He can label the story, and the daughters' triumph; he has already associated the word "hum" with the word "bug." "Humbug" or not, however, he has relinquished the tale to them, as Bartleby did not his history nor his modest successor his "chimney" to their foes.

It is perhaps not unimportant that "The Apple-Tree Table" was Melville's last short magazine piece. He was writing another book, *The Confidence Man*, in reality a string of sketches intended for serialization in *Putnam's*, and in it he brought to a culmination all he had been trying to say, and not to say, in the shorter works.[46] The struggle for possession is past: Melville has in several senses given up the ship. The book ostensibly details a day (April Fool's) in the life of a crook aboard a steamer called the Fidèle; in his numerous disguises, the con man tries to talk various other passengers out of their money. In actuality, the work shows American society ravaged by a sentimentality whose underlying viciousness Melville almost celebrates. He is no longer interested in the ambiguities of the genteel narrator but rather in his appetites. A book without a hero or even a narrator—a book, most significantly, about a ship without a captain—*The Confidence Man* reveals the triumph of "affection" over "authority" in America: sentimentality is seducing and fleecing the nation. Melville is here intent on the realities of the market. Where the narrator of "Bartleby" or the wife and daughters of "I and My Chimney" and "The Apple-Tree Table," all absorbed by questions of ownership, had at least been arguing over matters of interpretation, this confidence man has finally reached his goal only when he has transferred the contents of someone else's pocket to his own.

Significantly, in two of his most important incarnations, as "the Man with the Weed" and "the Cosmopolitan," the confidence man is clearly close kin to the sentimental observer. With his emphasis on sweetness and light and good faith, he is the apotheosis of the religious liberal: he can succeed in distorting the Bible message to fit his own exploitative creed of "trust" precisely because, as he points out, no one in America reads the Bible anymore. There are two clergymen aboard, one Episcopalian, the other Methodist, and Melville paints a favorable picture of both; yet both are taken in by one or more of the confidence man's impersonations. As "the Man in Gray," the confidence man easily dupes a sentimental lady prone to reading her Bible and gazing devoutly at the sunset. As if to underscore this confidence man's similarities to the editors for whom Melville was writing, he makes him explain that he has invented a "Protean easy-chair so all over bejointed, behinged and bepadded, every way so elastic, springy, and docile to the airiest touch, that in some one of its endlessly changeable accommodations of back, seat, footboard, and arms, the most restless body, . . . the most tormented conscience must, somehow and somewhere, find rest" (32).[47] The pun on the "Easy Chair" column of *Harper's* is obvious. Exposing the ethic which underlay the "dreamer's" pose, the ethic which exploited weakness as the basis for a power-play, Melville is pointing at the fundamental irresponsibility of the feminized sentimental observer and of the magazine culture which was his milieu. The Cosmopolitan's final sham is, tellingly, his defense of the press—of course several of the confidence men are tract and poem distributors and readers: " 'I hold the press to be neither the people's ... paid fool nor conceited drudge. I think interest never prevails with it over duty. The press still speaks for Truth' " (197).

The confidence man fundamentally has neither opponents nor competitors; he does not meet even with custodian figures, for there is nothing to preserve. Melville acknowledges here that America has only one spokesman, because it has only one culture, precisely that of "the press." The issue is simply whether or not to believe or disbelieve it. But this is a book of vanishing conflicts, and even this one dissolves into a hopeless paradox. To trust is to be a fool; perpetually to distrust is to be alone, crippled, unnourished. Both sides lose in so far as genuine human development is concerned. The world of *The Confidence Man* is one of handy-dandy; like that of Twain's *Pudd'nhead Wilson*, it is arid. Nowhere is there a possibility of the atmosphere in which ideas, or art, can flourish. This is appropriately the first story Melville has located on shipboard in which we hear next to nothing about the water on which the craft presumably floats. The boat itself is a kind of masquerade. Melville has anticipated that the final and archetypical locale of the anti-culture which had destroyed him will be the Hollywood set, flat, painted, imperishable in its very flimsiness. There is no boat, there are no people, there is no water, no life: we are not just becalmed, we are horribly grounded. The absence of any genuine culture, Melville suggests in the slickest, driest nightmare penned by an American author, is the absence of reality itself.

The Confidence Man is Melville's most elusive work: it marks his final dispossession of his readers. There is something vindictive at work here: the confidence man has Melville's stage because Melville recognizes that he is there. "*This* is what you've chosen," he tells his readers: "how do you like it?" But he realizes that "this" is also the only role he has left to utilize, and he does not like it either. I have said that Melville's Americanness consisted in part in his awareness that he could not be significantly better than his culture; never before did he feel the constraints of this theorem so bitterly. If his readers are dispossessed, so is Melville.

The Late Prose: The Independent Vision

After the publication of *The Confidence Man* in 1857, Melville underwent some sort of nervous collapse. None of his books were selling; he had no coterie of adoring disciples to compensate for popular neglect. He and Hawthorne were no longer close, if indeed they ever had been. His family did not understand or believe in his work. Lemuel Shaw, Melville's brother-in-law, could refer casually in a letter to "that horribly uninteresting class of nonsensical books he is given to writing." Melville at this time underlined a passage in the work of a French author which aptly summed up his own mood of profound discouragement: "the literary career seems to me unreal, both in its essence and in the rewards which one seeks from it."[48] Somewhat in the spirit of the narrator of "I and My Chimney," Melville, according to a friend's report, was wont to "pat great trees," as if to remind himself that strength existed although he no longer felt he had access to it.

In 1857, acting on the advice of his family and his doctor, Melville took a trip abroad, spending most of his time in the Middle East. He was tortured by the heat, the flies, his relentless inability to sleep. In the journals he kept during his travels, Melville throws out image after image of isolation and non-communication absolutely terrifying in the pain they suggest. After visiting a cemetery in Para, he notes:

> saw a woman over a new grave—no grass on it yet. Such abandonment of misery! Called to the dead, put her head down as close as possible to it; as if calling down a hatchway or cellar; besought "Why don't you speak to me? My God!—It is I! Ah,—speak—but one word!"—all deaf. So much for consolation.—This woman and her cries haunt me horribly.[49]

Melville too has been unable to raise his dead.

His peculiar pilgrimage reached its apotheosis in Judea: "one accumulation of stones—stony mountains & stony plains; stony torrents & stony roads .. stony homes & stony tombs.... Before you & behind you are stones." He actually tasted the Dead Sea and found it "bitter," adding, in the bleak repetitiousness, the more-coals-to-Newcastle principle which marks the style of these entries, "bitter is it to be poor & bitter to be reviled."[50] He has found an objective correlative, the geographic analogue to his state of mind; yet what makes the journal so wrenching to read is precisely Melville's inability to find his suffering interesting. The extraordinary almost unique quality of the writing comes from its combined intensity and flatness. Melville has come close to believing that no one—but no one—will ever read his pages. He has, at least momentarily, abandoned the secret cherished illusion which makes all of us, great novelists or unknown diarists and correspondents, write: the imaginary audience. His strength here is indeed the strength of stones. Melville's pain creates of necessity its own literature —stiff, jerky, stitched sentences sticking to the facts they must convey, the bleached skeleton of rhetoric—but it baldly sidesteps inspiration. Inspiration, Melville everywhere implies, has misled him; he has no more use for it.

When he returned home, Melville embarked, without enthusiasm, on a series of lectures to make money. Oliver Wendell Holmes regarded the lecturer as a "literary strumpet," and said so at a party in 1857 which Melville attended;[51] no prostitute ever minimized her charms more punitively than did Melville in his unpopular talks on "Statuary at Rome" and "The South Sea Islands." If to lecture was to dramatize the dependence of the writer or intellectual on the public, Melville made his dependency fall on his patrons like a lethal mass of lead. As one reviewer reported, "He makes no attempt at eloquence"—this about the creator of Ahab, this about the man who kept Hawthorne up half the night talking. We have a report of the "South Sea Islands" lecture.[52] Melville begins by telling his audience that he will cover nothing about which he has written in *Typee* or *Omoo*, although those books are presumably the incentives which drew his audience in the first place. The lecture makes it strikingly clear that Melville is no longer goading or satirizing his public as he did in *The Confidence Man*; he has come very close to giving up. Melville wrote no more prose for thirty years.

Melville did experience, however, a brief period of renewed hopefulness about his writing career, and it is worth discussing precisely because it reveals so clearly what Melville considered the causes of his defeat. At the outbreak of the Civil War, Melville began to write poetry, extraordinary poetry, about the conflict between the states. He published the resulting group of war poems as *Battle-Pieces* in 1866. On every page Melville's quickened faith in his nation is evident. He apparently believed that the stern realities of war would destroy the sentimental culture he detested: "Nothing like a bullet can undeceive," he writes. Hearing Sumter's cannon, his countrymen will surely realize "how tame the Nation/ In the age that went before." The war must prove a foe to domesticity:

> The appealings of the mother
>   to brother and to brother
> Not in hatred so to part—
> And the fissure in the hearth
>   Growing momently more wide.

The "optimist" will flee, for the Calvinist Deity reasserts his supremacy and "confirms his deep decree"; the "code" of battle corroborates "Calvin's Creed." Heroism has become possible once again, masculinity is an option: "nothing can lift the heart of man/ Like manhood in a fellow man."[53] Melville's war poems show little of the concern for the wounded, for the values of nurture and healing which characterize Whitman's response in

Drum-Taps; the older man is not interested in finding an outlet for his maternal feelings.[54] Melville dedicated *Battle-Pieces* appropriately to the northern soldiers who died for "the flag of their fathers." Not surprisingly his rough, irregular, and forceful poetry found little praise among American critics who considered Tennyson's verse the *beau idéal*. Melville continued to write and publish poetry, fine poetry, after 1866; his later poems never evinced, however, the felt spirit of expectancy, of summons to a waiting audience, which characterizes *Battle-Pieces*.

It is one of the good fortunes of American letters that Melville's thirty-year enforced silence in his chosen medium, prose, did not stifle him altogether, but rather prepared and disciplined him for a statement for a kind of public balancing of accounts whose powers of condensation have seldom been equaled. In *Billy Budd*, Melville is not a combatant; he is, as never before, at a distance, having calmly assumed the authority he has not officially been granted. We are back at sea in a world of men, we are back in the narrative form, we are back with Calvinism, but with important differences. Probably written in the late 1880s, *Billy Budd* is set, as only *Israel Potter* and "Benito Cereno" were among Melville's earlier works, in the past; and this narrative is uniquely conscious, as its two predecessors were not, of itself as history. Melville's tone is dignified, balanced, formal, legalistic, above all judicious. Despite Melville's frequently stated awareness in the tale that his audience is unfamiliar and uncomfortable with the Bible and with Calvin, theological discussion and definition are here as never before, on their own terms: Melville is explicit on the point that officer Claggart's hatred of the handsome sailor Budd, on which the plot turns, can be explained only by the doctrine of depravity (75–79).[55] Captain Vere's rationale for his decision to punish Budd for the unwitting murder of Claggart—" 'Struck down by the Angel of God, but the Angel must die!' " (101) draws meaning from a text often used by Calvinist thinkers and repeated by Lincoln in the spare theological cadences of the Second Inaugural Address: "it is impossible but that offenses will come, but woe unto him through whom they come" (Luke 17:1). In the austere literary form which Melville has evolved here, he has apparently discovered an analogue, perhaps a substitute, for the theological discourse which was the substance of America's primarily intellectual tradition. In *Billy Budd*, all experience is ultimately to be marshaled before the faculties of judgment and assessed by them.

This is a narrative not only of the mutual comprehension between two "phenomenal men," a son and a "father,"—the "handsome sailor" Billy Budd and his abstract, intellectual, but fair-minded superior, Captain Vere—but of the understanding between *the* son and *the* father (115). It is not simply that Budd is compared to Christ, and to Adam, and Vere is cast as his paternal superior, i.e. God. Whether or not he consciously intended it,

Melville has given us in *Billy Budd* something close to an allegory of the older Calvinist gubernatorial theory of the Atonement. Just as, in this view, God sacrificed Christ, his innocent son, to dramatize his hatred of man's sin, so Vere suppresses the "fatherly" feeling he has for Billy and becomes the "stern disciplinarian" intent on demonstrating to the rest of the crew the quickness and fierceness with which he will put down any effort at rebellion. Captain Vere refuses to listen to sentiment. Vere's primary concern is not the happiness or even the just deserts of his men as they understand these things. He urges the jury to rule out "the heart," the "feminine in man," and even the "private conscience" in the interest of the "imperial" conscience of their public duties (110–113). There are no Bushnellian elements in this Atonement process; Vere sacrifices Budd to instruct his crew and to keep his distance from them, not to win their affection by a display of his love of them.

I am not suggesting that Melville wrote *Billy Budd* as a conscious allegory of the older doctrine of the Atonement; I am suggesting that critics, in denouncing Vere's injustice or in viewing it as evidence of Melville's belief in God's malignity, are in part guilty of just the liberal heresy which Melville opposed—and opposed even in its highest form when it is closely linked, as it is in *Billy Budd*, to "charity." Such critics are like the readers Melville addresses whom he knows are no longer familiar with Calvinist doctrines (75), the chief of which is that God rules men according to his needs, in the interest of his honor, not in consideration of their desires. Again, it is not that Melville believes literally in these principles, but that he adheres to the rigor of the structures they create. No one could deny that *Billy Budd* is a testament of loss. Billy Budd dies. The re-established father-son relation is damaging as well as sustaining to both participants. Budd is partially speechless, even childish. He feels his fraternal ties less forcibly than his filial ones, and we resist the simplification of justice he finds congenial and perhaps easy. Captain Vere is of course a man, and the human drama is enormously important here. As a man, he suffers from Budd's death: not from "remorse," as Melville is at pains to emphasize, but from grief and loss (129). As a man, Vere's motives cannot be altogether pure; although Melville stresses his impartiality, his intellectuality, his extraordinary sensitivity, he also points out that Vere is perhaps ambitious, that others even question his sanity. Yet Vere's suffering and his imperfections do not alter the fact that his action in condemning Budd is *analogous* to the Calvinist Deity's in sacrificing Christ. Vere suffers in private for the fact that he has pulled off a totally public gesture: even those readers who condemn Vere can hardly feel that Melville suggests he was motivated by any personal animus against Budd. Since he is human, he pays a price for his determination to operate on the impersonal, even allegorical plane, but it is just this determination which creates the large, although painfully measured, spaces of the narrative. Psychology has given way to judiciousness; everything has its place. Injustice, as we, and even Melville, understand it, is undeniably present. The narrative is not, however, a protest against it. Melville's imaginative energy has unquestionably decreased; but his philosophical vision has gained precision.

Despite *Billy Budd*'s lack of dialogue, its refusal to penetrate the consciousness of the characters, the reader is given almost complete information about the situation in which the story is grounded. We are allowed no interior views, yet this is part of the essential fairness, as well as the remoteness, of the narrative: it is as if Melville can only fathom and bear his own story if presented in an extreme long shot. Yet one should add that Melville respects his characters' privacy as he could not respect Pierre's; Pierre's nightmare was that he had nothing but his privacy. In *Billy Budd*, decorum is the word. Within these limitations, there are no missing pieces of information comparable to the unknown fate of Toby in *Typee*, or the actual paternity of Isabel in *Pierre*, or the real identity of the confidence man; there are no symbols that precipitate and yet absorb events, such as the white jacket or the white whale; there is absolutely none of the sensuous detail which over-runs and destroys the narrative of *Pierre*; the action is not divided between narrative and story as in *Mardi*, *Redburn*, or *Moby Dick*. The process of judgment has become too important, the imperatives of rationalization too strong, for the case to rest on symbols or withheld information. As in no other of Melville's works, the tale simply proceeds, straightforwardly, chronologically; the reader is given whatever it is necessary he know.

The narrative is in some ways dry as a result, and its restraint is a testimony to its impulse toward edification. Because Melville so precisely acknowledges what can and what cannot be known, and because no one thing is less known or unknown than another—we learn as much, or as little, about Claggart's depravity as we do about Budd's innocence or Vere's authority—Melville presents an entire universe to the reader, all parts remote, all parts equally accessible. Melville assumes an audience in *Billy Budd* as he did not in the Dead Sea journals; yet it is not one he pretends to know particularly well. His very audience has become generalized by the unknown possibilities of history: we, the readers of the late twentieth century, are among Melville's rather indifferently hypothesized readers, yet Melville does not attempt to speak personally to us, as Whitman does in "Crossing Brooklyn Ferry." *Billy Budd* represents Melville's established distance from literature as an object to be consumed by a mass audience. The book is extraordinarily helpful to us precisely because Melville was not writing it *for* us, and I think Melville knew this. We may not possess the truth, the conflicting but equally false official and popular accounts of the incident appended at the story's close suggest its inaccessibility. We attain, however, a sense of its dimensions, of the space it occupies. Melville had always been imaginatively preoccupied with bigness, with size; now he is concerned with measurement. We the readers approximate to the "truth" simply because we are not deceived. We are kept to the actual facts and to those rather abstract statements and generalized scenes in which complex emotions and personalities can be presented with the solidity and impersonality of facts.

Despite its lack of dialogue, or perhaps because of it, *Billy Budd* is about communication, and the language and actions which can be trusted to accomplish it. In *Pierre*, where almost no real interaction takes place, incessant talking, singing, and attitudinizing occur among the characters. In *Billy Budd* genuine communication does occur although—and this is significant —only off-stage. Vere presumably explains Budd's fate and his own motivation to the young sailor in an interview whose "inviolable" privacy and "holy oblivion" Melville honors (115). We are told, however, that "in view of the character" of Vere and Budd, "each radically sharing in the rarer qualities of our nature," we may conjecture with the author that Vere explained himself to Billy, that Billy fully understood, that Vere embraced Billy with the passion Abraham felt for Isaac before offering him up "in obedience to the exacting behest" (115). Two men have met and spoken.[56] There is no doubt that in *Billy Budd* Melville has taken his final leave of abundance; he does not believe, as he once did, that he should try to have everything; he is no longer taking revenge on a public which helped to make such an attempt impossible. Melville has muted his material to master it, but the mastery is itself "phenomenal." Melville's very control becomes emblematic. He achieves what the sentimentalists with their unexamined fascination with process, with biology, failed to do; history, presented in its uncompromised detail, merges, no matter how inscrutably, partially, and ambiguously, with providence.

EPILOGUE

Melville worked on *Billy Budd* in the late 1880s and early 1890s, during the last decade of his life. At this time, many men, and women, were becoming deeply concerned about the "feminization" of American culture and the closing of the frontier, actual and metaphorical, which it suggested. Muscular Christianity was popular even in elite clerical circles. In less fashionable quarters, Billy Sunday was beginning the career which would culminate in the avowal that Jesus Christ was "no dough-faced, lick-spittle proposition. Jesus was the greatest scrapper that ever lived."[57] Movements were afoot in the field of education to control the still-proliferating and preponderant ratio of women to men among grade-school teachers, even to reverse the tide of co-education at the university level.[58] Violent collegiate sports, outdoor camping, hunting, and fishing grew rapidly in favor. Social Darwinism with its exaltation of the right of the strong to trample the weak dominated political practice and sociological theory. Naturalism with its emphasis on brute instinct and force influenced American novelists. Teddy Roosevelt was launched in the career that would lead him and his "Rough Riders" to San Juan Hill.

Melville was irrevocably apart from this militant crusade for masculinity even while he understood its deepest sources. The rhetoric of a Billy Sunday or even a Teddy Roosevelt was a signal, paradoxically, of the victory of the sentimental sabotage—a victory which was in a larger sense a defeat. For the point about the crusade for masculinity was the level at which the majority of its proponents conducted their campaign. It was a level no higher in an intellectual, spiritual, or political sense than Sarah Hale maintained in the veiled propaganda of the pages of *Godey's Lady's Book* or than Harriet Beecher Stowe descended to in *Lady Byron Vindicated*. The Teddy Roosevelts had learned much from the Purity Alliances, the temperance movement, even the ladies' magazines. T. R.'s "big stick" had something in common with Carrie Nation's hatchet. The forces of feminization were significant enough—they had tapped the increasingly formidable processes of industrialization, commercialization, and mass culture deeply enough— so that any opposition, even when waged by a Harvard graduate like T. R., had to be conducted on their terms. Certain forms of deprivation and exclusion had made middle-class American women, the readers and consumers of the nation, and the men who imitated, flattered, and exploited them, logical heirs to the anti-intellectual tradition in American culture; and they had conspired willy-nilly with changing historical circumstances to make anti-intellectualism the tradition in American culture.

It is hardly surprising that the long-overdue rediscovery of Melville took place in the 1920s, at a time when Neo-orthodox theologians and historians were noting and attempting to rectify the vitiation of serious intellectual and religious endeavor. It is especially fitting that *Billy Budd* was exhumed and published in 1924, as Karl Barth, Paul Tillich, and the Niebuhr brothers were beginning their careers. *Billy Budd*'s importance as a cultural document is not only in its creation of a structured arena for (masculine) discourse but also in the quality and form of that discourse. In taking his unnoticed leave of his audience, Melville reminds them of what Perry Miller has since called the "Life of the Mind in America."

This is not to say that nothing worthwhile is present in the mass culture which figures like Sarah Hale or Teddy Roosevelt helped to create and make the principal carrier of our political, cultural, and sexual identity; nor is it to imply that the formalism a work like *Billy Budd* partly suggests, fine as it is, is the only artistic good. Commercialism is, after all, inseparable from a minimal degree of vitality; some segment of lost productive energy resides in consumer appetite, even if it has hardly found there a safe home. Many intellectuals mistakenly if inevitably over-value formalism of a kind much more extreme than *Billy Budd* displays as the only available antidote to mass culture. At its worst, however, formalism can function simply as the unexplored reversal of mass stereotyping. A radical critique of society is confined, even nullified, in formalist works whose epistemology is punitively elitist.[59] Our current allegiance to the comforts of our televisions is not altogether a matter for embarrassment or shame. Mass culture rests on an enormous utopian promise, what Stendhal called "la promesse de bonheur," even if in practice it is largely engaged in the destruction of that hope. *Billy Budd* with its imaginative investment in the absolute poetry of conceptualization, is a great work; yet it is inferior to *Moby Dick*. *Moby Dick* represents Melville's most seriously hopeful engagement with his audience; it brings the sheer energy and fertility of the best of popular culture to the service of profound thought. In a country as diverse, as ideologically strained, as unmistakably materialistic as America, the "Life of the Mind" can be recorded but not finally defined. In *Billy Budd*, Melville is as conscious of the material he has lost as of that he has found abiding. In the most essential sense, Melville consistently produced a literature of inclusiveness. What his society would not allow him to conceive—sexual equality, a non-oppressive economic system, an honest culture—he also included by making his work a recognition of the price of their loss.

APPENDIX A

*Alphabetical Listing of Women and Ministers
in the Control Groups Discussed in Chapter 3*

WOMEN

1. Louisa May Alcott (1832–88)
2. Delia Bacon (1811–59)
3. Catharine Esther Beecher (1800–78)
4. Alice Cary (1820–71)
5. Lydia Maria Child (1802–80)
6. Emily Chubbuck Judson ("Fanny Forrester") (1817–53)
7. Maria Cummins (1827–66)
8. Dorothea Dix (1802–87)
9. Harriet Farley (1813–1907)
10. Charlotte Fillebrown (Jerauld) (1820–45)
11. Martha Finley (1828–1909)
12. Margaret Fuller (1810–50)
13. Sarah Josepha Hale (1788–1879)
14. Mary J. Holmes (1825–1907)
15. Lucy Larcom (1824–93)
16. Sara Clarke Lippincott ("Grace Greenwood") (1823–1904)
17. Mary Lyon (1797–1849)
18. Sarah Edgarton Mayo (1819–49)
19. Elizabeth Peabody (1804–94)
20. Elizabeth Stuart Phelps (1844–1911)
21. Elizabeth Prentiss (1818–78)
22. Catharine Maria Sedgwick (1789–1867)
23. Lydia Huntley Sigourney (1791–1865)
24. Elizabeth Oakes Smith (1806–93)
25. Ann Stephens (1810–86)
26. Harriet Beecher Stowe (1811–96)
27. Susan Warner (1819–85)
28. Adeline D. T. Whitney (1824–1906)
29. Emma Willard (1787–1870)
30. Sara Payson Willis ("Fanny Fern") (1812–72)

MINISTERS

1. Joseph H. Allen (1820–98)
2. Henry Bacon (1813–56)
3. Edward Beecher (1803–95)
4. Henry Ward Beecher (1813–87)
5. Joseph Buckminster (1784–1812)
6. Horace Bushnell (1802–76)
7. William Ellery Channing (1780–1843)
8. William Henry Channing (1810–84)
9. James Freeman Clarke (1810–88)
10. Theodore Cuyler (1822–1909)
11. Orville Dewey (1794–1882)
12. Bela B. Edwards (1802–52)
13. Ralph Waldo Emerson (1803–82)
14. Charles Follen (1796–1842)
15. Ezra Stiles Gannett (1801–71)
16. F. W. P. Greenwood (1797–1843)
17. James K. Hosmer (1834–1927)
18. Frederic Dan Huntington (1819–1904)
19. Sylvester Judd (1813–53)
20. Andrews Norton (1786–1853)
21. Edwards A. Park (1808–1900)
22. Theodore Parker (1810–60)
23. Edward Payson (1783–1827)
24. William Peabody (1799–1847)
25. Austin Phelps (1820–90)
26. Henry Soule (1815–52)
27. Joseph Tuckerman (1778–1841)
28. Henry Ware, Jr. (1794–1843)
29. William Ware (1797–1852)
30. Noah Worcester (1758–1837)

APPENDIX B

Biographical information on the women and ministers is here listed in chronological order.

WOMEN	FATHER'S OCCUPATION	SPOUSE
1. Emma Willard (1787–1870)	Samuel Hart, Connecticut farmer	m. 1809 Dr. John Willard, doctor (d. 1825); m. 1838 Christopher Yate, doctor (divorced 1843) 1 child
2. Sarah Josepha Hale (1788–1879)	Gordon Buell, New Hampshire farmer, tavern-keeper	m. 1813 David Hale, lawyer (d. 1822) 5 children
3. Catharine Maria Sedgwick (1789–1867)	Theodore Sedgwick, Massachusetts lawyer, politician	single
4. Lydia Huntley Sigourney (1791–1865)	Ezekiel Huntley, Connecticut gardener, hired man	m. 1819 Charles Sigourney, merchant 2 children
5. Mary Lyon (1797–1849)	Aaron Lyon, Massachusetts farmer	single
6. Catharine Esther Beecher (1800–78)	Lyman Beecher, Connecticut preacher, theologian, reformer	single

MAIN PLACES OF RESIDENCE	OCCUPATION	RELIGIOUS AFFILIATION
Berlin, CT	housewife*	(liberal) Congregationalist→
Middlebury, VT	teacher	Episcopalian
Waterford, NY	writer	
Boston	administrator	
Newport, NH	teacher	Congregationalist→
Boston	housewife	Episcopalian
Philadelphia	millinery-shop worker	
	editor	
	writer	
Stockbridge, MA	housewife	Congregationalist→
New York City	writer	Unitarian
Boston		
Lenox, MA		
Norwich, CT	teacher	Congregationalist→
Hartford, CT	writer	Episcopalian
	housewife	
Buckland, MA	housewife	Baptist
E. Derry, NH	teacher	
Ipswich, MA	revivalist	
S. Hadley, MA	administrator	
	writer	
Litchfield, CT	housewife	Congregationalist→
Hartford, CT	teacher	Episcopalian
Cincinnati, OH	administrator	
and extensive travels throughout the U.S.	writer	

*I have listed "housewife" as an occupation for any woman, married or unmarried, who devoted significant time and energy to the management of a home.

WOMEN	FATHER'S OCCUPATION	SPOUSE
7. Dorothea Dix (1802–87)	Joseph Dix, Massachusetts farmer, Methodist preacher	single
8. Lydia Maria Child (1802–80)	David Convers Francis, Massachusetts baker	m. 1828 David Lee Ch lawyer, politician, reformer, farmer no children
9. Elizabeth Peabody (1804–94)	Nathaniel Peabody, Massachuetts teacher, dentist	single
10. Elizabeth Oakes Smith (1806–93)	David Smith, Maine ship captain	m. 1823 Seba Smith, journalist, humorist 5 children
11. Margaret Fuller (1810–50)	Timothy Fuller, Massachusetts lawyer, politician	m. 1849 Angelo Ossoli Italian nobleman 1 child
12. Ann Stephens (1810–86)	John Winterbotham, Connecticut wool manufacturer	m. 1831 Edward Steph customs house clerk 2 children
13. Harriet Beecher Stowe (1811–96)	Lyman Beecher, Connecticut preacher, theologian, reformer	m. 1836 Calvin Stowe, theologian, teacher, author 5 children
14. Delia Bacon (1811–59)	David Bacon, Connecticut minister	single

MAIN PLACES OF RESIDENCE	OCCUPATION	RELIGIOUS AFFILIATION
Hampden, ME	housewife	Congregationalist/
Boston	teacher	Methodist→
Trenton, NJ	writer	Unitarian
and extensive travels	nurse	
throughout the U.S.	reformer	
Medford, MA	housewife	Congregationalist→
Watertown, MA	teacher	Unitarian
Boston	writer	(transcendentalist)
New York City	reformer	
	editor	
Salem, MA	teacher	Unitarian
Boston	writer	(transcendentalist)
Concord, MA	reformer	
Portland, ME	housewife	Congregationalist→
New York City	lecturer	Unitarian
	journalist and writer	
	minister	
Cambridgeport, MA	lecturer	Unitarian
Groton, MA	teacher	(transcendentalist)
Providence, RI	journalist	
Jamaica Plains, MA	writer	
New York City	revolutionary	
Rome, Italy		
Humphreysville, CT	housewife	Episcopalian
Portland, ME	editor	
New York City	writer	
Litchfield, CT	teacher	Congregationalist→
Hartford, CT	writer	Episcopalian
Cincinnati, OH	housewife	
Brunswick, ME		
Andover, MA		
Talmadge, OH	teacher	Congregationalist→
Boston	lecturer	Episcopalian
New Haven, CT	writer	
London, England		
Stratford, England		

WOMEN	FATHER'S OCCUPATION	SPOUSE
15. Sara Payson Willis ("Fanny Fern") (1812–72)	Nathaniel Willis, Maine deacon, editor	m. 1838 Charles Eldred, banker (d. 1847); m. 1849 A. D. Farringto merchant (divorced 1853); m. 1856 James Parton, historian, writer 3 children
16. Harriet Farley (1813–1907)	Stephen Farley, New Hampshire minister	m. 1854 John I. Dunlea engraver, inventor 1 child
17. Emily Chubbuck (Judson) ("Fanny Forrester") (1817–53)	Charles Chubbuck, New York farmer	m. 1846 Adoniram Juds missionary 2 children
18. Elizabeth Prentiss (1818–78)	Edward Payson, Maine teacher minister	m. 1845 George Prentis minister 6 children
19. Susan Warner (1819–85)	Henry Warner, New York lawyer	single
20. Sarah Edgarton Mayo (1819–49)	Mr. Edgarton, Massachusetts factory worker, manufacturer. First name unknown	m. 1847 A. D. Mayo, minister 1 child
21. Alice Cary (1820–71)	Robert Carey, Ohio farmer	single
22. Charlotte Fillebrown (Jerauld) (1820–45)	Richard Fillebrown, Massachusetts craft worker	m. 1843 L. W. Jerauld, occupation unknown 1 child

MAIN PLACES OF RESIDENCE	OCCUPATION	RELIGIOUS AFFILIATION
Portland, ME	seamstress	Congregationalist→
Boston	writer	(liberal) Congregationalist
New York City	housewife	
Claremont, NH	teacher	Congregationalist
Atkinson, NH	mill operative	
Lowell, MA	editor	
New York City	writer	
Eaton, NY	factory operative	Baptist
Utica, NY	teacher	
Burma	writer	
	missionary	
	housewife	
Portland, ME	writer	Congregationalist
Richmond, VA	teacher	
New York City	lay preacher	
	housewife	
Constitution Island, NY	writer	Presbyterian
	housewife	
Shirley, MA	writer	Universalist
Gloucester, MA	housewife	
Hamilton County, OH	writer	Universalist
New York City		
Boston	book-binder	Universalist
	writer	
	housewife	

WOMEN	FATHER'S OCCUPATION	SPOUSE
23. Sara Clarke Lippincott ("Grace Greenwood") (1823–1904)	Thaddeus Clarke, New York doctor	m. 1853 Leander K. Lippincott, clerk 1 child
24. Lucy Larcom (1824–93)	Benjamin Larcom, Massachusetts merchant, sea captain	single
25. Adeline D. T. Whitney (1824–1906)	Enoch Train, Massachusetts merchant, ship owner	m. 1843 Seth D. Whitney, wool and leather trader 4 children
26. Mary J. Holmes (1825–1907)	Preston Hawes, Massachusetts, occupation uncertain (uncle: Joel Hawes, Congregational minister)	m. 1848 Daniel Holmes, teacher, lawyer no children
27. Maria Cummins (1827–66)	David Cummins, Massachusetts lawyer	single
28. Martha Finley (1828–1909)	James B. Finley, Indiana doctor	single
29. Louisa May Alcott (1832–88)	Bronson Alcott, Massachusetts teacher, reformer	single
30. Elizabeth Stuart Phelps (1844–1911)	Austin Phelps, Massachusetts minister, teacher, theologian, writer	m. 1888 Herbert D. Ward, writer no children

MAIN PLACES OF RESIDENCE	OCCUPATION	RELIGIOUS AFFILIATION
Pompey, NY New Brighton, PA Washington, D.C. Philadelphia New York City	writer reformer	Congregationalist→ (liberal) Congregationalist
Beverly, MA Lowell, MA Godfrey, IL Norton, MA Boston	mill operative teacher writer editor housewife	Congregationalist→ Episcopalian
Boston Milton, MA	writer housewife	Congregationalist→ Unitarian→ Episcopalian
Brookfield, MA Versailles, KY Brockport, NY traveled widely	teacher writer housewife	Congregationalist→ Episcopalian
Salem, MA Springfield, MA Dorchester, MA	writer	Unitarian
South Bend, IN New York City Philadelphia Bedford, PA Elkton, MD	teacher writer housewife	Presbyterian
Concord, MA	seamstress servant teacher nurse writer housewife	Unitarian (transcendentalist)
Boston Andover, MA Gloucester, MA	writer reformer teacher	Congregationalist→ Episcopalian

MEN	FATHER'S OCCUPATION	SPOUSE
1. Noah Worcester (1758–1837)	Noah Worcester, New Hampshire justice of the peace	m. 1779 Hannah Brown (d. 1797); m. 1798 Hannah Huntington 8 children
2. Joseph Tuckerman (1778–1841)	Edward Tuckerman, Massachusetts merchant	m. 1803 Abigail Parkman (d. 1807); m. 1808 Sarah Cary 10 children
3. William Ellery Channing (1780–1843)	William Channing, Massachusetts minister	m. 1814 Ruth Gibbs 4 children
4. Edward Payson (1783–1827)	Seth Payson, Maine minister	m. 1811 Ann Shipman 8 children
5. Joseph Buckminster (1784–1812)	Joseph Buckminster, New Hampshire minister	single
6. Andrews Norton (1786–1853)	Samuel Norton, Massachusetts gentleman active in town affairs	m. 1821 Catharine Eliot 6 children
7. Henry Ware, Jr. (1794–1843)	Henry Ware, Massachusetts minister, theologian, teacher	m. 1817 Elizabeth Waterhouse (d. 1824); m. 1827 Mary Pickford 10 children
8. Orville Dewey (1794–1882)	Silas Dewey, Massachusetts farmer	m. 1820 Louisa Farnham 3 (?) children
9. Charles Follen (1796–1842)	Christoph Follenius, Giessen, Germany, judge	m. 1828 Eliza Lee Cabot 1 child
10. F. W. P. Greenwood (1797–1843)	William P. Greenwood, Massachusetts dentist	m. 1824 Maria Goodwin 5 children

MAIN PLACES OF RESIDENCE	OCCUPATION	RELIGIOUS AFFILIATION
Hollis, NH Thornton, NH Brighton, MA	teacher minister editor theologian	Unitarian
Boston	minister reformer	Unitarian
Cambridge, MA Boston	minister writer theologian	Congregationalist→ Unitarian
Rindge, NH Portland, ME	minister	Congregationalist
Portsmouth, NH Boston	minister writer	Congregationalist→ Unitarian
Hingham, MA Cambridge, MA	minister teacher scholar theologian	Unitarian
Hingham, MA Boston Cambridge, MA	minister teacher writer	Unitarian
Sheffield, MA Boston New York City	teacher minister writer lecturer	Congregationalist→ Unitarian
Giessen, Germany Cambridge, MA	teacher minister reformer	Unitarian (transcendentalist)
Boston	minister writer	Unitarian

MEN	FATHER'S OCCUPATION	SPOUSE
11. William Ware (1797–1852)	Henry Ware, Massachusetts minister, theologian, teacher	m. 1823 Mary Waterho... 7 children
12. William Peabody (1799–1847)	Oliver Peabody, New Hampshire lawyer, politician	m. 1824 Elizabeth Whi... 5 children
13. Ezra Stiles Gannett (1801–71)	Caleb Gannett, Massachusetts minister	m. 1835 Anna Tilden 3 (?) children
14. Horace Bushnell (1802–76)	Ensign Bushnell, Connecticut farmer	m. 1833 Mary Apthorp 3 children
15. Bela B. Edwards (1802–52)	Elosha Edwards, Massachusetts farmer, deacon	m. 1831 Jerusha Billings 3 children
16. Ralph Waldo Emerson (1803–82)	William Emerson, Massachusetts minister	m. 1829 Ellen Tucker (d. 1831); m. 1835 Lydia Jackson 4 children
17. Edward Beecher (1803–95)	Lyman Beecher, Connecticut preacher, theologian, reformer	m. 1829 Isabella Jones 11 children
18. Edwards A. Park (1808–1900)	Calvin Park, Rhode Island teacher	m. 1836 Ann Edwards 3 children
19. William Henry Channing (1810–84)	Francis Dana Channing, Massachusetts lawyer	m. 1836 Julia Allen 2 (?) children
20. James Freeman Clarke (1810–88)	Samuel Clarke, Massachusetts, no settled occupation	m. 1839 Anna Huideko... 3 (?) children
21. Theodore Parker (1810–60)	John Parker, Massachusetts farmer, mechanic	m. 1837 Lydia Cabot no children

MAIN PLACES OF RESIDENCE	OCCUPATION	RELIGIOUS AFFILIATION
Hingham, MA New York City	minister novelist editor	Unitarian
Exeter, NH Cambridge, MA Springfield, MA	teacher minister critic writer	Unitarian
Cambridge, MA Boston	teacher minister reformer	Congregationalist
New Preston, CT Hartford, CT	teacher minister writer theologian	Congregationalist
Southampton, MA Boston Andover, MA	minister editor	Congregationalist
Boston Concord, MA	minister writer lecturer	Unitarian→ (transcendentalist)
Litchfield, CT Boston Jacksonville, IL Galesburg, IL	teacher minister editor writer administrator	Congregationalist
Providence, RI Braintree, MA Andover, MA	teacher minister theologian	Congregationalist
Boston Liverpool, England	minister writer reformer	Unitarian (transcendentalist)
Newton, MA Louisville, KY Meadville, PA Boston	minister writer reformer	Unitarian (transcendentalist)
Lexington, MA Boston	minister writer reformer	Unitarian (transcendentalist)

MEN	FATHER'S OCCUPATION	SPOUSE
22. Henry Bacon (1813–56)	Robert Bacon, occupation uncertain (probably a craftsman or laborer in Boston)	m. 183? Eliza Monroe 3 children
23. Sylvester Judd (1813–53)	Sylvester Judd, Massachusetts antiquarian, editor	m. 1840 Jane Williams 3 children
24. Henry Ward Beecher (1813–87)	Lyman Beecher, Connecticut preacher, theologian, reformer	m. 1837 Eunice Bullard 4 children
25. Henry Soule (1815–52)	Clement Soule, New York farmer	m. 1843 Caroline White 5 children
26. Frederic Dan Huntington (1819–1904)	Dan Huntington, Massachusetts minister	m. 1843 Hannah Dana Sargent 4 children
27. Joseph H. Allen (1820–98)	Joseph Allen, Massachusetts minister	m. 1845 Anna Minot W 6 children
28. Austin Phelps (1820–90)	Eliakin Phelps, Massachusetts minister	m. 1842 Elizabeth Stua (d. 1852); m. 1854 Mary Stuart (d. 1856); m. 1858 Mary Johnson 3 children
29. Theodore Cuyler (1822–1909)	Benjamin Cuyler, New York farmer	m. 1853 Annie Mathiot children (number unknown)
30. James K. Hosmer (1834–1927)	George Washington Hosmer, Massachusetts farmer	m. 1863 Eliza Butler (d. 1877); m. 1878 Jenny Garland children (number unknown)

MAIN PLACES OF RESIDENCE	OCCUPATION	RELIGIOUS AFFILIATION
Boston	minister	Universalist
Cambridge, MA	writer	
Providence, RI	editor	
Philadelphia		
Northampton, MA	minister	Congregationalist→
Cambridge, MA	writer	Unitarian
Augusta, ME	reformer	
Litchfield, CT	minister	Congregationalist
Lawrenceburg, IN	writer	
Indianapolis, IN	lecturer	
Brooklyn, NY	reformer	
Utica, NY	minister	Universalist
Hartford, CT	writer	
Boston	editor	
Hadley, MA	minister	Congregationalist→
Boston	editor	Unitarian→
	writer	Episcopalian
Northboro, MA	minister	Unitarian
Jamaica Plains, MA	scholar	
Washington, D.C.	editor	
Bangor, ME	teacher	
Cambridge, MA		
Pittsfield, MA	minister	Congregationalist
Philadelphia	teacher	
Boston	writer	
Andover, MA		
Aurora, NY	minister	(liberal) Presbyterian
New York City	writer	
Brooklyn, NY	lecturer	
Northfield, MA	minister	Unitarian→ Liberal
Cambridge, MA	writer	
Antioch, OH	teacher	
St. Louis, MO		
Minneapolis, MN		

NOTES

INTRODUCTION:
THE LEGACY OF
AMERICAN VICTORIANISM

1. On American Victorian culture, see Meade Minnegerode, *The Fabulous Forties 1840–1850* (New York, 1924), and E. Douglas Branch, *The Sentimental Years 1836–60* (New York and London, 1934). For important efforts to define "Victorianism" as an American phenomenon, see the essays in the special issue of *American Quarterly*, 27 (1975) entitled "Victorian Culture in America," particularly the lead article by Daniel Walker Howe, "American Victorianism as a Culture."

2. See Susan Sontag, "Notes on 'Camp' " in *Against Interpretation and Other Essays* (New York, 1969), pp. 277–83.

3. See Edwin Wilbur Rice, *The Sunday School Movement 1780–1917 and the American Sunday School Union 1817–1917* (Philadelphia, 1917), pp. 42 ff.

4. Thoreau carefully told his readers in *Walden*, a rural narrative which is hardly a pastoral in any conventional sense, the monetary cost of his experiment in self-reliant solitude; and he never forgot the railroad whose cars thundered near his retreat. Cooper's Natty Bumppo, the hero of the Leatherstocking Tales, despite his religious adherence to conservation, is a hunter who kills more animals and Indians than he saves. Whether he likes it or not, Natty is the vanguard as well as the refugee of civilization, and his appearance in any forest prophesies its eventual demise. The great protagonist of Melville's *Moby Dick*, Ahab, whatever his spiritual quest, is a part of America's aggressive whaling industry, and as such, a proto-technocrat; if Natty's most intimate friend is his gun, Ahab's is his harpoon. The transcendental jingoism of Whitman's early Manhattan persona is not designed to conceal the fact that he is celebrating the proliferating population, self-propagating machinery, and randomly abundant materialism of the most ruthlessly expanding and constricting city in the world.

5. I am thinking here particularly of Hawthorne's treatment of the pure maiden figure: Priscilla in *The Blithedale Romance* (1852) and Hilda in *The Marble Faun* (1860).

6. I hope the reasons I have chosen this period (1820–75) as the crucial one for the development of Victorian sentimentalism in the Northeast will become clear in the course of this book. Recent historical opinion has minimized the importance of the Civil War as a crucial dividing line for American culture. I will make just a few further points here. First, the period 1820–1875 includes the initial

commercialization of culture, most notably the revolution in printing and the rise of nationally circulated magazines. Second, the most important work of the leading figures in the sentimentalization process (see Appendix A) seems to appear and, more significantly, to receive its highest valuation during these years. Elizabeth Stuart Phelps, for example, who was born late in the period (1844), produces her most characteristic work, *The Gates Ajar*, in 1868; thereafter, she repeats herself and receives steadily less critical attention and praise until her death in 1911. Third, the period marks the time when the majority of Protestants in the Northeast changed from a strict to a "liberal" creed and when the Protestant Church forged its relationship with the newly commercialized culture: both changes are still in force today. In Chapter Three, I try to break the period into smaller, defined units. In Chapter Seven, I discuss its culmination in the early 1870s with the late work of Henry Ward Beecher and Harriet Beecher Stowe.

7. In discussing what I am calling Calvinism, the older Protestant tradition of the Northeast, I am focusing throughout this study on its eighteenth- rather than its seventeenth-century New England exponents not because the former were greater than the latter but because they were inevitably more directly influential on the nineteenth-century Protestant clergymen whose reformulation of Calvinist thought will be my chief concern. I use the term "Calvinism," despite its partial imprecision, because it was the word the ministerial and feminine groups I am studying most commonly employed to describe the older, sterner creed of their forebears.

8. Martin Marty, in the "Foreword" to *Righteous Empire: The Protestant Experience in America* (New York, 1970), notes: "today seven out of ten citizens identify themselves as Protestants" (n.p.).

9. For an excellent introduction to Neoorthodoxy, see Sydney E. Ahlstrom, *A Religious History of the American People* (New Haven and London, 1972), pp. 932–48, and Martin E. Marty, *op. cit.*, pp. 233–43. For the most astute Neo-orthodox analysis of the American religious tradition, see Francis Miller, Wilhelm Pauck, and H. Richard Niebuhr, *The Church Against the World* (Chicago, 1935), and H. Richard Niebuhr, *The Social* *Sources of Denominationalism* (New York, 1929). Scholars like Perry Miller, who might be seen as the head of "Neo-orthodox" historiography, did not necessarily share the religious beliefs of those they studied, or of the Neo-orthodox theologians (the Niebuhr brothers, Paul Tillich, and others) who began to write in the 1920s. But they are "Neoorthodox" in the sense that they admire the Calvinist tradition and regret its passing.

10. This is the title of a novel published by Stowe in 1871.

11. My understanding of "influence" and how it functioned for the clerical and feminine groups under discussion was shaped by the work of Sigmund Freud and Heinz Kohut on narcissism as well as by the theories of a number of sociologists. I came to feel that, while Protestant ministers had been part of an elite group, they were increasingly joining middle-class women and becoming part of a special subculture. Such subculture groups, past and present, evince certain inherent patterns. Most simply, one might say that society forces members of a subculture at any moment of intersection with the larger culture into a constant, simplified, and often demeaning process of self-identification. The minister between 1820 and 1875 was beginning to experience the enforced self-simplification women had long known. In 1820 the statement "I am a minister" had a series of possible precise connotations, theological and political. By 1875, the statement meant roughly what it does today: it connotes vague church-bound efforts at "goodness." "I am a housewife," millions of American women have been explaining implicitly and explicitly for the last hundred and fifty years; yet, the term "housewife" is imprecise and obfuscating to an extreme. Surely there was (and is) as much difference between tending a childless urban apartment and running a fully populated farm household as there was between practicing law and selling merchandise. Yet just at the period when women were increasingly adopting a punitively generalized mode of self-description, men were labeling themselves in ever more specialized terms. The all-inclusive designation "lady" slowly gave way over the nineteenth century to the equally blank-check appellation "housewife." In contrast, the polite term "gentleman" had no real successor; it fragmented into a thousand parts,

personal, political, and professional. Why
have not men identified themselves by an
equally adequate, or inadequate, catchall
phrase such as "breadwinner"? Quite obviously, because society expresses its greater esteem for masculine occupations by honoring
them with a highly differentiated nomencla-
ture.

Naturally those belonging to a subculture will themselves be preoccupied with
who they are, often in equally simplistic and
distorted terms. They will struggle obsessively, repetitiously, and monotonously to
deal with the burden of self-dislike implied
and imposed by their society's apparently low
evaluation of them. In a sense, they will be
forced into some version of narcissism, by
which I mean to suggest not only a psychological process but a sociological and even a
political one. Narcissism is best defined not as
exaggerated self-esteem but as a refusal to
judge the self by alien, objective means, a
willed inability to allow the world to play its
customary role in the business of self-evaluation. Heinz Kohut has explained lucidly the
causes for the development of narcissism:
"Being threatened in the maintenance of a
cohesive self because in early life ... [the narcissist is] lacking in adequate confirming responses ... from the environment, [he] turns
to self-stimulation in order to retain [his] ...
precarious cohesion." The narcissist must always by definition be self-taught, because the
world's lessons are inevitably unacceptable to
his ego. He is committed not only to an un-
derestimation of the force of facts, but, in
Freud's words, to an "over-estimation of the
power of wishes and mental processes.... a
belief in the magical virtue of words and a
method of dealing with the outer world—the
art of magic." Narcissism can necessitate the
replacement of society by the self, reality by
literature. See Heinz Kohut, "Thoughts on
Narcissism and Narcissistic Rage," a paper delivered as the A. A. Brill Lecture of the New
York Psychoanalytic Society on November
30, 1971; Sigmund Freud, "On Narcissism: An
Introduction" in *A General Selection from the
Works of Sigmund Freud*, ed. John Rickman,
M.D. (New York, 1957), p. 106. For a defini-
tion of minority groups, see Helen Mayer
Hacker, "Women as a Minority Group,"
Bobbs-Merrill Reprint Series in the Social
Sciences, 5–108. The ministry had constituted

in the past what Suzanne Keller calls a "strategic elite"; see Suzanne Keller, *Beyond the Ruling Elite: Strategic Elites in Modern Society*
(New York, 1963).

12. See Henry James, "Anthony Trol-
lope," in *The Future of the Novel: Essays on the
Art of Fiction*, ed. Leon Edel (New York,
1956), pp. 247–8.

13. There are many interesting studies of
this aspect of the reading phenomenon.
Works that particularly stimulated my thinking are the "Introduction" in *The Oven Birds:
American Women on Womanhood 1820–1920*,
ed. Gail Parker (New York, 1972), pp. 1–56;
Roland Barthes, *The Pleasures of the Text*,
trans. Richard Miller (New York, 1975); and
Raymond Williams, "Base and Superstructure
in Marxist Cultural Theory," *New Left Review*
82 (1973), especially 12–16.

14. I am indebted for my understanding of
the positive side of sentimentalism to the superb study by Elaine Showalter, *The Female
Tradition in the English Novel: From Charlotte
Brontë to Doris Lessing* (Princeton, 1976). For
the J. S. Mill reference, see *The Autobiography
of John Stuart Mill* (New York, n.d.), pp. 103–
17.

15. Herman Melville, *White-Jacket, or the
World in a Man-of-War* (New York, 1967),
p. 141.

1

CLERICAL DISESTABLISHMENT

1. Quoted in F. W. Dupee, *Henry James:
His Life and Writings* (New York, 1956), p. 11.

2. H. Richard Niebuhr, *The Kingdom of
God in America* (New York, 1937), p. 193.

3. Winthrop S. Hudson, *American Protestantism* (Chicago and London, 1961), p. 136.

4. Perry Miller, *The Life of the Mind in
America* (New York, 1965), pp. 23, 25. For
other studies from a version of the "Neo-
orthodox" view, see William A. Clebsch, *From
Sacred to Profane America: The Role of Religion
in American History* (New York, 1968); Robert Handy, *A Christian America: Protestant
Hopes and Historical Realities* (New York,
1971), and "The Protestant Quest for a Christian America 1830–1930," *Church History*,
21–22 (1952–53), 8–20; Joseph Haroutunian,
*Piety Versus Moralism: The Passing of the New
England Theology* (New York, 1932); Win-

throp S. Hudson, *Religion in America* (New York, 1965); Martin E. Marty, *Righteous Empire: The Protestant Experience in America* (New York, 1970). A notable exception to the pervasive pessimism of current religious history is Sydney E. Ahlstrom's *A Religious History of the American People* (New Haven and London, 1972), which notably ignores the ministry itself and focuses on the richness of America's pluralist religious culture. For the classic and monumental study of the vitiation of nineteenth-century Protestantism, see Karl Barth, *Protestant Theology in the Nineteenth Century: Its Background and History* (London, 1972).

5. I am using "liberal" to describe the non-evangelical, non-revivalist wing of the northeastern Protestant Church; this included almost all Unitarians, many Congregationalists and Episcopalians, and some Presbyterians. For reasons which I hope will become clear in this chapter, I am primarily concerned with the Unitarians and Congregationalists, and to a lesser degree, the Episcopalians.

6. See Ahlstrom, *op. cit.*, p. 400; Henry Steele Commager, *Theodore Parker* (Boston, 1947), *passim;* Henry F. May, *Protestant Churches and Industrial America* (New York, 1949), p. 30. I have downplayed the reform aspect of liberal Protestantism in the period. Vital as it was, it does not seem to me Victorian Protestantism's central legacy; but it should not be forgotten.

7. *The Works of Charles Follen with a Memoir of His Life* (Boston, 1842), I, pp. 514, 515.

8. James Elliot Cabot, *A Memoir of Ralph Waldo Emerson* (Boston and New York, 1887), I, pp. 105, 167, 329.

9. James K. Hosmer, *The Thinking Bayonet* (Boston, 1865), pp. 17, 15, 54.

10. Joseph Henry Allen, *Our Liberal Movement in Theology* (Boston, 1882), pp. 190, 196.

11. William Henry Channing, *Memoir of William Ellery Channing with Extracts from His Correspondence and Manuscripts* (Boston, 1846), II, p. 266.

12. Elizabeth Palmer Peabody, *Reminiscences of Reverend William Ellery Channing, D.D.* (Boston, 1880), p. 259.

13. See *ibid.*, p. 302.

14. *The Works of William E. Channing, D.D.* (Boston and New York, 1849), VI, pp. 190 ff.; and see Peabody, *op. cit.*, pp. 203, 257.

15. Mary E. Dewey, ed., *Autobiography and Letters of Orville Dewey, D.D.* (Boston, 1884), pp. 88, 230, 231, 224.

16. See Milton Powell, ed., *The Voluntary Church: American Religious Life (1740–1865) Seen Through the Eyes of European Visitors* (New York and London, 1966), p. 90.

17. See Timothy Smith, *Revivalism and Social Reform: American Protestantism on the Eve of the Civil War* (New York, 1957), pp. 20, 21; Winthrop S. Hudson, *American Protestantism*, pp. 97, 98.

18. For discussion of disestablishment, see Daniel Calhoun, *Professional Lives in America: Structure and Aspiration 1750–1850* (Cambridge, Mass., 1965); Evarts B. Greene, *Religion and the State: The Making and Testing of an American Tradition* (Ithaca, N.Y., 1941); Sidney E. Mead, *The Lively Experiment: The Shaping of Christianity in America* (New York, 1963); H. Shelton Smith, Robert T. Handy, and Lefferts A. Loetscher, *American Christianity: An Historical Interpretation with Representative Documents* (New York, 1960), I, pp. 432 ff.; Anson Phelps Stokes, *Church and State in the United States* (New York, 1950), 3 vols.; Cushing Strout, *The New Heavens and New Earth: Political Religion in America* (New York, 1974). Also useful is H. Richard Niebuhr and Daniel D. Williams, eds., *The Ministry in Historical Perspective* (New York, 1956). For consideration of the broader problem of which the loss of ministerial status was a part, see Richard Hofstadter, *Anti-Intellectualism in American Life* (New York, 1962).

19. See Clebsch, *op. cit.*, Handy, *A Christian America*, and Mead, *op. cit.*

20. *The Autobiography of Lyman Beecher*, ed. Barbara M. Cross (Cambridge, Mass., 1961), I, p. 192.

21. *Ibid.*, p. 336.

22. Philip Schaff, *America: A Sketch of Its Political, Social, and Religious Character*, ed. Perry Miller (Cambridge, Mass., 1961), p. 80.

23. Andrew Reed and James Matheson, *A Narrative of the Visit to the American Churches by the Deputation from the Congregational Union of England and Wales* (New York, 1835), II, pp. 98ff.

24. Elwyn A. Smith, *Religious Liberty and the United States: The Development of Church-State Thought Since the Revolutionary Era* (Philadelphia, 1972), p. 107.

25. Greene, *op. cit.*, p. 97. See also M. Louise Greene, *The Development of Religious Liberty in Connecticut* (Boston and New York, 1905).

26. Strout, *op. cit.*, p. 343 and *passim;* James F. Maclean, " 'The True American Union' of Church and State," *Church History*, 28 (1959), 41–54, partially reprinted in John F. Wilson, ed., *Church and State in American History* (Boston, 1965), pp. 110–14.

27. Quoted in Wilson, *op. cit.*, p. 114.

28. *Ibid.*

29. Marty, *op. cit.*, p. 138. There are still relatively few good histories of the denominations under consideration here. For the history of Presbyterianism, see E. H. Gillett, *History of the Presbyterian Church in the United States of America*, 2 vols. (Philadelphia, 1864); Leonard Trinterud, *The Forming of an American Tradition: A Re-examination of Colonial Presbyterianism* (Philadelphia, 1949); William Warren Sweet, *Religion on the American Frontier, 1783–1840*, Vol. II: *The Presbyterians: A Collection of Source Materials* (New York, 1936); William Trice Thompson, *Presbyterians in the South*, 2 vols. (Richmond, Va., 1963); Elwyn A. Smith, "The Forming of a Modern American Denomination," *Church History*, 31 (1962), 74–99; and Fred J. Hood, "Presbyterianism and the New American Nation, 1783–1826: A Case Study of Religion and National Life," unpub. diss., Princeton University, 1968. On Methodism, see Wade C. Barclay, *Early American Methodism*, 2 vols. (New York, 1949); Emory Stevens Bucke, ed., *The History of American Methodism*, 3 vols. (Nashville, Tenn., 1964); William Warren Sweet, *Religion on the American Frontier, 1783–1840*, Vol. IV, *The Methodists* (Chicago, 1946); Walter Brownlaw Posey, *The Development of Methodism in the Old Southwest, 1783–1824* (Tuscaloosa, Ala., 1933); Wesley Gewehr, "Some Factors in the Expansion of Frontier Methodism, 1800–1811," *Journal of Religion*, 8 (Jan. 1928), 98–120. On the Baptists, see Norman A. Baxter, *History of the Freewill Baptists: A Study in New England Separatism* (Rochester, N.Y., 1957); Albert Newman, *A History of the Baptist Churches in the United States* (New York, 1894); Robert G. Torbet, *A History of the Baptists* (Philadelphia, 1950), *A Social History of the Philadelphia Baptist Association: 1707–1940* (Philadelphia, 1944), and *Venture of Faith: The Story of the American Baptist Foreign Mission*

Society (Philadelphia, 1955). On the Episcopalians, see Raymond W. Albright, *A History of the Protestant Episcopalian Church* (New York, 1964); S. D. McConnell, *History of the American Episcopal Church 1600–1915* (Milwaukee, 1916); William Wilson Manross, *A History of the American Episcopal Church* (New York, 1950). For general studies of the Congregationalists, see Gaius Glenn Atkins and Frederick L. Fagley, *History of American Congregationalism* (Boston, 1942), and Williston Walker, *Congregational Churches in the United States* (New York, 1894).

30. For distinctions and relations between Congregationalists and Old School and New School Presbyterians, see the excellent study by George M. Marsden, *The Evangelical Mind and the New School Presbyterian Experience: A Case Study of Thought and Theology in Nineteenth-Century America* (New Haven and London, 1970).

31. See Earl Morse Wilbur, *A History of Unitarianism in Transylvania, England, and America* (Cambridge, Mass., 1952), and Conrad Wright, *The Beginnings of Unitarianism in America* (Boston, 1955).

32. Evarts B. Greene, *op. cit.*, pp. 90 ff.

33. *Ibid.*

34. David D. Hall, *The Faithful Shepherd: A History of the New England Ministry in the Seventeenth Century* (Chapel Hill, N.C., 1972), pp. 146 ff. I am deeply indebted as well to David Hall's helpful comments on my work.

35. *Ibid.*, pp. 190–3.

36. Perry Miller, *Jonathan Edwards* (New York, 1949), p. 197.

37. Hall, *op. cit.*, p. 186.

38. Calhoun, *op. cit.*, pp. 120, 121.

39. Arethusa Hall, *Life and Character of the Reverend Sylvester Judd* (Boston, 1854), p. 231; William C. Gannett, *Ezra Stiles Gannett Unitarian Ministers in Boston 1824–1871* (Boston, 1875), p. 359.

40. Quoted in Calhoun, *op. cit.*, p. 174.

41. *Ibid.*, pp. 158–61.

42. William M. Thayer, *Spots in Our Feasts of Charity* (Boston and Cleveland, 1854), pp. 231, 232.

43. "The Shady and the Sunny Side of the Ministry," *Christian Examiner*, 55 (1853), 338–50. See also Rev. Amzi Benedict, "Ministerial Support," *National Preacher*, 29 (1855), 129–40, and Rev. T. S. Clark, "The Pulpit Worth

More than It Costs," *National Preacher*, 13 (1839), 161–76.

44. S. G. Goodrich, *Recollections of a Lifetime, or Men and Things I Have Seen* (New York, 1856), pp. 27, 99, 76.

45. J. H. Allen's astute observations on the state of the clergy can be found in two crucial articles he published in the late 1860s: "On Some Conditions of the Modern Ministry," *Christian Examiner*, 82 (1867), 51–63, and "On Some Results of the Voluntary System, Especially in Our Country Parishes," *Christian Examiner*, 84 (1868), 207–29.

46. See Roland H. Bainton, *Yale and the Ministry* (New York, 1957); Alice M. Baldwin, *The New England Clergy and the American Revolution* (New York, 1958); Alan Heimert, *Religion and the American Mind: From the Great Awakening to the Revolution* (Cambridge, Mass., 1966); J. Earl Thompson, Jr., "An 'Unnecessary, Unjust and Inexpedient' War: Congregational Clergy Dissent Against the War of 1812," *Andover Newton Quarterly*, 11 (1970), 33–47. Republicans at political banquets in Connecticut in the early nineteenth century made telling toasts like the following: "The Clergy of all Denominations—the Bible their constitution, their politics religion," "The Pulpit for the Priest not for the Politician." See Stokes, *op. cit.*, I, pp. 409, 410.

47. James Banner, *To the Federalist Convention: The Federalists and the Origins of Party Politics in Massachusetts, 1789–1815* (New York, 1970), pp. 150–65.

48. Quoted in Vernon Stauffer, *New England and the Bavarian Illuminati* (New York and London, 1928), p. 94.

49. *Christian Examiner*, 2 (1825), 2.

50. Marty, *op. cit.*, p. 69.

51. See David Hall, *op. cit.*, pp. 136, 144.

52. Stokes, *op. cit.*, II, pp. 15–17.

53. Charles Forrester Dunham, *The Attitude of the Northern Clergy Toward the South 1860–1865* (Toledo, Ohio, 1942), p. 53.

54. The leading opponent of slavery and the most severe critic of the northern clergy's lukewarm protest was of course William Lloyd Garrison. See *William Lloyd Garrison 1805–1879: The Story of His Life Told By His Children* (New York, 1885), 4 vols., *passim*, and John L. Thomas, *The Liberator: William Lloyd Garrison* (Boston and Toronto, 1963).

55. For this view of the southern clergyman's role, see Donald Mathews, "The

Southern Clergy as a Strategic Elite: 1780–1870," a paper delivered before the American Historical Association in 1970.

56. For discussion of this issue, see Gilbert Hobbs Barnes, *The Anti-Slavery Impulse 1830–1844* (New York; Chicago; and Burlingame, California; 1933); David Brion Davis, ed., *Ante-Bellum Reform* (New York, 1967); Louis Filler, *The Crusade Against Slavery 1830–1860* (New York, 1960); Daniel Walker Howe, *The Unitarian Conscience: Harvard Moral Philosophy 1805–1861* (Cambridge, Mass., 1970), pp. 270–305; Aileen S. Kraditor, *Means and Ends in American Abolitionism: Garrison and His Critics on Strategy and Tactics 1834–1850* (New York, 1967); Stokes, *op. cit.*, II, pp. 133 ff.; Bertram Wyatt-Brown, *Lewis Tappan and the Evangelical War Against Slavery* (Cleveland, 1969).

57. See Stokes, *op. cit.*, II, for a discussion of conflicts and breaks between anti- and proslavery groups in the various denominations.

58. My discussion of Bushnell is based on Charles C. Cole, Jr., "Horace Bushnell and the Slavery Question," *New England Quarterly*, 23 (1950), 19–30.

59. On Finney and slavery see Barnes, *op. cit.*, pp. 161 ff., and Wyatt-Brown, *op. cit.*, *passim*.

60. The Clerical Appeal of 1837, directed very specifically against Garrison and his followers, asserted that the church was the place "into which we flee from a troubled world for peace [not for] . . . doubtful disputation." The minister's task is "the promotion of personal religion." See *William Lloyd Garrison 1805–1879*, II, pp. 134–5. Andrew Peabody, a Unitarian divine from Harvard, writing a decade later in answer to another attack on clerical indifference, defensively listed all the good causes the American ministry *did* support: missions, prison reform, better conditions for the seamen, temperance—all of them causes whose immediate dimensions were private and personal. See *Christian Examiner*, 38 (1845), 369–70.

61. I base this remark on numerous primary and secondary sources to which I have already referred, but I am chiefly referring to what emerged as the semi-official reform (or anti-reform) line in several clerically dominated periodicals over the 1850s and 1860s. See most notably the Unitarian *Christian Examiner*, the liberal Congregationalist *New Eng-*

lander, and the more evangelical *National Preacher*.

62. Contemporary clerical awareness of the diminishing cultural power of church and pulpit was pervasive, but see especially J. H. Allen, "Liberalism in Church and State," *Christian Examiner*, 85 (1868), 82–98; H. W. Bellows, "On the Alleged Unattractiveness of the Christian Pulpit," *Christian Examiner*, 87 (1869), 28–38; Alvan Lamson, "A Plea for Theology," *Christian Examiner*, 39 (1849), 289–314; "True Work," *Christian Examiner*, 78 (1865), 165–84, and "The Pulpit," *Christian Examiner*, 29 (1840), 19–50.

63. Of the two hundred fifty Congregationalist ministers ordained between 1640 and 1740, all but twenty-five held a college B. A.; many of these had also followed a post-graduate course of divinity study in a qualified minister's home. Of the eight hundred Congregationalist ministers ordained between 1740 and 1810, fewer than twenty lacked a B.A., and by the end of this period ministerial candidates had several recognized divinity schools at which to pursue their clerical education. The Methodist sect, in contrast, until well into the nineteenth century asked only a conversion experience of its clergy, and gradually accelerating educational requirements were long fought by many of its most prominent members. See Mary Latimer Gambrell, *Ministerial Training in Eighteenth-Century New England* (New York, 1937); Niebuhr and Williams, eds., *op. cit.*, pp. 237–48.

64. *Autobiography of Peter Cartwright the Backwoods Preacher*, ed. W. P. Strickland (New York, 1856), pp. 79, 360, 371.

65. *The Autobiography of Lyman Beecher*, I, p. 47.

66. On the literary social scene in early nineteenth-century Boston, see Daniel Howe, *op. cit.*, *passim;* M. A. Dewolfe Howe, ed., *Journal of the Proceedings of the Society Which Conducts the Monthly Anthology and Boston Review* (Boston, 1910); Lewis P. Simpson, *The Federalist Literary Mind: Selections from the Monthly Anthology and Boston Review 1803–1811* (Baton Rouge, La., 1962); and Ronald Story, "Class and Culture in Boston: The Athenaeum, 1807–1870," *American Quarterly*, 27 (1975), 178–99.

67. Quoted in Louise Hall Tharp, *The Peabody Sisters of Salem* (Boston, 1950), p. 46. See also Tharp, *Until Victory: Horace Mann and Mary Peabody* (Boston, 1953), p. 47.

68. See "Lyman Beecher," *Christian Examiner*, 79 (1865), 177.

69. Quoted in William G. McLoughlin, Jr., *Modern Revivalism: Charles Grandison Finney to Billy Graham* (New York, 1959), p. 61.

70. Sedgwick's voluminous and revealing, if occasionally illegible, diaries are at the Massachusetts Historical Society.

71. For an excellent study of Bushnell and his congregation, see Barbara M. Cross, *Horace Bushnell: Minister to a Changing America* (Chicago, 1958).

72. See Reed and Matheson, *op. cit.*, II, p. 11, and also Schaff, *op. cit.*, pp. 94, 95.

73. William Henry Channing, *Memoir of William Ellery Channing*, I, p. 373.

74. Mary E. Dewey, ed., *Autobiography and Letters of Orville Dewey*, p. 36. Lewis Tappan left the Unitarians because of their lack of fervor; see Wyatt-Brown, *op. cit.*, pp. 34 ff.

75. John Ware, M.D., *Memoir of the Life of Henry Ware, Jr.* (Boston, 1846), pp. 53, 178, 179.

76. For negative readings of this phenomenon, see Ray Allen Billington, *The Protestant Crusade 1800–1860: A Study of the Origins of American Nativism* (New York, 1938); Charles C. Cole, *The Social Ideas of the Northern Evangelicals 1820–1860* (New York, 1954); Charles I. Foster, *An Errand of Mercy: The Evangelical United Front, 1790–1837* (Chapel Hill, N.C., 1960); Clifford S. Griffin, *Their Brothers' Keepers: Moral Stewardship in the United States 1800–1865* (New Brunswick, N.J., 1960). For more sympathetic, and in my view, more intelligent accounts, see Lois Banner, "Religious Benevolence as Social Control: A Critique of an Interpretation," *Journal of American History*, 60 (1973), 23–41; John A. Krout, *The Origins of Prohibition* (New York, 1925).

77. *The Autobiography of Lyman Beecher*, I, pp. 113–16.

78. See William R. Hutchison, *The Transcendental Ministers: American Reform in the New England Renaissance* (New Haven, 1959), pp. 1–3.

79. Many Unitarians crossed into the Episcopalian fold in this period or adopted a number of Episcopalian practices. See particularly F. W. P. Greenwood, *Social Services for Families and Sunday Schools With a Collection of Hymns for Private Use* (Boston, 1855), and

Arria S. Huntington, *Memoir and Letters of Frederic Dan Huntington* (Boston and New York, 1906). Huntington was a notable convert to Episcopalianism and his defection from Unitarian ranks caused consternation; see his *The New Discussions of the Trinity* (Boston, 1860). See also "Unitarian and Episcopalian Affinities," *New Englander*, 3 (1845), 556–61.

80. For a good account of early Episcopalianism, see Joseph J. Ellis, *The New England Mind in Transition: Samuel Johnson of Connecticut, 1696–1772* (New Haven and London, 1973).

81. Samuel Cutting, "The Inefficiency of the Church," *National Preacher*, 27 (1849), 14.

82. E. Thurston, "The Magnitude of the Ministerial Work," *National Preacher*, 19 (1845), 202. And see Rev. Henry R. Weed, "The Murder of a Faithful Minister," *American Preacher*, 8 (1834), 253–61.

83. "The Pulpit," *Christian Examiner*, 29 (1840), 30, 31.

84. Frederick Henry Hedge, "The Destinies of Ecclesiastical Religion," *Christian Examiner*, 82 (1867), 3.

85. See Niebuhr and Williams, eds., *op. cit.*

86. "An Andover Student," *New Englander* (1855), 236.

87. "The Pulpit," *Christian Examiner*, 29 (1840), 30, 31.

88. Powell, *op. cit.*, p. 85.

89. *Ibid.*, p. 90.

2

FEMININE DISESTABLISHMENT

1. Mary Bushnell Cheney, *Life and Letters of Horace Bushnell* (New York, 1880), p. 142.

2. *Ladies' Magazine*, 5 (1832), 308–15.

3. Cheney, *Life and Letters of Horace Bushnell*, p. 142. For the comments on women of Bushnell's clerical predecessors, see Laurel Thatcher Ulrich, "Vertuous Women Found: New England Ministirial Literature, 1668–1735," *American Quarterly*, 28 (1976), 20–40.

4. Aileen Kraditor in *The Ideas of the Woman Suffrage Movement, 1890–1920* (New York and London, 1965) documents the shift in the argument of the suffrage party over the course of the nineteenth century from a demand for women's "rights" to a plea for the wider exercise of their feminine influence; in other words, the conservative ploy of "influ-

ence" was so widespread and so accepted that the radicals were gradually forced to talk in its terms. I will discuss women and reform at greater length in Chapter Three. For the doctrine of "influence," the single most valuable source is *Ladies' Magazine*, 1828–36, edited by Sarah J. Hale. And see Norman Mezvinsky, "An Idea of Female Superiority," *Midcontinent American Studies Journal*, 2 (1961), 17–26; Glenda Gates Riley, "The Subtle Subversion: Changes in the Traditionalist Image of the American Woman," *The Historian*, 32 (1969–70), 210–27. I am indebted most heavily, however, to Nancy Osterud's undergraduate thesis, "Sarah Josepha Hale: A Study in the History of Women in Nineteenth-Century America," submitted to Harvard College in 1971. This thesis has been seminal for my work.

5. *Ladies' Magazine*, 3 (1830), 83, 84.

6. *Ladies' Magazine*, 9 (1836), 383–86.

7. Mrs. L. H. Sigourney, *Water Drops* (New York, 1848), pp. 49, 51. For other temperance literature, see Herbert Ross Brown, *The Sentimental Novel in America 1789–1860* (Durham, N.C., 1940). Of special interest are the following works by Timothy Shay Arthur: *Strong Drink: The Curse and the Cure* (Philadelphia, 1877); *Ten Nights In a Bar-Room, and What I Saw There*, ed. Donald A. Koch (Cambridge, Mass., 1964); *Woman's Trials or Tales and Sketches From the Life Around Us* (Philadelphia, 1869). See also *The Old Brewery and the New Mission House By Ladies of the Mission* (New York, 1834); Mary L. Fox, *The Ruined Deacon: A True Story* (Boston, 1851); Dr. H. A. Reynolds, *Minnie Hermon: or, The Curse of Rum* (New York and Cincinnati, 1878); Mrs. S. A. Southworth, *The Inebriate's Hut: or, The First Fruits of the Maine Law* (Boston, 1854); Emma Wellmont, *Uncle Sam's Palace; or The Reigning King* (Boston, 1853). For secondary sources, see Henry William Blair, *The Temperance Movement: or The Conflict Between Man and Alcohol* (Boston, 1888); Mrs. Annie Wittenmyer, *History of the Woman's Temperance Crusade* (Boston, 1882); Brian Harrison, *Drink and the Victorians: The Temperance Question in England 1815–1872* (Pittsburgh, 1971); John A. Krout, *The Origins of Prohibition* (New York, 1925). I wish to thank Christine Stansell for access to her unpublished paper, "Carrie Nation and the Temperance Movement."

8. Lydia Huntley Sigourney, *The Young Lady's Offering, or Gems of Prose and Poetry* (Boston, 1862), p. 222.

9. *Ladies' Magazine*, 8 (1835), 186. For evidence that Hale's paranoia was not altogether unfounded, see the case of the seduced and murdered Mahon Heberton as reported in *The New Englander*, 1 (1842), 442–551.

10. *Ladies' Magazine*, 7 (1834), 419. For an excellent paper on the implications for women of anti-Catholic literature, see David Bennett, "Anti-Catholic Movements and the Vision of the Victimized Woman," delivered before the American Historical Association in Atlanta, Ga., on Dec. 28, 1975.

11. Such articles by Hale are scattered throughout her first periodical, *Ladies' Magazine*, which she edited from 1828 until 1836.

12. See J. H. Allen, "On Some Results of the Voluntary System, Especially in Our Country Parishes," *Christian Examiner*, 84 (1868), 207–29.

13. For help in understanding the process of "disestablishment," see Mary R. Beard, ed., *America Through Woman's Eyes* (New York, 1933); Arthur W. Calhoun, *A Social History of the American Family*, Vol. 11 (Cleveland, 1918); Alice Clark, *The Working Life of Women in the Seventeenth Century* (New York, 1920); Arthur Harrison Cole, *The American Wool Manufacture* (Cambridge, Mass., 1926), Vol. I, *passim*; Elizabeth Anthony Dexter, *Colonial Women of Affairs* (Boston, 1911); Gerda Lerner, "The Lady and the Mill Girl: Changes in the Status of Women in the Age of Jackson," *Mid-continent American Studies Journal*, 10 (1969), 7, 8; Mary Ryan, "American Society and the Cult of Domesticity, 1830–1860"; Kathryn Kish Sklar, *Catharine Beecher: A Study in American Domesticity* (New Haven and London, 1973); Paige Smith, *Daughters of the Promised Land: Women in American History* (Boston, 1970). An important unpublished study is Nancy F. Cott, "In the Bonds of Womanhood: Perspectives on Female Experience and Consciousness in New England, 1780–1830," Ph.D. dissertation, Brandeis University, 1974.

14. On the southern women, see Lisabeth Cohen, "Beneath Cotton and Lace: The Plantation Legacy of the Southern Woman," an important essay submitted as an undergraduate thesis at Princeton University in 1973; Anne Scott, *The Southern Lady from Pedestal to Politics 1830–1930* (Chicago and London, 1970); William R. Taylor, *Cavalier and Yankee: The Old South and American National Character* (New York and Evanston, 1957).

15. I am basing my discussion here on the following works: Don E. Fehrenbacher, *The Era of Expansion 1800–1848* (New York, 1969); Douglas C. North, *The Economic Growth of the United States 1790–1860* (New York, 1966); Arthur M. Schlesinger, Jr., *The Age of Jackson* (Boston, 1945).

16. See Lerner, *op. cit.*; Smith, *op. cit.*, pp. 49–78.

17. Cole, *op. cit.*, p. 181.

18. *Ibid.*, pp. 192, 193.

19. *Ibid.*, pp. 97–110.

20. See Jeffrey Williamson, "Urbanization in the American Northeast, 1820–1870," in *The Reinterpretation of American Economic History* (New York, 1971), pp. 426–36.

21. Quoted in Schlesinger, *op. cit.*, p. 18.

22. Quoted in *ibid.*, p. 148.

23. Cole, *op. cit.*, p. 190.

24. See Richard B. Morris, *Studies in the History of American Law* (New York, 1930), Chap. III, "Women's Rights in Early American Law."

25. My comments here are based on an essay by Johnny Faragher, "Old Men and Old Women in Seventeenth-Century Wethersfield," forthcoming in *Women's Studies*.

26. See the widows in Mrs. Julia H. Scott, *The Blind Widow and Her Family* (Hudson, N.Y., 1837), and Bella Z. Spencer, *Tried and True; or Love and Loyalty* (Springfield, Mass., 1866).

27. Richard J. Purcell, *Connecticut in Transition 1775–1818* (Washington, D.C., and London, 1918), pp. 117–30.

28. Horace Bushnell, "The Age of Homespun" in *Litchfield County Centennial Celebration* (Hartford, 1851), pp. 114, 112, 124.

29. Cheney, *Life and Letters of Horace Bushnell*, p. 27.

30. *Ibid.*, pp. 29, 27.

31. *Ibid.*, p. 111. For Bushnell's views on women, see also *Woman Suffrage: The Reform Against Nature* (New York, 1869).

32. Beard, *op. cit.*, p. 80.

33. Cole, *op. cit.*, pp. 186–9.

34. See Johnny Faragher and Christine Stansell, "Women and Their Families on the Overland Trail, 1842–1867," *Feminist Studies*, 2 (1975), 150–66.

35. Nancy Cott, ed., *Root of Bitterness: Documents of the Social History of American Women* (New York, 1972), p. 235.

36. Thomas Woody, *A History of Women's Education in the United States* (New York and Lancaster, Pa., 1929), II, p. 3.

37. See Catharine Maria Sedgwick, *Home* (Boston, 1854); *Live and Let Live, or Domestic Service Illustrated* (New York, 1856); *Married or Single?* (New York, 1858); *Means and Ends: or Self-Training* (Boston, 1840).

38. Catharine E. Beecher, *A Treatise on Domestic Economy* (Boston, 1841).

39. *Ladies' Magazine*, 3 (1830), 42, 43.

40. Charles Butler, Esq., *The American Lady* (Philadelphia, 1842) and *The American Gentleman* (Philadelphia, 1836).

41. On women's education, see Barbara Cross, ed., *The Educated Woman in America: Selected Writings of Catharine Beecher, Margaret Fuller, and M. Carey Thomas* (New York, 1965); Willistyne Goodsell, *The Education of Women: Its Social Background and Problems* (New York, 1923); Mabel Newcomer, *A Century of Higher Education for American Women* (New York, 1959); Eleanor Wolf Thompson, *Education for Ladies 1830-1860* (New York, 1947); Ann Douglas Wood, "Women's Future in Higher Education," *University Magazine*, 52 (1972), 6–13; Woody, *op. cit.*

42. Quoted in Cross, *op. cit.*, p. 117.

43. *Godey's Lady's Book*, 20 (1840), 273.

44. See Catharine Esther Beecher, "Female Education," *American Journal of Education*, II (1827), 219–23, 264–9, and *Suggestions Respecting Improvements in Education Presented to the Trustees of the Hartford Female Seminary* (Hartford, 1829).

45. Mary E. Dewey, *Life and Letters of Catharine M. Sedgwick* (New York, 1871), pp. 56, 57.

46. Grace Greenwood, *Greenwood Leaves: A Collection of Sketches and Letters* (Boston, 1853), p. 29.

47. For the attitude of the ladies' magazines, see Thompson, *op. cit.*, *passim*.

48. On the educational work of these pioneers, see Alma Lutz, *Emma Willard: Daughter of Democracy* (Boston and New York, 1929); Beth Bradford Gilchrist, *The Life of Mary Lyon* (Boston and New York, 1910); Edward Hitchcock, *The Power of Christian Benevolence Illustrated in the Life and Labors of Mary Lyon* (Northampton, Mass., and Philadelphia,

1852); Marion Lansing, ed., *Mary Lyon Through Her Letters* (Boston, 1937); Mae Elizabeth Harveson, *Catharine Esther Beecher: Pioneer Educator* (Philadelphia, 1932); Sklar, *op. cit.* For clear evidence that they were often self-consciously aware of the need for a masculine front to dignify feminine enterprise, see Lutz, *op. cit.*, p. 27, where Willard determines to call her new school a seminary: "That word ... will not create a jealousy that we mean to intrude upon the province of men."

49. See especially Emma Willard, *A Plan for Improving Female Education* (Middlebury, Vt., 1818).

50. Isabelle Lucy Bird, *The Englishwoman in America*, ed. Andrew Hill Clark (Madison, Milwaukee, and London, 1966), pp. 152, 338.

51. Calhoun, *op. cit.*, pp. 236, 237.

52. Bird, *op. cit.*, p. 365.

53. *The Works of Charles Follen with a Memoir of His Life* (Boston, 1842), I, p. 108.

54. Smith, *op. cit.*, p. 78.

55. *Ladies' Magazine*, 1 (1828), 2.

56. Lydia Maria Child, *The Mother's Book* (Boston, 1831), p. 86.

57. *The Rose of Sharon* (Boston, 1849), p. 287.

58. For the lives of these women, see Mrs. E. R. Hanson, ed., *Our Women Workers: Biographical Sketches of Women Eminent in the Universalist Church for Literary, Philanthropic and Christian Work* (Chicago, 1882). Their writings appeared chiefly in the Universalist Giftbook, *The Rose of Sharon*, and the monthly *Universalist and Ladies' Repository*. For a fascinating study of the dependency of the ambitious rural girl on novels, see Mrs. A. D. T. Whitney's *Hitherto: A Story of Yesterdays* (Boston, 1869). This novel by one of the era's most popular writers for young ladies would repay extensive analysis.

59. On the increase in reading, see Carl Bode, *Antebellum Culture* (Carbondale and Edwardsville, Ill., 1959), pp. 109 ff.; Norman F. Cantor and Michael S. Werthman, eds., *The History of Popular Culture* (New York and London, 1968), pp. 84–94.

60. Elizabeth Wetherell, *The Wide, Wide World* (Philadelphia, 1888), p. 34. "Elizabeth Wetherell" was Susan Warner's *nom de plume*.

61. I am deeply indebted in my discussion of Stowe here and elsewhere to Elizabeth Kendall, "Secret Springs of Violence: A

Study of Margaret Fuller, Harriet Beecher Stowe, and Kate Chopin," an unpublished essay submitted as an undergraduate thesis at Harvard University in 1969.

62. David Potter, *People of Plenty: Economic Abundance and the American Character* (Chicago, 1954), pp. 173–5.

63. I have consulted the following sources on advertising: Daniel Boorstin, *The Image: A Guide to Pseudo-Events in America* (New York, 1972); J. A. C. Brown, *Techniques of Persuasion: From Propaganda to Brainwashing* (London, 1963); Revel Denney, *The Astonished Muse: Popular Culture in America* (New York, 1957); Frank Presbrey, *The History and Development of Advertising* (New York, 1929); Walter Dill Scott, "The Psychology of Advertising," *Atlantic Monthly*, 93 (1904), 29–36; E. S. Turner, *The Shocking History of Advertising* (London, 1952); James Pleysted Wood, *The Story of Advertising* (New York, 1958).

64. Presbrey, *op. cit.*, pp. 255, 256.

65. See Ann Douglas, "Art and Advertising in *A Connecticut Yankee:* The Robber Baron Revisited," *Canadian Review of American Studies*, 6 (1975), 182–95.

66. Presbrey, *op. cit.*, p. 259.

67. Potter, *op. cit.*, p. 169.

68. Quoted in Presbrey, *op. cit.*, pp. 276–8.

69. *Ibid.*, pp. 370 ff.

70. *Ibid.*, p. 318.

71. See Margaret Mead, "The Pattern of Leisure in Contemporary Culture," in Eric Larrabee and Rolf Meyersohn, eds., *Mass Leisure* (Glencoe, Ill., 1958), p. 14.

72. Catharine Esther Beecher, *An Essay on Slavery and Abolitionism with Reference to the Duty of American Females* (Philadelphia, 1837) and *The True Remedy for the Wrongs of Women* (Boston, 1851).

73. Emma Willard, *Via Media: A Peaceful and Permanent Settlement of the Slavery Question* (Washington, D.C., 1862).

74. For an analysis of Hale's politics, see Taylor, *op. cit.*, pp. 115–41.

75. See Hannah Josephson, *Golden Threads: New England's Millgirls and Magnates* (New York, 1949). I am indebted also to John Kasson, "The Factory as Republican Community: The Early History of Lowell, Massachusetts," a paper delivered before the American Studies Association in San Francisco on Oct. 19, 1973.

76. See Josephson, *op. cit.*, pp. 191 ff. Farley gives her account in the July and August

issues of the *Lowell Offering*, 5 (1845).

77. *Lowell Offering*, 5 (1845), 190.

78. Quoted in Josephson, *op. cit.*, p. 193.

79. *Lowell Offering*, 5 (1845), 56.

80. Quoted in Josephson, *op. cit.*, p. 188.

81. *Lowell Offering*, 5 (1845), 264.

82. Harveson, *op. cit.*, p. 231.

83. *Godey's Lady's Book*, 45 (1852), 283.

84. *Ladies' Magazine*, 1 (1828), 422, 423.

85. *The New Englander*, 11 (1953), 152.

86. For examples, see Rev. John S. C. Abbot, *The Mother at Home; or the Principles of Maternal Duty Familiarly Illustrated* (New York, 1833); Jabez Burns, D.D., *Mothers of the Wise and Good* (Boston, 1830); Margaret Conkling, *Memoirs of the Mother and Wife of Washington* (Auburn, Me., 1851); Marion Harland, *The Story of Mary Washington* (Boston and New York, 1892); *Our Mother: A Memorial of Mrs. S. C. Farley Maxwell* (Boston, 1860). Elizabeth Prentiss wrote a novel which is an extreme illustration of the motherhood cult, *The Home at Greylock* (New York, 1876). The classic example of medical support of the cult is Dr. Edward H. Clark, *Sex in Education: or a Fair Chance for Girls* (Boston and Cambridge, Mass., 1878). On the medical background, see Ann Douglas Wood, "The Fashionable Diseases: Women's Complaints and Their Treatment in Nineteenth-Century America," *Journal of Interdisciplinary History*, 4 (1973), 25–53, and *Clio's Consciousness*, ed. Louis Banner (New York, 1974).

87. John Hawksley, ed., *Memoir of the Rev. Jonathan Edwards Compiled Originally by Sam Hopkins* (London, 1815), p. 89.

88. Mrs. L. H. Sigourney, *Letters to Mothers* (Hartford, 1838), p. 10. See also Mrs. Sigourney's account of her relationship with her own son, Andrew, in *The Faded Hope* (New York, 1853).

89. Bernard Wishy, *The Child and the Republic: The Dawn of Modern American Child Nurture* (Philadelphia, 1968), p. 30. For a good discussion of motherhood, see Anne L. Kuhn, *The Mother's Role in Childhood Education: New England Concepts 1830–1860* (New Haven, 1947).

90. See Ann Douglas Wood, "The Fashionable Diseases," p. 49, and "The War Within a War: Women Nurses in the Union Army," *Civil War History*, 18 (1972), 197–212.

91. For Stanton's views and experiences of motherhood, see her autobiography, *Eighty Years and More (1815–1897): Reminiscences of*

Elizabeth Cady Stanton (London, 1898), pp. 108–25.

92. For the reaction, see Goodsell, *op. cit.*, *passim*.

3

MINISTERS AND MOTHERS:
CHANGING AND EXCHANGING
ROLES

1. I should stress that I have tried to re-search these sixty individuals carefully, reading all available works by and on them. I have consulted manuscript sources on the following: Catharine Esther Beecher and Harriet Beecher Stowe in the Beecher-Stowe Collection at the Schlesinger Library at Radcliffe College, Cambridge, Mass.; the Margaret Fuller papers at the Boston Public Library and Houghton Library, Harvard University; the letters of Sarah Edgarton Mayo and Mrs. L. B. J. Case at the Schlesinger Library; the Catharine Maria Sedgwick papers at the Massachusetts Historical Society; the Sigourney papers at the Connecticut Historical Society in Hartford, Conn.; the Fanny Fern (Parton) papers at the Sophia Smith Collection in Northampton, Mass.; and the Joseph Buckminster papers at the Boston Athenaeum. Although I am using these sixty persons as a "control group" in Chapter Three, here and elsewhere I have tried to check my conclusions against the data gathered by a wider if less thorough survey. For useful biographical information on the women of the period, see Edward T. James, Janet Wilson James, Paul S. Bryer, eds., *Notable American Women 1607–1950*, 3 vols. (Cambridge, Mass., 1971), and Frances E. Willard and Mary A. Livermore, *American Women: Fifteen Hundred Biographies*, 2 vols. (New York, Chicago, and Springfield, Ohio, 1897). Also useful are *Eminent Women of the Age* (Hartford, 1869) and *Our Famous Women* (Hartford, 1885). Nina Baym in a manuscript to be published by Cornell University Press, "Women's Fiction in America 1820–1870," provides a helpful study of many of the women I am considering. Where I am interested only in certain aspects of their production and in the underlying unity of their work, she treats their careers more broadly and examines the distinctive quality of each woman's effort. Baym furthermore sees their collective contribution in much more positive terms than I am able to do. On the ministers,

the invaluable source is William Sprague, *Annals of the American Pulpit*, 9 vols. (New York, 1837–69), which I have studied in its entirety. Also useful have been a number of magazines whose files I read through: *The Christian Examiner, The New Englander, North American Review, The National Preacher, Ladies' Magazine, Godey's Lady's Book, The Universalist and Ladies' Repository*, and the *Christian Parlor Magazine*. The important autobiographies, biographies, and literary productions by the sixty individuals under special consideration will be cited in the course of discussion.

2. *Christian Examiner*, 87 (1869), 29. Evangelicals of course also made extensive use of the press; indeed, non-evangelicals often urged or justified publishing in terms of catching up with the productivity of evangelical rivals. The difference is one in prestige and influence.

3. Lawrence C. Wroth and Rollo G. Silver, "Book Production and Distribution from the American Revolution to the War Between the States," in Hellmut Lehman-Haupt, ed., *The Book in America* (New York, 1951), p. 71.

4. I am drawing my information about the Harpers, unless otherwise stated, from Eugene Exman, *The Brothers Harper* (New York, 1965).

5. Charles A. Madison, *Book Publishing in America* (New York, 1966), p. 6.

6. William Charvat, *Literary Publishing in America 1790–1830* (Philadelphia, 1959), p. 26.

7. *Ibid.*

8. Exman, *op. cit.*, p. 45.

9. Charvat, *op. cit.*, p. 307.

10. *Ibid.*, p. 56.

11. Madison, *op. cit.*, p. 45.

12. *North American Review*, 56 (1843), 110.

13. Nathaniel Hawthorne suffered; see Charvat, *op. cit.*, pp. 57–9.

14. Quoted in Gordon S. Haight, *Mrs. Sigourney: The Sweet Singer of Hartford* (New Haven, 1930), p. 80.

15. *Eminent Women of the Age*, p. 87.

16. Quoted in Carl Bode, *The American Lyceum: Town Meeting of the Mind* (New York, 1956).

17. Sigourney wrote prolifically for a number of the magazines, most notably *Godey's, Graham's* and *Peterson's*. Henry Ward Beecher's work appeared in a newspaper he largely controlled, *The Independent*. Fern wrote almost exclusively for the *New York Ledger*.

18. Quoted in Matthew J. Bruccoli, ed., *The Profession of Authorship in America 1800–1870: The Papers of William Charvat* (n.p., 1968), p. 92.

19. *North American Review*, 41 (1835), 441–3.

20. *Christian Examiner*, 28 (1840), 119.

21. Awareness of the potential power of the press is evident everywhere in the articles in the *Christian Examiner* and the *New Englander*, but see particularly "The Pulpit," *Christian Examiner*, 29 (1840), 40–6.

22. For Norton's attitude, see the following reviews: "The Poetry of Mrs. Hemans," *Christian Examiner*, 3 (1826), 403–18, and "The Poetry of Mrs. Hemans," *Christian Examiner*, 3d series, 1 (1836), 328–62. See Elizabeth Stuart Phelps, *Austin Phelps: A Memoir* (New York, 1891), p. 224.

23. Earlier women did use literature at least occasionally for reform purposes. See L. Maria Child, *Philothea: A Grecian Romance* (Boston, 1845), which is concerned with the problem of slavery and women's place.

24. For the importance of feminine novels to the women reformers, see Gail Parker, ed., *The Oven Birds: American Women on Womanhood 1820–1920* (New York, 1972), pp. 1–56.

25. For a severe but accurate critique of the present state of the religious press, see Martin E. Marty, John G. Deedy, Jr., David Wolf Silverman, and Robert Latchman, *The Religious Press in America* (New York, 1963).

26. Mary Bushnell Cheney, *Life and Letters of Horace Bushnell* (New York, 1880), p. 2.

27. *Christian Examiner*, 3 (1826), 97.

28. *Ibid.*, 43 (1847), 189.

29. *Ibid.*, 38 (1845), 299.

30. Arethusa Hall, *Life and Character of the Reverend Sylvester Judd* (Boston, 1854), p. 138.

31. The best study of the Boston Unitarians from this point of view is Daniel Walker Howe, *The Unitarian Conscience: Harvard Moral Philosophy 1805–1861* (Cambridge, Mass., 1970).

32. Eliza Buckminster Lee, *Memoirs of Rev. Joseph Buckminster, D.D. and of His Son Rev. Joseph Stevens Buckminster* (Boston, 1851), p. 116.

33. J. H. Allen, *Our Liberal Movement in Theology* (Boston, 1882), p. 45.

34. Mary E. Dewey, ed., *Autobiography and Letters of Orville Dewey, D.D.* (Boston, 1844), p. 358.

35. Sprague, *Annals*, VIII, p. 174.

36. *Christian Examiner*, 28 (1840), 33.

37. Sprague, *Annals*, II, pp. 656, 657.

38. I make this statement on the basis of a study of Sprague's *Annals;* the shift toward a feminized descriptive vocabulary occurred in the pre–Civil War period covered by Sprague, most notably in reference to the Unitarian and non-evangelical Congregational ministry.

39. Greenwood, *Greenwood Leaves*, pp. 310–12.

40. *Physiology and Calisthenics for Schools and Families* (New York, 1856), p. 164. See also Catharine Beecher, "The American People Starved and Poisoned," *Harper's New Monthly Magazine*, 32 (1866), 771.

41. See Beecher, *Letters to the People on Health and Happiness* (New York, 1855), p. 124.

42. This paragraph is a summary of Ann Douglas Wood, "The Fashionable Diseases: Women's Complaints and Their Treatment in Nineteenth-Century America," *Journal of Interdisciplinary History*, 4 (1973).

43. *Ladies' Magazine*, 4 (1831), 3–4, and *Woman's Record*, p. 682.

44. For Sigourney's life, see Haight, *op. cit.*, and her own autobiography, *Letters of Life* (New York, 1866). For Hale's life, see Isabelle Webb Entrikin, *Sarah Josepha Hale and 'Godey's Lady's Book'* (privately printed, 1946), and Ruth E. Finley, *The Lady of Godey's: Sarah Josepha Hale* (Philadelphia and London, 1931).

45. I will come back to the uses of Episcopalianism for the feminine subculture in my discussion of Harriet Beecher Stowe in Chapter Seven.

46. In an earlier study of a smaller number of women sentimentalists, "The Literature of Impoverishment: The Women Local Colorists in America 1865–1914," *Women's Studies*, 1 (1972), 3–46, I found a higher percentage of marriages and assumed wrongly that this would hold true for a bigger sample. Much of my research and discussion here, however, confirms the research for the earlier study.

47. Henry James, *Partial Portraits* (London, 1905), p. 177.

48. James Hart, *The Popular Book: A History of America's Literary Taste* (New York, 1950), pp. 91–2.

49. Among the more important of the tracts these men produced, see Edward

Beecher, *The Conflict of Ages: or The Great Debate on the Moral Relations of God and Man* (Boston, 1853); Horace Bushnell, *God in Christ* (Hartford, 1849) and *Nature and the Supernatural* (New York, 1858); Andrews Norton, *Evidences of the Genuineness of the Gospels* (Boston, 1877); Edwards A. Park, *The Atonement* (Boston, 1839).

50. For examples, see Catharine Esther Beecher, *Common Sense Applied to Religion; or The Bible and the People* (New York, 1857); Lydia Maria Child, *An Appeal on Behalf of That Class of Americans Called Africans* (Boston, 1833) and *The Progress of Religious Ideas Through Successive Ages* (New York, 1835), 3 vols.

51. Alcott, Finley, Holmes, Phelps, Prentiss, Sedgwick, Sigourney, Smith, Stephens, Stowe, Warner, Whitney, and Willis ("Fern") were exceptionally prolific. Best-selling works of considerable interest by these authors are: Alcott, *Little Women* (1868); Finley, *Elsie Dinsmore* (1867); Holmes, *Lena Rivers* (1856); Phelps, *The Gates Ajar* (1868); Prentiss, *Stepping Heavenward* (1869); Sedgwick, *Hope Leslie* (1827); Sigourney, *The Young Lady's Offering* (1847); Smith, *The Newsboy* (1854); Stowe, *Uncle Tom's Cabin* (1852); Stephens, *Fashion and Famine* (1854); Warner, *The Wide Wide World* (1850); Whitney, *Faith Cartney's Girlhood* (1863); Willis ["Fanny Fern"], *Fern Leaves from Fanny's Portfolio* (1853) and *Ruth Hall: A Domestic Tale of the Present Time* (1854).

52. David D. Hall, *The Faithful Shepherd: A History of the New England Ministry in the Seventeenth Century* (Chapel Hill, N.C., 1972), pp. 271–2.

53. See "The Influence of the Gospel on the Character and Condition of the Female Sex," in *Sermons by the Late Joseph Buckminster* (Boston, 1841), pp. 383–410.

54. Daniel Wise, *The Young Lady's Counsellor* (New York, 1892), p. v.

55. Quoted in Milton Powell, ed., *The Voluntary Church: American Religious Life Seen Through the Eyes of European Visitors* (New York and London, 1966), pp. 125–6.

56. *The Universalist*, 2 (1833), 326.

57. F. D. Huntington, *Sermons for the People* (Boston, 1856), p. 350.

58. Rev. William L. Gage, *Trinitarian Sermons Preached to a Unitarian Congregation* (Boston, 1859), pp. v–xxi.

59. William Wilson Manross, *A History of the American Episcopal Church* (New York, 1950), p. 246.

60. Howard Allen Bridgeman, "Have We a Religion for Men?" *Andover Review*, 13 (1890), 388–96.

61. Aaron Ignatius Abell, *The Urban Impact on American Protestantism 1865–1900* (Cambridge, Mass., 1943), p. 214.

62. Paige Smith, *Daughters of the Promised Land: Women in American History* (Boston, 1970), p. 49.

63. William Henry Channing, *Memoir of William Ellery Channing, With Extracts from His Correspondence and Manuscripts* (Boston, 1846), I, p. 140.

64. Edmund S. Morgan, *The Gentle Puritan: A Life of Ezra Stiles 1727–1795* (New Haven and London, 1962), p. 188.

65. Sprague, *Annals*, I, p. 372.

66. *Ibid.*, p. 559.

67. *Life and Letters of Horace Bushnell*, p. 33.

68. See Mrs. E. A. Bacon, *Memoir of Reverend Henry Bacon* (Boston, 1857), *passim;* and Caroline A. Soule, *Memoir of Reverend H. B. Soule* (Boston, 1860), *passim.*

69. Theodore Ledyard Cuyler, D.D., LL.D., *Recollections of a Long Life: An Autobiography* (New York, 1902), pp. 4, 120–1, 119.

70. *Christian Examiner*, 62 (1857), 264.

71. Quoted in Frank Hugh Foster, *The Life of Edwards Amasa Park* (New York, 1936), p. 28.

72. Quoted in Powell, *op. cit.*, p. 127.

73. Quoted in *ibid.*, pp. 68–9.

74. Samuel Hopkins, *The Life and Character of Miss Susanna Anthony* (Portland, Me., 1810).

75. Ralph Emerson, *Life of Rev. Joseph Emerson* (Boston, 1834), pp. 74, 127.

76. Arethusa Hall, *Life and Character of the Reverend Sylvester Judd*, p. 148.

77. Charles Butler, Esq., *The American Lady* (Philadelphia, 1842), p. 36.

78. See Henry Steele Commager, *Theodore Parker* (Boston, 1947), *passim.*

79. Elizabeth Palmer Peabody, *Reminiscences of Rev. William Ellery Channing, D.D.* (Boston, 1880), pp. 41, 42.

80. William Henry Channing, *Memoir of William Ellery Channing*, I, p. 67.

81. On the development of the libraries, see Jesse H. Shera, *Foundations of the Public Library: The Origins of the Public Library Movement in New England 1629–1855* (Chicago,

1949), and Sidney Ditzion, *Arsenals of a Democratic Culture: A Social History of the American Public Library Movement in New England and the Middle States from 1850 to 1900* (Chicago, 1947).

82. Shera, *op. cit.*, p. 209.

83. Ronald Story, "Class and Culture in Boston: The Athenaeum," *American Quarterly*, 27 (1975), 178–99.

84. Shera, *op. cit.*, p. 166.

85. *Ibid.*, p. 140.

86. *Ibid.*, p. 94.

87. Ditzion, *op. cit.*, p. 83.

88. Parker Willis, *The Rag Bag: A Collection of Ephemera* (New York, 1859), p. 262.

89. Catharine E. Beecher, *Common Sense Applied to Religion*, p. xii, and *Letters on the Difficulties of Religion* (Hartford, 1857).

90. See Harriet Beecher Stowe, "The Minister's Housekeeping" in *Sam Lawson's Oldtown Fireside Tales* (Boston, 1871).

91. I will discuss ministerial biographies by women in Chapter Five.

92. Edwards A. Park, ed., *The Works of Samuel Hopkins, D.D., With a Memoir of His Life*, Vol. I (Boston, 1854), p. 28.

93. Sprague, *Annals*, I, p. 551.

94. *Selections from the Writings of Mrs. Sarah C. Edgarton Mayo with a Memoir By Her Husband* (Boston, 1849), p. 88.

95. "Illustrations of Female Education," *Universalist and Ladies' Repository*, 8 (1840), 15.

96. Catharine E. Beecher, *The True Remedy for the Wrongs of Women with a History of an Enterprise Having That for Its Object* (Boston, 1851), p. 49.

97. See Emily Noyes Vanderpoel and Elizabeth C. Barney Buel, eds., *Chronicles of a Pioneer School from 1792–1833, Being the History of Miss Sarah Pierce and Her Litchfield School* (Cambridge, Mass., 1903); Vanderpoel, ed., *More Chronicles of a Pioneer School from 1792 to 1833 Being Added History on the Litchfield Female Academy* (Cambridge, Mass., 1927).

98. Mae E. Harveson, in *Catharine Esther Beecher: Pioneer Educator* (Philadelphia, 1932), includes her correspondence with Zilpah Grant in Appendix A, pp. 257–9.

99. All page references to Lyon's career here, unless otherwise stated, are to Edward Hitchcock, *The Power of Christian Benevolence Illustrated in the Life and Labors of Mary Lyon* (Northampton, Mass., and Philadelphia, 1852).

100. See Mrs. Sarah D. (Locke) Stowe, *History of Mt. Holyoke Seminary, South Hadley, Mass. During Its First Half Century* (Springfield, Mass., 1887).

101. Lucy Larcom, *A New England Girlhood* (New York, 1961), p. 223.

102. L. T. Guilford, *The Use of a Life: Memorials of Mrs. Z. P. Grant Bannister* (New York, n.d.), p. 348.

103. R. Pierce Beaver, *All Loves Excelling: American Protestant Women in World Mission* (Grand Rapids, Mich., 1968), pp. 13–48.

104. Catharine E. Beecher, *Suggestions Respecting Improvements in Education Presented to the Trustees of the Hartford Female Seminary* (Hartford, 1829), p. 7.

105. For examples of popular biographies of popular women missionaries, see Daniel C. Eddy, *Daughters of the Cross or Woman's Mission* (New York, 1855); Emily C. Judson, *Memoir of Sarah B. Judson* (New York, 1849); James D. Knowles, *Memoir of Ann H. Judson* (Boston, 1847).

106. Mrs. A. D. T. Whitney, *The Gayworthys: A Story of Threads and Thrums* (Boston and London, 1865), p. 287.

107. See Michael Davitt Bell, *Hawthorne and the Historical Romance of New England* (Princeton, 1971).

108. All page references are to Eliza Buckminster Lee, *Naomi; or Boston Two Hundred Years Ago* (Boston, 1848).

109. Mary Alice Wyman, ed., *The Autobiography of Elizabeth Oakes Smith* (Lewiston, Me., 1924), pp. 22, 85, 216.

110. All page references are to Elizabeth Oakes Smith, *Bertha and Lily; or The Parsonage of Beech Glen: A Romance* (New York, 1855).

111. Sarah Josepha Hale, *Woman's Record: or Sketches of All Distinguished Women From the Creation to A.D. 1854* (New York, 1855), p. 328.

112. Hart, *op. cit.*, p. 15.

113. Shera, *op. cit.*, p. 113.

114. *Ibid.*, pp. 117–18.

115. *Ibid.*, p. 120.

116. Ditzion, *op. cit.*, p. 132.

117. *Ibid.*, and Shera, *op. cit.*, pp. 146 ff.

118. Quoted in Fred Lewis Pattee, *The Feminine Fifties* (New York, 1940), *op. cit.*, pp. 55–6.

119. *The Writings of Mrs. Sarah C. Edgarton Mayo,* p. 32.

120. *The Works of William E. Channing, D.D.* (Boston and New York, 1849), VI, p. 162.

121. *Ibid.,* II, p. 280.

122. *Christian Examiner,* 21 (1836–7), 399.

123. *Ibid.,* 80 (1866), 360.

124. *Ibid.,* 56 (1854), 33–4.

125. Horace Bushnell, *Moral Uses of Dark Things* (New York, 1868), p. 27.

126. Quoted in William G. McLoughlin, *The Meaning of Henry Ward Beecher: An Essay on the Shifting Values of Mid-Victorian America 1840–1870* (New York, 1970), p. 88.

127. Edwards A. Park, *The Theology of the Intellect and of the Feelings* (Andover, Mass., 1850), pp. 3–4.

128. Wise, *op. cit.,* p. 87.

129. For several classic statements of the anti-feminist clerical position, see "The Pastoral Letter" of 1837 provoked by early feminist activity included in Aileen Kraditor, ed., *Up From the Pedestal: Selected Writings in the History of American Feminism* (Chicago, 1968), pp. 50–2, and Horace Bushnell, *Woman Suffrage: The Reform Against Nature* (New York, 1869).

130. See Beaver, *op. cit., passim.*

131. Sarah Hale, *Manners or Happy Homes and Good Society All the Year Round* (Boston, 1868), p. 53.

132. See particularly Catharine Maria Sedgwick, *Home* (Boston, 1854).

133. I base my remarks here on Robert W. Lynn and Elliott Wright, *The Big Little School: Sunday Child of American Protestantism* (New York, 1971); Edwin Wilbur Rice, *The Sunday School Movement 1780–1917 and the American Sunday School Union 1817–1917* (Philadelphia, 1917); Joanna Bethune, *The Power of Faith Exemplified in the Life and Writings of the Late Mrs. Isabella Graham* (New York, 1843).

134. Lynn and Wright *op. cit.,* p. 128.

135. *Christian Examiner,* 78 (1862), 178.

136. *National Preacher,* 3d series, 1 (1862), 109. See Calhoun, *op. cit.,* p. 109.

137. *The Miscellaneous Writings of Henry Ware, Jr.,* IV (Boston, 1846), p. 338.

138. *Christian Examiner,* 34 (1845), 136–7.

139. "The Poetry of Mrs. Hemans," *Christian Examiner,* 3d series, 1 (1836), 335, 341.

140. See Daniel Howe, *op. cit.,* pp. 189–204. See W. B. O. Peabody, "The Waverly Novels," *North American Review,* 32 (1831), 386–421; Orville Dewey, "On the Religion of Life" in *Discourses on Human Nature, Human Life and the Nature of Religion,* I (New York, 1847), 292–3.

141. See "Jane Bouverie," *Christian Examiner,* 50 (1831), 178–89.

142. "Dr. Furness and Dr. Bushnell: A Question of Words and Names," *Christian Examiner,* 66 (1859), 115.

143. "Miss Bremer's Novels," *North American Review,* 37 (1845), 128. See also W. B. O. Peabody, "Paul de Kock's Novels," *ibid.,* 36 (1843), 276–300.

144. "Duty in Regard to Reading," *New Englander,* 10 (1852), 188–97.

145. *Sermons by the Late William B. O. Peabody With A Memoir by His Brother* (Boston, 1849), p. cviii.

146. "Miss Bremer's Novels," p. 135.

147. "New Books of Piety," *Christian Examiner,* 74 (1863), 428.

148. *Sermons by the Late William B. O. Peabody,* p. 133.

149. Almira H. Lincoln Phelps, *Lectures to Young Ladies Comprising Outlines and Applications of the Different Branches of Female Education* (Boston, 1833), pp. 171, 172.

150. "Novels and Tales," *Christian Examiner,* 66 (1859), 297.

151. H. T. T., "Mr. Thackeray As a Novelist," *ibid.,* 60 (1856), 103.

152. Dewey, *Discourses,* pp. 261–4.

153. Elizabeth Stuart Phelps, *Austin Phelps: A Memoir,* p. 224.

154. "Dante's Beatrice as a Type of Womanhood," *Christian Examiner,* 64 (1858), 49. And see J. W., "The Woman Question," *Christian Examiner,* 56 (1854), 1–34.

155. William Ware, *Zenobia; or the Fall of Palmyra* (New York, 1854), I, p. 196.

4

THE LOSS OF THEOLOGY: FROM DOGMA TO FICTION

1. All page references are to Joseph Bellamy, *True Religion Delineated* in *The Works of Joseph Bellamy With a Memoir of His Life and Character,* ed. Tyron Edwards (Boston, 1853), I.

2. See Frank Hugh Foster, *A Genetic History of New England Theology* (New York, 1963), pp. 200 ff.; Joseph Haroutunian, *Piety*

Versus Moralism: The Passing of the New England Theology (New York, 1932), pp. 164–79.

3. See "My Grandmother's Blue Book" in Harriet Beecher Stowe, *Oldtown Folks*, ed. Henry F. May (Cambridge, Mass., 1966), pp. 391–412.

4. The best discussion of this theological problem is still the "Introductory Essay" in Edwards A. Park, ed., *The Atonement: Discourses and Treatises* (Boston, 1859), pp. vii–lxxx. The documents included here are essential to an understanding of the range of the Edwardsean position on the Atonement. See also Stephen West, D.D., *An Essay on Moral Agency* (Salem, Mass., 1794). For an excellent recent study on the idea of sin and human agency, see H. Shelton Smith, *Changing Conceptions of Original Sin: A Study in American Theology Since 1750* (New York, 1955), which sheds light on a closely related problem.

5. See particularly Nathaniel Emmons, "God's Hatred of Sinners," "The Heavenly Hosts Praise God for His Justice," and "Saints Desire God to Punish Sinners," in Jacob Ide, ed., *The Works of Nathaniel Emmons* (Boston, 1842), VI, pp. 111–22, 181, 152–7.

6. See *ibid.*; Hopkins apparently got this idea from Jonathan Edwards' wife, Sarah Pierpont. See "Sin Through Divine Interposition, An Advantage to the Universe and Yet This No Encouragement for Sin" and "An Inquiry Into the Nature of True Holiness," in *The Works of Samuel Hopkins, D.D.* (Boston, 1852), II, pp. 493–545, and III, pp. 5–66.

7. Under pressure by the Universalists, Bellamy, like other prominent Edwardseans, was to move toward the idea of a general Atonement. In other words, God's sacrifice of Christ has made it possible for all men to be saved, although all men will not be able to avail themselves of this opportunity. See Haroutunian, *op. cit.*, pp. 164, 165.

8. Quoted in Edwards, ed., *The Works of Joseph Bellamy*, I, p. lix.

9. All page references are to Hosea Ballou, *A Treatise on the Atonement* (Boston, 1860).

10. Quoted in William Sprague, *Annals of the American Pulpit* (New York, 1837–69), VIII, p. 197, and Henry Ware, Jr., *Memoirs of the Reverend Noah Worcester* (Boston, 1844), p. 127. See also William E. Channing, *A Tribute to the Memory of the Rev. Noah Worcester, D.D.* (Boston, 1837).

11. All page references are to Noah Worcester, *The Atoning Sacrifice: A Display of Love Not of Wrath* (Cambridge, Mass., 1830).

12. Odell Shepard, *Pedlar's Progress: The Life of Bronson Alcott* (Boston, 1937), p. 169.

13. See Horace Bushnell, *The Vicarious Sacrifice, Grounded in Principles of Universal Obligation* (New York, 1866), pp. 279–83. And see Horace Bushnell, "Loving God is But Letting God Love Us" in *Sermons on Living Subjects* (New York, 1877), p. 37.

14. See "Review of Current Literature," *Christian Examiner*, 80 (1866), 278–9.

15. See the excellent discussion in H. Shelton Smith, ed., *Horace Bushnell* (New York, 1965), *passim*.

16. Excerpts from this work and *The Vicarious Sacrifice* are included in Smith, ed., *Horace Bushnell*, pp. 277–359. The original *Forgiveness and Law* was published in New York in 1874.

17. Smith, ed., *Horace Bushnell*, pp. 281, 280, 282.

18. Sarah Josepha Hale, *Woman's Record; or Sketches of All Distinguished Women From the Creation to A.D. 1854* (New York, 1855), pp. xxxvii, xxxix.

19. Smith, ed., *Horace Bushnell*, pp. 302, 307.

20. Christopher Crowfield [Harriet Beecher Stowe], *Little Foxes* (Boston, 1866), p. 36.

21. This essay is in *National Preacher*, 13 (1839), 65–80.

22. This essay is in *ibid.*, 20 (1846), 169–79. See also Bushnell, "The Efficiency of the Passive Virtues," *Sermons for the New Life* (New York, 1858), p. 339, and "The Little Coat" in Arethusa Hall, *Life and Character of the Reverend Sylvester Judd* (Boston, 1854), pp. 274–6.

23. *Selections from the Writings of Mrs. Sarah C. Edgarton Mayo with a Memoir By Her Husband* (Boston, 1849), p. 57.

24. Hall, *op. cit.*, pp. 459–60.

25. For a brilliant critique of the newly humanized Christ, see Charles Hodge, reviewing Bushnell's *God in Christ* in *Essays and Reviews* (New York, 1879), pp. 436–43. Hodge, a strict Calvinist, points out that in Bushnell's interpretation, Christ's act in the Atonement is "a work of art [which] produces an impression more powerful than a formula" (p. 437).

26. Park, ed., *The Works of Samuel Hopkins*, I, 434.

27. Edwards A. Park, ed., *Memoir of Nathaniel Emmons* (Boston, 1861), I, p. 434.

28. *The Autobiography of Lyman Beecher*, ed. Barbara M. Cross (Cambridge, Mass., 1961), p. 28.

29. *Ibid.*, II, p. 133.

30. For examples of Lyman Beecher's exhortations to his eldest sons William and Edward, see *ibid.*, I, pp. 278–80, 288–9.

31. For this correspondence, see *ibid.*, pp. 355–86.

32. See Kathryn Kish Sklar, *Catharine Beecher: A Study in American Domesticity* (New Haven and London, 1973), *passim*.

33. Quoted in William G. McLoughlin, *The Meaning of Henry Ward Beecher: An Essay on the Shifting Values of Mid-Victorian America 1840–1870* (New York, 1970), p. 15.

34. *Autobiography of Lyman Beecher*, I, pp. 224–6.

35. *Ibid.*, pp. 55–7. Harriet Beecher Stowe used this letter as the basis of her heroine's theology in *The Minister's Wooing* (New York, 1859).

36. Frank Hugh Foster, *The Life of Edwards Amasa Park* (New York, 1936), pp. 52–3.

37. Elizabeth Stuart Phelps, *Austin Phelps: A Memoir* (New York, 1891), pp. 23–5.

38. Mary E. Dewey, ed., *Autobiography and Letters of Orville Dewey, D.D.* (Boston, 1884), p. 33. See Sylvester Judd, *A Young Man's Account of His Conversion from Calvinism* (Boston, 1838).

39. Williston Walker, *Congregational Churches in the United States* (New York, 1894), pp. 216 ff.

40. See "The Design, Rights and Duties of Local Churches" in *Works by Lyman Beecher* (Boston and Cleveland, 1852), II, pp. 221–2.

41. See the seventeenth-century treatise by the New England minister Thomas Shepard, *The Parable of the Ten Virgins* (London, 1660), a work very influential on the Edwardseans.

42. William Henry Channing, *Memoir of William Ellery Channing, with Extracts from His Correspondence and Manuscripts* (Boston, 1846), I, pp. 375–6.

43. Horace Bushnell, *Views of Christian Nurture* (Hartford, 1847), p. 11.

44. For Judd's views, see *The Church in a Series of Discourses* (Boston, 1854). For a favorable review of Judd's book which links it with Bushnell's *Christian Nurture*, see E. E. H.,

"Judd's Discourses on the Church," *Christian Examiner*, 56 (1854), 428–45.

45. See Bushnell, *Christian Nurture*, *passim*.

46. Judd, *A Young Man's Account*, p. 21.

47. Hall, *op. cit.*, p. 223.

48. *Ibid.*, p. 187.

49. [Susan Warner], *Daisy Plains* (New York, 1885), pp. 102–22.

50. Quoted in "Judd's Discourses on the Church," *Christian Examiner*, 56 (1854), 437.

51. Henry Ward Beecher, *Yale Lectures on Preaching* (Boston and Chicago, 1872, 1873, 1874), pp. 181–6.

52. See Richard Huber, *The American Idea of Success* (New York, 1971); Donald Meyer, *The Positive Thinkers: A Study of the American Quest for Health, Wealth and Personal Power* (New York, 1965); and Gail Thain Parker, *Mind Cure in New England: From the Civil War to World War I* (Hanover, N.H., 1973).

53. "How to Spend Holy Time" can be found in *The Works of Henry Ware, Jr.* (Boston, 1846), I, pp. 87–106.

54. Henry Ward Beecher, *Norwood or Village Life in New England* (New York, 1868), pp. 301–2, v–vi.

55. Horace Bushnell, *Work and Play* (New York, 1883), pp. 10–16.

56. Henry Ward Beecher, *Yale Lectures*, p. 186.

57. Mary Bushnell Cheney, *Life and Letters of Horace Bushnell* (New York, 1880), p. 537.

58. *Ibid.*, p. 517.

59. *Ibid.*, p. 60.

60. Quoted in Smith, ed., *Horace Bushnell*, p. 281.

61. Cheney, *op. cit.*, p. 518.

62. *Ibid.*, p. 532.

63. Richard Hofstadter in his classic study, *Anti-Intellectualism in American Life* (New York, 1962), speculates that the root of the American disrespect or distrust of the mind lies in the sentimentalization of its religious faith. "to the extent that it becomes accepted in any culture," he writes, "that religion is largely an affair of the heart or of the intuitive qualities of the mind and that the rational mind is irrelevant or worse, so far it will be believed that the rational faculties are barren or perhaps dangerous" (p. 47).

64. Horace Bushnell, *Woman Suffrage: The Reform Against Nature* (New York, 1869), pp. 65, 66, 24. For a study of the problem of

anti-intellectualism and nineteenth-century women, see Barbara Welter, "Anti-Intellectualism and the American Woman: 1800–1860," *Mid-America*, 48 (1966), 258–70. Also of importance for this problem is Barbara Welter, "The Feminization of American Religion 1800–1860" in *Clio's Consciousness*, eds. Mary S. Hartman and Lois Banner (New York, 1974), pp. 137–57.

65. Harriet Beecher Stowe, *My Wife and I or, Henry Henderson's History* (New York, 1872), pp. 189–91.

66. Harriet Beecher Stowe, *We and Our Neighbors or, the Records of an Unfashionable Street* (New York, 1875), p. 39. Italics mine.

67. See Vivian C. Hopkins, *Prodigal Puritan: A Life of Delia Bacon* (Cambridge, Mass., 1959), p. 100.

68. All page references are to Catharine Esther Beecher, *Truth Stranger Than Fiction* (Boston, 1850). For negative responses to the book, responses which sensed the source of Beecher's hostility, see *The Knickerbocker*, 36 (1850), 464–5, *Holden's Magazine*, 8 (1851), 29–30, and *The Literary World*, 7 (1850), 133–4.

69. Quoted in H. Richard Niebuhr and Daniel D. Williams, eds., *The Ministry in Historical Perspective* (New York, 1956), p. 244.

70. Quoted in *ibid.*, p. 279.

71. Daniel Calhoun, *Professional Lives in America: Structure and Aspiration 1750–1850* (Cambridge, Mass., 1965), p. 152.

72. *National Preacher*, new series no. 2 (1859), 186.

73. Niebuhr and Williams, eds., *op. cit.*, p. 279.

74. *Ibid.*, p. 45; Mary Latimer Gambrell, *Ministerial Training in Eighteenth-Century New England* (New York, 1937), p. 27.

75. Emmons said, "Diversions, properly so called, have no foundation either in reason or religion. They are the offsprings of a corrupted heart and nourished by vicious example." See Park, ed., *Memoir of Nathaniel Emmons*, I, pp. 106–7.

76. Sprague, *Annals*, VIII, p. 45.

77. Charles E. Cunningham, *Timothy Dwight* (New York, 1942), pp. 44–7.

78. George P. Fisher, *A Discourse Commemorative of the History of the Church of Christ in Yale College During the First Century of Its Existence* (New Haven, 1858), p. 26.

79. Daniel Day Williams, *The Andover Liberals: A Study in American Theology* (New York, 1941), pp. 6–13.

80. Foster, *Edwards Amasa Park*, pp. 233–5.

81. See "Subjects for the Pulpit," *Christian Examiner*, 41 (1846), 381–92.

82. Rev. Asa Cummings, *A Memoir of the Reverend Edward Payson, D.D.* (New York, n.d.), p. 311.

83. See *Christian Examiner*, 43 (1847), 324–44. For a discussion of the failure of Biblical criticism at this time, see Jerry Wayne Brown, *The Rise of Biblical Criticism in America 1800–1870: The New England Scholars* (Middletown, Conn., 1969). For American scholars in Germany, see Jurgen Herbst, *The German Historical School in American Scholarship: A Study in the Transfer of Culture* (Ithaca, N.Y., 1965).

84. Quoted in Kermit Vanderbilt, *Charles Eliot Norton: Apostle of Culture in a Democracy* (Cambridge, Mass., 1959), p. 7.

85. Andrews Norton, "A Discourse on the Latest Form of Infidelity" in *Tracts Concerning Christianity* (Cambridge, Mass., 1852), p. 293.

86. Andrews Norton, *A Statement of Reasons for Not Believing the Doctrines of Trinitarians Concerning the Nature of God and the Person of Christ* (Boston, 1867), p. 37.

87. Quoted in Perry Miller, *The Transcendentalists: An Anthology* (Cambridge, Mass., 1967), p. 221.

88. Edwards A. Park, *A Discourse Delivered at the Funeral of Professor Moses Stuart* (Boston, 1852), p. 5.

89. See particularly Edward Beecher, "The Nature, Importance and Means of Eminent Holiness Throughout the Church," *National Preacher*, 10 (1835), 193–223. Beecher insists the true Christian must possess both the military and pacific virtues. See also Henry A. Nelson, "The Gentleness and Energy of Christianity," *National Preacher*, new series 4 (1861), 223–31, and F. D. Huntington, "The Religion That Is Natural," in *Sermons for the People* (Boston, 1856), pp. 362–99.

90. Edwards A. Park, *Duties of a Theologian: An Anniversary Address* (New York, 1839), p. 25.

91. Edwards A. Park, *The Theology of the Intellect and of the Feelings* (Andover, Mass., 1850), pp. 5, 3, 34.

92. "The Andover and Princeton Theologies," *Christian Examiner*, 52 (1852), 31.

93. Charles Hodge, "The Theology of the Intellect," *Essays*, pp. 543, 572. For Hodge's life, see A. A. Hodge, *The Life of Charles Hodge* (New York, 1880).

94. Park, ed., *Memoir of Nathaniel Emmons*, I, p. 296.

95. Ide, ed., *The Works of Nathaniel Emmons*, I, p. lxiii.

96. Park, ed., *Memoir of Nathaniel Emmons*, I, p. 76.

97. Park, *The Theology of the Intellect and of the Feelings*, p. 8.

98. *Ibid.*, pp. 21-2.

99. Charles Hodge, *op. cit.*, p. 625.

100. Walker, *op. cit.*, pp. 597-9.

101. Rev. Albert E. Dunning, D.D., *Congregationalists in America: A Popular History of their Origin, Belief, Polity, Growth, and Work* (New York, 1894), pp. 467-88.

102. J. H. Allen, "On Some Effects of the Voluntary System, Especially in Our Country Parishes," *Christian Examiner*, 84 (1868), 222.

103. Daniel T. McColgan, *Joseph Tuckerman: Pioneer in American Social Work* (Washington, D.C., 1940), pp. 9, 10, 19, 32. My discussion of Tuckerman's life is based on this biography.

104. Joseph Tuckerman, *The Principles and Results of the Ministry at Large in Boston* (Boston, 1838), pp. 135, 139, 37.

105. Henry Ward Beecher, *Yale Lectures*, pp. 187, 189, 192, 193, 215, 3, 173.

106. William C. Gannett, *Ezra Stiles Gannett, Unitarian Minister in Boston 1824–1871* (Boston, 1875), p. 387.

107. *The Works of William E. Channing, D.D.* (Boston and New York, 1848), VI, pp. 209-10.

108. *The Works of Charles Follen with a Memoir of His Life* (Boston and New York, 1887), V, p. 254.

109. Sumner Ellis, *The Life of Edwin H. Chapin* (Boston, 1882), pp. 87-103.

110. For anti-professionalism, anti-intellectualism, and anti-institutionalism among early women nurses and doctors, see Ann Douglas Wood, "The War Within A War" and "The Fashionable Diseases." See also Lydia Maria Child, *The Progress of Religious Ideas Through Successive Ages* (New York and London, 1855), 3 vols., for a veiled attack on theology.

111. Helen E. Marshall, *Dorothea Dix: Forgotten Samaritan* (Chapel Hill, N.C., 1937), p. 54.

112. Francis Tiffany, *Life of Dorothea Lynde Dix* (Boston and New York, 1891), p. 11.

113. *Ibid.*, p. 19.

114. *Ibid.*, p. 272.

115. Marshall, *op. cit.*, p. 101.

116. *Ibid.*, p. 104.

117. Marshall, *op. cit.*, p. 115.

118. See Tiffany, *op. cit.*, pp. 53 ff.; David J. Rothman, *The Discovery of the Asylum: Social Order and Disorder in the New Republic* (Boston and Toronto, 1971); Agatha Young, *The Women and the Crisis: Women of the North in the Civil War* (New York, 1959), p. 60; Sylvia G. L. Dannett, ed., *Noble Women of the North* (New York and London, 1959), pp. 88-104.

119. Tiffany, *op. cit.*, p. 358.

120. Marshall, *op. cit.*, pp. 206, 210.

121. Quoted in Young, *op. cit.*, p. 104.

122. See Young, *op. cit.*, pp. 308-9; Tiffany, *op. cit.*, p. 141.

123. Marshall, *op. cit.*, p. 57.

124. Fanny Fern, *Rose Clark* (New York, 1856), pp. 15-21.

125. The popular novelist Elizabeth Stuart Phelps, for example, was passionately interested in anti-vivisection. Yet she never lets the heroines of her anti-vivisection fiction join anti-vivisection societies or even be aware of their existence. See *Though Life Do Us Part* (Boston, 1908), and *Trixy* (Boston, 1904).

126. Tuckerman, *op. cit.*, p. 324.

127. Calhoun, *op. cit.*, p. 183.

128. Park, *Duties of a Theologian*, p. 5.

129. Edwards A. Park, *The Indebtedness of the State to the Clergy* (Boston, 1851), p. 11.

130. *Ibid.*, p. 22.

131. Gannett, *Ezra Stiles Gannett*, pp. 30, 76, 500.

132. John Ware, M.D., *Memoir of the Life of Henry Ware, Jr.* (Boston, 1846), pp. 99, 46.

133. *Ibid.*, pp. 46, 466, 87, 469.

134. *Ibid.*, pp. 321-3, 474.

135. *Ibid.*, p. 331.

136. Henry Ware, Jr., *On the Formation of the Christian Character* (Cambridge, Mass., and Boston, 1831), pp. 288, 318, 390, 293, 391.

137. *Ibid.*, pp. 165, 53, 67-8.

138. [Catharine Maria Sedgwick], *A New England Tale* (New York, 1822), pp. 214, 252.

139. Elizabeth Wetherell [Susan Warner], *Queechy* (Philadelphia, 1892), I, p. 69.

140. *Ibid.*, II, pp. 213-14.

141. Henry Ware, Jr., *Progress of the Christian Life* (Boston, 1847), pp. 67, 69, 68, 85.

5

THE ESCAPE FROM HISTORY: THE STATIC IMAGINATION

1. Daniel J. Boorstin, *The Image: A Guide to Pseudo-Events in America* (New York, 1972). A "pseudo-event," in Boorstin's definition, is an event which is made to happen, or seem to happen, because it is covered by the media, indeed *so that* it can be covered by the media. Boorstin suggests that many of the "events" of modern mass life are not actualities but fabrications; that attention-getting substitutes for experience. I have found this analysis greatly helpful for my own thinking.

2. I am not using the term "ideology" in the Marxist sense of that cluster of concepts by which a ruling class perpetuates and solidifies its hegemony. I rather mean to suggest by the term a coherent body of doctrine to which groups and individuals give their allegiance and which opposes as well as supports their apparent self-interest. Both Marxism and Christianity have at different points functioned as an ideology in this sense. For two crucial discussions relating to this issue, see Georg Lukács, *History and Class Consciousness: Studies in Marxist Dialectics,* trans. Rodney Livingstone (Cambridge, Mass., 1968), and Karl Mannheim, *Ideology and Utopia: An Introduction to the Sociology of Knowledge,* trans. Louis Wirth and Edward Shils (New York, n.d.).

3. There were exceptions, of course, although they lie largely outside this study. See the openly feminist revisionist studies of Christianity by Sarah M. Grimké, *Letters on the Equality of the Sexes and the Condition of Women* (Boston, 1838), and Elizabeth Cady Stanton, *The Woman's Bible* (Seattle, Wash., 1974). Both documents were disavowed, not simply by the sentimentalists with whom I am concerned, but by most of the suffragists themselves. On Sarah Grimké's life, see Gerda Lerner, *The Grimké Sisters from South Carolina: Rebels Against Slavery* (Boston, 1967).

4. For an interesting although not fully comprehensive study of the feminist movement from its inception until the present, from the perspective of this ideological failure, see William O'Neill, *Everyone Was Brave:* *The Rise and Fall of Feminism in America* (Chicago, 1969).

5. George H. Callcott, *History in the United States 1800–1860: Its Practice and Purpose* (Baltimore and London, 1970), p. 35.

6. *Ibid.,* pp. 57–9.

7. Whitman of course argues this in his "Preface to 1855 Edition of *Leaves of Grass*" in Walt Whitman, *Leaves of Grass and Selected Prose,* ed. Sculley Bradley (New York, 1960), pp. 453–72. For similar arguments from the turn of the nineteenth century, see *The American Literary Revolution, 1783–1837,* ed. Robert E. Spiller (New York, 1967).

8. Callcott, *op. cit.,* p. 195.

9. Quoted in *ibid.,* p. 139.

10. For the biographies and studies on which my discussion of the lives of these four men are drawn, see Van Wyck Brooks, *The Flowering of New England* (New York, 1936); David Levin, *History as Romantic Art: Bancroft, Prescott, Motley and Parkman* (Stanford, 1959); Harvey Wish, *The American Historian: A Social-Intellectual History of the Writing of the American Past* (New York, 1960); Marcus Cunliffe and Robin W. Winks, eds., *Pastmasters: Some Essays on American Historians* (New York, 1969); Russell B. Nye, *George Bancroft: Brahmin Rebel* (New York, 1943); Oliver Wendell Holmes, *John Lathrop Motley: A Memoir* (Boston, 1879); Howard Doughty, *Francis Parkman* (New York, 1962), and "Parkman's Dark Years: Letters to Mary Dwight Parkman," *Harvard Library Bulletin,* 4 (1950), 53–85; George Ticknor, *Life of William Hickley Prescott* (Philadelphia, 1863).

11. On the birth and meaning of the "historicist" viewpoint, see Callcott, *op. cit.;* R. G. Collingwood, *The Idea of History* (New York, 1956); Mircea Eliade, *The Myth of the Eternal Return: Or, Cosmos and History,* trans. Willard R. Trask (Princeton, 1954); G. P. Gooch, *History and Historians in the Nineteenth Century* (New York, 1913); Paige Smith, *The Historian and History* (New York, 1964); Hayden White, *Metahistory: The Historical Imagination of Nineteenth-Century Europe* (Baltimore and London, 1973).

12. The historian is Leopold von Ranke, quoted in Gooch, *op. cit.,* p. 87.

13. I speak of Calvinism here, but of course my remark is equally applicable to the Pauline or Augustinian tradition in Catholi-

cism on which the Protestant reformers drew so heavily.

14. Georg Wilhelm Friedrich Hegel, *The Philosophy of History*, trans. J. Sibree (New York, 1956), p. 21.

15. Callcott, *op. cit.*, pp. 9–11.

16. Quoted in Walter Kaufmann, *Hegel: A Reinterpretation* (New York, 1965), p. 1.

17. Quoted in White, *op. cit.*, p. 91.

18. Quoted in Kaufmann, *op. cit.*, p. 251.

19. I am indebted in my discussion of Hegel to Larry Gross.

20. *Life, Letters, and Journals of George Ticknor*, ed. George S. Hillard (Boston, 1877), I, p. 120.

21. Quoted in Nye, *op. cit.*, p. 41.

22. *Ibid.*, p. 63.

23. Paul Revere Frothingham, *Edward Everett: Orator and Statesman* (Boston and New York, 1925), pp. 272–3.

24. Quoted in *ibid.*, p. 66.

25. Doughty, *Francis Parkman*, pp. 5–6.

26. Ticknor, *op. cit.*, *passim*.

27. Quoted in John Lothrop Motley, *The Rise of the Dutch Republic: A History* (London, Toronto, and New York, 1920), I, p. 5.

28. Quoted in Holmes, *op. cit.*, p. 26.

29. On von Ranke, see Smith, *op. cit.*, pp. 50–6, and Gooch, *op. cit.*, pp. 76–100.

30. William H. Prescott, *Biographical and Critical Miscellanies* (Philadelphia, 1890), p. 77.

31. Quoted in Ticknor, *op. cit.*, p. 135.

32. Quoted in Herbert Baxter Adams, *The Life and Writings of Jared Sparks* (Boston, 1893), I, p. 32.

33. See David D. van Tassel, *Recording America's Past: An Interpretation of the Development of Historical Studies in America 1607–1884* (Chicago, 1960), pp. 115–17. Van Tassel is excellent on the political motivation of early nationalist history.

34. Quoted in *ibid.*

35. Bancroft's analysis of the witchcraft controversy of the late seventeenth century as the outcome of the attempt by certain groups of the New England clergy to regain their rapidly waning power in community affairs is both keen and unfair. Bancroft's anti-clericalism is apparent in such statements as "the ministers, desirous of unjust influence, could build their hope of it only on error"—hardly an adequate summation even of the complex role of the Mathers in the witchcraft crisis. See George Bancroft, *The History of the United States of America from the Discovery of the American Continent* (Boston, 1844), III, p. 74.

36. See Prescott, *The Conquest of Mexico, The Conquest of Peru and Other Selections*, ed. Roger Howell (New York, 1966), pp. 200–6.

37. Quoted in Nye, *op. cit.*, p. 108.

38. See *The Library of American Biography*, 25 volumes, ed. Jared Sparks (New York, 1835–48).

39. [William B. O. Peabody and George S. Hillard], *Lives of Alexander Wilson and Captain John Smith* (New York, 1856), pp. 177, 391.

40. Adams, *op. cit.*, I, p. 385.

41. Convers Francis, *Life of John Eliot: The Apostle to the Indians* (New York, 1860), p. 12.

42. On the treatment of Indians, see Levin, *op. cit.*, pp. 158–9. The classic example among the historians themselves is Francis Parkman, *The Conspiracy of Pontiac and the Indian War After the Conquest of Canada* in *Parkman's Works* (Boston, 1891–7), II.

43. Quoted in George Bancroft, *The History of the United States*, ed. Russell B. Nye (Chicago and London, 1966), p. xviii.

44. Francis Parkman, *La Salle and the Discovery of the Great West* in *Parkman's Works*, III, p. 125.

45. Motley, *op. cit.*, I, p. 59.

46. *Ibid.*, p. 35.

47. Edward Everett, *Orations and Speeches on Various Occasions* (Boston, 1870), III, p. 200.

48. Parkman, *The Conspiracy of Pontiac*, pp. 312–13.

49. I am indebted in this discussion to Eliade, *op. cit.*

50. On the continuing high reputation at home and abroad of the romantic historians, see John Higham with Leonard Krieger and Felix Gilbert, *History* (Princeton, 1965), especially pp. 3–72. See also Callcott, *op. cit.*, pp. 21–3.

51. Callcott, *op. cit.*, pp. 33–4.

52. See Higham, *op. cit.*, pp. 3–72.

53. See Daniel Calhoun, *Professional Lives in America: Structure and Aspiration 1750–1850* (Cambridge, Mass., 1965), p. 195. For the more general climate of nostalgia in the ante-bellum period, see Arthur P. Dudden, "Nostalgia and the American," *Journal of the History of Ideas*, 22 (1961), 515–30; Neil Harris, *The Artist in American Society: The Formative Years 1790–1860* (New York, 1966); Michael B. Katz, *The Irony of Early School Reform: Educational Innovation in Mid-Nineteenth-Century Massachu-*

setts (Boston, 1968); Marvin Meyers, *The Jacksonian Persuasion: Politics and Belief* (Stanford, 1957); Fred Somkin, *Unquiet Eagle: Memory and Desire in the Idea of American Freedom 1815–1860* (Ithaca, N.Y., 1967); Bernard Wishy, *The Child and the Republic: The Dawn of Modern American Child Nurture* (Philadelphia, 1968).

54. See Callcott, *op. cit.*, pp. 69–70, for a sociological profile of the more distinguished historians of the period, and pp. 111–15 for a discussion of the antiquarian impulse. He makes no mention of the conflict between romantic and antiquarian history I am discussing.

55. Callcott, *op. cit.*, pp. 112–15.

56. *New Englander*, 12 (1854), p. 194.

57. "The Religion of the Present," *Christian Examiner*, 67 (1859), 55.

58. See Arethusa Hall, *Life and Character of the Rev. Sylvester Judd* (Boston, 1854), pp. 121, 193, 211, 290–3 for his views on war.

59. *Friend of Peace*, 1 (1815), 39.

60. Horace Bushnell, "Barbarism the First Danger," *National Preacher*, 21 (1847), 218.

61. Edwards A. Park, *Duties of a Theologian: An Anniversary Address* (New York, 1839), p. 29.

62. Edwards A. Park, *The Indebtedness of the State to the Clergy* (Boston, 1851), p. 11.

63. Quoted in *ibid.*, p. 11.

64. Horace Bushnell, *Moral Uses of Dark Things* (New York, 1868), p. 76.

65. Park, *The Indebtedness of the State to the Clergy*, p. 11.

66. Quoted in Frank Luther Mott, *A History of American Magazines* Vol. II, *1850–1865* (Cambridge, Mass., 1938), p. 51.

67. Ellet here strikingly anticipated the French historian Lucien Febvre. See his essay "Sensibility and History: How to Reconstitute the Emotional Life of the Past," in Lucien Febvre, *A New Kind of History and Other Essays*, trans. K. Folca (New York, 1973), pp. 12–26.

68. Quoted in Sarah Josepha Hale, *Woman's Record; or Sketches of All Distinguished Women From the Creation to A.D. 1854* (New York, 1855), pp. 645–6.

69. For examples of typical reviews of Sedgwick's historical novels which single out for praise their ahistorical qualities, see [William Cullen Bryant], *"Redwood," North American Review*, 20 (1825), 245–69; Timothy Flint,

"Hope Leslie," Western Monthly Magazine, I (1827–28), 289–95; [F. W. P. Greenwood], *"Hope Leslie," North American Review*, 26 (1828), 403–20. For later, also inadequate, evaluations, see Richard B. Gidez, *A Study of the Works of Catharine Maria Sedgwick* (Columbus, Ohio, 1958), and Sister Mary Michael Welsh, *Catharine Maria Sedgwick: Her Position in the Literary Thought of Her Time Up to 1860* (Washington, D.C., 1937).

70. Catharine Maria Sedgwick, *The Linwoods; or Sixty Years Since in America* (New York, 1835), I, p. xii.

71. See Ann D. Wood, "The 'Scribbling Women' and Fanny Fern: Why Women Wrote," *American Quarterly*, 23 (1971), 3–24.

72. On pacifism, see Roland H. Bainton, *Christian Attitudes Towards War and Peace: A Historical Survey and Critical Re-evaluation* (New York and Nashville, 1960); Peter Brock, *Radical Pacifists in Antebellum America* (Princeton, 1968); Merle Eugene Curti, *The American Peace Crusade 1815–1860* (Durham, N.C., 1929); Alice Felt Tyler, *Freedom's Ferment: Phases of American Social History from the Colonial Period to the Outbreak of the Civil War* (New York, 1944), pp. 396–423.

73. Curti, *op. cit.*, p. 22.

74. Henry F. May, *Protestant Churches and Industrial America* (New York, 1949), pp. 26–7. See also Tyler, *op. cit.*, p. 399, and Curti, *op. cit.*, p. 48.

75. Curti, *op. cit.*, pp. 201–2.

76. *Ibid.*, pp. 23–4.

77. *Ladies' Magazine*, 9 (1836), 215–19.

78. *Ladies' Wreath*, 1 (1847–8), 50–3.

79. *Ladies' Album*, 10 (1848), 109–13.

80. See Alice M. Baldwin, *The New England Clergy and the American Revolution* (New York, 1958).

81. *Friend of Peace*, 1 (1815), 24–5.

82. *Ibid.*, 5.

83. "War: Discourses Before the Congregational Ministers of Massachusetts" in *The Works of William E. Channing, D.D.* (Boston and New York, 1848), III, pp. 40–1, 50. For a more ambivalent response to pacifism, see Ralph Waldo Emerson, "War," in *Emerson's Works* (Boston and New York, 1878), XI, pp. 177–201.

84. *Ladies' Album*, 10 (1848), 109.

85. Elizabeth Stuart Phelps, *Chapters From a Life* (Boston and New York, 1897), p. 98.

86. Adams, *op. cit.*, II, p. 191.

87. The exception, appropriately, is "A Memoir of Lucretia Davidson" by Catharine Maria Sedgwick, in *The Library of American Biography*, VII (New York, 1860), pp. 219–98. Lucretia Davidson was a young, consumptive, pious poet, entirely different from the usual subjects of the Sparks biographies, and Sedgwick's account of her is in the tradition of the clerical-feminine memoirs as I will be describing it.

88. I am referring to the contemporary work of the historian Fernand Braudel and of the psychologist-historian Erik Erikson. See particularly Braudel, *Capitalism and Material Life 1400–1800*, trans. Miriam Kochan (New York, 1967), and Erikson, *Young Man Luther: A Study in Psychoanalysis and History* (New York, 1958). Dramatically different as Braudel and Erikson of course are, they are among the most distinguished representatives of the modern school which has questioned and overcome the abstract and political quality of traditional history—Braudel by stressing the material and environmental aspects of the human experience, Erikson by exploring the psychological and spiritual development and influence of prominent historical figures. One should also mention in this context the recent work of the French anthropologist Claude Lévi-Strauss, whose expressed antagonism to the historicist view would have won some allegiance among the ministers and women I am discussing. See particularly Lévi-Strauss, "The Kyong," *Tristes Tropiques*, trans. John and Doreen Weightman (New York, 1974), pp. 405–15.

89. For an excellent essay on a more recent example of this phenomenon, see Leo Lowenthal, "The Triumph of Mass Idols" in *Literature, Popular Culture, and Society* (Palo Alto, Calif., 1961), pp. 109–40.

90. See Samuel Hopkins, *The Life and Character of Miss Susanna Anthony* (Portland, 1810).

91. *New Englander*, 24 (1845), 387.

92. Marie Howland, *Papa's Own Girl* (New York, 1874), pp. 64–5.

93. William Sprague, *Annals of the American Pulpit* (New York, 1837–39), I, pp. 659, 655.

94. *Ibid.*, p. 556.

95. Mary Bushnell Cheney, *Life and Letters of Horace Bushnell* (New York, 1880), pp. 465, 468.

96. Hall, *op. cit.*, p. 510.

97. Cheney, *op. cit.*, p. 2.

98. Rev. Daniel D. Addison, *Lucy Larcom: Life, Letters and Diary* (Boston and New York, 1895), p. v.

99. Henry Bacon, *Poetry and Prose by Mrs. Charlotte A. Jerauld* (Boston, 1850), pp. 17–19. See also *Selections from the Writings of Mrs. Sarah C. Edgarton Mayo with a Memoir by Her Husband* (Boston, 1849), pp. 9–10.

100. Cheney, *op. cit.*, pp. 549, 510.

101. *The Works of Charles Follen with a Memoir of His Life* (Boston and New York, 1887), I, pp. 7, 325, 414, 534.

102. Mary Clemmer Ames, *A Memorial of Alice and Phoebe Cary With Some of Their Later Poems* (New York, 1874), pp. vi, 97.

103. Bacon, *op. cit.*, pp. 9, 74, 76–7.

104. Ralph Waldo Emerson, describing his uneasy relations as a child with his rather stern and harsh minister father, compared himself to Adam hiding in the garden at the sound of the Lord's voice. See James Elliot Cabot, *A Memoir of Ralph Waldo Emerson* (Boston and New York, 1887), I, p. 35. In a sense, the liberal minister of Emerson's generation did indeed wish to hide from the father and the command to historical responsibility he suggested and take refuge in the garden, a place rich in Biblical, sexual, and feminine connotations. Another Unitarian, a convert from Episcopalianism, explaining his new sense of freedom, wrote in 1852: "Nature has recovered the bloom of her lost Eden; and the Lord God walks again in his garden in the cool of the day; and I no longer tremble at the sound of his voice, but listen to it, as to the melodious whisperings of the wind amid fragrant arbors." See *How I Became a Unitarian Explained in a Series of Letters to a Friend By a Clergyman of the Protestant Episcopal Church* (Boston, 1852), p. 192. Unlike Emerson, this man has achieved a reconciliation with God: he has found a milder and kindlier Deity who is now a part of the soft scenery of the Garden rather than an admonishing intruder in it. The Garden, rather than God, has become the primary reality; the Fall, which marked the beginning not just of mortal alienation but of human history, has been obviated. Guilt and the threatening paternal presence have disappeared together.

The garden was the chosen and consecrated terrain of the feminine sensibility in mid-nineteenth-century American culture. Lady-litterateurs like Sarah Hale and Mary Griffin respectively turned out books with coy titles: *Flora's Interpreter and Fortuna Flora* (Boston, 1848) or *Drops from Flora's Cup or the Poetry of Flowers* (Boston, 1852). These volumes were often extremely petite in size; their femininity seemed to dictate their smallness, and one remembers Sarah Edgarton Mayo, who loved the "little." They usually consisted of poeticized, moralistic, and sentimental descriptions of the various flowers, whose pretty appearance and sweet scent were clearly to symbolize and suggest a kind of transfigured female "influence." Ladies' magazines and gift annuals of the day, commonly edited by women or by ministers, often drew their titles from favorite flowers: *The Ladies' Wreath, The Lily, The Violet, The Amaranth, The Rose of Sharon, The Lily of the Valley* among such popular floral offerings. Girls were frequently named after flowers: Bushnell called one of his daughters "Lily." As we have seen, many women authors selecting *noms de plume* took floral or at least vernal names. Fictional heroines, if possible, had flowers in their hands; Mary Scudder in Stowe's *A Minister's Wooing* first appears framed in a bower of apple blossoms.

105. Edwards A. Park, ed., *Memoir of Nathaniel Emmons* (Boston, 1861), I, pp. clxxiii–ix. For a similar fascination with the aged minister, see Rev. Edwin Pond Parker, ed., *The Autobiography of the Rev. Enoch Pond* (Boston, 1883). Parker, Pond's grandson, a minister and a literal follower of Bushnell, softens the older man's rugged militant Calvinism by focusing on his gentle old age. I should add here that aged men were precious not simply because they were fragile but because they were in some sense feminized. Hannah Gould, a New Hampshire poet, trying to explain her reverence for the elderly, wrote to Mrs. Sigourney:

Walking the streets, and in the most exuberant spirits, talking with a companion, if a trembling, white-haired aged man passes before me, I feel the tears gushing hot and rolling down to quench the smile upon my lips, before I am aware of the change in my emotions. But it is not mourning nor sorrow that does this. I can only call it melting. (Quoted in Gordon

S. Haight, *Mrs. Sigourney: The Sweet Singer of Hartford* [New Haven, 1930], p. 5.)

Mrs. Sigourney was the perfect confidante in this case. In 1856, she published a book entitled *Past Meridian* (New York and Boston, 1854), on the "beauty of age"; in later life she exulted, "the overmastering force of the passions [is] broken." In a long passage in *Letters to Mothers*, she elaborated further:

Entire resignation is probably the highest attainment of our faith.... Protracted debility gives leisure for meditation.... If the deafened ear no longer excites the mind, if the right hand forgets its cunning ... it is because those weary laborers have need of repose. The Sabbath of existence has come. It brings with it a season of silence, in which to meditate, to release the soul from earthly ties.... The far-off past is more vivid than the moving current of things. Memory reverses her tablet. (*Letters to Mothers* [Hartford, 1838], pp. 224–8.)

Gould and Sigourney are moved by the elderly because the aged are by definition close to the feminine ideal: they are pious creatures of the Sabbath destined to embody the virtues of debility, pensioners of memory unfit for competition with the world. Gould's tears flow in a kind of excess of self-love; she pays the old man the tribute which in part is her own due.

106. Maturin M. Ballou, *Biography of Rev. Hosea Ballou* (Boston, 1852), pp. 212–13.

107. Quoted in Richard Eddy, *The Life of Thomas J. Sawyer and of Caroline M. Sawyer* (Boston and Chicago, 1900), p. 336.

108. A. A. Miner, *A Discourse, Delivered in School St. Church, Boston at the Funeral of the Rev. Hosea Ballou* (Boston, 1852), pp. 16, 17, 21, 33, 40.

109. Indeed, the sentimental literature of early religious liberalism makes stock villains out of the "father" and the Calvinist minister to whom he is symbolically allied. *The Universalist and Ladies' Repository* was launched in 1833 under the editorship of the Streeter brothers simply as *The Universalist.* As such it was filled with sermonizing non-fictional articles on the advantages of the Universalist faith. Within the year, it changed editors and became a magazine for Universalist ladies,

dedicated to the proposition that true women instinctively find Calvinism repugnant "to the kindness of their nature and [their] . . . amiable sympathies" (II, 29 [1833], 230). The new magazine tried to win a female readership, interestingly enough, by mingling religious fiction with scathing attacks on Calvinist clergymen. Such men have "passed all bounds of decency," one contributor warns luridly, to secure feminine converts. Even more significantly, the first piece to appear by a woman (who calls herself "Fidelia") was entitled "Letter from a Young Lady to Her Father" (*ibid.*, 243–4). The daughter firmly announces her new allegiance to Universalism and defies her tyrannical and orthodox parent. From 1833 on, the *Ladies' Repository* regularly ran stories about cruel Calvinist fathers and pure Universalist daughters. A title like "The Vampyre: or the Legitimate Fruits of Calvinism" (4 [1836], 17–23) speaks for itself. Fathers with names like "John Calvin, Jr.," oppress and even murder their wayward daughters, but all in vain. Whether he resorts to seduction or violence, the father-figure finally exerts his authority only as a gesture of impotence: the daughter-figure remains true to the precepts and examples of her gentle Universalist pastor and her own trusting heart.

110. Lydia Huntley Sigourney, *The Young Lady's Offering, or Gems of Prose and Poetry* (Boston, 1862), p. 10.

111. *Ibid.*, pp. 253, 247.

112. Compare Lydia Huntley Sigourney, *Letters of Life* (New York, 1866), or *Sketch of Connecticut, Forty Years Since* (Hartford, 1824), or *The Lovely Sisters Margaret and Henrietta* (Hartford, 1846), with *Lucy Howard's Journal* (New York, 1858).

6

THE DOMESTICATION OF DEATH:
THE POSTHUMOUS
CONGREGATION

1. *Christian Examiner*, 62 (1857), 114.

2. *Sermons by the Late William B. O. Peabody with a Memoir by His Brother* (Boston, 1849). p. xxv.

3. Rufus Wilmot Griswold, ed., *The Poets and Poetry of America* (New York, 1874), p. 266.

4. *Sermons by the Late William B. O. Peabody*, p. xlvii.

5. *Ibid.*, p. xc.

6. The causes of this literary, and in some part actual, magnification of mourning in America between 1820 and 1875 are complex and elusive. The historian's first instinct is to turn to demography and to consider the possibility of an unusually high death rate in this period. There was of course the Civil War, which took a million lives (James G. Randall and David Donald, *The Civil War and Reconstruction* [Boston, 1961], p. 531). Massive, even national, need for consolation and curiosity about the destination of the departed during and after the war seems inevitable. Elizabeth Stuart Phelps claimed that she wrote her bestselling novel *The Gates Ajar* (1868), a fictionalized mourning manual, because ' she was touched by the grief of the thousands who had lost beloved sons and husbands in the war. See Phelps, *Chapters From a Life* (Boston and New York, 1897), p. 97. Yet the shock imparted by the Civil War merely dramatized and accelerated a trend already well under way. Phelps's own father had felt for years that only his "conception of heaven as a place . . . not unlike this world," an idea which is the key to the appeal of *The Gates Ajar*, made living tolerable to him. (Elizabeth Stuart Phelps, *Austin Phelps: A Memoir* [New York, 1891], p. 18.) Writers in both England and America had anticipated Elizabeth Phelps's preoccupation with death and the afterlife; *Heaven Our Home* (Boston, 1864) and *Life in Heaven* (Boston, 1865) by the Englishman Peter Branks went through dozens of editions in England. And *The Gates Ajar* was even more successful in England, which had had no civil war, than in America.

Many cultural historians have assumed or implied that nineteenth-century American children died of more or less natural causes in staggering numbers. In this view, the copious consolation literature, so largely concerned with deceased children, was a sentimental but viable way to cope with a widespread and valid sense of loss and deprivation. Recently, however, scholars, most notably Maris Vinovskis of the University of Wisconsin, have begun to demonstrate that the mortality rate of the period was not so high as once supposed. Although no final results are in, it is at least uncertain that the death rate for infants increased from the eighteenth to the nineteenth century in the northern United States; it may have decreased. The outpouring of mourners' manuals needs further explanation. The answer may well lie in contemporary perceptions or misperceptions of demographic data, perceptions shaped by economic and social factors. Northern middle-class families by mid-century were beginning to "plan" their families; women hoped to have three or four children, rather than keep three or four. In a period of increasing prosperity and incipient scientific investigation, expectations were perhaps raised beyond the level of available medical competence.

7. Mrs. Sigourney's poem has been reprinted in Gail Parker's anthology *The Oven Birds: American Women on Womanhood 1820–1920* (New York, 1972), pp. 59, 60.

8. George C. Prentiss, *The Life and Letters of Elizabeth Prentiss* (New York, 1882), p. 295.

9. Perry Miller and Thomas H. Johnson, eds., *The Puritans* (New York, Evanston, and London, 1963), II, p. 475.

10. See *The Works of Anne Bradstreet*, ed. Jeannine Hensley (Cambridge, Mass., 1967), p. 235.

11. Theodore Cuyler, *The Empty Crib* (New York, 1873), pp. 81–2. Cuyler also produced two other very popular mourning manuals, *Beulah Land: or Words of Cheer for Christian Pilgrims* (New York, 1896), and *God's Light on Dark Clouds* (New York, 1882).

12. Eunice Hale Cobb, *Memoir of James Arthur Cobb* (Boston, 1852), pp. 24, 30, 111.

13. *Sermons by the Late William B. O. Peabody*, pp. xlvii, xc, lxxiv.

14. Lydia Huntley Sigourney, *Zinzendorff and Other Poems* (New York and Boston, 1835), p. 111.

15. Lydia Huntley Sigourney, *Letters of Life* (New York, 1866), p. 408.

16. Lydia Huntley Sigourney, *The Lovely Sisters Margaret and Henrietta* (Hartford, 1846), p. 238.

17. Sigourney, "A Record of My School," unpublished MS in The Sigourney Collection at the Connecticut Historical Society.

18. I am basing my interpretation of spiritualism on the brilliant work in progress by R. Lawrence Moore of Cornell University. See his articles, "The Spiritualist Medium: A Study of Female Professionalism in Victorian America," *American Quarterly*, 27 (1975), 200–21, and "Spiritualism and Science: Reflections on the First Decade of the Spirit Rappings," *American Quarterly*, 29 (1972), 474–500.

19. For accounts of the "Rural Cemetery" movement, see Thomas Bender, "The 'Rural' Cemetery Movement: Urban Travail and the Appeal of Nature," *New England Quarterly*, 47 (1974), 196–211; John Brinckenhoff Jackson, *American Space: The Centennial Years 1865–1876* (New York, 1972), p. 70; Stanley French, "The Cemetery as Cultural Institution: The Establishment of Mt. Auburn and the 'Rural Cemetery' Movement" in *Death in America*, ed. David E. Stannard (Philadelphia, 1975), pp. 69–91; Neil Harris, *The Artist in American Society: The Formative Years 1790–1860* (New York, 1970), pp. 200–8; Barbara Rotundo, "The Rural Cemetery Movement," *Essex Institute Historical Collections*, 109 (1973), 231–40; Peter J. Schmitt, *Back to Nature: The Arcadian Myth in Urban America* (New York, 1969), pp. 67–8.

20. Harriette Merrifield Forbes, *Gravestones of Early New England and the Men Who Made Them 1653–1800* (Boston, 1927), pp. 63–7. On cemetery art, see also Edwin Dethelson and James Feete, "Death's Heads, Cherubs, and Willow Trees: Experimental Archaeology in Colonial Cemeteries," *American Antiquities* 31 (1966), 502–10; and Edmund Gillon, Jr., *Victorian Cemetery Art* (New York, 1972).

21. Moses King, *Mt. Auburn Cemetery* (Cambridge, Mass., 1839), pp. 46–8.

22. Theodore Cuyler explained that no phrase was as popular for tombstone inscriptions as "asleep in Jesus"; see *God's Light on Dark Clouds*, p. 164.

23. Cuyler, *The Empty Crib*, pp. 158, 173.

24. Arethusa Hall, *Life and Character of the Reverend Sylvester Judd* (Boston, 1854), p. 523. On flowers, see Jessica Mitford, *The American Way of Death* (New York, 1963), pp. 198–9.

25. Nehemiah D. D. Adams, *Agnes and the Key of Her Little Coffin By Her Father* (Boston, 1857), p. 15.

26. Quoted in Mitford, *op. cit.*, p. 222. See also Robert Haberstein and William Lamers, *The History of American Funeral Directing* (Milwaukee, 1955).

27. Hall, *op. cit.*, p. 131.

28. Quoted in Rotundo, *op. cit.*, p. 238.

29. Quoted in *ibid.*, p. 237.

30. Harris, *op. cit.*, is excellent on this aspect of the cemetery movement. For the cemetery as utopia, see Sylvester Judd's extraordinary romance, *Margaret: A Tale of the Real and Ideal: Blight and Bloom* (Boston, 1845), in which the hero and heroine set up an ideal liberal religious community called Mons Christi which is laid out exactly like the new cemeteries, with floral names, marble statuary, etc.

31. Quoted in French, *op. cit.*, p. 87.

32. Quoted in *ibid.*, p. 79.

33. See *The Picturesque Pocket Companion and Visitor's Guide Through Mt. Auburn* (Boston, 1839), pp. 3 ff.

34. Philip Aries, *Western Attitudes Toward Death: From the Middle Ages to the Present,* trans. Patricia M. Ranum (Baltimore and London, 1974), p. 72.

35. Quoted in French, *op. cit.*, p. 83.

36. *Christian Examiner*, 26 (1836), 338–9.

37. Rev. Samuel Phillips, *The Christian Home* (Springfield, Mass., 1860), p. 15.

38. *Christian Examiner*, 31 (1841), 151.

39. Quoted in George B. Tatum, "The Beautiful and the Picturesque," *American Quarterly*, 3 (1951), 36–51.

40. N. Parker Willis, *The Rag-Bag: A Collection of Ephemera* (New York, 1855). p. 124.

41. Harris, *op. cit.*, p. 209.

42. For a discussion of "picturesque" domestic architecture, see Carl Bode, *Antebellum Culture* (Carbondale and Edwardsville, Ill., 1959), pp. 38–50.

43. *Picturesque Pocket Companion*, pp. 22–3.

44. William Holcombe, *Our Children in Heaven* (Philadelphia, 1868), p. 24.

45. Ralph Waldo Trine, *In Tune With the Infinite or Fullness of Peace, Power, and Plenty* (New York, 1897).

46. Elizabeth Phelps, *Austin Phelps: A Memoir*, pp. 127, 100.

47. Austin Phelps, *My Portfolio: A Collection of Essays* (New York, 1882), p. 263.

48. Elizabeth Phelps, *Austin Phelps: A Memoir*, p. 227.

49. Austin Phelps, *The Still Hour: or, Communion With God* (Boston, 1860), p. 96.

50. Austin Phelps, *My Portfolio*, p. 23.

51. *Ibid.*, p. 240.

52. Rev. Asa Cummings, *A Memoir of the Rev. Edward Payson, D.D.* (New York, n.d.), p. 246.

53. George C. Prentiss, *Life and Letters of Elizabeth Prentiss*, pp. 11–12, 142, 60, 510.

54. *Ibid.*, p. 281.

55. Elizabeth Prentiss, *Stepping Heavenward* (New York, 1880), pp. 23, 425–6.

56. For the development of American hymnology and its context, see Louis F. Benson, *The English Hymn: Its Development and Use in Worship* (Philadelphia, 1915), and *The Hymnology of the Christian Church* (Richmond, Va., 1927); Henry Wilder Foote, *Three Centuries of American Hymnology* (Cambridge, Mass., 1940); Edward S. Ninde, *The Story of the American Hymn* (New York and Cincinnati, 1921); H. W. Stephenson, *Unitarian Hymn Writers* (London, 1931). For the most important nineteenth-century study of hymns, see Austin Phelps, Edwards A. Park, and Daniel L. Furber, *Hymns and Choirs* (Andover, Mass., 1860).

57. Foote, *op. cit.*, pp. 42, 44, 48.

58. *Ibid.*, p. 61.

59. See "Hymns and Hymnbooks," *Christian Examiner*, 8 (1832), 163–81.

60. Theodore Cuyler, *Recollections of a Long Life: An Autobiography* (New York, 1902), p. 37.

61. See Foote, *op. cit.*, pp. 181–2, and Benson, *op. cit.*, pp. 46ff.

62. Phelps, Park, and Furber, *op. cit.*, pp. 82, 52, 123, 79.

63. *Ibid.*, pp. 81–2.

64. Quoted in Ninde, *op. cit.*, p. 66.

65. Phelps, Park, and Furber, *op. cit.*, pp. 84, 64–5, 85.

66. *Ibid.*, p. 82.

67. Quoted in Ninde, *op. cit.*, pp. 165, 168, 173, 347.

68. Austin Phelps, *The Still Hour*, p. 45. And see George C. Prentiss, *Life and Letters of Elizabeth Prentiss*, p. 60, for a similar expression of confidence.

69. Elizabeth Stuart Phelps, *Between the Gates* (Boston, 1887), p. 223.

70. For a study of these monastic visions, their development and themes, see Ann Douglas Wood, "*Piers Plowman* and the Monastic Vision Tradition," Ph.D. dissertation, Harvard University, 1970. The common pattern I discovered in these visions was one in which the dreamer, after a tour of hell, is given a glimpse of heaven; ravished with delight, he wishes to stay but is forced by his guide to return instead to a better performance of his earthly duties. It should be stressed that this vision tradition persisted in various guises until modern times. For American examples, see

Some Remarkable Passages in the Life of Dr. George De Benneville (Germantown, Pa., 1890); David Lord, *Visions of Paradise: An Epic* (New York, 1867). In the monastic visions, such dreams heralded a conversion experience; this link persisted in life and literary tradition among nineteenth-century American evangelical groups. See William Sprague, *Annals of the American Pulpit* (New York, 1837–69), VI and VII on the Baptists and Methodists, *passim.*

71. For general discussion of the developing ideas of heaven and the millennium, see James P. Martin, *The Last Judgment in Protestant Theology from Orthodoxy to Ritschl* (Grand Rapids, Mich., 1963); Ulrich Simon, *Heaven in the Christian Tradition* (New York, 1958); Ernest Lee Tuveson, *Millennium and Utopia: A Study in the Background of the Idea of Progress* (Berkeley, Calif., 1949).

72. See Ira V. Brown, "Watchers for the Second Coming: The Millenarian Tradition in America," *Mississippi Valley Historical Review,* 39 (1952), 44–58; J. A. De Jong, *As the Waters Cover the Sea: Millennial Expectations in the Rise of Anglo-American Missions 1640–1810* (n.p., 1970); and Ernest Lee Tuveson, *Redeemer Nation: The Idea of America's Millennial Role* (Chicago and London, 1968). The millennial impulse was very fundamental to the utopian movements in America; see Arthur Beston, *Backwoods Utopias: The Sectarian Origins and the Owenite Phase of Communitarian Socialism in America 1663–1829* (Philadelphia, 1970), pp. 6–8; and Maren Lockwood Carden, *Oneida: Utopian Community to Modern Corporation* (New York, 1969), p. 12.

73. Nathaniel West, ed., *Premillennial Essays of the Prophetic Conference* (Chicago, 1879), p. 7.

74. *Sermons by F. W. P. Greenwood* (Boston, 1844), I, pp. 41, 35.

75. George Duffield, *Dissertations on the Prophecies Relative to the Second Coming of Jesus Christ* (New York, 1842), p. 381.

76. Rev. J. W. Brooks, *Essays on the Advent and Kingdom of Christ and the Events Connected Therewith* (Philadelphia, 1840), p. 17.

77. West, ed., *Premillennial Essays,* p. 17.

78. See Martin, *op. cit.,* pp. xiii, 17–70; H. Richard Niebuhr, *The Kingdom of God in America* (New York, 1937), *passim;* and Simon, *op. cit.,* pp. 20–37.

79. Henry F. Hill, *The Saint's Inheritance; or the World to Come* (New York, 1853), pp. 178,

135, 50, 15, 253, 10. For other examples, see John Lillie, *The Perpetuity of the Earth; a Discourse Preached Before the Premillennial Advent Association* (New York, 1842), and Anna Siliman, *The World's Jubilee* (New York, 1836).

80. Jacob Ide, ed., *The Works of Nathaniel Emmons* (Boston, 1842). I, p. 187.

81. George B. Cheever, *The Powers of the World to Come* (New York, 1853), pp. 108, 221, 250. For other examples of this ambivalent attempt to enforce the older theocentric heaven, see Rufus W. Clark, *Heaven and Its Spiritual Emblems* (Boston, 1857); Peter Grant, *Light on the Grave* (New York, 1869); C. F. Hudson, *Debt and Grace As Related to the Doctrine of a Future Life* (Boston, 1858); John Williams Kimball, *Heaven* (Boston, 1857); Thomas L. Shipman, "No Communications from the Dead to the Living," *National Preacher,* 30 (1856), 246–54; and Augustus C. Thompson, *The Better Land; or The Believer's Journey and Future Home* (Boston, 1854).

82. See William Henry Channing, *Memoir of William Ellery Channing with Extracts from His Correspondence and Manuscripts* (Boston, 1846), II, p. 18; Charles Follen, "On the Future State of Men" in *The Works of Charles Follen with a Memoir of His Life* (Boston and New York, 1887), V, pp. 12–96; F. W. P. Greenwood, "Recognition of Friends," "Voices from Heaven," "The Good Revealed," "Peaceful Sleep," and "Seeing the Departed" in *Sermons of Consolation* (Boston, 1842) pp. 216–62, 312–21, and "Heaven a Place of Rest" in *Sermons* II, pp. 109–21; Andrew Peabody, "Identity of the Earthly and Heavenly Life" and "A Door in Heaven" in *Christian Belief and Life* (Boston, 1875), pp. 160–8; Henry Ware, *An Inquiry Into the Foundation, Evidences and Truths of Religion* (Cambridge, Mass., 1842), II, pp. 263–70.

83. Of course the big influence here was Emanuel Swedenborg, *Concerning Heaven and Its Wonders and Concerning Hell: From Things Heard and Seen* (New York, 1863). For an example of heavenly scenes from consolation literature, see Thomas Baldwin Thayer, *Over the River, or, Pleasant Walks Into the Valleys of Shadows and Beyond: A Book of Consolation for the Sick, the Dying, and the Bereaved* (Boston, 1862). For a more learned version, see Rev. H. Harbaugh, *Heaven; or An Earnest and Scriptural Inquiry Into the Abode of the Sainted Dead* (Philadelphia, 1853), 3 vols.

84. The most interesting is George Wood's *Future Life,* which he published to little effect in 1858; then, capitalizing on Elizabeth Stuart Phelps's best-selling *The Gates Ajar,* he republished the novel as *The Gates Wide Open: or Scenes in Another World* (Boston, 1869).

85. See "Extract from Captain Stormfield's Visit to Heaven," in *The Complete Works of Mark Twain* (New York, 1922), vol. VIII, pp. 223–78.

86. See Mary Angela Bennett, *Elizabeth Stuart Phelps* (Philadelphia, 1939), p. 2. For a more recent interpretation of Phelps, see Christine Stansell, "Elizabeth Stuart Phelps: A Study in Female Rebellion," *The Massachusetts Review,* 13 (1972), 239–56.

87. See Elizabeth Stuart Phelps, "A Woman's Pulpit," *Atlantic Monthly,* 26 (1870), 11–22.

88. Elizabeth Stuart Phelps, *The Gates Ajar,* ed. Helen Sootin Smith (Cambridge, Mass., 1964), p. 108.

89. Elizabeth Stuart Phelps, *The Struggle for Immortality* (Boston and New York, 1889), pp. 55, 61.

90. Elizabeth Stuart Phelps, *Songs of the Silent World* (Boston and New York, 1885), pp. 11–12.

91. Elizabeth Phelps, *Gates Ajar,* pp. 48–9.

92. Elizabeth Stuart Phelps, *Beyond the Gates* (Boston, 1883), pp. 125–6, 128.

7

THE PERIODICAL PRESS: ARENA

FOR HOSTILITY

1. N. Parker Willis, *The Rag-Bag: A Collection of Ephemera* (New York, 1855), p. 70.

2. Frank Luther Mott, *A History of American Magazines,* Vol. II, *1850–1865* (Cambridge, Mass., 1938), pp. 141, 10–11, 60.

3. Frank Luther Mott, *A History of American Magazines,* Vol. I, *1741–1850* (New York and London, 1930), pp. 303–12.

4. *New Englander,* 2 (1844), 96.

5. *Christian Examiner,* 42 (1847), 395, 397, 393, 394.

6. See Lawrence L. Buell, "Unitarian Aesthetics and Emerson's Poet-Priest," *American Quarterly,* 20 (1968), 3–21, and "The Unitarian Movement and the Art of Preaching in Nineteenth-Century America," *American Quarterly,* 24 (1972), 166–90. See also Daniel Dulany Addison, *The Clergy in American Life and Letters* (London, 1900). This was a period which saw a marked refinement and secularization of sermon style, especially among the Unitarian and non-evangelical Congregational groups. Revivalist leaders like Charles Grandison Finney, who found it impossible to believe that "a person who has ever known the love of God can relish a secular novel" (quoted in William G. McLoughlin, Jr., *Modern Revivalism* [New York, 1959], p. 118), denounced preaching which was but the "reading of elegant literary essays" (Finney, *Lectures on Revivals of Religion,* ed. William G. McLoughlin [Cambridge, Mass., 1960], pp. 176–8). Joseph Buckminster, in contrast, had demonstrated that the pulpit could and should induce "gratification of the taste as well as . . . improvement of the character" (Eliza Buckminster Lee, *Memoirs of Rev. Joseph Buckminster, D.D. and of His Son Rev. Joseph Stevens Buckminster* [Boston, 1851], p. 356), and most non-evangelicals followed his lead. When Austin Phelps inquired, a half century after Buckminster's death, "why should not a Christian sermon be a work of intellectual art?" (Elizabeth Stuart Phelps, *Austin Phelps: A Memoir* [New York, 1891], p. 69), he was clearly posing a rhetorical question. That sermons could be art, and popular art, was amply demonstrated by the constant appearance of the flowery effusions of men like F. W. P. Greenwood and E. H. Chapin in the ladies' albums and magazines of the day. Yet, during the same period, the Unitarian minister Ezra Stiles Gannett lamented that the opinion that "the sermon is not entitled to rank as one of the highest forms in which genius may give expression to its thought" (*Christian Examiner,* 45 [1848], 429) had gained wide currency. The sermon, no matter how literary and sentimentalized, had limited intellectual and commercial value. The contrast between Emerson's pulpit performances and his lectures reveal the strictures even a very liberal clergyman felt the sermon form imposed (Buell, "Unitarian Aesthetics," 9). Moreover, while a reviewer for the *New Englander* could boast in 1868 that the publication of sermons, as of hymns, had greatly increased, proving that such works were "popular reading" (27 [1868], 190), other clerical commentators were aware that both sermons and hymns, at least those written in the mid-nineteenth century, were perilously close to the domain of

journalism: their very effort to be topical, appropriate, and attractive doomed them to be ephemeral in a way even a novel was not ("New Hymn Books," *Christian Examiner*, 40 [1846], 29–47). Furthermore, Henry Ware, Jr., reviewing a collection of Greenwood's sermons for the *Christian Examiner* in 1843, was forced to admit that the sermon was still, no matter how polished, basically an oral form, unlike the novel: as a result, Ware laments, only a "small ... part of the sermon can be brought before us by the printed page" (34 [1843], 85).

7. Mott, *op. cit.*, I, pp. 42, 131, 198.

8. William Warren Sweet, *Religion in the Development of American Culture 1765–1840* (New York, 1952), pp. 184–5.

9. Mott, *op. cit.*, II, p. 62.

10. Lee, *op. cit.*, pp. 152, 84.

11. Buckminster's journals and papers are in the Athenaeum in Boston. The entry I refer to is Aug. 18, 1804.

12. Lewis P. Simpson, *The Federalist Literary Mind: Selections from the Monthly Anthology 1803–1811* (Baton Rouge, La., 1962), pp. 88, 174. See also Lewis P. Simpson, "A Literary Adventure of the Early Republic: The Anthology Society and the *Monthly Anthology*," *New England Quarterly*, 27 (1957), 168–90.

13. See Mott, *op. cit.*, I, p. 56.

14. Theodore Cuyler, *Recollections of a Long Life: An Autobiography* (New York, 1902), p. 93.

15. See, for example, *The Rose of Sharon* (Boston, 1841) which includes sermons, sketches, or essays by Universalist ministers Thayer, Bacon, Chapin, Skinner, Adams, Grosh, and Thomas. This degree of clerical participation is typical of the annual until its demise in the late 1850s.

16. Isabelle Webb Entrikin, *Sarah Josepha Hale and Godey's Lady's Book* (Philadelphia, 1846), p. 14.

17. *New Englander*, 2 (1844), 96–101.

18. *Ibid.*, 1 (1843), 112.

19. *Ibid.*, 11 (1853), 210–22.

20. *Ibid.*, 17 (1859), 277, 275.

21. *Universalist and Ladies' Repository*, 2 (1833), 184.

22. *Ibid.*, 291–2.

23. See *The Ladies' Repository*, 25 (1857), for example. Note, first, the changed title. The editor is Mrs. E. A. Bacon, the assistant editor

Mrs. N. T. Munroe, the corresponding editor Mrs. C. A. Soule.

24. *Christian Parlor Magazine*, 3 (1846–7), 155, 13, 16, 113–15. Frank Luther Mott says, "The *Christian Parlor Magazine* was a part of the movement by which the religious press attempted to compete with the lady's books and popular family magazines of the times" (*op. cit.*, I, p. 745).

25. This sketch is included in *The Miscellaneous Writings of Henry Ware, Jr., D.D.* (Boston and London, 1846), I, pp. 139–46.

26. Mary E. Dewey, ed., *Autobiography and Letters of Orville Dewey, D.D.* (Boston, 1884), p. 176.

27. I will treat the critical response to Melville in Chapter Nine. A clerical reviewer could complain of Richard H. Dana's *Two Years Before the Mast*, a book Melville was to admire greatly, that it showed a "sombre hue"; Dana does not "extract a kindly lesson from all things and all men." He shows no " 'motherly spirit' " (*New Englander*, 9 [1851], 33).

28. *Christian Examiner*, 36 (1844), 284.

29. *New Englander*, 6 (1848), 556. An anonymous reviewer for the *United States Magazine* in 1856 summed up the dire influence of the American female writer on her male peers:

> The magnetism produced by her out-given heart-throbs has warmed into vitality a vast number of womanly men, who, without manly force or manly vigor of intellect, have given way to unmanly mawkishness and morbid complainings ... prettiness and sentimentalisms, quite to the shame of manhood.... Our literature is growing rather fine than forceful. We are tired of the whole school of mosaic workers like Longfellow, and imitators like Bayard Taylor and Curtis (III [1856], 242).

Those who accommodated themselves to the feminine sentimental vogue succeeded, but often at the cost of genuine artistic achievement and sometimes at the cost of their self-respect. Willis presumably spent little time lamenting his current reputation as a "namby-pamby writer in twaddling albums," but Longfellow, that apogee of Victorian poetic piety, felt frequently trapped by the demands of his public for innocuous, cheerful, morally uplifting verse. The work he prided himself on—vigorous poems like "Michael Angelo," abstract narratives like *Christus*—met with little approval. The bitter aphorism that appears in his early novel *Kavanagh*—"This country is not priest-ridden but press-ridden" (*Longfellow's Prose Works* [London and New York, n.d.], p. 238)—was in a sense prophetic of the difficulties of Longfellow's own career. For the best discussion of this aspect of Longfellow, see Matthew J. Bruccoli, ed., *The Profession of Authorship in America 1800–1870: The Papers of William Charvat* (n.p., 1968), pp. 106–67.

30. Quoted in William L. Hedges, *Washington Irving: An American Study 1802–1812* (Baltimore, 1965), p. 14. Donald Mitchell, later to be known under the pseudonym of "Ik Marvel," long hesitated to go into a literary career because, in his words, "the literary men of our country have impoverished themselves by their labors" (Waldo H. Dunn, *The Life of Donald G. Mitchell* [New York, 1922], p. 116). The career of the poet Sumner Lincoln Fairfield (1801–44) may be used as an illustration of Mitchell's observation. In *The Autobiography of Jane Fairfield* (Boston, 1860), his wife Jane, whose love for the "sentimental" (18) had impelled her from a girlhood of suburban dreariness in New Jersey into a marriage with a poet and a city life, told his genuinely touching tale.

In her biography, Jane Fairfield has two major points to make. Her husband, whose talents even she in her most critical moments (and they were legion) was astute enough not to doubt, was in her opinion "a genius." As such, he was hopelessly unstable, unsuited to domestic life. She concluded that "a creative and poetical mind was a fatal gift" (53). She did not add "in America," but she probably should have. Fairfield was a man who "found literature a miserable dependence, and he was utterly without business faculties, or a profession of any kind" (35). His futile attempt at an acting career (his wife helped laugh him off the stage), his tragic period as a teacher, his increasing insanity, his growing reliance a la Edgar Poe on drugs and alcohol to help him endure miseries he had no real resources to alleviate, are painfully detailed in Jane Fairfield's account, a narrative more painful for the evident lack of sympathy displayed by the author for her subject. Jane Fairfield,

however, and here lay her second point, was distinctly of stronger stuff. When the couple's only son died, and the poet-father was weeping over his grave, the mother saw "the finger of fate pointing to me as the only deliverer" (96). Then and there was conceived the *North American Magazine*, an enterprise which her husband's talent made distinguished but which only Jane's acumen could have brought into being. She was writing an exemplary moral tale of how to succeed in American letters, casting herself in the virtuous apprentice's role. In contrast to her husband, she demonstrated well-calculated aggressiveness as she combed the country for money, patrons, and subscribers. By all accounts a strikingly handsome woman, she used her feminine charms for masculine purposes: the long-suffering wife with her two helpless little girls and her helpless husband could open purses closed to pleaders from the supposedly self-reliant sex. Perhaps she lacked genius (so much the better! she implies throughout her bitter narrative), but she knew how to find readers for genius, and without these, what was genius worth anyway?

31. Unpublished undated latter in the Parton Collection in the Sophia Smith Collection in Northampton, Mass.

32. Quoted in Cortland P. Auser, *Nathaniel P. Willis* (New York, 1969), p. 59.

33. I have also examined the lives and works of a number of other members of the genteel or Irvingesque school (broadly conceived), practitioners of a kind of witty yet sentimental journalism; most particularly Lewis G. Clark (1803–73), Willis G. Clark (1808–41), Oliver Wendell Holmes (1809–94), H. W. Longfellow (1807–82), James Russell Lowell (1819–91), Henry Tuckerman (1813–71), and Charles Dudley Warner (1829–1900). The personal and professional patterns I outline for Curtis, Irving, Mitchell, and Willis do not hold true for all these men, though there are strong affinities of literary style and subject.

34. Washington Irving's sire was a New York businessman and a Presbyterian deacon who demanded daily family worship at home and church attendance three times on Sundays. Mr. Irving distrusted Washington's emotional nature; Washington in turn disliked his father and always preferred his more kindly tempered mother. (See Stanley T. Wil-

liams, *The Life of Washington Irving* [New York, 1935], I.)

Nathaniel Willis' ancestors included a number of ministers as well as several journalists. His father, also called Nathaniel Willis, edited the *East Argus* paper in Portland, Maine, and later the *Boston Recorder* and *Youth's Companion*, and served as a deacon in "Brimstone Corner," the Park Street Church which was the stronghold of evangelical fervor in Boston. One of Willis' earliest biographers, summing up contemporary impressions of the older Willis, described him as "a rather wooden person," subscribing to "the formal and narrow piety of the ... evangelicals of that day, revolting against the latitudinarianism of the Boston churches" (Henry A. Beers, *Nathaniel Parker Willis* [Boston and New York, 1885], p. 11). Willis never got on with his father, although he, like his sister "Fanny Fern," adored his devout, affectionate, and playful mother. He liked to believe he inherited from her the "quick-silver spirit" which was his distinguishing characteristic. Willis was sent to Congregationalist Andover Academy and Yale. Although he later joined Edward Beecher's church in Boston, he became increasingly convinced that he had never experienced a saving change. Evangelical protestations were also a hindrance in the elite Unitarian circles to which Willis aspired. In 1829, he was officially excommunicated from the Park Street Church for "absence from ... communion ... and attendance at the theatre" (*ibid.*, p. 95).

Donald Mitchell was the son of an Andover-trained Congregationalist minister very much oriented toward revivals; despite a love for the beautiful, Reverend Mitchell was, in his son's words, "a very severe disciplinarian, too severe to kindle a child's best love" (Dunn, *op. cit.*, p. 24). Mitchell, like Willis and so many liberal ministers, claimed emotional descent only from his charming, consumptive Episcopalian mother; he was to be an admirer of Horace Bushnell (*ibid.*, p. 55).

35. Not one of them was genuinely healthy: Irving, Willis, and Mitchell spent good portions of their lives struggling with consumption. Willis in his later years wrote frankly and profusely about various remedies for tuberculosis; he received many letters of inquiry from his readers, especially from clergymen, "the class oftenest stricken by con-

sumption" (*Outdoors at Idlewild* [New York, 1855], p. 459). Chronic ill-health functions with the male sentimentalists, as with the non-evangelical ministers, as part of a sociological pattern: the frail boys who were perforce kept closer to mother were more likely to pick a life of writing and talking than their stronger peers.

36. For Curtis' life, see Edward Cary, *George William Curtis* (Boston and New York, 1894).

37. Willis was proud to announce his status as a kind of lapdog in chic feminine circles. Even as an undergraduate at Yale, he could write his mother: "I was much flattered in vacation by the attentions of literary men and women, the latter more particularly who seemed to consider it quite the thing to find a poet who was not a bear and who could stoop so much from the *excelsia* of his profession as to dress fashionably and pay compliments" (Beers, *op. cit.*, p. 57).

38. Dunn, *op. cit.*, p. 161.

39. *Life and Works of Washington Irving*, ed. Richard Henry Stoddard (New York, 1880), pp. 372, 379, 391.

40. See George William Curtis, *Lotus-Eating: A Summer Book* (New York, 1852); "Ik Marvel," *Fresh Gleanings or A New Sheaf from the Old Fields of Continental Europe* (New York, 1907); N. Parker Willis, *Pencillings by the Way* (New York, 1852).

41. Quoted in Auser, *op. cit.*, pp. 23–4. Moreover, Willis had been something of a literary prodigy in his youth, and he always disavowed hard labor. In 1855, answering his critics, who had been warning him for twenty years that his "light and flippant" work could not outlive him, he explained that he had no desire for posthumous fame. He wished only "*to* LIVE, *as variedly, as amply, and as worthily as possible*"; "literature—periodical literature—offered him the readiest means for this —the least confining mode of subsistence, the freest access to contemporary mind and society, the most influence and power" (*Outdoors at Idlewild*, pp. v–vii).

42. For other important examples of the "sketch," see Louis Gaylord Clark, *Knick-Knacks* (New York, 1852) and *The Literary Remains of the Late Willis Gaylord Clark* (New York, 1843); H. T. Tuckerman, *Leaves from the Diary of a Dreamer* (London, 1853), *The*

Optimist (New York, 1850), and *Rambles and Reveries* (New York, 1841).

43. The four writers in discussion ended their days presiding over carefully planned and dearly cherished semi-country retreats: Irving's Sunnyside in Tarrytown, New York; Willis' Idlewild outside New York City; Mitchell's Edgewood near New Haven; Curtis' retreat in Ashfield, Massachusetts. All these homes were "picturesque" in Andrew Jackson Downing's best style (both Willis and Mitchell were avowed followers of the architect); they represented their owners' desire not just to be landed gentry in the English style, but to duck out of the arena of masculine ambition into the safe shelter of feminine domesticity. Irving, a bachelor until his later days, ended his life surrounded by a bevy of adoring nieces; the other three men cherished an exalted ideal of family life which their behavior mainly supported. Like their liberal clerical counterparts, they were moved by their occupation into feminine society and toward feminine values.

44. *Life and Works of Washington Irving*, pp. 447–50.

45. "Paul Pry" is the title of the first chapter in Mitchell, *Fresh Gleanings*.

46. Donald Mitchell, *Reveries of a Bachelor: or, A Book of the Heart by Ik Marvel* (New York, 1888), p. 33.

47. The *locus classicus* for this encounter is Laurence Sterne's description in *A Sentimental Journey* of the meeting between Yorick and the abandoned insane Maria, a scene which was to inspire a host of imitations in England and America. Yorick has heard of Maria and seeks her out as a kind of sentimental sideshow. When he finds her, she is dressed in white, with hair hanging loosely about her shoulders; she is tearfully imploring her little dog not to desert her. Yorick immediately, in a symbolic gesture, attempts to appropriate her wounded sensibilities for his own:

> I sat down close by her; and Maria let me wipe them [her tears] away as they fell, with my handkerchief. I then steeped it in my own, and then in hers, and then in mine, and then I wip'd hers again, and as I did it, I felt such indescribable emotions within me as I am sure could not be accounted for from any combinations of matter and motion.
>
> I am positive I have a soul.

Yet his parasitic reliance on her breeds another conflicting impulse. When Maria offers to dry his handkerchief in her bosom, he leers tenderly at her, " 'And is your heart still so warm, Maria?' " Thus reminded of her sorrows, she pipes a response to his unspoken question in a "service to the virgin." Still, he tells us coyly:

> So much was there about her of all that the heart wishes or the eye looks for in woman, that could the traces be ever worn out of her brain, and those of Eliza out of mine, she should ... be in my bosom, and be unto me as a daughter (*A Sentimental Journey; The Journal to Eliza* [London and New York, 1960], pp. 122, 124).

48. George William Curtis, *Prue and I* (New York, 1893), p. 48.

49. Mitchell, *Reveries of a Bachelor*, p. 9.

50. William G. McLoughlin makes *Norwood* central to his recent re-evaluation, *The Meaning of Henry Ward Beecher: An Essay on the Shifting Values of Mid-Victorian America 1840–1870* (New York, 1970).

51. See Henry Ward Beecher, *Norwood, or Village Life in New England* (New York, 1868), pp. 211–16.

52. Quoted in Robert Shaplen, *Free Love and Heavenly Sinners: The Story of the Great Henry Ward Beecher Scandal* (New York, 1954), pp. 53, 33.

53. The scandal was one of a series involving the ministry. For contemporary attacks on the subject, see W. F. Jamieson, *The Clergy, A Source of Danger to the American Republic* (Boston, 1874); and *The Drama of Deceit: A Satire in Verse on The Rev. Henry Ward Beecher* (Worcester and Clinton, Mass., and Rochester, N.Y., 1875) by an anonymous author.

54. *The Beecher-Tilton Scandal: A Complete History of the Case* (Brooklyn, N.Y., 1874), p. 184.

55. See most notably Tilton's extraordinary romance, *Tempest-Tossed* (New York, 1874), and his tract, *The True Church* (Philadelphia, 1867).

56. Quoted in Paxton Hibben, *Henry Ward Beecher: An American Portrait* (New York, 1927), p. 183.

57. *The Beecher-Tilton Scandal*, pp. 54, 91.

58. *Ibid.*, p. 92.

59. Quoted in Hibben, *op. cit.*, p. 195.

60. Quoted in *ibid.*, p. 269.

61. Quoted in Shaplen, *op. cit.*, p 193. .

62. *Ibid.*, p. 266.

63. Shaplen, *op. cit.*, p. 99.

64. Quoted in Emanie Sachs, *"The Terrible Siren": Victorian Woodhull (1838–1927)* (New York, 1920), p. 174.

65. Quoted in *ibid.*, p. 193.

66. Quoted in *ibid.*, p. 236.

67. Quoted in *ibid.*, p. 262.

68. Quoted in Lyman Beecher Stowe, *Saints, Sinners, and Beechers* (Indianapolis, 1934), p. 154. Biographical studies of Stowe I have found useful are: Annie Field, ed., *The Life and Letters of Harriet Beecher Stowe* (Boston and New York, 1897); Johanna Johnston, *Runaway to Heaven: The Story of Harriet Beecher Stowe* (New York, 1963); Constance Rourke, *Trumpets of Jubilee*, ed. Kenneth Lynn (New York and Burlingame, 1963), pp. 67–112; Charles Edward Stowe, *Life of Harriet Beecher Stowe Compiled from Her Letters and Journals* (Boston and New York, 1889); Edmund Wilson, *Patriotic Gore: Studies in the Literature of the American Civil War* (New York, 1966), pp. 3–98; Forrest Wilson, *Crusader in Crinoline: The Life of Harriet Beecher Stowe* (Philadelphia, London, and New York, 1941). The best critical works are Alice Crozier, *The Novels of Harriet Beecher Stowe* (New York, 1969); Charles Foster, *The Rungless Ladder: Harriet Beecher Stowe and New England Puritanism* (Durham, N.C., 1954). See also Carol V. R. George, "Harriet Beecher: Suffering and the Feminization of Jesus," an unpublished paper delivered before the Association of American Historians in Atlanta, Ga., on Dec. 28, 1975.

69. Forrest Wilson, *op. cit.*, p. 232.

70. For notable examples, see Harriet Beecher Stowe, *The Mayflower and Miscellaneous Writings* (Boston, 1855), and *Sam Lawson's Oldtown Fireside Stories* (Boston, 1871).

71. Harriet Beecher Stowe, *Sunny Memories of Foreign Lands* (Boston, 1854), II, p. 166.

72. *Ibid.*, p. 388.

73. *Ibid.*, I, p. 281.

74. *The Autobiography of Lyman Beecher*, ed. Barbara M. Cross (Cambridge, Mass., 1961), I, pp. 393–4. When Byron died in 1824, Lyman told the young Harriet, " 'I'm sorry that Byron is dead. I did hope he would live to do something for Christ. What a harp he might have swept!' " He preached a sermon on Byron and closed, in Harriet's words, "with a most eloquent lamentation over the wasted life and misused powers of the great poet." He saw Byron as tormented by a dark religious faith and wished he might have talked with him and helped him.

75. Harriet Beecher Stowe, *Lady Byron Vindicated: A History of the Byron Controversy* (Boston, 1870), p. 395.

76. See *ibid.*, pp. 118–19. In protesting the dumb and silent fidelity Byron's friends thought appropriate for the much-abused Lady Byron to evince, Stowe exclaims passionately that a woman's affection should not be expected to resemble that of a devoted dog: "The dog is ever-loving, ever-forgiving, because God has given him no high range of moral faculties, no sense of justice." She bitterly protests "that *utter deadness to the sense of justice* which the laws, literature and misunderstood religion of England have sought to induce in women as a special grace and virtue."

77. Charles Edward Stowe, *op. cit.*, p. 471.

78. James Thayer Addison, *The Episcopal Church in the United States 1789–1931* (New York, 1951), pp. 192–8.

79. *Ibid.*, p. 207.

80. All page references are to Harriet Beecher Stowe, *My Wife and I: or, Henry Henderson's History* (New York, 1872).

81. Christopher Crowfield [Harriet Beecher Stowe], *Little Foxes* (Boston, 1866), p. 69.

82. Harriet Beecher Stowe, *Household Papers and Stories* (Boston and New York, 1896), p. 85.

83. Crowfield, *Little Foxes*, p. 238.

84. All references here and elsewhere are to Harriet Beecher Stowe, *We and Our Neighbors: or, The Records of an Unfashionable Street* (New York, 1875).

85. Stowe was also producing more serious, if not original work, in *Sam Lawson's Oldtown Fireside Stories, Poganuc People: Their Loves and Lives* (New York, 1878), and *Women in Sacred History: A Series of Sketches* (New York, 1874), as well as trivia like *Betty's Bright Idea* (New York, 1876), and *Little Pussy Willow* (Boston, 1870).

86. Mary Bushnell Cheney, *Life and Letters of Horace Bushnell* (New York, 1880), p. 168.

87. See R. A. Yoder, "The Equilibrist Perspective: Toward a Theory of American Romanticism," *Studies in Romanticism*, 12

(1973), 705–40, on the special problem of American romanticism. See also Morse Peckham, *The Triumph of Romanticism* (Columbia, S.C., 1970), and Quentin Anderson, "Practical and Visionary Americans," *American Scholar,* 45 (1976), 405–18.

88. Mrs. L. H. Sigourney, *Select Poems* (Philadelphia, 1854), p. 13.

8

MARGARET FULLER AND THE DISAVOWAL OF FICTION

1. *Journals of Ralph Waldo Emerson,* ed. Edward Waldo Emerson and Waldo Emerson (Boston and New York, 1912), VIII, p. 116. Hereafter referred to as *Journals.*

2. *The Letters of Elizabeth Barrett Browning,* ed. Frederic G. Kenyon (New York, 1897), I, p. 460.

3. The standard biographies of Margaret Fuller, none of which are fully adequate, are as follows: W. H. Channing, J. F. Clarke, and R. W. Emerson, *Memoirs of Margaret Fuller Ossoli* (Boston, 1852), 2 vols. (hereafter referred to as *Memoirs*); Thomas Wentworth Higginson, *Margaret Fuller Ossoli* (Boston, 1884); Julia Ward Howe, *Margaret Fuller* (Boston, 1883); Katharine Anthony, *Margaret Fuller: A Psychological Biography* (New York, 1920); Arthur M. Brown, *Margaret Fuller* (New York, 1967); Faith Chippenfield, *In Quest of Love: The Life and Death of Margaret Fuller* (New York, 1957); Joseph Jay Deiss, *The Roman Years of Margaret Fuller* (New York, 1969); Mason Wade, *Margaret Fuller: Whetstone of Genius* (New York, 1940). Fuller's papers are in Houghton Library of Harvard University and Boston Public Library.

4. Henry James, *William Wetmore Story and His Friends* (Boston, 1903), I, p. 127.

5. F. W. Dupee, *Henry James: His Life and Writings* (New York, 1956), p. 97.

6. James's standard defenses of fiction are "The Art of Fiction" and "The Future of the Novel," collected in *Henry James: The Future of the Novel,* ed. Leon Edel (New York, 1956).

7. James, in idealizing the mid-nineteenth-century Italy of Story and his friends, seems to have been vindicating his own courage in confronting a vastly changed and modernized Europe a half century later: expatriation, he implies, is no longer an evasion.

8. *Margaret Fuller, American Romantic: A Selection from Her Writings and Correspondence,* ed. Perry Miller (New York, 1963), pp. xxv–xxvi.

9. James, *William Wetmore Story,* I, pp. 127–8.

10. *Memoirs,* I, p. 234.

11. *The Letters of James Freeman Clarke to Margaret Fuller,* ed. John Wesley Thomas (Hamburg, Germany, 1952), pp. 78–9.

12. *Memoirs,* II, p. 39.

13. For recent biographies, see Wayne Andrews, *Germaine: A Portrait of Madame de Staël* (New York, 1963), and André Maurois, *Lelia: A Life of George Sand,* trans. Gerrod Hopkins (New York, 1953).

14. *Memoirs,* I, p. 229.

15. She left Italy for America in 1850, for example, because she could not earn the money she needed to support her family outside the United States. There were a number of young men with whom Fuller was in love as a young woman, most notably Samuel Ward, who married Fuller's closest friend, Anna Barker. Faith Chippenfield stresses (indeed, over-stresses) Fuller's love-life in her sentimental biography. What strikes a modern reader of Fuller's letters and journals is the gallantry with which she handled her isolation. At times she felt her loneliness to be unbearable, that she had "no real hold on life, no real permanent connection with any soul," and recorded with horror: "This thought envelops me as a cold atmosphere. I do not see how I shall go through this destiny. I can, if it is mine; but I do not feel that I can" (*Memoirs,* II, pp. 167–8). Yet she held herself to a high tone of magnanimity which she was scrupulous enough to distinguish rigorously from a spirit of martyrdom (*Memoirs,* II, p. 167). While it is clear that this high tone served a compensatory function—she would be admired if she could not be loved, she would predict destinies if she could not dictate affection—it is also clear that she demanded generosity of thought from herself as a basic precondition of self-respect. She struggled ruthlessly to live in altitudes where breathing is difficult. Repeatedly, she faced ruthlessly the waste of her emotions. She strove for "humility" (*Memoirs,* I, p. 166); she prayed, "Would that love like knowledge could be its own reward" (Higginson, *op. cit.,* p. 180).

16. Fuller once wrote that those who live

without love and support "are thrown upon themselves," and if they do not find "peace and incessant life," at least they are honest; "there is none to flatter them that they are not very poor and very mean" (*Woman in the Nineteenth Century and Kindred Papers* [Boston, Cleveland, and New York, 1835], p. 97. Hereafter referred to as *Woman*).

17. Caroline W. Healey, *Margaret and Her Friends, or, Ten Conversations with Margaret Fuller* (Boston, 1895), p. 156.

18. T. W. Higginson in his biography of Fuller noted that Fuller, influenced by her father, had turned "from the weak side of American intellect, which then was literature, to the strong side, which was statesmanship" (*op. cit.*, pp. 132–3).

19. *Memoirs*, I, pp. 31–2.

20. Quoted in Chippenfield, *op. cit.*, p. 82.

21. Higginson, *op. cit.*, p. 22.

22. *Memoirs*, I, p. 18.

23. *Ibid.*

24. *Ibid.*, p. 154.

25. Fuller, *Woman*, p. 41.

2⁶. *Memoirs*, II, p. 65.

27. *Memoirs*, I, p. 303.

28. *Memoirs*, I, p. 20.

29. Fuller, *Woman*, p. 387.

30. *Ibid.*, I, p. 297.

31. Thomas Carlyle, to pick one example of many, praised her "chivalrous nobleness à toute épreuve" and thought her work "the undeniable utterances ... of a truly heroic mind; altogether unique ... among the writing women of this generation, rare enough ... among the writing men" (quoted in Howe, *op. cit.*, p. 186).

32. John Wesley Thomas, *James Freeman Clarke: Apostle of German Culture to America* (Boston, 1949), p. 28.

33. See the early correspondence in *James Freeman Clarke to Margaret Fuller.*

34. This poem is included in *The Poetical Works of James Russell Lowell* (London, n.d.), pp. 140–80. Lowell was mocking a real attitude of Fuller's. In 1839, she wrote a friend: "I was proud that I was to test myself in the sternest way, that I was always to return to myself, to be my own priest, pupil, parent, child, husband and wife" (*Memoirs*, I, p. 99). What Lowell failed to understand was that Fuller had no other option.

35. *Memoirs*, I, p. 231.

36. Quoted in Wade, *op. cit.*, pp. 280–2.

37. After the birth of her child, Fuller drew much closer to her mother. She hoped to bring her family to live with Mrs. Fuller on her return to America in 1850.

38. *The Young Lady's Friend By a Lady* (Boston, 1836), pp. 327, 323. See Higginson, *op. cit.*, pp. 35 ff., for Fuller's relations with other older women.

39. See Alexander E. Jones, "Margaret Fuller's Attempt to Write Fiction," *Boston Public Library Quarterly*, 6 (1954), 67–73.

40. Margaret Fuller, *Literature and Art* (New York, 1832), II, pp. 130–1. Hereafter referred to as *Literature*. It is interesting that as a critic writing for the *New York Tribune* in the mid-1840s, Fuller had utter scorn for the common run of children's books coming into popularity. She disliked the "Peter Parley" style of narrative which put "instruction" over "development," "the moral" over "the nature in which it must find its root" (*Woman*, p. 311). The works fit for children, she believed, were not such specially tailored and truncated "thin and baseless fictions" but the classics which speak of "great realities" (p. 312). As a girl, she had read for pleasure Molière, Cervantes, Shakespeare, all of whom "loved the *natural history* of man. Not what he should be, but what he is" (*Memoirs*, I, p. 30).

41. Fuller, *Woman*, pp. 130 ff.

42. Margaret Fuller Ossoli, *At Home and Abroad, or Things and Thoughts in America and Europe* (Boston and London, 1836), pp. 171–2. Hereafter referred to as *Home and Abroad*.

43. Quoted in Andrews, *op. cit.*, p. 97.

44. *Memoirs*, I, p. 55.

45. Quoted in Maurois, *op. cit.*, p. 113.

46. *Memoirs*, II, p. 195.

47. *Woman*, p. 94.

48. *Memoirs*, I, pp. 248–9.

49. Alcott's school, which was an important influence on Fuller, is described in Elizabeth Peabody, *Record of Mr. Alcott's School* (Boston, 1874). See also Dorothy McCuskey, *Bronson Alcott, Teacher* (New York, 1940).

50. *The Letters of Ralph Waldo Emerson*, ed. Ralph Rusk (New York, 1939), II, p. 202. Hereafter referred to as *Letters*.

51. Healey, *op. cit.*, pp. 139–40.

52. See *ibid.*, pp. 67 ff., where Fuller deliberately enjoys an anecdote of cruelty (Apollo's flaying of Marsyas) in most unfeminine fashion, to the dismay of one of her more conservative students.

53. *Memoirs*, I, p. 329.

54. Quoted in Higginson, *op. cit.*, p. 117.

55. *Memoirs*, II, p. 160.

56. Howe, *op. cit.*, p. 85.

57. See, for example, "The Magnolia," included in Margaret Fuller Ossoli, *Life Without and Life Within, or Reviews, Narratives, Essays, and Poems* (Boston, 1960), pp. 333–5.

58. *Memoirs*, I, p. 238.

59. Quoted in Chippenfield, *op. cit.*, p. 197.

60. See Madame de Staël, *Corinne; or Italy*, trans. Emily Baldwin and Paulina Driver (London, 1890), *passim*.

61. See F. O. Matthiessen, *American Renaissance: Art and Expression in the Age of Emerson and Whitman* (London, Toronto, and New York, 1941), p. 17, and pp. 3–75 *passim*.

62. For contemporary views, see William Wirt, *The Letters of the British Spy*, ed. Richard Beale Davis (Chapel Hill, N.C., 1970), especially pp. 132–47, and *The Life of Patrick Henry* (Hartford, 1848), *passim*.

63. Elizabeth Barrett Browning, for example, remarked: "If I wished anyone to do her [Fuller] justice, I should say ... 'Never read what she has written'" (Letters of Elizabeth Barrett Browning, I, p. 59).

64. *Letters*, IV, p. 222.

65. *Journals*, VIII, p. 250.

66. *Memoirs*, I, p. 295.

67. James, *William Wetmore Story*, I, p. 171.

68. *Memoirs*, II, p. 24.

69. *Ibid.*, I, p. 294, and see Wade, *op. cit.*, p. 130. Edgar Poe was aware of Fuller's confusion between life and literature at this time. He wrote perceptively: "her personal character and her printed book are merely one and the same thing. Her acts are bookish, and her books are less thoughts than acts" (quoted in Wade, *op. cit.*, p. 155).

70. Healey, *op. cit.*, p. 137.

71. *Memoirs*, II, p. 11.

72. For two fine articles on the Fuller-Emerson relationship to which I am indebted, see Carl Strauch, "Hatred's Swift Repulsions: Emerson, Margaret Fuller and Others," *Studies in Romanticism*, 7 (1968), 63–103; and Harry R. Warfel, "Margaret Fuller and Ralph Waldo Emerson," *Publications of the Modern Language Association*, 30 (1935), 376–94.

73. Higginson, *op. cit.*, p. 85.

74. *Memoirs*, II, p. 75.

75. Quoted in Higginson, *op. cit.*, p. 62.

76. Quoted in Warfel, *op. cit.*, p. 382.

77. *Letters*, I, p. 32.

78. *Ibid.*, pp. 351, 245, 239. Fuller was capable of taunting Emerson with his failures of creativity: "But, Waldo, how can you expect the Muse *to come to you?* She hovers near, I have seen her several times, especially near night. Sometimes she looks in at your study windows when she can get a chance, for they are almost always shut" (*Letters*, III, p. 284). Emerson, notoriously cold-blooded, liked a fire even in summer. It takes little imagination to realize that Fuller, then (July 1844) on her way to New York, saw herself as Emerson's vanishing Muse. When he heard of her death six years later, he wrote in his journal, "I have lost my audience" (*Journals*, VIII, pp. 115–19). What he meant probably was that after her death no one would again address the "overwhelming question" to him with such force. And no one did.

79. *Letters*, I, p. 32.

80. See Ann Wood, "Emerson's *Representative Men,*" *New Republic*, Jan. 1–8, 1972, p. 29.

81. *Letters*, II, p. 322.

82. Higginson, *op. cit.*, pp. 166, 167.

83. *Literature*, II, pp. 2–3.

84. *Letters*, III, pp. 19–20, 29.

85. Her fascination with Goethe had stemmed largely from the fact that this emphasis on the outward world was his central message. See Frederick Augustus Brown, *Margaret Fuller and Goethe* (New York, 1910).

86. *Letters*, III, p. 180.

87. I am indebted for this point and for much of my thinking on the Fuller-Emerson relationship to Michael Davitt Bell of Williams College.

88. Quoted in Higginson, *op. cit.*, p. 165.

89. Quoted in Perry Miller, *The Transcendentalists: An Anthology* (Cambridge, Mass., 1950), pp. 307–8.

90. *Memoirs*, II, p. 58.

91. Odell Shepard, *Peddlar's Progress: The Life of Bronson Alcott* (Boston, 1937), pp. 155–6.

92. *Memoirs*, II, p. 29.

93. *Memoirs*, II, pp. 151 ff. See also Horace Greeley, *Recollections of a Busy Life* (New York, 1868), pp. 169–91. For Greeley's career, see Frank W. Scott, "Newspapers 1775–1860" in *The Cambridge History of American Literature*, II (New York, 1918), pp. 177–95; Henry Luther Stoddard, *Horace Greeley, Printer, Editor, Crusader* (New York, 1946); Glyndon Garlock Van Deusen, *Horace Greeley: Nine-*

teenth-Century Crusader (Philadelphia, Pa., 1953).

94. Fuller, *Woman*, p. 103.

95. *Memoirs*, II, p. 156.

96. Fuller, *Woman*, pp. 119, 172.

97. Quoted in Wade, *op. cit.*, p. 143.

98. *Memoirs*, II, p. 151. Fuller's friendship with Greeley was not the only sign of the change taking place in her, however. She had an unpromising relationship with a German Jew called James Nathan, an evasive and weak man whose presence in Fuller's life at first glance tells more about her hunger for affection than about her ability to read character. After a few months he fled to Europe, and another woman. Yet she was attracted to Nathan at least in part because he worshiped Margaret the "Muse" only intermittently, if at all. While she wrote him that she was one of "the few in whose lot the meaning of the age is concentrated," she also confessed that she lacked "humility." On one occasion she recoiled from insults he had hurled at her, yet she liked his telling her, "little girl, you are a fool" (quoted in Wade, *op. cit.*, pp. 164–5). In responding positively to this apparently degrading remark, she was recording not simply her desire to be treated as a woman even when that involved belittlement, as it often by definition did, but also her half-conscious instinct for self-demythification. (See also Julia Ward Howe, ed., *The Love Letters of Margaret Fuller 1844–1845* [New York, 1903], for Fuller's letters to Nathan.)

99. Quoted in Wade, *op. cit.*, p. 153. It is important to note, moreover, that the newspaper was a natural offspring of the American oratorical tradition. Even its greater informality was a logical modification of a tradition which maintained that the most "sublime" eloquence was spontaneous and even untutored.

100. *Letters*, III, p. 183.

101. Fuller, *Home and Abroad*, p. 62.

102. *Ibid.*, p. 232.

103. Fuller, *Home and Abroad*, p. 214.

104. *Ibid.*, p. 243.

105. The best account of the Fuller-Ossoli relationship is in Deiss, *op. cit.* Anthony, *op. cit.*, pp. 154–70, is also useful.

106. She wrote a friend, "Our relation covers only a part of my life, but I do not perceive that it interferes with anything I ought to have or be" (quoted in Deiss, *op. cit.*, p. 295).

In a dark moment, she could refer to Ossoli's love as "all fondness, but no help" (*Memoirs*, II, p. 233). She had reservations about the institution of marriage (*ibid.*, p. 278), and gave a great deal of thought to the freedom the much younger Ossoli might one day need (Deiss, *op. cit.*, p. 295).

107. Fuller, *Home and Abroad*, pp. 162, 166.

108. See Paul P. Baker, *The Fortunate Pilgrims: Americans in Italy 1800–1860* (Cambridge, Mass., 1964); Edgar P. Richardson and Otto Wittman, *Travellers in Arcadia: American Artists in Italy 1830–1895* (Detroit, Ill., 1951); Natalie Wright, *American Novelists in Italy* (Philadelphia, Pa., 1965).

109. Quoted in Baker, *op. cit.*, p. 42.

110. A. William Salomone, "The 19th-Century Discovery of Italy: An Essay in American Cultural History," *American Historical Review*, 173 (1968), 1360–2. See also Howard R. Marraro, *American Opinion on the Unification of Italy 1846–1861* (New York, 1932).

111. Fuller, *Home and Abroad*, p. 218.

112. *Ibid.*, pp. 331, 334.

113. *Ibid.*, p. 367.

114. Deiss, *op. cit.*, p. 222. Fuller's estimate of the gap between reportage and fact was not exaggerated. The dramatically changing opinions of Louis Cass, the American attaché who arrived in Rome in the spring of 1849, testify to the same phenomenon. Pleading with his government to empower him fully to recognize the young republic, he summed up the issue at stake: this is "not, as the European press has so constantly insinuated, [a conflict] between anarchy and order, [but one] between constitutional, representative government and the most benumbing despotism" (Joseph Rossi, *The Image of America in Mazzini's Writings* [Madison, Wis., 1954], p. 71). For Fuller's Roman journal, see Leona Rustenberg, "Documents: Margaret Fuller's Roman Diary," *Journal of Modern History*, 12 (1940), 209–70.

115. Fuller, *Home and Abroad*, p. 248.

116. *Ibid.*, p. 327.

117. *Ibid.*, pp. 305–6.

118. *Ibid.*, p. 420.

119. *Memoirs*, II, p. 310.

120. *Ibid.*, p. 209.

121. See *James Freeman Clarke to Margaret Fuller*, p. 102, where Clarke praises Mrs. Sigourney.

122. James Freeman Clarke, *Autobiography, Diary and Correspondence*, ed. Edward Everett Hale (Boston and New York, 1891), pp. 171, 179.

123. *Memoirs*, II, p. 235.

124. Leopold Wellisz, *The Friendship of Margaret Fuller Ossoli and Adam Mickiewicz* (New York, 1947), p. 34.

125. Fuller, *Woman*, p. 177.

126. Quoted in Anthony, *op. cit.*, pp. 82–3.

9

HERMAN MELVILLE AND THE REVOLT AGAINST THE READER

1. *Margaret Fuller: American Romantic: A Selection from Her Writings and Correspondence*, ed. Perry Miller (New York, 1965), pp. 222–3.

2. Quoted in Jay Leyda, *The Melville Log: A Documentary Life of Herman Melville 1819–1891* (New York, 1951), I, p. 390, II, p. 651.

3. Perry Miller makes the point that the New York literary circle Melville joined in the later 1840s was self-consciously looking for a "genius." See *The Raven and the Whale: The War of Words and Wits in the Era of Poe and Melville* (New York, 1956), *passim*.

4. Leyda, *op. cit.*, II, p. 519.

5. Quoted in Julia Ward Howe, *Margaret Fuller* (Boston, 1883), p. 186.

6. On Melville's reading, see M. M. Sealts, Jr., *Melville's Reading: A Check List of Books Owned and Borrowed* (Cambridge, Mass., 1950).

7. For another author who became increasingly fascinated with the detective mode and for similar reasons, see Mark Twain, most notably *Pudd'nhead Wilson* and *Tom Sawyer, Detective* in *The Writings of Mark Twain* (New York and London, n.d.), Vols. XIV, XX.

8. The feminine members of Melville's family read Mrs. A. D. T. Whitney's works aloud in the 1850s. See Leyda, *op. cit.*, I, p. 676. His wife attended the New York church of the liberal Unitarian Henry Bellows, a close friend of Orville Dewey's. See William Braswell, *Melville's Religious Thought: An Essay in Interpretation* (New York, 1959), p. 8.

9. All page references here and elsewhere to *Pierre* are to Herman Melville, *Pierre, or, the Ambiguities* (New York, 1957).

10. Merrell R. Davis and William H. Gilman, *The Letters of Herman Melville* (New Haven, 1960), p. 93.

11. *Ibid.*, p. 138.

12. *Ibid.*, p. 92.

13. Melville quickly became bitter at the public's insistence that he simply reduplicate his first two successful travelogues, *Typee* and *Omoo*. His dislike of such stereotyping led him to refer to himself in cruel parody as the "Author of *Peedee, Hullabaloo* and *Pog Dog*" (quoted in Matthew J. Bruccoli, *The Profession of Authorship in America 1800–1870: The Papers of William Charvat* [n.p., 1968], p. 227). He could later refer to *Redburn*, which he wrote to answer popular demand that he return to his original material after the failure of *Mardi*, as "nothing but cakes & ale" and "a nursery tale" (quoted in *ibid.*, p. 237).

14. Herman Melville, *Omoo: A Narrative of Adventure in the South Seas* (Chicago, 1968), p. xiii.

15. *Ibid.*, p. 108.

16. Herman Melville, *Typee* (New York, 1961), p. 175.

17. Herman Melville, *White-Jacket, or, the World on a Man of War* (New York, 1959), pp. 118, 164.

18. Herman Melville, *The Apple-Tree Table and Other Sketches* (Princeton and London, 1922), p. 107.

19. See particularly "The Paradise of Bachelors and the Tartarus of Maids" in *The Apple-Tree Table*, pp. 167–210. For an interesting article on the social and sexual implications of "Tartarus," see Marvin Fisher, "Melville's 'Tartarus': The Deflowering of New England," *American Quarterly*, 23 (1971), 79–100.

20. Certain of Melville's works, most notably *The Confidence Man*, do not include women as prominent characters; yet I classify it as "Freudian" and feminine because, as I will try to show later, the consciousness of the male protagonists is determined by an essentially feminized culture whose off-stage presence Melville keeps us aware of.

21. Herman Melville, *Redburn: His First Voyage* (New York, 1957), p. 12.

22. For an example of the cult of boyhood, see Thomas Bailey Aldrich, *The Story of a Bad Boy* (Boston and New York, 1869).

23. Melville, *Omoo*, p. 184.

24. Melville, *White-Jacket*, pp. 49, 289.

25. *Ibid.*, p. 270.

26. Interestingly enough, when Melville in *Redburn* is being genuinely informative in the style of *Omoo*—about life at sea, or conditions

in Liverpool—he is clearly talking to an imaginary audience which is either male or shares male interests. When he condescends by explaining terms like "microcosm, or little world" (102), shows off by using archaic words like "wight" (104), and satirizes his readers by mocking Redburn's naive adherence to the causes of temperance or purity, he is apparently addressing genteel readers. It is important to keep in mind that *Redburn* is in form a hybrid. Two types of narratives about life at sea were common in Melville's day. There was the straight adventure chronicle, whether fact or fiction, such as Richard Henry Dana's *Two Years Before the Mast* (1840) and Melville's first two books, which were clearly designated as reading for boys and men. There was also the sentimental sobstory of the sailor's trials at sea propagated by societies for the relief of seamen and tailored to the tastes of a religious and feminine audience. Sigourney belonged to such a society, and in tales like "The Widow and Her Son" (*Water-Drops* [New York, 1848], pp. 44–73) she depicted the unrepentant sailor's wild life at sea as an unjust protest against female authority. Melville dismissed *Redburn* as a "little nursery tale"; more accurately one might say it is a confused parody of a little nursery tale. In *Redburn*, Melville is writing in deliberate consciousness of the sentimental sea tracts. While the character Redburn's meaning (as a vehicle of class-consciousness) is clear, his formal identity, what part he is to play, is not. Redburn is an odd cross between the conventional virtuous lad of pious sea literature, exposed but resistant to maritime temptation, and the tough sailor of the adventure narratives. To further complicate the confusion of the book, like *Mardi* (although less conspicuously so), *Redburn* is divided between a narrative, about young Redburn's adventures at sea, and a rather improbable "story," which peaks with Redburn's mysterious, perhaps decadent, escapades with the English boy Harry Bolton in London. Melville is not in control of the dichotomy between the book's two formal modes, narrative and "story." He nominally finishes off the "story"—Melville always rounds out his stories, as he never does his narratives—by telling the reader what he or she presumably wants to know, most particularly the sad fate of Harry Bolton. He can't end the narrative; we only learn that

Redburn "survives," although not happily. So *Redburn* stands, painful in the revealed, self-mocking tension between Melville's awakened but unsatisfied intention and his conventional reader's aroused but unfulfilled interest.

27. Newton Arvin, *Herman Melville* (n.p., 1950), p. 265.

28. William Charvat, in one of the finest essays to date on Melville and one which has guided my own approach, remarks that "*Moby Dick* . . . [is] the work of a writer who was in a state of creative tension with a reading public whose limitations he had at last defined" (Bruccoli, *op. cit.*, p. 240).

29. All page references here and elsewhere are to Herman Melville, *Moby Dick* (New York, 1948). On the connections between Melville and Calvinism, see particularly Braswell, *op. cit.*; Arthur M. Schlesinger, Jr., and Morton White, *Paths of American Thought* (Boston, 1963), p. 84, where the authors state in connection with Melville and Hawthorne that "the emotions of Calvinism thus persisted in literature after the structure of theology had begun to fall to pieces"; Randall Stewart, *American Literature and Christian Doctrine* (Baton Rouge, La., 1958); Lawrance Thompson, *Melville's Quarrel with God* (Princeton, 1952). On Melville's reception in the religious press, see Mentor L. Williams, "Some Notices and Reviews of Melville's Novels in American Religious Periodicals 1846–1849," *American Literature*, 22 (1950), 119–27.

30. Melville is of course enormously aware of the economic realities and significance of the whaling industry, however. See Warner Berthoff, *The Example of Melville* (New York, 1962), pp. 78–84, and Leo Marx, *The Machine and the Garden: Technology and the Pastoral Ideal in America* (London, Oxford, and New York, 1964), pp. 277–319. I should add that I am indebted to Berthoff's book, the finest study of Melville we have, not only for a number of particular points, but for my general understanding of Melville's supreme importance and value.

31. For further information on Melville's intention with *Pierre*, see William Braswell, "Melville's Opinion of Pierre," *American Literature*, 23 (1951), 246–50. For an interesting interpretation of the artistic and sexual difficulties revealed in *Pierre*, see Lewis Mumford, *Herman Melville: A Study of His Life and Vision*

(New York, 1956), pp. 151 ff. Another helpful interpretation is William Ellery Sedgwick, *Herman Melville: The Tragedy of Mind* (Cambridge, Mass., 1945), pp. 127 ff.

32. Bruccoli, *op. cit.*, p. 276.

33. For these views, see Hershel Parker, ed., *The Recognition of Herman Melville: Selected Criticisms Since 1846* (Ann Arbor, Mich., 1967), pp. 49–60; Hugh W. Hetherington, *Melville's Reviewers British and American 1846–1891* (Chapel Hill, N.C., 1961). On the unreliability of Hetherington, see Hershel Parker, "A Re-examination of *Melville's Reviewers*," *American Literature*, 42 (1970), 226–32.

34. Quoted in Bruccoli, *op. cit.*, p. 239.

35. See Leon Howard, *Herman Melville* (Berkeley and Los Angeles, 1951), p. 221. Mitchell, Curtis, and Melville shared the same publisher, Harper's. See Eugene Exman, *The Brothers Harper* (New York, 1965), p. 245. For Melville's relations with Harper's, see *ibid.*, pp. 282–302. Melville perhaps saw the comparisons critics in the early 1850s liked to draw between his own atheistic, materialistic, sensual, chaotic productions and the writing of Mitchell, praised for writing "from the heart," or the tasteful, "moderate, judicious, and experienced" work of Curtis. See Parker, ed., *Recognition*, pp. 63, 93.

36. For this and other favorable reactions, see Howard, *op. cit.*, pp. 211 ff.

37. Richard D. Mosier, *Making the American Mind: Social and Moral Ideas in the McGuffey Readers* (New York, 1947), p. 130.

38. See George William Curtis, *Prue and I* (New York, 1892), p. 111.

39. For modern recognition that Melville was working in the Sterne-Irving-Mitchell-Curtis tradition in his magazine tales, see Richard Harter Fogle, *Melville's Shorter Tales* (Norman, Okla. 1960), p. 46; Edward H. Rosenberry, *Melville and the Comic Spirit* (Cambridge, Mass., 1955), pp. 146 ff.; Sedgwick, *op. cit.*, p. 193; Judith Slater, "The Domestic Adventurer in Melville's Tales," *American Literature*, 37 (1965), 267–79.

40. For interpretations of "Bartleby" which I found helpful, see John Gardner, "*Bartleby:* Art and Social Commitment," *Philological Quarterly*, 43 (1964), 87–98; Liane Norman, "Bartleby and the Reader," *New England Quarterly*, 44 (1971), 21–39.

41. Page references to "Bartleby" will be to Herman Melville, *Billy Budd and Other Tales* (New York and Toronto, 1961).

42. Quoted in Howard, *op. cit.*, p. 224.

43. Page references to "I and My Chimney" and "The Apple-Tree Table" will be to Herman Melville, *The Apple-Tree Table and Other Sketches*. For useful studies of "I and My Chimney," see Merton M. Sealts, "Herman Melville's 'I and My Chimney,'" *American Literature*, 13 (1941), 142–54; Stuart C. Woodruff, "Melville and His Chimney," *Publications of the Modern Language Association*, 75 (1960), 283–92.

44. See Vicki Halper Litman, "The Cottage and the Temple: Melville's Symbolic Use of Architecture," *American Quarterly*, 21 (1969), 630–8.

45. See Carolyn L. Karcher, "The 'Spiritual Lesson' of Melville's 'The Apple-Tree Table,'" *American Quarterly*, 23 (1971), 101–9.

46. See Charles N. Watson, Jr., "Melville and the Theme of Timonism: From *Pierre* to *The Confidence Man*," *American Literature*, 44 (1972), 398–413.

47. All page references are to Herman Melville, *The Confidence Man: His Masquerade* (New York, 1949).

48. Leyda, *op. cit.*, II, p. 574.

49. *Ibid.*, p. 542.

50. *Ibid.*, p. 547.

51. *Ibid.*, p. 579.

52. See "The South Seas" in *The Portable Melville*, ed. Jay Leyda (New York, 1952), pp. 575–83. See also Merton M. Sealts, *Melville as Lecturer* (Folcroft, Pa., 1970).

53. *Selected Poetry of Herman Melville*, ed. Hennig Cohen (New York, 1964), pp. 7, 24, 32. For a negative response to *Battle-Pieces* by Charles Eliot Norton, see Leyda, *Melville Log*, II, p. 683.

54. For an interesting contrast of these two works, see John P. McWilliams, Jr., "*Drum-Taps* and *Battle-Pieces*: The Blossom of War," *American Quarterly*, 23 (1971), 181–201.

55. All page references are to *Billy Budd Sailor: An Inside Narrative*, ed. Harrison Hayford and Merton M. Sealts, Jr. (Chicago, 1962).

56. I am indebted for the spirit of my interpretation to the superb discussion of *Billy Budd* in Berthoff, *op. cit.*, pp. 183–203. For a differing and penetrating analysis, see Edgar

A. Dryden, *Melville's Thematics of Form: The Great Art of Telling the Truth* (Baltimore, 1968).

57. Quoted in Richard Hofstadter, *Anti-Intellectualism in American Life* (New York, 1962), p. 116.

58. The University of Wisconsin, the University of Chicago, Tufts, and Wesleyan University all tried to reverse or modify their policies on co-education at the turn of the twentieth century. See Thomas Woody, *A History of Women's Education in the United States* (New York and Lancaster, Pa., 1929), II, pp. 268–98.

59. I am referring to the phenomenon which Georg Lukács described as the "Grand Hotel Abyss," the "coupling of 'left' ethics with 'right' epistemology"; see *The Theory of the Novel*, trans. Anna Bostock (Cambridge, Mass., 1971), p. 22.

INDEX